HANDBOOK OF MIDDLE AMERICAN INDIANS

EDITED AT MIDDLE AMERICAN RESEARCH INSTITUTE, TULANE UNIVERSITY

ASSEMBLED WITH THE AID OF A GRANT FROM THE NATIONAL SCIENCE FOUNDATION, AND UNDER THE SPONSORSHIP OF THE NATIONAL RESEARCH COUNCIL COMMITTEE ON LATIN AMERICAN ANTHROPOLOGY

HANDBOOK OF MIDDLE AMERICAN INDIANS, VOLUME 3

Archaeology of Southern Mesoamerica, Part 2

HANDBOOK OF MIDDLE AMERICAN INDIANS

ROBERT WAUCHOPE, General Editor

VOLUME THREE

Archaeology of Southern Mesoamerica

PART TWO

GORDON R. WILLEY, Volume Editor

UNIVERSITY OF TEXAS PRESS AUSTIN

Published in Great Britain by the
University of Texas Press, Ltd., London

Library of Congress Catalog Card No. 65–10316

The preparation and publication of the
Handbook of Middle American Indians
has been assisted by grants from
the National Science Foundation.

Typesetting by G&S Typesetters, Austin, Texas
Printing by Meriden Gravure Company, Meriden, Connecticut
Binding by Universal Bookbindery, Inc., San Antonio, Texas

CONTENTS *(Continued from Vol. 2)*

HANDBOOK OF MIDDLE AMERICAN INDIANS, VOLUME 3

Archaeology of Southern Mesoamerica, Part 2

GENERAL EDITOR'S NOTE

The manuscripts for the following articles were submitted at various dates over a period of two and one-half years. Because of revisions and minor updatings made from time to time, it is difficult to assign a date to each article. In some cases, an indication of when an article was completed can be had by noting the latest dates in the list of references at the end of each contribution.

21. Jades of the Maya Lowlands

ROBERT L. RANDS

JADE, among both the highland and lowland Maya, was a highly prized stone, often subject to artistic embellishment. Considerable diversity is present in the raw material, which constitutes forms of jadeite, diopside-jadeite, and chloromelanite. In addition, various jadelike minerals were sometimes fashioned into objects similar to those made of jade. Nevertheless, jade itself was normally used in the finest carvings, indicating that greater intrinsic value was placed on this hard, often lustrous gemstone.[1]

As shown by the waterworn appearance of their uncut surfaces, many jade objects were worked from stones found in stream beds. Numerous slices had been sawed from such a boulder excavated at Kaminaljuyu (Kidder, Jennings, and Shook, 1946, fig. 154,*c*,*d*). A single outcrop of jade-bearing stone is known, from Manzanal, near the Motagua River in Guatemala. Ground near the outcropping is littered with angular fragments of jadeite and associated albite, showing breakage on all sides but no signs of natural wear, an indication that these materials had been quarried. Foshag (1957) compares the jade from Manzanal to the pale greenish jadeite found frequently in carvings from the Quiche region and recognizes six other types of jade in objects from Guatemala. Among these, the so-called "blue" or "Olmec" jadeite is of limited occurrence, known only in Preclassic and Early Classic contexts. Favored emerald-green to apple-green jadeite occurs widely, although it is not typical at many of the sites where it is found. This fine-quality jade dates from the Preclassic through Late Classic periods, perhaps extending into early Postclassic, and is especially characteristic of Kaminaljuyu. Another jadeite, gray-green in color, is present in the form of well-shaped celts, and the dark green chloromelanite occurs frequently as utilitarian objects (celts, chisels, and reamers). The occurrence of still other types of jade is traced by Foshag, who warns, however, that their source of origin may not be in distinct localities; consider-

[1] Acknowledgments are made to Elizabeth Easby and Tatiana Proskouriakoff, who have read the manuscript and offered helpful suggestions.

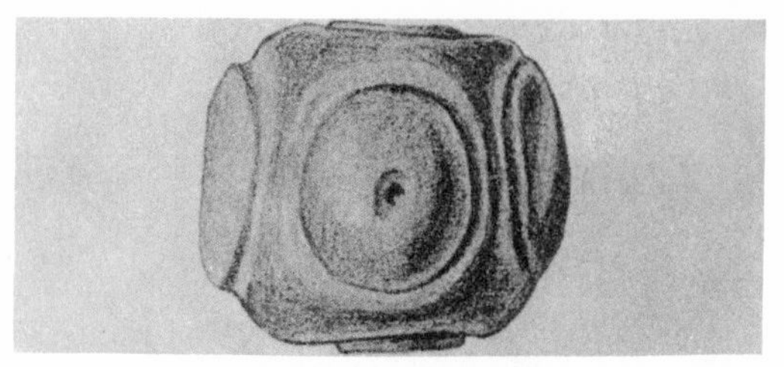

Fig. 1—LOBED GLOBULAR JADE BEAD, KAMINALJUYU. Early Classic tomb. Diameter 2.6 cm. (After Kidder, Jennings, and Shook, 1946, fig. 148,*d*.)

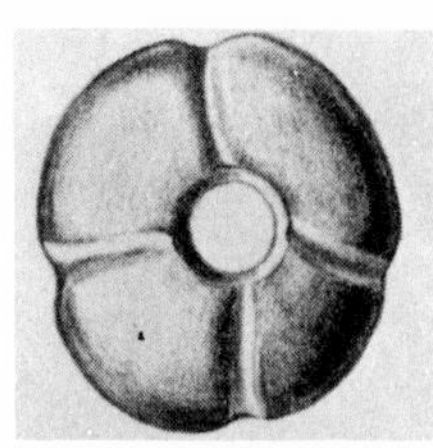

Fig. 2—GROOVED GLOBULAR JADE BEAD, ZACULEU. Early Classic tomb. Diameter 2.6 cm. (After Woodbury and Trik, 1953, fig. 283,*b*.)

a

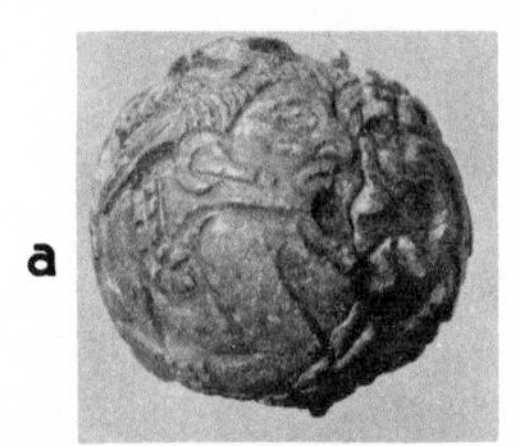

b

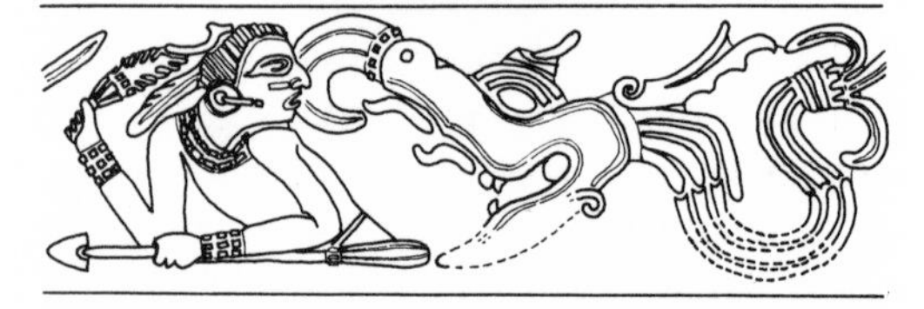

Fig. 3—CARVED GLOBULAR JADE BEAD, CHICHEN ITZA. Postclassic (Toltec) style. Diameter 4 cm. (*a*, courtesy, Peabody Museum, Harvard University; *b*, after Tozzer, 1957, fig. 564.)

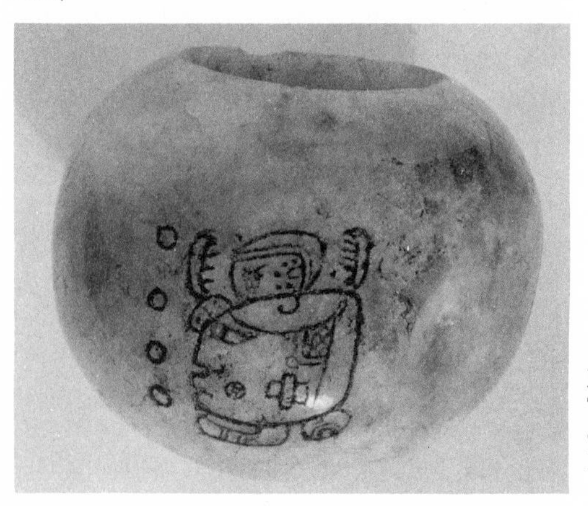

Fig. 4—INCISED GLOBULAR JADE BEAD, TONINA. Late Classic inscription. Diameter 5.5 cm. (Courtesy, American Museum of Natural History.)

Fig. 5—SPIRALLY GROOVED BARREL-SHAPED JADE BEAD, CHICHEN ITZA. Length 3.5 cm. (Courtesy, Peabody Museum, Harvard University.)

Fig. 6—BANDED RECTANGULAR JADE BEAD, PIEDRAS NEGRAS. Late Classic burial. Length 9.7 cm. (After W. R. Coe, 1959, fig. 47,*d*.)

Fig. 7—ELONGATED CARVED JADE BEAD, GUATEMALA HIGHLANDS. Early Classic style. Length 14.3 cm. (After Kidder, 1949a, fig. 2,*e*.)

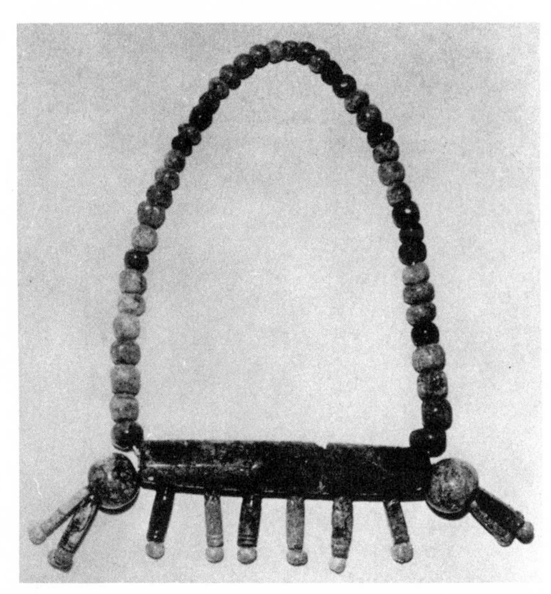

FIG. 8—JADE NECKLACE ASSEMBLED FROM SACRED CENOTE, CHICHEN ITZA. Globular beads, banded tubular beads, and bar ornament. Late Classic style. Length of bar 36.2 cm. (After Tozzer, 1957, fig. 624.)

able gradation of one type into another is known (Foshag, 1957, p. 23).[2]

FORMS

An adequate typology of jade objects has yet to be worked out for the Maya area as a whole.[3] A number of basic forms exist. These show important variations, especially in the ornamental objects. Beads, earplug assemblages, "buttons" and spangles, carved effigy pendants, and mosaics are relatively common, although the latter are rarely found intact. Dental and other inlays of jade occur widely, whereas nose buttons, finger rings, carved circlets, incised superficially worked jades, and incised jade pebbles have more limited distributions. Several forms of silhouette carvings exist, though none is common. Statuettes and unperforated plaques are rare. Low-relief or incised pendants, varying in shape and subject, attain the climax of Maya jade-working in the well-known seated-figure plaques. The following remarks can only suggest the nature and range of elaboration present within each category. Bracketed dates, subject to revision, indicate temporal range or concentration of the form if known, and sites where unusual forms occur are noted.

Beads (Preclassic–Postclassic) are normally undecorated and constitute the most common object of jade. A globular shape is frequent, and includes lobed, grooved, and other decorative examples (figs. 1, 2). Certain globular beads from the Sacred Cenote at Chichen Itza are carved with Toltec motifs (fig. 3). A large globular bead from Tonina bears an incised inscription (9.15.0.0.0?) (fig. 4). Spiral grooving occurs on cylindrical beads (tubular and barrel-shaped), and rectangular beads are often banded (figs. 5, 6). Several carved elongated beads or pectorals, of Early Classic date, depict standing human figures or heads (fig. 7). Beads assembled from the Sacred Cenote to form a necklace with this type of elongate bar ornament are shown in figure 8. Long tubular beads, unknown from the extensive excavations at Mayapan, may be especially characteristic of the Classic period.

Various parts of the demountable *earplug assemblage* (Preclassic – Late Classic or beyond) were made of jade. Following Kidder (1947), the nomenclature of this assemblage is given in figure 9. Flares are usually circular or irregularly rounded, although square examples are known. Type

[2] Additional references to the mineralogical aspects or occurrence of jade from the Maya area include Washington, 1922; Ball, 1941; Foshag, 1954; Foshag and Leslie, 1955; Lothrop, Foshag, and Mahler, 1957; Barbour, 1957.

[3] In addition to citations in the text, discussions of jade objects from the Maya area include Squier, 1870; Spinden, 1913; Gann, 1925b; Willard, 1926; Mason, 1927; Kelemen, 1939; Beyer, 1945; Satterthwaite, 1946; Lothrop, 1950b; Morley, 1956. Shook (1945) and Shook and Kidder (1952) are of interest for well-documented early occurrences of jade, Proskouriakoff (1962b) for Postclassic jade, and Sáenz (1956) for the quantities of excavated jade objects.

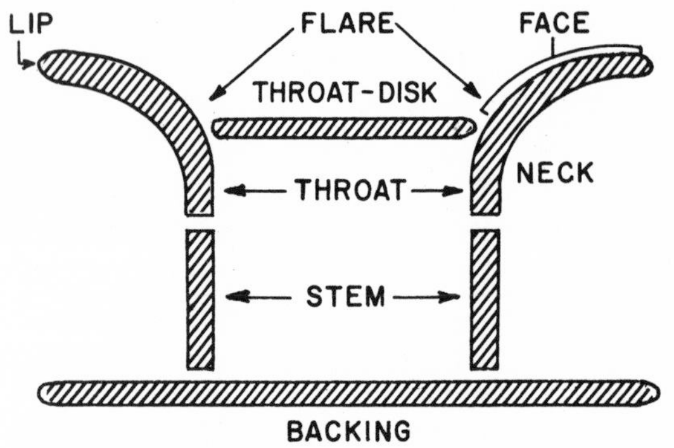

Fig. 9—NOMENCLATURE OF THE COMPOUND EARPLUG. (After Kidder, 1947, fig. 26.)

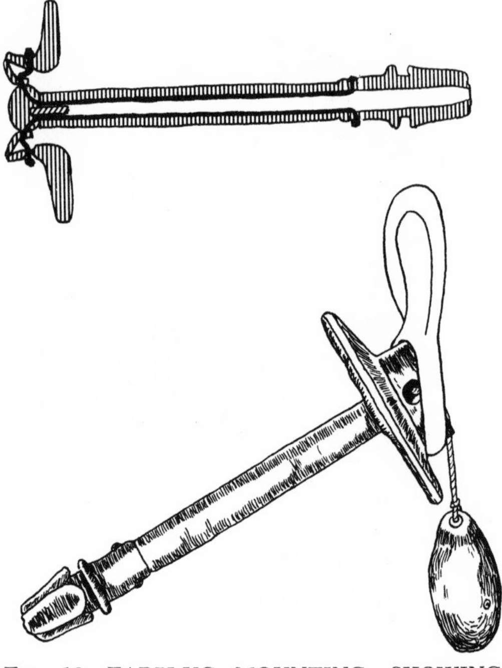

Fig. 10—EARPLUG MOUNTING, SHOWING USE OF LONG TUBULAR JADE BEAD, PALENQUE. Late Classic tomb. Length (assembled), approx. 13 cm. (After Ruz Lhuillier, 1955a, fig. 13,*a,c*.)

a b c d e

Fig. 12—JADE SPANGLES, FROM DIADEM, PALENQUE. Late Classic tomb. Maximum height 2.4 cm. (After Ruz Lhuillier, 1955a, fig. 11,*a–e*.)

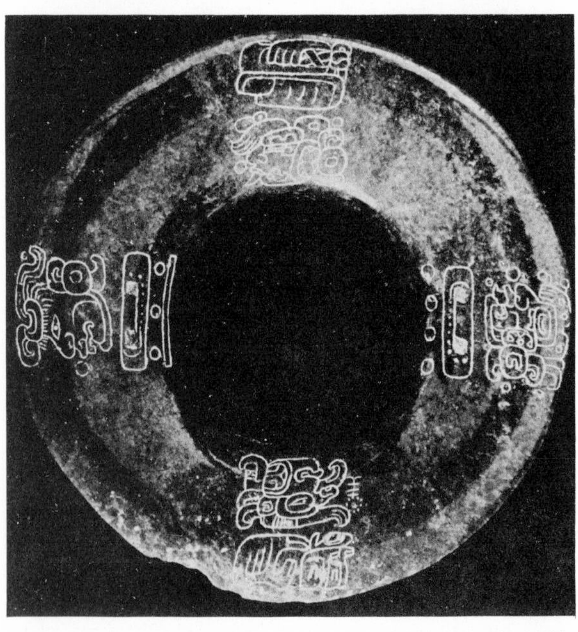

Fig. 11—LARGE INCISED JADE EARPLUG FLARE, POMONA, BRITISH HONDURAS. Early Classic tomb. Diameter 18 cm. (After Kidder and Ekholm, 1951, fig. 2.)

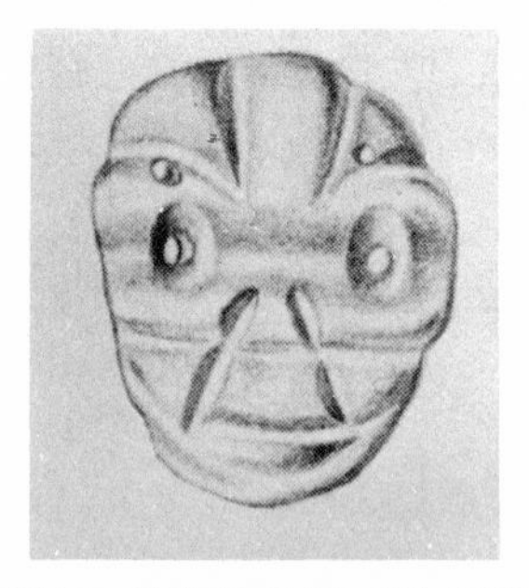

Fig. 13—HEAD PENDANT OF JADE, ZACULEU. Early Classic tomb. Height 4.9 cm. (After Woodbury and Trik, 1953, fig. 281,*b*.)

FIG. 14—HEAD PENDANT OF JADE, CHICHEN ITZA. Late Classic inscription. Height 8.5 cm. (After Proskouriakoff, 1944, fig. 1.)

A flares, with face curving gradually to a wide throat, and the less common Type B flares, in which a relatively wide face narrows abruptly into the neck, have been recognized (Kidder, Jennings, and Shook, 1946). The throat was often closed by a disc of jade or jade mosaic, or a long tubular jade bead might protrude from it. The latter arrangement is seen in figure 10, where the distal end of the plain jade tube is attached to a shorter, flower-shaped bead. Most flares are plain, but a few square examples have petal-like designs or other motifs in low relief. Flares from Pomona, British Honduras (fig. 11), Palenque, and Kaminaljuyu bear incised glyphs.

As a generic term, *spangles* refer to small jade ornaments perforated in a way that suggests they were attached or sewn, rather than suspended. Some are thin and flat, others button-like. Burial 5, Piedras Negras, illustrates the range of forms which may be present in a single headband, re-used or miniature earplug flares occurring along with countersunk, cup-shaped and dish-shaped ornaments of jade (W. R. Coe, 1959). Additional shapes appear in the diadem from the tomb beneath the Temple of the Inscriptions, Palenque (ca. 9.13.0.0.0) (fig. 12). Such decorations were probably used extensively, not being restricted to a particular part of the costume.

Effigy pendants carved in the round or semiround are usually small and of crude, sketchy workmanship (mostly Classic). The back may be hollowed or left flat. Human heads predominate. Features are often suggested by the minimal use of straight lines and drilled circles and pits (fig. 13), but a few outstanding examples of Late Classic lapidary art occur. Such pieces are a human head from the Sacred Cenote at Chichen Itza, with incised hieroglyphic inscription referable to 9.13.7.13.1 on the back (fig. 14), and a grotesque "Chac" of unknown provenience (fig. 15). Crude full-figure pendants also appear in the semiround (fig. 16). A unique seated figure with large grotesque head, from the Inscriptions tomb at Palenque, exhibits monumental qualities (fig. 17).

The jade in *mosaics* (Preclassic? – Postclassic) is usually of fine quality. The thin plates, often less than 1 mm. in thickness, are highly polished on the upper face. Backing materials include shell, potsherd discs, stucco, possibly pyrites, and undoubtedly wood. Jade mosaic was applied as

Fig. 15—HEAD PENDANT OF JADE. Late Classic style. Height 8.3 cm. (Courtesy, American Museum of Natural History.)

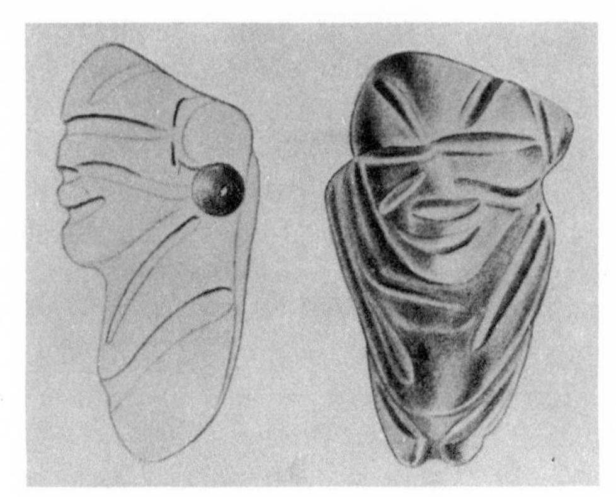

Fig. 16—FULL-FIGURE PENDANT OF JADE, ZACULEU. Early Classic tomb. Height 14.8 cm. (After Woodbury and Trik, 1953, fig. 281,*a*.)

Fig. 17—FULL-FIGURE PENDANT OF JADE, PALENQUE. Late Classic tomb. Height 9 cm. (Courtesy, Instituto Nacional de Antropología e Historia, Mexico.)

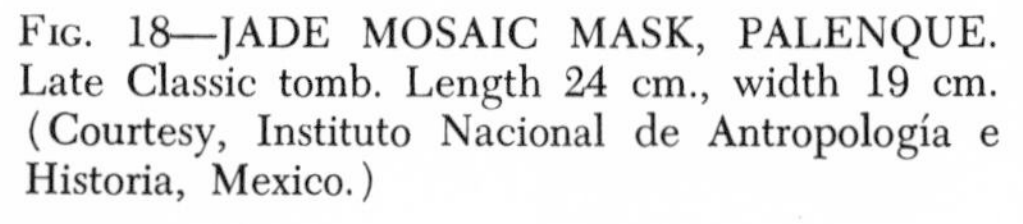

Fig. 18—JADE MOSAIC MASK, PALENQUE. Late Classic tomb. Length 24 cm., width 19 cm. (Courtesy, Instituto Nacional de Antropología e Historia, Mexico.)

Fig. 19—MOSAIC FIGURINE HEAD, TIKAL. Early Classic tomb. Height 4 cm., width 4.5 cm. (Courtesy, University Museum, University of Pennsylvania.)

Fig. 20—JADE-INLAID JAGUAR THRONE, CHICHEN ITZA. Postclassic structure. Length 84 cm., height 68 cm. (After Kelemen, 1943, pl. 92,*b*.)

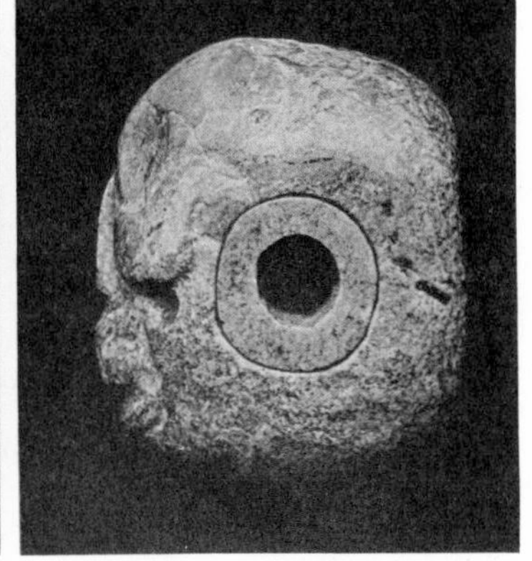

Fig. 21—JADE DEATH'S-HEAD WITH CAREFULLY FITTED JADE PLUGS, NEBAJ. Early Classic tomb. Height 3.5 cm. (After A. L. Smith and Kidder, 1951, fig. 56.)

Fig. 22—JADE NOSE BUTTON, NEBAJ. Early Classic tomb. Length 2.5 cm. (After A. L. Smith and Kidder, 1951, fig. 58,*b*.)

Fig. 23—CARVED JADE FINGER RING, PALENQUE. Late Classic tomb. Diameter (back to nose) 4.4 cm. (Courtesy, Instituto Nacional de Antropología e Historia, Mexico.)

Fig. 24—JADE CIRCLET, CHICHEN ITZA. Postclassic (Toltec) style. Diameter (as reconstructed) 12.5 cm. (Courtesy, Peabody Museum, Harvard University.)

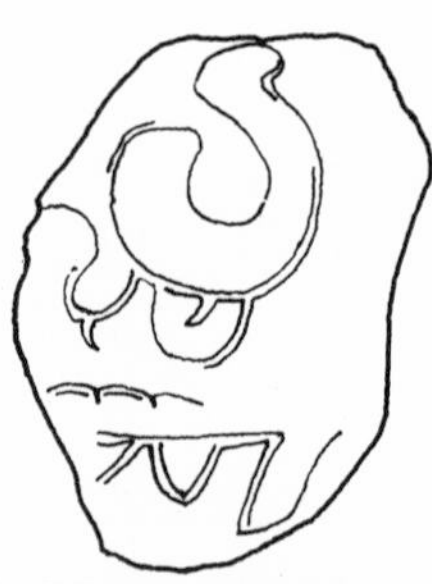

Fig. 25—INCISED JADE, PIEDRAS NEGRAS. Late Classic cache. Height 5 cm. (After W. R. Coe, 1959, fig. 46,*r*.)

Fig. 26—INCISED JADE PEBBLE, COPAN. Classic cache. Height 3.5 cm. (Courtesy, Peabody Museum, Harvard University.)

Fig. 27—PARROT-PROFILE BEAD OR PENDANT, ZACULEU. Early Classic tomb. Height 2.5 cm. (After Woodbury and Trik, 1953, fig. 280,*l*.)

Fig. 28—TWO-SIDED PLAQUE, CHICHEN ITZA. Late Classic style. Height 9 cm. (Courtesy, Peabody Museum, Harvard University.)

Fig. 29—SILHOUETTE JADE CARVING. Late Classic style. Width 8 cm. (After Kelemen, 1943, pl. 239,*f*.)

minor decoration to many objects, occurring frequently in the earplug assemblages. Its most spectacular use, however, was in masks. The life-size mask from the Inscriptions tomb at Palenque (fig. 18) is composed of some 200 pieces of jade and has eyes of shell with irises of obsidian. The miniature Early Classic head from Tikal (fig. 19) was found almost intact, accompanied by mosaic elements suggesting that it had been attached to a body. In addition to plates of dark green jade, this colorful object includes elements of red and yellow shell. Eyes are of white shell, black paint being used to indicate the pupils.

Apart from its use in mosaics, *jade inlay* was set with an adhesive into human teeth, shell and stone. A spectacular example of the latter is the Postclassic red-painted jaguar throne at Chichen Itza, on which jade discs represent the spots and eyes of the animal (fig. 20). In some instances, jade plugs were carefully fashioned to fit into a larger jade object of corresponding color. This was sometimes done to hide perforations in a reworked jade. A different purpose is evident in figure 21, a carved jade death's-head from Nebaj. Transversely perforated plugs of jade fit perfectly into the head at the region of the ears, being so precisely shaped that they can be pinned in place through corresponding holes in the cheeks. The virtuosity of the Early Classic lapidary is well attested to in this remarkable piece.

Certain jade objects have limited distributions. Crescent-shaped *nose buttons* appear at Nebaj (fig. 22) (Early Classic), possibly Kaminaljuyu (Early Classic), and, more frequently, Chichen Itza. At the latter site, they are related to the Toltec by Tozzer (1957, p. 155). *Finger rings* (Late Classic) form an unusual part of the lavish jade accoutrements in the Inscriptions tomb at Palenque. The 10 rings include plain and grooved examples, one of them carved to depict a crouching human (fig. 23). *Circlets* of jade are known only from Chichen Itza. Human sacrifice is portrayed, as well as the apparent subjugation of the Maya by Toltec conquerors (fig. 24). *In-*

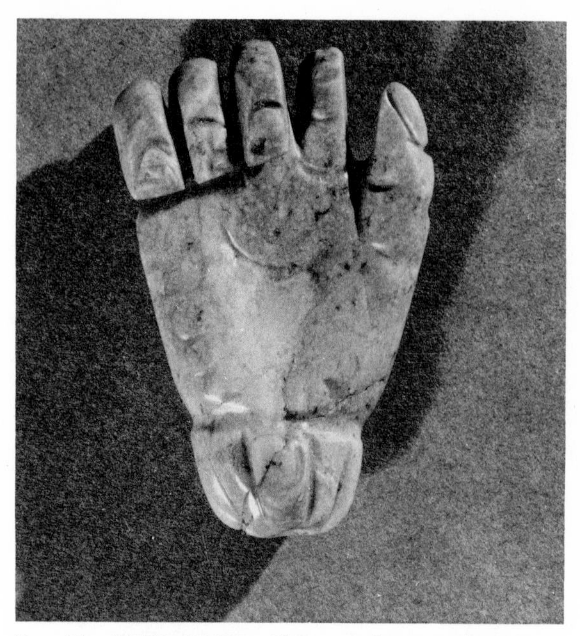

FIG. 30—JADE HAND. Classic style. Length 6.5 cm. (Courtesy, American Museum of Natural History.)

FIG. 32—UNPERFORATED JADE PLAQUE, COPAN. Classic cache. Height 13.9 cm. (Courtesy, Peabody Museum, Harvard University.)

FIG. 31—JADE STATUETTE, COPAN. Classic style. Height 19.5 cm. (After Kelemen, 1943, pl. 242,*a*.)

FIG. 33—UNPERFORATED JADE PLAQUE, COPAN. Classic cache. Height 16.6 cm. (Courtesy, Peabody Museum, Harvard University.)

FIG. 34—STANDING FRONTAL-FIGURE JADE PENDANT, SAN SALVADOR. Early Classic style. Height 11 cm. (After Kelemen, 1943, pl. 236,*d*.)

cised, superficially worked bits of jade occur in caches at Piedras Negras (Classic, beginning prior to 9.12.5.0.0). Surfaces are unpolished, and incising is often scratchy. Full figures, profile heads of deities, and plaited bands appear among the designs on these unique objects (fig. 25). A group of more deeply *incised pebbles* from Copan (fig. 26) shows human and animal subjects, including "kneeling, hunched-up men, with very large heads" (Longyear, 1952, p. 107) ("Full Classic"?).

Jade *silhouette carvings* take several forms. The most distinctive of these employ openwork, achieved through string-sawing. This is seen in the Early Classic *parrot-profile beads or pendants* from Zaculeu (fig. 27) and Kaminaljuyu. The treatment reappears in ornate *two-sided plaques* (Early and especially Late Classic), which Easby (1961) has identified as diadem or headdress ornaments. Grotesque heads are carved on both sides of these plaques (fig. 28), found at Nebaj, Tonina, Palenque, and Chichen Itza. Miscellaneous carvings, though not done in the openwork technique, maintain the silhouette quality. Figure 29 shows one of a small number of Early and Late Classic jades which combine a profile head and other object, such as grotesque face or hand, into a composite representation. The hand, in unelaborated form, may also have a silhouette-like treatment (fig. 30).

Large unperforated figurines or *statuettes* are known from Copan (fig. 31) ("Full Classic"). Stylistically related to the Copan statuettes are *unperforated jade plaques*, incised or decorated in low relief, which occur at the same site (fig. 32). A profile serpent head and involved composition distinguish one of these plaques (fig. 33).

Low-relief pendants of jade comprise several major categories. The *standing frontal figure pendant* (Early and Late Classic) is sometimes shown with hands brought stiffly together over the chest (figs. 34, 35). A second group is *frontal face pendants* (Early Classic – Postclassic?), often having prominent circular earplugs, a semicircular element above the head, and scrolls or necklace below the chin (figs. 36, 37). The head and jaw of a jaguar-like monster (fig. 38) or elaborate scrollwork (figs. 39, 40) serves to enclose the face in related designs. Less commonly, the face is flanked by additional profile heads (fig. 41). Late Classic *seated frontal figure pendants* ("plaques") form a third group (fig. 42). These jades are proportionately wide, as plumes or scrollwork in the headdress extend far to each side. A frame is sometimes present. This form of pendant has a limited occurrence with examples of known provenience from Nebaj, Palenque, and Chichen Itza. Unusually elaborate compositions occur in a fourth group, *seated figure pendants with head turned in profile* (mostly Late Classic). Features confined to this group or particularly characteristic of it are well seen in the famed Nebaj Plaque (fig. 43) and include framing bands

FIG. 35—STANDING FRONTAL-FIGURE JADE PENDANT, CHICHEN ITZA. Late Classic style. Height 11 cm. (Courtesy, Peabody Museum, Harvard University.)

FIG. 36—FRONTAL-FACE JADE PENDANT, COPAN. Late Classic cache. Height 5.1 cm. (Courtesy, American Museum of Natural History.)

FIG. 37—FRONTAL-FACE JADE PENDANT, GUATEMALA HIGHLANDS. Late Classic style. Width 7.1 cm. (After Kidder, 1949a, fig. 2,*a*.)

FIG. 38—FRONTAL-FACE JADE PENDANT. Classic style. Height 8.7 cm. (Courtesy, Metropolitan Museum, Bishop Jade Coll.)

FIG. 39—FRONTAL-FACE JADE PENDANT, TONINA. Late Classic style. Height 6.8 cm. (Courtesy, American Museum of Natural History.)

FIG. 40—FRONTAL-FACE JADE CARVING, CHICHEN ITZA. Postclassic style. Height 11 cm. (Courtesy, Peabody Museum, Harvard University.)

Fig. 41—FRONTAL-FACE BAR PENDANT OF JADE, GUATEMALA HIGHLANDS. Early Classic style. Length 17.6 cm. (After Kidder, 1949a, fig. 1,*b*.)

of ornate scrollwork, thrones, and subsidiary dwarflike figures. Hierarchal aspects are pronounced. A number of these pendants were found in the Sacred Cenote (fig. 44 and, atypical for its Toltec style and subject, fig. 45). Other known occurrences in the Maya area are Uxmal and Tonina. The rare *incised pendants* are exemplified by the Leyden Plate (fig. 46) with its elaborately costumed standing profile figure and Baktun 8 inscription.

Techniques of Manufacture

Techniques used in Maya jadeworking have been examined in greatest detail by Kidder (Kidder, Jennings, and Shook, 1946, pp. 118–24) and Foshag (1957, pp. 44–57). Abrasives probably consisted of crushed jade and quartz sand. These have been found together in a grave at Kaminaljuyu, apparently placed in a perishable container (Kidder, Jennings, and Shook, 1946, p. 120). Tools, often of chloromelanite, probably included hammerstones; grinding stones; rasps; saws of hardwood or bamboo; cords for string-sawing; solid drills, which Foshag believes were of chloromelanite; tubular drills made of bamboo, reed, or bird bone; reamers; gravers; and—for polishing—jade celts, hard wood, or bamboo (Foshag, 1957, pls. 1, 2,*l*). *Pecking* was apparently confined to jade of lesser quality, so as not to deface the preferred emerald-green stones. *Grinding* was employed where minor modifications were necessary but seemingly was little used otherwise. *Rasping* was practiced in manufacturing mosaic plates. *Sawing* with a

Fig. 42—SEATED-FRONTAL-FIGURE JADE PENDANT. Late Classic style. Height 8 cm. (After Kelemen, 1943, pl. 238,*c*.)

Fig. 43—SEATED-FIGURE JADE PENDANT WITH HEAD TURNED IN PROFILE, NEBAJ. Late Classic cache. Width 14.5 cm. (After A. L. Smith and Kidder, 1951, fig. 59,*b*.)

rigid implement served to cut large pieces of jade into slabs and to preform various objects. Except in thin pieces, sawing was usually done from both sides. The pieces were then broken apart, leaving the rough remains of the septum between the cuts. *String-sawing* produced slits and openwork carving (figs. 27, 28). The string was often passed through a drilled hole to commence

Fig. 44—SEATED-FIGURE JADE PENDANT WITH HEAD TURNED IN PROFILE, CHICHEN ITZA. Late Classic style. Width 12.5 cm. (After Kelemen, 1943, pl. 240,*f*.)

Fig. 45—SEATED-FIGURE JADE CARVING WITH HEAD TURNED IN PROFILE, CHICHEN ITZA. Post-classic (Toltec) style. Height 9.2 cm. (Courtesy, Peabody Museum, Harvard University.)

the operation. *Drilling* was accomplished with solid and tubular tools. The former were employed for perforating beads and for making small, cuplike depressions. Hollow drills removed large cores in the manufacture of earplug flares. Smaller tubular drills cut circles or, if tilted, arcs. The use of the tubular drill for these effects is seen in the earplugs, chin, eyes, and other features on many frontal-face pendants (figs. 37, 39). Tubular drilling also came to be used to achieve relief as part of the general carving process. Due to the hardness of jade, Kidder (Kidder, Jennings, and Shook, 1946, p. 123) believes that a bow-drill or similar device must have been required. Very small jades were sometimes worked from one side only, though for the most part pieces were drilled biconically. *Reaming* was a means of enlarging drilled holes and was used extensively in earplug flares. *Deep cutting or grooving*, the basis of Maya relief carving, may have been done with hard stone gravers or hardwood tools and abrasives. Finer *incising* was apparently accomplished with jade, quartz, or flint tools. Although incising was of limited occurrence, glyphic inscriptions on jade were in this technique (figs. 4, 11, 14, 46). Foshag (1957, p. 56) has shown that *polishing* was accomplished with jade tools, or possibly hardwood or bamboo plus an abrasive, for unlike modern lap-polished objects the intergrain depressions are rough. Polishing to bring out the lustrous quality of the jade was widely employed, although the back of many objects was left in a smooth but dull state.

Temporal Styles

Time distinctions in Maya jadeworking are better understood than regional differences. On the basis of stratified tomb material at Nebaj, Kidder (1949a; A. L. Smith and Kidder, 1951) was able to demonstrate the basic differences between Early and Late Classic Maya jade carving. Proskouriakoff (1944) has discussed corresponding stylistic features in jadework and monumental Maya sculpture. Stylistic insights have been further developed through Easby's (1961) searching comparative study of the Squier Collection of jades from Ocosingo (Tonina).

Early Classic jade carving is executed in soft low relief. Elements are gently and evenly rounded, little attempt being made

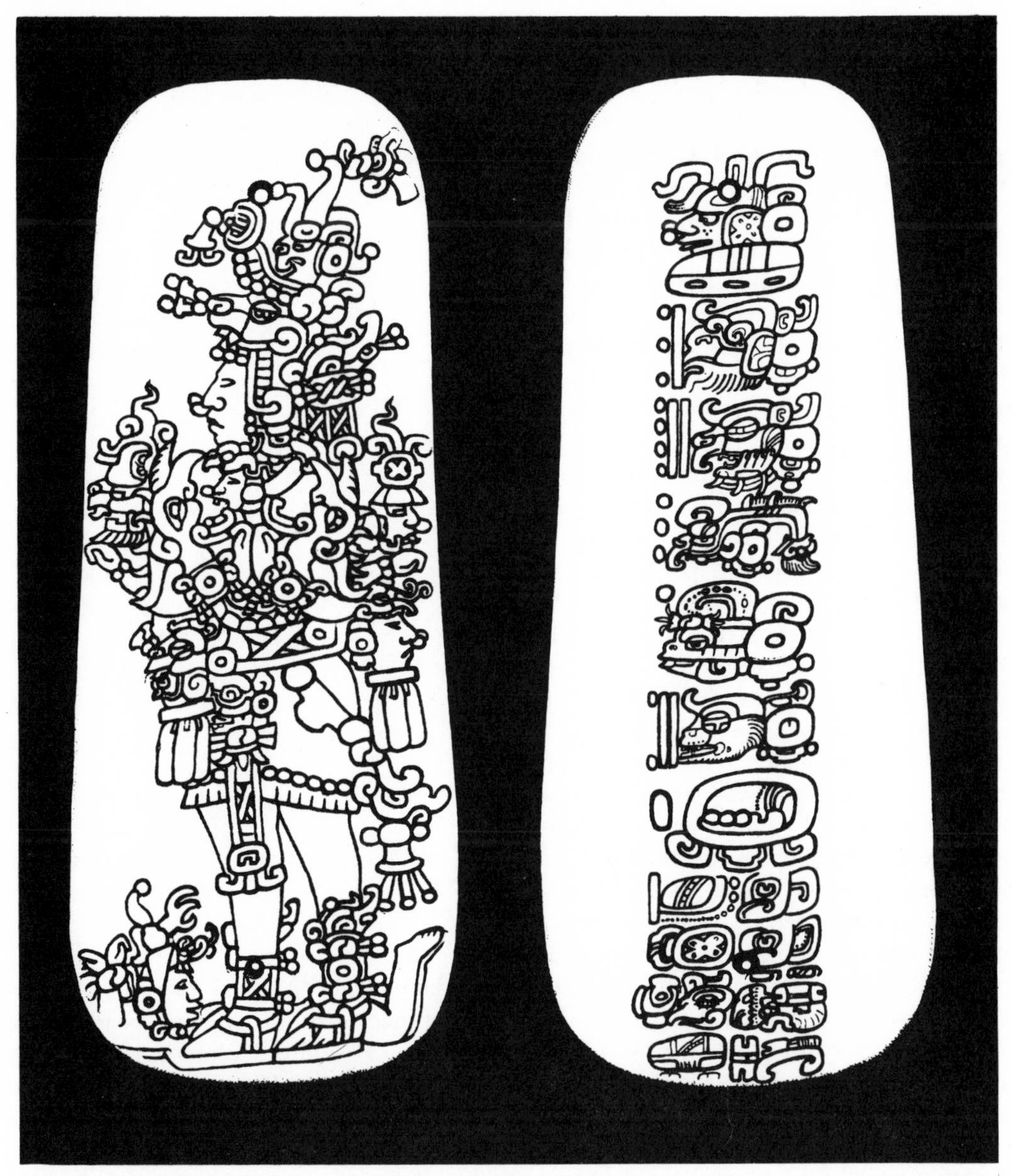

Fig. 46—LEYDEN PLAQUE, PUERTO BARRIOS, GUATEMALA. Early Classic inscription. Height 21.6 cm. (After W. R. Coe *in* Shook, 1960, p. 34.)

to emphasize portions of the design by varying the depth, detail or sharpness (figs. 7, 34, 41). Polishing occurs equally on low and raised surfaces. Early Classic lapidaries tended to preserve the original outline of the stone and follow the prized green layer, at the expense of an even surface in the finished piece. Carved jades are comparatively thick with smooth, rounded backs. Designs sometimes extend from the front of the object slightly onto the top, bottom and sides. The head and torso are disproportionately large in the Early Classic human figure (fig. 7). The nose is T-shaped, its lines turning outward to form eyebrows or the tops of the eyes (figs. 7, 34). The mouth is a horizontal bar, sometimes slightly depressed at the corners; a single line within it differentiates the lips (figs. 34, 41).

In contrast, Late Classic jades tend to be carved in sharp, crisp relief. Concentrically drilled earplugs are characteristic. The design may appear in several planes. Important features are brought out by higher relief and deep vertical cutting, with subsidiary elements more gently rounded. Raised parts of the designs are sometimes more highly polished than the low areas. In the frequently ornate compositions, contrasting lines and masses are achieved by such techniques, directing and focusing attention (figs. 15, 28, 37, 39, 42, 43). The human figure shows changes from Early Classic norms. In full-face portrayals the mouth droops in a semicircular arc, achieved by the use of the tubular drill. The long nose widens toward the base. The lines of the nose may arch at the top to suggest eyebrows, but they no longer enter into the formation of the eye itself. The eye is characteristically straight across the top and curved or angular at the bottom (fig. 37). Profile representations have the prominent hooked nose, drooping lower lip, almond-shaped eye, and receding forehead (fig. 43) typical of Classic monumental sculpture. Poses of the human figure show greater variety than in the Early Classic. Cross-legged figures are occasionally seated in front view but with heads turned in profile. Arms show greater freedom, one hand often resting on the leg for support while the other is held before the chest in a stylized gesture (figs. 42, 43). The leaning posture in figure 43 combines with the swirl of plumage and undulating scrollwork to give a dynamic composition that is lacking in Early Classic portrayals. The same sense of motion is achieved by the rhythmic play of the scrolls in the Tonina face pendant (fig. 39).

Additional features help to distinguish Early and Late Classic carvings. "Petalled" necklaces (fig. 39), scrolls (fig. 37), or bar pendants (fig. 42) tend to replace close-fitting necklaces of circular beads (figs. 34, 36). Headdress plumes are a Late Classic diagnostic (figs. 42, 43). Elongated Early Classic beads are perforated longitudinally, the carved human figure probably being worn in a horizontal position (fig. 7). In general, Late Classic pendants were perforated along the axis which is horizontal in respect to the carved figure. It should be stressed that many of the temporal distinctions can be equated with Early and Late Classic periods in only a general way; it is not known to what extent these changes are internally synchronous or are correlated with developments in other media such as monumental sculpture or ceramics.

FIG. 47—TUXTLA STATUETTE, SAN ANDRES TUXTLA, VERACRUZ. Height 15 cm. (After Morley, 1956, pl. 14,*a*.)

Little can be said about Preclassic and Postclassic Maya styles of jadeworking. A number of jade and other greenstone carvings may be of Preclassic date but are best related to the Olmec tradition. Whatever its origin and chronological position, the Tuxtla Statuette (fig. 47) lies outside the Maya style. Of the many jade pieces dredged from the Sacred Cenote at Chichen Itza, the great majority have affiliations with Late Classic materials. Some, however, show unmistakable Toltec motifs and rendition (figs. 3, 24, 45). Plumed or disc-incrusted serpents, atlatl, warrior with head turned behind, "bird" or "butterfly" pectoral, "celestial eye" skirt, and scenes of capture or sacrifice appear in the Toltec manner so familiar on sculptures and gold discs from Chichen Itza (Tozzer, 1957; Lothrop, 1952). The face in a circular field surrounded on all sides by tightly coiled scrolls is also non-Mayan in concept (fig. 40). The sharply cut tapering curvilinear masses, so often found on terminal Classic jades, are absent. The paucity and simplification of still later material make impossible an adequate definition of a Late Postclassic style of jadecarving.

STYLISTIC RELATIONSHIPS

Regional schools of jadeworking are little understood, for jades, small and highly valued, might be traded far from their points of manufacture. Nevertheless, possible relationships in style or motif, among the jades or with other media, merit attention.

Tooth-shaped jade pendants are known in Preclassic and Early Classic horizons at Kaminaljuyu, Finca Arizona, and Zaculeu (fig. 48). Similar forms appear in shell from Maya sites, and jade counterparts exist in the Olmec area (Drucker, 1952a, pl. 57).

The Leyden Plate (fig. 46), bearing an incised 8.14.3.1.12 inscription, relates stylistically to stela sculpture. Close relationships to Tikal are indicated (Morley and Morley, 1938; Shook, 1960, p. 35). Proskouriakoff (1950, p. 105), while graphing the Leyden Plate at 9.3.0.0.0, feels that the position of the feet, one behind the other, is a confirmation of its Baktun 8 origin. Other jade pendants with incised glyphs, in cartouches, have been attributed to early times (Kelemen, 1943, pl. 235,*b*, p. 289; Lothrop, Foshag, and Mahler, 1957, pl. 68).

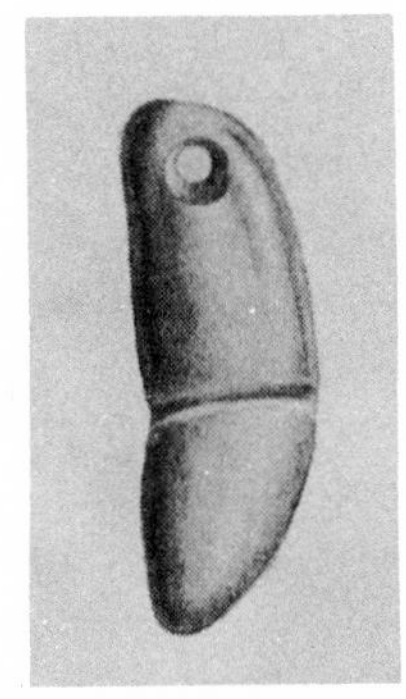

FIG. 48—TOOTH-SHAPED JADE PENDANT, ZACULEU. Early Classic tomb. Height 3.7 cm. (After Woodbury and Trik, 1953, fig. 282*e*.)

Carvings at Copan may pertain to a regional Early Classic school, overlap the Early and Late Classic periods, or form a later, somewhat isolated group with retention of Early Classic features. A triangular structure of the face exists in figure 36, lines extending from the root of the nose to the corners of the mouth. This contrasts with the rectangular facial features characterizing the traditional Early Classic style (figs. 7, 34, 41), as well as the flaccid face of later times (figs. 37, 39). The triangular composition within the face occurs on many crude Early Classic effigy jades from Zaculeu (fig. 13, and Woodbury and Trik, 1953, fig. 281), whereas the Copan jade, cached below Stela 3, has a minimal date of 9.11.0.0.0. T-shaped nose and bar mouth appear on several Copan jades (fig. 32), yet these rectangular features are strongly modified or absent in closely comparable jades from the site (fig. 31). Early Classic jade figures often stand with arms placed horizontally across the body, hands close together (fig. 34). A similar position of arms and hands occurs on various stelae and the Leyden Plate (fig. 46), but arms are upraised holding a ceremonial bar (Proskouriakoff, 1950, figs. 7, 8 [I-A1, I-A3, I-D1, I-E1]). Copan jades, unlike the Early Classic norm, usually show the arms upraised and hands far apart (figs. 31, 32). With the addition of the ceremonial bar, the identical arm-and-separated-hand position was long a favored motif on Late Classic stelae at Copan (Proskouriakoff, 1950, figs. 49, 50). This could be taken as the retention of a once more widely spread trait at Copan, where it was perpetuated on both stelae and locally carved jades. Incised pebbles, statuettes, and unperforated plaques also point to the existence of a Copan school of jadeworking.

It has been traditional to look to the Usumacinta for centers of the jadeworking industry, Proskouriakoff combining impressive stylistic and epigraphic data to assign the manufacture of one of the Cenote jades (fig. 14) to Piedras Negras, around 9.14.0.0.0 (Proskouriakoff, 1944; A. L. Smith and Kidder, 1951, p. 36; J. E. S. Thompson, 1950, p. 27). Remarkable correspondences exist between figure 14 and an object sculptured on Stela 10, Piedras Negras (9.15.10.0.0), as well as between the poses in figure 43 and on Lintel 7, Piedras Negras (9.12.0.0.0?), Stela 12, Piedras Negras (9.18.5.0.0?), and Sculptured Stone 1, Bonampak (9.12.0.0.0?). Nevertheless, W. R. Coe (1959, pp. 47, 53) has noted that similar jade objects have not been found archaeologically at Piedras Negras, leading him to doubt that the site was an influential jade-producing center. Hastily incised jades from Piedras Negras caches (fig. 25), while resembling votive offerings of incised obsidians from Tikal and Uaxactun, provide evidence that raw jade was worked at least to this extent locally. Except perhaps for Burial 5, rich tombs have not been found at Piedras Negras, and the discovery of such tombs might yet reveal elaborate jade pieces in the style of figures 14 and 43.

Differences exist in the type of headdress shown on seated frontal-figure pendants and seated figures with head turned in profile (figs. 42, 43). The former depicts a jaguar-like creature, which with varying degrees of conventionalization appears on Maya jades from earliest times (figs. 14, 35, 38, 46). Particularly in figure 35, similarities to many Piedras Negras sculptures, such as Stelae 7, 26, 31 (9.9.15.0.0? – 9.14.-10.0.0), are once again striking. Departing sharply from the tradition of a jaguar helmet which may encase the head, a serpentine head, characterized by long nose rather than arching mouth, is worn on most of the profile jade plaques (fig. 43). It, too, has its counterparts on the monuments.

Even the seated profile-figure pendant, which was probably manufactured for a relatively short period of time, was subject to different technico-stylistic approaches. Figure 43 is crisply carved, participating in a general trend of Late Classic development (compare fig. 42). On the other hand, figure 44, from the Sacred Cenote at Chichen Itza, has lines so soft and rounded as to resemble modeling. Many of the Cenote jades, which otherwise are in the Late Classic tradition, have this feature. The homogeneity of these carvings is underscored by the fact that they occur frequently in a speckled, opaque stone.

The possibility has been suggested of jadeworking schools at Copan, Piedras Negras, and Chichen Itza, where local lapidaries, all participating in fundamentally similar patterns, varied their productions noticeably. Detailed analysis would probably reveal important distinctions in other localities. This is not to deny the existence of far-flung trade in luxury items of jade but to direct attention to the more localized output that may sometimes loom larger in the assemblages from a particular site. Toltec motifs carved on jades indicate that

Chichen Itza was a place of jadeworking in the Early Postclassic period (finished jade pieces may have been imported and recarved), but it is not known if a region as distant from the source of the raw material as northern Yucatan would have worked its own jades at other, less prosperous times.

Presumed Functions

Some idea of the way in which the Maya regarded jade may be obtained from scattered hints in the documentary sources, broad comparisons with central Mexico, and detailed epigraphic studies (Tozzer, 1941a; J. E. S. Thompson, 1950). On such bases, jade can be assumed to have been considered a sacred substance, associated primarily with water and having a chain of secondary symbolic attributes. Among these were the more mundane concepts of preciousness and wealth. Jade beads were apparently used as a form of money and were sometimes placed in the mouth of the dead. Teeth of the living might be inlaid with jade. Mostly, however, the material was used for jewelry or other costume accessories; its primary role in utilitarian objects may, indeed, have been as tools hard enough to work other jade into ornaments (Foshag, 1957). Jade was probably not confined exclusively to the aristocracy (Willey, 1956b, p. 779), but the great quantities of jade accompanying important burials (Ruz Lhuillier, 1955a) suggest that it was concentrated heavily in the hands of an elite class.

Certain archaeological indications exist that jade had a direct religious import. Worked jades were ceremonially broken or burned with copal as part of the Cenote cult (Tozzer, 1957). Votive offerings of jade objects are known from a number of Maya sites. Carved jades sometimes occur in substela caches (Stromsvik, 1942b). Unworked jade pebbles and bits of crystal in small caches suggest that the material itself had a magical or religious significance. On the other hand, jade carvings of grotesque anthropomorphic figures which can with confidence be identified as supernaturals are extremely rare (figs. 15, 17, 28)—less common, as a matter of fact, than one might suppose from the frequent representation of such objects as accoutrements adorning the principal figure in monumental Maya sculpture.

Summary

To judge from the archaeological record, a distinctively Maya tradition of jadecarving was elaborated only in Classic times. Remains from Preclassic horizons which can be related stylistically to this tradition are not numerous, although a number of carvings with Olmecoid features suggest the early importance of jade and jadelike stones. The Tuxtla Statuette, controversial as it may be, is another possible indication of the importance of jade in the Maya background. On the other hand, the beautifully incised Leyden Plate shows affiliations with monumental art, and it is possible that Maya lapidary techniques of jadecarving had not been developed at this early time. Following the Classic period, a number of Toltec artistic concepts are set forth in jade—a sharp break in the tradition—and Maya jadeworking seems to have suffered a severe decline in the centuries prior to the Spanish conquest. References ascribable to jade in the 16th-century accounts are limited (Tozzer, 1941a), in striking contrast to the rich documentation surrounding the material in central Mexico (Foshag, 1957).

Jades are fairly abundant in the highlands, close to their presumed natural source, and excavated materials from Kaminaljuyu, Zaculeu, and especially Nebaj have provided our best knowledge of stylistic change in Classic Maya jadeworking. Tonina, also in the uplands, is the source of an imposing jade collection. With important exceptions, however, jade is poorly represented in the north. Extensive digging at Uaxactun and Mayapan, for example, yielded only limited quantities. On the other hand, spectacular tombs at Palenque and Tikal were richly stocked with jade ornaments, and dredging in the Sacred Cenote at Chichen Itza—a place of pilgrimage and sacrifice—produced the largest collection of this material known from the Maya area. Due mostly to differences in time but also to regional styles, each of the large collections has its individual stamp. Recognition of such distinctions, however, should not obscure the essential unity of Maya jadeworking or, for that matter, the close resemblances which extend even beyond the Maya area, to the relatively late jade carvings of Oaxaca.

REFERENCES

Ball, 1941
Barbour, 1957
Beyer, 1945
Coe, W. R., 1959
Drucker, 1952a
Easby, 1961
Foshag, 1954, 1957
—— and Leslie, 1955
Gann, 1925b
Kelemen, 1939, 1943
Kidder, 1947, 1949a
—— and Ekholm, 1951
——, Jennings, and Shook, 1946
Longyear, 1952
Lothrop, 1950b, 1952
——, Foshag, and Mahler, 1957
Mason, J. A., 1927
Morley, 1956
—— and Morley, 1938
Proskouriakoff, 1944, 1950, 1962b
Ruz L., 1955a
Sáenz, 1956
Satterthwaite, 1946
Shook, 1945, 1960
—— and Kidder, 1952
Smith, A. L., and Kidder, 1951
Spinden, 1913
Squier, 1870
Stromsvik, 1942b
Thompson, J. E. S., 1950
Tozzer, 1941a, 1957
Washington, 1922
Willard, 1926
Willey, 1956b
Woodbury and Trik, 1953

22. Garments and Textiles of the Maya Lowlands

JOY MAHLER

Doubts have been expressed that the textile skill of the Mexican-Mayan areas attained the complexity and refinements of preconquest Peru. Yet, if the surviving textiles were as few as in Mesoamerica, and if we judged solely on their representation in other media, surely we would underestimate their variety, especially in technique and use of color.

Although dependent almost entirely on sculpture, figurines, painted pottery, murals, and codices for our knowledge of clothing and textile designs, we do, in fact, have sufficient actual textile fragments to support a claim for considerable technical ability, at least, through the evidence of the Sacred Cenote in Chichen Itza and some other scattered remains. The relationship between representations of textiles and actual samples of material, however, is difficult to demonstrate with any certainty. This is partly due to the fact that a large percentage of published illustrations are worthless for the study of detail. Also, certain local styles, especially at Copan and Quirigua, often so overburden the human figure with ornamental details that it is virtually impossible to detect any garments.[1] Hence our data are limited to the recognizable vestments.

In a discussion of garments, several facts must be considered. First, a loincloth is so basic to men's clothing that it probably was always worn, although not necessarily visible in the art styles. Second, from the earliest times, there is a tremendous preoccupation with headdresses. Such is the variety that an attempt to classify them might amount to a description of each one individually. Third, the activity and rank of the personages portrayed influence the type of garment worn. A warrior in battle can scarcely be expected to fight with 60 lbs. of beads around his neck and a full-length

[1] The problem of identifying specific techniques of weaving on nontextile material is seriously limiting for several obvious reasons. First, there often exists confusion or doubt as to the weaving method of an actual fabric, e.g. brocade vs. embroidery. Second, identical designs may be reproduced in more than one technique, e.g. warp float and weft float. Third, the plastic or representative arts may be freed of some restrictions inherent in weaving and be expressed as impressions or selection of design or technique.

FIG. 1—YAXCHILAN, LINTEL 26. Reading 9.14.15.0.0. (After Spinden, 1957b.)

ceremonial robe. Fourth, the depiction of Mexicans with two-fingered, fur-covered spearthrowers and circular back-shields appears at an early date (9.0.10.0.0 on Stela 31 at Tikal). A truly comprehensive discussion of garments and textiles therefore covers far more than space permits in this article.

PRECLASSIC PERIOD

Information about costumes during the Preclassic period comes only from pottery figurines which usually are broken and incomplete (Ricketson and Ricketson, 1937, pls. 74, 75). Normally no clothing at all is represented, but there are a few examples of very short kilts, a type of garment worn by the Maya up to the time of the conquest (fig. 1). Headdresses include caps, some with disks attached to them.

Early Classic Period[2]

Knowledge of Early Classic dress styles comes from effigy jars, bas-reliefs, stelae, and the Leyden Plate, but during this period figurines were not manufactured.

Two-part effigy jars from Uaxactun (R. E. Smith, 1955b, fig. 5,*e,h*) represent human figures decorated with a narrow headband tied in a bow in front and sometimes clothed in a V-necked cape, showing zigzag or rectangular incised patterns. The lower bodies are also incised, but the type of clothing cannot be determined. A form on a similar jar from Kaminaljuyu wears a narrow string-width breechclout, tied in a single bow in back (Kelemen, 1956, pl. 127,*b*).

Sculpture, in general, presents a vast amount of decorative detail, but the two oldest stelae now known, Stela 29 at Tikal (8.12.14.8.15; Shook, 1960), and Stela 9 at Uaxactun (8.14.10.13.15) are either too fragmentary or too eroded to give any information on dress. The Leyden Plate (8.14.3.1.2), an incised jade slab, represents a heavily ornamented figure wearing a loincloth and a short skirt or kilt, beaded and fringed. This is supported by a massive belt. Stela 31 at Tikal (9.0.10.0.0; W. R. Coe, 1962b, figs. 6–8) is so broken that no details of dress can be seen on the principal figure. The two lateral figures wear circular back-shields, such as are seen in Tula-Toltec art, with three pendant monkey (?) tails. They also wear loincloths, one with parallel stripes and a fret motif at the end. This loincloth is supported by a belt which is knotted in front. Stela 23 at Tikal (9.3.16.8.4; Shook, 1958, fig. 20) pictures a knee-length fringed skirt and shoulder cape. Stela 25 at Tikal (9.4.3.0.0; *ibid.*, fig. 25) introduces a capelike garment of tubular beads (jade?) strung in a diamond pattern. This is the earliest example of a clothing technique which survived into historic times, both in the Maya area and in central Mexico. The beaded garment, as a long skirt reaching to the ankles, appears at Tulum in 9.6.10.0.0. Many examples of later date may be seen at Palenque.

Classic Period

It is probable that by this period all basic types of garments were in existence and were, in fact, similar from Mexico to Peru. In general, clothing was constructed of square or rectangular fabrics, several of which might be combined by sewing to add details such as sleeves, border patterns, and fringes. Cloth was not cut and tailored in the European fashion. The usual clothes were breechclouts, kilts or short skirts, long skirts, shirts, and mantles. It is possible that socio-political or religious demands on the individual affected his wearing apparel.

Stone Carvings and Bas-Reliefs

Loincloths. A loincloth was probably worn by all ranks and classes, but at times it is obscured by what Proskouriakoff (1950, p. 70, figs. 24–26) calls a second apron, which may reach as low as the ankles. Examples also are illustrated in Spinden (1957b, fig. 15) and Morley (1956, fig. 7). Obviously these are not all necessarily textiles, as some stronger material must have been needed to sustain the weight of the many ornaments attached to them.

Short Skirts and Kilts. Garments of this description were worn until the conquest. They were made of jaguar skins, tubular beads, and textiles. The basic type reached

[2] The dates are taken from Proskouriakoff, 1950, which are based chiefly on readings by Morley and Thompson. Most references to illustrations have been omitted if they can be found in Proskouriakoff. For details, original sources should be consulted, e.g. Maler (1901–03, 1908b) and Maudslay (1889-1902). Also some art books, and many Mexican publications, e.g. Marquina (1951) and Cook de Leonard (1959c) are of great value.

FIG. 2—YAXCHILAN, STELA 11. Reading 9.16.5.0.0. (After J. E. S. Thompson, 1954a.)

approximately to the knees, and sometimes can be identified as a wrap-around garment (fig. 7,*h*; Morley, 1956, pl. 78). The lower edges may be fringed, or decorated with rows of shell or beads. In some cases the entire skirt may consist of parallel stripes of beads (fig. 1).

Variants occur when the skirt covers the hips behind but is short in front. There is no evidence that this is a specially woven fabric, such as a *quexquemitl*, but it may be a result of gathering and tying the four ends of the material. This can be seen more clearly in frescoes (Villagra Caleti, 1949,

Cuarto 1). Sometimes the skirt comes to a point in front, such as on Stela 2 at Piedras Negras (9.13.15.0.0; Maler, 1901, pl. 15,*l*) and on Lintel 12 at Yaxchilan (9.15.10.0.0; Maler, 1903, pl. 65).

LONG SKIRTS. Skirts reaching from waist to ankle were worn by men on ceremonial occasions. They probably first appeared on Stela 1 at Tulum (9.6.10.0.0); they certainly are present on Stela 1 at Coba (9.12.0.0.0).

BELTS. Belts shown in sculpture rarely seem to have been made of textile materials as they are frequently adorned with massive modeled heads, below which hang heavy shell-like pendants. Even the earliest examples appear stiff and unyielding.

CAPES. The upper portion of the body is so obscured by characteristic ornaments that it is difficult to learn the nature of the garments underneath. As we have seen, a suggestion of a cape, made of tubular beads assembled to form a diamond pattern, was present in Tikal as early as 9.4.3.0.0. This continued in use, but was most prevalent later at Palenque. It is not known whether or not these had a textile base. Stela 23 at Tikal (9.3.16.8.4) is eroded in the upper portion, but what appears to be a fringe across the mid-arm strongly suggests a true textile cape. Beyond this, however, they cannot be identified until 9.14.5.0.0 on Stela 30 at Naranjo. An apparently unique cape, short over the arms and waist-length in back, also bordered with a fringe, is seen on Stela 10 at Yaxchilan (9.16.15.0.0; Maler, 1903, pl. 73). Others which may have a textile base are feathered, as on Stela 21 at Naranjo (9.13.15.0.0; Maler, 1908b, pl. 35). We do not discuss the over-size beaded collars which drape over the shoulders and upper arms like a cape because there is no evidence that they have a fabric base.

SHIRTS. This was a tight-fitting garment reaching from shoulder to waist with holes for the arms and head. The bottom usually is embellished by tabs, a fringe, or a row of shells. Very occasionally a textile pattern is represented (Proskouriakoff, 1950, fig. 103,*a,b.*) or two vertical rows of discs are attached (*ibid.*, fig. 74; our fig. 1).

Shirts were fashioned from textiles and from jaguar skins. The wearers of shirts usually either carry a large spear or appear in a battle scene. Evidently the garment is associated primarily with high-ranking warriors. The time range covers the Classic period.

MANTLES. This is a covering which falls from shoulders to ankles and is usually draped over the arms, apparently the largest single article of clothing worn by the Maya of the Classic period. Although it is often seen in sculpture, we cannot be certain of the actual shape or how it was worn because the artists had difficulty in representing folds and draping in low relief.

Wearers of mantles often can be identified as high officials, although subordinate to a more important personage. Usually they appear in profile and often a long skirt can be detected hanging below the bottom of the mantle (Stela 2 at Bonampak, 9.17.0.0.0). Rarely, except at Yaxchilan, are the wearers shown full face; it can be seen in such cases that the mantle is open from top to bottom in front.

TEXTILE ACCESSORIES. There are three types of additional pieces of apparel (1) A chasuble-like garment, which hangs from shoulders to knees and is sometimes adorned with feathers, is shown on Stela 7 at Piedras Negras (9.14.10.0.0). Stela 9 at La Florida (9.15.0.0.0) may have a textile pattern. These may represent a cloak, which is swung in front of the body, as is shown in painted media, or they may hang front and back like a poncho. (2) A "stole," which encircles the neck and is joined near the waist to form a single element (fig. 1), is shown only on Lintel 26 at Yaxchilan (fig. 1) (9.14.15.0.0) and on Stelae 18 (Maler, 1903, pls. 58, 77) and 20 (9.12.0.0.0). This has not been identified except by Maler, who considers the adornment to be shells (Maler, 1903, p. 181). (3) A series of at-

FIG. 3—DECORATIVE MOTIFS ON A CLOAK. Piedras Negras, Stela 33, reading 9.10.0.0.0. Width 25 cm.

tendant figures from the well-known Palenque bas-reliefs from the Temple of the Cross, the Temple of the Foliated Cross, and the Temple of the Sun (Maudslay, 1889–1902) wear a heavy twisted textile around the neck and spiraling down the back. The purpose of these is unknown.

DESIGNS. It is from the long mantle, which is particularly characteristic of several Usumacinta sites, that most, if not all, textile designs can be detected. Stela 33 from Piedras Negras (9.10.0.0.0), now in the National Museum of Guatemala City, has been incised to show details of the textile decoration (fig. 3). The principal motif is a band of interlocking heads flanked by crosshatched triangles. The angularity of the design suggests a tapestry technique. The border pattern (fig. 3, *top*) has been identified as a star symbol.

Both these designs have a long history. The angular face motif is represented on Maya garments throughout the Classic period. The diagonal border pattern also persisted in Maya art. Its appearance in central Mexico, both in textiles and other media, has been discussed by I. W. Johnson (1954).

Some other designs (Spinden, 1957b, pt. I, fig. 207; pt. II, pls. 8, 58, 59) have been drawn principally from Yaxchilan, where the greatest concentration of both mantles and patterns occurs. All resemble one another in consisting of geometric squares, arranged horizontally or diagonally, in a possible brocade technique (fig. 1). Some fanciful interpretations or reconstructions have been published, such as the paintings by H. M. Herget (*in* Mason, 1935) or by Du Solier (1950).

Frescoes

Uaxactun, Str. B-XIII, dated towards the end of the Early Classic (A. L. Smith, 1950, p. vi), contains frescoes which present no new features of dress. Some figures wear a broad breechclout and belt, others skirts, and one group wears mantles.

By far the most outstanding Maya frescoes, which call for many years of study, are those of Bonampak (Villagra Caleti, 1949; Ruppert, Thompson, and Proskouriakoff, 1955). The whole Classic range of garments is repeated in the frescoes, but with more variation and realistic detail. The abundant use of color, which has disappeared on the sculpture, gives us our best picture of the ancient Maya, both as individuals and in groups. A number of activities, including battle scenes, ceremonials and preparation for them, call for many different costumes.

Plain breechclouts are worn by prisoners and by persons who may be slaves or servants. In battle, several costumes are worn: very short kilts or shirts which come to the hips and are belted; shoulder capes which are longer in the back than front. Some shirts are of jaguar skin, belted and with a long tab in front. All these are shown in large detail especially from Room 2, by Villagra.

The musicians and singers (?) are all bare above the waist. They wear back-skirts or skirts which reach mid-calf. As a group they are distinguished by their enormous belts.

Two assemblages of personages of high rank are dressed in long white cloaks, open in front to reveal kilts and elaborate front

FIG. 4—DETAILS OF DRESS SHOWN ON FIGURINES. Lubaantun, British Honduras. (After Joyce, 1933.)

Fig. 5—DESIGN FROM POLYCHROME JAR. Chama. (After Morley, 1956.)

tabs. At least three skirts wrap around so that a triangular edge hangs down to one side. Only one of the 25 men wears a long skirt over which a shorter skirt (?) criss-crosses in front. Textile patterns are shown particularly in this group.

The most unusual scene concerns the dressing in full regalia of three top-ranking chiefs or priests. They wear long tiger-skin skirts painted red on the inside and have multicolored belts: red, blue, yellow, black, and white with long ends. Attendants are in the act of attaching tremendous frames fringed with long quetzal feathers.

One of the major scenes is a terraced pyramid on which a sacrificial ceremony and dance are being performed. There are 10 dancers with immense headdresses of quetzal feathers and with huge projecting wings attached to the belt. These flare horizontally, as if the dancer were spinning. This is a unique costume. The ends and bottoms of the wings are fringed or feathered, and the main portions are embellished with polychrome patterns. Unfortunately, the bodies are quite marred.

A few women appear at Bonampak, clad in long white "Mother Hubbards" (loose fitting white gowns), which seem to cover the arms. One wears a red stole over her arms, another a collar (?).

Figurines

Figurines are not common in Classic times, except on the Island of Jaina and the adjacent coast of Campeche and at Lubaantun in British Honduras. Scattered examples have been found along the Usumacinta and in the highlands of Guatemala. The figurines do not show the same emphasis on religious ceremonies as do the stelae and frescoes. They probably represent the life of the common people rather than the ruling classes. At Lubaantun (Joyce, 1933) many headdresses are made of cloth and include turbans, ribbons twisted into the hair, and large mushroom-like arrangements which look as if they were stuffed with cotton (fig. 4,*l-o*). Men's clothing consists of a breechcloth with front tab (fig. 4,*a*), sometimes with an apron over it (fig. 4,*b*), a short back-skirt (fig. 4,*d,e*) or an ankle-length skirt (fig. 4,*b*). Only one figure wears a shoulder cape (fig. 4,*c*), possibly of feathers. Others have large cloaks or mantles. What appears to be a fabric

FIG. 6—DESIGN FROM POLYCHROME JAR. Uaxactun. (After Morley, 1956).

hangs like a bib around the neck. Other male costumes consist of special paraphernalia for ball-players.

Women's skirts are long, often with a broad decorated band running down the front (fig. 4,*f*,*h*). They also are girdled with a very broad garment extending from the hip to just beneath the breasts. This has not previously been described. It invariably is completely decorated (fig. 4,*g*,*h*). Possible textile techniques may include tapestry (fig. 4,*f*); tie-dyeing is suggested by the arrangement of dots in figure 4,*i*; and the diamond patterns in *j* and *k* may be related to the tubular beading discussed elsewhere.

Although many hundreds of beautiful figurines are known from Jaina and the adjacent mainland, they are widely scattered and no classification or comprehensive study has yet been published. They are so highly individualistic that they do not readily fall into groups. Some are moldmade and others are sculptured; still others are a combination of both. The same basic garments already discussed appear on these figurines, but there are some types which do not occur elsewhere. The tabs of wide breechclouts, for instance, may reach all the way to the ground. Wrap-around garments are common, both kilt-length and longer. Most unusual is an open-fronted cape (Lothrop, Foshag, and Mahler, 1957, pl. 74) or a jacket reaching to the waist (*ibid.*, pl. 68) or to the knees (*ibid.*, pl. 69). Some of these have projecting cone-shaped tabs, the nature of which is not clear. A possible example of a "stole" (p. 585) is seen on one figure (Stendahl, 1957). Women frequently wear a curious garment which has a wide neck opening and which hangs as long as a mantle in back but is short and rounded in front—much like many Zapotec garments (Caso and Bernal, 1952, figs. 125,*b*; 126; 230).

Textile patterns seem to be limited to the moldmade figurines. Some stepped frets might be of tapestry. Other curvilinear motifs surely must be embroidery.

Painted Pottery

Polychrome pottery with painted human figures which add to our knowledge of Classic textiles is not common. In general additional details stem from greater realism, whereby drapes and folds, especially in the large breechclouts, are clearly visible (fig. 5). Textile designs include diamond shapes with central dots, stripes, or the so-called

FIG. 7—SKIRTS. *a–c,* Dresden Codex. *d,* Tro-Cortesiano Codex. *e–g,* Perez Codex. *h,* Comalcalco bas-relief. (After Blom, 1926, fig. 100.)

planet motif, first seen at Piedras Negras (fig. 3). Others suggest painted cloth (Gordon and Mason, 1925–43, pl. 30). Chama and Nebaj jars depict turbans which obviously are of woven material.

Only one type of garment calls for special mention (fig. 6), a front cloak, shown on standing figures in profile, which hangs from the neck and seems to end in a point below the knees. This may be an attempt to present a side view of the rounded front cloak of Classic Maya sculpture, as on Stela 9 at La Florida and on Stela 7 at Piedras Negras. Similar front cloaks are also illustrated in the codices.

POSTCLASSIC

Frescoes

Tulum (Lothrop, 1924) is a site contemporaneous with Mayapan, and the ceramics indicate only a very late settlement. Existing frescoes are on the most recent layers

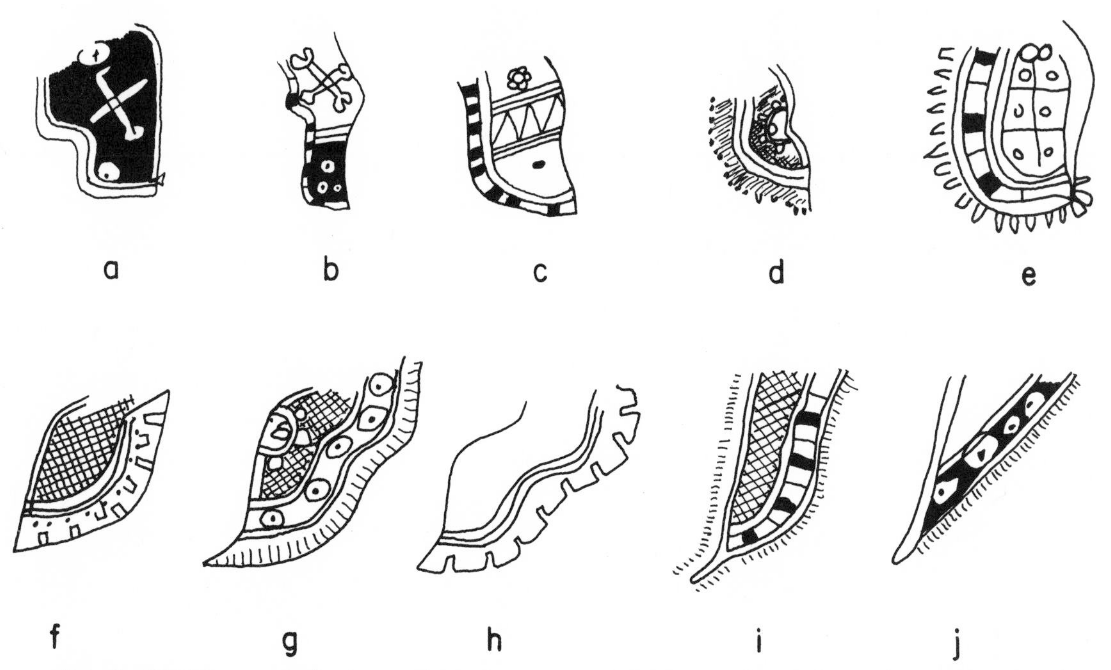

FIG. 8—CAPES. *a–e,* Back capes; others, front capes. *a–d,f–h,* Dresden Codex. *e,i,j,* Tro-Cortesiano Codex.

of plaster and therefore date from about 1500 or later. There seems to be a strong Mixtec influence.

Men wore a short back-skirt with front (?) and back ties, and either what appears to be a neck accessory similar to the stoles on stelae (see above) or a back-cloak. One figure, a woman using a metate, wears a long plaid (?) skirt with a stepped-fret border (Lothrop, 1924, pl. 7). Other figures, probably priests, clad in skirts, wear around their necks a pointed object which bears much resemblance to a *quexquemitl.* The clearest textile pattern (*ibid.,* pl. 6, lower left) on a cloak consists of flower-like motifs on the main cloth, which is bordered with short tabs, possibly of tapestry. These frescoes, like those at Mitla, are shown against a black background with blue the only added color.

The Santa Rita frescoes (Gann, 1900) are, we believe, too Mixtec in style to be discussed in this paper. In regard to the Chichen Itza frescoes and bas-reliefs, one might assume they should be linked with the Cenote textiles (p. 592) but it is uncertain as to what is Toltec and what is Maya attire.

Codices

In the latest manifestations of Maya art, traditional garments persist. The Dresden Codex shows most variety: short back-skirts (fig. 7,*e-g*), long skirts on men and women (fig. 7,*a-d*) and front and back capes (fig. 8,a-j). Perhaps an innovation is, in the case of priests, a skirt of narrow swinging panels hung from the waist. Textile techniques may include painting, tapestry, brocade, plain and tab fringes. Net-making for burden-frames is actually depicted, but it is not known whether or not netting is represented by the crisscross patterns on clothing.

Surviving Textiles

THE SACRED CENOTE. The largest lot, about 600 fragments, comes from the

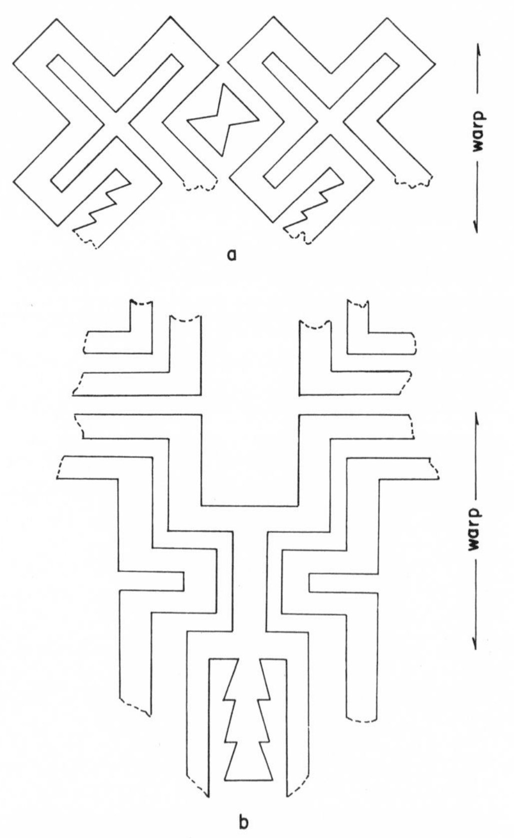

Fig. 9—DESIGN MOTIFS FROM BROCADED FABRICS. Sacred Cenote, Chichen Itza. Scale: abt. ½.

Fig. 10—DESIGN MOTIFS FROM EMBROIDERED FABRICS. Sacred Cenote, Chichen Itza. Scale: abt. ½.

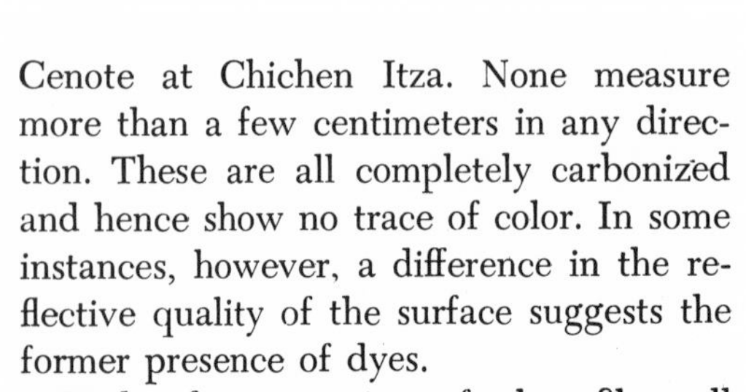

Cenote at Chichen Itza. None measure more than a few centimeters in any direction. These are all completely carbonized and hence show no trace of color. In some instances, however, a difference in the reflective quality of the surface suggests the former presence of dyes.

With a few exceptions of a bast fiber, all the specimens are made with cotton yarn, used either Z-spun single ply or S-doubled. There are, however, over a dozen combinations of spinning direction, doubling, pairing, etc., of warps and wefts for the base fabric. In the case of supplementary yarns, as in brocades and embroidery, these yarns usually differ from the base cloth. If present, the heading cords may also differ from the base fabric, and usually warps along the side selvage are the same as the rest. There is great variety in the quality of spinning, and in the desired compactness of the weave.

Except for four types of twills, all fabrics are technically plain weaves. Within the the plain-weave category, it has been possible to detect warp stripes, weft stripes, plaids, embroidery, brocade, gauze, openwork, weft pile, warp floats, and tapestry, mostly kilim.

Decorative motifs are few and still exist only in the brocades or on embroidery. Design elements consist typically of crosses, lozenges, and frets, but the over-all pattern of any one of them is lost because the fragments are so small. The general appearance of these designs, however, perhaps is approximated by the well-known relief patterns on the walls at Mitla (Seler, 1904a, pl. 31). Some motifs are shown in figures 9 and 10.

Basketry consists of a few coiled fragments, and imprints on large masses of copal.

MAYAPAN. The Mayapan fragments that I have examined were preserved through contact with copper, and retain the original tawny color of the cotton. A similar color of cotton is still used in the highlands of Guatemala. Two fragments are of plain weave, one of which has been published (Thompson, 1954b, p. 78). Another is a double cloth with warp floats on one face (Thompson, *loc. cit.*). The other is a warp float (Proskouriakoff, 1962b). All are Z-spun, single-ply cotton.

Some plain-weave textile impressions have been found on sherds, probably not differing greatly in age, as Mayapan was occupied for a comparatively brief span.

OTHER REMAINS. Textile fragments from Chiapas have been published by O'Neale (1942), Johnson (1954), and King (1955). Additional examples are given by Johnson (*in* Cook de Leonard, 1959c).

SUMMARY

Basic clothing changed little throughout Maya history. Landa's description (Tozzer, 1941a, p. 89) might well have been applicable at almost any date. Garment types and the manner of wearing them are often obscure, however, as the Maya tended to overburden their figures with a wealth of jewelry and ornamental details. Textile designs, apparently frequently symbolic in nature, are difficult to translate into terms of weaving, but it is clear from some surviving textiles that throughout the Mexican-Maya lowland area, skill and variety in technique were greater than generally supposed.

REFERENCES

Blom, 1926
Caso and Bernal, 1952
Coe, W. R., 1962b
Cook de Leonard, 1959c
Du Solier, 1950
Gann, 1900
Gordon and Mason, 1925–43
Johnson, I. W., 1954, 1959
Joyce, 1933
Kelemen, 1956
King, 1955
Lothrop, 1924
——, Foshag, and Mahler, 1957
Maler, 1901–03, 1908b
Marquina, 1951
Mason, J. A., 1935
Maudslay, 1889–1902
Morley, 1956
O'Neale, 1942
Proskouriakoff, 1950, 1962b
Ricketson and Ricketson, 1937
Ruppert, Thompson, and Proskouriakoff, 1955
Seler, 1904a
Shook, 1958, 1960
Smith, A. L., 1950
Smith, R. E., 1955b
Spinden, 1957b
Stendahl, 1957
Thompson, J. E. S., 1954a, 1954b
Tozzer, 1941a
Villagra C., 1949

23. Artifacts of the Maya Lowlands

WILLIAM R. COE

Lowland Maya artifacts stand for the most part as isolates. Collections of tools have emerged incidentally in investigation of ceremonial architecture. The recovery of a shattered celt from the hearting of a temple structure, with fragments of obsidian flake-blades and an incomplete mano stone, hardly allows much insight into an artifact assemblage at any given moment. There is the strong possibility of redeposition of one or more items as well as the unexplained presence of a broken mano (if not redeposited) in the fill of some elaborate, far from domestic building. The dating of such implements largely depends on ceramic associations. Yet, the fact that a mano occurs, for instance, at Uaxactun in fill containing Tepeu 2 pottery provides no more than the probable latest date for the implement.

Studies of lowland artifacts, however, both primary tools and their products (Kidder, 1947; Proskouriakoff, 1962b; W. R. Coe, 1959; Thompson, 1931, 1939a, 1940; Longyear, 1952), substantiate the concept of lowland Maya culture, as well as indicating potentially significant discrepancies from site to site. Nevertheless there are not enough data for classifying confidently a Formative or Preclassic assemblage or one of Late Classic times. The delineation of lithic complexes at a given site (Smith, Willey, and Gifford, 1960, p. 331) is surely a desideratum but as surely a distant one until implements are as conscientiously recovered as ceramics.

Here we are more concerned with the actual implements of the lowland Maya than with the personal ornaments and ritual paraphernalia which tools produced. It is the fact that certain objects do not conform to opulent standards that classifies them as utilitarian, regardless of our frequent inability to assign definite utilitarian functions to them.

Raw materials include flint, obsidian (imported), limestone, quartzite and granite (the igneous areas of British Honduras being likely sources), clay, bone, and presumably local hardwoods. Flint occurs in nodule form and even as substantial exposures (as at Tikal) throughout the limestone comprising the lowlands.

In the Peten–British Honduras regions

during Classic times the following inventory (culled from printed reports and unpublished field data from Tikal) appears to have existed:

CORE, BIFACED, PERCUSSION-FLAKED IMPLEMENTS OF FLINT (occasionally of limestone)

These have been considered by Kidder (1947) to be general utility tools. The outstanding form (fig. 1,*e*), found widely and persistently in the lowlands (W. R. Coe, 1959), is petaloid and superficially comparable to many Acheulian hand axes. Specific function is problematic. Many examples (Uaxactun, Tikal, Benque Viejo, Piedras Negras, Puuc sites) have polished bits (fig. 1,*e*, left), but the opposite or poll end never seems to show the wear that would be expected had this implement been used as a chisel; nor do any signs of hafting appear (though this is hardly conclusive in view of the toughness of the material.) The polish is likely the result of use rather than an intentional finish; possibly earth-polish implies an agricultural rôle. It has also been proposed that this implement may have served as a chopper. Whatever its use, this tool is a hallmark, admittedly minor, of lowland culture and one which carried through Preclassic, Classic, and even early Postclassic times. An apparent workshop for these tools has been recently reported near the Guatemala–British Honduras line (Bullard, 1960b, pp. 363–64).

Other implements of this general kind, elongated with more or less parallel sides, are on record at Uaxactun, San Jose, and in current excavations at Tikal. Technically comparable to the preceding, these tools do not show polish. According to Kidder (1947, pp. 5–6), they occurred in Preclassic and Classic deposits at Uaxactun. A pecking-pounding function is presumed; specific use as a pick is a possibility.

Lowland sites abound in relatively large, percussion-flaked core implements. Their frequency and battered or fragmentary condition suggest they were important mundane items in subsistence activities. No other tool seems to have had such everyday usefulness. Or perhaps these implements were employed in the work of dressing stone and general masonry in the construction of ceremonial architecture.

SCRAPING AND ABRADING TOOLS

These are common items, principally flint, though not infrequently obsidian. Most scraping tools were not specially made but merely preparatory flakes put to use with little or no modification. Specially made, oval, unifacially flaked scrapers of flint have been encountered at Uaxactun (Kidder, 1947, fig. 62) and at Tikal, double-ended and thumbnail scrapers at Tikal, possibly a bone flesher at San Jose (Thompson, 1939a, pl. 30,*a*,4). Other tools could have been used secondarily for scraping. Abraders, even polishing tools, are not easily identified. Ones of pumice are recorded for Piedras Negras (W. R. Coe, 1959, p. 36). Mano stones could have been re-used as polishers and plaster smoothers.

DRILLING AND PERFORATING TOOLS

Objects of appropriate form and wear to suggest their having been used as drills are recorded principally at Uaxactun (Kidder, 1947, p. 6). Simple flint flakes, bilaterally notched to form a tapered point with deliberate retouching, have appeared at Tikal and Uaxactun (Ricketson and Ricketson, 1937, pl. 55,*b*). A possible obsidian drill is known from Piedras Negras (W. R. Coe, 1959, p. 14). At Uaxactun and Tikal, some drills were likely handled as awls; others, such as a set from Uaxactun (Kidder, 1947, fig. 1), could have been inserted in a wooden shaft and probably turned with a bow device. A hollow drill (with proper abrasive) is to be inferred from jadeite ornaments; but here we are uncertain whether such ornaments were in all cases locally produced. The lowland use of the hollow drill, however, is conclusive at Tikal where

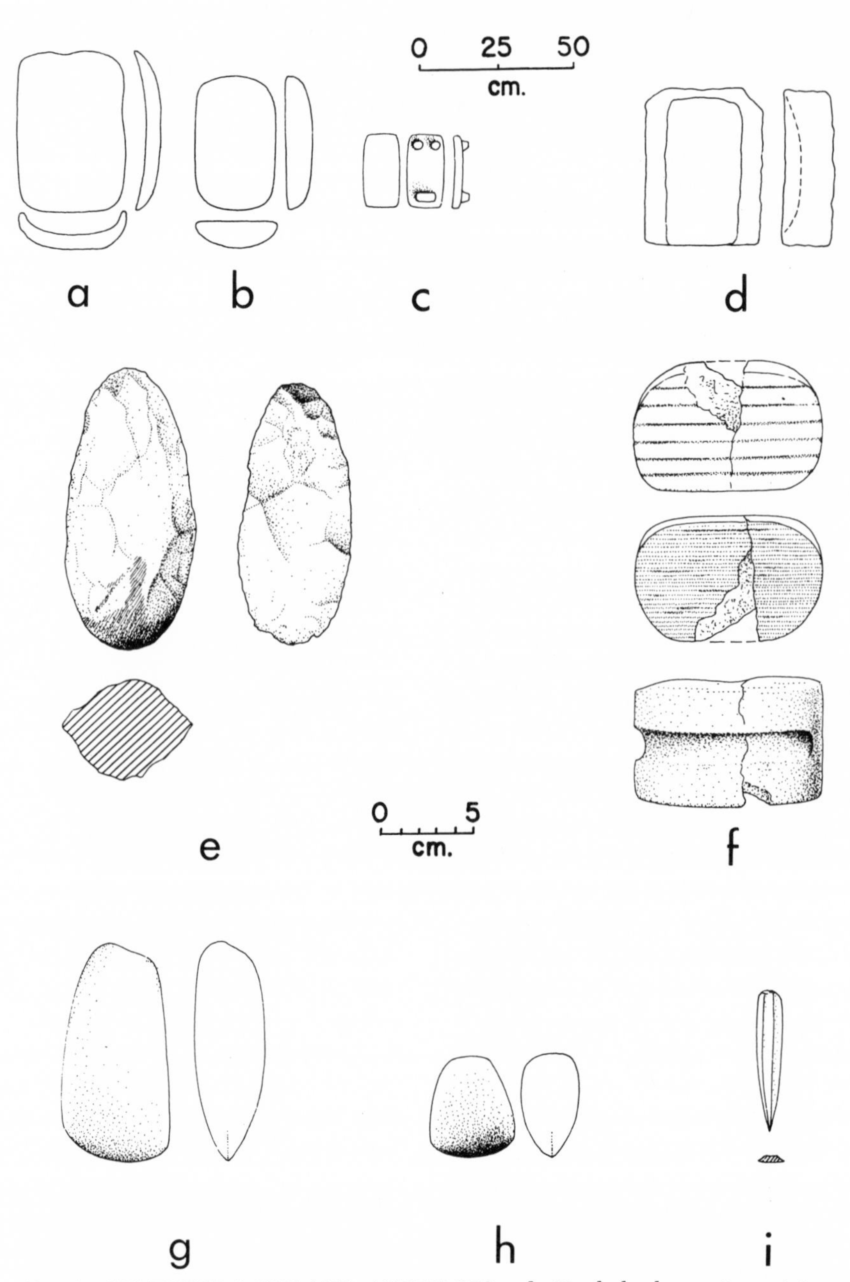

FIG. 1—SELECTED LOWLAND ARTIFACTS. *a,b,* Turtle-back granite metates from Uaxactun. *c,* Small tripod, sandstone metate, from Piedras Negras. *d,* Typical limestone metate from Chichen Itza. *e,* Two flint bifacially flaked implements, from Piedras Negras; hatching of left example indicates area of polish. *f,* Bark beater of limestone, from Uaxactun. *g,h,* Large and small examples of celts from Uaxactun. *i,* Obsidian flake-blade, from Uaxactun, with probable cross-section added. (After Kidder, 1947; W. R. Coe, 1959; Stromsvik, 1931.)

plain and incised flakes of obsidian (all ritual, cache items) were occasionally perforated and necessarily so with a drill of this type (W. R. Coe and Broman, 1958, p. 44; as subsequent finds leave no doubt that they were hollow-drilled, the suggestion of reaming may now be discarded). The hollow drill seems to have been used principally in making or finishing exotic items and was likely a very specialized implement.

Bone awls, commonly of deer metapodials, have been discovered at most Classic lowland sites where large-scale excavations have been conducted, as were needles, the outstanding feature of which is the scraped and, at times, drilled eye (see Kidder, 1947, p. 56 for discussion).

Knives and Primary Cutting Tools

Leaf-shaped blades of flint and, less frequently, of obsidian are not uncommon. But, due to the ceremonial elaboration of these sites and general ritual context of many specimens, one would hesitate to ascribe these blades to any lithic complex encompassing farmers, priests, and artisans. Such blades could well have been lanceheads, an object depicted in Classic sculpture. Almost any flint or obsidian flake is serviceable as a knife. Certain keen-edged apparent scrapers could conceivably have doubled as knives. The single implement completely suited as a knife was the obsidian core-struck flake-blade (fig. 1,*i*). These small, fragile tools were struck from prepared cores; the flakes thrown off in core preparation became blanks for scrapers, even for simple knives, and for probably most of the ritualized eccentric and incised obsidians. The obsidian was necessarily imported, probably in rough blocks. Recent work at Tikal affords likelihood of local core production and blade-striking. The presence of exhausted or nearly exhausted blade-cores at Tikal and other lowland sites has always implied full knowledge and application of the nearly universal technique in Mesoamerica of producing such blades (for discussion and distribution see Kidder, 1947, pp. 14–16; Kidder, Jennings, and Shook, 1946, p. 135; W. R. Coe, 1959, pp. 14–15; Woodbury and Trik, 1953, pp. 229–31). Flint blades, comparably narrow with parallel sides and prismatic cross-sections, are appearing at Tikal but as a very minor item.

Projectiles

Certain artifacts are by necessity classified as blades or points. Was a laurel-leaf blade 10 cm. long a knife or a spearpoint? Were stemmed specimens dartpoints, arrowheads, or even hafted knives?

Preponderantly of flint and obsidian, artifacts so classifiable have not appeared in great quantity at any lowland Classic site. Collections of any consequence are on record for Uaxactun (Kidder, 1947), Piedras Negras (W. R. Coe, 1959), San Jose (Thompson, 1939a), and Copan (Longyear, 1952). Despite relative scarcity, such objects now show diversity in form and size, but as excavations continue it may be found that this present diversity is deceptive and that lowland Classic material falls into a few basic types. Some idea of the range may be gained from figure 2. Size and, probably more significantly, weight should be kept in mind when evaluating the probability of darts and spearthrowers in Classic times (an atlatl is seemingly depicted on the quite early Uaxactun Stela 5) as well as the probable absence of the bow and arrow during these same times (see Kidder, 1947, p. 12 for excellent discussion of this point).

As yet no formal typology has been attempted on projectile material. Like so many basic artifacts, they have appeared incidentally in investigation of fills and debris of ritual structures; many are incomplete. They have been dated only in a general way (i.e., as Early Classic, Late Classic).

As Kidder has pointed out (1947), the

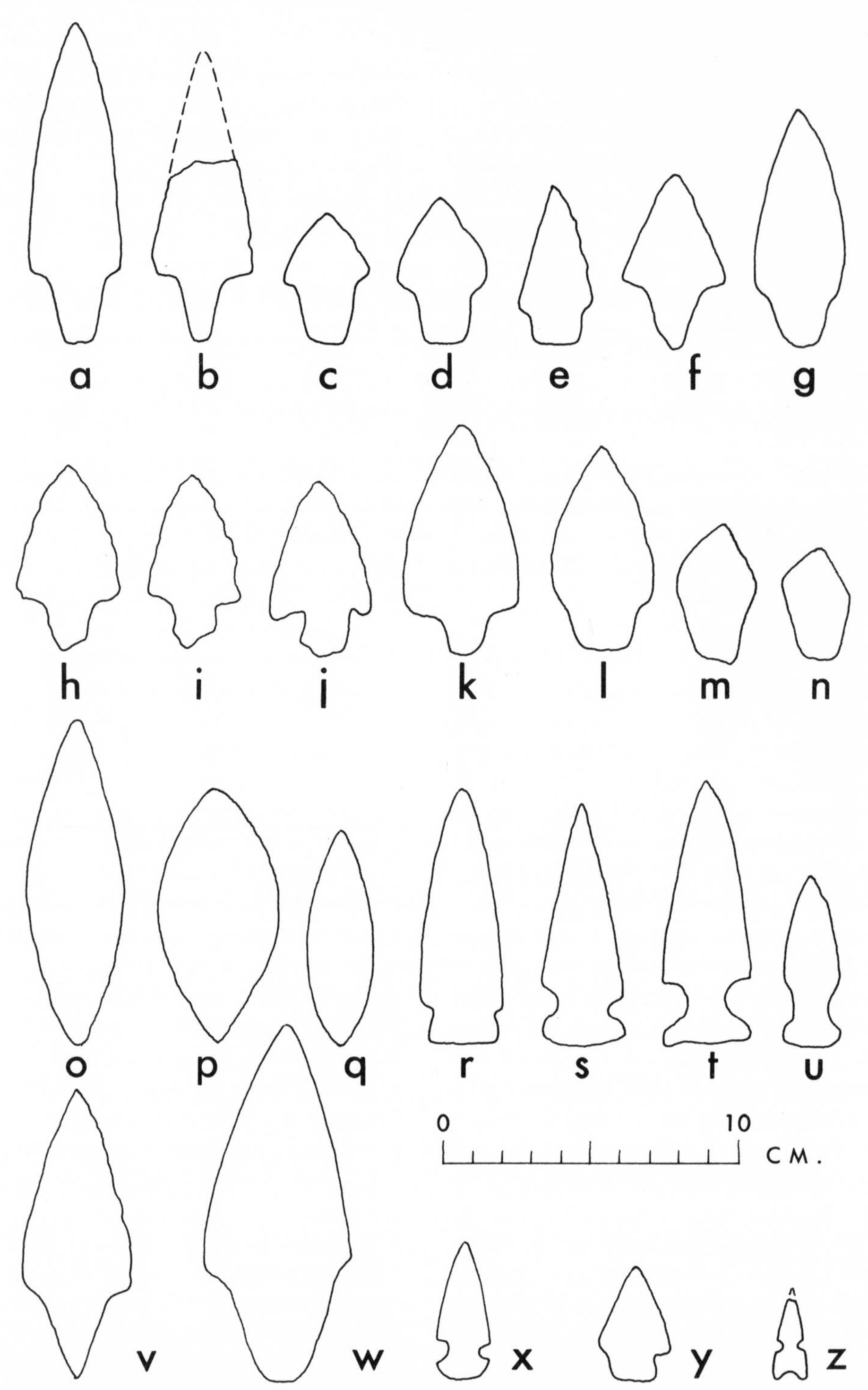

Fig. 2—OUTLINE OF LOWLAND MAYA PROJECTILE POINTS AND BLADES WHICH MAY HAVE SERVED AS POINTS. All flint except those of obsidian in *h–j,r,z*. Uaxactun: *a,d,e,g,h,j,k,m,q*. Piedras Negras: *b,c,f,o*. San Jose: *l,p,r;* Copan: *i*. Chichen Itza: *s–v*. Mayapan: *w–z*. All Classic except *s–z* and possibly *r* (San Jose V) which are Postclassic. (From Kidder, 1947; W. R. Coe, 1959; J. E. S. Thompson, 1939a; Longyear, 1952; Adams, 1953; Shook, 1953, 1954a; Shook and Irving, 1955.)

outstanding characteristic of the Classic Maya lowland collections is the practical absence of expanding-stem points or blades. The latter attribute, exemplified in part by side-notching, is basically Postclassic (fig. 2,*s-u*). This conclusion will undoubtedly be tested as investigation of Postclassic remains develops in the Peten–British Honduras regions.

Pounding Tools

Randomly use-shaped and intentionally spherical hammerstones served a variety of uses at such sites as Uaxactun (Kidder, 1947, pp. 37–38). Amorphous specimens could have served as crumbling tools in preparation of masonry blocks (A. L. Smith, 1950, pp. 69–70).

A pounding implement of seemingly specialized function is the one referred to as a "bark beater" (fig. 1,*f*). In the lowlands this tool is generally oval or with approximately parallel long sides and rounded ends, with two opposed flat working surfaces scored with closely set parallel grooves. Most show a groove encircling three of the sides by which the implement was bound to a handle. These bark beaters are widely distributed (San Jose, Uaxactun, Piedras Negras, Tikal) but to date appear to have been absent in Preclassic times (Kidder, 1947, p. 38; Kidder, Jennings, and Shook, 1946, p. 142; W. R. Coe, 1959, pp. 37–38). The two-part type, just noted, is to be contrasted with the one-piece, "monolithic" beater (W. R. Coe, *ibid.*), a type not evidently used in this region although the present-day Lacandon are said to have a wooden form of it. The head portion of the two-part beater may at times have relatively elaborate designs on the working surfaces, as, for instance, crosshatches and drilled depressions and incised triangles (e.g. Kidder, 1947, fig. 78,*j*).

Metates and Manos

Three basic types of metates were employed for grinding corn in the lowlands during Classic times (Kidder, 1947, pp. 33–35; W. R. Coe, 1959, pp. 34–36): a large rectangular limestone block in which end-to-end grinding produced a deep trough; a tripodal metate, usually of granite, sandstone, and other imported stone, with a laterally flat grinding surface; and the so-called "turtle-back" or legless metate with an initially flattish grinding surface which deepened with use. Grinding appears to have been done with a mano shorter than the width of the metate, but a longer mano may have been used with laterally flat tripodal metates (producing the "overhanging" mano). The turtle-back metate (fig. 1,*a,b*) is the common form at sites in the eastern Peten and in central British Honduras; recent excavations at Tikal corroborate this distribution. At Piedras Negras, however, the common metate was the large, legless limestone "trough" type. Here, legged metates (fig. 2,*c*) are rare, as they are at Uaxactun and other sites to the east. Tripodal metates are curiously plentiful at Lubaantun in southern British Honduras (Kidder, 1947, p. 35). Yet the metates of the not overly distant Copan are described as "simple, legless troughs of volcanic stone" (Longyear, 1952, p. 105).

The fact that the turtle-back type is preponderantly of granite may be significant in view of the relative proximity of granite in the Pine Ridge areas of British Honduras. This regionally typical metate nevertheless does occur in limestone at times (San Jose, in Thompson, 1939a, Table 13); Thompson has noted a possible shift in time from limestone to granite in this same form.

It is difficult to assess the importance of these discrepancies from site to site in metates and implied preferences. They might be considered significant with respect to basic, tradition-bound attitudes and activities. Some metates were portable and could be placed on a table; others were massive and probably required the grinder to kneel. Close attention to metates and other elementary, day-to-day items from site to site may provide a useful viewpoint in evaluating the somewhat overwhelming nonsecular products of lowland Classic culture.

Gouges and Celts

Elongated, hard stone implements adapted for gouging (bit end unifacially grooved) have been noted for Piedras Negras and Lake Peten Itza (distribution given in W. R. Coe, 1959, p. 39). These probably were not commonly used. It has been suggested that such gouges were used as percussion tools in the working of jade (Foshag, 1954). For Uaxactun, Kidder (1947, p. 6) discusses a possible type of percussion-flaked, elongated gouging tool of flint.

The celt is one of the most puzzling tools in the lowlands. It is a fairly expectable item at Classic sites but not in any quantity. Some are small and wedge-shaped (the "cuneate" type; Thompson, 1939a, p. 174); others, more surely Classic in date, may be as much as 17 or 18 cm. in length (fig. 1,*g,h*). Generally speaking, the greatest width occurs across the curved bit. The pecking scars may be obliterated by what would seem to be use-polish, beginning at the cutting edge and continuing onto the body. The question is whether these tough green or dark stone items were hafted as axes or were intermediate tools such as chisels or gouges. The absence of a grooved provision for hafting together with the often battered state of the poll would suggest the latter possibility. However, small celts could have been inserted in a handle in line with the celt itself. Observation of celts found to date at Tikal allows that the polished areas could have resulted from use at quite acute angles to the object altered. On the other hand, in Classic sculpture celtlike objects are depicted as inserted in appropriately perforated handles, with friction alone securing the object (Proskouriakoff, 1950, fig. 34,*w,x*). A large, magnificently flaked ritual artifact of obsidian from San Jose depicts a hafted celt (Thompson, 1939, pl. 28,*a*; Willey, 1956, p. 779 notes an object of comparable shape from Barton Ramie); a few tiny eccentric obsidians from Piedras Negras share this same form (W. R. Coe, 1959, figs. 26,*g*; 36,*d*).

It seems likely that celts were imported in finished form, most probably from the highlands, where these items are comparatively common and apparently of much greater antiquity (for general discussion, see W. R. Coe, 1959, pp. 40–42). The majority of specimens at such sites as Uaxactun and Piedras Negras appear to be Late Classic. They do not seem to have been a common household item. The fact that various lowland celts are of jadeite (as at Piedras Negras) would tend to confirm this view. Moreover, there are instances of comparatively large, inscribed celts, suggestive of imports, which have appeared in certain burials (summary in W. R. Coe, 1959, p. 40). In light of the heavy trade from highlands to lowlands, it is curious that the celt did not diffuse earlier and in quantity if highland function was applicable in the lowlands.

Weaving Implements

Spindle whorls were of stone and pottery but, if correctly interpreted, more commonly in the form of perforated, round-cut potsherds (Kidder, 1947, pp. 39–49, 67–68; W. R. Coe, 1959, pp. 39, 69). As Kidder notes, formed whorls seem to have appeared towards the end of Classic times. At San Jose, formed pottery whorls all pertain to Period V of the site and give every indication of being imports from Veracruz. (Thompson, 1939a, p. 153).

Ceremonial Artifacts

These objects are in many ways far better known than the basic implements just discussed. Principal sources are burials and cached offerings; monumental sculpture and frescos help to illustrate the range and elaboration of personal ornaments and ritual paraphernalia.

Techniques of their manufacture included primary and secondary flaking, sawing, drilling with solid and hollow drills, incision, grinding and polishing. The results were carved and drilled jade ornaments; beads of shell, jadeite and other stones; extravagant items decorated with inlaid mosaics of jadeite, shell, hematite, and pyrite elements (a jade mosaic mask is shown in Article 21, fig. 18, p. 566); large quantities of exotically chipped flint and obsidian objects for offerings; obsidian flakes, pieces of shell, and lumps of jade or pseudo-jade incised with the symbols and figure of deities for offertory use. Dental inlays were delicately worked from jadeite and hematite, even from obsidian. Jadeite, crystal, and jade-shell mosaics were used to form and decorate elaborate ear ornaments. Wood was used to fashion at least two types of drums; trumpets were made from wood and conch shells; other drums as well as whistles were made from clay; pieces of longbone were notched to form rasping sticks. Rare pyrite mosaic plaques were probably imported along with the obsidian, jadeite, amazonite, and other materials lacking in the lowlands but necessary for adornment and ritual regalia. It is practically impossible to enumerate all the items that were produced in this category and all that were traded into the lowland region. The basic range of material is well illustrated and described for Uaxactun (Ricketson and Ricketson, 1937; Kidder, 1947), San Jose (Thompson, 1939a), the Mountain Cow sites (Thompson, 1931), Piedras Negras (W. R. Coe, 1959), Palenque (Ruz, 1955a, 1958, among other reports), Copan (Longyear, 1952), and Tikal (reports in preparation).

Utilitarian implements from the lowland Postclassic period are best known from deposits of the principal occupation at Mayapan, in northern Yucatan, and to a lesser extent from Chichen Itza during the phase of Toltec domination or influence. Brief description and substantial illustration of the Mayapan artifacts are to be found in Carnegie Institution's *Current Reports*. A full study of artifacts of Mayapan and data on those from Chichen Itza and Puuc sites (considered to be Late Classic)[1] has been published by Miss Proskouriakoff (1962b), whom I wish to thank for permission to summarize from her manuscript in the following paragraphs.

Despite profound changes in other aspects of culture, a continuity in basic artifacts is evident in collections from Puuc sites, Chichen Itza, and the Late Postclassic Mayapan. In these collections there are few obvious tool types that would be out of place in any Classic site to the south. An unusual artifact at Chichen Itza, however, is the grooved hammer. At Mayapan, quality markedly dropped with the use of local limestone and chert although the repertory of tools employed for abrading, smoothing, and rubbing increased, but often through the re-use of tools originally designed for other purposes (e.g. manos, bark beaters). By the time of the florescence of Mayapan, a perhaps more striking change occurred with the disappearance of the common biface core tool of flint (fig. 1,*e*). As Proskouriakoff notes, if this tool was used in cultivation, its absence at Mayapan might possibly reflect a basic change in agricultural practices.

In northern Yucatan, Toltec times saw the introduction of a new weapon in the form of a small dart propelled by the atlatl. Side- and corner-notched points of flint and obsidian corroborate sculptural evidence for this weapon. With the subsequent shift of power to Mayapan, the bow and arrow may have eventually superseded such darts. Side-notched points are decidedly rare at Mayapan but are typical of Chichen Itza; the side-notched examples at Mayapan are moreover distinctive (fig.

[1] Ed. note: Or Pure Florescent (Andrews, Article 12).

2,*x*). Various points of Postclassic date from Yucatan[2] are shown in figure 2,*s-z*.

Limestone metates, presumably locally made (as opposed to imported ones of volcanic stone), are essentially the same at both Chichen Itza and Mayapan (fig. 1,*d*). These were roughly rectangular, relatively thick slabs. Grinding was end-to-end with manos shorter than the widths of the metates (cf. Stromsvik, 1931). Grinding produced deep concavities which at times opened at one end of the metate. Such metates have flat bases, an additional feature which sets them apart from the turtle-back type encountered at Classic Uaxactun, Tikal, and San Jose. The tripodal, flat (side-to-side) metates at Chichen Itza (Stromsvik, 1931) are believed by Proskouriakoff to date to a time after the collapse of Mayapan (traditionally about A.D. 1450) or even to early colonial times. Tripods did nevertheless occur at Mayapan but in lava, with presumption of importation.

Ritual items at Mayapan were meager, owing to the evident ancient disturbance and robbery of cached offerings and burials. Copper ornaments and gold, beads and stylistically diverse pendants of jadeite, as well as celts of jadeite, ritual blades of flint, etc., are the substantial residue of what must have been extensive trade relations.

Irrespective of the complexity of lowland hierarchic culture, the inventory of tools seems small when compared with those of various other American peoples. The appearance of metal in Postclassic times hardly altered the basic neolithic frame of artifacts. Priestly introspection and preoccupation with celestial happenings gave way to the militarism and secular, urban trends of late times. In the midst of fundamental change (which must have affected all social levels) tools remained much the same. Those interested in artifacts of this nature must search hard to point to evolution of any consequence. However, as excavations continue in the lowlands, substantial changes may be found to have occurred in this category, particularly as knowledge of the Formative or Preclassic period grows.

[2] Ed. note: Or Florescent and Decadent (Andrews, Article 12).

REFERENCES

Adams, R. M., 1953
Bullard, 1960b
Coe, W. R., 1955, 1959
—— and Broman, 1958
Foshag, 1954
Kidder, 1947
——, Jennings, and Shook, 1946
Longyear, 1952
Proskouriakoff, 1950, 1962b
Ricketson and Ricketson, 1937
Ruz L., 1955a, 1958
Shook, 1953, 1954a
—— and Irving, 1955
Smith, A. L., 1950
Smith, R. E., Willey, and Gifford, 1960
Stromsvik, 1931
Thompson, J. E. S., 1931, 1939a, 1940
Willey, 1956b
Woodbury and Trik, 1953

24. Calendrics of the Maya Lowlands

LINTON SATTERTHWAITE

THE CALENDAR SYSTEM was an exceedingly important element in the culture of the ancient lowland Maya. It is here considered mechanistically, with only superficial attention to its deeper meaning. The literature goes back more than a century and is very extensive. Although much of it is opinion and interpretation, established fact has been steadily increasing.

The authoritative synthesis (J. E. S. Thompson, 1950, 1960) stresses a "burden of time" philosophy behind the time machine, but it includes full expositions of the machine and its parts. A less ambitious text is S. G. Morley's *An Introduction to the Study of the Maya Hieroglyphs* (1915), founded on *The Numeration, Calendar Systems and Astronomical Knowledge of the Mayas,* by C. P. Bowditch (1910), but these and numerous shorter descriptions of the system are no longer adequate. Morley's *The Ancient Maya* (1946; and as revised by G. W. Brainerd, 1956) perpetuates an important early misconception of his noted later on.

The area of the lowland Maya languages (fig. 1) is unique in its wealth of date-bearing inscriptions on stone and in the complexity of its calendar system. Some of these elements were widely distributed in the Maya highlands and in ancient Mesoamerica generally. The hieroglyphic writing system is treated elsewhere in this Handbook. Thompson (1950) gives the best drawings of calendrical glyphs, which we shall mention only by name.

We first attempt to provide general background, terminology, and a superficial picture of calendrical mechanics, which do not differ in principle from our own Christian calendar. Then we consider particular time-counts in some detail and discuss the astronomy which can be inferred from recorded positions or dates in some of them, with final emphasis on the problem of correlating Maya and Christian dates.

The paper is not only descriptive but offers some criticism of published interpretations and a modicum of new inferences, in the hope that if a nonspecialist fails to follow the latter fully, nevertheless he will obtain a general idea of why correlation hypotheses have differed by over a millen-

FIG. 1—MAP OF THE MAYA AREA SHOWING ARCHAEOLOGICAL SITES WITH HIEROGLYPHIC TEXTS AND MAIN LINGUISTIC DIVISIONS AS THEY PROBABLY WERE IN THE SIXTEENTH CENTURY. Som minor sites in Yucatan and Campeche are omitted to avoid crowded lettering. Broken line marks approximate area c lowland Maya speech. Note that all sites with hieroglyphic inscriptions are within that area. (Map and caption afte J. E. S. Thompson, 1950.)

nium, with the "leading" Spinden and Thompson ones differing by about 260 years. He should also be able to judge claims that "the Maya calendar" was "more accurate" than that of their conquerors, and realize the limited sense in which their astronomy was "accurate."

Mesoamerican calendars are best viewed as pseudoscientific tools of shamans and priests for divination and the regulation of rituals addressed to a multitude of supernaturals. Specific gods "ruled" during cyclically repeating short or long periods, to which they were assigned. The resulting complexity exceeds the needs of time measurement in affairs of daily life, or the recording of history in the ordinary sense, though such uses of the calendar were not precluded. The number of cycles running concurrently suggests growth of the complete system by accretion. Jakeman (1947) and Thompson (1950, pp. 150–53) speculate on stages in such a process. Kelley (1960) investigates possible Old World connections, which are generally denied.

Calendars may be represented by purely numerical models, so that an "arithmetic approach" has permitted "decipherment" of hieroglyphically recorded Maya dates, though not necessarily implying knowledge of spoken Maya words. The decipherments rest on inferences of many scholars, foremost Thompson, who also calls the roll of his predecessors and contemporaries (1950, pp. 28–34). He makes full use of the arithmetic approach, but uses it as a control, not only in seeking decipherments but also in translating noncalendrical glyphs, some hundreds of which are not understood. Others are now following his lead.

The most ancient deciphered dates have immediate value for archaeologists because they date associated objects on an accurate time-scale covering about 600 years. They will be more valuable when the correlation is settled, a prerequisite for a fuller understanding of Maya achievements in astronomy. Maya calendrics form a significant chapter in the history of science, not yet fully exploited.

Throughout the Maya complex the basic time unit is the day, whether a specific segment of time was labeled as the date, or "distance numbers" expressed the interval between a pair of dates. There were no formal divisions of the day, such as hours, minutes, and seconds. Presumably one day ended and another began at the same time in all counts, probably either at sunset or sunrise, i.e., at about 6 P.M. or 6 A.M. in local as opposed to Greenwich Mean Time. In recording a position or date in a particular cycle the designation of the day or longer period was one of a repeating sequence or cycle of numbers, names, or combinations of these, as in the Christian calendar. It is probable that dates involving names were converted to numerical form for calculation purposes, such as determining when an esoterically significant combination of dates in different cycles would occur in future or had occurred in the past.

Special terms and the chronological framework require comment. The raw Maya calendrical data are spread through a considerable period of time. We use "Protoclassic" for the last portion of the Preclassic or Formative period and "Classic" for the next era, probably from A.D. 300 to 900 (Morley and Brainerd, 1956, Table 3). "Postclassic" covers the period from then to the conquest, officially completed in Yucatan in 1542.

The provisional limits for the Classic period depend on an unproved but probable "Thompson" correlation of Initial Series or Long Count dates with Christian dates. Other solutions of the correlation problem move the Classic period forward or backward in Christian chronology by as much as 260 years. Initial Series dates are Long Count dates recorded in a special style characteristic of the Classic period, Long Count being preferred when referring to structure and function. It involves counting periods of time from a common

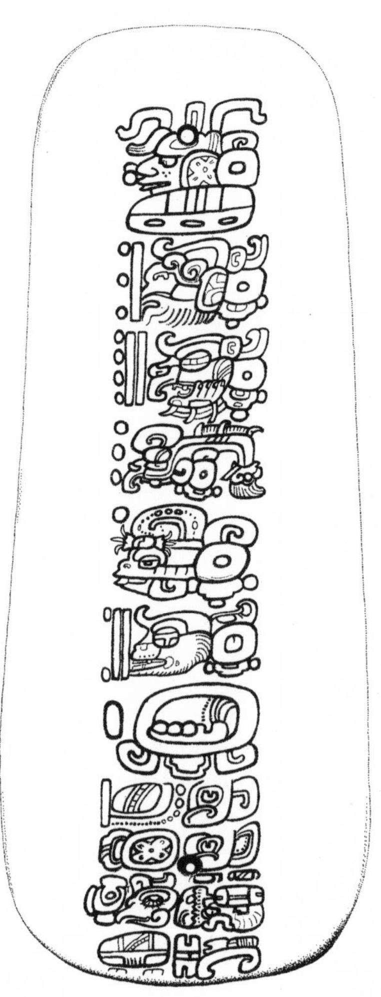

FIG. 2—INSCRIPTION ON BACK OF LEYDEN PLAQUE. Text records Initial Series date 8.14.3.1.12 1 Eb G5 0 Yaxkin, followed by five noncalendrical hieroglyphs. (Drawn from photograph by W. R. Coe; after Shook, 1960.)

fixed date in the past, as we do with "A.D. 1960."

The periods of the Long Count appear to have been a Protoclassic addition to those of the Calendar Round, the accepted term for the more widely distributed Mesoamerican calendar in its Maya manifestations. The term "round" implies the permutation of dates or positions in separable cycles, as in our "Monday, January 4." Each "round" cycle covers a period after which the same date combination appears again. In the Calendar Round cycle the constituent cycles are a 365-day vague year and two weeklike cycles of 13 and 20 days. The latter alone form a period of 260 days, here called "Sacred Round." Thompson's term is "Sacred Almanac"; other terms are "Tzolkin" and the Aztec "Tonalamatl," now replaced in Mexican contexts by "Tonalpohualli," avoiding the implication of a written "almanac." The permutation of the Sacred Round with the vague year, which lacked leap days, produced the Calendar Round cycle of 52 vague years, or 18,980 days.

The earliest evidence for the Sacred Round count, and possibly for the larger Calendar Round cycle, is non-Maya. Caso (1958b, p. 73) finds it on stone at Monte Alban in Oaxaca, placing it in the 6th century B.C. at least. Because calendar systems may be unwritten, or recorded only on perishable materials, their origin must remain unknown. But it evidently lay well back in the Preclassic period; certainly thereafter the Calendar Round was always of basic esoteric importance. A date in the shorter Sacred Round is often referred to as "the day."

The earliest surviving Maya dates are those of the Classic period, with the Long Count increment. They appear in hieroglyphic texts, most commonly carved on large stone monuments, especially stelae, related to ceremonial buildings, and involve an elaborate iconography of priests or gods. I shall refer to the corpus of Classic texts as "the inscriptions," though texts were sometimes painted on plastered walls or on pottery. Figures 2 and 4 show a text incised on a small jade object and another carved on wooden lintel beams of a temple.

Calendrical names were recorded in alternative styles, one called "symbolic" or "normal," the other "personified" or "head variant." Mesoamerican counting was normally vigesimal, with 20 as the radix, so there was need for digits from 1 to 19. These could be written with head-variant glyphs, but the easy-to-read normal style was with dots and bars. In decimal notation, each dot represents 1, each bar, 5. For example, reading down in figure 2, the first five numbers to the left of the head-variant glyphs are 8, 14, 3, 1, 12. If, as in this example, a series of numerals are related as digits of a multiterm number above 20, we transcribe them with points or points and dashes marking off the places. In this case we have an Initial Series number transcribed as 8.14.3.1.12 or as 8.14-3-1-12. Figures 2 and 4 illustrate the usual arrangement of number and glyphs in glyph blocks forming columns or columns and rows. For reference, columns are lettered, rows are numbered. Normally one reads down in a column, or from left to right across two columns and down to the next row.

Figure 1 locates most known ceremonial centers with inscriptions, but others are continually being discovered. The earliest Classic texts are concentrated in the vicinity of Uaxactun and Tikal, in northeastern Peten, Guatemala, about the middle of lowland Maya area. It is likely that the Long Count originated here and developed into a glyphic system, its earliest recordings having vanished on perishable materials in Protoclassic times. There is a disputed claim, however, that the earliest contemporaneous Long Count dates are non-Maya, witness the Tuxtla Statuette from Vera Cruz (fig. 3).

A Classic inscription may record one date only, usually followed by noncalendrical glyphs; but other dates also associated with noncalendrical glyphs may appear in the same text, with time-distance-measuring numbers showing the intervals between the dates. The patterning of the dates is different from that in another corpus of dates and distant numbers, found in three paper Postclassic manuscripts which have survived: the Dresden (Dresdensis), Paris (Peresianus), and Madrid (Tro-Cortesianus) codices. These are filled with tabulations roughly analogous to our almanacs.

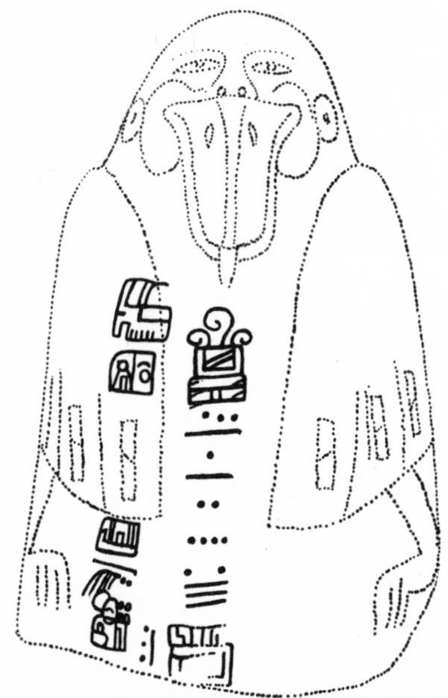

FIG. 3—NON-MAYA INSCRIPTION ON FRONT OF TUXTLA STATUETTE. Note absence of period glyphs with digits of a number 8.6.2.4.17, with reliance on position-value notation. (After Holmes, 1907.)

Clearly, one looked things up in these tables of sequences of dates and distance numbers to be repeated cyclically, with descriptive glyphs and often with pictures of gods. Individual gods have been designated by letters.

Each codex is a long strip of paper folded screen-wise into numbered "pages." A single table or group of related ones may extend across several pages. In the Dresden Codex only, some tables are supplied with "introductions" containing Long Count dates. Here we are concerned only with certain of these, and references to "the codex" are confined to the Dresden Codex. All three codices show a remarkable flair for horizontal-vertical tabulation, and functional use of red and black color. It is not unreasonable to suppose that the calendar complex developed in Preclassic times, with paper as the principal medium for recording. With the exception of the three codices, nothing survives from preconquest times except what was thought

Fig. 4—LEFT PANEL OF INSCRIPTION ON UNDERSIDE OF LINTEL 3, TEMPLE 4, TIKAL. Text opens with Period End date equivalent to Initial Series date 9.15.10.0.0 3 Ahau 3 Mol, followed by Secondary Series date (After J.E.S. Thompson, 1950.)

worth recording on stone or other relatively imperishable materials, and much of that is damaged. There is evidence that codices were buried with the priestly owners in Classic times.

We come to another category of lowland Maya calendrical material: Yucatecan Maya dates, date-tabulations, and descriptions of the calendar. These are in postconquest documentary sources, which are here called "historical." It is here that the question of Maya-Christian correlations enters the picture, but unfortunately the Long Count of the ancient texts is absent, though there is a related "Short Count," to be described later. This term is fairly well established as an alternative for the Maya "U kahlay katunob" and does not refer to the 52-year Calendar Round as recently discussed by Lizardi Ramos (1959, p. 235).

We have writings by the Spanish and by educated Maya who used the alphabet of their conquerers. The most important Spanish source is Bishop Diego de Landa's *Relación de las cosas de Yucatan,* ca. 1566. The Books of Chilam Balam, as late as the 18th century, show that the old calendrics went underground. These books relate to different towns and contain duplications and disagreements. Some materials may have been transcribed from more ancient originals. Historical chronicles reach far back of the conquest, events being dated in terms of the Short Count.

Valuable to a study of the correlation problem are historical sources of the Maya highlands, as are also modern survivals of Maya calendars, correlated with the Christian count.

A sampling of accessible sources will indicate the character of the raw calendrical data of the various periods. Morley (1920, 1937–38) published a great wealth of chronological decipherments, site by site, with illustrations or references. These are supplemented by invaluable tabulations and appendices, and by site maps relating the inscription-bearing monuments to architecture. Villacorta and Villacorta (1933) reproduced drawings of all three codices, page by page, with facing explanations in Spanish. The great pioneer Förstemann gave the basic analysis of the Dresden Codex, converting Maya numbers to decimal form (1906, an English translation of the 1901 German original). Tozzer's (1941a) translation of Landa's *Relación* is equally valuable for its commentary. R. L. Roys (1933) issued the Maya text of an important Yucatecan historical source, with translation into English. LaFarge (1931) listed and discussed Maya-Christian date equations in the Maya highlands, both historical and modern.

Table 1—EQUIVALENT DAY NAMES, LOWLAND AND HIGHLAND MAYA

I	*II*	*III*	*IV*	*V*	*Yucatec*	*Quiche (1722)*
A					Imix	Imox
	B				Ik	Ikh
		C			Akbal	Akhbal
			D		Kan	Kat
				E	Chicchan	Can
F					Cimi	Ceme
	G				Manik	Ceh
		H			Lamat	Khanil
			I		Muluc	Toh
				J	Oc	Tzih
K					Chuen	Batz
	L				Eb	Ee
		M			Ben	Ah
			N		Ix	Iix
				O	Men	Tzicin
P					Cib	Ahmac
	Q				Caban	Noh
		R			Etz'nab	Tihax
			S		Cauac	Caoc
				T	Ahau	Hunahpu

Note: Lists of day names from Thompson, 1950, Table 3. Letters added as cross-tribal symbols for equivalent day names.

Calendar Round and Related Cycles

We have noted that the Calendar Round is formed by the permutation of three cycles of 13, 20, and 365 days, the two shorter weeklike cycles forming a shorter Sacred Round, also called Sacred Almanac or Tzolkin. The days of the 13-day cycle were simply numbered, but the 13 day numbers were apparently regarded as deities. The 20-day cycle was one of 20 day names, very fully discussed by Thompson (1950). Our Table 1 compares his list of Yucatecan day names with one of his lists from the Maya highlands, to bring out the important fact that equivalent day names can be traced cross-tribally. Much use has been made of the Aztec names.

The letters A–T at the left of Table 1 are

TABLE 2—EQUIVALENT MONTH NAMES, LOWLAND AND PROBABLY LOWLAND MAYA

	Yucatec	*Chol (?) (Kekchi ??)*
1st	Pop	?
2nd	Uo	Icat
3rd	Zip	Chaccat
4th	Zotz	?
5th	Zec	Cazeu
6th	Xul	Chichin
7th	Yaxkin	Ianguca
8th	Mol	Mol
9th	Ch'en	Zihora
10th	Yax	Yax
11th	Zac	Zac
12th	Ceh	Chac
13th	Mac	Chantemat
14th	Kankin	Uniu
15th	Muan	Muhan
16th	Pax	Ankiku
17th	Kayab	Kanazi
18th	Cumku	Olh
	UAYEB	MAHI IKABA

Note: Lists of month names from Thompson, 1950, Table 8. In vague year all months of 20 days, with 5-day period between 18th and 1st months.

a convenience to cross-tribal comparisons. For example, we say that Day T is *Ahau* in Yucatecan Maya, *Hunahpu* in a Quiche calendar of 1722, and *Xochitl* in Aztec. Adding day numbers of the 13-day cycle, we may say that "Day 13 T" was regarded as the last day of the Sacred Round cycle in Yucatecan and Aztec, "Day 1 A" as the first. The day names and other calendrical terms represented by hieroglyphs in the inscriptions are always "translated" in the literature as if the authors were Yucatecans.

The 365-day vague year was called *haab* in the historical sources, but this term was also used for a 360-day *tun* period, basic in time-distance measuring numbers and the Long Count, discussed later. Thompson renders differing glyphs for that period as tun and haab. Lacking leap days, the vague year slipped slowly back in the solar or seasonal year, a fact which must have been known. Thus it has an artificial character, presumably for esoteric reasons. Like the 20-day cycle of named days, the year reflects vigesimal counting, for it is divided into 18 20-day months, plus a 5-day period "outside" the year proper, a period of supernatural dangers. Table 2 compares the Yucatecan month names with the one other known list probably applicable to a lowlands Maya group. There are enough similarities to show that the arrangement (from Thompson, 1950) is one of equivalent month names, one from the north, the other from the south of our area. Such equivalences are less easily traced than with day names, suggesting that the latter were more fundamental.

It will be helpful to restrict the term *month* to the 20-day divisions of the year, *uinal* to the 20-day divisions of the 360-day tun, though they appear in the literature interchangeably. In the inscriptions and the Dresden Codex position within the current month was fixed by numbering its days (and those of the 5-day period) in "elapsed time" style. This is analogous to our measuring the passage of a current day with numbered hours, entering the numbers so that the current hour designation becomes, say, 11 o'clock when the 11th hour has been completed. In the same way, when a Maya year date such as 19 Xul became the current one, the 19th day of Xul had ended. Logically one would expect 20 Xul to enter one day later, but the last day of the month was indirectly designated by one of two alternative non-numerical glyphs. At the end of the 20th day of Xul the next month Yaxkin begins. Normally, for our example, a glyph connoting the idea of beginning, and probably meaning "seating," would appear with the glyph for Yaxkin. Instead, in another and very rare style, one might find another glyph with that for Xul. This must mean "end of Xul," necessarily at the end of its 20th day.

We owe discovery of the behavior of these glyphs to Thompson (1950, pp. 120–21). "Seating of Yaxkin" is doubtless recorded with an early variant form of the "seating" glyph on the Leyden Plaque (fig. 2) and is universally transcribed as O Yaxkin. The zero or cipher sign is an unfortunate choice, but it is too well established to be discarded. The seating glyph enters at what could be described as the "zero point" of Yaxkin, but there is no "zero day." The glyph reflects the current-time entry of the complete named months.

There appears to be a fair presumption that in the ancient texts the *days* of all cycles entered in elapsed-time style whether named or numbered, in conformity with the periods of the Long Count, including its smallest unit, the day. There seems to be no good evidence for elapsed-time entry elsewhere than in the inscriptions and the Dresden Codex.

Combining the Sacred Round and vague-year cycles produces the 52-year Calendar Round cycle, covering 18,980 days, each day distinguished by a different combination of dates in the constituent cycles. In the inscriptions Thompson has distinguished a third weeklike 9-day cycle of nine "Lords of the Night," known also in Mexico at the conquest. It was not then running indefinitely, as in the Maya inscriptions of the Classic period. Glyphs for the Lords are labeled G1-G9, or G1-G8 and G0. Position in this cycle is recorded by the G5 form on the Leyden Plaque (fig. 2) immediately after the Sacred Round date 1 Eb, a normal position. Thompson also finds evidence but not proof of a fourth 7-day weeklike cycle of "Lords of the Earth."

When cycles are added which are not aliquot parts of others, they automatically generate larger rounds of individual date combinations. Adding the well-established 9-day cycle to the Calendar Round creates a round of 468 years. If, in some contexts, position in a 7-day cycle was added, the round covered 3,276 vague years. Thus, it is not impossible that proliferation of small weeklike cycles first led to interest in large segments of time.

Year Bearers and Calendar Round Types

Tables in the three Postclassic codices show a "year bearer" pattern found also in Yucatan and highland Maya historical sources, and in modern survivals in the latter area, first discovered by La Farge. A year bearer is one of a cycle of 52 Sacred Round days which coincides with the first day of the vague year. The bearers determined or indicated esoteric prognostications for the 52 years of the cycle and presumably for this reason they were used as names for the years themselves. However, the day numbers in these naming Sacred Round dates seem to have been of subordinate importance. Only four day names were involved, and "year bearer" may also refer to these only, as in the following discussion. These day names function as bearers in a cycle of only four years, and are spaced five days apart in the 20-day cycle itself.

In Table 1 letters A–T are arranged in five sets of four labeled with Roman numerals. Members of any set can fall only on a corresponding set of month positions in the year, as 1, 6, 11, 16; 2, 7, 12, 17, etc. If Set I (Days A, F, K, P) is tied to month positions 1, 6, 11, 16, the days of that set are the bearers. But this depends on how the Sacred Round and vague-year cycles are correlated. In spite of an undoubted common origin for all Calendar Round counts, there are differences in this respect, in the lowlands as well as in the highlands. We can use the Roman numerals as classificatory labels, and this is more convenient than spelling out Yucatecan equivalent day names as bearers, as has been customary.

The Calendar Round "typology" is independent of the naming function of the bearers. All one needs is a recorded day name, its position in our lettered scheme of cross-tribal day-name equivalences, and its position in some month of the vague year. For example, Caso (1939a) reconstructs an Aztec Calendar Round in which the day names of Set III name the years; but those

TABLE 3—CALENDAR ROUND TYPES OF MAYA HIGHLANDS AND LOWLANDS

Highlands	*CR Type*	*Calculated Year-Bearer Equations*		
Quiche (1722)	II	7 B	Mar. 11 1941	JDN 2,430,065
				0
Ixil (1941)	II	7 B	Mar. 11 1941	JDN 2,430,065
				1
Kanhobal (1932)	III	8 C	Mar. 12 1941	JDN 2,430,066
				29
Quiche (1854)	II	11 L	Apr. 10 1941	JDN 2,430,095
				235
Cakchiquel (1685)	II	12 G	Dec. 1 1941	JDN 2,430,330

Lowlands	*CR Type*
Classic Maya inscriptions, Dresden and Paris codices	III
"Shifted Classic" Maya inscriptions, Madrid Codex, Yucatecan historical sources	IV

Note: Yucatecan equivalents of highland year bearers are 7 Ik (7 B), 8 Akbal (8 C), 11 Eb (11 L), 12 Manik (12 G). See Table 1 for letters representing day names.

of Set IV are the bearers, as in the Calendar Round of 16th-century Yucatan. Both are Type IV Calendar Round calendars.

Table 3 summarizes the known highland and lowland Maya Calendar Round types. The process of differentiation in the highlands has been studied by LaFarge (1931). There reliable historical and modern ethnological correlations of year bearers and Christian dates are available. In the table four equations from LaFarge are projected to 1941, the year of the Ixil equation which is taken from Lincoln (1942). The latter is added to show its complete agreement with Quiche of 1722. The bearers at the calculated dates are shown with the letters of Table 1 representing the day names. Christian dates are followed by corresponding Julian Day Numbers (JDN) in the chronologist's count from January 1, 4713 B.C. In this column distance numbers 1, 29, and 235 measure the discontinuities in four Calendar Round counts in a restricted area within which they presumably once functioned simultaneously. The numbers connect Julian Day Number "dates" analogous to Long Count dates.

The tabulation illustrates important points made by LaFarge, the most significant of which is that the differentiation did not involve any breaks in the Sacred Round count. The four systems show the same Sacred Round correlation, which LaFarge labeled the "Intertribal Tzolkin." Granting a common origin, the 5-day period of the year must have been shifted among the named months, resulting in the overlapping of at least some equivalent months. Some shifts of the 5-day period must have been by distances which were multiples of five days, producing three variant Type II Calendar Rounds. On the other hand, if Quiche-Ixil was derived from Kanhobal, or vice versa, there was a 1-day shift of the whole year pattern. A shift from some third count, however, might have had the same effect (Satterthwaite, 1947, pp. 157–63).

Brainerd follows Morley in specifying the Type II bearers Ik, Manik, Eb, and Caban for the inscriptions, postulating two 1-day shifts, first to Type III and then to Type IV (Morley and Brainerd, 1956, pp. 253–54). Thompson specifies Akbal, Lamat, Ben, and Eznab for inscriptions and the Dresden Codex. These Type III bearers are required by his convincing interpretation of the so-called "zero" month position. However, Proskouriakoff and Thompson (1947) demonstrate a few sporadic shifts from a Type III Calendar Round to Type IV in inscriptions confined to the Campeche and Usumacinta regions. In Table 3 we label these "Shifted Classic." Long Count control shows that the Sacred Round count was unbroken, as in the highlands, and that the shift in the year was definitely a 1-day one. This is strong confirmation of LaFarge's thesis that the Intertribal Tzolkin was universal in preconquest times.

On this assumption LaFarge proposed that Landa was mistaken by one day in placing a Type IV bearer 12 Kan 1 Pop at July 16, undoubtedly in 1553, July 15 being required. An alternative explanation is a "freezing" of the Maya to the Christian year in 1552, by introducing leap days or equivalent double-counting so that bearers always fell at July 16, as Landa himself specifies, and as they do in later equations in the Yucatecan historical sources. Correlationists of the Long Count have long assumed a 1-day spread between the normal Type III Calendar Round of the inscriptions and Landa's Type IV Calendar Round. The evidence for it is very strong, but with the discontinuity in the year count, not the Sacred Round count, as assumed in Thompson's original correlation, though not in that of Spinden. Thompson now accepts the LaFarge reasoning, as noted later.

Long Count Dating and Time Measurement

In the inscriptions and the Dresden Codex pairs of Sacred Round or Calendar Round dates are associated with numbers which measure the quantity of elapsed time between them. Because such dates recur cyclically this quantity may exceed the minimum which one may calculate from the dates themselves. The quantity may be visualized as a "time distance," and any such number is then logically classed as a distance number. Various types may be distinguished, among them the "Secondary Series" of the inscriptions. Thompson seems to restrict "distance number" to these, but Long Count or Initial Series numbers measure time distances with the same system of small to very large periods. These periods are listed in Table 4, the smallest being the kin, the Maya term for "day."

The table brings out the special unitary character of the 360-day tun period. Twenty tuns are converted to 1 katun, and so on with the higher orders on the vigesimal principle. But the tun itself is formed of only 18 uinals. It appears to be a "calculator's year," of which the kins and uinals are divisions. However, in adding or subtracting numbers formed on this plan all distance numbers may be regarded as giving a modified vigesimal count of single days, analogous to our chronologist's decimally expressed Julian Day Count. With Table 4 one may easily convert a Maya distance number to decimal notation. For example two baktuns are 288,000 ($2 \times 144{,}000$) days; they also equal 800 (2×400) tuns, closer to our habit of thinking in terms of years. Note that 1 kinchiltun, the period of the eighth order, is equal to 3,200,000 tuns, and the system could be logically expanded.

An Initial Series or Long Count date is a Sacred Round or Calendar Round date supplied with a Long Count distance number. Normally this is counted forward from a special "normal" date 4 Ahau 8 Cumku, projected into the mythological past when the count was inaugurated. It is also convenient to think of the Long Count number alone as an Initial Series or Long Count "date," though in the texts the Sacred Round or the full Calendar Round date reached is always stated after the number.

In Maya place-value notation, periods are always recorded in descending order of their values. If the count of any period has reached completion, say 18 uinals or 20 tuns, this is indicated with a sign probably meaning completion, though it is called

TABLE 4—PERIODS FORMING MAYA LONG COUNT AND DISTANCE NUMBERS AND THEIR DECIMAL-NOTATION VALUES IN TUNS AND DAYS

1 kinchiltun	=	3,200,000 tuns	=	1,152,000,000 days	(very rare)
1 calabtun	=	160,000 tuns	=	57,600,000 days	(very rare)
1 pictun	=	8,000 tuns	=	2,880,000 days	(rare)
1 baktun	=	400 tuns	=	144,000 days	
1 katun	=	20 tuns	=	7,200 days	
1 tun	=	1 tun	=	360 days	
1 uinal	=	20 kins	=	20 days	
1 kin	=	1 kin	=	1 day	

Note: Tun also called haab in some contexts; baktun, pictun, calabtun, and kinchiltun also called cycle, great cycle, great-great cycle, and great-great-great cycle.

"zero" and we transcribe it thus. As an example a Long Count date on page 70a of the codex is fully transcribed by 4 Ahau 8 Cumku 10.11.4.0.14 9 Ix. Eighteen uinals have been "carried" as one more tun, leaving the uinal term "at zero." We depend on position in deciding that the digit 4 is the coefficient or multiplier of the tun, and not of some other period. Entry of the zero sign is necessary to keep the places straight. The codex uses this position-value notation for all types of distance numbers. The "zero of completion" sign serves as place-indicator whenever needed, precisely as in our "A.D. 1960" or as in "1960 days" in the Julian Day Count.

The Maya positional notation is generally regarded as a major intellectual advance, without stimulus from the Old World. In the Classic inscriptions it was almost never exclusively relied on, since glyphs for the periods normally follow the coefficients. Perhaps this is because Secondary Series numbers leading directly or in sequence from Initial Series dates to Secondary Series dates were recorded in the reverse or ascending order of period values. Presence of period glyphs in both types of number makes this clear, and permits occasional abbreviation by omitting a period count, which is then understood to be at zero. A very few Secondary Series distance numbers fail to show the reversed order.

The Long Count dates of the inscriptions are called "Initial Series" because they usually open the text. They begin with an often oversize "Initial Series introducing glyph" with a variable element first shown by Beyer to indicate the patron god of the month to be reached. The base date of the Long Count is implicit, not expressed as in the codex. The Leyden Plaque (fig. 2) shows the earliest complete and probably contemporaneous Initial Series, with period glyphs of the head-variant type. Ignoring these, this is transcribed as IS 8.14.3.1.12 1 Eb 0 Yaxkin. Had the scribe wished to advance to another Calendar Round date, say 3 Ahau 8 Mol, 28 days later, he would have also recorded the Secondary Series "8 (kins) 1 uinal 3 Ahau 8 Mol." In Secondary Series the kin glyph was usually omitted as indicated by the parentheses. Secondary Series are usually transcribed in the descending order, necessary when adding or subtracting to obtain the Long Count position which is implicit, as in the transcription below.

IS 8.14.3.1.12	1 Eb 0 Yaxkin	(1,253,912 days)
1. 8		(28 days)
(8.14.3.3. 0	3 Ahau 8 Mol	(1,253,940 days)

The Long Count and Secondary Series numbers are repeated in decimal day-count form at the right, converting with the aid of Table 4. The "secondary" nature of the smaller number is obvious. There is no satisfactory explanation for the reversed order of the periods of Maya Secondary Series numbers.

If the lowest terms of a Long Count number are at zero, including at least the two lowest, the date is classed as at a "period end"; otherwise it is a "non-tun-ending" or "odd" date in terms of the Long Count. Most texts of the inscriptions contain a period-ending date. A Period End statement may substitute for the Initial Series, but from the context that can be calculated. For example, the text on the Tikal lintel (fig. 4) opens with 3 Ahau 3 Mol, half period of katun. The Long Count position of the Calendar Round must be 9.15.10.0.0. A Secondary Series number 2.2.2 leads immediately to the Secondary Series date 11 Ik 15 Chen, which therefore must be at Long Count position 9.15.12.2.2, an odd Long Count date. In the complete text, not illustrated, two other Secondary Series lead farther forward in a sequence or "chain." The complete chronological structure of this text is given in Thompson, 1950, figure 52.

In several inscriptions the Normal Date 4 Ahau 8 Cumku is given as a Period End, the statement being deciphered as "end of 13 baktuns." At Palenque there is an IS 12.19.13.4.0 8 Ahau 18 Zec and at Quirigua an IS 13.0.0.0.0 4 Ahau 8 Cumku. Both are counted from a base-date 4 Ahau 8 Zotz, 13 baktuns earlier than the normal Long Count base 4 Ahau 8 Cumku. Evidently Long Count numbers gave positions in repeating 13-baktun cycles, and could not exceed 13.0.0.0.0, just as a day number in the 13-day cycle could not exceed 13, which is the "zero" of the next count. Presumably there was special esoteric significance in the round of the Long Count baktun with the Sacred Round, as there surely was in the round of the katun, described later under "Short Count."

By Initial Series or Long Count one usually means the count from 4 Ahau 8 Cumku, in the 13-baktun cycle current when a present-time "inaugural" Calendar Round date must have been first assigned a Long Count position. Thompson (1950, pp. 150–53) reviews and rejects proposed specific inaugural dates, but suggests 7.0.0.0.0 to 8.5.0.0.0 as probable limits. In an article (1961a) I have since suggested 8.6.1.9.0. The inaugural date was, by definition, the earliest recorded Long Count date which was approximately contemporaneous with its recording.

The earliest known contemporaneous Maya Long Count date is 8.12.14.8.15, on the incomplete Stela 29 at Tikal (Shook, 1960); the latest in the inscriptions is 10.3.0.0.0. These, in Long Count terms, define the presently known spread of the Classic or Initial Series period in our area. Long Count dates in the Dresden Codex which may have been contemporaneous when first recorded range from 8.6.16.7.14 to 10.17.13.12.12, both appearing with others on page 70 of the codex. We bypass a possible reconstruction of 10.19.6.1.8 on page 58 (Satterthwaite, 1951a). The codex dates, like those of the inscriptions, show an interest in "Maya historical" as well as mythological past time.

The 8.6.16.7.14 date cited is the Long Count equivalent of what is actually stated. A distance number 8.6.16.12.0 is counted forward from Sacred Round date 9 Ix to another suppressed 9 Ix. A ring number, 4.6, is counted forward from the same early 9 Ix to the normal date 4 Ahau 8 Cumku. Subtracting the ring number 4.6 from the longer recorded distance number 8.6.16.12.0 gives the Long Count position of its terminal date. Failure to fully understand this and other ring numbers led Morley (1937–38, 4: 271) and his predecessors to list erroneous Initial Series dates for the codex, in this case 8.6.16.12.0.

In the codex there are eight 6-term numbers counted forward from a fixed base-date 9 Kan 12 Kayab, analogous to the fixed base of the Long Count. One of these counts, on page 62, transcribes as 9 Kan 12 Kayab 4.6.9.15.12.19 13 Akbal 1 Kankin. Nearby is the "ring-and-distance-numbers" equivalent of Long Count date 10.6.10.6.3 13 Akbal (1 Kankin). It has been reasonably inferred that the terminal dates are identical, in which case the 9 Kan 12 Kayab base was earlier than the normal date by 3.16.3.5.6.16. Subtractions of this constant from the Serpent Numbers give the highly probable Long Count positions for their terminal dates, all being Baktun 9 or Baktun 10 dates. That cited is the latest. But only in that one case is there evidence that the position of a single terminal date in both counts might be needed.

It should be clear that mere existence of a multiterm number does not prove it to be a Long Count number. This is claimed, however, for the number on the non-Maya Tuxtla Statuette (fig. 3). The theory assumes a combination of position-value notation, as in the codex, and substitution of the introducing glyph for the base date as in the inscriptions. It further assumes that this base was 4 Ahau at 8 Cumku, not at 8 Zotz. Granting all this, the illegible terminal day name must be the equivalent of Yucatecan Caban. Morley accepted decipherment as IS 8.6.2.4.17 8 Caban, but not as a contemporaneous date. Thompson makes a very plausible case for seeing a 5-term number connecting two non-Maya Sacred Round dates, of which only the day numbers (10 and 8) can be read by inspection. These are correct if the period values are in descending order, but in a logical *unmodified* vigesimal system, for which there is other evidence (Thompson, 1941a). Wauchope (1950, pp. 237–38) and M. D. Coe (1957b) support the Long Count interpretations of Stirling and others, seeing these as contemporaneous recordings. It is an important link in an argument that the La Venta Olmec originated the Long Count with a Baktun 7 inauguration date and, by implication, positional notation with its necessary written zero sign.

Additions and subtractions of all types of distance numbers were probably made with physical counters on a flat surface, with spaces for the periods and empty spaces for those at zero (Long, 1948; Thompson, 1941b, designs a hypothetical abacus). Archaeology can give no clue to the time and place within Mesoamerica for the origin of the position-value concept, as opposed to its use in recording results. It would be useful as soon as there was need for manipulating multiterm numbers of anything. Thompson cites evidence for an abacus in Peru, and empty spaces on Inca quipus seem to have recorded zero in a decimal system (Locke, 1923, fig. 3).

In judging the claim for a Long Count record on the Tuxtla Statuette it should be remembered that in the inscriptions the introducing glyphs, with its variable patron-indicating element, was apparently essential. On Stela 10 at Tikal it appears with an 8-term number, the only known case. This has led to theories of an "expanded" Long Count, with positions not limited to 13.0.0.0.0 or less. For differing speculations see Morley (1937–38, 1: 308–26) and Thompson (1950, App. 4). Morley assumes a base date 5 Ahau 8 Yaxkin, 1.11.19.0.-0.0.0.0 before the normal date 4 Ahau 8 Cumku. Thompson's version calculates to 9 Ahau 3 Kankin as a base 1.13.0.0.0.0.0.0 before the normal date. Another count at Quirigua, if I understand him, calculates to a base date 7 Ahau 8 Xul, 1.0.1.13.0.0.0.-0.0.0 (10 terms) before the normal date. These inferred early bases are not logical expansions of the 13-baktun cycle system since the base dates are not at 4 Ahau. In this respect they are comparable to the Serpent Numbers of the codex.

Morley recognizes an apparent expanded Initial Series on Stela 1 at Coba, transcribed as 13.13.13.13.0.0.0.0 4 Ahau 8 Cumku. It is a count forward to the normal date by vigesimal multiples of 13 baktuns. But there is no introducing glyph. Morley also notes a clear Secondary Series

13.13.13.1.1.0.11.14 on the Stone of Chiapa. The tun, doubtless at zero, is suppressed. The base for the expanded Coba Initial Series, if real, is 4 Ahau 3 Pop, the earliest vague-year position for Ahau. The number equals 43,789,200 tuns.

We turn from such stupendous distance numbers to ordinary inscriptions recording Long Count dates with baktun coefficients of 8, 9, or 10, and without higher periods. Except for the earliest texts there is usually a tun-end date which reflects a time-marking pattern governing the time of carving and erection of the monuments bearing most of the texts. Subject to exceptions the "contemporaneous," "commemorative," or "dedicatory" date is at a tun-end of the Long Count, and is the latest date if others are given. The latter are usually odd, non-tun dates. In descending order of frequency the dedicatory dates are at ends of katuns, of half-katuns or "lahuntuns," of first or third quarters of katuns, of the 13th tun, or of other tuns (Morley, 1937–38, 4: Tables 138, 139). The last two are very rare and the others are classed as "hotun-ends." A special importance of the katun is thus demonstrated. Stylistic analyses of accompanying "scenes" are important controls in determining dedicatory dates. Spinden (1913, reprinted in 1957b) and Proskouriakoff (1950) are major contributors in that field.

The spread of recorded odd dates in a given text may reach back from the dedicatory date by many katuns or even baktuns, but usually by less than a katun or two. Recording of future dates is very rare. Explaining the recorded nondedicatory dates is an important problem. The best evidence of esoteric calculations is an 819-day cycle discovered by Thompson (1950, pp. 213–17). Various astronomical meanings have been postulated. Barthel (1951) has made a recent study in this tradition. A solar year "determinant" theory is discussed later as is a lunar count in a "Supplementary Series" appearing with many Initial Series. Proskouriakoff (1944) questions recording of dates of eclipses or other dramatic celestial events, noting that the same odd date was seldom recorded at more than one site. Her 1960 study breaks new ground with a radical hypothesis that recording of many odd dates may have involved the histories of local rulers. There is reason to expect future progress in this difficult field, which requires analysis of recorded distance numbers, of noncalendrical glyphs, and of accompanying scenes.

Calculation from Long Count Epochs in the Dresden Codex

The numerous and varying tables comprising the three codices cannot here be described in detail. Their basic common features are tabulated sequences of Sacred Round dates which are stations in repeating esoteric cycles. Distance numbers show the structures of the cycles and glyphs and usually pictures describe the stations. The periods of these described cycles are normally 26, 52, or 65 days, but in the Dresden Codex they are not always aliquot parts of the Sacred Round period and they may cover more than 260 days. Provision is always made for following the described cycle through at least one round with the all-important Sacred Round period.

Two tables of the Dresden Codex are unique in dealing respectively with the planet Venus and with eclipses, though obviously with esoteric overtones. These and several purely esoteric tables are engaged in the Long Count. Below we give a partial model of one of these, on pages 69–73 of the codex. It is analyzed by Thompson (1950, pp. 253–54) as the "5×13" table because there is an 1820-day cycle of 28 described stations, the latter spaced evenly at 65-day intervals. In the model we save space by using decimal equivalents of Maya numbers, and the letters of our Table 1 for day names. Glyphs describing the stations are not represented. The last station is 4 Eb (4 L).

A. Epoch	1,567,332 4L					
B. Period Multiples	109,200 4L		94,640 4L		72,800 4L	etc. to 3640 4L
C. Stations	65 4Q	130 4B	195 4G	260 4L	325 4Q	390 etc. to 1820 4C 4L

An epoch at 4 Eb (A) is supplemented by a sequence of distance numbers which must also reach 4 Eb (B). These are multiples of the 1820-day period number of the cycle, which ends on 4 Eb (C). The complete series of period multiples consists of the 60th, 52nd, 40th, 36th, 28th, 24th, 20th, 16th, 12th, 8th, 3rd, and 2nd multiples. The epoch and the multiples are in an "introduction" to the described cycle (C). Each station of the latter is associated with another special type of distance number which we may label "position number." For example, the position of the fifth station is Day 325, counting from the end of the last prior cycle at Day 1820.

By adding one of the multiples or a combination of them to the epoch, later epochs at 4 Eb can be obtained. It is also arithmetically possible to reach earlier epochs by subtraction. Given some distance forward or backward from the epoch, that distance can be divided by the period number 1820, subtracting the highest possible given multiple, repeatedly if necessary. The remainder gives the net change in cycle position at the given distance from the epoch. Below we solve a hypothetical problem by dividing in this manner, using Maya as well as decimal numbers and actual day names as well as letters for them. Assuming special interest in the tun-end Long Count date 11.12.18.0.0 1 Ahau, we want its precise position in the 1820-day 4 Eb cycle.

The answer is that our Long Count date 11.12.18.0.0 is at Cycle Position 348 which is 23 days after the fifth station at 4 Caban. We searched the recorded series of multiples and position numbers, choosing the highest possible in each case. Though we subtracted, we were really working forward in time from the recorded epoch, passing a later epoch not recorded.

There is a presumption that the recorded epoch lay in past time for the calculator because in the inscriptions distance numbers usually, though not universally, lead forward through past time. One would expect such tables as this to cover past, present, and perhaps future time without backward counting from the epoch. Put differently, one would expect the earliest epoch likely to be needed to appear with the table, though not necessarily the latest one.

This is an important inference because our epoch 10.17.13.12.12 4 Eb is the latest sure Long Count date in the codex. If it lay in past time for the user of the table, it is an approximate early limit for the painting of this copy of the codex. The much earlier Long Count dates which appear to be epochs for the astronomical tables must then have been far in the past

	LC 11.12.18. 0. 0	1	Ahau	LC 1,676,880	1	A
A. Epoch	−10.17.13.12.12	4	Eb	−1,567,332	4	L
	15. 4. 5. 8			109,548		
B. 60th Multiple	− 15. 3. 6. 0	4	Eb	− 109,200	4	L
	17. 8			348		
C. Station	− 16. 5	4	Caban	− 325	4	Q
	1. 3			23		

for the user of the codex. Thompson (1950, p. 24), citing the 4 Eb date, places the *end* of the eclipse table "apparently" somewhat earlier, at 10.14.10.0.8. The epoch, if not recorded, can be advanced farther as far as positive controls are concerned, so that all calculating tables of the codex cover the user's present time. The calculated "current" epoch may be much later than the recorded one. It is here suggested that present-time coverage of all such tables should be assumed with forward counting only. In that case 10.17.13.12.12 is only an early limit for the contemporaneous date of the codex.

Astronomy

Much has been written on this subject, and I am no astronomer. On the other hand, interpretations of those skilled in modern astronomy do not all agree, so one must dodge the problems or attempt to judge. An astronomer may overproject his knowledge into the Maya record.

As with the calendar system, one is faced with cycles but they involve fractions of a day and time distances between sequent recurrences of the same event may vary by many days. Nevertheless the Maya could easily record the dates on which the celestial events had been observed to occur. In our ignorance of the meaning of most noncalendrical glyphs there is difficulty, however, in deciding when they did so. The basic method must be the "arithmetic approach"–analyzing for patterns in dates and distances while seeking confirmation in patterns among associated noncalendrical glyphs. There are many recorded dates and many astronomical phenomena—and therefore danger of failing to allow sufficiently for the long arm of coincidence. In this area of investigation there have been many disagreements as to what was intended by the Maya.

With Long Count control and availability of paper on which to write, the way was open for Maya calculators to analyze recorded dates of the same observed astronomical event. If they discovered patterns in the dates and/or the intervals between them, it would be natural to project the patterns into the future as predictions. On this level a high degree of caution seems appropriate.

We confine ourselves to the astronomical phenomena dealt with in Teeple's fundamentally important 1930 study: the solar year, the phases of the moon, a solar-eclipse-predicting pattern of same moon-age days, and the cycle of appearances and disappearances of the planet Venus as morning and evening star. The eclipse data are on pages 51–58 of the Dresden Codex in a table sometimes called the "Lunar Series," here simply called the "eclipse table." This follows a Venus table on pages 24, 46–50. These two tables provide the best basis for judging intellectual achievements of the Maya. If Long Count epochs for these tables can be agreed on, they provide precise checks on correlation hypotheses, for which reason considerable space is devoted to the matter of epochs. The eclipse table presupposes moon-age calculation as well as observation. Teeple showed that moon ages were recorded in the inscriptions; in a few cases they were certainly calculated though he thought that most of them reflected observation.

He gives the length of the solar year as 365.2423 days at A.D. 600 and 365.2422 days at present. Apparently there was no appreciable variation in year length throughout Maya history. Accurate baseline observations of equinox day or of a nearby day taken for it appear to be easy (Merrill, 1945; Long, 1948). It seems fair to presume that the Maya measured the backward slip of their uncorrected 365-day year in the true solar year, and with considerable accuracy. This would require a basic whole-day equation of 1461 days for four solar years as in our Julian and Gregorian calendars. The error in this equation is 0.0308 days, which accumulates to 0.2464 days at the eighth repetition. The next common 365-day year cancels this accumulated error almost exactly. Thus, granting a recording of accurate equinox-day observations over two or three generations, the need for correcting a 1461-day solar year period to 1460 days should have been apparent. For long-distance calculation one would expect adoption of a Maya rule for secondary corrections analogous to those of our Gregorian calendar.

A "determinant theory" of Teeple has been developed by Thompson (1950, App. 5) and is widely accepted. This theory assumes that many dates in the inscriptions record the net slips of the vague year as of the time of selected contemporaneous dates, calculating from the time of the Long Count base date 4 Ahau 8 Cumku. It is assumed that the results were expressed in differing ways and also that differing solar-year formulae were used so that accepted results vary from Gregorian calculations by as much as ± 3 days. No confirmatory pattern has emerged among the noncalendrical glyphs. For me it is difficult to imagine such a spread of error in solving what appears to have been the simplest Maya astronomical problem. I have questioned (1947, pp. 125–42), with given reasons, the only formula proposed, which yielded Teeple's "Copan year" with an average length of 365.2420 days. The formula involves equating 149 moons with 4400 days, for which (it is claimed) there is no convincing evidence.

The determinant theory does not affect the correlation problem, nor the presumption that a slip of one day in four years was normally allowed in regulating agricultural and other seasonally determined activities.

When we turn to the phases of the moon, we have an average cycle of 29.53059 days and face the complicating factor of variations from this average moon of up to 0.06 days (Andrews, 1940, p. 154, quoting Ludendorf). I have reviewed (1947) various attempts to work out Maya lunar predicting cycles and indicated that an experimental approach shows additional possibilities but not proved Maya schemes.

It is clear that they were based on alternating formal 29-day and 30-day moons, with rules for primary and secondary corrections of the basic 59-day equation, which rapidly accumulates error at the rate of 0.06118 days. There is little doubt that at Palenque such a scheme of whole-day "formal" moons completed its cycle in 11,960 days as the value for 405 moons—or possibly in one-fifth of this, the equation being 2392 days for 81 moons. The latter is Teeple's "Palenque Formula," which does not specify the internal formal moon pattern of the period. The 11,960-day period is written 1.13.4.0 and is equal to 46 periods of 260 days. Hence, as a distance number it always connects the same Sacred Round days at the same formal moon age, obviously an esoteric reason for choosing it.

Assuming that one knew the internal pattern or structure of formal moons, one could calculate formal moon ages at any date. These would deviate within limits from ages which may be calculated with the average value for one moon. The 11,960-day period is about 0.11 days longer than 11,959.88835 days for 405 average moons. The average error may be expressed as a deviation of −0.11 days, counting back as a correction from the larger Maya whole-day value to the average or mean value. A plus deviation would be counted forward to a larger mean value.

On repeating the 11,960-day period as a cycle, the error accumulates to just over a full day at the ninth repetition, and this is reflected in two Palenque moon-age calculations far into the mythological past. The calculations were made at about 9.13.0.0.0 in the Long Count, suggesting that greater accuracy with corrections of this period was then a matter for the future, in that region at least.

If predictions were made with this period, it is reasonable to suppose they were checked later by observation, and the results recorded. In spite of lunar variation from average and mistakes in observation, an archive of Long Count dates showing when a given Sacred Round date fell at a given moon age would show eventually that the 11,960-day yardstick was too long for long-distance prediction. As an average value for 405 moons its error accumulates to about 0.666 days at the sixth repetition (71,760 days). This accumulated error compares with one of 0.654 days for the fifth multiple of 260, i.e. for 1300 days for 44 moons. It follows that ideally the 6th 11,960-day period should be shortened by this amount if one wishes to reach the same Sacred Round day with a correcting period. The result is a 70,460-day corrected cycle covering nearly a half-baktun (9.15.-13.0), in which the proportion of short to standard lunar periods is 1:5 and the average error only 0.012 days. It would be easier to learn the need for such corrections than to fix on the correct ratio. Thompson proposed the use of the method as a likely hypothesis, but doubted that the ideal 1:5 ratio was known even in the relatively late codex. He notes (1950, pp. 235–36) the similar method of correcting the Venus table, discussed later.

His most cogent evidence in the codex is the interval between Long Count date 9.16.4.10.8 and an emended date 9.19.7.7.8, both at 12 Lamat in the introduction to the eclipse table. The interval between them equals 11,960 + 10,660 days. This seems good evidence for the method and for the end of the cycle at 9.19.7.7.8. It appears possible that the earlier of the two dates was at the end of the 4th standard period in a 1:5 scheme. Lacking evidence, we turn elsewhere for a hint that this may have been the case.

On pages 61–62 of the codex there are eight terminal dates reached by four black and four red 6-place "Serpent Numbers," and though emendations are required, all have been firmly fixed in the Long Count. Four of these dates are tabulated below, with average moon ages calculated from a single arbitrary base, in parentheses. For any Long Count correlation these would be changed by a constant amount.

In our arrangement the dates on the left are reached by black numbers, those on the right by red numbers. In the upper row the dates are late Baktun 9 dates, in the lower row they approach the middle of the next baktun. All are at Day Number 3, and all are within 0.60 days of being at same average moon age. A fifth (red) Serpent Number date, 3 Chicchan 13 Pax, is associated by the codex itself with the earlier of our two 3 Chicchan dates and belongs at 10.11.5.14.5, where the arbitrary moon age is 0.38. One suspects that moon ages played a part in selection of these five dates. It may be that four were calculated as at day of first visibility after conjunction, and the fifth as at day of last visibility before it. If these moon-age relationships are more than remarkable coincidences, then the 9.15.13.0 interval between two 3 Chicchan dates seems fair evidence of use of the 1:5 ratio lunar correction scheme. If that was set to 12 Lamat at 9.19.7.7.8 (or elsewhere), it would of necessity calculate the same age for any two dates separated by the 9.15.13.0 interval.

Use of the 1:5 ratio 70,460-day correction cycle in the codex appears to be at least a reasonable hypothesis. We have a hint

9.17. 8. 8.5	3 18	Chicchan Xul	(3.31)	9.18.4.8.4	3 17	Kan Uo	(3.84)
9.15.13.0							
10. 7. 4. 3.5	3 13	Chicchan Yaxkin	(3.32)	10. 8.5.0.6	3 14	Cimi Kayab	(3.55)

that it was engaged in the Long Count at 9.19.7.7.8 and that this was at day of last visibility (arbitrary age is -0.72 days).

Even with an ideal structure keeping the deviations of the predicting scheme to an absolute minimum, and with assumed perfect observation, an allowance of ± 1 day is necessary to cover the observations when made. As noted later, this seems to have been provided for in the eclipse table; in the inscriptions a greater allowance was probably made, but how large it was is a matter of uncertain inference.

Morley (1916) first discovered a lunar count of some sort in the inscriptions, as part of Supplementary Series frequently accompanying Initial Series dates, with specifications of 29-day or 30-day moons. Teeple discovered a day-by-day moon-age count, with "zero age" replacing Age 29 or 30. He considered a further count of numbered complete moons to be an elapsed-time-count. This is questionable, particularly in view of the current entry of months of the vague year. The moon numbers never rise above six and absence of a coefficient corresponds to Number 1.

If moon ages for the accompanying Initial Series dates are calculated with the average lunation value from a recorded zero age at 9.17.0.0.0, allowances of ± 3 days are required to cover all accepted recorded ages. Variable factors at different times and places probably account for this since otherwise "Teeple's limits" seem excessive. These factors may include shifts in the precise phase of the moon taken as at zero age, at different times and places. Possibilities are the day of last visibility, of first visibility or a day between these on which eclipses were feared. I have twice explored the question (1948, 1951a). Full-moon day as the zero day has been postulated by Spinden and supporters of his correlation, but this seems to be safely ruled out (Thompson, 1950, pp. 78–80; Andrews, 1940, pp. 150–56). Granting this, the eclipse table was set for solar eclipses though it may have been projected from a lunar eclipse pattern. Since the eclipse table deals with lunar intervals in a single system, it provides a more satisfactory check on correlation hypotheses than do the moon ages of the inscriptions.

In the Lunar Series of the latter Teeple isolated a "Period of Uniformity," better called a "Period of uniform moon-numbering" because slightly differing moon ages for the same day at different sites are not ruled out. During the period the moon numbers almost everywhere reflect a continuous count of 6-moon cycles. A rapid spread of the system is indicated but there is now evidence that it may have had greater antiquity in the Peten–British Honduras region (Satterthwaite, 1958c, taking advantage of an extensive table of Lunar Series decipherments in Andrews, 1951).

The eclipse table of the Dresden codex has often been reproduced. Guthe (1921) gives a complete description and corrects various mistakes in the original, most probably due to a copyist. At first glance the table appears to describe a repeating 11,960-day cycle of 69 Sacred Round stations, departing from a day 12 Lamat and covering 405 moons. Intervals between the stations, given in days, show that a lunar correction scheme was used to select 60 dates at intervals of 6 moons, in a sequence interrupted by nine dates at intervals of 5 moons, forming a pattern of 6-moon and 5-moon groups. The pattern can be experimentally set at various positions in time so as to predict 69 sequent solar eclipses, a large proportion of which were invisible to the Maya. For them it must have been a table of potential eclipses calling for ceremonial precautions, which seemed successful in most cases. If properly set, no visible eclipse would catch them unprepared.

Assuming a repeating cycle, as has been usual, the period is 11,960 days from one 12 Lamat epoch to another. But the total coverage was limited by the function of the whole-moon pattern. At a setting in actual time once proposed by Makemson, if repeated more than four times the table would begin to miss visible eclipses (1943, p. 194). The position of the 5-moon groups among the 6-moon groups must be changed from time to time, and this must have been known. But it does not follow that an infallible rule was known for changing it ahead of time.

Teeple showed that construction of the table depended on the coincidence that three "eclipse seasons" equal 520 days, twice the SR period. I have shown (1947, pp. 142–47) on an operational level how the Maya might have proceeded, though I failed to duplicate the record completely.

The sequence of 69 Sacred Round stations must have been calculated from a 12 Lamat, each station at same-moon age though this need not have been zero-moon age. Above each such entry is the preceding Sacred Round day, and below it the following Sacred Round day, the vertical three-day groups forming three horizontal lines. An explanation of the three lines (perpetuated in Andrews, 1940, p. 156) is untenable with a cycle of limited coverage in respect to the whole-moon pattern. Thus it seems obvious that the three-day groups functioned as stated ±1-day allowances for errors in the lunar correction scheme used, and for the lunar variation. This seems to have been assumed by Guthe, Teeple, and Makemson, but it has not been emphasized.

There are reasons for doubting that the given sequence of stations was to be repeated at all. If it was, the central line of days proceeding from 12 Lamat should have reached another 12 Lamat 11,960 days later; actually it reaches 11 Manik 11,959 days later. This is not likely to have been a copyist's mistake, nor a calculator's. It is as if a katun was said to end on Cauac instead of on Ahau. It is not impossible that the lunar scheme had a period of 2 × 11,960 days covering 810 lunations and placed the 405th moon at the 11,959th day. In that case, even if the whole-moon pattern for the next 405 lunations was unchanged, the composition of the three-day groups would vary in some cases at least.

In line with this possibility, the first multiple of 11,960 is absent in both a red and a black series of multiples of that lunar period set to 12 Lamat. The introduction gives, in the red series, the 39th, 6th, 5th, 3rd, and 4th multiples; in the black series the 18th multiple first appears in its own column, then the 17th, 16th, 4th, 3rd, and 2nd multiples, interwritten with red numbers. One additional red and one additional black number fails to be a multiple of 11,960 as well as of 260, but neither can be reasonably restored as the first multiple. Presumably these multiples of 11,960 are related to the lunar calculation scheme; at the 18th multiple the period would call for a lunar correction of almost exactly two days. The apparent epoch for the described sequence or limited cycle of 69 stations is a recorded 9.16.4.10.8 12 Lamat, long before our supposed early limit for current coverage of codex tables at 10.17.13.12.12 4 Eb. But one of the given multiples may have been understood to lead forward to the eclipse-pattern epoch. Later we suggest that this could have been the 18th multiple, which is first encountered in the normal order of reading, and is emphasized by appearing alone in its own column.

The Venus table of the codex is a masterpiece of vertical-horizontal tabulation which provides the one reasonably clear picture of a Maya astronomical prediction scheme. Thompson (1950, pp. 217–29) transcribes and fully explains this table. Again we owe fundamental insights to Teeple (1930). We follow his basic interpretations, not certain departures from them by Makemson (1943, 1946), which seem unconvincing. Ignored also is Thompson's expansion of the Teeple findings which depends on changing a recorded distance number.

In terms of whole days the Venus cycle varies from 580 to 587 days, the average length being 583.98 days. A formal whole-day cycle of 584 days is divided by Calendar Round stations into parts of 236, 90, 250, and 8 days, corresponding approximately to appearances and disappearances of the planet as morning and evening star. The cycle in theory ends at heliacal rising after inferior conjunction during the eight days of disappearance. For actual appearances and disappearances, plus or minus allowances of at least four days would seem to have been necessary, but these are not indicated, perhaps for lack of space.

The 584-day cycle accumulates an error of 0.08 days at each repetition. The described stations cover five of these cycles, giving the 20 stations for each of its parts as they make the round with the 20 day names and with the vague year, at eight vague years and 2920 days. The vague-year stations are in a separate line, which is used over and over again as multiples of 2920 days; 13 lines of Sacred Round stations carry one through the round with the complete Calendar Round at 65 Venus cycles, 104 vague years, and 37,960 days. By this time the average error has accumulated to the wholly unrealistic amount of 5.2 days. Yet the 4th, 3rd, 2nd, and 1st multiples of 37,960 days seem to provide for later epochs. Using the highest multiple once gives a coverage of 260 cycles and 416 years. In the introduction we find the ring-and-distance-numbers equivalent of Long Count date 9.9.9.16.0 1 Ahau 18 Kayab, repeated in Long Count style with 18 Uo replacing the expected 18 Kayab. This is obviously an epoch for calculating in the uncorrected 2920-day round of the 584-day cycle in the manner of our example with the 1820-day cycle at 4 Eb. The Venus stations are provided with position numbers and also "counters" giving the varying intervals between the stations.

Teeple showed that various features having no function in such a context reflect a correction scheme imposed on the uncorrected 584-day cyclical count. Only one epoch, at 1 Ahau 18 Kayab, could be shared by the uncorrected and the corrected systems, and this we shall hereafter mean by the simple term "epoch." It was desired that the corrected periods should also end on 1 Ahau, though a new set of vague-year stations was needed whenever a correction was made, and four days instead of one day were required as the correcting unit. Counting from the common 1 Ahau 18 Kayab epoch, the 57th cycle was shortened by eight days, reducing 57 cycles from 33,288 to 33,280 days, and reaching 1 Ahau 18 Uo. These eight days overcorrected an accumulated average error of 4.56 days. The net error is +3.44 days, counting forward from 33,280 days to the average value of 57 cycles, 33,283.44 days. Thereafter, the 61st formal cycle was shortened by only four days thus undercorrecting accumulated errors of 4.88 days, with net errors of −0.88 days. These latter corrected periods first reached the year position 13 Mac, then 3 Xul. Alternative sets of vague-year stations reaching 13 Mac and 3 Xul are provided, but the set reaching 18 Uo after an eight-day correction is missing. It seems to be referred to by the misplaced 18 Uo in the introduction; the table itself was not available for calculating purposes. Thompson sees evidence for the logically required proportion of four four-day correcting periods to one eight-day correcting period.

The coverage for corrected calculation, including the 18 Uo gap, extends 19.9.5.0 (139,140 days) forward from the epoch. Teeple did not rule out the recorded date 9.9.9.16.0 1 Ahau 18 Kayab as the epoch but he suggested 10.10.11.12.0 1 Ahau 18 Kayab as a late alternative, 416 years later. Only that epoch will give a function for a recorded distance number 1.5.14.4.0 in the introduction. Counted from Long Count date 9.9.9.16.0, this reaches 1 Ahau 18 Uo as the end of the first correction period. Thus there is specific evidence for a corrected Venus cycle coverage from 10.10.-11.12.0 1 Ahau 18 Kayab as epoch, extending forward by the distance 19.9.5.0 to Long Count date 11.10.0.17.0 1 Ahau 18 Pax. In confirmation, this allows for a calculator's present time being after our supposed early limit for it, i.e. 10.17.13.12.12 4 Eb, the latest sure date in the codex and an epoch for another table. The Baktun 11 date at 18 Pax (not recorded) is a late limit for the user's present time since he would then begin to need an 18 Pax set of stations in the 2920-day cycle, which is not given.

Our reasoning requires that the eclipse table also be functional within these limits, and from a single epoch if the stations were not repeatedly used as a cycle, as seems probable. Further, some one of the given multiples of the 11,960-day period presumably led to the epoch, counting from the recorded 9.16.4.10.8 12 Lamat. Under these assumptions we have three possibilities only, listed below. We add two sets of Christian year equivalents which are respectively according to the 12-9 and 11-16 correlation variants of Table 5. But note that the reasoning is equally valid for any correlation.

The leeway in interpretations of the astronomical data has resulted in differing "astronomical" correlation proposals founded on such data only. These cannot be used alone to obtain a generally acceptable correlation but they ought to make sense in a correct correlation founded on other evidence. Various astronomical tests have been proposed. It appears to me that the true correlation ought to conform to the minimum of conditions listed below. These are founded on the assumptions that predicted Venus and lunar dates did not deviate from mean or average positions by much more than the amounts required by the respective predicting patterns; and that average deviations or errors and actual variations from average were covered by plus and minus whole-day allowances.

1. The ideal setting of the Venus epoch at 1 Ahau 18 Kayab is 5.72 days after the mean position for inferior conjunction, hence 1.72 days after assumed heliacal rising four days later. The deviation or error in terms of the average heliacal rising "age" is then +1.72 days; at the end of the first correction period reaching 1 Ahau 18 Uo the error becomes −1.72 days, since the net effect of an eight-day correction of the 57th cycle is 3.44 days in the early direction. Logically, four four-day correction periods should follow. The "age" errors at the beginnings of the five periods, with the ideal setting, are +1.72, −1.72, −0.84, +0.04, +0.92, +1.80 days. Changing the signs will convert these deviations to required corrections of the Maya positions.

2. Ideally the eclipse table epoch should be quite close to a mean position for lunar conjunction, the deviation being such that 69 actual conjunction days are covered by the sequence of 69 three-day groups.

3. Ideally these conjunction days should include all days of potentially visible solar eclipses occurring within the 405-moon period covered.

4. The foregoing need not hold for repetitions of the eclipse stations as an 11,960-day cycle.

One may consider what degree of conformity to ideal situations ought to be required, particularly in the matter of not missing any visible eclipses. Determining in advance when the positions of the 5-moon intervals should be changed must have been difficult, and actual failures might be missed for some time because of bad weather. In respect to calculated deviations in Greenwich Mean Time

At 16th multiple:	11.2.16. 2.8	12 Lamat	A.D. 1019 (??)	A.D. 1279 (?)
At 17th multiple:	11.4. 9. 6.8	12 Lamat	A.D. 1052 (??)	A.D. 1312 (?)
At 18th multiple:	11.6. 2.10.8	12 Lamat	A.D. 1085 (??)	A.D. 1345 (?)

according to a given correlation, time-of-day adjustments may be in order. It seems highly improbable that the eclipse table was set with great lunar accuracy and the Venus table with gross inaccuracy, as required by two correlations noted in the final section of this article. Obviously the Long Count positions of the two astronomical epochs are vital factors. Good reasons, short of proof, recommend the view that both epochs were much later than the Baktun 9 dates recorded with the tables, and we have tried to narrow the field to Teeple's late Venus epoch and to three alternatives for the eclipse table, all later than a 1943 proposal of Makemson, who then was using the Thompson correlation labeled B4 in Table 5.

Short Count Dating: Historical Controls on Correlations

In the 16th-century and later historical sources for Yucatan one finds Maya dating in terms of a Type IV Calendar Round, usually by placing events within years named by their bearers, and there are lists of bearers correlated with Christian years. In addition there was an "U kahlay katunob" or "Short Count" of tuns and katuns set to end on days Ahau, like those of the Long Count. The tuns were numbered but, like the years, the katuns were named. These katun names were the Sacred Round days at their ends, not at their beginnings, a distinction which also recalls the numbered elapsed-time periods of the Long Count. From an arbitrary start at the end of Katun 13 Ahau, the day numbers in the names, always Ahau, change in the cycle 11, 9, 7, 5, 3, 1, 12, 10, 8, 6, 4, 2, 13, an easily memorized sequence. The Books of Chilam Balam give differing prophecies for each katun, which is thus shown to have had esoteric value like a year of the Calendar Round.

The chronicles systematically list the katun names in sequence, placing historical events within various of the named katuns. Although there is no accompanying numeration, by repeating the cycle there was no limit to the coverage, which extended from long before the conquest to well after it. Christian datings for some of these events give imprecise controls on Long Count correlation hypotheses.

The ancient Long Count was essentially a time-distance count, in no way incompatible with a co-existing Short Count, using names for the same katuns which were numbered as periods in the Long Count. It appears in the Paris Codex, and Thompson (1950, pp. 197–293) has demonstrated its existence as early as 9.6.10.0.0 in an inscription at Tulum.

It appears at Caracol as early as 9.3.0.0.0 (Satterthwaite, 1954, p. 31). The clearest evidence is later, in Thompson's now surely acceptable "Yucatecan Method' of recording Baktun 10 dates, most of them at Chichen Itza (1950, pp. 197–203). As an example, "9 Lamat 11 Yax, Haab (Tun) 13, 1 Ahau" places the Calendar Round date 9 Lamat 11 Yax within the 13th tun of the katun which will end on Sacred Round Day I Ahau. With such full Short Count dating the corresponding Long Count position can be calculated as 10.2.12.1.8 9 Lamat 11 Yax. Unfortunately the later documentary sources do not provide any surely reliable and complete examples of this method.

As a possible origin, since a Long Count number normally gave position in what may have been a 13-baktun round of named baktuns, the Long Count itself may have been a superstructure on a more ancient Short Count of 13 katuns, which had greater survival value. Logically the 13-katun cycle could have been an outgrowth of an original 13-tun cycle of named tuns which, dealing with still shorter periods, had the greatest viability of all.

Pertinent to this speculation, the historical sources include two corrupt but essentially agreeing lists of sequent year bearers and stated or implied tun ends, correlated with Christian years. These have been compared independently by Schulz (1944) and Proskouriakoff (1952b). Page 66 of the Chronicle of Oxcutzcab covers 1533–45, while pages 124–25 of Codex Perez cover 1758–74. The 18th-century list shows features which are not fully understood. Nevertheless it affords strong evidence for tun-counting as well as year-counting during the unrecorded interval between 1545 and 1758, or a late revival of the older count. This has a bearing on the correlation problem, since one list authenticates the other, partially at least. Further, persistence of tun-counting argues for no preconquest break in it. Proskouriakoff finds confirmatory evidence in the Chilam Balam of Kaua.

The Oxkutzcab list of Christian years seems to place the year bearer 11 Ix at 1 Pop and the tun-end 13 Ahau at 7 Xul within 1540, but the Perez list and the weight of other year-bearer evidence indicates that the Maya years *ended* in the given Oxkutzcab Christian years, so that 1539 was the current year for 11 Ix 1 Pop and 13 Ahau 7 Xul. The Oxkutzcab correlation is generally stated with this interpretative emendation, though it may be required because of a systematic one-year mistake. The only proposed Long Count correlations conforming to this evidence are members of a Goodman-Thompson-Martínez family of variant proposals listed in Table 5. These make the tun-end 13 Ahau a katun-end in the Long Count, at 11.16.0.0.0 13 Ahau 8 Xul (Calendar Round Type III). Dropping the zeros, such variants may be classed as 11-16 correlations. All other proposals reject the Oxkutzcab evidence, now stronger than ever.

In other historical sources one may read or reconstruct other Maya-Christian equations of varying degrees of precision, but there are mistakes and disagreements and the necessity of judging what is reliable by the weight of the evidence. Among those who admit historical controls on the correlation at all, however, there is a consensus that a Katun 13 Ahau ended and a Katun 11 Ahau began not far from 1542, when Merida was officially founded. Unfortunately the sources disagree as to the Christian year of the katun-end. Other evidence than that above cited for 1539 indicates 1536, or even 1542. The years 1536–42 thus appear to be limits for the Katun 13 Ahau of the late Yucatecan Short Count. Spinden (1924, pp. 91–92) rejected the Oxkutzcab equation as unreliable, placing 12.9.0.0.0 13 Ahau 8 Kankin in 1536.

To convert a vague imprecise correlation to a day-for-day equation the historical control is a "typical year" of Landa, beginning with 12 Kan 1 Pop at July 16. This must have been in 1553 (Long in Thompson, 1935, p. 97), and therefore within Katun 11 Ahau. The yardstick measuring the intervals between alternative correlations becomes 260 vague years instead of 260 tuns. With this equation one may calculate back to a precise date for the end of Katun 13 Ahau—1300 days farther back for the 12-9 than for the 11-16 correlation.

Landa specified leap-days for his Yucatecan Maya year. One may emend his July 16 allowing for a freeze of the vague to the Christian year before 1553, or postulate misunderstanding and mistake as to the exact date. Thus there is a little leeway for variants of the same basic correlation. These are ignored in such terms as "*the* Goodman-Thompson" and "*the* Goodman-Thompson-Martínez" correlation.

In using Landa's equation one must remember that his 12 Kan 1 Pop (Calendar Round Type IV) is the equivalent of 12 Kan 2 Pop (Type III) in the year of the Long Count system. Further, in deriving Long Count correlations from it, one accepts the very good evidence that only a one-day break accounts for the differing Calendar Round types.

Some Proposed Correlations

It was noted earlier that one may found various correlations on the astronomical data; it has been indicated that the same is true for the historical equations of the Yucatecan documentary sources. In both categories there is considerable leeway for selection and interpretation. An acceptable solution must come by trial and error, using all possible lines of evidence, as Thompson has insisted. Archaeological implications should not be neglected, and this source of control is becoming more precise with the development of radiocarbon dating. One may expect that consensus will be achieved when only a single day-for-day correlation satisfies generally accepted requirements of each category of evidence, and this cannot be laid to coincidence.

Here we attempt to give a brief picture of the present status of the problem, which has been developing since Morley organized the Yucatecan historical data (1920, App. 2). Some later discussions involving new raw data, interpretations, and correlation hypotheses are: Spinden (1924; 1930; 1957b, epilogue), Teeple (1930), L. Roys (1933), Vaillant (1935c), Thompson (1935, with appendices by R. C. E. Long and L. Roys; 1950, app. 2; 1958a), Andrews (1940), Makemson (1943, 1946), Schulz (1936, 1944), Satterthwaite (1956b), Brainerd (1958), Satterthwaite and Ralph (1960).

The Long Count reaches a Katun 13 Ahau of the Short Count every 13 katuns or 260 tuns. If we merely require one of them to fall near 1542, we may postulate 12-9, 11-16, 11-3, and 10-10 alternative correlations. Each places Long Count dates later in time, in that order, and at intervals of 260 tuns. On ceramic evidence Vaillant (1935c) at one time preferred 11-3 or 10-10; very recently Brainerd (1958) preferred 11-16, 12-9, and 11-3, in that order. On the basis of art analysis Lothrop (1952, pp. 111–13) has suggested 11-3, or a somewhat earlier Kreichgauer astronomical correlation described by Andrews (1940). Day-for-day 11-3 and 10-10 correlations are listed by Satterthwaite (1956b), but three independent radiocarbon tests seem to make them definitely too late. These correlations are very dubious for other reasons (see Thompson, 1950, pp. 307–09 on Escalona Ramos and Weitzel correlations).

In Table 5 we list all variants proposed for the "leading" 12-9 and 11-16 correlations, some of them now definitely obsolete. The labeling system is that used in my 1956b article except that there the Goodman and Martínez correlations were improperly treated as identical. The "correlation constants" are also known as "Ahau

TABLE 5—COMPARISONS OF VARIANT 12-9 AND 11-16 CORRELATIONS OF THE LONG COUNT.

	Labels	*Constants*	*Katun 13 Ahau (1536 – 1542?)*	*12 Kan 1 Pop (Landa Jul. 16)*	*Av. moon ages (see note)*	
					A	*B*
A1	Makemson	489,138	12-9 in 1535	Nov. 12 1552	−0.32	+ 1.68
A2	Modified Spinden	489,383	12-9 in 1536	Jul. 15 1553	+8.43	+10.43
A3	Spinden	489,384	12-9 in 1536	Jul. 16 1553	+9.43	+11.43
BG	Goodman	584,280	11-16 in 1539	Jul. 12 1553	−5.88	− 3.89
B1	Martínez	584,281	11-16 in 1539	Jul. 13 1553	−4.88	− 2.89
B2	Modified Thompson 2	584,283	11-16 in 1539	Jul. 15 1553	−2.88	− 0.89
B3	Modified Thompson 1	584,284	11-16 in 1539	Jul. 16 1553	−1.88	+ 0.11
B4	Thompson	584,285	11-16 in 1539	Jul. 17 1553	−0.88	+ 1.11

Note: Constants or "Ahau equations" are Julian Day Numbers correlated with the base date of the Long Count. Average moon ages are at 9.16.4.10.8 (Column A) and 11.6.2.10.8 (Column B), supposed extreme Long Count limits for the epoch of the eclipse table of the Dresden codex. Calculations from Age 29.53 (= Age 0.00) at mean lunar conjunction point at JDN 1,874,463.8133 (Weitzel, 1949).

equations." They are the Julian Day Numbers equivalent to the Christian dates equated with 4 Ahau 8 Cumku, the normal base date of the Long Count. Adding the constant to any Long Count number in decimal form gives its equivalent Julian Day Number. The next two columns show how closely the historical controls have been followed, the dates being in the Julian calendar. Morley (1937–38, 4: Table 14) published Gregorian calendar equations for the dates of the Classic period, at 5-tun intervals, according to the Spinden (A3) and the original Thompson (B4) correlations.

Independently of correlations we have claimed a probability that the epoch of the eclipse table of the codex was later than the recorded Long Count date 9.16.4.10.8, and we inferred that 11.6.2.10.8 is a late limit for it. Columns A and B of Table 5 give, respectively, mean moon ages at these two dates as they change with differing correlations. Negative ages are backward deviations from Age 29.53 days, which becomes zero age whenever it is reached. Column A shows that with the early epoch only the Makemson (A1) and the original Thompson (B4) correlations probably can pass the precise lunar test as proposed earlier. The combined columns indicate that neither of the two variants of the Spinden 12-9 correlation (A2, A3) or the Goodman and Martínez variants of the 11-16 correlation can be caused to pass the lunar test by choosing one of our three late epochs. But they indicate that a late epoch may pass the lunar test with any of the three Thompson 11-16 variants (B2, B3, B4).

Let us briefly examine the Makemson (A1) and Thompson (B4) hypotheses, assuming recorded early epochs for both tables. According to Makemson, 9.9.9.16.0 as Venus epoch is 18 days after heliacal rising in her correlation and 18 days before it in Thompson's (1950, pp. 62–63). I am indebted to C. H. Smiley of Brown University for a table of Julian Day Numbers for inferior conjunctions of Venus, four days before the Maya heliacal rising day. Though extreme accuracy is not claimed for it, it yields Makemson's two deviations to within ± 0.5 days. Mean positions must be far outside our proposed limits for the deviation. Why should the Maya set the eclipse table with great accuracy, the Venus table with such gross inaccuracy? As to the Makemson correlation, it required an unacceptable explaining-away of Landa's July 16 equation (Thompson, 1950, pp. 306–07).

In her prior (1943) study of the Thompson correlation (B4) Makemson avoided gross inaccuracy by placing the Venus epoch at 10.5.6.4.0 which is 104 vague years earlier than Teeple's late epoch. Her late eclipse table epoch, 10.12.16.14.8, is far short of our proposed Baktun 11 alternatives. A detailed investigation of those epochs using the B2 variant seems called for, but some comment is appropriate here.

Schultz first adopted the 584,283 constant (B2) as the proper one for an 11-16 correlation, but without considering the late epoch possibilities (1936). In this correlation Teeple's late Venus epoch is at JDN 2,100,483. This is 8.2 days after JDN 2,100,474.8, an inferior conjunction point in the Smiley table, which does not claim great accuracy. The deviation back from the JDN position of the epoch to the approximate actual conjunction point is -8.2 days. Apparently the deviation to the mean conjunction point, if calculated, might be very close to -5.72 days corresponding to our ideal setting with average position $+5.72$ days.

We have labeled this B2 variant of the 11-16 correction as "Modified Thompson 2 correlation," distinguishing it from the B3 modification by one day, proposed by Beyer (1937a). Thompson has now accepted the two-day B2 modification, and there are two very cogent reasons for doing so. Evidence continues to accumulate to the effect that La Farge was correct in suggesting that there was never any preconquest break in the Maya 260-day count (Thompson, 1958a). The highland "Intertribal Tzolkin" places 12 Kan at July 15, 1553, and either Landa's July 16 was an easy mistake to make, or was due to a freeze of the vague to the Christian year in 1552. The second reason is a discovery of F. V. Scholes, described by Thompson (1950, p. 304). A Manche Chol vague year began in 1631, 1632, or 1633 in an area where it probably was a survival of the year of the Long Count system, beginning at 1 Pop or its equivalent, Calendar Round Type III. The Intertribal Highland Sacred Round places Type III bearers at July 4 in 1632 and 1633. If the Manche Chol year ended in either of those years, it was in line with 11 Akbal 1 Pop at July 14, 1553, and with 12 Kan 2 Pop at July 15. If this is a coincidence, it is a very remarkable one. The 10-day Gregorian correction must be allowed for in making the calculation.

It may be said that only the B2 variant 11-16 correlation, more formally labeled "Modified Thompson 2," conforms to the great weight of the best historical evidence. It probably will require only moderate and reasonable interpretative leeway in applying astronomical tests. It is at a central position within the present-day range of archaeological opinion.

In connection with the latter, however, we must notice two independent radiocarbon datings for inscriptions on wood from Tikal, including that of our figure 4 (Kulp, Feely, and Tryon, 1951; Libby, 1954). These seemed to throw the above picture into confusion since both call for acceptance of an astronomically unsatisfactory 12-9 correlation, or a satisfactory one without historical control, such as an unpublished solution of the problem by W. B. Dinsmoor. With his permission and that of the Wenner-Gren Foundation for Anthropological Research we give the Dinsmoor constant, 497,879. It places the Maya dates only 23 years later than the 12-9 correlation, within the Kulp and Libby one-sigma limits.

This situation led to a much more extensive series of radiocarbon datings of Long Count-dated Tikal samples, collected with great care as part of the Tikal Project of the University Museum, University of Pennsylvania. The radiocarbon datings of 17 beams from two temples are by Elizabeth K. Ralph of the University of Pennsylvania laboratory. They reverse the earlier radiocarbon picture, favoring an 11-16 correlation and excluding all earlier and later proposals by wide margins, including Dinsmoor's new early astronomical one (Satterthwaite and Ralph, 1960).

Since the foregoing was written Smiley (1960) has added another correlation based primarily on assumptions respecting Maya astronomy. The correlation constant places Maya Long Count dates some 41 years earlier than in the Dinsmoor proposal and 18 years earlier than in the Spinden correlation. Smiley's astronomical assumptions cannot be compared with those of Dinsmoor until the latter are published. However, not forgetting the Makemson solution, we note that astronomy has been used to find three correlations within a spread of less than 25 years on either side of the Spinden historically based 12-9 correlation. Clearly there is no single "astronomical approach," with general agreement on just what the astronomical controls really are.

The Smiley, Makemson, Spinden, and Dinsmoor correlations are all well within the 1-sigma radiocarbon limits as determined by Kulp and Libby for Tikal beams, but they are far outside those found since by Ralph, with extraordinary precautions against error, including measurements of duplicates of Kulp and Libby samples, and a special effort was made to supply her with samples representing only the latest growth of the beams. If her findings stand up, the case for an 11-16 correlation will be even stronger than it was before the radiocarbon method seemed to deny it. The Modified Thompson 2 variant, with 584,283 as the constant, appears to be the correct precise version. Surely it must continue to be reckoned with in judging present-day space-time schemes for Mesoamerican archaeology, and in attempts to refine our understanding of ancient Maya astronomy.

REFERENCES

Andrews, 1940, 1951
Barthel, 1951
Beyer, 1937a
Bowditch, 1910
Brainerd, 1958
Caso, 1939a, 1958b
Coe, M. D., 1957b
Förstemann, 1906
Guthe, 1921
Holmes, 1907
Jakeman, 1947
Kelley, D. H., 1960
Kulp, Feely, and Tryon, 1951
LaFarge, 1931
Libby, 1954
Lincoln, 1942
Lizardi R., 1959
Locke, 1923
Long, 1948
Lothrop, 1952
Makemson, 1943, 1946
Merrill, 1945
Morley, 1915, 1916, 1920, 1937–38, 1946, 1956
Proskouriakoff, 1944, 1950, 1952b, 1960
—— and Thompson, 1947
Roys, L., 1933
Roys, R. L., 1933
Satterthwaite, 1947, 1948, 1951a, 1954, 1956b, 1958c, 1961a
—— and Ralph, 1960
Schulz, 1936, 1944
Shook, 1960
Smiley, 1960
Spinden, 1913, 1924, 1930, 1957b
Tax, 1951
Teeple, 1930
Thompson, J. E. S., 1935, 1941a, 1941b, 1950, 1958a, 1960
Tozzer, 1941a
Vaillant, 1935c
Villacorta and Villacorta, 1933
Wauchope, 1950
Weitzel, 1949

25. Maya Hieroglyphic Writing

J. ERIC S. THOMPSON

THE POSSESSION by the Maya of a system of hieroglyphic writing and books in which to record it early excited the interest of Spanish intellectuals. The first account appears to be that of Peter Martyr (1612, dec. 4, ch. 8), who gave a good description of books sent from Veracruz by Cortés in 1519, probably a mixed consignment of Maya, Mixtec, and Totonac, including perhaps the best of the three surviving Maya hieroglyphic books, the Dresden Codex. Martyr says that innumerable books were found on the island of Cozumel, but his account is somewhat confused, and one may doubt that Cozumel held innumerable books.

The first to illustrate and describe Maya hieroglyphs was Bishop Diego de Landa, whose long-lost manuscript, written in or about 1566, gives the hieroglyphs for the 20 days and the 18 months, as well as a description of Maya hieroglyphic books, and his famed alphabet. However, his manuscript was lost and it was not until a century ago that an abstract of it was found and published (Brasseur de Bourbourg, 1864). A. Humboldt (1810) published five pages of Codex Dresden but without identifying them as Maya, and del Río (1822), who was at Palenque late in the 18th century, failed to identify its hieroglyphs as Maya. The first person to draw Maya hieroglyphs and describe them as such appears to have been Juan Galindo, who in his report dated 1834 on Copan (Morley, 1920, app. XI) recognized that they were not Mexican and assigned them to the Maya.

The Yucatecan scholar, Juan Pío Pérez (1843), working with the books of Chilam Balam (colonial compilations of Maya history, ritual, calendar, and medicinal recipes), initiated Maya studies connected with the hieroglyphs, although the Franciscan Avendaño y Loyola (1696, 29*v*, 35*r*; English version with important omissions in Means, 1917) seems to have had a good knowledge of the hieroglyphic codices and their contents, as well as the books of Chilam Balam, but, most unfortunately, his treatise on the matter has disappeared.

The subject received a tremendous impetus from the studies of Codex Dresden by Ernst Förstemann, who issued in 1880 a very accurate reproduction of that book, and in subsequent years made a number of most important contributions to decipherment of the glyphs (Förstemann, 1904, contains most of these; for others and a discussion of his work see Thompson, 1950, pp. 29–30 and bibliography). One may say with assurance that in the two decades subsequent to 1880 he brought to light the whole framework of Maya chronology as it concerns the written sources and, to a lesser extent, the sculptured monuments. J. T. Goodman (1897), devoting himself to the sculptured monuments thanks to the magnificent photographs and drawings of text published by Maudslay (1889–1902), has to his credit the identification of heads used as numbers and other glyphs. E. Seler (1902–23) made some significant contributions to the subject. S. G. Morley dedicated his life to the collecting of texts on monuments, spending part of every year save one from 1907 until his death in 1948 in the Maya area. He ransacked the Peninsula of Yucatan for unknown inscriptions, the greater part of which were published (Morley, 1920, 1937–38); a third volume covering the remainder was never written.

To J. E. Teeple, Maya scholarship is much indebted for his decipherment of the series of glyphs recording information on the age of the moon, as well as for his important findings on the tables for eclipses and the synodical revolution of Venus in the Dresden Codex (brought together in Teeple, 1930). Hermann Beyer instituted a new approach with his studies of the component elements of the glyphs, paying much attention to the affixes which hitherto had been largely ignored. He studied the "rules" governing their use, and, with a thoroughness new to the field, he noted variations of detail of great value to the understanding of the underlying significance of the signs. Many of his articles were short, but his papers on affixes and his one lengthy publication, *Studies on*

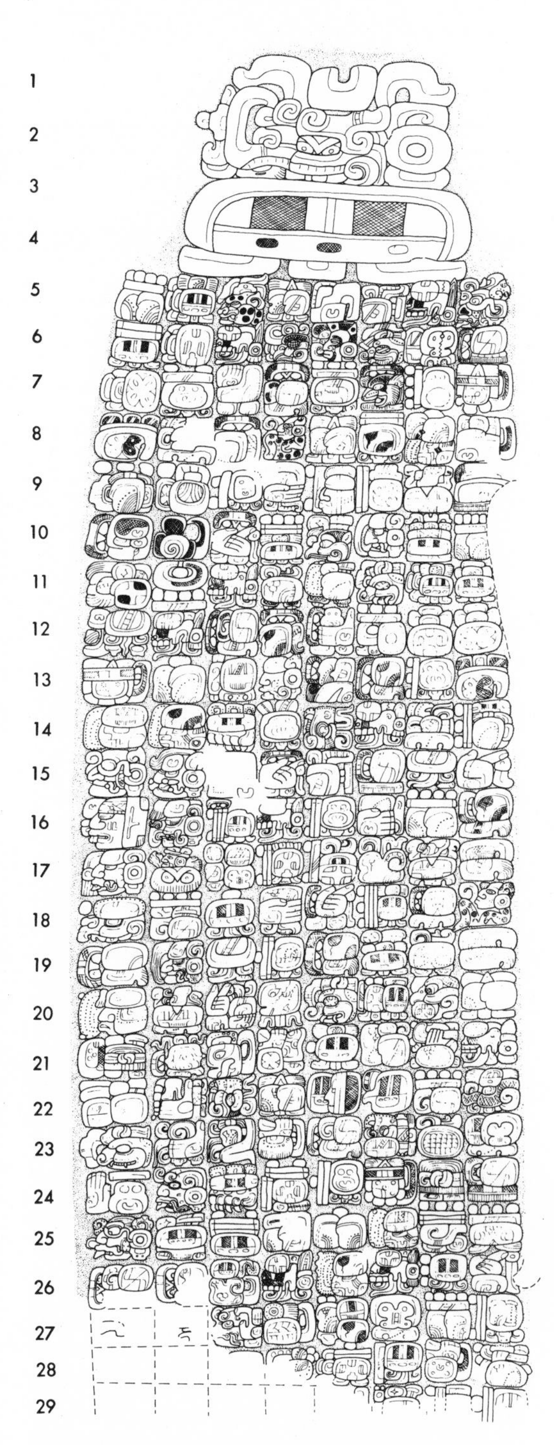

FIG. 1—EARLY GLYPHS, BACK OF STELA 31, TIKAL, GUATEMALA. CA. A.D. 500 (Courtesy, University Museum, University of Pennsylvania.)

FIG. 2—MIDDLE PERIOD GLYPHS, SUPPORTS OF ALTAR 2, PIEDRAS NEGRAS, GUATEMALA. A.D. 751. (After Morley, 1937, vol. 5, pl. 36,*c–f*.)

the inscriptions at Chichen Itza (Beyer, 1934–36, 1937b) typify his systematic handling of the problems.

It would be invidious to summarize the work of those whose harvest has yet to be fully reaped, but many of their individual writings are cited below. An exception must be made of the catalogue of hieroglyphs in the codices by Zimmermann (1956) because of its great importance to Maya research and, at the same time, its uncontroversial nature. Fuller details of the history of glyphic research are in Termer (1952, pp. 143–50) and Thompson (1950, pp. 28–34).

Sources of Texts and Subject Matter

Hieroglyphic texts fall into two main groups: those sculptured in stone or worked in stucco and those painted or written in books, on murals, and on pottery. There is a third, but smaller, group comprising inscriptions on bijoux, that is on bone, shell, semiprecious stone, and (very rarely) on metal.

Texts on stone occur on the large stone

FIG. 3—PANEL 96 GLYPHS, PALENQUE, CHIAPAS. A.D. 783. (Photo by Giles G. Healey, published in Thompson, 1950, fig. 55,*1*.)

shafts called stelae; altars, round or square, ball-court markers; and stones, often of huge size, shaped as mythological animals, generally two-headed monsters with celestial or terrestrial associations or turtles. In addition, they appear inside or outside buildings, on lintels, jambs, wall panels, columns, daises, moldings, capstones, stairways, single steps, balustrades, retaining walls, façades, and, in a single case, at Tikal, on a roof comb. The number of texts at a site varies enormously. The largest number occur at Copan—just over 100, counting the hieroglyphic stairway as a single text; Calakmul has 104 stelae and altars, but about 20 of those are unsculptured; some sites have only one, and many have none.

The subject matter of these texts generally is different from those which were painted. As a rule (but there are exceptions) they carry specific dates, frequently quite a number in a single text, as a framework for the information given.

The calendric glyphs and the calculations often form the bulk of a text and in a few texts there is little—in very short ones no—explanatory matter. Typical of this group is Altar S, Copan, which carries 18 glyphs, of which 12 (perhaps 14) are calendric. On the other hand, some early lintels at Yaxchilan have very little calendric data. A happy medium is supplied by the text on exterior panels on Temple XVIII, Palenque (Sáenz, 1956). This comprises 80 glyphs, of which 42 are calendric and 3 illegible.

The Maya had the custom of erecting one or more monuments or inscribing a text in a building at the end of every katun (20 years of 360 days), and in many instances also at the completion of the half- or quarter-katuns (10 or 5 or 15 tuns [360-day years]). This is the so-called dedicatory date of the monument. The glyphs associated with such period endings presumably are set in a ritualistic context. However, there are many dates, reached by distance numbers (i.e. by addition or subtraction) which fall into a different category. It was widely held that these dates which do not fall at the end of a period had an astronomical or ritualistic significance or were connected with Maya juggling with time, and that is certainly true of some, for instance of stations in the 819-day count (Thompson, 1950, pp. 212–17), and perhaps of those set far in the past.

Recently Tatiana Proskouriakoff (1960) has produced good evidence that a number of these non-tun-ending dates deal with

FIG. 4—CORNICE INSCRIPTION, STR. 1, QUIRIGUA, GUATEMALA. A.D. 810. (After Morley, 1937, vol. 5, pl. 175.)

dynastic history, births and accessions of rulers, and their commemorations after the lapse of one or more katuns, a situation roughly comparable to that found in the Mixtec codices (Caso, 1960). She has shown a relationship between glyphs and the subject matter of the associated scenes on the fronts of the monuments. For example, certain hieroglyphs occur when the scene shows an individual seated in a raised niche or doorway reached by a ladder marked with footprints, which Miss Proskouriakoff identifies with the inauguration of a ruler; another glyph can be construed as marking the birth of the ruler and is associated with a date a number of years before the individual's accession. With a somewhat different approach, Berlin (1958) has identified what he tentatively calls emblem glyphs. Each main glyph (the affixes are the same in every case) appears in a single city or region, but with rare appearances at other sites. He suggests that these emblem glyphs stand for the name of the city or region, its ruling dynasty, or some such local aspect. His case rests on very firm ground (fig. 10).

Neither in the case of Proskouriakoff's dynastic glyphs nor in that of Berlin's emblem glyphs have linguistic decipherments been made; a certain glyph can be associated with a particular city or event, but its actual Maya equivalent is not known. The same is true of the ritualistic glyphs associated with period endings. The meanings of the calendric glyphs and often the Maya terms for them are, in contrast known. The names of the days, months, and longer periods have come down to us from early sources; some terms, for instance those for 'count forward to' or 'count backward to,' can be reconstructed from their

FIG. 5—REGIONAL GLYPHS, TEMPLE OF THE THREE LINTELS, CHICHEN ITZA, YUCATAN. A.D. 889. (After Beyer, 1937b, pl. 3, no. II.)

component elements (Thompson, 1950, pp. 162–64).

Texts painted or written with a brush-pen appear in books and on capstones, on murals on the inner and outer walls of buildings, once (at Tikal) on the walls of a tomb, once (at Ixtelja, near Salto de Agua) on the walls of a cave, and on pottery. Only three hieroglyphic codices have survived. They are generally named for the city in which each now rests. They are the Dresden, Madrid (also called Trocortesiano), and the Paris (also known as the Perez, a confusing name since the volume of material from the books of Chilam Balam collected by Juan Pío Pérez is also called the Codex Perez). Maya books were made of the inner bark of a species of wild fig tree *(Ficus)* called *amatl* in Aztec, from which comes the Aztec term *tonalamatl*, 'book of days,' for the ritualistic books used in divinations. The Maya term is *huun*, which means both bark paper and book, and is used by the modern Lacandon for the bark of a tree, presumably the *Ficus*. In Yucatan, however, the name for *Ficus cotinifolia* is *copo*.

Long sheets of this bark cloth were given a surface coating of lime or stucco and were folded screen-fashion, each fold forming a page. Both sides of the screen were used: the pages were read from left to right; on reaching the end of the recto, the reader turned to the back and again read from left to right, so that the last page of the verso was the back of the first page of the recto. Codex Dresden is 3.5 m. long, 2.05 cm. high, and is folded into 39 leaves, of which four are blank on the verso; Codex Madrid is 6.55 m. long, with 56 leaves, and is a couple of centimeters higher. Codex Paris is a fragment consisting of only 11 leaves.

There is internal evidence that Codex Dresden is a copy of an older original presumably painted in the Classic period. The present edition was probably made between A.D. 1200 and 1300. Original base dates for calculations were brought forward from the Classic period to present time. There are also Mexican influences, particularly in the portraits of gods in the section dealing with the planet Venus. There is some linguistic evidence that the codex comes from Yucatan. Furthermore, it contains one or two glyphs, other examples of which have so far been found only at Chichen Itza. The year bearers are the same set used in the cities of the Central area,[1] the Peten-Usumacinta-Copan area, and also at Chichen Itza during the

FIG. 6—EXAMPLES OF MAYA HIEROGLYPHIC WRITING. *a–c,* Month sign Ch'en showing how hatched element, representing black, can be at left of, above, or inside the main element. *d, te,* sign for wood or tree. *e,f,* Glyph of the god Bolonyocte, composed of number 9 *(bolon),* the Oc sign, and *te* element. *f,* Month position 3-te Zotz'. *g,h,* Count forward to. The head of *xoc* fish represents count (*xoc* in Maya); or the water sign, the fish's environment, can be substituted. *i,f,* Count backward to. Forward sign replaced by element beneath. *k,* Fresh maize. *l,* Severe drought is the prospect for the year. *m,* Drilling fire with sticks. *n,* Very lucky. *o,* Misfortune. *p,* Rainy skies. *q,* Seed. *r,* Fainting spells. *s,* Moon goddess. *t,* Maize god. *u,* East. *v,* West. *w,* Red world-direction tree. (After Thompson, 1954a, fig. 13, *7–18,30–41.*)

[1] Ed. note: Thompson's "Central area" is referred to by some other writers as the "Southern Maya Lowland region."

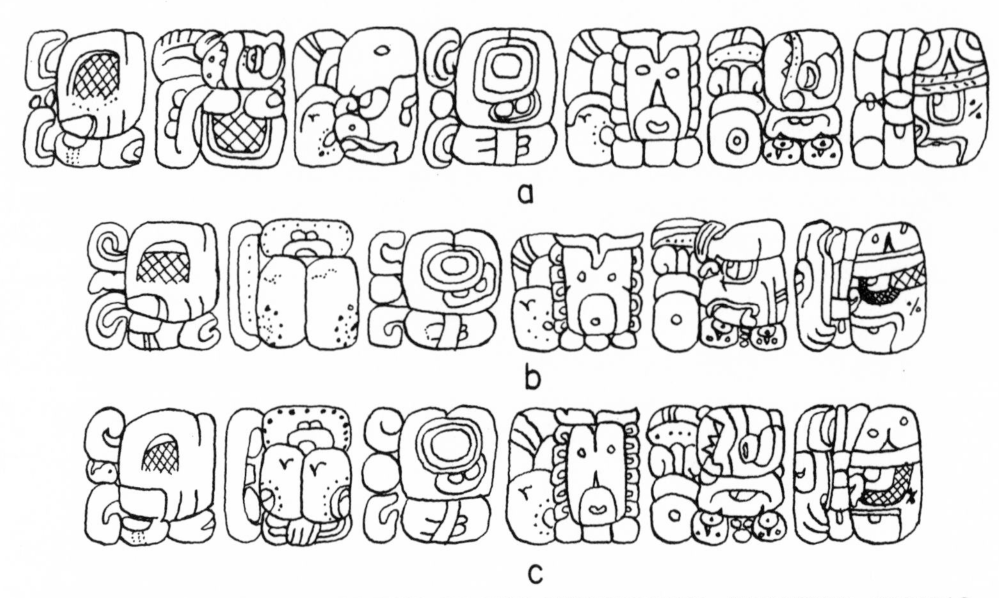

FIG. 7—MAYA PHRASES, TEMPLE OF THE INSCRIPTIONS, PALENQUE, CHIAPAS (After Thompson, 1950, fig. 3, *10–12.*)

Classic period. The delineation of glyphs and portraits is excellent.

Codex Madrid appears to be of late date (15th century?); workmanship is crude and careless. The use of the Yucatan-Campeche set of year bearers is a pretty clear indication of where it was composed. Codex Paris is of fine workmanship, although portraits are rather crude and are in a style comparable to those of murals at Tulum and the widespread Mayapan style. Year bearers are the same as those used in the Peten-Usumacinta-Copan area. There are illegible comments in Spanish. It may have come from Chetumal in view of the portraits and the occurrence of a very rare glyph (Thompson, 1962, Glyph 702) which appears elsewhere only on the murals of Santa Rita, British Honduras, as noted by Zimmermann (1956).

Codex Dresden has some pages devoted to astronomy (excellent tables of possible dates for eclipses and for synodical revolution of the planet Venus), data on new-year ceremonies according to the year bearer, which are found in the other two codices, and a large number of divinatory almanacs which give the glyphs for the gods and their influences—good, bad, and indifferent—for specified days in the 260-day sacred almanac. These cover such subjects as agricultural activities, weather, disease, and possibly birth. Usually each section has four glyphs of explanation and a picture to supplement the glyphs (figs. 12, 13, 15).

Codex Madrid is very largely confined to divinatory almanacs which include, in addition to the subjects covered in Codex Dresden, hunting, beekeeping, and idol making; it has no astronomical information. Codex Dresden was a dual purpose book, for it set forth material of meaning only to the small group of the hierarchy interested in problems of time and celestial influences, but it also contained the tools of divinations for the rank and file. Codex Madrid, in contrast, was the *vade mecum* of a parish priest who had it handy to indicate days suitable for undertaking everyday activities (fig. 14).

One side of Codex Paris carries pages for

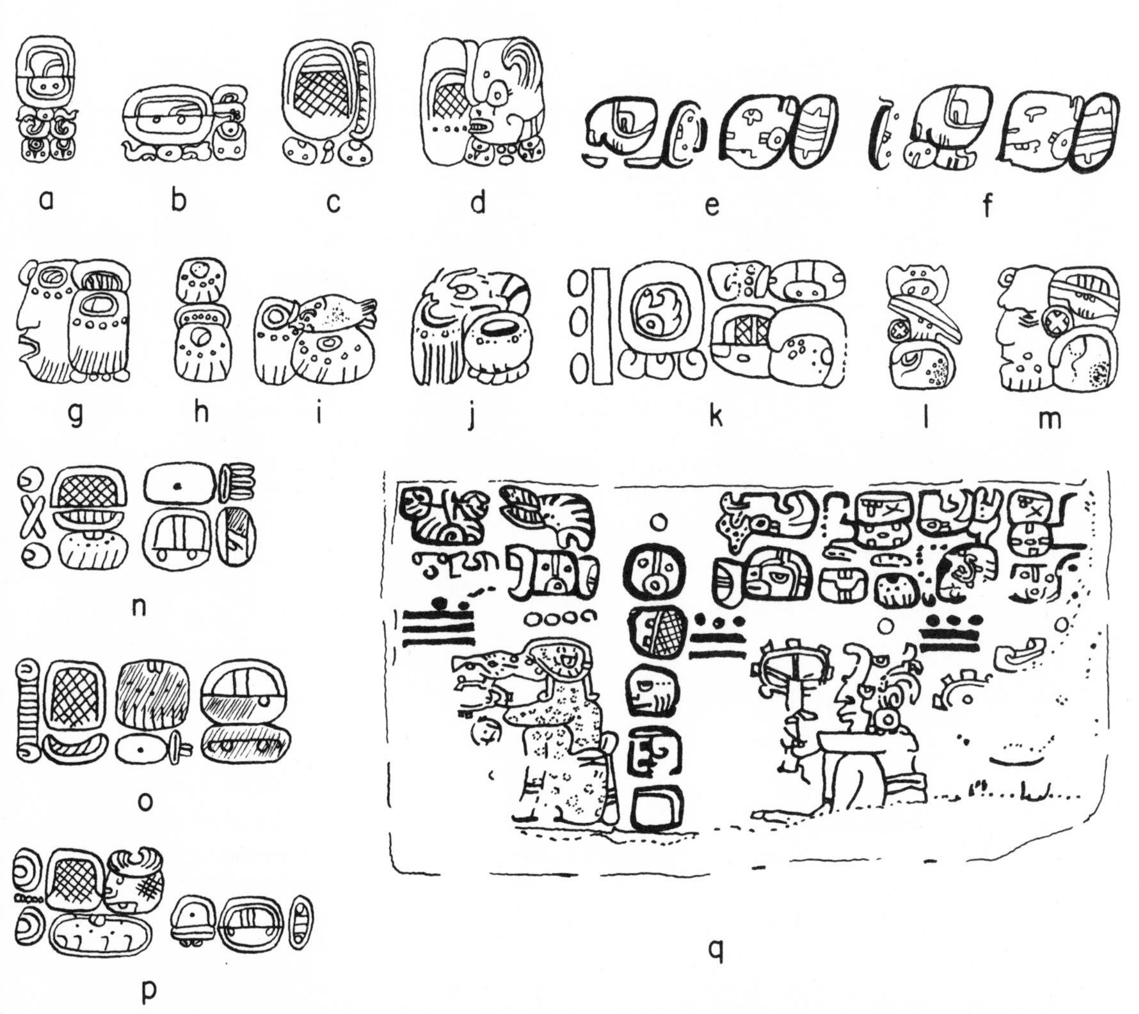

[F]IG. 8—MAYA GLYPH FORMATION. *a,b,* Shift of inverted Ahau affix from below to right and from double to [s]ingle without affecting meaning. Stela J, Copan. *c,d,* Comb postfix in *c* personified and changed to main sign in *d* [w]ithout change of meaning. Palace and Panel of Inscriptions, Palenque. *e,f,* Postfix of first glyph in *a* becomes prefix [i]n *b* without apparent change of meaning. Codex Dresden, p. 31*c*. *g–j,* Double Imix compound. Comb and line of [d]ots affixes in *g* and *h* replaced by naturalistic fish in *i* and *j*. Stela A, Quirigua; Lintels 56 and 2, Yaxchilan; and [N]ebaj vase. *k,* Tun sign as ending prefix. 8 Manik end of month Ceh. Miscellaneous Stone 16, Piedras Negras. *l,m,* [S]un at horizon glyph, *l* with Yax prefix which in *m* is personified as the head of the Chicchan god of number 9. [A]ltar R and Stela N, Copan. *n-p,* Flexibility in writing the same clause in three texts at Chichen Itza. Ti (59), super[f]ix of 679 in *n,* becomes suffix of preceding Imix (501) in *o,* and is inverted in *p.* The comb (25) suffix to the [h]atched spot (586) in *n, o,* is prefixed to Imix in examples not illustrated, and is personified as a fish (738b) in *p.* [S]hifting of affixes argues against syllabic decipherment. *q,* Codex Madrid, page 21d. *a-m,* after J. E. S. Thompson, [1]950. *n-p,* after Beyer, 1937.

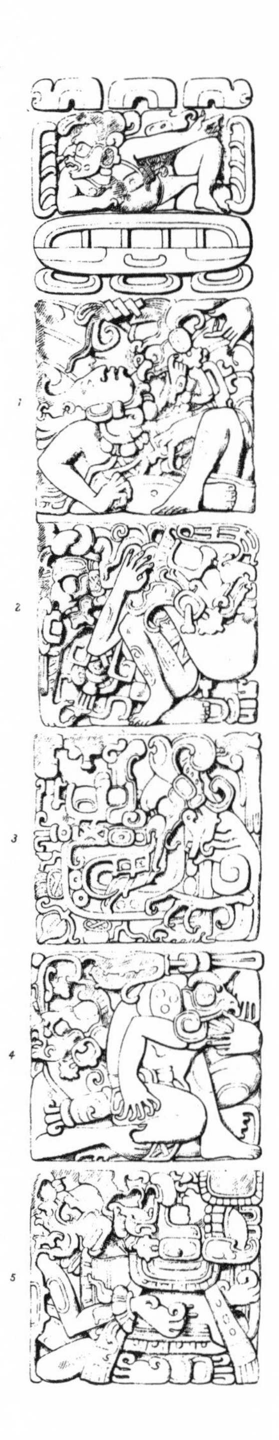

Fig. 9—FULL-FIGURE GLYPHS, STELA D, QUIRIGUA, GUATEMALA. The first glyph block records that the jaguar is patron deity of the month which follows. The pairs of intertwined figures in the following glyph blocks record respectively nine four-hundred-year periods, sixteen twenty-year periods, fifteen years, no months and no days and that the day is 7 Ahau. The years are of 360 days. The date reached corresponds to February 17, A.D. 766. (After Maudslay.)

the round of 13 katuns and also for tuns, and these were probably used for prophesying the "burden" or luck of the incoming katuns. As, however, the events of a katun were expected to repeat when that particular katun returned at the end of the round (that is, after 257 years), the prophetic material was, at the same time, an historical compilation.

One can be reasonably certain that the Maya also had maps (circular and with east at the top) with the names of the towns given in hieroglyphs, as on the Mixtec map of Teozacoalco (Caso, 1949a), but of those none has survived. Similarly, neither genealogical books nor tribute lists remain to us.

It is clear, therefore, that the subject matter of surviving codices is quite different from that of the monuments; divinatory almanacs never appear on stone sculptures, and texts built around a framework of dates are absent from the surviving hieroglyphic books.

Texts on murals vary. On the one hand, at Bonampak, the glyphs pretty clearly refer to the actions (dances, war, judgment of captives) except for a band of glyphs which include a date recorded by an Initial Series, and the same is true of the scene painted at Uaxactun. On the other, purely glyphic texts occur at Palenque and Uaxactun. There was a long text with the murals of Santa Rita, but most unhappily this was destroyed, the only long text of the Mayapan period ever found. The tomb mural at Tikal is purely glyphic and includes an Initial Series date (that of the death of the occupant?); the cave paintings of Ixtelja comprise figures and glyphs. Texts painted on pottery appear to be largely meaningless, copied from one pot to another (fig. 11; Thompson, 1962).

Glyphs inscribed on jade, shell, and bone for the most part fall into the same class as those on the monuments; that is to say, they are often associated with dates. The extremely rare glyphs on metal (all Postclassic period) would seem to be ornamental; they are crude affairs. Texts on some carved or molded pottery vessels—in particular carved brown ware of Copan—in contrast to those on painted vessels, appear to have meaning. The carved vessel with Initial Series and a position in the 819-day cycle is unique (Ruz, 1952b). It was either copied from a drawing made by a priest with a thorough acquaintance with the calendar or was carved by a priest, just as a clergyman in our culture might paint watercolors as a hobby. The latter explanation endows Maya priests with a touch of the common man, something they seem so often to lack.

Composition and Nature of Hieroglyphs

Maya hieroglyphs fall into two classes: main signs and affixes, the latter so called because they are affixed to the main signs.

Main signs normally are larger than affixes, and they are generally square with slightly rounded corners. However, the proportions can be varied according to available space. The surface of a monument was divided into approximate squares (glyph blocks), but as the number of glyphs to be engraved usually exceeded the number of glyph blocks, the latter frequently hold two glyphs placed side by side, with the result that both main signs are elongated. Sometimes, four glyphs occupy a glyph block; on occasions the glyph block is divided horizontally with consequent lateral elongation of glyphs. The attachment of affixes also distorts the ideal square outline. Generally speaking, the main sign corresponds to the more vital part of the message to be written, often the nouns, whereas affixes are the modifiers–adjectives, adverbs, and the affixes of the spoken language.

Affixes are usually narrow because they have to be squeezed into the available space, much of which is already in the possession of the main sign; their length corresponds to the length of the side of the main glyph to which they are attached.

Affixes fall into two main groups: prefixes and postfixes. Prefixes are placed to the left or above (when they are sometimes called superfixes) and postfixes which stand to the right or below (when they are sometimes called suffixes) of the main sign. Some affixes are only prefixes; others are only postfixes. Of the total of 370 affixes (Thompson, 1962) 125 occur as both prefixes and postfixes, 197 are prefixes only; 48 are postfixes only. Of course the discovery of more texts will change these numbers and proportions to a certain extent but will not affect the general picture. Of those that can be both prefixes and postfixes some are far more common in one position than the other (fig. 8,*a-f*).

Beyer (1934–36) established the general rule that "affixes of bilateral symmetry with vertical axis in the superfix . . . always adjoin their main signs with their bases"; that is to say, they rotate around the main sign so that a suffix is upside down. When there are prefixes or postfixes in both positions open to them, one is elongated so that its base rests against one side of the other, forming what one might term an outer and an inner affix. In such cases, or when two affixes are placed together in parallel positions, it would seem that the inner one usually has a more intimate connection with the main sign. For instance, in a record of so many katuns, the numeral is invariably outside the affix corresponding to the *ka* of katun.

There is no hard division between affixes and main signs; the former sometimes are promoted to main signs and vice versa. About one sixth of the affixes appear as main signs, but main signs serving as affixes are far fewer. Exchange of main signs and affixes distort the normal shapes of the elements. An elongated affix then has to fill a square space, and a square main sign has to be elongated to serve as an affix. Sometimes, to avoid this distortion, the element is doubled. Thus we find the comb elements (Affix 25)[2] doubled on Dresden 7c, 10b, and 25a; similarly, the inverted Ahau is frequently doubled when it serves as an affix. There is no change of meaning in such cases of duplication, as Beyer (1926) has pointed out.

Affixes can also be infixed in main signs. The black affix (95) is sometimes infixed in the cauac sign (528) to represent the month Ch'en, or in the Kin (544) to form Glyph G9 (545). Two main signs may be fused (i.e. one infixed in the other) to form a new sign. For example, Glyphs 644 and 528 are often fused to form a sign (Beyer, 1932a) which appears to mean the seating of the haab. Often an infix is a permanent part of a glyph; for example, Pop (551) invariably has Affix 281 infixed. Many of the main signs can be broken down into separate elements which appear also as affixes, but to see relationships in every stroke or simple design would be as dangerous as to regard our E as signifying F and a minus sign (figs. 6,*a-c*; 8,*a-d*).

Main signs fall into two main categories: symbolic and personified forms (in early

[2] This and subsequent numbers of glyphs are according to the catalog in Thompson, 1962.

Fig. 10—EMBLEM GLYPHS. *a*, Partitioned sky, emblem of Yaxchilan. *b*, Bat with cauac elements infixed, emblem of Copan. Lintel 16, Yaxchilan, and Stela 11, Copan. (After Maudslay.)

writings called normal and head variants). A number of glyphs can be written in both forms. For instance, there are symbolic and personified forms for all the common time periods, and for 15 of the 20 days. In a number of cases the connection between one form and the other is apparent. Thus, the moon and earth goddess of 1 is the personified form of the day Caban, 'earth'; the god of number 3, whose attribute is the Ik symbol, personifies the day Ik; the ear of a dog replaces the portrait of a dog as the symbol for Oc on the *pars pro toto* convention; the percentage sign, an attribute of the death god, replaces his head as the symbol for Cimi, 'death.' Sometimes a glyph is personified by giving the outline of the symbolic form a human profile (Thompson, 1950, fig. 40, *50*); very rarely it may be given a human body in addition to the profile. The Caban glyphs on Altar T, Copan, supply interesting examples of this imaginative treatment (Morley, 1920, p. 335).

Personified glyphs may be shown with complete bodies. The extremely elaborate glyphs of the Initial Series on Stela D, Copan, on Stela D, Quirigua, and on the Palace Panel, Palenque, with their contorted bodies of gods, birds, and animals, are elaborations of personified glyphs. The artist, given free rein, has dominated the epigrapher with magnificent splendor (fig. 9).

Affixes on occasions are also personified. Thus the Yax affix (16) is occasionally replaced by the head of the god of number 9 (Glyph 1003), one of whose attributes is this symbol. A little head of the death god is used as an affix (230, 232), but more often the symbolic form with "eyes" between a cross or a line of "hairs" (12) is substituted. Similarly, the comb affix (25) replaces affixes which depict a fish, natural (203) or conventionalized (204) or a portrait of the fish god (205). There are rare cases in which an affix, on becoming personified, changes places with the main sign

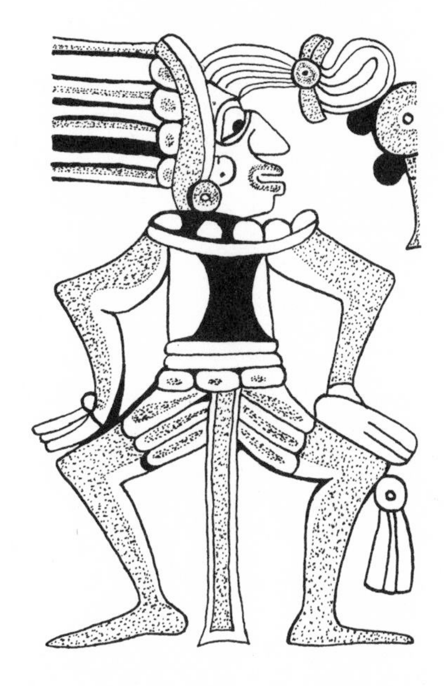

Fig. 11—GLYPHS ON POTTERY, COPAN, HONDURAS. (After Longyear, 1952, fig. 24*a,b*.)

(Thompson, 1950, fig. 34, *27*). The most obvious example of personification of affixes occurs in the case of numbers which appear with such frequency on the monuments (figs. 6,*g-j*; 8,*c,d,g-j*).

Numbers were usually shown by means of bars and dots, a dot for the numbers 1 to 4, a bar for 5. Quite frequently, however, the head of a god was substituted for a number. A sequence of days starting with

Fig. 12—GLYPHS FOR DISEASE, CODEX DRESDEN, PAGES 17b,18b

the day Caban was ruled by a series of gods with associations with each of those days. More correctly, one should say that the days were the gods, for they were so regarded, and, indeed, the personal male prefix *ah* is sometimes added to the day name in the books of Chilam Balam. Caban, for instance, was the earth, and was identified with the young moon goddess who was also a goddess of the earth. Indeed, her symbol, like our query mark and thought to represent a lock of hair, is the main element in the day sign Caban. Similarly, Ahau, fourth in the sequence, is the day of the sun; Kan, eighth in the sequence, is the day of maize; and Cimi, tenth in the sequence, is the day of death. The corresponding personification of the numbers 1, 4, 8, and 10 are the deities of the moon, the sun, the maize, and death. Above 13, personified numbers repeat with the addition of the death attributes of number 10. Thus 14 is shown as the god of the sun, for 4, with death symbols added to represent number 10; 19 is the portrait of the Chicchan god, patron of the ninth day, Chicchan, plus death symbols. The system has a strange parallel in our use of the termination *teen*. Indeed, the Maya number 13 is sometimes shown as the head of the god 3 with the 'teen' death symbol.

This personification of numbers derived from the sequence of deified days well illustrates the ritualistic basis of so much of Maya writing, mystical associations which, I feel, will never serve as material to feed into a computing machine; one can no more treat Maya mysticism in that way than one can reduce El Greco's Burial of the Count of Orgaz to a mathematical formula. That is a personal opinion; great advances in decipherment of the Maya codices with the aid of computing machines have been claimed recently in the U.S.S.R.

A feature of Maya writing is its extreme flexibility. Texts were inscribed or written in some instances to fill a given space. If unused space remained, a glyph compound which would normally occupy one glyph block could be expanded, if necessary, to occupy two or even three glyph blocks. An interesting example of this is the Maya compound for drought, kintunyaabil in Yucatec, which is formed of four glyphic elements corresponding to the four components of the word—the signs for *kin, tun, haab,* and *il.* Normally, these are arranged with kin over haab to the left and tun over il to the right (544, 528, 548, 24). On Dresden 72c, the scribe must have had an extra space to fill, and so he wrote tun over il in one glyph block and kin with the haab sign to its right. As he then had room to spare he inserted the tail (116) below the haab sign. This is a normal element of the haab sign, but is omitted on occasions, particularly in compounds, such as this, in which there was already some overcrowding (Thompson, 1950, fig. 46, *5,6*).

A fairly common compound includes the Ik (503) glyph with affix 179 which really corresponds to the main sign (533 Fancy Ahau). Normally this is written 1.179:503:-24 in one glyph block, but at Tonina on Monument 31 (altar now in National Museum, Mexico) the compound was expanded to two glyph blocks and affix 179 became Glyph 533 to read: 1. 533. 103 and 58:503:24; at nearby Santo Ton it becomes 1.533.103:? 1.58 [503]:24, that is 503 is infixed in affix 58. In the Dresden drought glyph and Tonina–Santo Ton compounds, the reader has to look ahead to get the complete meaning—"spelling out" one glyph block at a time will give a wrong interpretation. Beyer (1937b, figs. 108, 110) supplies another example of a glyph compound occupying one or two glyph blocks. Again, a postfix belonging with one glyph will sometimes be prefixed, instead, to the next glyph. Beyer (1937b, figs. 32–38) brings together seven examples of a clause at Chichen Itza. In six cases the *ti* affix (59) is prefixed to the forward sign (679); in the seventh it is postfixed to the previous glyph (501 or 558). We know the meaning of affix 59, it is the locative *ti*, 'at, to, or from.' Here then the transfer of the affix has no effect on the meaning; it is the equivalent of saying 'I went - to New York' or 'I went to - New York,' but it makes a great deal of difference if one attempts to read the passage by some system in which each element has a syllabic value.

Similarly, an affix which is normally a prefix can be added, instead, as a postfix without changing the meaning. For example, in Dresden the 59–19 M.S. (used as main sign) compound has the 59 affix above, but in the corresponding passage on Codex Madrid 94c–95c the affix is four

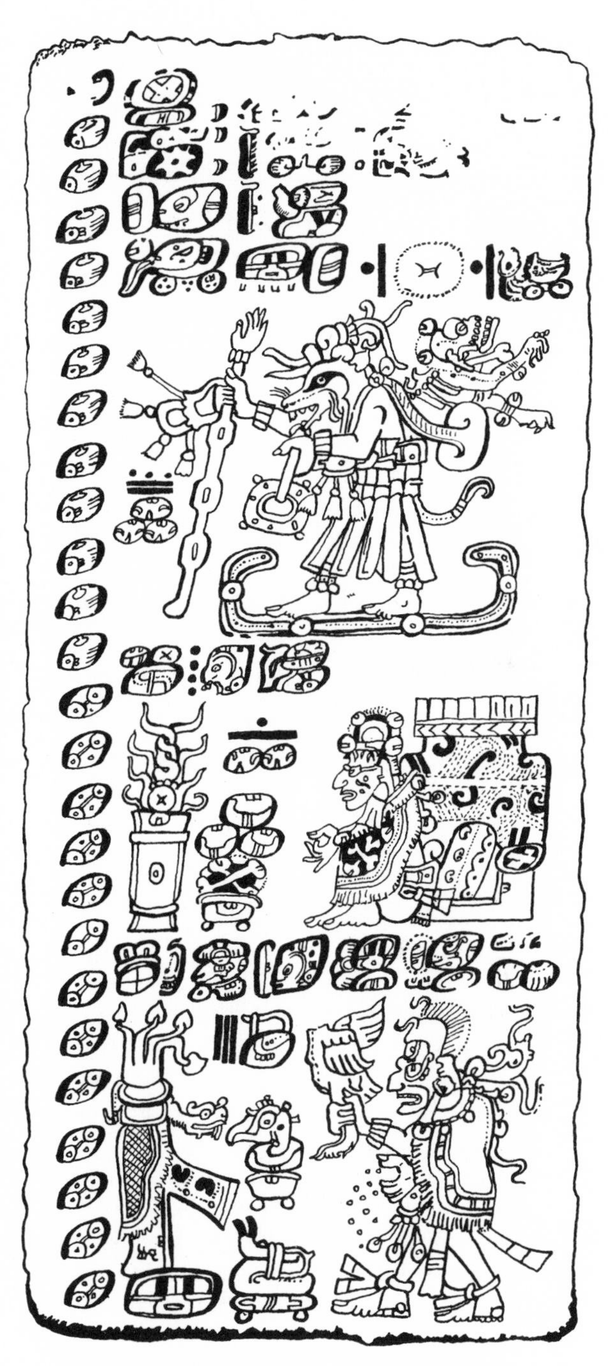

FIG. 13—NEW YEAR PROPHECIES, CODEX DRESDEN, PAGE 28

Fig. 14—FATE OF THE MAIZE CROP, CODEX MADRID, PAGES 26d,27d

times above and twice below 19 M.S. The meaning of this compound is, I think, established; it means *ti*, 'on or at,' and *koch*, the position of carrying on one's head or shoulders, which is what the accompanying pictures show. However, it is really a rebus picture and a rebus glyph for *koch*, illness or disease, particularly if sent by gods (Thompson, 1958b). The moon goddess, patroness of disease, bears on her shoulders the symbols of the diseases with which she afflicts mankind. Knowing this meaning of *koch*, for the glyph, it was immaterial whether the *ti* affix was placed above or below it, although it should be above. On the other hand, the position is vital if one is dealing with a syllabic writing (fig. 12).

These examples illustrate the flexibility in the arrangement of glyphic elements; their interchangeability is another direction in which pliancy in writing is evident. We have noted how the god of number 9, the Chicchan god, can replace the Yax affix (Thompson, 1950, figs. 49–51). Similarly the kin sign once replaces the number 4 because the sun god (*kin* means both sun and day) is god of the number 4.

The process can apparently be reversed: on Dresden 33b – 35b God B is depicted above the jaws of a serpent which encloses a mass of water, as usually, painted as a blue-green streaked mass. The corresponding glyph has the number 9 prefixed to a spiral, which is a common convention for water in Middle America. Below is affix 24 to which the sound *il* has been assigned. If the number 9, as is the cited case of the head for 9, is read as yax, one obtains the word Yaxilha or Yaxhail. Yaxila (the *h* of *ha* 'water' sometimes disappears after a consonant) is deep water, or water without a bottom according to the Motul dictionary; it can also be the first water. God B is Chac, the rain god. The Chacs were believed to have barrels or gourds of water which they sprinkled on the earth, and in a parallel passage in Codex Madrid 3a–6a the Chacs stand beside similar bodies of water enclosed in snakes (the snake is very closely connected with water). Accordingly, it is quite possible that here we have the glyph for *yaxila*, and that is the primaeval water in the sky from which the Chacs draw their supplies. If this interpretation is acceptable, we have a case of the number 9 expressed as bar and dots, standing for *yax*, 'new, green' or, in the case of *Yaxil*, 'first.' An irrefutable example of this process is on Dresden 40*b*, where four numerical dots express the kinich part of the glyph of Kinichkakmo, 'sun-parrot.' Four is the number of Kinich, the sun god.

Both space considerations and ritualistic associations militated against precision in writing; and, in addition, the great use of rebus writing, to be considered below, influenced the texts so that the reader had to have a good background of mythology and folklore to comprehend the texts. This is understandable when one bears in mind the many statements from early Spanish sources that the knowledge of the hieroglyphs was confined to a small group of nobles, presumably persons in the upper brackets of the hierarchy. On the other hand, merchants and tribute collectors and assessors probably had only a smattering of hieroglyphic knowledge, sufficient to allow them to make up their accounts or to read place names on maps. In contrast, the writers of the surviving texts on monuments and in books were writing only for others in their small circle who had the same educational background and the same outlook and, therefore, could readily comprehend mythological allusions.

Unity and Regionalism and Their Political Implications

Generally speaking, the hieroglyphs were the same from the Maya Dan to Beersheba; a Maya priest from, let us say, Copan would not, one may suppose, have had difficulty in reading the inscriptions of Xcalumkin, for instance, although to our eyes they seem decidedly different. Local expressions in the form of unusual compounds might have puzzled him for a moment or two, just as an American colloquialism might not be immediately intelligible to an Englishman and vice versa, but I do not think the meaning of a local compound would long escape him.

The emblem glyphs are examples of local glyphs but they carry the same set of affixes wherever they occur. There are other main signs which do not fall in this category, but are confined to one or two sites. There is also a very marked difference between the range of glyphs which appear on monuments and those found in the hieroglyphic codices, although many glyphs appear in both groups. Here the differentiation must mark the variations in subject matter, for the glyphs in the divinatory almanacs which give the luck of the days do not appear on the monuments which do

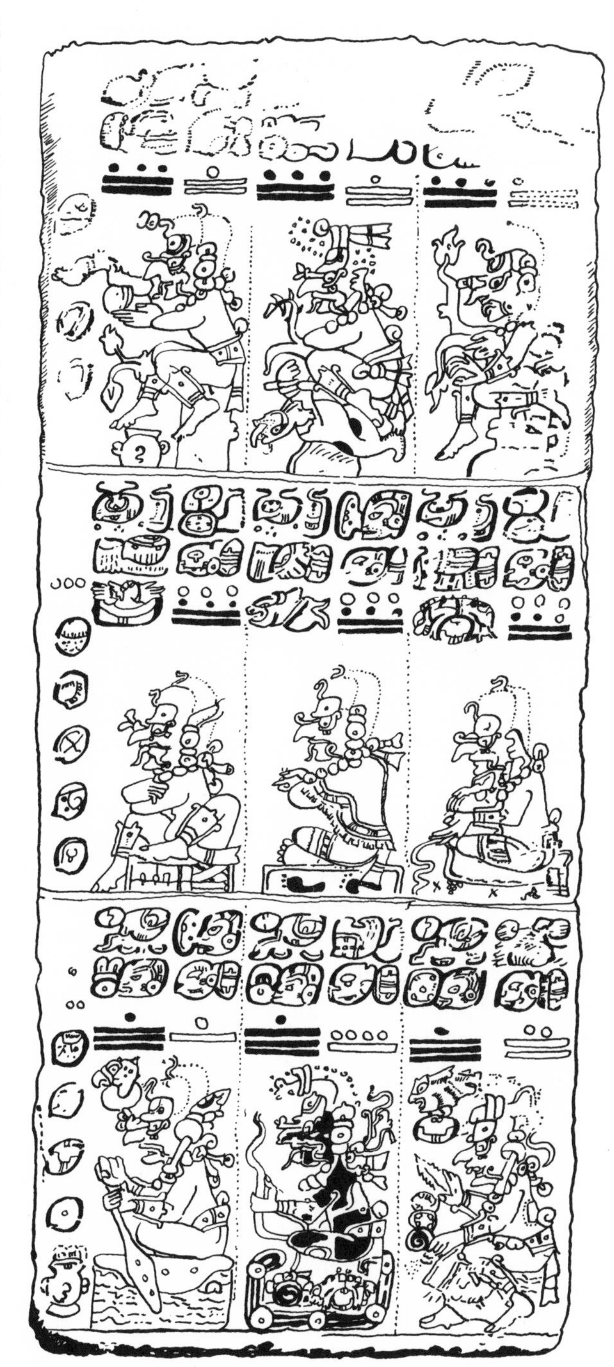

Fig. 15—ACTIVITIES OF THE CHACS, CODEX DRESDEN, PAGE 29

not deal with such trifles. Contrariwise, the subject matter of the monuments finds no place in the codices. Even where—as in the case of the lunar and Venus tables of Codex Dresden—written texts cover the same subjects as the monuments, the explanatory or associated ritualistic glyphs differ; the series of glyphs associated with positions in the eclipse and Venus tables are confined to Codex Dresden. Similarly, many of the glyphs with the series of katuns in Codex Paris are not found with the records of katun endings on the monuments. Nevertheless, the general unity of the whole central area, as far as hieroglyphic writing is concerned, is clearly demonstrable. It applies above all to the great body of calendric glyphs.

In some cases we can trace the spread of a new glyph. Glyph B of the lunar series is absent from the earliest inscriptions which record that group of glyphs giving the age of the moon, and its meaning seems to have been so general that it wasn't an essential element at any time (it is suppressed in some late texts, e.g. Quirigua, Stela A and F). Its first known appearance is on Stela 25, Piedras Negras, erected at 9.8.15.0.0. (Statements by two writers that it occurs on Stela O, Pusilha, are erroneous; the assumption that two weathered glyphs on the early Stela 16, Caracol, are X and B seems gratuitous in view of irregularities in the presentation of the lunar series on Stelae 14 and 29 at nearby Naranjo, with which, on glyphic evidence, Caracol was very closely connected.)

Naturally, one cannot give the precise date on which Glyph B was accepted at any given site because prior monuments may not have survived. The glyph appears in a text at Copan dated 9.9.0.0.0, and had reached distant Coba at 9.10.0.0.0. It is found at Naachtun, ten years later, at 9.10.10.0.0, at Pusilha and Xultun at 9.11.-0.0.0, at Uxul, Calakmul, and possibly Altar de Sacrificios at 9.11.10.0.0, at Etzna and possibly Yaxchilan (Stela 6) at 9.12.0.0.0, at Tonina at 9.12.10.0.0, and at nearby Tila at 9.12.13.0.0.

Piedras Negras started with the symbolic form of Glyph B, but Copan, after following that example, five years later, at 9.9.0.0.0, switched to the personified form at 9.9.5.0.0, and Piedras Negras did the same at 9.10.5.0.0. Whether this throws light on relations between sites is not clear; at least it shows that both the symbolic and personified forms of the glyph were known at an early date at widely separated cities.

An unusual variant of the baktun glyph (528.528:548) makes its appearance for the first time at Copan (Temple 11) in association with the date 9.18.0.0.0. This same glyph appears 20 years later on Stela 8, Caracol, and on Mountain Cow (Hatzcap Ceel) Altar 2, sites which are only a few miles apart. Here it would seem that influences from Copan made themselves felt in western British Honduras. On the other hand, some innovations never took. Stela 7, Aguateca, has a most unusual main element of the katun glyph. This consists of a bar and two dots, apparently representing the number 7, but a connection between the number 7, which is ruled by the jaguar god, and a katun is not apparent. No other city followed Aguateca's lead. Can it be that the substitution was based on an association so slender that other cities thought it too farfetched to follow?

The spread of the uniform system of counting moons in groups of six, as demonstrated by Teeple (1931, pp. 53–61), is an outstanding example of cooperation between the ceremonial centers of the Central area. As Teeple showed, this may have originated at Copan with the erection of Altars H′ and I′ at 9.12.10.0.0 or 9.13.0.0.0. Moons were standardized in groups of six so that if a moon carried the number 3 in one center, that same moon would bear the same number in other cities of the central area. Satterthwaite (1958b, p. 132) has made a case for the use of the uniform system at Tikal, nearly two centuries earlier, but as no lunar series for the intervening period exist there, the bearing of these on the spread of the uniform system is not clear.

The system was, by accident, extraordinarily simple, for 5 tuns are only a day or two less than 61 moons ($6 \times 10 + 1$) so that at each quarter-katun the group number increases by 1. The discovery of texts at Palenque since Teeple wrote has demonstrated that that city did in fact conform to the uniform system (Berlin, 1943; Thompson, 1952b). The tables published by Andrews (1951) and subsequent discoveries of new texts have extended the list of centers which conformed to the uniform system, but demonstrate a marked blowing hot and cold as to adopting the uniform system in southern Campeche; but, as we shall see, Campeche was nonconformist in other matters. The spread of the Maya uniform grouping of moons is roughly comparable to the spread of the Gregorian calendar.

Piedras Negras may have initiated the uniform system with Stela 6 (9.12.15.0.0), but Copan's claim is perhaps supported by the fact she took the trouble to explain the system, choosing a date just 144 moons (24 moon groups) before 9.13.0.0.0.

The general picture is one of exchange of ideas within most of the central area, but there is evidence of regional variations in outlying parts. Throughout the Peten, the Usumacinta drainage, and the eastern parts of the Maya lowlands the year bearers (the days on which the new year started on 1 Pop) were the days Akbal, Lamat, Ben, and Etz'nab; and, as a corollary, the day Ahau, on which all normal time periods ended, could be associated only with the month positions 3, 8, 13, and 18. For example, 9.13.0.0.0 ended on 8 Ahau 8 Uo; in the standard system it could not end on 8 Ahau 7 Uo. However, with a shift of year bearers to the next set of days—Kan, Muluc, Ix and Cauac—so that they occupy the position 1 Pop, Ahau comes to be associated with the month positions 2, 7, 12, and 17, one position earlier, the engaged day and month counts having slipped a cog. Such a slip may seem of small consequence to us, but to the Maya who regarded the calendar as divine and the very core of their ceremonial life, the existence of a rival system must have been of profound importance.

Etzna erected Stelae 19 and 20 at 9.12.0.0.0 and 9.13.0.0.0 respectively, and on those monuments the day Ahau falls on the positions 7 Yaxkin and 7 Uo respectively, that is, in the nonconformist system. Later monuments at other sites in Campeche and Yucatan (at Xcalumkin, Kabah, Oxkintok, and Uxmal) also follow this nonconformist tradition, which is also found in Codex Madrid, and in the system Landa gives in his report (from a Xiu source?). There are no earlier records at Etzna or elsewhere in Campeche. I had once supposed that this was a heresy which developed not long before 9.12.0.0.0, but it may have had its beginnings far earlier when the calendar first came into use in that area. It has been called the Puuc style of dating.

All of a sudden, Yaxchilan, deep in orthodox territory, erected a monument, Stela 18, giving a date (9.14.16.15.12) 3 Eb 14 Mol in the Puuc style. However, as the date had been given in the heretical Puuc manner, the priests of Yaxchilan, in explanation or in a spirit of repentance, gave the same month position on a step of Structure 44 in the orthodox system (9.14.16.15.11) 2 Chuen 14 Mol. Each date is followed by six identical glyphs, establishing the relationship between them (Thompson, 1952a). Stela 20 at Yaxchilan also carries a date in the Puuc system. Now it is of great importance to note that Proskouriakoff had independently noted Puuc influences in these two monuments. Thus epigraphic evidence and artistic analysis combine to give us a most important piece of information, namely, that for a short time Puuc influences, epigraphic and artistic, swayed Yaxchilan from her normal course. The heresy was short-lived; Yaxchilan, of her own will or because of outside pressure, kicked over the traces, but then returned sedately to the orthodox stable. The case is illustrative of how epigraphy can contribute to political history.

The style of glyphs and the subject matter of the monuments in certain Puuc sites and at Chichen Itza are in marked contrast with that obtained in ceremonial centers of the Peten-Usumacinta area. Individual glyphs are often different or differently carved. More important, the framework of dates which characterizes the inscriptions of the Central area are unknown in Yucatan and northern Campeche. There, the distance numbers which lead forward to, or backward from, the dedicatory date of a monument to string together a series of dates, an arrangement so typical of the Central area, are unknown. Instead, at Chichen Itza and, to a far lesser extent, in other northern ceremonial centers, dates are recorded by noting in what tun they fall and giving the day on which the current katun will end, e.g. the date given several times in the Temple of the Four Lintels at Chichen Itza: 9 Lamat 11 Yax, 13 tuns, 1 Ahau, which is 10.2.12.1.8 9 Lamat 11 Yax, falling in the 13th tun of the katun 10.3.0.0.0, which ends on 1 Ahau 3 Yaxkin (Thompson, 1937). In the cities of the Central area this would have been expressed by means of an addition.

10.2.12. 1. 8	9 Lamat 11 Yax
7.16.12	Count forward
10.3. 0. 0. 0	1 Ahau 3 Yaxkin, completion of 3 katuns

The distinctive style of date recording at Chichen Itza is in keeping with local style of sculpture (Proskouriakoff, 1951) and of pre-Mexican period architecture. Epigraphy here, too, is good evidence of regionalism with political implications (fig. 5). At Seibal non-Maya glyphs, together with non-Classic sculptural elements and arrangements, hint in no whisper at foreign penetration.

Stylistic Changes

Surviving Maya glyphs range in date from shortly before A.D. 300 to the 18th century (in the books of Chilam Balam), but both early and late texts are rare; the great bulk of monumental inscriptions fall in the 400 years between 9.3.0.0.0 and 10.3.0.0.0, when the Classic period was almost at its end. The codical glyphs, as already noted, are attributable to the two or three centuries prior to the Spanish conquest (Merida, the Spanish capital of Yucatan was founded in 1542). As is only natural, there are stylistic changes between early and late texts. Furthermore, new glyphs appear in later texts and some early glyphs drop out of use in the middle of the Classic period.

Both Morley (1920, p. 380; 1937–38, 2: 14; 4: 297–303) and Beyer (1932b) discuss stylistic changes in the history of hieroglyphic writing, but some of Beyer's conclusions on the chronological development seem to be vitiated by dubious assignments to divisions of Postclassic periods (Thompson, 1937). To the examples discussed by those authors may be added a most useful time-marker, the use of an *X* as filler in numerical coefficients in place of the usual crescent. This innovation seems to have made its appearance about 9.17.0.0.0, perhaps at Copan, and rapidly spread to many ceremonial centers (Ruppert, Thompson, and Proskouriakoff, 1955, p. 36). Replacement of curves by straight lines (e.g. late examples of Kan, Cauac, Cumku, Kankin, and the tun sign) is a sign of lateness. Very early texts are ornate and have much detail; later glyphs are more cursive. Some details of glyphs in the codices have been regarded as indicative of lateness, but may respond to the different media—paper versus stone—for Classic period painted glyphs sometimes seem to have affinities with those in the codices. The present editions of Codex Dresden have an interesting mixture of glyph styles; the scribe obviously copied some glyphs as they were in the prototype; others he painted as they were written when the present edition was prepared. Note for instance the jumble of early and late forms of the day signs Kan and Ahau on the pages of the Venus calendar.

Figures 1–5, arranged in chronological order, illustrate stylistic changes, but variation in figure 5 is also regional.

Origins of Maya Writing

As yet no Maya text has been found which can be described as representing an early stage of evolution of the writing. The text incised on the broken stela from Kaminaljuyu may be the earliest example of writing with what are clearly Maya glyphs; the sculpture certainly is not later than Miraflores (Late Formative). There are no glyphs unreservedly attributable to La Venta I–IV; the only ones so far found are on Monument 13, a surface find in an aberrant style. The Tuxtla Statuette we may style Olmec for the present, but its spiritual home may be nearer Cerro de las Mesas. Additional to those two texts and certain jades of questionable authenticity, there are not a dozen known Olmec glyphs. In contrast to the elaboration of early Maya glyphs and their cursive nature, those on the Tuxtla Statuette are very simple and markedly rectilinear (Holmes, 1907). How far this is due to the intractable character of the stone on which they are incised it is hard to say, but three portrait glyphs are fairly elaborate, suggesting that the rcetilinear character of the symbolic signs is characteristic of the writing. Among the glyphs are ones which resemble the Maya signs 188, 506, 511, 544, 732, and 772. One glyph also has little circles on the outside corners of the cartouche, a feature also found in some early Maya texts.

The same vague resemblances are apparent in comparing Maya with Zapotec glyphs, which lack the rectilinear treatment of Olmec writing; when the resemblance is specific, as in the case of Zapotec Glyph E (Caso, 1928, fig. 8) and Maya glyphs 585 and 721, the design is simple (here 5 circles in one form; a cross in the other). A connection may exist between the Zapotec tied-bag glyph (Caso, 1947, fig. 21,*a,b*) and Maya glyph 569, and there are resemblances in one or two portrait glyphs.

Since it is almost inconceivable that the 260-day almanac originated independently in more than one place, one would expect a reasonably close resemblance between the day signs in the three areas, but this is not apparent (there is, of course, no good example of an Olmec day sign except the reptile eye glyph at Piedra Labrada and the apparent day sign at the top of the Tuxtla Statuette with apparent coefficient of 10 below, but this was identified by Morley [in Holmes, 1907] from its position as an Initial Series introductory glyph, to which in fact it bears no resemblance). Simple glyphs which one might expect to have been spread from the original home of the sacred almanac may be represented by some of the signs just discussed. The wide divergence of the three writings, as we now know them, may perhaps be due to the absence of any really early Maya text.

In the matter of the place of origin of the nucleus of Middle American writing, the 260-day sacred almanac, it is well to ponder a point made by Gadow (1908, p. 303). He noted that several of the fauna which serve as day names and day glyphs –crocodile, jaguar, monkey, king vulture, and probably the iguana (*Iguana tuberculata*)— are foreign to the Mexican plateau and, one may add, to the highlands of Guatemala. The conclusion he drew is that the 260-day almanac originated in the lowlands.

Affixes, which are so common in Maya writing, are not common in what has survived in Olmec writing, and are still rarer in Zapotec texts. Moreover, the few recognizable examples are largely prefixes; one gets the impression that both Zapotec and Olmec inscriptions are less articulated than Maya writing and, in fact, hardly qualify as writing.

Comparisons with Mixtec and Aztec texts are dangerous since these are largely genealogical and historical, of which no examples have survived among the Maya. However, it is worth noting that ritualistic codices from central Mexico almost completely lack explanatory glyphs; one must depend on the pictorial matter to recognize the subject of the divinations. Possibly Maya glyphic writing was not the earliest in Middle America, but it soon forged far ahead of its rivals, who never came anywhere near overtaking it. Ciudad Real, who knew Middle America extremely well and was an acute observer, was justified in his remark that the Maya of Yucatan were praiseworthy above all the other peoples of New Spain for three things, the first of which was "in ancient times they had characters and letters with which they wrote their histories, their ceremonies and the sacrificial rites to their idols, and their calendar in books made of the bark of a certain tree" (Ponce, 1873, 2: 392). Ciudad Real had traveled extensively in Mexico and must have seen Aztec and Mixtec books, but he considered that only the Maya ones could be said to contain "characters and letters," an appraisal with which present-day scholarship would concur.

Nature of Maya Writing and Its Decipherment

The decipherment of the Maya hieroglyphs started with the publication of Landa's alphabet in 1864. Landa gave Maya symbols corresponding to the letters of the alphabet, together with a three-word sentence and a single word to explain how the system worked. It is now obvious that Landa named the letters of the alphabet to his informant who gave him a sign, one of the meanings of which corresponded to the name, not the sound, of its opening letters. However, it is clear that the alphabet (it was really a syllabary) was not of pre-Spanish type, the symbol for *b* (*be* in Spanish) was a footprint, the conventional symbol for a road or travel throughout Middle America, but footprints practically never appear in Maya texts although *be* is a common sound in spoken Maya. Landa had started up a hare and there were many joyful halloings as the pack gave chase. It was soon obvious that Landa's "alphabet" would not serve to translate the texts; the Maya Rosetta stone had become a millstone around the necks of decipherers. It was discarded but occasional students to this day have continued to use it, each adding his own dressing of new elements to Landa's mixed salad and, indeed, putting to one side of the plate any component of the original dish he could not digest. Others have gone far beyond Landa's explanation and have attempted to use Landa's alphabet as the basis of a syllabic writing. Recent advocates of a Maya syllabic system are Whorf (1933, 1942) and Knorozov (1952, 1955, 1958a, 1958b). For a discussion of this approach see Thompson, 1959a.

The glyphs themselves, I think, are not easily reconciled with a syllabic style of writing. Their number appears to argue against the idea. The total of glyphic elements (main signs, portraits, and affixes) in the catalogue is 862, but, deducting for duplications between main signs and affixes and of personified and symbolic forms (although their functions do not completely coincide in all cases), a total of 750 glyph elements seems reasonable (Thompson, 1962). This compares with 734 symbols listed in Gardiner's Egyptian grammar and 604 for the total of Egyptian symbols excluding ligatures and numbers, and is about a third above the minimum of signs estimated to be needed for an ideographic or pictographic script. On the other hand, glyphs for a syllabary may drop to about 100 (Diringer, 1948, p. 196). As noted, of the total body of affixes the majority are prefixes only: 53 per cent appear only in that position, 33 per cent can occur in both positions, and 33 per cent are postfixes only. Now, should Maya writing be syllabic, the proportions should be quite different; it would be natural to expect most affixes to occupy both positions, for if each element in a compound glyph represents a syllable or a syllable reduced to a consonant, as proponents of the syllabic nature of Maya writing assume was the Maya practice, it is hard to understand why so many consonants or syllables should appear only at the beginnings of words.

The four commonest glyphs used in noncalendric passages are of calendric origin; others of very frequent occurrence, such as the signs for sky, death, good tidings or perhaps abundance, and evil or misfortune, represent abstract ideas, still others (jaguar and vulture) are of ritualistic importance. If the Maya, conforming to Old World practice, developed an acrophonic system (use of a sign to represent the sound with which it begins), it is difficult to explain why three of the five most frequent signs (cauac, caban, and caan) start with the same syllable. A number of important Maya words commence with *ca*, but they are insufficient to account for such an overwhelming preponderance. In fact, there is good evidence that these signs in almost all their occurrences represent respectively the concepts: storm, possibly storm clouds, as well as god and adjectively divine; earth; and sky.

Moreover, if *caan*, for example, has a syllabic or consonantal value it is hard to understand why it is not used also as a prefix, for we must assume that in syllabic writing the order of reading would be prefix–main sign–postfix (a fixed order is practically essential, otherwise a glyph for our word *pat* could equally well stand for *tap* or *apt*). Similarly, affixes should appear very frequently as main signs. No consonant or syllable is very frequent in the middle of a word but absent at its start.

A strong argument against a syllabic writing is that many glyphs are confined to divinatory passages in the codices; others appear only on the monuments. Were the writing syllabic one could not expect such distinctions or, at least, the same main signs should appear in both kinds of texts with different affixes. Technical terms are to be expected, but the same syllabic or alphabetic elements should enter into their composition had such a system been employed. For the case for a syllabic system readers should consult the writings of Whorf and Knorozov already cited.

Although there is at present, in my opinion, no adequate reason for supposing that the Maya possessed a syllabic writing in pre-Spanish times, yet there is good evidence that grammatical particles were expressed as affixes. Examples of this practice are the particles *al* (Barthel, 1954), *il*, and *te*. Adjectives (e.g. the colors) and adverbs (*ti*) seem to be affixes. Some affixes—*zac*, *chac* and *te*—were also used rebus-fashion as noted below (fig. 6,*a-j*,*r*,*w*).

Rebus is applied to a method of writing, in which an easily depicted object stands for an abstract idea which is a homophone, as in children's pastimes in which "I can bear" is represented as pictures of an eye, a tin can, and a bear. Other examples are the punning names on mediaeval coats of arms. It was common among the Maya, and to a lesser extent in central Mexico where it received a tremendous impetus when it was extensively used by the friars to indoctrinate the Indians. Maya, which is largely monosyllabic, lends itself to that method of writing. Pictures of animals were much favored. Thus, we find pictures and glyphs of a dog, the general term for which in Yucatec is *pek*, used also to denote *pek*, 'worthless rains,' a term, accompanied by a drawing of a dog, used in the books of Chilam Balam in auguries of drought (Thompson, 1959a, p. 359). They appear in almanacs which treat of weather, and the drought aspect is emphasized by lighted torches in the dog's paws, a well-recognized symbol of scorching rainless days. The dog glyph also appears in texts treating of disease, and there the homophone is *pek*, a Yucatec name for a skin infection (Thompson, 1958b, p. 305).

Mac is the carapace of a turtle or tortoise, and a picture of it is sometimes used as the symbol of the month Mac, although there is no reason to suppose that that month has any connection with a tortoise or its carapace. *Ch'ich'* is the common Yucatec term for bird, but it is also applied to augury; *ch'ich' tun*, the augury of the tun, is an expression which occurs in the books of Chilam Balam. Accordingly when we find on pages of Codex Paris which treat of katun prophecies a compound showing a bird over a tun sign, it is reasonable to read it as *ch'ich' tun*, or *mut tun* (see below), the tidings of the tun.

In Codex Dresden the moon goddess is shown in passages which treat of disease with a lighted fire bundle on her back. In Yucatec *kak* is both fire and certain eruptions which nowadays include smallpox. Now the moon goddess, who in ancient times was the patroness of weaving, birth, and disease and was known as 'our mother,' has been confounded with the Virgin Mary, probably because of the mother aspect and because the Virgin Mary is often depicted standing on a crescent moon. In a discussion of disease in Dzitas, Yucatan, Redfield and Redfield (1940, p. 69) note that smallpox is called "smallpox of the virgin," which suggests that there was in ancient times a close association between that disease and the moon goddess, although she also has other diseases in her charge. Here, then, the fire on her back is rebus writing for *kak*, some form of skin eruptions.

A semi-mythological being was Xoc, a fish god, perhaps a whale, which resided in the sky. *Xoc* is also the Yucatec term for a count or to count. After the distance numbers on the monuments we find the head of a fish, sometimes partly anthropomorphized, with the locative postfix *ti*, 'to, at or from,' and a pair of affixes one of which is used if the count is forward, the other if it is a count backward by subtraction (Thompson, 1950, pp. 162–64). Here a rebus is clearly intended, but the matter goes farther than that, and well illustrates the complexity of Maya writing. As the carving of a recognizable fish head is not easy, the symbol of water or jade, used also as a glyph for the day Muluc, equivalent of the Aztec Atl, 'water,' often replaces it. In such cases water, in which the fish lives, is the symbol for its rebus, *xoc*, 'to count.'

Elsewhere this same water symbol combined with the drilling glyph appears to refer to the drilling of jade (jade is a symbol for water throughout Middle America; both are green and precious). The other Muluc symbol, changed from a horizontal to a vertical position, is the sign for the 360-day year, called tun. *Tun* is the Yucatec word for jade and, by extension, stone in general.

The ceremonies inaugurating a new year in Yucatan were largely performed at the heaps of stones which stood at the entrances of the town set at the four points of the compass. Idols connected with the new-year ceremonies were set up on, or close by, the piles of stone. Landa (Tozzer, 1941a, pp. 139–49) does not make the point clear, but it seems logical that they should be set on top of the pile, particularly since crosses are now placed on top of such stone piles at the entrances to the villages. In the pictures of the new-year ceremonies in Codices Dresden and Paris the gods are set on the tun sign (fig. 13, bottom left). Cyrus Thomas suggested 80 years ago that this must be a glyphic representation of the pile of stones (the plural affix in spoken Yucatec is often omitted and may have been always omitted with the glyphs). On page 25c of Codex Madrid which deals with divination for the maize crop, the maize god twice appears seated on the earth symbol and once on the tun sign. The fourth picture shows a raccoon scratching up the seed shallowly planted on the tun sign, to represent outcropping rock, a condition often found in the Maya area. An interesting parallel to the parable of the sower, "some fell upon stony places where they had not much earth."

Tun is an affix in spoken Yucatec which serves as an intensifier. *Kin* is sun, but in the Maya word for severe drought, *kintunyaabil, tun* is affixed to the kin sign to indicate scorching, or very strong, or dominating, sun. The complete word means 'scorching sun throughout the year.' In the glyph for this the affix *tun* is expressed by the regular tun glyph with the normal meaning of 360-day year (fig. 6,*l*).

Tun also has a meaning of 'final.' In the affix used for the 20th day, the last day of a month, the regular tun sign is used rebus-fashion with that value (fig. 8,*k*).

From the above it is clear that the reader had to choose the use of the word which fitted the text. In the case of *tun* it might signify year, stone, bedrock, final, or very. Sometimes a glyph has two quite different meanings, but a connection through rebus writing is not apparent. The cauac sign is a symbol of storms, rain and rain clouds, and also a *haab*, the year, which comprises the word for water, *ha* plus what may possibly be the instrumental affix *ab*. However, there are places in the codices where such meanings do not fit. In some of these the root *ku*, 'god,' or its adjectival form *kul*, 'divine, holy,' or the verbal root *kul*, 'to worship,' fit very well. The statues in the new-year ceremonies on Codex Dresden 26–28 carry the cauac symbol within the trunk, which is shown to be of wood (*che*) because of the symbol for wood on its exterior. *Kulche* is Yucatec for a wooden statue of a god. Frequently a deity is seated in a temple which carries the cauac sign. *Na* is house in Yucatec, with the addition of either *ku* or *kul*, it becomes *kuna* or *kulna*, temple, literally 'god house' or 'holy house.' Trays or flat supports for offerings may carry the cauac emblem, presumably to show their association with offering and worship. Cedar was much used for religious purposes—idols were invariably made of it—and so it was called *kuche*, 'god wood.' Objects of cedar wood may be identified by the cauac symbol. Landa gives to the cauac symbol the sound value *cu*. As his writings show that he was confused as to when a glottal stop was present, there is a possibility that he was given the cauac sign as corresponding to *ku* or to the opening letters of *kul*.

A tenuous connection between the usual meanings of the cauac glyph–storm, rain and clouds—and its apparent secondary value of ku or kul can be seen. The rain gods were the most important deities in Maya life, and there is some evidence, that they may sometimes have been known merely as *kuob*, 'the gods' (Redfield and Villa, 1934, p. 353, where the title of Dios precedes chac; Thompson, 1930, p. 115, where a Maya informant thought that the *kuh* were thundergods; Villa R., 1945, where the chief chac is called Kunku, 'chief god'). However, one must proceed with great caution in assigning two different and only loosely related concepts to a glyphic element. Yet the Maya link those two; the burgeoning cedar signals the rains.

Glyphs for gods and persons, apart from portraits, were until recently unrecognized or undeciphered. The German scholar Thomas Barthel (1952) has identified a name glyph, Zacakab, of one of the manifestations of the deity of the planet Venus at heliacal rising. The contributions of Barthel (1954, 1955a, 1955b) to glyphic decipherment have not received the attention they certainly merit. Since this article was prepared, Miss Proskouriakoff (1961) has carried decipherment a big stride forward by identifying a number of name glyphs, including those of women, on monuments of the Classic period.

Pictorial glyphs are found in the codices (identifiable birds and animals, haunches of venison, fish offered in sacrifice, etc.) and they also occur on the monuments, for instance Glyph 685 which is a naturalistic picture of a pyramid. However, such glyphs do not play an important part in Maya epigraphy (fig. 13).

Ideographic glyphs are not uncommon. The moon sign in its use as a symbol for 20 is an example; the employment of a hand as a symbol for completion is another. The various glyphs in the codices which depict action by means of hands in different positions and with variable affixes presumably fall in this same category. The sun glyph between the signs for sky and earth to represent sunrise (conceivably sunset), and hence a whole day, is ideographic, and so, probably, is the use of a shell as the sign for completion (possibly zero) in the codices and as an adjunct of other completion symbols on the monuments. Footprints for a road or travel, and the affixing of the symbols for smoke and sparks to the drilling glyph to form the symbol for fire-drilling are other examples (figs. 6; 8,*l,m*). Juxtaposition of the glyphs for earth and seed to give the sign for milpa (cornfield) is a frequent ideograph in divinatory almanacs for farming. Future research should expand this group.

In this connection mention should be made of pictorial ideograms. For example, on Codex Dresden 45c the augury is drought, confirmed by the presence of the drought glyph. The picture, however, is of a dying deer with God B crouching over it. A catch phrase for times of drought in Yucatec was *cimcehil*, 'when the deer die' (Roys, 1933, p. 122). The glyphs make no reference to a dying deer. A secondary point which this elucidates is that the pictures illustrate, amplify, and often paraphrase the text; the glyphs do not explain the pictures. Indeed, the greater importance of the text is demonstrated by the fact that where space is lacking, the illustrations are suppressed. The scenes are of great value in indicating the subject matter, but more than one decipherment has been shipwrecked on the false assumption that the glyphs interpret the picture.

Poetry, I think, plays its part in the arrangement of Maya texts on the monuments. To our way of thinking a number of the Maya glyphs are redundant. For example, a record of 1 Ahau 8 Kayab completion of 10th katun fixes a date, to all intents and purposes in all eternity. It cannot repeat for 18,980 tuns, about 18,700 solar years. Yet, the Maya add that this date falls at the end of a half-baktun and also that it ends a tun, two pieces of information which are quite unnecessary; they merely repeat in other ways what the compound completion of 10th katun has already told us. The glyph for seating of a tun which often accompanies such period endings is equally redundant. In Maya writings of the books of Chilam Balam a phrase in the second half of a sentence often repeats what has previously been said in the first half, a close parallel to Hebrew poetry, best exemplified by the psalter. Knowing that the Maya used that type of antiphonal poetry, it is best to ascribe the unnecessary glyphs on the monuments to it rather than to tautology.

The imagery which clothes the Maya philosophy of time plays a part both in the writings in the books of Chilam Balam and in the hieroglyphic texts. Time was conceived of as a sort of relay race in which the gods of the numbers bore the periods of time on their backs. At the end of each day, the bearers of the day and of the month set down their burdens and the gods of the next day took up the load. At the end of a tun there was of course a greater exchange of burdens. The whole concept is well illustrated on Stela D, Copan, which commemorates the date 9.15.5.0.0 10 Ahau 8 Ch'en. The gods of all those numbers bear their periods on their backs by means of tumplines across their foreheads in typical Maya fashion, such as one sees to this very day in Middle America. As they come to rest and set down their burdens, the god who rules the night rises with his burden, the night, shown as a rolled-up jaguar skin (the spots represent the stars). He is depicted with great realism with one hand on the ground to take the strain as he rises with his burden (Thompson, 1950, frontispiece and pp. 59–61). The same conception is seen in other texts, and burden glyphs are liberally scattered through the hieroglyphic books.

This concept of bearers of time periods coming to rest is expressed in a few texts by a glyph recently recognized by Berlin as the inverted head of a bat. Bats, it will be recalled, rest upside down. This striking metaphor, like that of the dying deer for drought, is an example of what I call metaphorgrams.

Developers of Maya Hieroglyphs

Wherever Maya hieroglyphic writing may have originated, its great development was in the lowlands. Apart from a very limited number of early texts, such as the Kaminaljuyu stela, the Guatemalan highlands are singularly lacking in hieroglyphic inscriptions. Indeed, the framework of Maya texts, the Long Count based on the tun of 360 days, may have been unknown in the mountain country, for the only Long Count to have survived is that of the Cakchiquel Maya which was based on a period of 400 days with its next highest unit one of 8,000 days, a structure perhaps shared with southern Veracruz (Thompson, 1943c, pp. 108–109). It may also be significant that the only account of hieroglyphic writing in highland Guatemala at the time of the Spanish conquest refers to a Mexican system (Fuentes y Guzmán, 1932–33, pt. 2, bk. 2, chs. 11, 12). In parenthesis it may be noted that name glyphs which accompany Maya Toltec sculptures at Chichen Itza are largely of Mexican origin.

Apart from the fact that the enormous bulk of Maya texts comes from the lowlands, practically all the known examples or rebus glyphs are based on lowland speech, principally Yucatec. The lowland languages or dialects—Yucatec, Chontal, Mopan, Palencano Chol, Manche Chol, and Chorti—are very close together lexically speaking, although there are differences in grammatical structure. The latter, however, are not so easily detected in the hieroglyphs because glyphic elements to represent such things as tenses and pronouns seem to be absent.

It would, therefore, seem probable that hieroglyphic writing was developed, although not necessarily invented, by lowlanders who spoke a language ancestral to those listed above, but which probably differed only to a small degree from those current in the 16th century, particularly when one bears in mind that the sacerdotal class which wrote the glyphs was probably more conservative in its speech than the rest of the population. The earliest noncalendric texts in the lowlands fall about 1500 years before the extinction of Maya culture; how much earlier they existed will probably always remain conjectural.

A point of some importance is that the affix *te*, originally the symbol for wood but also used rebus-fashion for homophones (e.g. as a numerical classifier), is used in Codex Dresden with the sound value *che*, for instance in the glyph of the ceiba tree (*yaxche* in Yucatec). The shift was from *t* to *ch* in the case of Yucatec as the retention of the *t* in compound words and ceremonial objects clearly demonstrates, linguists notwithstanding. There are also far rarer indications of a retention of *ch* which shifted to *c* in Yucatec (e.g. the god Lahun Chan, '10 sky,' and the day name Chicchan, 'snake'). Again the terms *mut* or *ch'ich'* used as the augury or tidings of a time period would indicate the conservation of an archaic term in Yucatec. *Mut* is no longer a general term for bird in Yucatec, but it survives as such in some of the other lowland dialects (Roys, 1933, p. 148).

These examples point to a development

of Maya glyphs in the southern Maya lowlands, which is, in fact, the area favored on archaeological grounds, and by a people which had not made the *t* to *ch* and *ch* to *c* shifts.

It is also worthy of note that some Maya day names in Chiapas and the northern highlands of Guatemala are closer to the original meanings of the days than are the Yucatec names. That might be regarded as support of the idea that the neighboring northern highlands witnessed the first differentiation of Maya glyphs from the common Formative growth, a view for which much may be said.

Schellhas (1945), in a pessimistic survey of the problem, concluded that Maya hieroglyphic writing would never be read, but since he wrote advances have been made. In the apparent absence of any form of syllabic writing, progress must be slow, for the solution of one glyph is often an isolated advance with little or no bearing on the decipherment of those of unknown meanings, such as the solution of a syllabic system entails. On the other hand, should there be a syllabic element in Maya writing, every new decipherment hastens the wresting of the sonic values of the remainder, and a computing machine might well solve the problem. My opinion, for what it is worth, is that the *gradus ad Parnassum* in the case of Maya script can never be a fast-moving escalator.

REFERENCES

Andrews, 1951
Avendaño y Loyola, 1696
Barthel, 1952, 1954, 1955a, 1955b
Berlin, 1943, 1958
Beyer, 1926, 1932a, 1932b, 1934–36, 1937b
Brasseur de Bourbourg, 1861
Caso, 1928, 1947, 1949a, 1960
Codex Dresden, 1880
Codex Madrid, 1869–70, 1892
Codex Paris, 1887
Diringer, 1948
Förstemann, 1904, 1906
Fuentes y Guzmán, 1932–33
Gadow, 1908
Goodman, 1897
Holmes, 1907
Humboldt, 1810
Knorozov, 1952, 1955, 1958a, 1958b
Martyr, 1612
Maudslay, A. P., 1889–1902
Means, 1917
Morley, 1920, 1937–38
Motul Dictionary, 1929
Pérez, 1843
Ponce, 1873
Proskouriakoff, 1951, 1960
Redfield and Redfield, 1940
—— and Villa, 1934
Río, 1822
Roys, 1933
Ruppert, Thompson and Proskouriakoff, 1955
Ruz L., 1952b
Sáenz, 1956
Satterthwaite, 1958b
Schellhas, 1945
Seler, 1902–23
Teeple, 1930
Termer, 1952
Thompson, J. E. S., 1930, 1937, 1943c, 1950, 1952a, 1952b, 1958b, 1959a, 1962
Tozzer, 1941a
Villa R., 1945
Whorf, 1933, 1942
Zimmermann, 1956

26. Lowland Maya Native Society at Spanish Contact

RALPH L. ROYS

The Yucatan Maya

Country and Population

LINGUISTIC AREA. Although the term *Maya* has long been employed to designate a much larger linguistic group, only those living in the Yucatan peninsula, so far as I know, have applied the name to themselves. When the Spaniards arrived, the southern boundary of this linguistic group extended from the Gulf of Mexico, not far south of Champoton, to a point a short distance southwest of Lake Peten, passing east of the Candelaria basin, which was then occupied by the Chontal-speaking Acalan. From here it ran east, south of Lakes Peten and Yaxha, to the Rio Mopan, and thence, skirting the northern slope of the Maya Mountains, to the Caribbean Sea, not far south of the Sibun River. This boundary is somewhat tentative, for Maya-speaking people were later found in lowland regions farther to the south; but I believe they came to these regions in post-conquest times. (Roys, 1957, p. 3; López de Cogolludo, 1867–68, bk. 12, chs. 3–7.)

COUNTRY. The northern part of the Yucatan peninsula is a limestone plain with a thin soil and for the most part is broken by low rocky hillocks and ridges. In conquest times, as now, this area contained nearly all the important towns and most of the population. The greater part of this region, when not under cultivation, is covered by a dry scrub forest. There are no rivers or streams on this plain, for nearly all the water seeps through the rock to the water table. The water of the few sedimented ponds is not considered potable.

From the coast the land rises about 18 cm. to the kilometer, so it was not usually possible to dig wells with stone tools for more than a limited distance inland. In deep natural hollows, however, I have found a number of artificial wells, apparently not excavated with metal tools, and what I thought were the vestiges of others which had been abandoned. Natural wells, caused by underground erosion and called cenotes (Maya, *dzonot*), are frequent. Some are open and others are in caves. I have found many small natural rock tanks, but the water in them rarely lasts throughout the dry season. On this plain the rainfall varies from 45.25 cm. in the northwest to

Fig. 1—MAP OF THE PENINSULA OF YUCATAN AT TIME OF SPANISH CONTACT

125.65 cm. near Chichen Itza. (Roys, 1943, pp. 4–7.)

South of the northern plain much of the country is hilly, the forests seem taller, and there is more rain. The land is so high above the water table, however, that artificial wells were impossible until the introduction of iron tools. The main dependence during the dry season was on man-made or natural reservoirs. Here pond water is potable, but there is not much of it. Archaeological remains are frequent, but in conquest times, as today, the population was scarce. Also, in the region south of the northern plain the forest changes, first to a tall dry forest, and then to a dense rain forest. (Ricketson and Kidder, 1930; Lundell, 1934, p. 262.)

Population. The population of the Yucatan Maya area at the time of Spanish contact is difficult to estimate. At present our best source is the 1549 tax list, which might approximate the number of Indians under Spanish control in northern Yucatan in 1545 or 1546 in 14 of the 16 provinces shown in the accompanying map. The Indians are listed in terms of tributaries, the able-bodied married men. In this area the document shows 57,000 tributaries. An estimate of four persons per tributary would give us 228,000 inhabitants. It does not, however, include the wealthy provinces of Uaymil and Chetumal; nor does it comprise either the Itza state around Lake Peten or the large but sparsely inhabited area in the center of the peninsula. Uaymil and Chetumal must have contained at least as many inhabitants as Ah Canul, which I would now put at 21,000. In 1690 the Itza population, which had remained undisturbed all this time, was estimated at 24,000 or 25,000; and I see no reason to believe that they were now more numerous than in the middle 16th century. True, they had given asylum to many individual refugees from the north, but they were hostile to larger groups, as they also were to the Cehache. The central area, inhabited by the Maya-speaking Cehache, contained few towns of even moderate size, so it seems possible that they numbered only some 5,000 or 6,000 persons. All these considerations give a rough estimate of not over 280,000. However, since many people were already fleeing to the forests in the 1540's and European diseases had for several years begun to take a heavy toll, the population at the time of Spanish contact may have been well over 300,000. (Archivo General de Indias, Seville, Guatemala 128; E. B. Adams, n.d.; Means, 1917, p. 22; Scholes and Roys, 1948, pp. 462–67; Roys, 1957, p. 10.)

Subsistence Activities. The Yucatan Maya, although great traders, were primarily an agricultural people. The principal crops were maize, black and Lima beans, squash, various root crops such as sweet potato and cassava, and cotton. Agriculture was also very general. The only important domestic animals were the dog and probably some turkeys, both of which were eaten. With a milpa system of farming, much of the land was either wooded or growing back into forest, so deer and other game were always plentiful. Many fish were caught in the sea or coastal lagoons and preserved by salting or drying. In these lagoons a vast quantity of salt was gathered, which, as we shall see, was one of the principal exports from the peninsula. (Landa, 1941, pp. 64, 97, 127, 204; RY, 1:63, 102, 110, 261; Motul dictionary, p. 495; Vienna dictionary, ff. 34*r*, 58*r*, 177*r*, 196*v*; Archivo General de Indias, Seville, México 72; Beltrán de Santa Rosa, 1859, p. 230; Tozzer and Allen, 1910; Standley, 1930; Thompson, 1930, pp. 41–42; 1936; Gann and Thompson, 1931, pp. 190–93; Roys, 1931, pp. 327–47; 1943, pp. 41–42; 1957, pp. 15, 103.)

Social Organization

Name Group. Underlying the entire social organization was an exogamous division which could have been called the name group; elsewhere I have called it a lineage group, for its members considered themselves to be related. It consisted of all the persons of both sexes who bore the same patronymic. I have found over 250 such groups; some comprised comparatively few members, others were numerous. (Roys, 1940.) Writers have differed as to whether or not this constituted a unilateral sib system. (Tozzer, 1941a, pp. 98–99; Beals, 1932; Eggan, 1934.) Most of such names as we can translate seem to be either flora or fauna names; a few are Nahuatl. Often a matronymic precedes the patronymic, but the significance of the former is obscure. Not only was intermarriage prohibited, but they were obligated to aid one another in time of need. It is difficult to understand how this worked out, when we find a noble, a commoner, and a slave, all in the same name group, or when its members took part in opposing war parties. In the early colonial tax lists we find members of the same name group distributed, though unequally, in different wards, or *barrios*, of the same town. (Roys, Scholes, and Adams, 1959.) I surmise that the local head of a numerous name group may have been entitled *holpop* ("head of the mat"), but we also find holpops exercising political authority. (Roys, 1933, p. 65; 1943, pp. 35, 63–64; 1940, p. 40.)

Social Classes. Both the social and political organizations were based on a division of the population into three classes: nobles, commoners, and slaves. (Roys, 1943, pp. 33–35.) The male nobles were designated *almehen*, implying known descent in both male and female line, or *ah ch'ibal* ("man of lineage") (Vienna dictionary, f. 151*r*). A noble woman was called *ix ik*, which is the common word for "woman" in Chontal. The nobles filled all important political and military offices. They had a preferred position in the use of agricultural and orchard land, exploited the salt beds, and monopolized the priesthood. They were the most important merchants, the ones who owned boats and slave carriers. (Landa, 1941, pp. 62–63; Roys, 1933, app. E; 1943, pp. 37, 196; 1957, p. 5.)

The commoners (*yalba uinic*, "plebeian"), who constituted the main body of the population, included the ordinary farmers, the small merchants, the artisans, and the poorer fishermen. Some men, entitled "rich man" (*ayikal*), are hard to place. The *açmen uinic* (Motul dictionary) is explained as being between a noble and a plebeian. Possibly he was the son of a noble and a plebeian, or even slave, woman (cf. Crónica de Calkini, p. 15). I can find little evidence of discontent during the last century of pre-Spanish times among commoners with the rulers or other nobles in their own province, whom they treated with great deference.

The slaves consisted largely of certain debtors, convicted thieves and homocides, and plebeian captives. Noble captives were usually sacrificed, though some were ransomed as were, apparently, a good many plebeian slaves. Children of slaves remained slaves, unless redeemed. Slaves worked as house servants, fishermen, carriers, canoe-paddlers, and also as farmers, although the long idle periods may have made slave-farming unprofitable. Cacao-growing, on the other hand, requires steady work during most of the year, and many slaves were exported to Honduras and Tabasco. The distinguishing mark of a slave was that his hair was cut short. Slaves were often purchased by the community for sacrifice. We are told that in the region of Chichen Itza when "a lord died his sons and daughters were sold as slaves," but I suggest that these were only his children by slave women. (Landa, 1941, pp. 63, 94–95, 116; Chi, 1941, pp. 231–32; Crónica de Calkini, p. 38; Roys, 1943; Díaz del Castillo, 1933–34, ch. 29; RY, 1:105, 2:38.)

Marriage. A man could not marry a person with the same patronymic, his brother's wife, his wife's sister, his stepmother, or his maternal aunt. "They married all their other relations on their mother's side, even though they were their first cousins" (Landa, 1941, p. 100). Evidence regarding polygyny is conflicting, but this may be due to the fact that it was not considered adultery to take a slave concubine. A man had a right to his own property, but Maya wives were recorded as being violently jealous (Landa, 1941, 100, 107, 127; Beals, 1932; Eggan, 1934.) A childless husband was, and indeed still is, looked down upon by others.

DIVORCE. Divorces were frequent; except for family protests, which were usually very strong, either spouse was free to leave the other. If the children were small, they remained with the mother; but if older, the father took the sons and the mother, the daughters. For a later alliance between widowed or divorced persons, the only formality was for the man to eat a meal in the home of the woman. (Thompson, 1930, p. 85; Landa, 1941, p. 100; RY, 1:80.)

ADULTERY. This was a serious offence. Landa tells us (1941, p. 32) that the husband might either crush the man's head with a stone or pardon him. For the woman, the disgrace was sufficient punishment. Gaspar Antonio Chi, a noble himself, reports (1941, p. 231) that this vice was especially condemned in persons of high rank, and both offenders were killed with arrows. He also notes that when a man was merely found under compromising circumstances, they stripped him and cut his hair, or they left him bound for some hours, a great dishonor. The woman's comparative immunity might be a relic of a very different social organization in earlier times.

MARRIAGE SERVICE. A son-in-law lived with and worked for his father-in-law for several years; three to six are recorded, and sometimes the latter compelled him to remain longer (Landa, 1941, p. 101; Ordinances of López Medel *apud* López de Cogolludo, bk. 5, ch. 17). Later he could return with his wife to his father's home or establish one of his own.

THE HOUSEHOLD. There is evidence of many multiple-family households. In 1548 Bienvenida reported that there was scarcely a house containing only a single citizen *(vecino)*. "On the contrary, every house has two, three, four, six, and still more; and among them is one paterfamilias, who is the head of the house. (Cartas de Indias, 1877, pp. 70–82; cf. Motul dictionary, *ah cuch nal.*) Although the actual house structure probably changed, during most of the 16th century we continue to find multiple-family households; but as time went on single-family homes became more numerous (Roys, Scholes, and Adams, 1940, 1959). The unmarried youths, however, slept in the municipal men's house; and sons-in-law, while performing marriage service, lived with their wives in small houses facing the parental domicile (Landa, 1941, pp. 41, 124–25).

In the 16th century colonial tax lists, large households are apparently composed, in part, of sons, daughters, sons-in-law, brothers, or nephews of the head. In Cozumel more rarely are there members of the same name group as the head's wife. At Pencuyut, in 59 multiple-family households we find many persons of the head's name group, but only six men and two women belonging to the name group of the head's wife. This is in sharp contrast to the multiple-family households of the Chontal-speaking people of Tixchel, where we note a strong tendency toward matrilocal residence. (Roys, Scholes, and Adams, 1940, 1959; Scholes and Roys, 1948, pp. 317, 475.) Among the smaller households in Cozumel and at Pencuyut we often find two or three apparently unrelated couples living together; one can only surmise that it was due to personal friendships.

THE HOME. The home, apparently that of a well-to-do household, is described as a pole-and-thatch structure with low eaves. A wall with several doors divided the house lengthwise into a back room where the beds stood, and a front room where guests were received and lodged. The front room was open the entire length of the house; here the men of the household usually slept in summer. (Landa, 1941, pp. 85–87.) Hammocks are listed in early colonial Maya dictionaries, but pole beds were still generally used as late as 1766. (Scholes et al., 1936–38, 3:20.) The missionaries disapproved of Maya sleeping arrangements, for from 1552 to 1655 we find ordinances that "each family live separately in its own house and not with others, however closely related." (Cogolludo, 1867–68, bk. 5, ch. 16; Roys, 1941, pt. II, doc. 41.) The early Spanish reports from Yucatan say little or nothing about the kitchen, servants' or slaves' quarters, or a household shrine.

Reports of excavations at Mayapan by the Carnegie Institution of Washington tell us much about domiciles at that city only about a century before the Spanish conquest. These descriptions of the residences of important nobles both confirm and supplement Landa's account. Here we find complexes, each of several structures around three sides of a court. Some had stone walls and a beam-and-mortar roof; and an open front room is supported by four stone columns. Stone houses were noted in conquest times, but they appear to have been rare. (Smith and Ruppert, 1953, 1956; Thompson, 1954a; Thompson and Thompson, 1955; Proskouriakoff and Temple, 1955.)

On the coast were a few really large towns, which depended largely on fishing, salt gathering, or cacao growing as at Chetumal; but the size of the agricultural towns was restricted by the exigences of milpa farming. Possibly not over 17 per cent of the land was under cultivation at any one time (Kempton, 1935). Not only was much of the population dispersed on farms and in small hamlets during the growing season; but as the larger towns grew or the land around them became overcultivated, colonies were leaving them and founding new villages or small towns (RY, 1:49). The Spaniards soon concentrated this scattered population to a great extent (Roys, 1939, pp. 73–77; 1957, pp. 76, 119–21). Oddly enough, such settlements were not spreading to the fertile Puuc area, so filled with ancient ruins; the Maya farmer still loves the proximity of a cenote or a well.

The 16th-century Maya town is best described by Landa (1941, pp. 62–64). It was not laid out in regular streets, but it had four ceremonial entrances at the cardinal points (RY, 1:50; Landa, 1941, p. 139). In the center stood the raised temple, set in a handsome plaza; around it were the houses of the "lords" and the priests, then those of the most important people. Next came the homes of the richest, then of those who were held in the highest estimation. At the outskirts were the houses of the lower class. However, we know that many towns were divided into *barrios*, or wards; it is altogether probable that the powerful head of each barrio lived in his own district, as we know he did in colonial times (Roys, Scholes, and Adams, 1959). The large men's house, "whitened with lime, open on all sides" surely must have been in the center of town. It served as a dormitory for the youths. Here also they prepared for religious ceremonies, held indoor games, and consorted with prostitutes, the last in strong contrast to the severe discipline among the Aztecs (Landa, 1941, pp. 124–25; Thompson, 1954a, p. 135). The yards with their gardens were large, but it is uncertain how they were enclosed. The Motul mentions fences of poles, wattle, and dry stone (like those of today); we also read of fences or hedges of gumbo limbo posts, which take root when planted. The last I have never seen, but they may still exist (RY, 1:167). The towns were not very compact; some parts, perhaps different barrios, were separated by thickets (Cogolludo, 1867–68, bk. 5, ch. 16).

LAND TENURE. Reports are conflicting.

Chi (1941, p. 230) tells us that unimproved lands were in common, with no boundaries to divide them except between one province and another. This seems to be refuted in the Mani land treaty of 1557, where we read: "this forest and their lands are not slave, which we leave to them that the nobles (*almehenob*) may sustain themselves, in order that they may farm it in time to come." Again: "It is for our nobles in order that they sustain themselves in time to come" (Roys, 1943, pp. 36–37, 191, 193–94). Elsewhere we find a strong suggestion of certain landholding organizations, though it is not conclusive. There is also a document showing the sale of a privately owned tract to the municipality of Ebtun not long after 1561 (Roys, 1939, pp. 21, 23, 121, 125, 241). Improved lands like orchards and cacao groves were privately owned (Chi, 1941, p. 250). A town lot (*solar*) was sold to the same municipality about 1670 for people to live on, and later we find the town buying other such lots (Roys, 1939, p. 207).

INHERITANCE. When a man died, his estate was divided among his sons, but somewhat in proportion to how much they had aided in its accumulation. Daughters, Landa tells us, received little, and even that only as a favor. Perhaps that was true in pre-Spanish times, but hardly a century later they were receiving substantial bequests of household goods, apparently with the full approval of the men in the community, and I could see no indication that it was an innovation. Besides clothing, ornaments, ritual accessories like masks, and weapons, these estates consisted of beehives, houses, and land improvements, such as gardens, orchards or isolated fruit trees, and cacao groves, of which there were some small ones in hollows in pre-Spanish times. For minors, guardians were appointed, usually relatives in the same name group. These helped the mother support the children and later restored the property to the sons but retained the usufruct. An accounting was made in the presence of the authorities. If a man died leaving no sons, his brothers or other closest male relatives in his name group inherited his property. (Landa, 1941, pp. 99–101; Libro de Cacalch'en, first part; Roys, 1939, pp. 56 and *passim*.)

Dress, Adornment, Customs, and Festivals

DRESS. For men the narrow loincloth (*ex*) was indispensable. It was wound around the waist and between the thighs; the ends, often embroidered, hung down before and behind. Upper-class men had a short sleeveless jacket (*xicul*, a Nahuatl loan word, but it was portrayed in pre-Mexican times). Sandals (*xanab*) of hemp or deerskin were often, though not always, worn. All women were attired in a somewhat short skirt (*pic*), sometimes slit on the sides; but many added a light scarf (*boch'*), which covered the breast and sometimes the head. In Bacalar and Campeche a folded cloth was tied over the breast. Both men and women wore or carried a square cloth mantle. (Landa, 1941, pp. 126–27; RY, 1:82, 149, 162–63, 245, 2:29, 154; Thompson, 1954b, pp. 181, 216.)

ADORNMENT. Men cut part of their hair closely and bound the rest so it hung down behind (RY, 1:82, 96, 123). They avoided growing beards (Landa, 1941, p. 88). Youths painted themselves black, as did older men during fasts; but older people seem to have usually painted themselves red. Youths tattooed themselves little but older people, much (Thompson, 1936). The head was flattened in infancy, and a squint was caused by hanging before the eyes a small disk suspended from the hair. Women filed their teeth, as men probably also did; both pierced the septum of the nose to insert a long topaz bead. Men and women wore earplugs. (RY, 1:41; Landa, 1941, pp. 88, 125). Head deformation must have been a deeply rooted custom, for the Toltecs did not practice it, and even after their long rule at Chichen Itza it prevailed in the 16th century; although many, perhaps most, of the Maya upper class considered themselves to be of Mexican descent.

ETIQUETTE. Hospitality to visitors was required; only merchants paid for their food and lodging. A visitor both brought and received a present. The humbler one listened attentively, replied in a low voice, and never said No, constantly repeating the superior's title name. (Chi, 1941, p. 230; Landa, 1941, pp. 97, 98, 128.) Women were of modest demeanor, spoke briefly, and never laughed with a man. At home they ate alone. They turned aside if they met a man on the road. At banquets, when they served a man a drink, they turned away until he finished it. At great festivals they drank alone and never as much as the husband. They had their own dances, one of them not too decent, and it was only rarely that a woman took part in any religious festival. To this day, when lime is burned, the presence of a woman can spoil the burn. (Landa, 1941, pp. 91, 97, 121, 127–28.)

FESTIVITIES. These were important. Probably all were connected with some phase of religion, as was the calendar itself. Not only did the ancestor cults enter into the matter, but every division of the calendar had its own deity (Thompson, 1950, *passim*). Landa (1941, pp. 151–66) gives us an annual calendar for the 18 20-day months, during which he mentions 13 religious festivals. Others are mentioned and described which we would consider real festivities. In most of both sorts the participants became intoxicated with *balche,* which was made of fermented honey and the bark of a tree so named. Some banquets among the upper class seem like a potlatch, for they were accompanied by gifts and had to be reciprocated by the guest or his heirs. The ancestor cult was also celebrated at such banquets given by a rich member of the name group. Toward the end of the year wealthy men gave drunken feasts to their fellow nobles, where violent brawls were customary among the guests, apparently a feature of traditional pattern. At another more general festival both men and women indulged in a wild saturnalia, in which sexual rules were suspended and houses even burned. (RY, 2:215; Landa, 1941, 91–92, 166.)

MUSIC. Martial music, or its equivalent, was produced by a tortoise shell struck with a deer antler (*culun-ac*) and bone whistles. Other instruments were a wooden kettle drum (*pax*) played by the hand, a hollowed log beaten with a rubber-tipped stick (*tunkul*), a gourd rattle (*zoot*), wooden trumpets of varying shapes (*hom*), a reed flute (*chul*), and a conch shell (*hub*). Most of these, though not the tunkul, appear in the frescos at Bonampak. (Landa, 1941, p. 93; López de Cogolludo, 1867–68, bk. 4, ch. 5; Motul dictionary; Roys, 1933, fig. 4; Ruppert, Thompson, and Proskouriakoff, 1955, figs. 27, 29.)

DANCES. These seemed innumerable to the first Spaniards. There was a reed-throwing dance (*hech*), a stilt dance (*ah ximib che*?). Other names could be translated as "cloud dance," "shield dance," "monkey dance," "grandfather's song," and "shadow of the tree." (Landa, 1941, pp. 94, 143, 145; RY, 2:185; Ciudad Real, 1932, p. 327; Vienna dictionary, ff. 25*r*, 127*r*; San Francisco dictionary, Spanish-Maya, p. 62.)

COMEDIES. An important feature of the festivals and much admired by the early Spaniards were the comedies, which were performed both indoors and out. The actors were often masked and sometimes impersonated birds. They had license to ridicule even wealthy or important people. A few names of these comedies have been recorded: "he who forces a sale," "the parasite," "the pot vendor," "the chile vendor," and "the cacao planter." (Motul dictionary, pp. 80, 101; Landa, 1941, pp. 158, 179; Roys, 1933, p. 5; 1943; López de Cogolludo, 1867–68, bk. 4, ch. 5.)

The Life Cycle

Birth, Childhood, and Adolescence. The deity of procreation and birth as well as medicine was the goddess Ix Chel, who was associated with the moon. At childbirth a sorceress was called in, who placed an image of the goddess under the bed, "enchanted" the mother, and received her confession. The child's head was flattened at an early age, and they called in a priest to forecast its destiny and, it is reported, to bestow a name. This might have been the "boy name" *(paal kaba)*, which we often find taking the place of the matronymic but also preceding the patronymic. The actual evidence, however, is conflicting. In the early 1560's the names of a number of sacrificed children aged from 5 to 12 were recorded; they all consist only of the patronymic preceded by the masculine prefix (*Ah*) or the feminine (*Ix*). This leads one to suspect that the "boy name" was not bestowed until baptism. In any case a bead was fastened to a boy's hair, and a small shell was hung below the girl's abdomen from a cord around her loins, a token of virginity. Later came the very important ceremony of baptism, performed by the priest and four assistants. Forehead, face, fingers, and toes were anointed with water; the children confessed carnal sins, if any; so-called "godparents" were appointed. Reports of their ages are again conflicting. It may have been a puberty rite, since the emblems of childhood were removed and they now might marry, although it seems to have been several years before they did so. (Thompson, 1939b, pp. 133–37; 1954a, pp. 135, 223; Landa, 1941, pp. 102–06, 125, 129; López de Cogolludo, 1867–68, bk. 4, ch. 6; López Medel, 1941, p. 226; Roys, 1940, p. 138; 1943, p. 25.

After puberty a youth spent most of the day with his father, helping him in the milpa or with other work. He ate at home and slept in the men's house. A girl remained at home with her mother, who taught her spinning and weaving and trained her strictly in household tasks, punishing her severely when she was lazy or even slightly misbehaved. (Landa, 1941, pp. 124–125, 127.) Higher education of youth is only briefly mentioned. The priests "taught the sons of other priests and the second sons of the lords, who brought them [up] for this purpose from their infancy, if they saw they had an inclination in this profession." We also read of certain nobles who were literate, which meant more than a little education. It would seem as though some equivalent of the Mexican *calmecac* must have existed, but I can find no reference to it. In view of the religious functions of the more important rulers, as we shall see further on, an extensive formal education would have been necessary. (Landa, 1941, p. 27; Thompson, 1954b, pp. 189–97.)

Marriage. Statements are conflicting as to the usual age of marriage, but in early colonial tax lists bachelors of 18 and spinsters of 16 or over are extremely rare, so I infer that people usually married by this time. A father sought a wife for his son, dealt through a matchmaker, and paid a small purchase price, which could be recovered, if the bride turned out to be childless. The groom's mother supplied clothing for the pair. A priest incensed the house and officiated at the marriage ceremony and feast, which was at the bride's home. The man's service to the bride's father has already been discussed. It was usual, but a refusal to complete it did not necessarily disrupt the marriage. (Landa, 1941, pp. 27, 100–01; Herrera y Tordesillas, 1941, p. 218; Roys, Scholes, and Adams, 1940, pp. 14, 15; 1959, p. 220; Thompson, 1930, pp. 79–80; 1954a, pp. 189–97.)

After marriage a man had a right to use his matronymic, to which the prefix Na- was added. Such a matronymic was called his *naal* and preceded his patronymic. Thus in Na-chi Cocom's name his *naal* was Chi and preceded his patronymic, Cocom. Obviously it would be inconvenient, if all the sons of the same father and mother constantly exercised this right. We find that only one son of the same parents usually availed himself of this privilege, and there is some indication that it was the eldest. The others continued to use their boy name. For example, on the Xiu family tree the first son of Ah Mochan Xiu is Na-cahun Xiu, and his name is followed by his younger brothers, Ah Çiyah Xiu, Ah Kukil Xiu, and Ah Cuate Xiu. On the other hand, two of the sons of Na-dzul Iuit had the Christian names Francisco Na-mo-n Iuit and Juan Na-mo-n Iuit. It is very possible that the pagan name of Lorenzo Cocom, who succeeded Nachi Cocom at Sotuta, was Ah Cuat Cocom. Ah Cuat is a familiar boy name. (Roys, 1940, pp. 37–39, 44–45; 1957, pp. 59, 65; Brinton, 1882, pp. 235, 237; Martínez H., 1926, pp. 28–29.) We do not have many women's names, but here the prefix Ix seems to take the place of the masculine prefixes Na- and Ah.

As the young married man grew older, he might fill various offices or dignities, most of which will be discussed in the section on political organization. Many of these called for title names. The title of a priest was Ah Kin; of a "great lord," Ahau; of a local ruler, Batab; of an *ah kulel*, Ah Kul; of a prophet, Chilan or Chilam; other such title names were Holpop, Nacom, Ayikal. Besides the names previously discussed, there was a "jesting name" (*coco kaba*), of which we have six examples. (Roys, 1940, pp. 39–41.)

Confession and Death. As a man grew older and his health sometimes suffered, he began to think of death and how to avoid the consequences of past sins. This could be done by confession. One put it off as long as one dared, for it could not be repeated and so subsequent sins could never be forgiven. One confessed to a priest, if available, but otherwise to a spouse or relative. The confession was usually of such sins as homicide, theft, and adultery, but not of relations with a slave concubine. If the confessor recovered, it could make trouble with his spouse both for himself and a former accomplice. (Landa, 1941, pp. 106-07.)

In the Cupul Province they sometimes broke a dying man's back, "that he might not suffer." Among the Itza on Lake Peten and the Cehache, it was reported, they killed men at the age of 50, "so that they shall not learn to be wizards and to kill"; but this rule did not apply to priests. (RY, 2:24; Means, 1917, 131–32).

Burial. Disposal of the dead varied greatly, possibly because of traditional differences between the upper class and the commoners. The body was put in a shroud for interment with game and other food and, sometimes, with implements of the deceased person's profession. Among certain noble families the body was burned; the skull and skin of the face were preserved and made into a sort of portrait head, which was kept in the oratories. Both ossuaries and oratories have been found in the finer residences at Mayapan. Many remains were buried beneath their homes. A small household might abandon the site, but a larger one would be more apt to remain. Secondary burials at Mayapan have been reported. Some highly valued possessions were still deposited with the remains in conquest times. In northeastern Yucatan skeletons lay with clay vessels containing beads, carved shells, obsidian points, and a steel penknife with a horn handle. (RY, 2:24; Smith and Ruppert, 1953, 1956; Thompson, 1954b; Thompson and Thompson, 1955; Stephens, 1843, 2:341–43.)

Mourning. Landa (1941, pp. 129, 107) tells us: "During the day they wept for them in silence; and at night with loud and very sad cries. . . . And they made abstinences and fasts for the dead, especially the husband or wife." "They did not marry again for a year after they became widowers, the custom being not to have carnal knowledge of man or woman during that time."

Political Organization

TERRITORIAL GOVERNMENT. Formerly a large part of the Yucatan Peninsula had been subject to centralized administration, called a joint government (*mul tepal*), with its capital at Mayapan. When this organization was dissolved by a revolution about the middle of the 15th century, it broke up into 16 independent states (see map), each of which the Spaniards called a "province" and the Maya loosely designated as *tzucubte* ("division") or *cuchcabal* ("jurisdiction"). Three types of territorial government are recorded. One was ruled by a *halach uinic* ("real man"), who was also the local chief, or *batab*, of his own town. He exacted a light tribute of foodstuffs such as produce, turkey hens, honey, game, and sometimes salt and fish (RY, 1:187). He owned slaves, cacao groves, and plantations. He declared war and exacted military service from all his towns (RY, 1:89, 95; Roys, 1933, App. E). One important duty was to keep track and even inspect the boundaries of his province (Roys, 1939, pp. 424–29). The position was inherited in the family, often from brother to brother and then to the sons (Roys, 1943, p. 60). The halach uinic is defined as a "bishop" as well as a "governor," and he had important religious duties (Motul dictionary; Chi, 1941, p. 230). Provinces of this type were Cehpech, Mani, Sotuta, Cochuah, Tazes, and probably Ah Kin Chel, Chetumal, and Chanpoton.

Another type of province, like Ah Canul and Cupul, consisted of towns ruled mostly by members of the same name group. In Ah Canul they usually acted in harmony; but in Cupul even members of the Cupul name group fought with one another and sometimes subjected and enslaved persons whom they considered their own kin. A third type, such as Chakan and Chikinchel, was little more than a loose alliance of independent towns, which kept their aggressive neighbors from absorbing them. (Crónica de Calkini, *passim;* RY, 2:161; Roys, 1957, p. 6.)

MUNICIPAL GOVERNMENT. In each town the batab was the administrative, judicial, and military head. He superintended building and repairs as well as agricultural activities of his townsmen. He could have inherited his post from a father or brother, or he might have been appointed by the halach uinic. Where such existed, the batab was subject to him, and his power was also limited in some respects by the town council. From early colonial times the town cultivated a farm for his support, built and maintained his home, and furnished domestic service. This was probably mostly a continuation of pre-Spanish practice, except for his servants, who may well have been personal slaves. He was treated at all times with great ceremony and deference. Some Cupul batabs, who were overlords of neighboring towns, exacted tribute from such subjects. (RY, 1:80, 2:44, 53, 103, 116, 208, 211; Crónica de Calkini, p. 11; Roys, 1933, App. E.)

In each barrio of the town the powerful head was called *ah cuch cab*. He had a seat and power of veto in the town council (Vienna dictionary, f. 169*r*; RY, 1:137–38, 2:211). Next in rank to the ah cuch cab were the deputies, often three, of the batab called *ah kulel;* their title was Ah Kul. They attended the batab on all occasions, and served him as assistants and advisers (Roys, 1943, pp. 62, 136). Another important official was the *holpop*, or *ah holpop* ("at the head of the mat"). In colonial times he was in charge of the *popolna,* a sort of municipal hall, which we know only from the Maya dictionaries. Here public affairs were deliberated and certain festivities like dances took place. In Hocaba and Sotuta, he was said to be like a *regidor* or a captain and an intermediary between local petitioners or foreign emissaries and the batab or halach uinic. In some small towns he took the place of the batab. I surmise that he was the local head of the most important name group. (RY, 1:92, 95, 187; Sánchez de Aguilar, 1937, p. 149; Roys, 1943, pp. 63–64; 1957, p. 76; Motul dictionary items ah holpop and popolna.)

At the bottom of the official scale was the *tupil* (Nahua *topil*, a borrowed word), who was a minor peace officer, handled the town stores, and sometimes even acted as a carrier for his betters. (Crónica de Calkini, p. 17; Roys, 1939, pp. 424–27.)

COURTS OF JUSTICE. The batab was the town magistrate and held court in his *palacio*. He received gifts from litigants but was considered impartial. The batab made his own decisions, but he was influenced by the ah kulels, whose opinions were seriously considered. Minor officers, apparently tupils, were in attendance. Damages were sought for unintentional injuries, such as accidental homicide or starting fires, and even for provocation which resulted in the suicide of a spouse. If compensation for such homicide was not paid, the relatives of the deceased could assassinate the defaulter. (Chi, 1941, pp. 230–32; Landa, 1941, pp. 87, 98, 124.)

In criminal cases the penalties were death or enslavement. Flogging and punitive confinement seem to be unknown, though prisoners could be fettered by a sort of yoke (Roys, 1933, fig. 21), and there were cages for victims awaiting sacrifice. The penalty for seduction or rape could be stoning to death. A noble, when convicted of theft, was tattooed conspicuously on the face. (Chi, 1941, pp. 230–31; Landa, 1941, pp. 32, 124.)

Commerce

FOREIGN COMMERCE. The first Spanish explorers recognized the area from northern Honduras to Tabasco as a vast commercial empire, its center occupied by the Yucatan Maya. On the periphery of this area its traders dealt with Nicaragua, the Guatemala highlands, the Zoque and other inhabitants of Chiapas, probably Oaxaca, and merchants from the Valley of Mexico. Commerce was a highly honored pursuit, followed by noble families with their great canoes and slave carriers, as well as plebeian peddlers carrying their own packs. (Vienna dictionary, f. 145v; Morris, Charlot, and Morris, *apud* Roys, 1943, fig. 12; Landa, 1941, p. 39; RY, 1:87, 125–26, 208, 2: 37–38.)

Exports from Yucatan consisted largely of salt, cotton cloth, slaves, honey (scarce in Tabasco), and probably flint tools (hard to obtain in Honduras). Imports were cacao from both Tabasco and Honduras, bells, small axes and sheets of copper, obsidian, a little jade but more inferior hard green stone. Other imports were skeins of rabbit hair for embroidery, perhaps from Oaxaca, nose beads of yellow topaz apparently from Chiapas, and carved gourd cups from Honduras. They also brought in macaw feathers from Honduras, a few quetzal feathers and a little gold. Honduras was called "the land of gold, feathers, and cacao." (Herrera y Tordesillas, 1725–26, 4:133; RY, 1:369; Roys, 1943, pp. 51–56; 1957, pp. 28–29, 36, 44, 103; Scholes and Roys, 1948, p. 391n.; Tozzer, 1941a, p. 44.) The media of exchange were cacao beans, red shell beads, hard green stone beads, and small copper hatchets and bells.

Trade from Tabasco was by water. We are told that Chontal pilgrims, presumably traders, skirted the coast at least as far as Cozumel Island. Bacalar in Uaymil was a center for canoe construction; and both Cochuah and Chetumal had trading factories on the Ulua River in Honduras. Traders crossed the base of the Yucatan Peninsula on foot and by river. Along the latter route on the Rio Candelaria the Chontal-speaking Acalan had a large commercial city named Itzamkanac and a factory on the Rio Dulce in what is now Guatemala. The commerce between Tabasco and the west coast of Yucatan was carried on by merchants of Potonchan and Xicalango in Tabasco and by those of Chanpoton and probably Campeche in

Yucatan. In northeastern Yucatan the Spaniards found large commercial towns at Chauaca, Sinsimato, Conil, and the unidentified site of Cachi not far east from Sinsimato. They were much impressed by the markets and the courts which regulated them. Cachi especially appears to have been an entrepot, where the importers met the merchants from the interior. The markets of the interior towns seem to have aroused no such interest among the early Spaniards. (Roys, Scholes, and Adams, 1940, p. 5; RY, 2: 54; Herrera y Tordesillas, 1725–26, 3:346–48; Oviedo y Valdés, 1851–55, bk. 32, ch. 8, bk. 33, ch. 6; Blom, 1932b, p. 546; Torquemada, 1943, bk. 3, ch. 41.)

Domestic Commerce. Salt and fish, the latter dried, salted, or slowly roasted, were carried into the interior from the western and northern coasts. In the northwest outsiders could gather salt by paying a royalty in kind or other products to the local ruler. Farther east, in Ah Kin Chel and Chikinchel, they tried to exclude people of Sotuta and Cupul, causing economic warfare and sometimes even wars. Copal gum for incense was exported to other provinces from Sinsimato in Chikinchel. Cacao was carried regularly overland from Bacalar in Uaymil to the Province of Mani. In return the inland provinces shipped cotton cloth, game, fruit, slaves, and some maize to those on or near the coast, where the land was often poorer and fishing and salt gathering were more profitable than farming, cotton growing, or manufacturing. Business was sometimes done on credit; contracts were only oral but made in the presence of witnesses. (Documentos de Tabi; Thompson, 1930, pp. 185–86; Landa, 1941, pp. 14, 40, 89, 94–96, 190; Roys, 1957, pp. 35–36, 44, 46, 159, 168–69.)

Warfare

Causes of War. The Yucatan Maya were divided into 16 separate states, most of which were often at war with one another for various reasons. The fighting was usually between different states. Only between Chauaca and Sinsimato in Chikinchel and between Ekbalam and some of its neighboring towns in Cupul have we found internal wars within the same province. For the most part people made war only in November, December, and January, when agricultural duties were light. A warrior captive was especially desirable for sacrifice. Not only were there frequent boundary disputes, but farmers near a frontier were sometimes tempted to trespass on the neighboring state, cut the forest, and harvest a crop before it was practicable to interfere. The upper class needed to recruit its slave labor from time to time, and slaves were always wanted for export. Sometimes merchants were abused or killed in another state in quarrels over debts or other disagreements; and finally in some of the coast provinces outsiders were not allowed to come and gather salt in the lagoons. (RY, 1: 80–81, 89, 2: 86, 90, 186, 208; Roys, 1939, pp. 40, 43; 1957, pp. 104, 129.)

Weapons. These were a bow of medium length of *chulul* (*Apoplanesia paniculata* Standley and Gaumer) and a reed arrow with its flint or bone point set in a wooden tip; a dart, often with a fire-hardened point, propelled by a throwing stick; a short flint-pointed spear; a broad wooden sword with flint blades set in its edges; a short dagger of chulul with a flint point; and an axe, sometimes of copper but more often, stone. Stones were hurled from a sling (*yuumtun*) or by hand. (Landa, 1941, pp. 32, 35, 121; RY, 2: 186; Vienna dictionary, f. 125r.)

Armor and Costume. Armor consisted of a small round shield made of two layers of chulul rods bound together and faced with leather. Firmly quilted cotton jackets falling to the mid-thigh gave some protection. Only a few "lords" or captains wore helmets, which were of wood. Important personages also wore jaguar or puma skins, necklaces of red shell and greenstone beads, and sometimes a breast ornament into battle. The ordinary warrior seems to have worn only a loincloth but he was adorned with feathers and paint (Landa, 1941, p. 122; Crónica de Calkini, p. 15; RY, 1: 41, 80, 89, 2: 186; Follet, 1932, pp. 375–402.)

BATTLES. The commander was the batab, but active operations were conducted by a war chief (*nacom*). He held the position for three years, during which he lived austerely and apart from others. Military service was general, but we find certain picked warriors (*holcan*), who bore the brunt of the fighting and were paid, besides receiving much of the spoils. An attacking force was preceded by scouts ("road weasels"). The advance was made with insulting shouts and much noise of whistles, conch shells, and beating turtle carapaces with deer antlers. (RY, 1: 81, 257, 2:5; López de Cogolludo, 1867–68, bk. 2, ch. 6; Landa, 1941, p. 122–23; Gann and Thompson, 1931, pp. 181–82.)

FORTIFICATIONS. We are told of few towns surrounded by ramparts, except for Champoton and an occasional one in Uaymil. Defences were likely to be constructed of wood, with stations for shooting arrows. They were often set at a strategic spot on a trail or at the entrance to a town. Chamberlain and I found a ditch and the apparent banking for a rampart at Dzonotake in the northeast. Campaigns were usually of short duration. (RY, 1: 43, 138, 2: 48, 162.)

Religion

TEMPLES. The temple proper was a small structure, often with masonry walls and apparently often thatched, though many of them probably had flat beam-and-mortar roofs. I surmise that some of the ancient stone-vaulted structures were still in use. It was erected on a pyramidal base with a ceremonial stairway and set in a parklike plaza, which must have been surrounded by a wall, for we read of its patio, or court. We are told of a somewhat small room and an altar, which may not always have been inside, for when Cortés transformed one into a Christian chapel, he had to supply an altar. The interior walls were sometimes decorated with religious frescos; in the room were idols, chests of votive objects, bones of important rulers, incense burners, and shallow clay bowls. Many important ceremonies, such as human sacrifices, were performed either on the platform in front of the door or in the patio below. In some cases, at least, the platform outside was large enough to hold many people. (Díaz de Castillo, 1933–34, chs. 3, 27; Oviedo y Valdés, 1851–55, bk. 17, ch. 8; RY, 1:130, 2:19; Roys, 1943, pp. 71–72; Tozzer, 1941a, p. 305.)

ORATORIES. Although the temples and their grounds were imposing and the scenes of widely attended public ceremonies, much of the worship was conducted in or around private shrines and oratories. The name groups had their own deities. The upper classes, many of whose members considered themselves the descendants of foreign conquerors, had gods and ancestor cults of their own, such as were associated with the disposal of their dead. Some of their oratories uncovered at Mayapan are impressive; those of the Itza at Tayasal on Lake Peten, described by Avendaño, were "very large buildings," one even larger than the reception hall of the ruler. Even the latter place may have sometimes served a similar purpose, for it contained a very large stone "table of sacrifice" on stone columns with 12 seats for the priests around it. (Tozzer, 1957, p. 80; R. M. Adams, 1953; Thompson, 1954a; Smith and Ruppert, 1953, 1956; Thompson and Thompson, 1955; Proskouriakoff and Temple, 1955; Means, 1917, pp. 18–19, 137.)

IDOLS. The Spaniards were astounded by the incredibly large number of idols they saw everywhere, not only in the oratories, shrines, and temples, but also on the temple steps and in the streets. Some were of wood or stone, but most were of clay, and I surmise that many of them were effigy censers.

The Maya *lac*, the usual name of a shallow clay bowl, was also defined as a clay idol (Motul dictionary). The Europeans were also appalled by the hideous appearance of many of these; their descriptions remind us of the devils portrayed on the walls of the Campo Santo at Pisa. Besides the great deities of the sky, earth, and underworld, every calling or profession had its own patron. Deified ancestors were worshipped, and we are told: "there was not an animal or insect of which they did not make a statue" (Landa, 1941, p. 110). Surely this is referable to the patronymics of the name groups, or so-called lineages, many of which are fauna names, comprising those of mammals, birds, fishes, reptiles, and insects. The last included even the tick (Pech) and the gnat (Us). I surmise that some of the many patronymics that were flora names were also represented, but in too symbolic a form to be easily recognized. We know (RY, 2:181) that in Cochuah at Kanpokolche (also the Maya name of a shrub, *Durante repens* L.) there was an idol of the same name. (RY, 2: 28: Means, 1917, p. 135; Landa, 1941, pp. 9, 108–10, 131; Roys, 1940; Tozzer, 1941, p. 60.)

The Indians claimed that they had not always been idolaters, but that idolatry had been introduced some centuries before by Kukulcan, the captain of certain Mexican invaders. Deities had been portrayed in Classic times, but their worship apparently was that of natural features and forces, like that of the eastern Chol. Idolatry has almost ceased in Yucatan today, although some pagan deities are still worshipped. (RY, 1: 270–71; Thompson, 1938, p. 594; Tozzer, 1957, p. 208.)

Priests. Various costumes of the clergy are mentioned. The most usual was a long white sleeveless robe of bark cloth ornamented with small snail shells; the headdress was a miter-like crown. The hair was unkempt and smeared with blood from sacrifices, which would account for the name of one, Teppanciz ("enveloped in stench"). At baptismal ceremonies the priest wore a red feather-work jacket and a crown of feathers. (RY, 1:51, 162, 2: 27; López de Cogolludo, bk. 4, ch. 7; Roys, 1933, p. 74; Landa, 1941, p. 105.)

We read of a high priest (*ahaucan*, "chief speaker") at Mayapan and a later one at Mani, who examined applicants and appointed the lesser clergy. The halach uinic also had important sacerdotal duties. The ordinary priest officiated at sacrifices, weddings, baptisms, and other ceremonies. He heard confessions, preached sermons, enforced religious rules, and kept track of the religious and agricultural calendars. In a special class was the *chilan*, or *chilam*, literally "mouthpiece," who went into a trance and delivered prophecies. Another category was that of the priest who specialized in human sacrifices (*nacom*, also the name of the war chief). The famous Chilam Balam was also called Nacom Balam. Only nobles could enter the priesthood, which was the repository of all science and learning. Their compensation seems to have consisted only of fees and voluntary offerings. (Landa, 1941, pp. 27, 102–06, 112; Motul dictionary, item *halach uinic;* RY, 2: 183–84, 210; Roys, 1933, p. 182; Codex Pérez, p. 65.)

Cosmology. Above the earth were 13 heavens and below it, nine underworlds, and we find frequent references to "13 gods" and "9 gods" in colonial Maya manuscripts. At the cardinal points in sets of four were certain trees, birds, and "fixed stones" (*acantun*), each associated with one of the four sacred colors: red with the east, white with the north, black with the west, and yellow with the south. The world had once been destroyed by a flood and would be again some time by fire. (Roys, 1933, pp. 31–33, 99–101, 165; Thompson, 1934.)

Deities. Many of the gods were also in groups of four, each associated with its particular color and cardinal point. Most gods had both a good and a bad aspect. The rain gods might send either good rains or hailstorms.

The head of the pantheon was the sky god, Itzam-na ("lizard house"); but an incorporeal deity, Colop-u-uich-kin ("he who robs the sun of his face," apparently an eclipse god) was his superior. Itzamna had two principal aspects: Kin-ich Ahau ("sun-eyed lord") and Itzamna Kauil ("Itzamna the food-giver"). Sometimes they prayed to him for rain, though there were also four rain gods. In one ritual we read of four Itzamnas. Other sky gods were the planet Venus and a number of constellations. (Vienna dictionary, f. 129*r*; Motul dictionary, p. 404; Ritual of the Bacabs, *passim;* Roys, 1943, p. 96; 1954, pp. 30–31, *passim.*)

At the four cardinal points were the four Chacs, or rain gods, four Pauahtuns, probably wind gods, four bee gods called Musencabs, and the four Bacabs who held up the sky. (Thompson, 1934; Gann and Thompson, 1931, pp. 124–26; Landa, 1941, pp. 135–39; López de Cogolludo, 1867–68, bk. 4, ch. 8.)

The mother of the gods was Ix Kan-le-ox ("yellow-leaf breadnut"), of whom we know little, though the Maya still pray to her. The moon goddess, who appears to have been the wife of the sun, was Ix Chel. She was the deity of women, childbirth, medicine, and illicit love. As the patroness of weaving, she was associated with the spider and divination. Divining stones were called *am* ("spider"). Ix Chel had a famous shrine on Cozumel Island, where both Maya and Chontal pilgrims sought forgiveness of sin. (López de Cogolludo, 1867–68, bk. 4, ch. 8; Ritual of the Bacabs, pp. 157–60; Thompson, 1934, 1939b; Landa, 1941, pp. 9, 129, 154; Roys, Scholes, and Adams, 1940, pp. 5–6.)

The most prominent of the earth gods was the handsome young maize god. Also important were the lords of the forests and Ekchuuah, the god of cacao planters and merchants. (Gann and Thompson, 1931, pp. 120–24; Thompson 1954b, pp. 230–31; Landa, 1941, p. 107.)

Of the gods of the underworld we have details only of its dread ruler, whom everybody feared. His realm was *mitnal,* a Nahuatl word. It was a cold dismal place that smelled like a charnel house. A few people escaped, such as sacrificed warriors, and suicides who hanged themselves. Among his various names were Cumhau, Ah Puch, Xibalba, and Cizin ("the stinking one"). (Gann and Thompson, 1931, p. 129–30; Thompson, 1950, index under Underworld; 1954a, pp. 230–31; RY, 1: 121; Landa, 1941, p. 132; Vienna dictionary, f. 64*r*; Roys, 1943, pp. 75–76.)

MEXICAN DEITIES. The worship of Xipe, Tlazolteotl, and other Mexican deities is evident from the remains at Mayapan; but in the 16th-century accounts and the Books of Chilam Balam the references to Mexican religious cults, although such still existed in conquest times, lead us to believe that they had become less popular. (Thompson, 1957; Roys, 1933.)

SACRIFICES. Sacrifices were made of one's own blood and of dogs, wild turkeys, other wild animals, and even some reptiles. In times of public calamity human sacrifice was considered necessary. War captives were preferable, but slaves or children were often sufficient. The last were especially acceptable to the rain gods, and sometimes their bodies were thrown into a cenote. The famous sacrifices to the rain gods in the great cenote at Chichen Itza need no mention here. Of especial interest is an account of an arrow sacrifice, which must have been a fairly late innovation in Yucatan. (Landa, 1941, pp. 115–21; RY, 1:276; Scholes and Roys, 1938, pp. 611–16; Scholes and Adams, 1938, 1: 78–80, and *passim;* Roys, 1933, App. B.)

Science and Learning

MAYA SCHOLARSHIP. Maya scholarship, especially in the fields of chronology, mathematics, and astronomy, was truly impressive; but our own knowledge of their attainments is drawn not so much from colonial Maya manuscripts and information by the early Spaniards as from the Dresden codex and certain inscriptions which dated from a time long before the Spanish conquest (see Satterthwaite, Article 24, and Thompson, Article 25). It seems possible that much of their science and learning had been forgotten by the middle of the 16th century. The educated class could still read and write, but neither letters nor important contracts were written.

Nevertheless, the priests still knew the tun and katun endings and how to reconcile the 365-day vague year with the true solar year, so they could advise the farmers when to burn or plant their fields. Although the Long Count appears in the Dresden codex, it seems to have gone out of use. A historical event was usually recorded in terms of its position in the katun round, a period of about 256 years (13 × 7200 days). In the colonial Maya chronicles we sometimes find it hard to determine in which katun round an event occurred, because it was not recorded with sufficient detail. It must be admitted, however, that in colonial times some people were still reported to know, at least by name, such numerical terms as *pic* (8000), *calab* (160,000), *kinchil* (probably 3,200,000), and even the *alau* (64,000,000). Some of these might have been employed in counting cacao beans, but it seems hard to associate the last two with concrete objects. (Roys, 1943, pp. 88–89; Beltrán de Santa Rosa, 1859, p. 203.)

Since most educated persons were priests, it would seem that their most important branch of learning, aside from theology and ceremonies, must have been a knowledge of the complicated religious calendar. Religious activities were timed, not always by the position of a day in the 365-day vague year, but sometimes by its position in the 260-day ritual period, the 360-day *tun*, or even the 7200-day katun. Attention was paid to the moon, the morning star, the north star, and some of the constellations. (Landa, 1941, pp. 27–28, 151–66; Thompson, 1930, p. 63; Roys, 1943, p. 96; Motul dictionary, pp. 66, 237, 254, 292, 311, 916; RY, 1: 52.)

Divination and Prophecy. The proper days for certain activities of ordinary life and their good or bad luck generally depended on the name and number of the day. These determined its position in the 260-day period. This 260-day cycle with its prognostics was evidently very popular, for we find it and the 18 20-day *uinals* correlated with the Spanish annual calendar. In this manner it served the Maya as an almanac throughout the colonial period. (Stephens, 1843, 1:449–58; Solís Alcalá, 1949, pp. 2–49, 102–29, 188–95, 276–97; Roys, 1949a; Thompson, 1950, pp. 297–302.)

Almost equally popular were the katun prophecies. A number of these, written only in Maya, have also come down to us from colonial times. Although they contain some postconquest material, they correspond closely to the hieroglyphic books of prophecy of the Itza on Lake Peten, which were described at a time when they were still unaffected by Spanish influence. The latter were reported to be "a book like history which they call analte [*anahte*]." These prophecies are apparently based on a belief that whatever had occurred in the past would be likely to recur in another katun of the same name. The latter could only return after a little over 256 years or a multiple of that period. Consequently their historical allusions are a supplement to the legendary history that has come down to us. Most of their prognostics are unfavorable. Each katun was ruled by a celestial patron, often unfriendly, who was responsible for the evils which would occur. I feel sure that at least some of these patrons were deified stars or constellations.

Even as late as 1670 large groups of fugitives from northern Yucatan were proclaiming that according to the prophecies the time was approaching when the Maya should depart from under Spanish rule. We also have an example of prophecies for the 20 tuns of a Katun 5 Ahau, but the historical allusions are more obscure. (Roys, 1933, pp. 144–63; 1943, pp. 89–92; 1949a; 1954; Scholes and Roys, 1948, pp. 308–09.)

MEDICINE. This was an important science, and the Spaniards were impressed by Maya knowledge of the medical uses of the local flora and fauna. The 16th-century Motul dictionary cites the names and healing properties of many plants, and a large body of medical literature, both in Maya and Spanish, has survived from colonial times. Sickness was considered to be either a divine punishment for sin or the work of a sorcerer, who could "throw" a certain disease. The latter might be cured either by medical treatment or by an incantation. Some diseases were ascribed to mythical birds or reptiles. Not only were there hieroglyphic books of curative incantations, but one large Maya manuscript in Spanish script has come down to us, in which Ix Chel, the goddess of medicine, and other deities are invoked. It has been named The Ritual of the Bacabs, and here the disease is often apparently personified, its birth or origin is cited, and it is cursed to make it go away. In the Motul dictionary (p. 110) both the medical doctor and the reciter of incantations, often probably the same person, are called *ah dzac yah* ("he who cures sickness"). The evil sorcerer was called *ah pul yah* ("he who throws sickness"). (Landa, 1941, pp. 27–28, 112, 154–55; RY, 1: 62, 66–67; Thompson, 1958b.)

Not only could snake bites be cured, but the snakes themselves could be bewitched: "and they had their books to conjure and charm them; and these sorcerers, with the few words which they recited, charmed and tamed poisonous serpents. They caught them and took them in their hands without their doing them any harm" (RY, 1: 66–67.)

I have as yet found no reference to "evil winds" as a cause of disease in any of the books or reports from colonial times.

GENEALOGY. Much attention was paid to lineage and descent. I infer that a real noble had to be of noble descent on both his father's and his mother's sides; and one of the proofs of noble status was a knowledge of one's ancestry. It was important, if an ancestor had had a home at Mayapan; but we know from the Crónica de Calkini that the son of a noble father and a plebian mother could achieve a position of considerable importance. Francisco Pech, cacique of Telchac, had a book telling the names of various deified lineage ancestors, one of whom was recorded elsewhere as a Mexican invader of Yucatan. (Landa, 1941, pp. 28, 98; Scholes and Adams, 1938, 1: 153; Roys, 1933, p. 92; Brinton, 1882, p. 115.)

MYTHOLOGICAL NARRATIVES. In the Books of Chilam Balam, so named because of their frequent mention of a famous prophet of that name, we find mythological stories about the creation, the great flood, and early times on earth. Apparently they are derived from hieroglyphic manuscripts, for Sánchez de Aguilar tells of his familiarity with such books and states elsewhere that he once confiscated a *cartapacio* containing "prejudicial fables and histories." It is possible, however, that this particular book was written in the Maya language but in European script. (Roys, 1933, pp. 99–106; Sánchez de Aguilar, 1937; pp. 142, 181; Thompson, 1932.)

THE MAYA CHONTAL

The name Chontal is Nahuatl ("foreigner") and was also applied to non-Maya people in Nicaragua and Oaxaca. The language of the Maya Chontal is closely related to the Yucatan Maya and is even more similar to Chol and Chorti. In Yucatan it was called Putunthan. This linguistic area covered most of Tabasco and a part of southwestern Campeche including the Candelaria basin. Much of this region is low and swampy, covered by a network of creeks and rivers, so there was little travel by land.

In this area only eight towns were Nahuatl-speaking, but there is much evidence of wide Nahua influence. Most of the place names, except in the basins of the Usumacinta and Candelaria Rivers, and a very considerable proportion of the personal names that have come down to us are Nahuatl. In Acalan, in the Calendaria region, 76 Chontal place names were recorded. (RY, 1: 313–15, 320, 331–41, 352; Scholes and Roys, 1948, pp. 383–89, 481–90.)

We know little about their social organization, but an early tribute list of the Chontal-Acalan indicates neither patronymics nor matronymics. Certain prefixes occur before many names, but I am unable to discern their significance. They lived in multiple-family households, which display a strong tendency toward matrilocal residence; for the members were more likely to be relatives of the wife of the head than of the head himself. In contrast to this evidence, however, the ancestry of the ruler is traced for seven generations in the male line. When a ruler died, he was succeeded by his brothers in turn, if any, before his oldest son succeeded. Only two or three of these had a Nahuatl name. (Scholes and Roys, 1948, App. C.) In Tabasco multiple-family houses are indicated by comparing the number of tribute payers with the number of houses in a given area. (Roys, 1943, p. 103.)

We know little of the Tabasco Chontal towns. Potonchan was fortified by a palisade of thick tree trunks. Apparently at its center was a large square, around which were three temples and some "large halls." Probably the latter were the tecpan and an unmarried men's house, such as we know existed at Xicalango. Descriptions of the finest houses indicate flat beamed roofs. There was no stone in Tabasco, but the country was unique in producing burned brick, which was used with shell mortar and earth. Most houses had thatched roofs with pole or wattle walls. An unusual feature in the Maya area was the existence of large handsome country houses with gardens outside of the towns. (Díaz del Castillo, 1933, ch. 31; Ximénez, 1929–31, bk. 2, ch. 37; López de Gómara, 1931, p. 31; Anghiera, 1912, 2:35.)

Itzamkanac, the Acalan capital, was a large town of thatched houses, many of them with stone walls. All Cortés' Spanish soldiers and their horses were quartered in a single large building. (Roys, 1943, p. 103; Scholes and Roys, 1948, pp. 53, 110; Herrera y Tordesillas, 1725–26, 3: 360.)

Itzamkanac was divided into four quarters, each headed by its own subchief. These men, no doubt supported by a council, were able to depose the ruler and put his young son in his place. The ruler was the most important merchant in conquest times; and his brother governed the Acalan quarter at Nito, a distant commercial center on the Río Dulce in Guatemala. (Scholes and Roys, 1948, pp. 389–90, 392.)

Tabasco had no native metals or stone, but it was wealthy, both from its cacao plantations and its commerce. The latter was largely along the lines already noted for Yucatan Maya, which it surpassed. Besides its export of cacao to Yucatan and the Mexican highlands, all Yucatan imports from Mexico and Chiapas had to pass through Tabasco. Other specialties were canoe building, tanning, and fine work in metals and tortoise-shell. (Oviedo y Valdés, 1851–55, bk. 17, ch. 3; Herrera y Tordesillas, 1725–26, 2: 127–28; Scholes and Roys, 1948, pp. 3, 15, 28–34.)

Idolatry was general, and all but one of the gods we know correspond to those of Yucatan. Both human sacrifice and ceremonial cannibalism were reported. The worship of Ix Chel, goddess of medicine and childbirth, seems to have been general, but of the other deities we know only those recorded at Itzamkanac. Here the ruler had a temple to Cukulchan (Maya Kukulcan, Mexican Quetzalcoatl), and each of the four quarters of the town had its own place of worship. The deities of these were apparently the ones named Ykchaua (Ekchuuah, the Maya god of merchants and cacao growers), Tabay (a Maya god of hunters), Ix Chel, and Cabtanilcabtan (unidentified). (RY, 1: 364–65; Scholes and Roys, 1948, pp. 57, 158, 395.)

REFERENCES

Adams, E. B., n.d.
Adams, R. M., 1953
Anghiera, 1912
Archivo General de Indias, Seville, 1548–51, 1604–07
Bacabs, Ritual of, n.d.
Barrera V., 1957
Beals, 1932
Beltrán de Santa Rosa, 1859
Blom, 1932b
Brinton, 1882
Cacalch'en, Libro de, n.d.
Calkini, Crónica de, n.d.
Cartas de Indias, 1877
Chi, 1941
Ciudad Real, 1932
Cogolludo, *see* López de Cogolludo
Díaz del Castillo, 1933–34
Eggan, 1934
Follett, 1932
Gann and Thompson, 1931
Herrera y Tordesillas, 1725–26, 1941
Kempton, 1935
Landa, 1941
López de Cogolludo, 1867–68
López de Gómara, 1931
López Medel, 1941
Lundell, 1934
Martínez Hernández, 1926, 1929
Means, 1917
Morris, Charlot, and Morris, 1931
Motul, Diccionario de, *see* Martínez H., 1929
Noyes, 1932
Oviedo y Valdés, 1851–55
Pérez, Codex, 1837
Proskouriakoff and Temple, 1955
Relaciones de Yucatan, 1898–1900
Ricketson and Kidder, 1930
Roys, R. L., 1931, 1933, 1939, 1940, 1943, 1941, 1949a, 1949b, 1954, 1957
——, Scholes, and Adams, 1940, 1959
Ruppert, Thompson, and Proskouriakoff, 1955
RY, *see* Relaciones de Yucatan
Sánchez de Aguilar, 1937
San Francisco, Diccionario de, n.d.
Scholes and Adams, 1938
——, Menendez, Rubio Mañé, and Adams, 1936–38
—— and Roys, 1938, 1948
Smith, A. L., and Ruppert, 1953, 1956
Solís Alcala, 1949
Standley, 1930
Stephens, 1843
Tabi, Documentos de, n.d.
Thompson, D. E. and J. E. S., 1955
Thompson, J. E. S., 1930, 1932, 1934, 1936, 1938, 1939b, 1950, 1954a, 1954b, 1957, 1958b
Torquemada, 1943
Tozzer, 1941, 1957
—— and Allen, 1910
Vienna Dictionary, n.d.
Ximénez, 1929–31

27. Archaeological Synthesis of Southern Veracruz and Tabasco

MICHAEL D. COE

Area and Environment

THE ARCHAEOLOGICAL AREA described in this paper lies about 350 km. long in southeastern Veracruz and western Tabasco and extends no more than 100 km. inland from the shore of the Gulf of Mexico (fig. 1). On the northwest it is bounded by the upper reaches of the Rio Blanco and by the western shore of the Laguna de Alvarado, on the east by the lower Grijalva River and the Barra de Tupilco. This generally low-lying, tropical region was the *locus classicus* of the ancient Olmec civilization. It is certainly one of the richest archaeological zones of the world, probably having the highest density of pre-Columbian sites per square kilometer in Mesoamerica. Almost all these are relatively unplanned groups of earthen mounds dotting the humid coastal plains, the majority of them totally unexplored. The frequency of such groups is so great that one may drive for 11 km. along the road passing through the sugar fields near Angel Cabada and Lerdo de Tejada and never be out of sight of mounds.

Geographically, southern Veracruz and the adjacent part of Tabasco consist of one broad, low, rainy coastal plain, which is continuous with the coasts of eastern Tabasco and Campeche. The only break in the monotony of continuous tropical forest and open pasture land is the Tuxtla Mountains (Los Tuxtlas), an upland cluster of volcanoes occupying approximately the center of the area, near the sea. The annual rainfall is quite high, and where it has not been removed for grazing land, the forest is high and dense, although extensive open savannas flank some parts of the coast and are found inland. As is usual in this part of Mesoamerica, almost all the rain falls in the summer months.

A multitude of sluggish, meandering rivers originating on the slopes of Orizaba and in the Sierras of Oaxaca and Chiapas have created this alluvial plain. Toward the coast, they often lose themselves in swamps, mangrove-lined estuaries, and lagoons. The most important of these rivers are, from east to west, the Rio Blanco, which empties into the enormous Laguna de Alvarado; the Papaloapan, originating

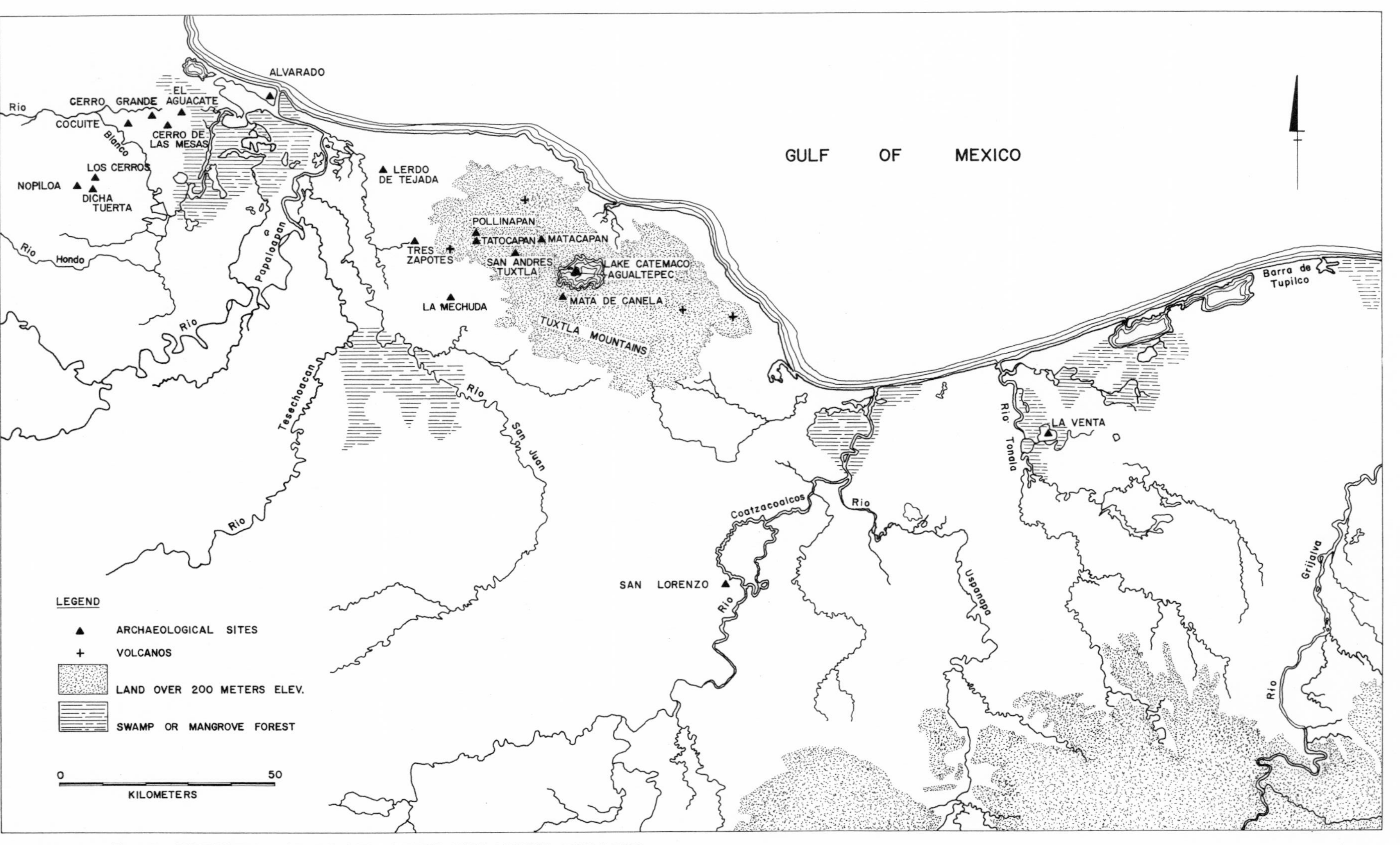

Fig. 1—PRINCIPAL SITES OF LOWER VERACRUZ–TABASCO

near Tehuacan, Puebla, and also flowing into the Laguna de Alvarado after traversing a maze of estuaries and swamps in the Tlacotalpan region; the Coatzacoalcos, which drains most of the Isthmus of Tehuantepec, and which must have provided the major route across that great constriction in the waist of Mesoamerica; the Tonala, providing the border between Veracruz and Tabasco; and the Grijalva (or Rio Grande de Chiapa), which leaves the Central Depression of Chiapas through a series of impassable gorges before it winds across the plains of Tabasco to join the Usumacinta and meet the Gulf of Mexico.

It must not be thought, however, that the southern Veracruz – Tabasco area was completely uniform, either ecologically or culturally. For one thing, the amount of annual precipitation varies considerably over the region: the lower Coatzacoalcos and Tonala drainages receive more than 2500 mm. annually, whereas most of our area receives about 2000 mm., and a zone in which under 1500 mm. falls extends down along the coast from the city of Veracruz to the Papaloapan drainage (Tamayo, 1949). As the ancient peoples were slash-and-burn maize farmers, such variations in the environment must have been accompanied by different patterns of cultural adaptation.

On the basis of geography and cultural remains, several subareas are here defined.

1. *The Mixtequilla* (Stirling, 1943, p. 31; Drucker 1943a, pp. 1–2), a small region about 25 km. west of the Laguna de Alvarado, consists of a low sandy plateau or series of "islands" of aeolian origin above periodically flooded pasture lands and swamps. Although this subarea is much drier than any other part of southern Veracruz–Tabasco, mound groups, including Cerro de las Mesas, are extremely abundant. For the sake of convenience, sites around the Laguna de Alvarado are here grouped with the Mixtequilla.

2. *The Tuxtlas* comprise the Tuxtla Mountains and that portion of the coastal plain fringing them. The volcanic peaks of these mountains rise to over 1400 m. and can be seen for many kilometers away; the lava flows on their flanks provided the single source of basalt so prized by the ancients. In the center of the Tuxtla Mountains, at a height of 338 m., lies Lake Catemaco, from the surface of which rise two small islands of volcanic origin, Agaltepec and Tenaspi. The lands around Catemaco and throughout the valleys, basins, and plains of this subarea are highly fertile and are dotted with ancient mound groups.

3. *Northern Isthmian Plain*, comprising the lower reaches of the Coatzacoalcos and Tonala Rivers, has extensive flatlands of clayey alluvium, mangrove forests and swamps, and a very high annual rainfall. Here, ancient and modern occupation is often confined to "islands" of higher ground above the frequently inundated plain. Tropical rain forest was once the dominant floral type, and still is in many places. This is the homeland of the Olmec civilization.

Naturally, there are extensive territories within our area not covered by this classification, but they are unknown archaeologically and so not necessary to our discussion.

Archaeological Sites and Excavations

The early explorations of the area by such archaeologists as J. M. Melgar, the Selers, Strebel, and Weyerstall have been described by Stirling (1943, pp. 7, 48–49). The most important reconnaissance prior to 1938, however, was that undertaken by Blom and LaFarge (1926–27), who in 1925 traversed Los Tuxtlas subarea and visited the site of La Venta in the northern isthmian plain. Our first real knowledge of southern Veracruz – Tabasco is entirely based on the explorations and excavations carried out under the direction of M. W. Stirling in the years since 1938 at several sites of great importance. Other excavations undertaken in subsequent years have enlarged our picture of the prehistory of this area, but it is still only fragmentary.

All of these are summarized below, for it is upon them that the present paper is based.

1. MIXTEQUILLA
   a. *Cerro de las Mesas* (Stirling, 1943, pp. 31–48; Drucker, 1943a). This site is but one of many strung out along a ridge of high ground extending from the modern village of Cocuite to Ignacio del Llave, but it is the largest. It consists of some dozens of earthen mounds, with little evidence of planning, but there is some clustering into groups. The Central Mound Group comprises several closely set high mounds, the tallest of which is between 15 and 18 m. high and 60 m. square at the base, and some platform mounds, arranged to form four large plazas in which stood stone monuments. Another group of large mounds is 0.4 km. to the southwest, and groups of scattered small mounds were strewn at random over other parts of the site.

      Of the 43 trenches dug in the site during 1940–41 the majority were exploratory cuts within or outside mounds connected with the search for monuments, caches, or architectural features, or were pits made to determine depth of deposit. Only three were actually stratigraphic tests (Drucker, 1943a, Table 1). The major significance of the site lies in its 15 stelae and 8 monuments, described by Stirling (1943, pp. 33–47).
   b. *Cerro del Gallo* (Stirling, 1943, pp. 31–32), near Cerro de las Mesas but never excavated, has a large mound resting on a platform base, together measuring about 30 m. high, and a single crude stela.
   c. *Dicha Tuerta* (Medellín Zenil, 1960a, pp. 194–95) is an earthen-mound site. Several cuts were made by Medellín Zenil, apparently stratigraphic, one of which is stated to have been in an ancient pottery dump.
   d. *Los Cerros* (Medellín Zenil, 1960a, pp. 191–94) is a mound group not far from Dicha Tuerta. At least one trench was made, in a mound, excavated in arbitrary levels of 70 cm.
   e. *Nopiloa* (Medellín Zenil, 1960b), a large and important site excavated by Medellín Zenil in 1957 and 1958, consists of mounds (one of which is 18 m. tall), platforms, and plazas, as well as a huge monolith of basalt which Medellín (p. 38) identifies as the Earth Monster. A cut was made where the monument stood; three stratigraphic pits were sunk in a midden deposit; and, on the summit of a mound contiguous to the midden, a trench was excavated 10 m. down to sterile deposits. Back-dirt from a pit made by pothunters in another mound was explored, and explorations were undertaken in the undisturbed mound fill.
   f. *Alvarado*. Near the modern port of Alvarado, in the Cerro de las Conchas, several stratigraphic pits were made by Medellín Zenil (1960a, pp. 189–90). According to J. L. Lorenzo (1961, p. 16), excavations in this shell mound were halted when nonceramic levels were encountered even though the base of the deposit had not been reached.

2. LOS TUXTLAS
   a. *Tres Zapotes* (Stirling, 1943, pp. 4–30; Weiant, 1943; Drucker, 1943b) lies nearly at the foot of the Tuxtla Mountains near the Arroyo of Hueyapan. The approximately 50 earthen mounds, strung out along the flood plain of the arroyo for about 3 km., are on a kind of eroded plateau consisting of sandstone overlaid by clay. The mounds are nucleated in irregular groups with no real orientation; on a slight south-to-north rise are Mound Group 1, the Ranchito Group, the New Lands Group, and Mound Group 3; closer to the arroyo are Mound Group 2 and the "Burnt Mounds." Most of the mounds are 3–4.5 m. high, but two are over 12 m. Besides a few pieces of columnar basalt, a fair number of extremely significant stone monuments have been found at Tres Zapotes: five stelae, two colossal heads, two large stone boxes (one elaborately carved), two large, tenoned stone heads, three seated figures, a carved owl, a relief-carved bar-and-dot numeral, and various miscellaneous monuments.

      Excavations carried out by Stirling and Weiant in 1938–39 were nonstratigraphic exploratory trenches around monuments and into various mounds, but some materials were separated out by gross level. In the winter of 1939–40 Stirling and Drucker undertook more extensive digging of the site: 19 nonstratigraphic pits to test the depth of deposits, and six nonstratigraphic mound cuts. The Tres Zapotes sequence as outlined by Drucker (1943b) is based on five stratigraphic trenches covering various parts of the site; the deepest was Trench 26, which reached a level of 6.63 m., well below a thick layer of volcanic ash, but the average depth of deposit was between 1.50 and 1.80 m. The results of field work in this site and at Cerro de las Mesas are of the utmost importance in understanding the cultural development of southern Veracruz – Tabasco.

b. *San Andres Tuxtla* (Valenzuela, 1945a, pp. 85–91). Extensive reconnaissance and excavations were accomplished by Juan Valenzuela and Karl Ruppert in 1937 and 1938 in the Tuxtlas subarea, particularly around San Andres Tuxtla, Santiago Tuxtla, and at Lake Catemaco, but the results have never been fully published. In the first-named town cuts were made in midden deposits below Maclovio Herrera Street, as well as test pits in a small mound in the same ward. Also on the outskirts of San Andres test excavations were made on the land of Carlos Figueroa.

c. *Matacapan* (Valenzuela, 1945a, pp. 91–101) is a very large group of more than 70 mounds between Lake Catemaco and the slopes of San Martin Tuxtla volcano, on a well-watered plain with fertile soils. Unlike other sites of our area, the mounds at Matacapan are regularly laid out on an orientation slightly east of north, which is typical for Classic sites in Mexico.

Stratigraphic trenches were cut down from the summits of three mounds in the western part of the site (Mounds 1, 3, 4), producing evidence for cultural change; the overburden of a fourth (Mound 2) was cleared to reveal a stone-faced platform pyramid beneath.

d. *Agaltepec* (Valenzuela, 1945a, pp. 102–04). In Lake Catemaco just east of the modern town is the small island of Agaltepec, described by Blom and La Farge in 1925, who drew a sketch-map. The narrow island lies west-east; its entire length has been altered for ancient constructions of various sorts: mounds, plazas, sunken courts, and retaining walls. I visited the island in 1962 and noted a long causeway on the eastern tip of the island, from the terminus of which a series of rock-cut steps descends to the water. Four excavations were made by Valenzuela in a sunken court near the eastern extremity, and a cut made into the principal mound bordering the court, but no stratigraphic sequence is described.

e. *Tatocapan* (Valenzuela, 1945b) is a site of approximately 60 earthen mounds, clustered into distinct groups, located about 2 km. north of Santiago Tuxtla. One group surrounds a sunken patio with several small "adoratories" in the center, in which three test pits proved sterile. About 50 m. east of these mounds three further cuts in another adoratory gave better results. In a second mound group, other adoratories were excavated.

f. *Pollinapan* (Valenzuela, 1945b) is another mound site in the Santiago Tuxtla region, in which three adoratories near Mound 1 were excavated.

g. *La Mechuda* (Valenzuela, 1945b) is a mound group lying some 2 km. west of the Tilapam railroad station on the southwestern slopes of the Tuxtla Mountains, only 14 km. from Tres Zapotes. A carved stone column in the center of a plaza had been much destroyed by treasure seekers. A brief excavation was made at this site.

h. *Mata de Canela* (Valenzuela, 1945b) is a large site south of Lake Catemaco, on the road to Acayucan. The mounds are arranged in planned groups; largest are two north-south mounds forming a ball court, closed on the north by a great conical mound and on the south by a low, long one. (A very similar ball court was noted by Kent Flannery and me in 1962 at Arroyo Agrio, a large site just north of Lake Catemaco.) Several carved stones were once associated with Mata de Canela

(Blom and LaFarge, 1926–27, pp. 24–25). Trenches were dug by Karl Ruppert, and a test pit cut into a platform mound.

3. NORTHERN ISTHMIAN PLAIN
   a. *San Lorenzo group* (Stirling, 1957) comprises three sites near San Lorenzo Tenochtitlan: San Lorenzo, Rio Chiquito, and Potrero Nuevo. All lie on a ridge of high land near the flat bottoms of the Coatzacoalcos River. Like all sites of our area, they are complexes of earthen mounds enclosing courts. Numerous carved monuments were discovered by Stirling at the San Lorenzo group, including five colossal heads of great beauty, as well as "altars" and other sculptures. Test excavations were made by Drucker but have never been published.
   b. *La Venta* (Stirling, 1943, pp. 48–60; Drucker, 1952a; Drucker, Heizer, and Squier, 1959). The coastal plain of western Tabasco is so low-lying and the coast itself prograding to such a degree that rivers and streams are tidal and lined with mangrove forests well inland. The bottomlands are swampy, with a few eroded sandstone hills rising above the surrounding alluvium. La Venta is one of these "islands," between systems of streams and sloughs draining into the Tonala River, about 19 km. from the actual coast. It is surrounded by swamp and covered by a windblown, sandy soil. The dimensions of the island are 6–7 km. from north to south and 4.5 km. wide. The major archaeological feature is the great Central Group, a mound complex at approximately the center of the island, which represents the type site for the Olmec culture. Because it apparently belongs to a single period, it will be described in detail below. Other, smaller, mound clusters are also known on the island; some at least can be ascribed to much later cultures.

      In 1940 Stirling spent 10 days excavating stone monuments in the Central Group so that they could be photographed and he recorded 17. Stratigraphic excavations were undertaken by Drucker in 1942 (Drucker, 1952a); 40 trenches were dug to test various parts of the site, but they were nonstratigraphic and nothing but figurines were saved. He made three stratigraphic trenches, by 30-cm. arbitrary levels, in midden debris. Architectural investigations were carried out by Drucker and Stirling in 1942, by Stirling and Wedel in 1943, and, on a massive scale, by Drucker, Heizer, and Squier in 1955, all largely in Complex A of the Central Group. (The charcoal samples recovered by the latter investigators have provided the only radiocarbon dates thus far for the southern Veracruz – Tabasco area.)

Methodology and Assumptions of the Present Synthesis

Detailed studies and final reports have been published for only three sites of the area: Cerro de las Mesas, Tres Zapotes, and La Venta. As noted above, C14 determinations are almost absent. On the basis of his stratigraphic trenches at these sites, Drucker (1943b, pp. 114–23; 1943a, pp. 76–87; 1952a, pp. 204–40) has established a sequence of phases and attempted to correlate them with other regions on a basis which seems to me untenable (see also Wauchope, 1954, note 40), particularly in the light of more recent work in the rest of Mesoamerica. Furthermore, his conclusions disagree with those of Weiant (1943) over the sequence at Tres Zapotes, a key site.

At Tres Zapotes, for instance, probably the most complex and long-enduring of all sites in the area, the wares have been grouped by Drucker into six gross classes, some of which (like his "Polychrome") may cut across dozens of distinct varieties of slip, color, design motif, and shape. On the basis of the stratigraphic distribution of these "wares" and of figurine types (none of which were ever numerous enough to preclude a wide sampling error), he has made a correlation of his trenches and from this defined three broad phases: Lower, Middle, and Upper Tres Zapotes (Drucker, 1943b, pp. 100–02).

The same method has been applied to Cerro de las Mesas and to La Venta. On this basis, an obviously early deposit of material assigned by him to the Lower phase at Tres Zapotes has been aligned with Late Preclassic cultures in the Maya area (with which I do not disagree); a "transitional" phase called by him Middle Tres Zapotes, still with the solid, handmade figurines of the Lower phase and discoverable only through his "correlation" of trenches, is equated with Tzakol of the Peten and therefore with the Early Classic (in spite of there being no resemblances to Tzakol [cf. Wauchope, 1954, note 40; see Drucker, *ibid.*, note 43]); finally, by a canceling-out process, Upper Tres Zapotes must be Late Classic. An obviously intrusive complex of cremation vessels called "Soncautla" is with reason seen as postdating the Upper phase.

Drucker's correlations between Tres Zapotes and other sites in our area may be summarized as follows. La Venta is said to be a single-period site. Although no typical Tres Zapotes figurines occur at La Venta and although the La Venta ceramic complex is quite unlike that of Tres Zapotes, Drucker (1952a, pp. 147–51, 210–11) equated that site with Middle Tres Zapotes. Since the latter had already been identified as Early Classic, then La Venta also must be Early Classic. The chronology for Cerro de las Mesas is determined from the stratigraphic distribution of 21 wares and subwares in two trenches (Drucker, 1943a, pp. 69–76), and thus is probably somewhat more reliable than that at Tres Zapotes. Four phases were abstracted from this material and aligned with those of Tres Zapotes:

Cerro de las Mesas	*Tres Zapotes*
Upper II	Soncautla complex
Upper I	Upper Tres Zapotes
Lower II	Middle Tres Zapotes
Lower I	Lower Tres Zapotes

Thus, the earliest ceramics of Cerro de las Mesas must, by this token, again be considered as coeval with the Early Classic of the Maya area (Wauchope, 1954, note 40), and, by analogy, Lower II through Upper II must all postdate that period.

The synthesis presented here has been reached through entirely different means. Since in neither the Tres Zapotes nor the Cerro de las Mesas reports are there indications of which illustrations of Drucker's broad ware categories are to be considered as typical of a particular phase, his stratigraphic data have temporarily been ignored. Instead, new approaches have been sought. The basic method has been to work out from known associations in caches, burials, and offerings not only in Drucker's reports but in others as well; once these were established, a tentative sequence was postulated for each site, in the light of cultural development as now known for other areas within Mesoamerica. As a final check, these sequences were then compared with the stratigraphic data already presented by Drucker, Weiant, and others.

Naturally, behind this new synthesis there are certain assumptions, one or more of which, if proved untrue, would undermine its validity. The first is that trends in artifact manufacture, art styles, and other traits here follow more or less the same lines of development as elsewhere in Mesoamerica: that southern Veracruz – Tabasco is not atypical. Second, that the Goodman-Martínez-Thompson correlation of the Maya and Christian calendars is essentially correct, with the Classic period beginning about A.D. 300 and ending around 900. Last, that Classic Teotihuacan (Teotihuacan III) was destroyed at the end of what otherwise might be considered the Early Classic period, that is, at approximately A.D. 600; no valid arguments have ever been proposed that there really *is* a "Teotihuacan IV" occupation at that great site, and recent stratigraphic investigations

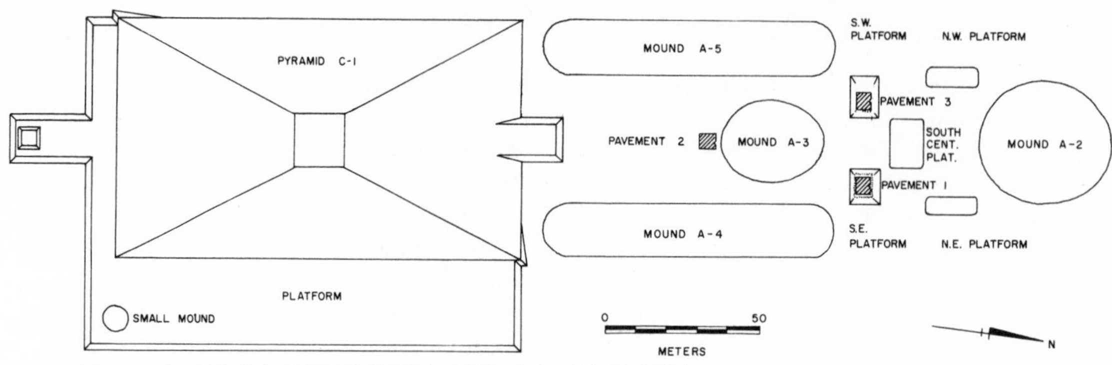

FIG. 2—PLAN OF COMPLEXES A AND C AT LA VENTA

are against it (R. E. Smith, personal communication). Thus, any strong influence from Classic Teotihuacan on southern Veracruz – Tabasco must be confined to the Early Classic period.

In the new scheme, five phases have been postulated for Tres Zapotes and four for Cerro de las Mesas; there seems to be little doubt that the occupation of the Central Group at La Venta represents a single cultural phase. At Tres Zapotes, these correspond roughly to the published sequences of Weiant and Drucker in this fashion:

Synthesis	*Weiant*	*Drucker*
Tres Zapotes V	Part of Upper phase	"Soncautla complex"
Tres Zapotes IV	Part of Upper phase	Part of Upper II phase
Tres Zapotes III	Part of Upper phase	Parts of Upper I and Lower II phases
Tres Zapotes II	Middle B phase	
Tres Zapotes I	Middle A phase	Lower I phase

Likewise, the correlation for Cerro de las Mesas is as follows:

Synthesis	*Drucker*
Cerro de las Mesas IV	Upper phase
Cerro de las Mesas III	Part of Lower II phase
Cerro de las Mesas II	Parts of Lower II and Lower I phases
Cerro de las Mesas I	Part of Lower I phase

For the entire area a sequence has been devised which begins with the Middle Preclassic (800–300 B.C.)—that is, the Olmec period—and continues through Late Preclassic (300 B.C. to A.D. 100), Protoclassic (A.D. 100–300), Early Classic (A.D. 300–600), Late Classic (A.D. 600–900), Early Postclassic (A.D. 900–1200), and Late Postclassic (A.D. 1200 to conquest).

MIDDLE PRECLASSIC PERIOD

Olmec Phase

The earliest culture in our area of which we have any knowledge and, paradoxically, the oldest civilization in Mesoamerica, is that called "Olmec." A recent series of radiocarbon dates suggests a placement for the climax of the civilization between 800 and 400 B.C. The type site of the Olmec culture is La Venta, specifically the Central Group on that island, and it is on this site that the definition of the Olmec phase is based (see also Greengo, 1952).

Its characteristics as a phase are: (1) the Olmec art style in its "classic" form, (2) a spatial restriction to the Northern Isthmian Plain, (3) a temporal restriction to the Middle Preclassic period, (4) predominant use of clay and earth in the construction of platforms and great pyramids, (5) highly advanced techniques in the transport and carving of stone, particularly of basalt, (6) columnar basalt used for "fences" and for construction of tombs, (7) sophisticated techniques in the working of jade and serpentine, (8) massive offerings of large mosaic pavements and layers of stone, (9) concave mirrors, (10) handmade clay figurines, and, (11) a ceramic pattern that includes a high percentage of flat-bottomed dishes and neckless jars (*tecomates*), along with such decorative techniques as rocker-stamping and the "double-line break" (see below).

If we restrict the phrase "Olmec culture" to the above definition, there is little chance of falling into the trap which has caught so many: the fallacy of using the concept as a *tradition* which is only vaguely defined. For instance, some authors even refer to the smiling figures of Late Classic Veracruz as "Olmec," stretching the term to a point where it has no meaning.

La Venta

The Central Group (fig. 2) on La Venta island is an alignment of mounds and plazas extending approximately 750 m. north-south (actually, the centerline or axis is about 8 degrees west of true north). The group is dominated by Pyramid C-1 (Great Mound), a huge earthen or adobe mound 32.3 m. high, elongated along its north-south axis. North of this is Complex A, comprising, first, two long, low mounds on either side of the centerline, each about 1 m. high, with a low mound (A-3) in the center between them. Just north of this is a broad, rectangular court or plaza (A-1), surrounded by kind of fence of upright, columnar basalt pillars, set side by side in the top of a low wall made from adobe bricks. This enclosure is not complete, and Wedel (in Drucker, 1952a, p. 78) believes that it was robbed for tomb construction. Last, along the centerline is a large earthen mound (A-2). Well to the south of Pyramid C-1 is Complex B, not as important as the foregoing and not quite on the main axis, consisting of a group of four small mounds, an east-west line of basalt columns, and a long, north-to-south mound. The excavated mounds of the Central Group show that the favored method of construction was the employment of heavy clay fills, floors and platform sides being surfaced with colored clays (especially red, yellow, and purple). Adobe bricks

Fig. 3—STELA 3, LA VENTA. (From Drucker, Heizer, and Squier, 1959, fig. 67.)

were generally used to overlay massive offerings.

The monuments of La Venta are more fully treated in Article 28. Most are of basalt, but many are of gneiss or schist. The style is purely "Olmec," a highly evolved art centered on the cult of a were-jaguar with infantile features and a snarling mouth (see M. D. Coe, Article 29). Of the four stelae, Stela 3 (fig. 3) is particularly outstanding; on it two elaborately garbed men face each other, one of whom has aquiline features and a goatee, while chubby were-jaguars float above. The "altars" are large basalt blocks of which the tops are flat; one side often has a human figure seated in a niche. Most striking,

FIG. 4—MONUMENT 1, LA VENTA. (Copyright, National Geographic Society.)

however, of the La Venta monuments are the four colossal heads, which measure up to 2.5 m. high: great thick-lipped human faces, topped by "football helmet" headgear (fig. 4). The source of basalt for the heads and other monuments was near Soteapan, on the southeastern slopes of the Tuxtla Mountains, 90 km. west of La Venta as the crow flies (Robert Heizer and Howel Williams, personal information). Since the heads weigh up to 20 tons and Stela 3, for instance, weighs about 25, the engineering operation required to get the basalt to La Venta must have been staggering. Presumably the stone was floated by raft down to the sea at Coatzacoalcos, then to the mouth of the Tonala River and upstream to the site.

The massive offerings are among the most peculiar features of La Venta. They include three rectangular pavements (fig. 5), each formed of about 485 serpentine blocks set in colored clays above a deep foundation of stones and clay (underlying each pavement are about 1000 tons of stone; see Drucker, Heizer, and Squier, 1959, p. 97). These pavements are mosaics representing highly stylized jaguar masks, the features of which were left open to be filled with colored clays or sands. They are interpreted as offerings by Drucker, Heizer, and Squier (1959, pp. 128–33), since they were covered over soon after construction by platforms of adobe brick and clay, and two of them had been placed in deep pits. Two further "massive offerings" consist of numerous layers of serpentine blocks placed at the bottom of deep pits and later buried.

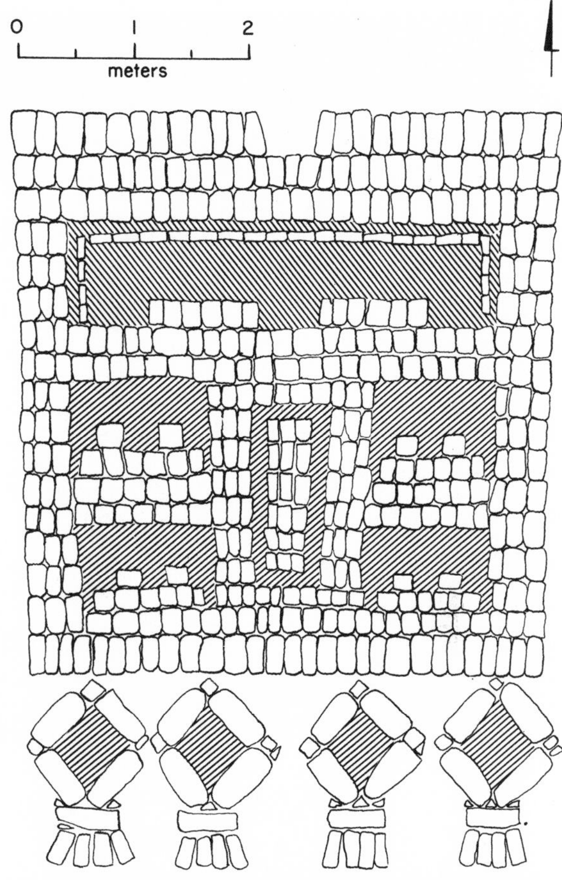

Fig. 5—MOSAIC PAVEMENT IN SOUTHWEST PLATFORM, LA VENTA. (From Drucker, Heizer, and Squier, 1959, fig. 29.)

Some 21 small dedicatory offerings have been discovered in the Central Group. An offering of this sort is generally a group of jade and serpentine celts laid in rows, although figurines of highly anthropomorphic were-jaguars may also be included. Offering 4 (fig. 6) consisted of six celts and 16 standing figures of jade and serpentine arranged in a sort of scene (Drucker, Heizer, and Squier, 1959, pp. 152–61). Other things placed in offerings are earspools, pendants in the shape of jaguar teeth (probably intended to dangle from the spools), bead necklaces, masklike pendants, and punches or awls, all made from jade; rock-crystal pendants (very rare); and concave mirrors of magnetite or ilmenite, drilled for suspension as pendants, and certainly worn as pectorals, on the evidence of Olmec figurines.

Human interments at La Venta are difficult to distinguish from offerings, owing to the poor state of bone preservation. Of the probable tombs, the one in Mound A-2 was the most spectacular (Drucker, 1952a, pp. 23–27), surrounded and roofed with

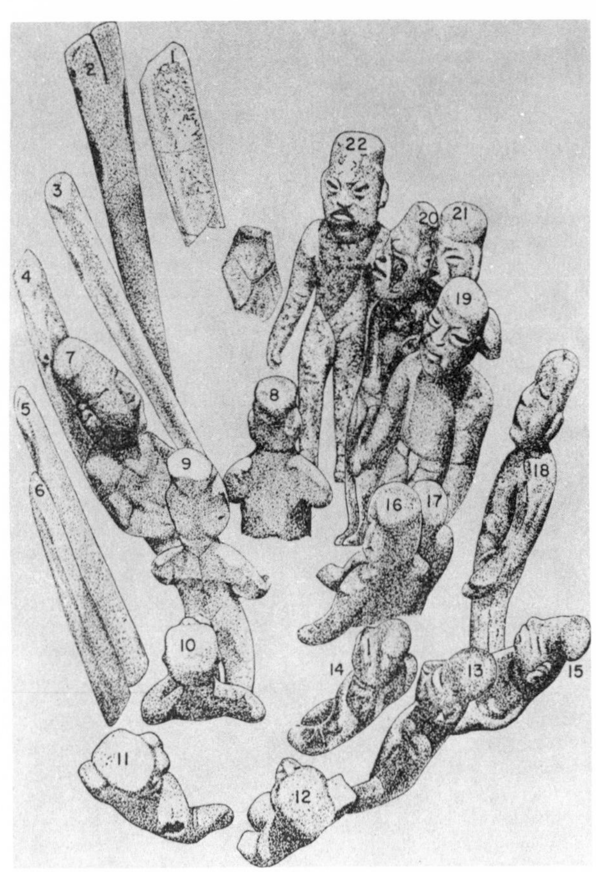

FIG. 6—OFFERING 4, LA VENTA, LOOKING SOUTH (From Drucker, Heizer, and Squier, 1959, fig. 38.)

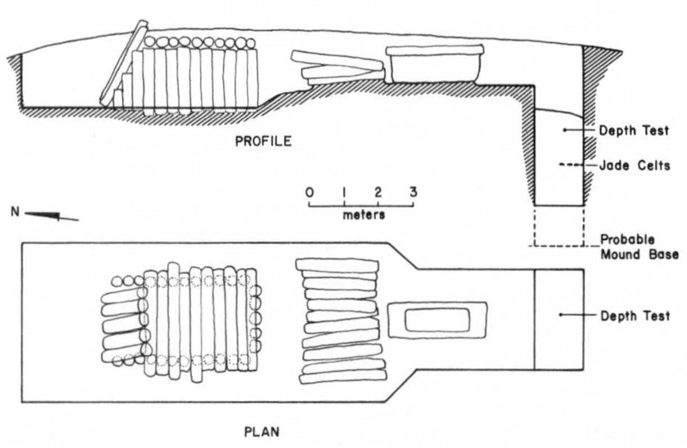

FIG. 7—ELEVATION AND PLAN OF TOMB AND SARCOPHAGUS IN MOUND A-2, LA VENTA. (Drucker, 1952a, fig. 9.)

pillars of columnar basalt and deliberately filled with clay (fig. 7). On a floor of limestone slabs were laid the bundled remains of two juveniles, heavily coated with cinnabar pigment and accompanied by figurines, beads, a pendant in the form of a clam shell, and a sting-ray spine, all of jade. To the south of the tomb in A-2 was a sandstone "sarcophagus" with tiger-mask relief and a cover, but, other than some jade objects on the bottom, nothing was found within but clay fill.

In terms of what is now known about Mesoamerican ceramic sequences, the pottery of La Venta (Drucker, 1952a, pp. 80–132) is Middle Preclassic (M. D. Coe, 1961, p. 125). The complex (fig. 8) as a whole is related to Tlatilco, Chiapa II, Mamom, and Conchas; nothing exactly comparable to the Early Preclassic phases of Chiapa I and Ocos has yet been published. The commonest vessel is a flat-bottomed dish with flaring sides and simple rims (fig. 8,*c*). Just under the rim on the interior or exterior, and encircling the vessel, are usually engraved or incised two parallel lines, the bottom of which may be turned up to meet the upper ("double-line break," a horizon-marker for the Middle Preclassic, see M. D. Coe, 1961, p. 133). This dish can also have a thick, beveled rim. Next in frequency are tecomates (fig. 8,*l*) of coarse brown ware, followed by dishes with slightly incurved sides in coarse red, black or fine paste ware. Other forms include deep bowls or vases, bottles with gadrooned bodies (fig. 8,*n*) very much like those from Tlatilco, and so-called "pot stands" (fig. 8,*o*), which are probably pottery seats. The few available supports are nubbin; loop and strap handles occur only on jars.

Decorative techniques (fig. 9) include plain rocker-stamping, zoned red painting, some crude painted lines in thick red or black (asphalt?) paint, simple incising of curvilinear parallel lines or opposing diagonals, and zoned punctation. True poly-

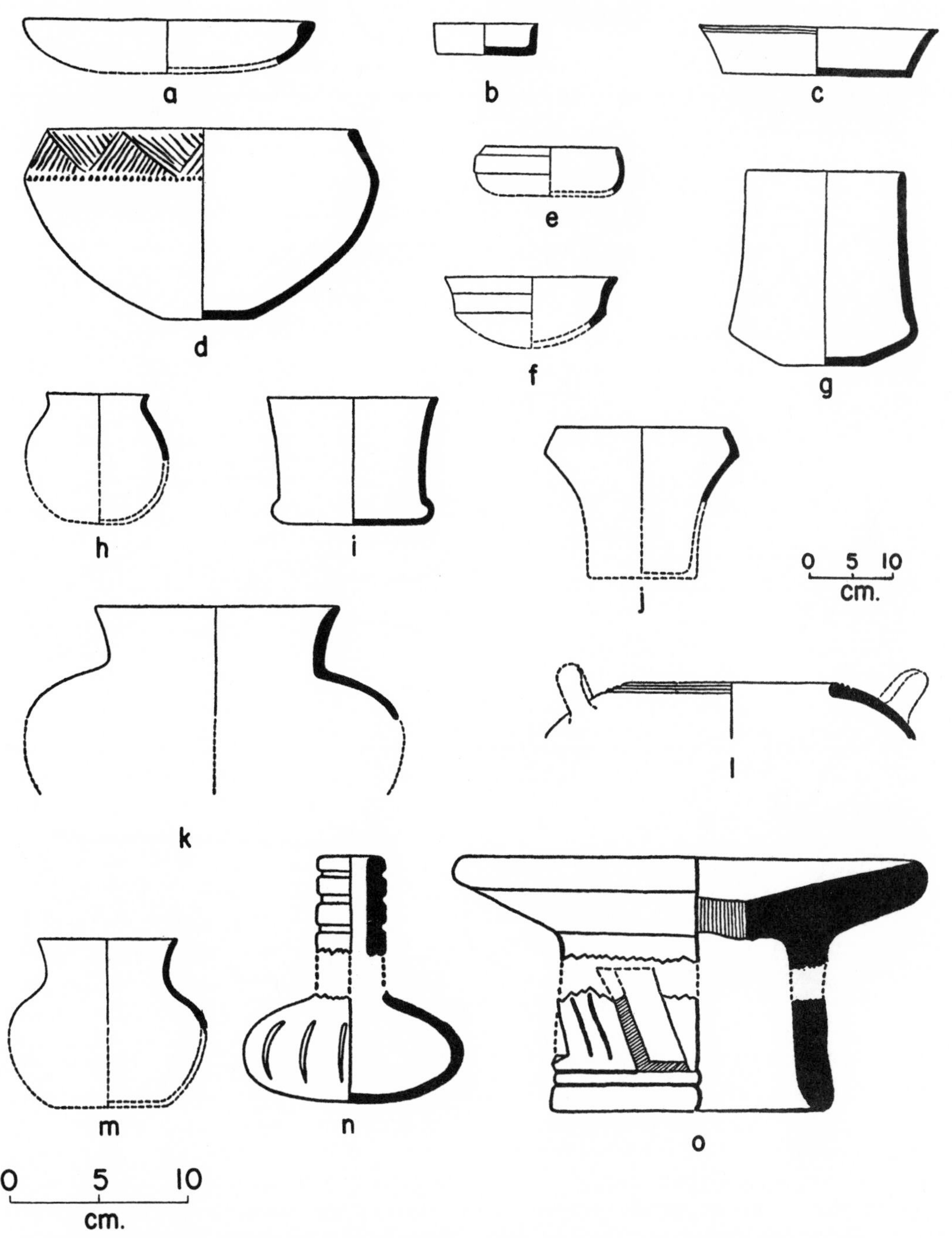

Fig. 8—ASSEMBLAGE OF VESSEL SHAPES FROM LA VENTA. A pottery seat is shown in *o*. Upper scale applies to *a–m*, lower to *n,o*. (From Drucker, 1952a, various figures.)

FIG. 9—DECORATIVE TECHNIQUES ON LA VENTA POTTERY. *a–c,* Plain rocker-stamping. *d–k,* Incision. *l–o,* Punctation. (From Drucker, 1952a, various figures.)

chrome painting is totally absent. The very important technique responsible for white-rimmed black ware is already present at La Venta: differential firing of rim and body, so that the rim is oxidized white. This technique is a tradition that persists in southern Veracruz – Tabasco through the Early Classic.

The ceramic complex at La Venta is quite different from anything known at Tres Zapotes, where rocker-stamping and the "double-line break" are apparently absent.

Clay figurines from the Central Group are small, solid, and handmade. Most represent plump but flat-chested human females, sometimes pregnant; these are generally nude, although a few wear simple pubic coverings. A handful of male figurines includes a bearded and helmeted type (Drucker, 1952a, pl. 28,*l*). The typical La Venta figurine face is quite round, the eyes and mouth indicated by horizontal slits and the pupils by a very small punctation. Some have larger punches for the pupils and closely resemble the typical figurine of the Conchas phase in Guatemala. None of the typical Tres Zapotes figurines occur here, nor do the other types from that site as defined by Drucker (1943b).

Other artifacts at La Venta are carved cylindrical stamps of clay; biconical clay objects with grooves around both axes (interpreted by Drucker, 1952a, p. 142, as weights for fishing gear or for looms, but which could be bolas weights); notched sherds (net weights?), reworked sherd disks, and sherd "abraders"; pumice abraders; prismatic blades and flakes of obsidian; legless metates and manos of basalt; hammerstones; and basketry or matting, probably close-twined, preserved as an impression on a sherd.

Four major building phases have been determined for Complex A of the Central Group, and seven radiocarbon dates on these have enabled Drucker, Heizer, and Squier (1959, pp. 264–67) to place the Olmec occupation of the site from about 800 to 400 B.C. The site was destroyed by unknown hands at the end of this occupation, 24 of the monuments being severely mutilated. The Central Group was abandoned, to be covered by drifting sands. New people came to the site and plundered it for stone and probably for jade; offerings were made, however, and continued to be placed even into colonial times (see Offering 23, a Spanish olive jar, Goggin, 1960, p. 17).

This great site is viewed by Drucker, Heizer, and Squier (1959, pp. 267–71) as a mighty cult center, the swamp island perhaps having been chosen for its very inaccessibility, like Mont-Saint-Michel in France. Since midden material is extremely scarce on the island, there probably was never a larger population than the elite staff needed to keep the place running, as well as the more humble persons who were the actual construction workers. La Venta could have been supported by food and labor supplied by a fairly large hinterland population farming the land between the Tonala and Coatzacoalcos Rivers. Its destruction could be equally well explained as the result of internal revolt as by outside conquest.

San Lorenzo Group

Another manifestation of the Olmec phase is the San Lorenzo group on the Coatzacoalcos River, which has previously been described. Although no report of Drucker's excavations there has been published, a collection of sherds made by Gareth W. Lowe from the bank of a ravine is pertinent (Lowe, personal information). The very top of the site has typically Late Classic pottery, especially thin, fine paste wares. However, the major deposits, which are very deep, are Preclassic and include white-rimmed black ware, rocker-stamping, and even cord-marking (known in Mesoamerica principally in the Early Preclassic Ocos phase, see M. D. Coe, 1961). The magnificent basalt Olmec monuments from San Lorenzo almost certainly belong with this ceramic complex.

Olmec Diffusion

Olmec-style sculptures, even very large ones, are not confined to the Northern Isthmian Plain. In fact, they are very widely distributed not only throughout the southern Veracruz – Tabasco area but as far away as El Salvador. I believe that a great Olmec diffusion, perhaps even a missionary movement, took place in the Middle Preclassic (see M. D. Coe, Article 29). To be explained, however, are the three

Olmec monuments at Tres Zapotes, for it is thought that the occupation of this site does not begin until the Late Preclassic. One of these is a relatively small sculpture (Monument M, in Stirling, 1943, pl. 11) that could have been easily transported from another site. The other two, however, are colossal heads (*ibid.*, pl. 4); either Tres Zapotes begins earlier than claimed in this paper, or else Olmec techniques of heavy transport persisted and these heads were brought in from elsewhere.

Problem of Olmec Origins

Olmec civilization appears at La Venta full-blown, with its art style in full development, its people already capable of creating great structures. Whence did it come? Where are its beginnings? La Venta is a small, sandy island, and it is hardly likely that the Olmec genesis is to be sought there, no matter how deep one digs. There is no other civilization of comparable age in Mesoamerica, so that the problem of the origin of civilized life here is important. Quite probably earlier manifestations of Olmec culture, or even its roots, will be found when the Northern Isthmian Plain is better known. San Lorenzo, for instance, has hardly been touched, and there must be many less spectacular sites awaiting excavation which might well have Early Preclassic levels containing, at least, partial answers to this question.

LATE PRECLASSIC PERIOD

Definition of the Late Preclassic in the southern Veracruz – Tabasco area is largely based on the material subsumed in Weiant's "Middle Tres Zapotes A" as well as on a good deal of the ceramics in his "general Ranchito collection" from that site (Weiant, 1943), together with the sub-ash deposit in Trench 26 labeled as "Lower Tres Zapotes" by Drucker (1943a, pp. 118–20). Strong continuities with the Middle Preclassic of the area are evident, but in general most resemblances lie with

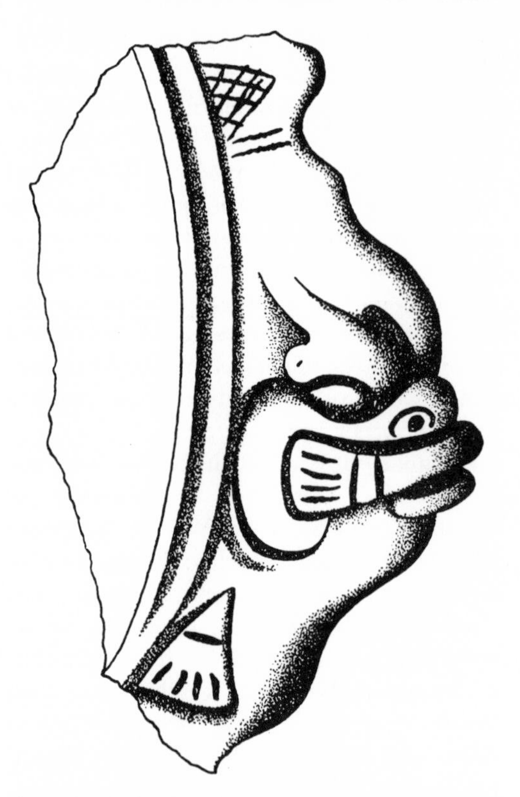

FIG. 10—MODELED RIM IN IZAPAN STYLE ON TRES ZAPOTES I BLACK WARE BOWL. (From Ducker, 1943a, fig. 33.)

other Late Preclassic phases of Mesoamerica, such as Chicanel of the lowland Maya area, Chiapa IV and V at Chiapa de Corzo, and terminal Preclassic manifestations in the Valley of Mexico. Olmec and other Middle Preclassic phenomena are either absent or very weak, such as rocker-stamping, the double-line break, and the tecomate, although some Olmecoid clay figurines are still being manufactured. In the place of the Olmec art style is a new one, Izapan, which has a wide representation at this time in southern Mesoamerica.

Tres Zapotes I

The site of Tres Zapotes in the Tuxtlas subarea has already been described. The ceramics here considered as Tres Zapotes I are generally monochrome, with some bichrome but no polychrome. White-rimmed black ware, showing a Middle Preclassic heritage, is present, in simple-silhouette bowls and flat-bottomed dishes; as in La Venta, there is a tan-rimmed variety. Black-slipped bowls with flat bases and flaring rims have simple engraving in parallel lines and arcs; in the same ware are bowls with wide-everted rims which often are modeled (see fig. 10 for a modeled rim in Izapan style). Black ware composite-silhouette bowls are simple incised. Very common are brown ware bowls with flat bases and wide-everted, grooved rims like those in the Chicanel phase of Peten Maya culture, incurved-side bowls with tapered-everted or short vertical rims, simple-neck jars, and composite-silhouette bowls and dishes, all in brown ware and often with simple engraved designs. Also not uncommon are necked ollas with striated bodies and a white slip on neck and shoulder. Somewhat rarer is white-slipped ware: flat-bottomed bowls with flaring sides, incurved bowls with short vertical rims, and composite-silhouette bowls. Very rare are flaring-sided bowls with white-slipped exterior and red interior, and a polished red-slipped ware. Jars with unsupported spouts are present, a trait which disappears from the Tres Zapotes record, only to crop up again in the Early Postclassic. In general, the various forms exhibited by this complex (wide-everted and grooved rims and composite-silhouette bowls), as well as the notable absences, leave little doubt as to the Late Preclassic affiliation of the phase (Wauchope, 1954, note 40).

Clay figurines are solid and handmade, as in La Venta. Practically all are female. The considerable variation in their style has been organized by Drucker (1943b, pp. 76–81) into five types. Types A to C are the most common in Tres Zapotes I and are quite uniform among themselves: heads with eyes formed by two punches to make an inverted V with a third punch for the pupil, punched mouths, and earspools; the

Fig. 11—FRAGMENTARY LONG COUNT DATE ON STELA C, TRES ZAPOTES. (Drawing by Avis Tulloch.)

female figurines are nude except for a pubic covering, and the males wear a loincloth. Figurines in such style have been found in very late Conchas deposits at La Victoria, Guatemala (M. D. Coe, 1961, fig. 55,*p*). Other styles are Type D (Weiant's "Morelos type"), vaguely Olmecoid with simple features and high, peaked headdresses; Type E, which is strongly Olmecoid and emphasizes modeled "baby faces"; and Type F, very rare, which is rather La Venta-like but diverges from the typical figurine type of that site.

Other artifacts include worked sherd discs, both perforated and unperforated, prismatic obsidian blades, and probably clay roller stamps.

The only architectural construction that can with confidence be ascribed to Tres Zapotes I is Mound G (Stirling, 1943, pp. 25–26, pl. 13,*b*; Weiant, 1943, Maps 9, 10), a rectangular platform of earth faced with cut stone, and fronted by stairs formed of flat sandstone slabs. No lime mortar was used in the construction.

Already mentioned are a number of stone monuments found at Tres Zapotes, three of them definitely Olmec. The majority of the carved monuments, however, are in the Izapan style, named for a type site near Tapachula, Chiapas. The hallmarks of this style are the baroque, cluttered scenes depicted and the presence of a long-lipped god derived from the Olmec were-jaguar (see M. D. Coe, Article 29). Recent work at Izapa has demonstrated that the style is a Late Formative phenomenon (Gareth W. Lowe, personal information), and there can be little doubt that at Tres Zapotes such monuments are to be ascribed to that period. Also to be assigned to Tres Zapotes I are Monument E, a bar-and-dot numeral carved into the living rock, in association with the sub-ash deposit in Trench 26 (Drucker, 1943b, p. 34), and the famous Stela C (fig. 11), with an epi-Olmec mask and a Long Count date which, if read in the Goodman-Martínez-Thompson correlation, would read 31 B.C., exactly within the period with which we are concerned.

La Mechuda

At this site, also in the same subarea, a brief excavation by Valenzuela (1945b) produced a number of typical Tres Zapotes I figurine heads in association with a deep bowl of polished gray ware with a pronounced rim flange, a good Late Preclassic trait (M. D. Coe, 1961, p. 133).

Cerro de las Mesas I

The deposits excavated in the deeper levels of Trench 42 at Cerro de las Mesas in the Mixtequilla are considerably different from other materials at the site, and probably represent a very light occupation during the Late Preclassic (Wauchope, 1950, p. 242). These include handmade, punctate figurines like the Tres Zapotes Type A (Drucker, 1943b, pl. 27,*a-j*), as well as Type D of that site (*ibid.*, pl. 27,*k,l*); these lack the asphalt paint used to touch up details on later Cerro de las Mesas figurines. Cerro de las Mesas I ceramics would include white-slipped open bowls with incised rims, white-rimmed black ware, black-slipped ware, red-on-brown ware, and red ware. It might well be that some of these persist into the Protoclassic (Cerro de las Mesas II).

PROTOCLASSIC PERIOD

A period transitional between the Preclassic and Early Classic of Mesoamerica, and as yet little understood, is the Protoclassic. Although in many respects its ceramics and figurines are a projection of the Preclassic past, developmentally it is already "Classic" (Wauchope, 1950, pp. 219–20). For instance, the tremendous Pyramid of the Sun at Teotihuacan is largely a product of the Protoclassic Teotihuacan II (R. E. Smith and F. Jacobs-Müller, personal information), and the evolved Building J at Monte Alban, with its advanced inscriptions, is also of this date. The apparently southern affiliations of the period, above all in ceramics, have long been noticed: this is the famous Q-complex of Vaillant and Lothrop, with its pottery traits being swollen, mammiform supports, bridged spouts, spool-shaped pot stands, and lavish use of polychromed stucco. This complex is very well represented in the more luxurious tombs of the period in Mesoamerica (see the tombs of Chiapa VI—the Horcones phase—at Chiapa de Corzo, Lowe, 1962), but is hardly to be found in the refuse deposits of more humble persons. The foregoing situation is very much that seen in our area.

Cerro de las Mesas II

The Protoclassic is strongly represented at this Mixtequilla site, especially in the mound cut by Trench 30 (fig. 12), which is entirely of this period. The mound is 2.5 m. high and has two phases of con-

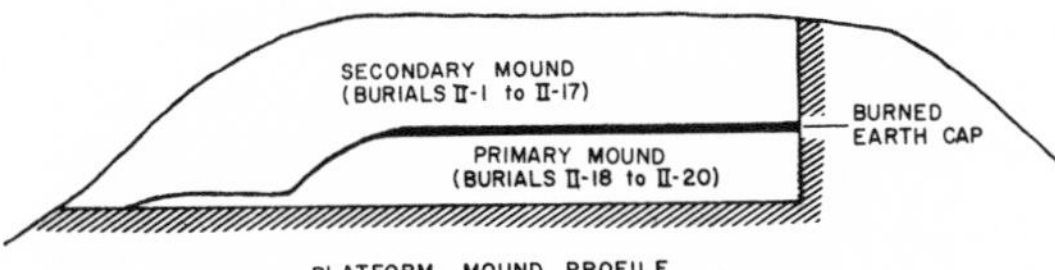

FIG. 12—TRENCH 30, PROFILE OF NORTH WALL, CERRO DE LAS MESAS. (From Drucker, 1943b, fig. 2.)

struction, both of which contain a number of burials. Within the lower, primary mound, which was covered with a floor of baked clay, was the burial (II-18) of a great personage (Stirling, 1941, pp. 282-86; Drucker, 1943a, pp. 8–9; Covarrubias, 1947, pp. 104–05). The body was tightly flexed and laid on its side in the center of the mound; the skull was separated and placed face down on a large marine shell filled with red pigment. The skull showed extreme fronto-occipital flattening; the incisors and canine teeth were inlaid with circular pieces of pyrite. Offerings near the head included a large pearl, jade beads, jade tubes, ornaments of pelecypod shell and tinklers of some gastropod, shell beads, and a magnificent turtle shell engraved with a head in profile surrounded by two Izapan-style serpents (fig. 13). By the knees of this person were 11 pottery vessels of typical Protoclassic shape and decoration; north of his head was a polished stone yoke, beside which lay an Olmec-style seated pottery figurine (apparently an heirloom) holding another figure in its lap. Associated with the burial and contained in the overlying mound were other interments, but especially notable is the placing of sawed-off facial skeletons inside pots; five of these were found in the secondary mantle. Almost all other Cerro de las Mesas II burials are flexed, with the same kind of skull deformation; cinnabar pigment is lavishly used; and the deceased is usually accompanied by a river clamshell over or near the mouth and by jade ornaments.

The pottery vessels found with the above-mentioned burials can be compared with other pieces from the same site and a complex defined (fig. 14). This would include spool-shaped pot stands, stuccoed and painted in rose, green, red, blue, yellow, and black; vases with bulbous, flattened bases, slightly gadrooned, with vertical walls, slipped either brown monochrome or red-on-brown; black ware jars with tall spouts joined by a bridge to the neck; tall, slender-necked vases, carved in curvilinear designs and also with bridged spouts; polished black vessels—vases on tall, annular bases and cylinders—engraved with complex geometric designs emphasizing hachured triangles, opposed areas of parallel lines, and crisscrossed squares; and simple-silhouette as well as composite-silhouette bowls in brown ware. Probably white-rimmed black and negative-painted wares (Drucker, 1943a, figs. 139–40) belong here as well. The complex as a whole is closely related to the patently Protoclassic Lower Remojadas phase of central Veracruz (Medellín Zenil, 1960a,

FIG. 13—DESIGN ENGRAVED ON TURTLE CARAPACE, BURIAL II-18, CERRO DE LAS MESAS II PHASE. (From Covarrubias, 1947, figure on p. 105.)

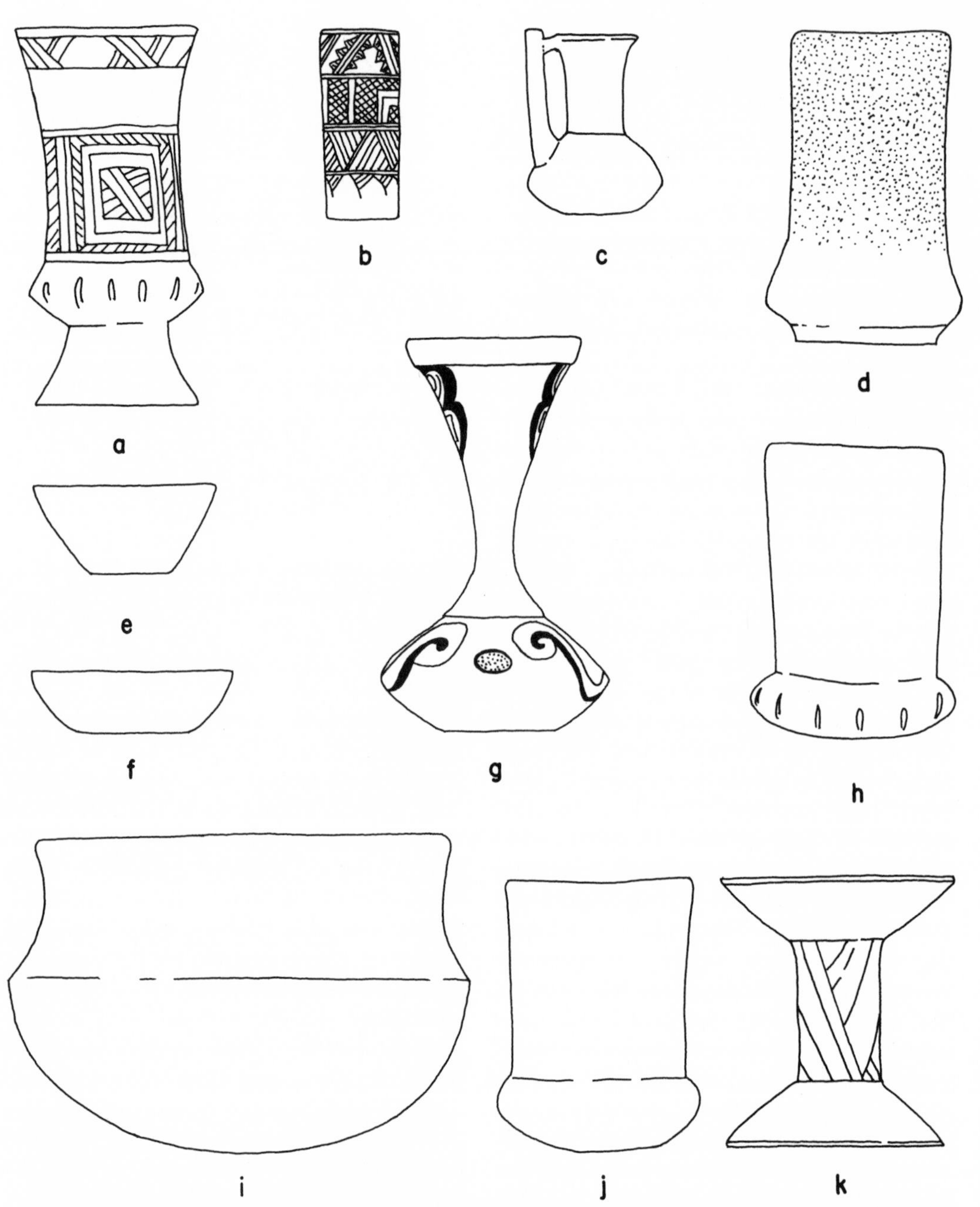

FIG. 14—CERAMIC ASSEMBLAGE OF THE CERRO DE LAS MESAS II PHASE. *a–c,* Black ware. *d,* Red-on-brown. *e,f,* Brown. *j,k,* Stuccoed ware (*k* is a pot rest). Height of *g,* 22.2 cm., others to scale. (Based on various plates in Drucker, 1943b.)

pp. 7–51), which also has a wide range of vessels with bridged spouts.

If this correlation with central Veracruz is correct, then it is likely that the crudely handmade figurines (fig. 15) usually touched up with asphalt paint, found in such abundance at Cerro de las Mesas (Drucker's Types G and H), are likewise Protoclassic, for they are very similar to those of Lower Remojadas.

The affiliations of Cerro de las Mesas II are with other Protoclassic phases of Mesoamerica, especially with those of the south: Holmul I, Matzanel, Chiapa VI, and Monte Alban II. The most interesting aspect of the phase is the evidence for the stone yoke, already present at this date. Although it has not yet developed into its final form, the roots of the well-known central Veracruz yoke-*palma-hacha* complex extend back to an early period. It might also be that some of the carved stelae and other monuments of Cerro de las Mesas are to be placed in the second phase of the site; this is a possibility, but the two stelae with Long Count dates, if the GMT correlation is valid, are certainly later.

Other Sites of the Mixtequilla

The site of Los Cerros also is said to have a deep deposit closely related to Lower Remojadas (Medellín Zenil, 1960a, pp. 191–94), with the same kind of incised pottery motifs filled with cinnabar pigment that were found in that central Veracruz site.

In the lower ceramic levels of the Cerro de las Conchas at Alvarado, there was a predominance of white-rimmed black ware, polished white ware, and what the excavator (Medellín Zenil, 1960a, pp. 189–90) identifies as Lower Remojadas types. It may well be that some of this material must be considered Protoclassic.

In the undisturbed fill of a substructure within a looted mound at Nopiloa, Medellín Zenil (1960b) uncovered a secondary burial of extraordinary richness, with 140

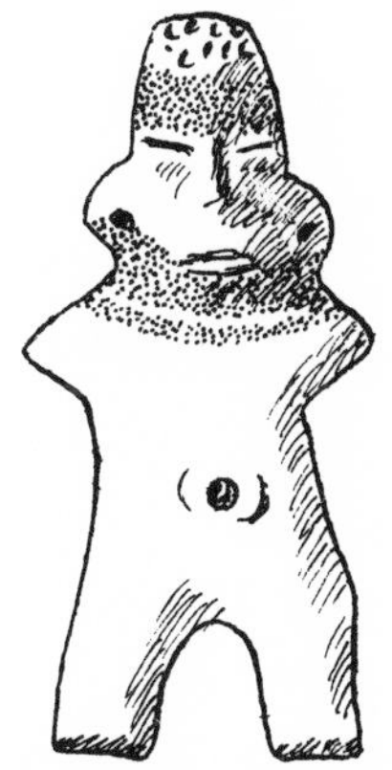

Fig. 15—CLAY FIGURINE, PAINTED WITH ASPHALT, PROBABLY OF THE CERRO DE LAS MESAS II PHASE. Height 12.5 cm. (Drawn from Drucker, 1943b, pl. 52.)

Fig. 16—POTTERY FIGURINE OF STANDING FEMALE, NOPILOA I PHASE. (From Medellín Zenil, 1960b, foto 8.)

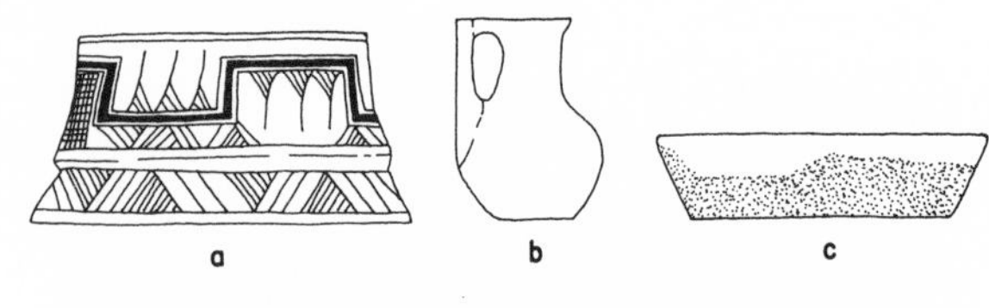

FIG. 17—REPRESENTATIVE POTTERY OF THE TRES ZAPOTES II PHASE. *a*, Incised black ware bowl. *b*, Black ware vessel with supported spout. *c*, White-rimmed black ware bowl. Not to scale. (Drawn from Drucker, 1943b, pl. 20,*d*; Weiant, 1943, figs. 8,*b*; 11,*d*.)

objects as offerings. These included a tripod vessel of typically Teotihuacan II form, filled with a mixture of earth and asphalt, containing jade beads, a shell ring, and six anthropomorphic stone figures (a serpentine figurine of very Teotihuacan II appearance with incrusted shell teeth, an alabaster mask also Teotihuacanoid, a nude female figurine of bone, a seated jade figurine of obvious Olmec manufacture, and a small stone representation of a hunchback). Another vessel was a small, globular olla with a spout. Also associated were 10 clay whistle figurines of large size (fig. 16), marking the beginning of a long tradition in the Mixtequilla and in central Veracruz; the eyes of these anthropomorphic figures, most of which are female, sometimes have button-appliqué pupils painted with asphalt, resembling in many details figurines of Lower Remojadas and foreshadowing Early Classic production in Veracruz. The entire find should be ascribed, therefore, to the Protoclassic.

Tres Zapotes II

Based on comparisons with the well-established pottery associations at Cerro de las Mesas, there was a fairly important Protoclassic occupation of Tres Zapotes (Wauchope, 1950, p. 242); these conclusions are also based on the cache in Trench 4 (Drucker, 1943b, p. 17), Burial R-2 (Weiant, 1943), and certain typological considerations. Apparently the deep urn burials of the 1939 excavations belong in this period, as well as certain small earthen mounds like that cut by Trench 4.

The ceramics of Tres Zapotes II (fig. 17) are very much like those of Cerro de las Mesas II. Shared are the identical black ware with complex geometrical engraving and complicated profile, necked jars with supported spouts, and white-rimmed black ware. Also present are the beginnings of polychrome painting, in bold, geometric designs on a cylindrical vase, as well as multiple-brush painting in positive, wavy patterns on an open bowl with tripod nubbin feet. Probably also to be associated are orange ware bowls with large, mammiform supports; brown ware flat-bottomed bowls with wedge-shaped, hollow tripod supports and complex engraving; and, as a holdover from Tres Zapotes I, composite-silhouette bowls with simple incising.

EARLY CLASSIC PERIOD

Diffusion of the Teotihuacan Pattern

The tremendous city of Teotihuacan, in a pocket-like valley to the northeast of the Valley of Mexico, had a profound influence on the rest of Mesoamerica during the Early Classic period. The well-known site of Kaminaljuyu, on the outskirts of Guatemala City, was during its Esperanza phase apparently a cultural satellite of Teotihuacan, perhaps even a conquest state (Kidder, Jennings, and Shook, 1946, pp. 254–55). Much weaker influences, but still discernible, are to be seen in other important areas of Mesoamerica, such as Puebla, Oaxaca, Guerrero, and the Peten. Nevertheless, it is usually supposed that a culture so Teotihuacanoid as Esperanza is not to be found elsewhere. That the southern Veracruz-Tabasco area had an occupation as provincially Teotihuacan as that at Kaminaljuyu is generally not realized. The mysterious migration route of Early Classic culture from the Valley of Mexico into highland and lowland Guatemala may well have traversed our area.

This Teotihuacanoid diffusion, or horizon (Lathrap, 1957, pp. 59–61, has termed it the "X-T" horizon after the Xolalpan-Tlamimilolpa complexes of Teotihuacan III), comprises the following traits: (1) the cylindrical tripod with slab or hollow-rounded legs, (2) the *florero*-shaped vase, (3) Thin Orange ware, (4) *candeleros,* one- or two-holed clay objects perhaps used for containing blood-spattered paper, (5) in some cases, Teotihuacan III-style (and "Teotihuacan IV") moldmade figurines, (6) hollow effigy heads on bowl rims, (7) Teotihuacan painting style, and (8) an architectural style featuring *talud-tablero* construction, the tableros being supported by a layer of thin stone slabs. Most of these are present in certain sites which are to be considered below.

Added to this, as will be seen, are certain local traditions and developments which give the southern Veracruz – Tabasco area its distinctive regional flavor, but the Teotihuacanoid element is omnipresent.

Fig. 18—JADE PLAQUE WITH LIGHTLY ENGRAVED DESIGN, FROM CACHE IN TRENCH 34, CERRO DE LAS MESAS III PHASE. (From Drucker, 1955, fig. 3.)

Cerro de las Mesas III

The Early Classic period probably marks the major occupation of the Cerro de las Mesas site, following which it is abandoned until the Late Postclassic. During this time, the Central Group reached its present form, and a number of stone monuments were carved and set. Three major elements may be discerned in Cerro de las Mesas III: (1) a sculptural style which is strongly traditional, with traits derived from an Olmec and Izapan past, (2) a pottery complex under Classic Teotihuacan influence, and (3) a large pottery figure complex which represents a local development.

The associations on which the definition of this period is based are principally found in the large mound of the Central Group cut by Trench 34, lying just east of the monument plaza (Drucker, 1943a, pp. 11–14). This mound had gone through extensive rebuilding, with the superimposi-

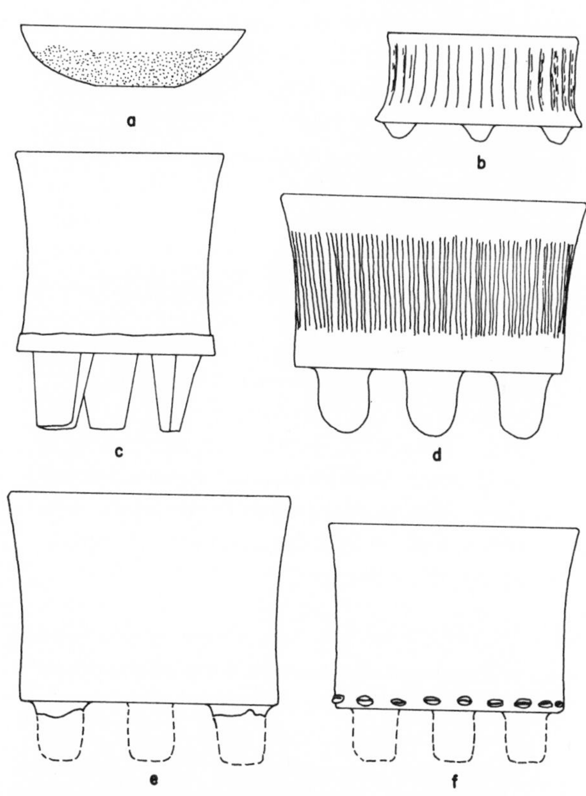

Fig. 19—CERAMIC ASSEMBLAGE OF THE CERRO DE LAS MESAS III PHASE. *a,* White-rimmed black ware; others, brown ware. Height of *d,* 20 cm.; all except *c* to scale. (Drawn from various plates in Drucker, 1943b.)

Fig. 20—LARGE CLAY FIGURE OF THE FIRE GOD FROM TRENCH 34, CERRO DE LAS MESAS III PHASE. (From Covarrubias, 1957, pl. 38, right.)

tion of floors of burned clay or stucco, as well as stucco-faced stairs. On the basis of close resemblances of the associated pottery to that of Teotihuacan III, all the offerings, caches, and the mound itself are to be assigned to the Early Classic period. These include the famous cache found at the front of the mound (Drucker, 1955), consisting of about 800 objects of jade, serpentine, calcite, and other materials. A number of the pieces in the cache are clearly Olmec heirlooms: two were-jaguar figurines (*ibid.*, pls. 27, 28), an incised, canoe-shaped plaque (pl. 38), "stilettoes" (pl. 50), and perhaps other objects. Many of the other pieces in this great find are probably Early Classic, but undoubtedly from far-flung centers of manufacture, such as a plaque with an incised Maya profile resembling that on the Leyden Plate (fig. 18). The many earspools associated are in the shape of squared circles, an Early Classic trait which subsequently died out.

The whole vessels from Trench 24 (fig. 19) are principally tripod cylinders of highly Teotihuacanoid appearance, either in brown or red-on-brown ware. The walls are slightly concave, and the supports may be cylindrical, bulbous, or hollow-slab, the latter with L- or T-shaped openings. One also notes the presence of fluting or zoned striation on the exterior, and the use of coffee-bean appliqué around the base. Also associated with these vessels in the same trench are white-rimmed black ware bowls (fig. 19,*a*) and bowls in red ware.

On the top of a stair in a buried structure cut by Trench 34 was discovered a large hollow clay figure of the fire god (fig. 20) in the form of a flabby old man with sunken chest, satanic goatee, and peculiarly wrinkled face, carrying on his head a bowl embellished with kan crosses. Elsewhere in the same trench were found similar large figures, and there is no doubt that huge clay sculptures of this type (Drucker's "Monumental Ware") as well as the extremely similar modeled figurines called "Lirios" are of the Early Classic period, both here and at other sites in the area.

What the usual kind of smaller figurine was is not clear. At this time in the Maya area, figurines were absent, and none may have been produced at Cerro de las Mesas. Two characteristically Classic Teotihuacan, clay, moldmade heads, however, were found at the site (Drucker, 1943a, pl. 49,*c-d*).

There is a good deal of sculpture at Cerro de las Mesas, most, if not all, Early Classic. An hacha is said to have been found in Trench 24; the only example illustrated in the report (Drucker, 1943a, pl. 58, not identified as to provenience)

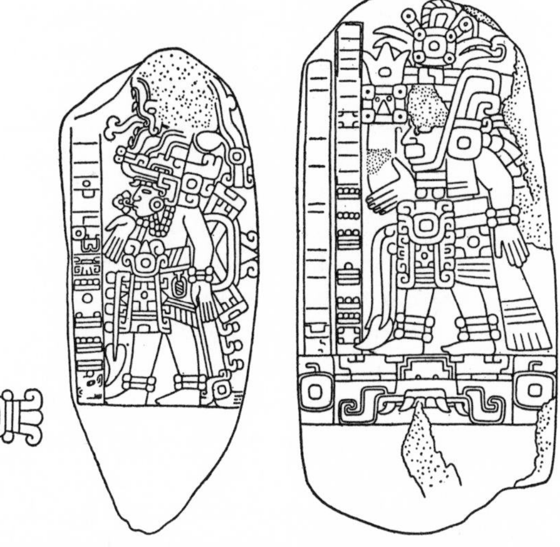

FIG. 21—STELAE OF THE CERRO DE LAS MESAS III PHASE. *a*, Stela 6. *b*, Stela 8. (From Stirling, 1943, fig. 11,*b*,*c*.)

FIG. 22—MONUMENT 5, CERRO DE LAS MESAS. (From Stirling, 1943, fig. 14,*b*.)

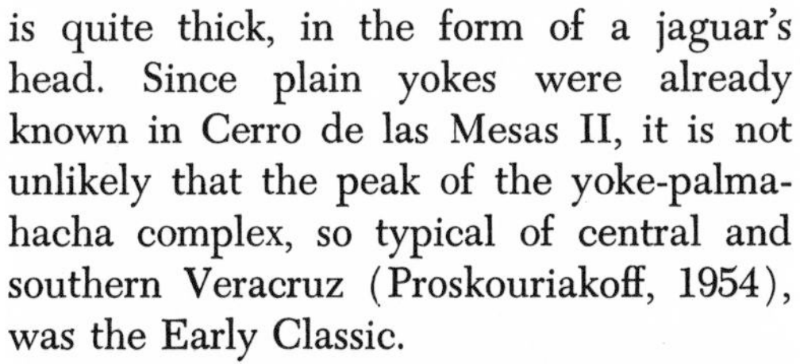

is quite thick, in the form of a jaguar's head. Since plain yokes were already known in Cerro de las Mesas II, it is not unlikely that the peak of the yoke-palma-hacha complex, so typical of central and southern Veracruz (Proskouriakoff, 1954), was the Early Classic.

Two of the 14 known stelae have Long Count dates: Stela 6 (fig. 21,*a*), with 9.1.12.14.10 (A.D. 468) and Stela 8 (fig. 21,*b*), with 9.4.18.16.8 (A.D. 533) (Stirling, 1943, fig. 11), falling within the A.D. 300–600 span of the period. The style of all the stelae is very archaistic and quite Izapan, with figures stiffly posed to the left; the elaborate headdresses sometimes have glyphic elements like ahau or the "precious" element; a few personages wear sandals and one carries an incense bag; and earspools are generally squared circles, like those in the jade cache. The were-jaguar masks worn by two personages over their faces are highly Olmecoid. There is not enough stylistic difference between any of the stelae to consider them products of another cultural phase. However, Monument 5 (fig. 22) is really aberrant—a crude, phallic, duck-billed figure like the Tuxtla Statuette—and may be considerably earlier than the others.

It should also be noted that on these monuments are many unreadable glyphs which are noncalendrical, and writing was probably well advanced during Cerro de las Mesas III.

Alvarado II

A few tantalizing scraps of information are provided by Medellín Zenil on the upper levels of Pit 1 and on the whole of Pit 2 at the site of Cerro de las Conchas. Here we are told that some ceramic types are Upper Remojadas; others (Medellín Zenil, 1960a, p. 190) are said to be imports from Classic Teotihuacan. Without more detailed data, it is impossible to segregate what might be a Late Classic occupation of this strategic location at the mouth of the Laguna de Alvarado, for two smiling figures of definitely late type are illustrated (*ibid.*, figs. 42, 50).

Tres Zapotes III

The Early Classic period at Tres Zapotes was probably never very important, but it was closely related to that of Cerro de las

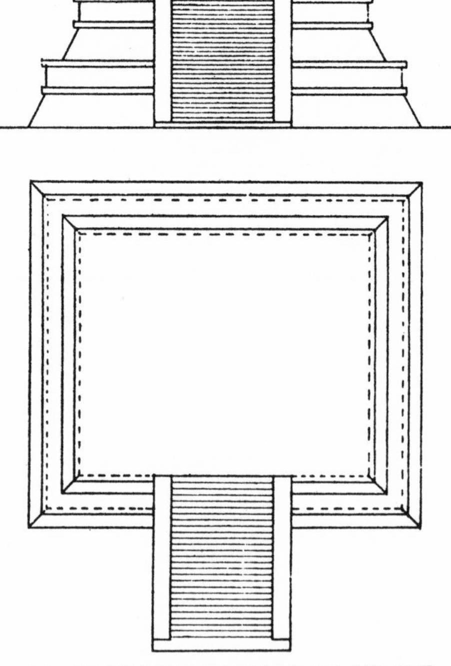

FIG. 23—ELEVATION AND PLAN OF STR. 2, MATACAPAN. Height 6.8 m. (From Valenzuela, 1945a, Map II.)

Mesas, and it was highly Teotihuacanoid. Unfortunately, there are no caches or offerings which contain such material, so that the following inventory is basically typological. Those traits which can be so segregated include slab-footed, tripod cylinders in black or orange monochrome, with T-shaped perforations made in the feet; hollow effigy heads from bowl rims, especially Xipe heads; *floreros* (Weiant, 1943, pp. 10–11); stick-polishing of vessels; two-holed *candeleros*; and possibly incensarios with vertical molded flanges (Drucker, 1943b, pls. 25,*g-i*; 64). The Teotihuacan "Fat God" (Weiant, 1943, pl. 41, no. 7) appears, as do jointed figurines (*ibid.*, pl. 61), but these two traits are known to continue well into Late Classic times both here and in Campeche.

As noted for Cerro de las Mesas, this probably also marks the beginning, perhaps the apogee, of the large, modeled, grotesque clay figurines of the Lirios type: wrinkled old men like that at Cerro de las Mesas (the spider-webby appearance of the wrinkles is identical at both sites), men with open mouths, bageyed and bearded men. All are hollow, usually with large, hollow irises. It is likely that in some cases molds were used for the faces, although modeling is the major technique. The completely moldmade figurines that are said to be of the San Marcos (Late Classic) type found in association with these (Drucker, 1943b, pl. 61,*f*) are, rather, Teotihuacanoid. As will be seen, the later San Marcos productions are Mayoid. The early smiling figures known at Remojadas and at Cerro de las Mesas are apparently absent.

Matacapan I

Nowhere on the Gulf coast is Teotihuacan influence so apparent as at this site in the Tuxtla mountains. The one structure that was completely cleared is in the purest Teotihuacan style (fig. 23), with two bodies or tiers in talud-tablero construction, the tableros resting on thin stone layers. This temple platform is faced with rude stones coated with red-painted clay, and has a front stairway flanked by balustrades (Valenzuela, 1945a, pp. 94–96). Teotihuacanoid artifacts came from the overlying debris on this structure as well as from pits cut down into two other mounds at the site: cylindrical vases with pierced, hollow, slab legs, bowls on low ring bases (Thin Orange?), one- and two-holed candeleros, sherds with Teotihuacanoid glyphs (including the Teotihuacan year sign and what may be *Ojo de Reptil*), an eyed bone needle, and Classic Teotihuacan figurine heads. The local ceramic tradition seems to be represented by red-on-cream (or -orange) bowls with simple, Teotihuacanoid glyphic designs (*ibid.*, pl. 3).

If this site is ever investigated with the thoroughness bestowed on the mounds near the Roosevelt Hospital at Kaminaljuyu, it seems highly probable that evidence would indicate Matacapan as an important way station on the road that the Teotihuacanos took to the highland Maya area.

Late Classic Period

With the disappearance of Teotihuacan influence over Mesoamerica at the close of the Early Classic, entirely new cultural alignments on a more regional basis can be discerned. One of these alignments takes in most of the Gulf coast between central Veracruz and western Campeche. This new "macrostyle" is highly Mayoid, under the cultural shadow of Late Classic Maya culture in Yucatan. Its salient traits are: (1) fine-paste figurines completely moldmade and often polychromed in blue, white, and other colors, with many Maya iconographic features, (2) fine-paste polychrome pottery, and (3) clay flutes, ocarinas, Panpipes, and other musical instruments. It is true that there are within this macrostyle definite local variations, such as the developed smiling-figure complex of the Mixtequilla and central Veracruz, but the entire coast is in great contrast to the rest of Mesoamerica at this time.

Mixtequilla Sites

While Cerro de las Mesas continues abandoned throughout the Late Classic, other sites of the Mixtequilla reach great importance, such as Nopiloa, Los Cerros, and Dicha Tuerta. Typical of this period in the Mixtequilla are the smiling figures of clay (fig. 24). These evolved from the Early Classic pottery figures of Upper Remojadas I of central Veracruz (Medellín Zenil, 1960a, p. 77), which are hand-modeled, hollow whistles depicting smiling individuals, often with a sort of mask over the lower face and with filed teeth, details of the features being touched up with asphalt paint. The Late Classic type is usually a standing figure of either a boy or a girl with outstretched arms, largely moldmade with extra details added by hand (as in Classic Maya figurines from

FIG. 24—"SMILING FIGURE," LATE CLASSIC PERIOD, FROM CENTRAL OR SOUTHERN VERACRUZ. (From Groth-Kimball, 1953, pl. 63.)

Jaina, Campeche). The extraordinary expression displayed by these figures borders on the idiotic: a wide, foolish grin revealing filed teeth. Strong fronto-occipital head deformation is exhibited, and a kind of flattened pillbox hat with molded relief decoration is worn. The girls are attired in skirts and have simple bandlike brassières; the boys either are nude or wear the breechcloth. On rare occasions, the smaller figurines have jointed limbs. The use of as-

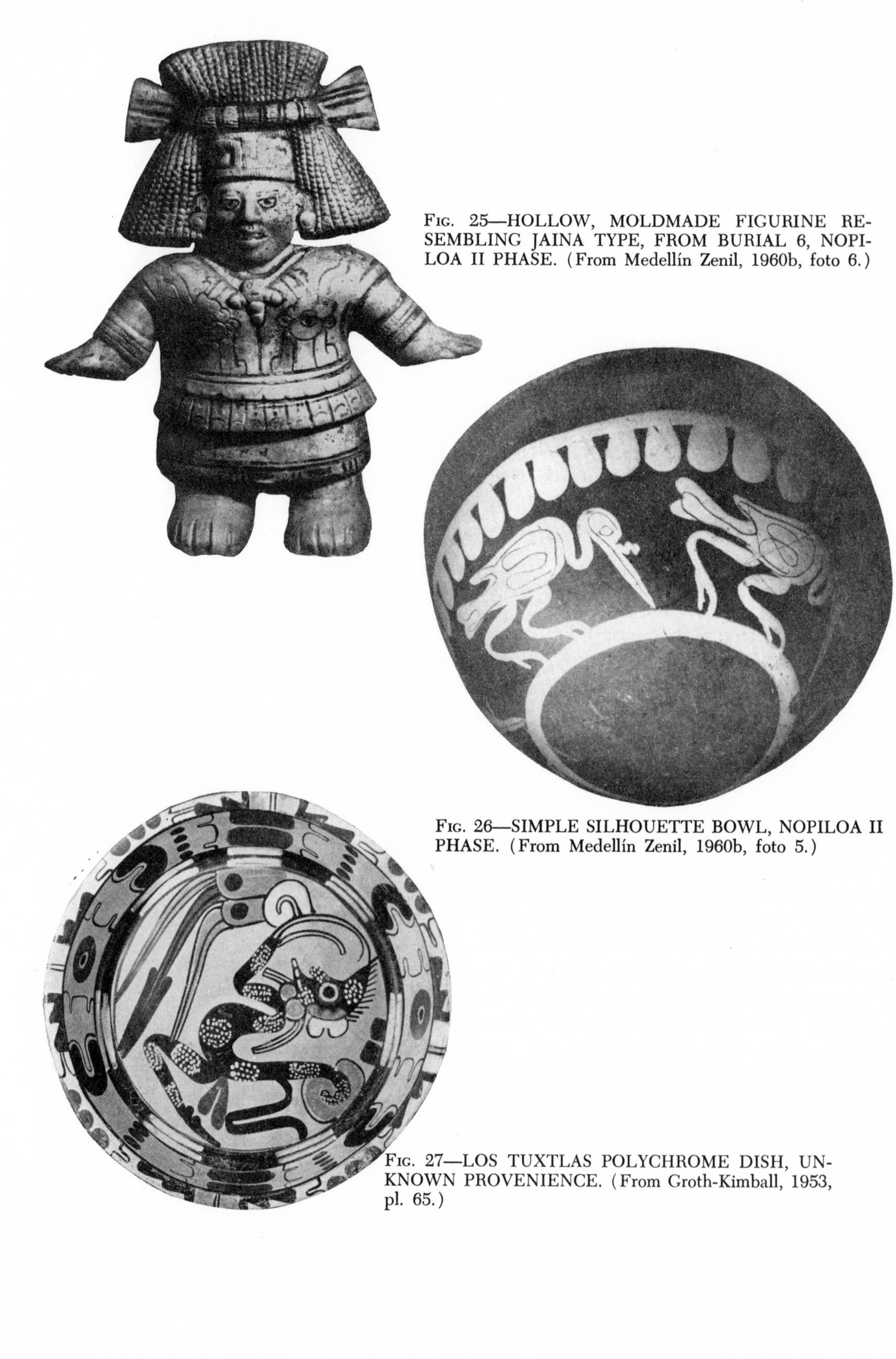

Fig. 25—HOLLOW, MOLDMADE FIGURINE RESEMBLING JAINA TYPE, FROM BURIAL 6, NOPILOA II PHASE. (From Medellín Zenil, 1960b, foto 6.)

Fig. 26—SIMPLE SILHOUETTE BOWL, NOPILOA II PHASE. (From Medellín Zenil, 1960b, foto 5.)

Fig. 27—LOS TUXTLAS POLYCHROME DISH, UNKNOWN PROVENIENCE. (From Groth-Kimball, 1953, pl. 65.)

phalt is absent, but postfire polychroming present. In general, close relationships can be seen with Maya figurine styles of the Late Classic.

Two further figurine styles of this period in the Mixtequilla are almost indistinguishable from certain Jaina types. The first is a completely moldmade female personage (Medellín Zenil, 1960, pl. 55), dressed in a skirt and pullover huipil with a large and elaborate hairdo; she often carries a child *hetzmek* fashion. Figurines of this type have a cream slip and postfired painting, in colors which include "Maya blue." In the second type, only the face is moldmade, the rest of the body and its dress being hand-modeled, and immediately calls to mind the famous portrait-figurines of Jaina (fig. 25).

The upper levels of Trench I at Los Cerros (Medellín Zenil, 1960a, pp. 191–94) contained a number of secondary burials with abundant pottery offerings of Late Classic type, including smiling figures and Jaina-like figurines.

Within the midden area of Nopiloa (Medellín Zenil, 1960b) were discovered nine secondary burials, of which eight were contained within pairs of large funerary urns, the bottom vessel being covered by its inverted counterpart; these urns are composite-silhouette with slightly convex bases and are slipped red. The bones had been covered with cinnabar, and two individuals had had their teeth painted with asphalt. Again, Jaina-like and smiling figurines were encountered (fig. 25). The pottery vessels used as offerings are almost all of a fine-paste, orange-red ware; two are simple-silhouette bowls (fig. 26) with beautiful designs, apparently carried out in negative technique; several others are said to resemble Z Fine Orange of Uxmal and Y Fine Orange of Uaxactun.

A further Mixtequilla site briefly reported (Medellín Zenil, 1960a, pp. 194–95) is Dicha Tuerta, where investigations in an ancient pottery dump produced smiling figures, rattle and whistle figurines of Maya type, and various ceramic types said to be characteristic of central Veracruz during the Late Classic.

Tres Zapotes IV

Tres Zapotes also shared in this pan-coastal, Late Classic macrostyle, but, of course, with certain local traditions present as well. This phase at the site, which apparently marks an intensive occupation, has been formulated on the basis of a great cache of pottery vessels and figurines in Trench 23 (Drucker, 1943a, p. 29) and on typological considerations.

Polychrome ceramics reach the peak of their popularity in Tres Zapotes IV. Definitely of the period are flat-bottomed dishes with flaring sides, and with designs in red and black over an orange slip; the figures represented look like very crude long-billed birds, but there also may be serpents with hairlike feathers sprouting from the heads. This type is found elsewhere at sites in the Tuxtlas subarea. Another distinctive kind of decorated pottery is Los Tuxtlas Polychrome (fig. 27), but its placement within the Late Classic is not so certain as that of the above: this is a cream-slipped, flat-bottomed dish with low walls and projecting rims, and with bold, naturalistic interior painting in black, red, yellow, and white. A frequent design element on Los Tuxtlas Polychrome consists of a fattened U turned on its side and facing the other member of its pair, both with the open ends toward each other. Also present are various fine-paste, thin-walled, polychrome bowls with cascabel feet.

Monochrome pottery is still abundant, however, as seen in the large number of flat-bottomed bowls with outflaring rims recovered from the Trench 23 cache, as well as gray-slipped, hemispherical bowls with three small, solid ball-feet. It is possible that Tepeu 3–like carved ware (Drucker, 1943b, pl. 22) also is Late Classic; some of the illustrated sherds look moldmade.

Whether or not Lirios-style figures were still being manufactured is doubtful, but certainly the moldmade figurines of San Marcos type were now dominant (Drucker, 1943a, pl. 48). These are the same sort of whistle or rattle figurines that we have already encountered in the Mixtequilla: fine-paste, with a white slip and often postfire polychroming, and highly Mayoid. They include ballplayers, with protective gloves and belt; Amazon-like females wearing warriors' eagle headdresses; standing and seated females with Mayoid headdresses and garb; and standing individuals closely resembling the portrait-like figurines of Jaina and Jonuta in the Maya area. A number of dog effigies with the feet joined to axles were found in Trench 23; this unusual trait of wheeled toys, the only use of the wheel principle in pre-Columbian America, apparently first appears in Upper Remojadas I of central Veracruz, an Early Classic phase (example in American Museum of Natural History). Also present are small smiling figures of very poor type—we are here on the southern limit of this trait.

Other artifacts can be assigned to this phase with less confidence. These include flutes, Panpipes, and whistles of clay, and perhaps moldmade spindle whorls and flat clay stamps. The common metate seems to have been a type with two nubbin feet and bar support.

Neither at this site nor anywhere else in the southern Veracruz – Tabasco area are there stone monuments of the Late Classic period. Whether or not there are smaller sculptures in the Tres Zapotes IV phase is unknown. A cache of plain open and carved closed yokes was unearthed in Mound F of the Ranchito Group (Weiant, 1943, pl. 66, 67), which also contained a deposit of Late Classic smiling figures, but there seems to be a possibility that the yokes came from a deeper level than the latter. Because of the wide divergence between style motifs displayed on the relief carvings of the yoke-palma-hacha complex and those on the Late Classic moldmade figurines of Veracruz (Proskouriakoff, 1962c), a time difference between the two would seem likely; perhaps the complex belongs entirely within the Early Classic (although heirloom pieces may have been redeposited in later times).

The Late Classic may have seen the major mound-building at the site. The information on burial type is ambiguous, but it probably was primary interment.

Other Sites of the Tuxtlas Subarea

A scattering of sites in the Tuxtla mountains can be shown to have had Late Classic occupations very similar to Tres Zapotes IV, characterized by the same types of polychrome pottery and identical figurines.

The upper levels of the excavations in Maclovio Herrera Street in San Andres Tuxtla produced fine examples of Los Tuxtlas Polychrome along with large, cream-slipped, necked jars embellished with designs of cranelike birds and step-and-fret motifs in black or red (Valenzuela, 1945a, pls. 1, 2), as well as moldmade (San Marcos) figurines of Mayoid aspect (*ibid.*, figs. 1–3).

The mound groups of Tatocapan and Pollinapan, both in the vicinity of Santiago Tuxtla, were characterized by the presence of small earthen "adoratories," sometimes covered with volcanic rocks or river boulders, located within plazas (Valenzuela, 1945b). These adoratories proved to be of Late Classic date on the basis of the numerous caches or offerings which many of them contained. In the caches were moldmade, Mayoid figurines, some of them jointed; a flat clay stamp in the form of a double-headed bird; small, necked jars with simple red-and-black-on-cream painting; fine, cream-slipped vessels, incised through the slip with representations of Mayoid personages or of the *cipactli;* a barrel-shaped vase of reddish clay, closely resembling certain Tepeu 3 examples, with

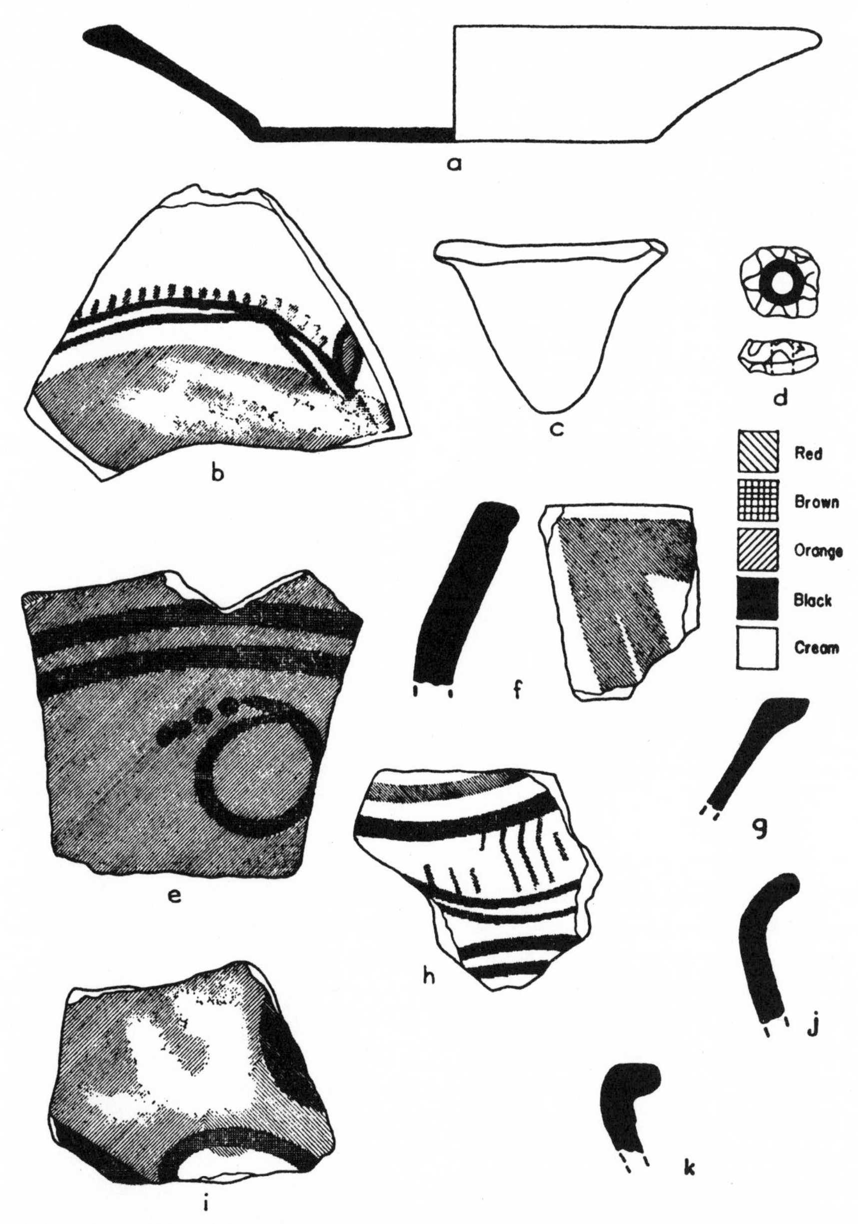

Fig. 28—RESTORED VESSEL, SHERDS, VESSEL FOOT, AND MOLDMADE SPINDLE WHORL FROM CERRO DEL ENCANTO SITE, LA VENTA ISLAND. Not to scale. (From Drucker, Heizer, and Squier, 1959, fig. 74.)

molded panels showing a seated Maya god with a foliated nose. In one cache, well associated with this sort of material, were a fine, simple hacha (thin stone head) without any relief carving, and a small, very crude palma. The hacha bears a far greater resemblance to the type known on the Pacific coasts of Guatemala and El Salvador than it does to thin stone heads from Veracruz, and it may be a late product.

At the large mound site of Mata de Canela, with its ball court, test excavations likewise produced Late Classic moldmade whistle figurines, besides an offering of

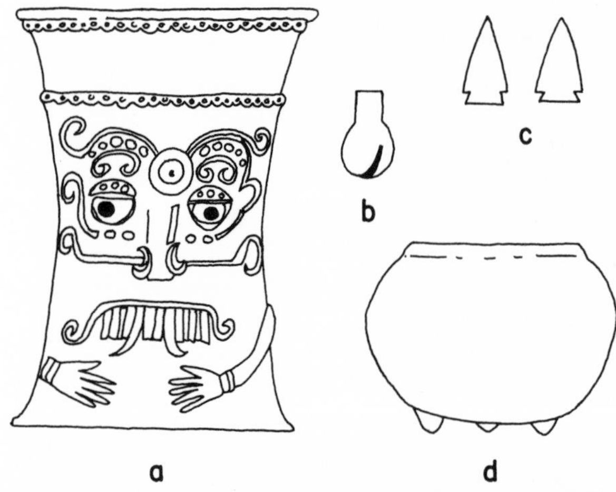

Fig. 29—POTTERY AND ARTIFACTS OF THE MATACAPAN II PHASE. *a*, Large appliqué-decorated incensario. *b*, Copper bell. *c*, Projectile points of white flint. *d*, Alabaster vase. Height of *a*, 45 cm.; others not to scale. (Drawn from figures in Valenzuela, 1945a.)

jades, which although not exactly Maya are in the Late Classic tradition of that culture.

Northern Isthmian Plain

Located about 0.5 km. north-northwest of the Central Group on La Venta island is the Cerro del Encanto mound group reported by Drucker, Heizer, and Squier (1959, pp. 237–40). A sherd collection (fig. 28) made when the mounds were in the process of being destroyed is markedly different from the Olmec ceramics of the Central Group, being largely polychrome. There is a cream-slipped type with curvilinear decoration in red and black, and several other kinds of polychrome. Conical vessel supports and a moldmade spindle whorl (touched up with asphalt) were also present. The authors see close affiliations with pottery from the upper levels of Mound I, Matacapan, which may be a transitory Late Classic occupation overlying the important Early Classic culture found there; there are also strong suggestions, to me, of connections with the Late Classic ceramics of Tatocapan and Pollinapan.

Early Postclassic Period

It is generally agreed that a Mexican people known as the Toltec, coming from the city of Tula, Hidalgo, and led by a semidivine personage called the Feathered Serpent, conquered the Maya of Yucatan and built their new capital at Chichen Itza (for an opposing view, see Kubler, 1961). Toltec Chichen is held to postdate the fall of Classic Maya civilization, and the Toltec period, both here and in the Mexican highlands, is synonymous with the Early Postclassic.[1]

From the myths recorded about the flight of the Feathered Serpent and his followers from Tula, it would seem that this group of Toltec made their way to the Gulf coast of Mexico, thence by water to the Yucatan peninsula; it is significant that at Chichen the gold plaques from the Sacred Cenote and the murals of the Temple of the Warriors show Toltec attacks on the Maya being made from the sea. If true, the foregoing would suggest that Toltec remains might be found in the region of southern Veracruz – Tabasco, in association with locally made artifacts of the Early Postclassic period.

Tres Zapotes V

The vessels and other artifacts found by Weiant and Drucker with cremation burials near the uppermost levels of Tres Zapotes are, as Drucker (1943b, p. 123) has stressed, distinctly different from everything that precedes them at the site, and have been grouped as the "Soncautla Complex." This complex is, as will be seen, related to the Toltec horizon in Mesoamerica, but lacking are some traits which are on this time level in the Maya area: metallurgy, Tohil Plumbate, and X Fine Orange. Relationships are particularly close between Tres Zapotes V and other Early

[1] Ed. Note: This is Andrews' Modified Florescent (see Andrews, Article 12).

Postclassic phases of Veracruz, such as Tres Picos I and Isla de Sacrificios I. As yet inexplicable, there are in this pottery a number of recrudescences of forms which are quite typical of the Preclassic, such as the teapot-shaped vessel with unsupported spout and composite-silhouette bowls with corrugated sides. This archaism is also a feature of Plumbate ware, and the whole phenomenon would bear further investigation.

Vessels within the Tres Zapotes V, or Soncautla, complex are: (1) red-and-black-on-cream necked jars with unsupported spout and superior strap handle (very similar to vessels of Period V in the Huasteca and to Quiahuiztlan I ceramics from central Veracruz and Isla de Sacrificios, see Medellín Zenil, 1960a, pl. 82), (2) monochrome "teapots" with unsupported spout, (3) a shoe-shaped vessel, monochrome, with one vertical handle, (4) a "cream pitcher," (5) composite-silhouette bowls as described above, (6) a wide-mouthed cooking vessel with horizontal strap handles, (7) small, crude jars with three vertical loop handles, plain or rudely polychromed, (8) a double dish with strap handle, and, (9) bowls with fine-line incising. This incising comprises representations of a Toltec-style warrior and of Feathered Serpents.

Two amazingly crude, hand-modeled female figurines and some asphalt-painted spindle whorls were associated.

The presence of cremation burials, previously nonexistent in the area but known in the Mexican highlands as far back as Classic Teotihuacan, along with Toltec iconography and an entirely aberrant pottery complex, certainly suggests a foreign intrusion onto the Gulf coast.

Matacapan II

A pit excavated down from the summit of Mound 4 at Matacapan, in the Tuxtlas subarea (Valenzuela, 1945a, pp. 97–100), encountered first a burned floor made of shell-lime stucco, on the surface of which was a large, smashed, hourglass-shaped incensario of red clay (fig. 29,*a*). The Taloc face modeled with appliqué fillets on its exterior is highly Toltec, and the entire piece is comparable to an incensario at Tula (Dutton, 1955, pl. 20,*a*). Below the floor was a cache containing a number of important objects (fig. 29,*b-d*), all, like the overlying incensario, to be ascribed to the Early Postclassic period. Outstanding among them was a globular, marble (onyx) vessel on three nubbin feet, which contained 6 jade beads, 41 shell beads, and a copper bell. Marble or onyx vases are on the Toltec horizon in Veracruz, as at Isla de Sacrificios (Medellín Zenil, 1960a, p. 136). Several shell fragments bear incised scenes in Toltec style, including a rabbit seated in front of a fragmentary headdress, a personage in profile, and tree motifs (fig. 30). A group of fine, corner-notched projectile points of white flint were also associated with the cache. A Teotihuacanoid sherd and figurine can be interpreted as pit fall, as the cache is probably intrusive into an older Matacapan I mound.

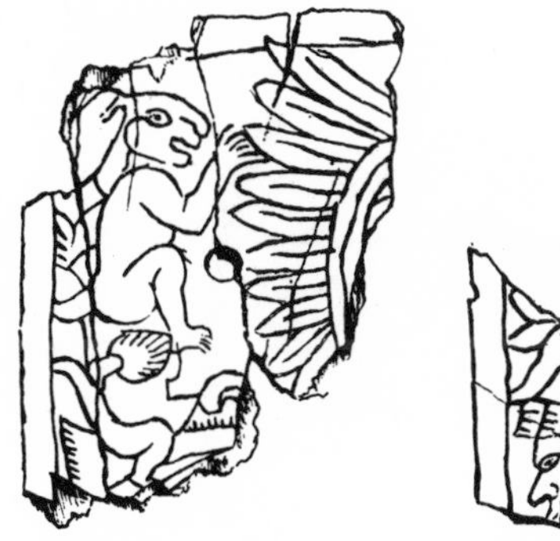

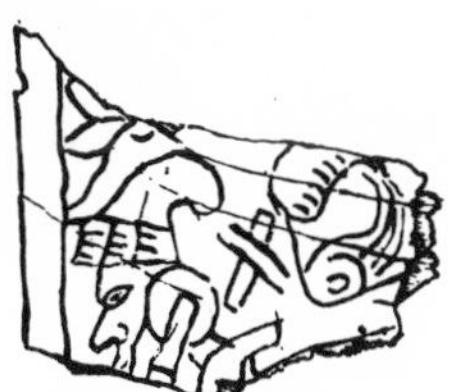

Fig. 30—INCISED SHELL FRAGMENTS OF MATACAPAN II PHASE, ASSOCIATED WITH OBJECTS SHOWN IN FIG. 29. (From illustration in Valenzuela, 1945b, p. 82.)

Agaltepec

As previously mentioned, the entire surface of Agaltepec island in Lake Catemaco

FIG. 31—POLYCHROME SHERDS FROM THE TORRES SITE, LA VENTA ISLAND (From Drucker, Heizer, and Squier, 1959, fig. 75.)

has been altered by aboriginal constructions. Excavations in shallow burial shafts (Valenzuela, 1945a, pp. 103–04) brought to light a copper earspool with flaring end and three vessels which clearly belong with the Tres Zapotes V (Soncautla) complex: a necked jar with unsupported spout, and two composite-silhouette bowls, one of which has simple incising near the break of the wall. A surface collection that Kent Flannery and I made on the island in 1962 includes a piece of Tohil Plumbate pottery. There probably is a Late Classic occupation of Agaltepec, but the site was certainly in use during the Early Postclassic.

LATE POSTCLASSIC PERIOD

The very few sites within our area that can be considered as Late Postclassic demonstrate that southern Veracruz – Tabasco was at this time participating to a certain extent in the widespread Mixteca-Puebla horizon style that seems to be centered at Cholula, Puebla. Aztec or Aztecoid ceramics are totally lacking in this part of the Gulf coast, but this may be merely a result of admittedly inadequate knowledge; Aztec influences begin farther north, in central Veracruz, about A.D. 1450 (Medellín Zenil, 1960a, pp. 142–43). So scanty is our information on the period as a whole that hardly one example of architectural construction can be ascribed to it.

Cerro de las Mesas IV

A polychrome ceramic complex closely allied with Isla de Sacrificios and similar sites and in large part derived from late Cholula can be seen in the upper levels of Cerro de las Mesas, which was now reoccupied following a long hiatus (see Drucker, 1943a, pp. 45–56, for a description of these wares). "Complicated Polychrome" is identical with the beautiful *polícroma laca* of Cholula, and is either a direct import from that site or a very good imitation. This fine ware has a wide distribution in Veracruz, extending at least as far north as Cempoala. "Brown Polychrome" (flat-bottomed bowls with stamped bases, painted in red, black, white, and orange on a brown slip) is the same as the *cerámica sellada* of Medellín Zenil (1960a, pp. 138–40), and is known at Quauhtochco and Cuetlaxtlan in central Veracruz. "Dull Buff Polychrome" (the *trícroma* of Medellín Zenil) is one of the most abundant here and at other Veracruz sites; "Black-on-Red-Incised," with its incised spirals and circles, is also well represented at Cerro Montoso. Medellín Zenil (*ibid.*, p. 147) believes the "Black-and-White-on-Red" polychrome of Cerro de las Mesas IV to be a direct import from the Mixteca.

The usual design motifs of these polychrome vessels are geometric and precise —step-and-fret, circle-and-dot, feathers. Tripod supports are either animal-head effigies or stepped-down slab in form.

Small, flat figurines very similar to those of Cerro Grande in central Veracruz (Medellín Zenil, 1960a, p. 144) are common in the phase. These are crude and entirely moldmade. Type II figurines resemble those of Cholula; they usually represent recognizable Mexican deities, such as Xochiquetzal, Xipe, Tlaloc, and Michtlantecuhtli. The faces are quite naturalistic, the bodies less so. Far more schematic are Type III figurines (Drucker, 1943b, pl. 39), which are always female, with the features indicated in a very abstract, linear relief. Moldmade spindle whorls and flat clay stamps are also of the period.

The tortilla is apparently a latecomer to southern Veracruz – Tabasco, for not until Cerro de las Mesas IV are comales found. Presumably maize was previously eaten only in other forms, such as tamales and atole.

The small mounds lying northwest of the Central Group seem to belong to this late horizon. Leading down the sides from the top of two of these mounds are large pottery tubes formed from telescoped sections. They have no known function.

Northern Isthmian Plain

As the result of its destruction by bulldozers, a shallow occupation site was found on La Venta island about 250 m. southwest of Pyramid C-1 (Drucker, Heizer, and Squier, 1959, pp. 240–46), the Torres site. A high frequency of polychrome sherds (fig. 31) was collected: designs in red, orange, blackish-brown, black, and white on a cream, orange, or white slip. The painted motifs are complex and vaguely like those on the "Complicated Polychrome" of Cerro de las Mesas IV and Cholula, but there are differences. Simple handmade spindle whorls were picked up. The only figurines at the Torres site were solid, handmade Olmec examples, which

TABLE 1—ARCHAEOLOGICAL CHRONOLOGY OF VERACRUZ-TABASCO

Period	*Central Veracruz*	*Mixtequilla*	*The Tuxtlas*	*Northern Isthmian Plain*
Late Postclassic A.D. 1200	Isla de Sacrificios II-III, Quiahuiztlan II-III, Tres Picos II-III	Cerro de las Mesas IV		Torre site
Early Postclassic A.D. 900	Isla de Sacrificios I, Quiahuiztlan I, Tres Picos I		Tres Zapotes V ("Soncautla"), Matacapan II, Agaltepec	
Late Classic A.D. 600	Upper Remojadas II	Nopiloa II, Los Cerros II, Dicha Tuerta	Tres Zapotes IV, Tatocapan, Pollinapan	Cerro de Encanto
Early Classic A.D. 300	Upper Remojadas I	Cerro de las Mesas III	Tres Zapotes III, Matacapan I	
Protoclassic A.D. 100	Lower Remojadas	Cerro de las Mesas II, Nopiloa I, Los Cerros I	Tres Zapotes II	
Late Formative 300 B.C.		Cerro de las Mesas I	Tres Zapotes I, La Mechuda	
Middle Formative 800 B.C.				Olme

must have been redeposited with Postclassic potsherds (for an opposing interpretation see *ibid.*, pp. 245–46).

SUMMARY

Although it has been described as "the Olmec area," the southern Veracruz – Tabasco region has no great unity throughout its long development; there is neither an "Olmec" nor any other kind of persistent tradition. Rather, the area moves through a series of stages each of which displays considerable internal uniformity as the result of certain widespread currents of diffusion.

The first of these great horizon phenomena is the Olmec culture, an apparently autochthonous civilization centered on the Northern Isthmian Plain which had an enormous influence on the rest of Mesoamerica; the Olmecs, who may have invented writing and the Long Count, created the "mother culture" from which are derived all others both here on the Gulf coast and elsewhere. The outstanding unsolved problem of southern Veracruz – Tabasco archaeology is the origin of this great civilization of the Middle Preclassic.

In the late Preclassic the important Izapan monumental style crystallizes, almost certainly from an Olmec base, and it is in this context that the first known date in the Long Count system is recorded.

A cultural complex, perhaps a burial cult, of considerable significance spreads throughout the area in the Protoclassic period. Its origins seem to lie to the south, within or beyond the Maya area.

The Early Classic is essentially a Teotihuacan horizon, with certain continuities from the native Gulf coast past. These continuities are mainly to be seen in the epi-Izapan monuments of Cerro de las Mesas, and in the survival of the Long Count, although both traits subsequently disappear from the area forever. Teotihuacan civilization had a profound influence on these native cultures, not only in pottery and other artifacts but also in architecture, and it might be asked whether or not thoroughly Teotihuacanoid phases like Matacapan I might represent way stations along the route to Kaminaljuyu from highland Mexico.

An entirely different cultural alignment is seen in the Late Classic, following the fall of Teotihuacan. There is now a kind of "super-culture," a Gulf coast horizon which links all the peoples of the area with coastal Campeche and which is under the cultural shadow of the Late Classic Maya. Curiously enough, these Mayoid influences are confined to such things as moldmade figurines and polychrome ceramics; the really significant Maya traits such as the construction of stone-masonry temples (of course, building stone is rare on the Gulf coast plain) and the erection of dated stone monuments are absent. It is as though the peoples of our area had become too provincial to move the stones and do the work which had made possible the great Olmec civilization. Because of this, the Late Classic of southern Veracruz – Tabasco strikes one as a peasant phenomenon, with no great art but with some amusing clay figurines.

Some very scattered information on a Toltec horizon is available for the area, but it is hardly complete enough to offer conclusions. Metallurgy, marble vases, a curious ceramic complex, and Toltec art are introduced, and it may be that the Toltec held southern Veracruz – Tabasco in their control before setting off on the conquest of the Yucatan Maya. In the Late Postclassic, all that we know is that influences from the Mixteca-Puebla region were strong, and that there are yet no archaeological data on the Aztec occupation of this coastal region.

REFERENCES

Blom and LaFarge, 1926–27
Coe, M. D., 1961
Covarrubias, 1947, 1957
Drucker, 1943a, 1943b, 1952a, 1955
——, Heizer, and Squier, 1959
Dutton, 1955
Goggin, 1960
Greengo, 1952
Groth-Kimball, 1953
Kidder, Jennings, and Shook, 1946
Kubler, 1961
Lathrap, 1957
Lorenzo, 1961
Lowe, 1962
Medellín Zenil, 1960a, 1960b
Proskouriakoff, 1954, 1962c
Stirling, 1941, 1943, 1957
Tamayo, 1949
Valenzuela, 1945a, 1945b
Weiant, 1943
Weyerstall, 1932

28. Monumental Sculpture of Southern Veracruz and Tabasco

MATTHEW W. STIRLING

THE RIVER COURSES of southern Veracruz – Tabasco are dotted with large archaeological sites, marked by groups of earth mounds of great size and extent. Stone architecture is almost entirely lacking, although it occurs throughout the surrounding area. One of the most interesting archaeological features is the relative abundance of stone monuments. Although the making of these continued to some extent up to the time of the Spanish conquest, at least half of the known examples belong to the early Olmec culture of the Preclassic period, which began approximately 1000 B.C. and may have lasted for 500 years or more. Among these are the majority of the more striking pieces. Although the archaeology of this rich area is still imperfectly known, enough work has been done in recent years at a few key sites to give a general idea of the chronology and sequence of the cultures and art styles.

The most important Olmec sites are Tres Zapotes and San Lorenzo Tenochtitlan in southern Veracruz, and La Venta in northern Tabasco. The majority of the best Olmec monuments are found in these three sites. Two other sites of importance are Cerro de las Mesas, in southern Veracruz, and Izapa, which lies in Chiapas, outside the southern Veracruz – Tabasco region. Cerro de las Mesas is significant as a late Olmec and post-Olmec center with stone carvings which show a retention of earlier Olmec features. Izapa is best known for its monuments which may provide a link between the Olmec style and related styles of the Preclassic period of the Guatemalan highlands.

Because the art style of the Olmecs is distinctive and easily recognized, and because a large proportion of the monuments fall in this period, I have for the sake of convenience divided the discussion into the Olmec and the post-Olmec.

MONUMENTS OF THE OLMEC PERIOD

Greatly admired by present-day artists for its high aesthetic merit, stone monument carving of the Olmec style is also of interest because of its great age. In this style are to be found the prototypes of virtually all features in later Mesoamerican stone-

Fig. 1—OLMEC COLOSSAL HEAD, MONUMENT 4, LA VENTA. (Copyright, National Geographic Society.)

Fig. 2—OLMEC COLOSSAL HEAD, MONUMENT 4, SAN LORENZO TENOCHTITLAN. (Copyright, National Geographic Society.)

Fig. 3—OLMEC COLOSSAL HEAD, MONUMENT 5, SAN LORENZO TENOCHTITLAN. (Copyright, National Geographic Society.)

Fig. 4—OLMEC ANTHROPOMORPHIC JAGUARS AND PUMA. *a (above, left),* Monument 11, La Venta. *b (above, right),* Monument 10, San Lorenzo Tenochtitlan. *c (below),* Puma, Monument 7, San Lorenzo Tenochtitlan. (*a,b,* copyright, National Geographic Society.)

FIG. 5—OLMEC BASIN IN FORM OF DUCK, MONUMENT 9, SAN LORENZO TENOCHTITLAN. (Copyright, National Geographic Society.)

work. A feature of Olmec art is its powerful simplicity. Lacking the rigidity and somewhat rococo quality of most later products, the art of the Olmecs in general is not only the earliest but the best in Mesoamerica.

It is probable that the Olmecs became proficient in the carving of small figures in jade and other materials, and in modeling with clay before undertaking the more formidable task of shaping large monuments in stone. Once embarked in this new field, they seemed to take pride in tackling subjects of truly colossal size, where they exhibited the same artistic skill seen in the jade figures.

In the southern Veracruz – northern Tabasco region, there are no known examples of Olmec art on natural rock exposures, such as are found at Chalcacingo, Morelos, San Isidro Piedra Parada, Guatemala, and Chalchuapa, El Salvador. While rock carvings, small carvings in jade and other stones, and ceramic pieces in true Olmec style spread far and wide from the valley of Mexico and Guerrero to El Salvador, true monument carving remained near its place of origin.

Basalt, which is abundant in the volcanic mountains near the coast, was the favorite material of the Olmec sculptors. Handicapped by only stone tools, the artists handled this rather intractable material as though it were a plastic. Stones weighing 30 tons or more were transported for distances up to 75 miles to such sites as La Venta and San Lorenzo Tenochtitlan, probably floated there on rafts.

In addition to figures in the full round, there were many subjects carved in low or high relief. When he wished, the Olmec artist could be fully realistic, but for certain effects conventionalizations were freely used. Features on the colossal heads, for example, are almost completely realistic, but the ears are somewhat conventionalized as is the area at the base of the nose, which the artist altered in order to obtain the expression desired. The portrait quality of these carvings is quite evident. The bulk of Olmec representative art consists of human and anthropomorphic beings. Animals and birds are rare but well within the artists' capacity, as evidenced by the beautifully carved puma (fig. 4,*c*), the snarling jaguar (Stirling, 1955, pl. 3), and the duck basin of San Lorenzo Tenochtitlan (fig. 5), (*ibid.*, pls. 17, 18). In depicting anthropomorphic beings the sculptors exhibited a high quality of imagination; most of these figures, both in relief and in the round, are intensely dynamic.

Utilitarian objects, stone columns, cylindrical bowls, stone spheres, and the troughlike seats or aqueduct sections of San Lorenzo were not embellished with carved decorations, although they were carefully shaped and finished. The Olmec artist seldom felt the need to fill the open areas in his carvings.

Although the kinds of objects were fairly numerous and the things represented rather diverse, the art style remained constant over a long period of time, and the subjects were definitely limited. No doubt religion was the inspiration for much of the art work and frequently determined the subject matter. Olmec art, however, was far less hampered by religious symbolism than was that of the later high cultures.

The frequent depicting of the jaguar indicates that it was the most important deity of the Olmecs. The rattlesnake and the fer-de-lance, the harpy eagle, the monkey (fig. 7), and the sting ray were also apparently deified; some of these were given anthropomorphic form, as gods.

Fig. 6—OLMEC STONE SNAKE, POTRERO NUEVO

Even floral elements appear. Nevertheless, the majority of monuments carry human figures, male and female, in what appear to be historic or mythologic scenes, but none of them warlike. The colossal heads so characteristic of this region may well be portraits of prominent leaders.

On the human figures are sometimes quite elaborate headdresses, but in general costumes are simple though accurate. Feathers are portrayed, but not in the sweeping style of the later Maya. Olmec figures are especially notable for their dynamic quality, almost invariably striding, crouching, kneeling, leaping.

Monuments of the Post-Olmec Period

Although the archaeology of the southern Veracruz–northern Tabasco region is poorly known except for the Olmec culture and period, there are many monuments clearly not products of the Olmec. Except at Cerro de las Mesas (Stirling, 1943) virtually none of these have been found in a recognized archaeological context, and their chronological position can be determined only on stylistic grounds.

FIG. 7—OLMEC ANTHROPOMORPHIC MONKEY IN GREEN SERPENTINE, LA VENTA (Copyright, National Geographic Society.)

A number of monuments from the vicinity of Alvarado, in the misnamed "Totonac" style, are probably early post-Olmec (fig. 18,*b*).

Piedra Labrada (Blom and LaFarge, 1926–27, pp. 40–42), on the coastal side of the Tuxtla Mountains, contains a group of monuments difficult to appraise. In addition to a few small animal carvings there is the upper portion of a female figure, realistically formed and vaguely suggesting the Olmec style (*ibid.*, fig. 40). The most interesting piece is a stela set into a rectangular base and decorated on one face with a column of glyphs and what may be bar-and-dot numerical elements. This is probably an early post-Olmec site (*ibid.*, fig. 38).

At Matacanela (*ibid.*, pp. 23–25), near Lake Catemaco, relatively small stone carvings in the form of animals (fig. 8) and stone boxes are numerous. A site on the southern side of Santiago volcano has produced many small human heads and frogs, snakes, and rabbits. Although mostly well done, these carvings are entirely non-Olmec in style and are probably quite late, possibly dating from Aztec or pre-Aztec times.

A very interesting though bizarre figure of a crouching man holding a head on his hands was recently found at Matalapan, near Lake Catemaco. This piece, in a style all its own, is probably quite late (fig. 9).

Near Tlacotalpan on the Papoloapan river have appeared a number of human figures carved in typical Aztec style (figs. 10, 11). It is known that this region was under the domination of the Aztecs during the latter half of the 15th century, and before the time of the Spanish conquest Nahuatl had become the prevailing language. Therefore it is not surprising to find Aztec stone carving in this lowland region (Stirling, 1943, pp. 5–7).

The monuments of the southern Veracruz – Tabasco region, as well as Olmec

FIG. 8—LATE STYLE CARVINGS, LAKE CATEMACO REGION.
a,b, Rodents. *c,* Snake head.

and later styles, will be discussed in more detail under the following headings.

Stelae

The Olmecs were evidently the first Mesoamericans to erect stelae, probably as commemorative monuments. This practice began in southern Veracruz and spread across southern Mexico into Guatemala and, probably by way of the Guatemalan highlands, into the Peten and Yucatan. The custom also spread to the north, where related monuments are found as far as northern Veracruz.

The Long Count calendar, with the same beginning date as that of the Maya, probably had its origins in Olmec culture. Early dates in this system were occasionally recorded on stone. The Olmecs also developed a system of glyphic writing which was sometimes put on stone.

In keeping with the importance of the jaguar, the earliest stelae were in the form of semirealistic jaguar heads with open mouth, such as Stela D, Tres Zapotes (fig. 13,*a*), and Monument 2 (Stirling, 1943, pl. 53), Izapa. Next in stylistic evolution were stelae in which both upper and lower jaws project but are more conventionalized, as in Stela A, Tres Zapotes (Stirling, 1943, pl. 12) and Stela 1, La Venta (fig. 13,*b*). Following this, only the lower jaw projects, forming a ledge near the base, as in Stela 3, La Venta (fig. 14,*b*; and Stirling, 1943, pl. 39), and Stelae 3 and 6 at Izapa (Stirling, 1943, pl. 50). Eventually both projecting ledges are abandoned, being replaced by a transverse band or bands, and the

Fig. 9—LATE STYLE CARVING, LAKE CATEMACO REGION

Fig. 10—AZTEC PERIOD CARVINGS REPRESENTING GOD XIPE, VICINITY OF TLACOTALPAN (Copyright, National Geographic Society.)

Fig. 11—AZTEC PERIOD CARVINGS, VICINITY C TLACOTALPAN. (Copyright, National Geographic S ciety.)

FIG. 12—OLMEC STONE SCULPTURE. *a (above, left),* Stela C, Tres Zapotes. Jaguar mask panel on reverse of dated monument. *b (above, right),* Sarcophagus, La Venta. Jaguar face on the end. *c,* Altar 1, La Venta, in the form of anthropomorphic jaguar. (*b,c,* copyright, National Geographic Society.)

jaguar motif is indicated by the conventionalized jaguar mask panel. At Izapa the mask panel is usually placed above the design; at Cerro de las Mesas, at the base. A recently discovered stela from Kaminaljuyu, Guatemala, carries the mask panel at the base in the identical form as that on Stela 4, Izapa.

From the Guatemalan highlands the stela cult apparently spread to the Peten, where the jaguar element became de-emphasized and eventually lost, although it shows up occasionally as mask panels on stelae, as at the Classic Maya sites of La Honradez and Yaxchilan, and sometimes as an architectural feature.

A number of very interesting stelae occur at the large site of Cerro de las Mesas, which apparently was established in late Olmec times and continued to be occupied for a very long period. At least one of the stone carvings, Monument 5 (Stirling, 1943, pl. 28), may be Olmec as it bears a rather striking resemblance to the Tuxtla statuette. The best of the Cerro de las Mesas stelae belong to the Early Classic period and at least two of these bear glyphs and dates in the Long Count calendar (figs. 15, 16), one in Katun 1 and the other in Katun 4 of the Cycle 9. Stylistically, they closely resemble early Maya stelae of the same period (Stirling, 1943; Proskouriakoff, 1950), but their location so far from the Maya area presents an interesting and important problem. There are two possible explanations: either, the art style developed locally from Olmec antecedents along with the Olmec practice of occasionally putting dates and glyphs on monuments, and from here spread to the Maya area; or, it represents a diffusion to the north from the Maya area in Early Classic times.

Other Cerro de las Mesas stelae clearly

Fig. 13—OLMEC CARVINGS OF HUMANS IN OPEN MOUTHS OF JAGUARS. *a (left)*, Stela D, Tres Zapotes. *b (right)*, Female figure, Stela 1, La Venta (Copyright, National Geographic Society.)

Fig. 14—OLMEC STELAE, LA VENTA. *a (left)*, Stela 2. *b (right)*, Stela 3 (copyright, National Geographic Society).

FIG. 15—EARLY CLASSIC STELAE WITH INITIAL SERIES DATES, CERRO DE LAS MESAS *a (left)*, Stela 6, reading 9.1.12.14.10 1 Oc. *b (right)*, Stela 8, reading 9.4.18.16.8 9 Lamat. (Copyright, National Geographic Society.)

belong to a much later period. Two of them, Stelae 4 and 15 (fig. 17), bear Mixtec style dates. One represents a man seated on a "throne" and holding a fan, the other is a Tlaloc-like figure apparently holding a piece of shredded rope. Stela 7 (Stirling, 1943, pl. 26) and Stela 11 (*ibid.*, pl. 25) are difficult to place stylistically, but they are probably Postclassic.

A stela from Huilotitzintla in the vicinity of Tuxpan bears relief carving somewhat in the style of Cerro de las Mesas, but surely later than most of these stelae: a striding figure representing Quetzalcoatl, or his antecedent, in the penitential act of drawing a stick through his tongue. The Quetzalcoatl symbol is shown as the cross section of a conch shell, in the style used by the Aztecs; but the carving itself is more Huastec than Aztec in style. This stela is probably fairly early and antedates the later typical Huastec carvings.

Four stelae in the neighborhood of Alvarado seem to constitute a separate group. Three are made from large natural basalt columns, each representing a male figure, with pointed beard, standing on a decorated panel. On the Alvarado stela (fig. 18,*b*), which apparently once had a column of glyphs, the standing figure faces a seated bound captive. The example from El Meson (Stirling, 1943, pl. 16) is very similar although much of the design is obscured. The so-called Matisse stela (Covarrubias, 1957, pl. 17) shows a ball-player with hands upraised in front of his face. On the fourth from Tepatlaxco (fig. 18,*a*), a more conventional rectangular slab, a

Fig. 16—EARLY CLASSIC STELAE, CERRO DE LAS MESAS. *a (left)*, Stela 5. *b (right)*, Stela 3.

Fig. 17—LATE CLASSIC STELAE, CERRO DE LAS MESAS. *a (left)*, Stela 4, seated figure with fan. *b (right)*, Stela 15.

ball-player is being helped with his gear by an attendant.

All of these appear to be in a style closely related to the so-called "Totonac." The carving of the faces is reminiscent of the circular slate mirror backs from Veracruz. They have certain Olmec features, however, and what might be highly conventionalized mask panels. They give the impression of being early, but are certainly post-Olmec since as far as we know the ball game was not known in Olmec times.

The large El Meson stela from this area (Covarrubias, 1957, fig. 68) shows in typically Olmec dynamic fashion an elaborately costumed standing figure, facing a seated personage as though in argument. The standing figure is on a jaguar mask panel flanked on either side by a serpent head. The mask panel suggests those on the Early Classic stelae of Cerro de las Mesas, and is strikingly like that on the face of Stela C from Tres Zapotes, which bears a Baktun, or Cycle, 7 date. Since this date must occur near the end of the Olmec period, the El Meson stela is probably late Olmec, a conclusion further confirmed by the two-headed serpent design and other features closely similar to those at Izapa where these occur in an art style also bearing Baktun 7 dates. Because of the linkage it suggests between Tres Zapotes, Izapa, and Cerro de las Mesas, the El Meson stela is of special significance.

Fig. 18—STELAE CARVED IN EARLY STYLE, VERACRUZ. *a (left),* Ball player, Tepatlaxco. *b (right),* Alvarado. (Copyright, National Geographic Society.)

Altars

A typical Olmec invention was the tabletop altar. The principal center for these was La Venta, where seven have been found. There is one at San Lorenzo Tenochtitlan and another at nearby Potrero Nuevo.

They consist of a rectangular block supporting a massive tabletop which projects at the front and both ends but not at the back. In those examples whose upper portions are undamaged, a smaller raised rectangle is superimposed on the top surface. All the altars of this class are rather elaborately decorated. The most typical have in front a deep arched niche in which is seated a human figure in the full round; on the ends other human figures in action are carved in low relief. Not all altars, however, follow this theme. Altar 1 at La Venta (Stirling, 1943, pl. 36) is in the form of the typical jaguar, with an opening which passes from one ear to the mouth. Altar 7 at La Venta (Drucker, 1952a, pl. 65) has in the niche a large head wearing a duck-bill mask over the lower part of the face,

Fig. 19—OLMEC ATLANTEAN ALTAR, MONUMENT 2, POTRERO NUEVO. (Copyright, National Geographic Society.)

like that on the Tuxtla statuette. On the sides, carved in high relief, are several nocturnal animal or bird heads and in low relief a number of human figures in action.

Monument 2 at Potrero Nuevo (fig. 19) has two chubby atlantean figures standing in front, with up-raised arms supporting the tabletop. Pairs of conventionalized jaguar eyes are on the front and ends. This very early occurrence of atlantean figures may be a precursor to their use in later Middle American art.

Altars 2 (Stirling, 1943, pl. 38) and 5 (fig. 20,*a*) at La Venta show the seated figure in front holding an infant on his lap. Altar 5 is the finest of all, and one of the best examples of Middle American carving extant. On the ends of this altar, carved in low relief, are four adults each holding a struggling figure with infantile body and adult face (fig. 21,*a*).

Altar 4 at La Venta (fig. 20,*b*) and Monument 14 at San Lorenzo (Stirling, 1955, pl. 21) are of truly enormous proportions, being 11½ feet long, and 5 feet 3 inches and 6 feet high, respectively. At the other end of the size range is Altar 6 at La Venta, which is 4 feet 6 inches wide and 3 feet 9 inches high. Although belonging to the class under discussion, the art style is different, the carving being angular, somewhat crude, and without relief. It is difficult to say whether this represents an early or a decadent phase. I am inclined to feel that Altar 1, the anthropomorphic jaguar, is an early type and that the majority of the remainder belong to the florescent period of Olmec stone carving, contemporaneous with the colossal heads.

There are a few other Olmec monuments which possibly should be classed as altars. Monuments F and G at Tres Zapotes (fig. 22) are figures in the form of a head with shoulders and flexed arms and a long flat

FIG. 20—OLMEC ALTARS, LA VENTA. *a (above)* Altar 5. *b (below)*, Altar 4. (Copyright, National Geographic Society.)

FIG. 21—OLMEC RELIEF CARVING. *a (left),* Altar 5, La Venta (copyright, National Geographic Society). *b (right),* Monument 14, San Lorenzo Tenochtitlan.

FIG. 22—OLMEC TENON ALTARS, TRES ZAPOTES. *a (left),* Monument F. *b (right),* Monument G. (Copyright, National Geographic Society.)

FIG. 23—OLMEC COLOSSAL HEAD, MONUMENT Q, TRES ZAPOTES. At Santiago Tuxtla.

tenon-like projection instead of a body. The former has a cup-shaped depression in the top of the head as though to receive offerings. It is probable that Monument 6 from San Lorenzo (Stirling, 1955, pl. 14) was of this type although the flat projection has been broken away.

Monument 13 from La Venta (Drucker, 1952a, pl. 63) is a roughly cylindrical stone with a flat upper surface, on which are carved four glyphs and a striding human figure carrying a banner. This might well have served as an altar. Monument 15 from La Venta (Drucker, 1952a, pl. 64 and fig. 54), now only two fragments, was evidently a low table supported by a foot at each of the four corners. On the upper surface a jaguar mask panel was carved in high relief. This too may have served as an altar.

Colossal Heads

Among the most characteristic of Olmec stone carvings are the colossal heads. At the present time 11 typical examples are known: five from San Lorenzo (Stirling, 1955), four from La Venta (Stirling, 1943) and two from Tres Zapotes (fig. 4; Stirling, 1943). An incomplete and somewhat atypical specimen comes from the Olmec site at San Miguel, Tabasco (Stirling, 1957, pl. 50).

They range from a height of slightly less than 5 feet, Monument Q from Tres Zapotes (fig. 23), to 9 feet 6 inches, Monument 1 at San Lorenzo (fig. 24,*b*). All are carved from basalt. The realistic treatment of the features depicts men rather than gods. Although in all examples the racial type is the same—wide face, thick lips, broad flat nose—each has an individual quality and was probably the portrait of a prominent leader. The expressions differ; some are stern, some are placid, one is smiling. In two instances at least, the teeth are shown; usually the iris is indicated by a circle in low relief on the eyeball. All wear a close-fitting, helmet-like headdress, some rather elaborately decorated, some plain. Since such things as feathers, jaguar paws, or teeth are represented, perhaps the round helmet is an artistic con-

Fig. 24—OLMEC COLOSSAL HEADS, SAN LORENZO TENOCHTITLAN. *a (left),* Monument 3 (copyright, National Geographic Society). b *(right),* Monument 1.

Fig. 25—OLMEC ANTHROPOMORPHIC JAGUARS. *a (left),* Seated on human figure, Rio Chiquito, near San Lorenzo Tenochtitlan. *b (right),* With snake, Monument 1, Potrero Nuevo, near San Lorenzo Tenochtitlan. (Copyright, National Geographic Society.)

vention for the purpose of eliminating protruding parts, which would be fragile and difficult to carve and would require the removal of a great quantity of material in the carving. The majority have ear ornaments: a circular earspool or a rectangular bar through the lobe.

All heads share one feature; a perfectly flat, plain surface a foot or more in width extending vertically up the middle of the back. This might indicate that the heads were meant to be set up against a wall, a possibility borne out by the fact that in most cases they were designed to be viewed from in front or at a three-quarter angle. The features appear rather flat when seen in full profile.

The heads at Tres Zapotes and La Venta were found upright and *in situ.* At San Lorenzo they had been overthrown and some rolled into ravines. They appear to have been set up with no particular orientation or relation to other structures on the sites, save that all were part of the ceremonial establishment.

At Cerro de las Mesas a basalt head, evidently representing a tear-streaked rain god related to the later Tlaloc, was made to lie on its back looking upwards. It is Early Classic in style and contemporary with the Early Classic stela of the same site.

Seated Figures

Basalt monuments in the form of human or anthropomorphic seated figures occurred at the three principal Olmec sites. Four such figures were Monuments I, J, K, and M at Tres Zapotes (Stirling, 1943). All were broken; the head remains only on Monument M. Apparently all represented males. They were relatively small, not exceeding 4 feet in height.

Six such monuments come from La Venta. Monuments 9, 10, and 21 (Drucker, Heizer, and Squier, 1959) are men sitting cross-legged; 8 and 11 are anthropomorphic jaguars; the head is broken from Monument 23 (Drucker, Heizer, and Squier, 1959) but it was probably human. This figure is wearing on the chest a concave hematite mirror, a motif also on some of the relief carvings at La Venta.

Monuments 10, 11, and 12 (Stirling, 1955) at San Lorenzo are seated figures, as is Monument 1 at nearby Potrero Nuevo (Stirling, 1955). Monument 11 holds a cylindrical bar on the lap; Monument 12 holds in the same position an infant with a jaguar face. Both pieces lack heads but probably represent men. Monument 10 (fig. 4,*b*) represents the classic anthropomorphic jaguar clasping two cestus-like objects to his chest. Monument 1 of Potrero Nuevo (fig. 25,*b*), although headless, is undoubtedly also an anthropomorphic jaguar, supporting a serpent on his knees.

FIG. 26—OLMEC BAS-RELIEF ON LARGE STONE BOX, MONUMENT C, TRES ZAPOTES

On the top of San Martin Pajapan vol-

Fig. 27—OLMEC SANDSTONE SARCOPHAGUS WITH LID, LA VENTA. Monument 6, carved in form of crouching jaguar. (Copyright, National Geographic Society.)

Fig. 28—OLMEC TOMB OF BASALT COLUMNS, LA VENTA. Monument 7. Stone sarcophagus in background. (Copyright, National Geographic Society.)

cano is an elaborately carved, seated human figure wearing a headdress in the form of the classic Olmec jaguar face (Blom and LaFarge, 1926–27, fig. 43) and at one time holding a bar across the knees. Under it had been placed an offering of pottery and jade.

Human figures on Olmec altars, whether in the round or in relief, are usually though not always seated, whereas on the stelae they are standing or striding. There is no standard sitting position.

The magnificent Olmec carving called "the wrestler" (Art. 29, fig. 36), a nearly nude figure, is seated with one leg thrust forward, the other bent to the rear.

Kneeling Figures

Kneeling is a position not commonly seen in Middle American art. Monument 5 from La Venta, a figure holding a rectangular offering bowl, rests on both knees. One of the figures carved in relief on the early Stela D from Tres Zapotes is also in this position.

The figure on Stela 9 (Stirling, 1943, pl. 21) at Cerro de las Mesas, an early but non-Olmec carving rests on one knee.

In Veracruz a few figures dating from the late Aztec period are also on both knees, such as the female figure from the vicinity of Tlacotalpan (fig. 11,*a*).

Standing Figures

There is no Olmec monument of a standing figure carved in the full round, although this was the most common position for small figures of jade or serpentine. The Olmec frequently carved standing or striding figures in both low and high relief.

During the Aztec and pre-Aztec periods, standing figures in the round were frequent, usually mounted on a flat stone base. The elbows are bent and the hands held forward. The majority are in the vicinity of Tlacotalpan (fig. 10).

A standing figure at Atasta (Stirling,

1957, pl. 70) in northern Tabasco is interesting because it may be a relic of the Toltec invasion which reached Yucatan.

Stone Boxes

At Tres Zapotes are two large stone boxes, whose use is unknown. Although incomplete, each was about 5 feet long, 4 feet wide. The upper parts of both are broken away but originally they were probably about 4 feet high. The sides flare out slightly giving them a "bathtub" shape. Monument B (Stirling, 1943, pl. 7) had a well-smoothed but undecorated surface. The outer surface of Monument C (fig. 27) was covered with elaborate designs in relief, deities apparently engaged in combat amidst an elaborate series of scroll-like figures. The art style in many respects is reminiscent of Izapa.

At San Lorenzo is a fragmentary stone box very similar to Monument B of Tres Zapotes. Monument 8 at San Lorenzo (Stirling, 1955, pl. 15) is also probably the bottom of a somewhat larger box. The sides are broken away, but the interior surface of the bottom is carved in a systematic series of celt-shaped depressions.

The sandstone sarcophagus from La Venta (fig. 28) can be considered in this category since it is in effect a box. It was in the form of a conventionalized jaguar in typical Olmec style and was covered with a lid on which was carved a large shallow rectangular depression. Although the bones had disappeared, the box was of the proper size and shape to receive a human body; jade earspools and other jade ornaments were in position as though they had been placed on a body.

At a much later date, probably in pre-Aztec times, smaller stone boxes were made in the Tuxtla Mountain region in the vicinity of Lake Catemaco. Two examples are illustrated, one decorated with a row of circles, the other with a shell design (fig. 29).

FIG. 29—LATE PERIOD STONE BOXES, VICINITY OF LAKE CATEMACO

Cylindrical Offertories

Two of these were found at Tres Zapotes. Monument N was a true cylinder with a circular depression on top. Monument D was similar but somewhat rounded toward the base (Stirling, 1943, pl. 10).

Another cylinder, Monument 14, at La Venta (Drucker, 1952a, pl. 15) was similar in size and shape to Monument N, but the perforation passed completely through. Later, however, it had been neatly plugged at the base and when found was standing upright, *in situ*. This may have been originally a roller for smoothing floors in the stone palisaded court and later converted into an offertory.

At Tres Zapotes another well-worked cylinder (Stirling, 1943, pl. 15) lacks the basin on top. It, too, may have been a roller.

A similar object, circular but bowl-shaped rather than cylindrical, was found near Lake Catemaco (Blom and LaFarge, 1926–27, fig. 26). It apparently dates from pre-Aztec times and was contemporary with the stone boxes found in the same locality.

Stone Balls

A stone ball, Monument 13, 115 inches in diameter, was found at the Olmec site of San Lorenzo Tenochtitlan (Stirling, 1955, pl. 11), two other examples at Cerro de las Mesas (Stirling, 1943, pl. 30). Since the beginnings of Cerro de las Mesas fall in late Olmec times, it is probable that all are of Olmec origin. One of the Cerro de las Mesas examples has a plane surface ground on one side. The purpose of these balls is unknown but they are reminiscent of the larger specimens from southwestern Costa Rica. It is just possible that they may have been astronomical symbols.

REFERENCES

Blom and LaFarge, 1926–27
Coe, M. D., 1957b
Cook de Leonard, 1959c
Covarrubias, 1957
Drucker, 1952a
——, Heizer, and Squier, 1959
Greengo, 1952
Jiménez Moreno, 1942
Proskouriakoff, 1950
Stirling, 1940, 1943, 1955, 1957

29. The Olmec Style and its Distributions

MICHAEL D. COE

ALTHOUGH OBJECTS of what we now designate the Olmec art style have been known for many years in collections from Mexico (see Saville's 1929 study of votive axes), its distinctive features and unity were first recognized by Vaillant (1932), who christened it "Olmec."

Vaillant recognized that the provenience for most of the objects in this peculiar style was the region of southern Veracruz and neighboring Tabasco. Blom and La-Farge (1926–27, 1: 81–90) visited La Venta and other Olmec sites, but were inclined to ascribe the monuments to the Maya. It was not until Stirling's field excavations at Tres Zapotes from 1938 to 1940 and at La Venta in 1939–40 and 1942–43 that the full splendor of Olmec civilization was revealed, in a series of colossal stone heads and larger sculptured monuments, as well as fine jade figurines and other artifacts. From his analyses of the ceramics from stratigraphic cuts at these sites Drucker (1943a, b; 1952a) believed at that time, as did the majority of American archaeologists concerned with the Olmec problem, that the style may have begun as early as the Preclassic period but reached its height during the Early Classic. Nevertheless, Stirling, influenced by the Cycle 7 date on Stela C at Tres Zapotes, a monument in a derived Olmec style, believed that the peak of Olmec culture came in the Preclassic. He was backed in this by such Mexican archaeologists as Caso and Bernal, who had found Olmec-influenced carvings in the definitely Preclassic Monte Alban I, and by Covarrubias, who had collected purely Olmec figurines at the Preclassic site of Tlatilco, outside Mexico City.

An attempt to resolve these conflicts of judgment was made at the Mesa Redonda in Tuxtla Gutierrez (Sociedad Mexicana de Antropología, 1942). At this time, Caso and Covarrubias presented important definitions of the Olmec style and its distribution in space and time, the latter listing a number of important elements which make up the style. The conference concluded that the Olmec culture was confined to the Preclassic, in spite of its remarkably high development.

FIG. 1—STELA, PADRE PIEDRA, CHIAPAS. Height 2.20 m., width 1.10 m. (Courtesy, Carlos Navarrete.)

FIG. 2—PETROGLYPH 1, CHALCATZINGO, MORELOS. (From Covarrubias, 1957, pl. 13, top.)

FIG. 3—PETROGLYPH 2, CHALCATZINGO, MORELOS. (From Piña Chan, 1955, p. 69.)

FIG. 4—STONE OBJECT, TLACOTEPEC, GUERRERO. (From Covarrubias, 1946, p. 26.)

Further important contributions to the understanding of the Olmec style were made by Covarrubias in his article of 1946 (which has a much fuller compendium of traits), in his book *Mexico South* (1947), and, above all, in his posthumous *Indian Art of Mexico and Central America* (1957), which contains the best statement in print about Olmec art and its characteristics. Drucker's 1952a report was an objective study of the style, but was hampered by a faulty placement of Olmec culture in time, the author still insisting on an Early Classic date. Greengo (1952) admirably summed up what was then known about the Olmec problem, but shed no new light on the chronology. Wauchope (1954, p. 34, n. 40) presented ceramic evidence for assigning La Venta to the Preclassic ("Late Formative") period.

The most significant development in recent years has been the publication (Drucker, Heizer, and Squier, 1959) of the 1955 excavations at La Venta. A long series of radiocarbon dates firmly anchors the florescent Olmec art of La Venta to the Preclassic, placing the Olmec style at the very base of all other known Middle American great styles. Furthermore, the authors discuss Olmec problem in detail, especially yet-unanswered questions about the ultimate origins of the style.

MATERIALS OF OLMEC ART

The Olmec art style appears on a very wide range of objects that vary tremendously in size and material. These objects may be divided into monumental and portable, an important distinction because large and extremely heavy monuments may be presumed to have been carved *in situ* and therefore testify to the actual presence of the bearers of the Olmec style. On the other hand, portable objects, being relatively light and small, could have been traded across Olmec boundaries to distant peoples (as seems to have been the case), where they could have been treasured as heirlooms for centuries or millennia. It may be reasonably inferred, however, that where these small objects are concentrated, to the near exclusion of objects in other contemporaneous styles, there may have been an actual Olmec population.

Monumental Art

The most striking of Olmec monuments are the colossal heads of basalt which may be as much as 3 m. high and sometimes weigh more than 10 tons. These appear to be restricted to the climax region of Olmec art, in lower Veracruz and neighboring Tabasco, and have been found so far only at La Venta, Tres Zapotes, and San Lorenzo. They are somewhat divergent in style from the usual Olmec canon, being rather Negroid in physiognomy; most Olmec faces are noticeably "Oriental."

FIG. 5—PETROGLYPHS ON BOULDER AT LAS VICTORIAS, EL SALVADOR. (From Boggs, 1950, fig. 1.)

Fig. 6—JADE FIGURINE, PROVENIENCE UNKNOWN. Height 17.8 cm. Bliss Coll. (Courtesy, S. K. Lothrop.)

Stelae also are concentrated in the climax region and are very rare elsewhere. The granite stela of Padre Piedra in Chiapas is an unusual exception (fig. 1). More recently Medellín Zenil (1960c) describes a large stela with two figures in Olmec style from Viejon, near Actopan, Veracruz; this may be considered, like Padre Piedra, a "colonial Olmec" site. What Stirling has labeled as altars, rectangular blocks of basalt usually elaborately carved, seem to be restricted to La Venta, San Lorenzo, and Potrero Nuevo. Bas-reliefs or pictographs, carved on large boulders or rock outcrops, are particularly characteristic of the climax region, but are also found in Chalcatzingo, Morelos (fig. 2, 3); Tonala, Chiapas (Ferdon, 1953, pl. 23b); San Isidro Piedra Parada, Guatemala (Thompson, 1943c); and Las Victorias, El Salvador (fig. 5). Large stone sculptures in the round are a trait mainly of the climax region.

Portable Art

The great majority of the smaller objects in Olmec style, either from excavations or in collections, are of stone—usually jade or serpentine, but occasionally basalt or another coarse-grained rock. The style very seldom appears on pottery vessels or figurines, unlike the pieces by the Classic Maya, who applied their art to every kind of pottery artifact. Olmec jade is very often of high quality and is bluish green to bluish gray; it may be readily distinguished from Classic Maya jade, the best quality of which is of a more yellowish hue, usually apple-green. Only one example of the style on a wooden object has been discovered (fig. 26), but it may be that sculpture in wood was not uncommon.

The most common portable art objects are the small stone figurines (figs. 6–16), usually in jade or some other greenish stone like serpentine, but also in various black stones. One hematite figurine is known. These objects vary widely in quality of stone and fineness of carving; many appear to be rather simple replicas of pottery figurines, but some are unusually fine. A few have been pierced at the back for use as pendants.

Second in frequency are decorated celts of jade, serpentine, and black slate (figs. 17–19). The engraving on these sometimes ranks with the finest productions of Olmec art, as on the celt from Simojovel, Chiapas (fig. 17).

Various kinds of plaques (figs. 20–24) were almost certainly used as pectorals, for most are pierced for suspension; they appear as such on Stela 3 at La Venta. These are made from jade, fine-grained basalt, porphyry, and several other kinds of stone, are usually shaped somewhat like

FIG. 7—JADE FIGURINE, PROVENIENCE UNKNOWN. Brooklyn Museum Coll.

FIG. 8—JADE FIGURINE, SAN CRISTOBAL TEPATLAXCO, PUEBLA. Height 11.1 cm. Bliss Coll. (Courtesy, S. K. Lothrop.)

FIG. 9—JADE FIGURINE, PROVENIENCE UNKNOWN. Height 10 cm. Bliss Coll. (Courtesy, S. K. Lothrop.)

FIG. 10—SERPENTINE FIGURINE, XICO, VERACRUZ. Height 11 cm. (Courtesy, Chicago Natural History Museum.)

FIG. 11—DANCING FIGURE OF SERPENTINE, SAN CRISTOBAL TEPATLAXCO, PUEBLA. Length ca. 11 cm. Bliss Coll. (Courtesy, S. K. Lothrop.)

FIG. 12—JADE FIGURINE, PROVENIENCE UNKNOWN. Height 10.9 cm. (Courtesy, Cleveland Museum of Art, J. H. Wade Coll.)

FIG. 13—JADE FIGURINE, NECAXA, PUEBLA Height ca. 7.5 cm. (Courtesy, American Museum of Natural History.)

FIG. 14—FRAGMENTARY FIGURINE OF BLACK STONE, PROVENIENCE UNKNOWN. Height ca. 12.5 cm. (Courtesy, American Museum of Natural History.)

a rounded rectangle, and are decorated with engraving or a combination of this with excising. An unusual example from Cerro de las Mesas is canoe-shaped (fig. 23). Many of the so-called "masks" of stone are also to be regarded as pectorals, since they are too small to have been worn over the face. Other objects suspended on the body are small pendants, like the fine duck-billed effigy in the Bliss Collection (fig. 25).

Some masks were undoubtedly just that. The miraculously preserved wood mask encrusted with jade, from Cañon de la Mano, Guerrero, is the outstanding example (fig. 26).

Effigy axes of jade, basalt, or other stone, have been known in collections for many years. Drucker, Heizer, and Squier point out that these have so far never been encountered at La Venta; some probably come from far afield, beyond the borders of the climax area. Occasionally these are so thin and so completely useless as axes that they are little more than plaques, with the axe outline.

Miscellaneous small stone objects with Olmec-style decoration include a spoon-like artifact of jade from Guerrero (fig. 29), finely engraved jade ear spools from La Venta, an engraved obsidian core from the same site (fig. 38), jade "stilettos" in the

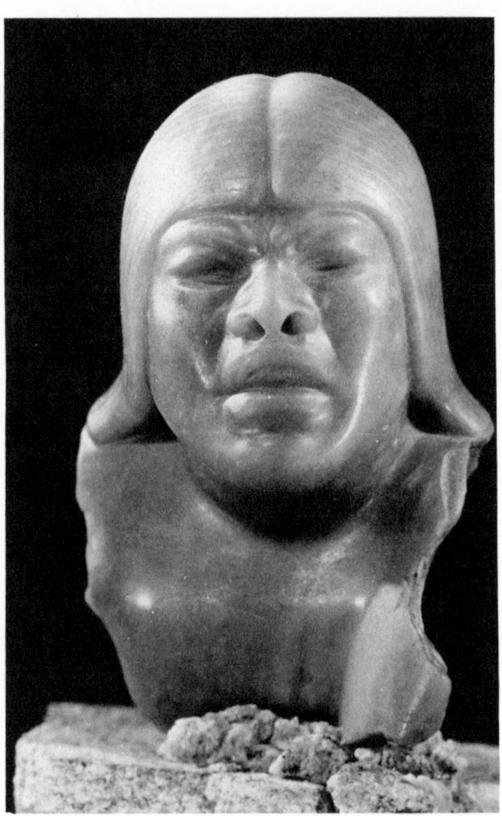

Fig. 15—FRAGMENTARY JADE FIGURINE. Height 6 cm. Bliss Coll. (Courtesy, S. K. Lothrop.)

Bliss Collection (fig. 32), and a unique jade bead in the form of a head, now in the Berlin Museum.

As mentioned above, pottery objects in the Olmec style are exceedingly rare, even at such sites as La Venta and Tres Zapotes. One can only conclude that the ceramic art was in the hands of persons who did not participate to any extent in the mystic symbolism of the Olmec style. Two hollow figurines in a thorough-going Olmec tradition were excavated by the Vaillants (1934) at Gualupita, Morelos (fig. 33), but such fine examples are almost nonexistent elsewhere except at Tlatilco and Tlapacoya. From the latter site we also have a carved roller stamp bearing three Olmec glyphs or signs. The beautifully decorated flat-bottomed bowl in a private collection in Mexico (fig. 34), and some Tlatilco and Tlapacoya examples, comprise the only vessels in Olmec style, unless one includes the fine effigy incense burners from Monte Negro (fig. 35) and Monte Alban I, which have very Olmec characteristics.

Finally, mention should be made of small stone sculptures which probably were transportable. One of the finest examples of Olmec art is the "Wrestler" from the Corona collection (fig. 36). Other small sculptures of basalt have been found in the climax region.

Definition of the Olmec Style

The qualities of the art style considered here are those which are characteristic of Olmec culture as it has been revealed in the climax region, spanning approximately 800–400 B.C. As Drucker realized, whether this is the Olmec "heartland" or not, a pre-

Fig. 16—JADE FIGURINE OF A WERE-JAGUAR WITH BAT WINGS, GUANACASTE PROVINCE, COSTA RICA. Brooklyn Museum Coll.

cise definition of the style must be limited and not allowed to range over the map, absorbing every known piece which looks the least bit Olmec. Outside the climax region only those objects which fit this definition will be regarded as belonging to the Olmec style. The highest achievements of Preclassic Middle America were attained in the Olmec climax region, and it would be difficult not to agree with Drucker, Heizer, and Squier that this was the *fons et origo* of the style and its ramifications.

Formal Qualities

The Olmec style is strongly contrasted with all other Middle American styles not only in its iconographic content of baby-faced, snarling were-jaguars and cleft heads but in its formal qualities of shape, line, and space. In the sense that it eschews geometric abstraction for curvilinear natu-

Fig. 17—BLACK SLATE CELT, SIMOJOVEL, CHIAPAS. Length 31.2 cm. (Courtesy, M. W. Stirling and National Geographic Society.)

Fig. 18—CAST OF JADE CELT. Length 21 cm. Formerly in Humboldt Coll., Berlin Museum. (Courtesy, Smithsonian Institution.)

Fig. 19—JADE CELT, PROVENIENCE UNKNOWN. Length 35.5 cm. (From Covarrubias, 1957, fig. 33, right.)

ralism, the style is "realistic"; in fact, it is more "realistic" than even the Classic Maya, if one takes into account that the Olmec artists were depicting creatures that they believed actually existed, no matter how monstrous or farfetched. The extraordinarily sensitive treatment of the human form in such sculptures as the Corona "Wrestler" or Altar 5 (the "Quintuplet Altar") at La Venta is not matched by any known Maya sculpture. This is not to say that the treatment of monstrous forms is not grotesque; it is, but it is never reduced to abstraction.

Fig. 20—JADE PLAQUE, PROVENIENCE UNKNOWN. Height ca. 15 cm. (From Groth-Kimball, 1953, pl. 21.)

Fig. 21—JADE PLAQUE, PROVENIENCE UNKNOWN. Glyphs in early Maya style are incised on back. (Courtesy, American Museum of Natural History.)

Fig. 22—JADE PLAQUE, PROVENIENCE UNKNOWN. Height ca. 8.3 cm. (Courtesy, British Museum.)

In spite of the over-all realism and interest in faithful depiction of the well-fed human form, there are certain archaic, somewhat primitive features which show up. Among these is the general adherence to profile depiction of the body, from head to toe, in bas-relief sculptures and in engraved designs. The feet usually point in the same direction, and the shins are characteristically concave; only the shoulders and torso face the onlooker, as in Egyptian tomb reliefs. This profile treatment, with concavity of the shins, is a trait of several early art syles of Middle America, as seen in the Late Preclassic art of Izapa and Loltun cave, and in the Early Classic art of the Maya (Proskouriakoff, 1950).

On a more formal level, we can examine the Olmec treatment of space. Classic Maya sculpture has a notorious horror vacui; the idea is to fill up everything, rather than leave blanks. The Olmec utilized space to give three-dimensional depth to bas-reliefs, by establishing a tension between forms; clutter would have destroyed this effect. Another Olmec feature is the emphasis on curved lines; perhaps the basis of the Olmec canon was that rectangles and squares must always be rounded and slightly leaned into parallelograms, and circles avoided. The combination of tension in space and the slow rhythm of the lines produces the overwhelmingly monumental character of Olmec art. No matter how small the object, it always looks much larger than it really is. The Olmec emphasized this property by not overloading the forms with a baroque pro-

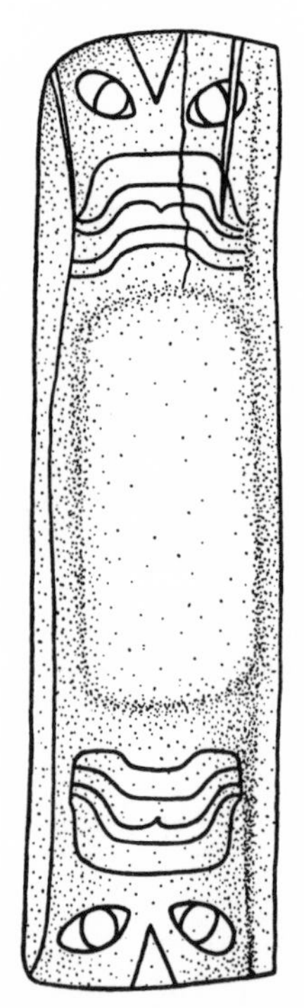

Fig. 23—CANOE-SHAPED PLAQUE OF JADE, CERRO DE LAS MESAS CACHE. (From Drucker, 1955, fig. 5.)

Fig. 24—DIORITE MASK-PLAQUE, PROVENIENCE UNKNOWN. Height 13.2 cm. Bliss Coll. (Courtesy, S. K. Lothrop.)

fusion of costume details and by concentrating on the solid qualities of body.

A further development of this idea of external space is seen in the great frequency of sculpture in the round. This is true not only of monumental art (cf. the colossal heads, the figures in the niches of the La Venta altars, and other climax region sculptures) but also of small sculptures and even of jades. Again, this contrasts notably with the Maya area, where three-dimensional sculpture or carving is extremely rare; even the small Classic pottery figurines from Jaina and elsewhere are to be seen really only from the front. In part, the full carving of Olmec jades may be a function of the greater availability of jade in the Preclassic, since most Maya jades are mere bas-reliefs on thin plates of the material. The monumental quality of Olmec art may also be seen in these smaller sculptures. By avoiding costume and other surface details and by carefully posing the muscular seated figure in *contrapposto*, the sculptor of the Corona "Wrestler" created a piece of great power which appears to be bigger than life size although it is only 65 cm. high.

The wide use of engraved lines either by themselves (as on the decorated celts) or in common with excision and bas-relief is a characteristic of the Olmec style. Many smaller objects such as the effigy axes, the plaques, or jade figurines, have extensive engraving which often is hard to see in most published photographs. This may represent actual tattooing when present on faces, but generally engraved details give additional iconographic information (such as were-jaguar heads in profile or fullface). Very rarely, what are probably true hieroglyphs are inscribed on jade objects in this manner.

It has been stated above that the Olmec artists were uninterested in producing abstract or geometric forms, but this is not

FIG. 25—JADE PENDANT, DISTRITO DE BALSAS, GUERRERO. Bliss Coll. (Courtesy, S. K. Lothrop.)

FIG. 26—WOODEN MASK INCRUSTED WITH JADE, CANON DE LA MANO, GUERRERO. Height 18 cm. (Courtesy, American Museum of Natural History.)

completely true. Certain iconographic elements are so reduced that in some cases they are represented by almost entirely geometric symbols (see the four-dots-and-bar symbol, below fig. 43,*c*, as shown in the mosaic pavements of La Venta). This is uncommon, however.

Iconography

The Olmec style cannot be separated from its content, or iconography, for its weird jaguar-baby symbolism is the hallmark of the style. We have no definite knowledge in tradition and no inscriptions to guide us in seeking out the mythical basis of Olmec iconography. Nevertheless, in the climax region, and in that alone, a number of sculptures found by Stirling and others at the Olmec sites of La Venta, Tres Zapotes, San Lorenzo, Potrero Nuevo, and Rio Chiquito, seem to point to what we might term the central myth underlying the Olmec religion and its art. There is no way to prove this, but our interpretation of these representations may not be so far wrong, in the account that follows.

The Olmec evidently believed that a jaguar had copulated with a woman in the mythical past. One sculpture, discovered by Stirling and recognized by him as depicting this event (Stirling, 1955, p. 19, pl. 25), is Monument 3 at Potrero Nuevo; the realism of the monument leaves no question about his interpretation. Whether the woman was a mortal or a goddess of some sort cannot be answered. Women are rarely depicted in Olmec art (even the simple pottery figurines at La Venta are largely sexless or androgynous); but Stela 1 at La Venta shows a woman, with the typical short skirt of the Middle Preclassic, standing in a niche, above which is the stylized face of a jaguar. This may be related to the same concept. The jade head from the Bliss Collection and the "spoon" from Guerrero both depict women with long coiffures, but these have the slightly heavy and downturned mouths of the were-jaguars. The jaguar, in pure form, is also somewhat rare; most show contamination with the were-jaguar concept. Monument 2 at Rio Chiquito (Stirling, 1955, pl. 3,*a,c*)

FIG. 27—JADE EFFIGY AXE (THE "KUNZ AXE"), PROVENIENCE UNKNOWN. Height 28 cm. (Courtesy, American Museum of Natural History.)

is in the form of a crouching, quite lifelike jaguar; Monument 7 from San Lorenzo (Stirling, 1955, pl. 17,*a*) may show the same subject. A porphyry mask in the Bliss Collection also seems untouched by anthropomorphism.

It is reasonable to conclude that this union resulted in a race of infants combining the features of the jaguar and man in varying degrees. These are usually shown as somewhat infantile throughout life, with the puffy features of small fat babies, snarling mouths, fangs, and perhaps even claws. The heads are cleft at the top. There is something so completely abnormal about these were-jaguar babies that an origin of the concept in observed births of defective infants with some such syndrome of traits is not unlikely. *Spina bifida,* for instance, results in stillborn individuals with open crania and often with snarling, idiot-like faces; it would be a quick step from these to the cloven-headed were-jaguars. On Altar 5 at La Venta each of five of such creatures is held by what seems to be an attendant priest; here the clefts look like real deformities. Another good depiction of the were-jaguar baby is on a jade from Olinala, Guerrero (fig. 37). They are always quite sexless, with the obesity of eunuchs.

These were-jaguar babies evidently became sky gods or perhaps rain gods. A number of them are shown flying through the air, carrying weapons, above the central figures on Stela 3 at La Venta (Drucker, Heizer, and Squier, 1959, fig. 67). The attributes of the adult were-jaguar are the cleft, the snarling mouth with jaguar fangs, sometimes the flamelike element for brows, and occasionally a small, pointed beard. These are among the most common iconographic motifs in Olmec art, showing up in figurines, effigy axes, jade plaques, and monuments. They may have been thought of as carrying on a kind of "war in heaven" among themselves, as seen on Stela 3, and at Chalcatzingo in Petroglyph 2 (fig. 3), where they are carrying war clubs; or perhaps they battled together in behalf of the Olmec. Covarrubias (1957, fig. 22) has convincingly demonstrated the stylistic evolution of the Monte Alban, Teotihuacan, Tajin, and Maya rain gods from the Olmec were-jaguar, so that there can be little doubt of its role in Olmec religion.

A bearded were-jaguar may have been the lord of all these little creatures, for some important pieces of Olmec art depict such a monster. The most impressive example is the polished black stone fragment (fig. 14) in which the being carries something which may be a ceremonial bar. A plaque from the Mixteca in Oaxaca (Covarrubias, 1947, pl. 7) has a very jaguar-like face, but is bearded. The purely Olmec figure (Thompson, 1943c, p. 111*a*) of a running (?), bearded were-jaguar carved on a boulder at San Isidro Piedra Parada, on the Pacific slope of Guatemala, is iconographically close to both the figures on Petroglyph 2, Chalcatzingo, and on Stela 3 at La Venta.

Two very similar figurines, one of serpentine from San Cristobal Tepatlaxco, Puebla (fig. 11), and the other of jade found at San Geronimo, Guerrero (Covarrubias, 1947, pl. 8), show a very anthropomorphic were-jaguar dancing, evidently doing an *entrechat* with one arm raised to the head. They are reminiscent of the Olmecoid "dancing" were-jaguars on bas-reliefs of Monte Alban I date.

Two small jade figurines of a were-jaguar with upraised, batlike wings from Guanacaste, Costa Rica, are so far unique (fig. 16).

Although the overwhelming bulk of objects in Olmec style is confined to the were-jaguar motif, certain other motifs are not uncommon. A bird or, more correctly, a bird-monster is shown on a number of objects, and is derived from some raptorial creature like the eagle. The clearest depiction is on the engraved obsidian core from La Venta, which shows the bird with outstretched wings (fig. 38); in spite of the presence of a kan cross in the eye, this is an eagle. The bird-monster appears in several other La Venta objects, such as on an engraved celt from Offering No. 2 (where it is much anthropomorphized) and on engraved ear spools of jade. The figure with an eagle-claw hat at San Lorenzo is described below. A celt from the Cerro de las Mesas offering (fig. 40) is also the bird-monster, as Drucker notes, and is in Olmec style. A duck-monster different from the raptorial bird just mentioned appears twice in Olmec art: on Monument 9 at San Lorenzo, which is in the shape of a hollow duck and has carved on it a small duck flapping its wings, and on the jade pendant from the Bliss Collection in the form of a human face with a duck bill (fig. 25). The latter when looked at as a whole is also a cicada, the duck's bill serving as the wings of the insect. Duck-billed figures persist into the Early Classic, when they

FIG. 28—STONE EFFIGY AXE, PROBABLY FROM OAXACA. Height ca. 21.5 cm. (Courtesy, Smithsonian Institution.)

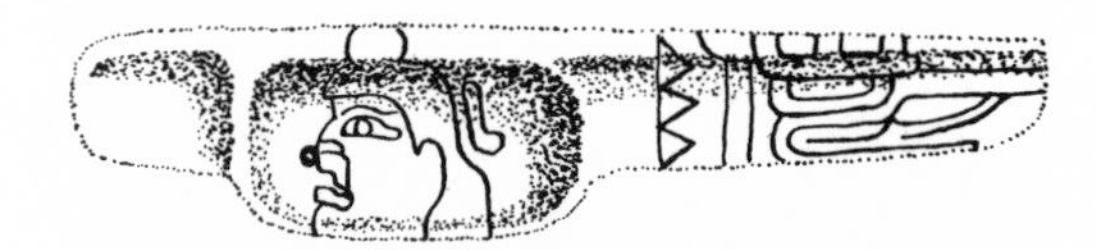

Fig. 29—JADE "SPOON," DISTRITO DE BALSAS, GUERRERO. Length 10.6 cm. Private collection. (From Covarrubias, 1946, fig. 24.)

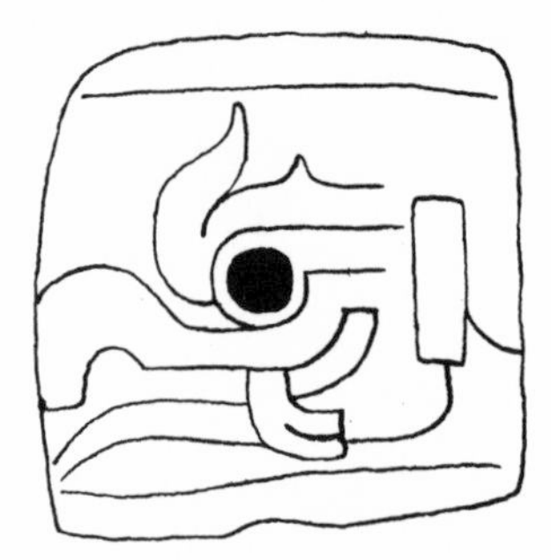

Fig. 30—INCISED JADE EARPLUG, LA VENTA. (From Covarrubias, 1947, p. 94, right.)

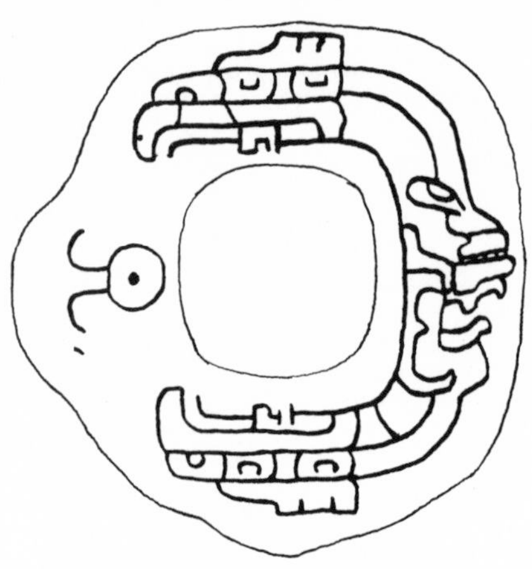

Fig. 31—INCISED JADE EARPLUG, LA VENTA. (From Covarrubias, 1947, p. 94, left.)

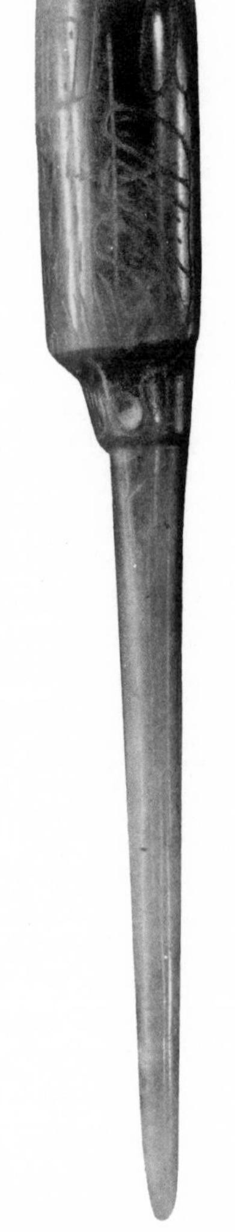

Fig. 32—INCISED JADE "STILETTO," PROVENIENCE UNKNOWN. Length ca. 17 cm. Bliss Coll. (Courtesy, S. K. Lothrop.)

are found at Cerro de las Mesas and notably on the Tuxtla Statuette.

Other animals are seldom encountered in Olmec art. An almost unique motif can be seen on Monument 19, La Venta, as a human figure seated in the curve formed by the undulating body of a rattlesnake. Drucker, Heizer, and Squier identify this beast as the Feathered Serpent, but it is difficult to see any indication of feathers. The face of the snake has no jaguar features. At Potrero Nuevo is a serpent carved in the round; the body is arranged in intricate convolutions, but the head is missing (Stirling, 1955, pl. 26,*b*). The single representation of a monkey yet discovered in Olmec style is Monument 12 at La Venta (Drucker, 1952a, pl. 62), and even this is not within the usual Olmec canon; the engraved were-jaguar on the belt of the animal, however, is purely Olmec. A monstrous fish appears on the headdress of the "Uncle Sam" figure of Stela 3, La Venta. Drucker, Heizer, and Squier (1959, fig. 56, pl. 50) tentatively identify Monument 20 at La Venta as a whale.

In the Preclassic art styles of Middle America, what seems to be symbolic representations of the sky, or clouds, are delineated by volutes with or without raised edges (see the monuments at Izapa, El Baul, and Colomba). Such a representation also occurs in Olmec art, on the upper portion of Monument 26, La Venta (Drucker, Heizer, and Squier, 1959, fig. 60, pl. 53). Above the seated personage of Petroglyph 1, Chalcatzingo, who seems to be associated with sky volutes, is the same device repeated twice, three tiers of cloudlike volutes below which stream vertical parallel lines (fig. 41). This must represent a rain cloud, not unlike that known in Pueblo art of the American Southwest.

Humans without noticeably jaguar or baby-like characteristics do occur on the monuments of the climax region, but seldom on the portable art and hardly anywhere outside the area. It is of course not beyond probability that the Olmec artists tended to look at everybody as having a little bit of jaguar-baby in him, but it would be safer to consider as portraits only those depictions without such an aspect. The individuality of some of these human portraits is so strong that they must represent historical personages. Most of these are bearded, like the famous "Uncle Sam" figure on Stela 3, La Venta, and like this, often have hooked noses. Two individuals are seated conversing on Altar 3, La Venta, and are clearly portraits of different men. The same might be said of Monument 13 at La Venta (Drucker, 1952a, pl. 63, fig. 61), showing a man walking with what seems to be a flag in one hand; this is quite portrait-like, and what may have been his name was carved and probably painted in three glyphs next to the figure.

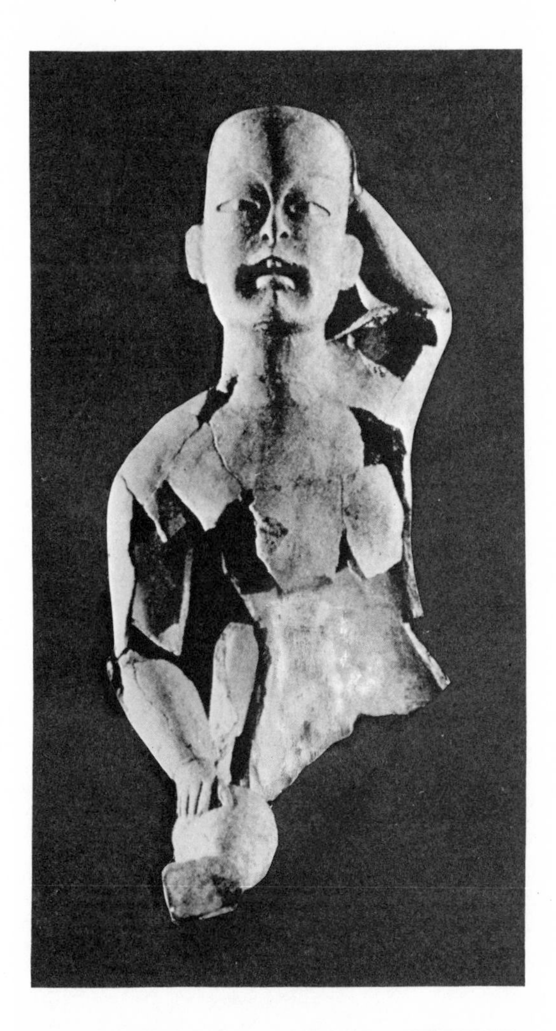

FIG. 33—HOLLOW POTTERY FIGURINE, GUALUPITA, MORELOS. (From Vaillant and Vaillant, 1934, fig. 14, no. 3.)

It is more difficult to decide whether the figure in bas-relief on the south end of Monument 14 at San Lorenzo, wearing an eagle-claw hat with broad and tasseled brim, is a portrait or not, for there is a suggestion of were-jaguar in the profile face. The Corona "Wrestler" must have been a real person, in spite of a trace of the were-jaguar mouth.

The Olmec were deeply interested in deformity, as were almost all Preclassic peoples in Middle America; a small serpentine hunchback was found in the Cerro de las Mesas offering (Drucker, 1955, pl. 28).

Fig. 34—POTTERY VESSEL, PROVENIENCE UNKNOWN. Height 20 cm. Private collection. (From Groth-Kimball, 1953, pl. 22.)

Fig. 35—POTTERY INCENSE BURNER, MONTE NEGRO, OAXACA. Height 15.7 cm. (From Groth-Kimball, 1953, pl. 34.)

The most horrific depiction is a chinless baby or dwarf of black serpentine, bought by Covarrubias in Iguala, Guerrero (Covarrubias, 1947, fig. 12, below). Potbellied dwarfs in the role of atlantean figures appear on Monument 2 at Potrero Nuevo (Stirling, 1955, pl. 23).

Symbols

Although it is often stated that the Olmec had hieroglyphic writing (see for instance Coe, 1957b; Knorosov, 1958a), the evidence for this is admittedly slim. It cannot be denied, however, that real hieroglyphs resembling those of the Maya occasionally are found inscribed on small objects, so that we may guess that these people had more extensive records written on perishable materials which have not survived. The Long Count date in bar-and-dot numerals on Stela C, Tres Zapotes, although certainly to be considered Cycle 7 (Coe, 1957b), is associated with a face mask of the were-jaguar which is in an epi-Olmec style and probably later than the Olmec style itself, but it is not unlikely that the use of written numerals goes far back into the Olmec past.

In spite of the paucity of hieroglyphs in Olmec art, a fairly extensive use is made of a symbolic system which apparently had religious meaning. Many of these symbols, such as the cleft, appear over and over again, but some occur only once or twice in the whole corpus of Olmec art. Regarding the Humboldt celt (fig. 18), on which are engraved many symbols, we are in doubt whether hieroglyphic writing is involved or whether this is a symbolic "language" without real linguistic reference—merely to be "read" like the symbols which indicate the Trinity, for instance, in Christian churches. It may be that later hieroglyphic systems originated in such symbols.

Symbols relating to the were-jaguar are relatively common, as might be expected. Most frequently encountered are variations of the cloven-head concept, found not only on certain monuments at La Venta but on all sorts of other objects, and frequently by itself as a sort of swallowtail-shaped element. On some engraved celts, what appear to be shoots of a plant like corn sprout from the cleft, perhaps indicating that the were-jaguar was also connected with maize fertility. Eyebrows expressed as flamelike scrolls are also a were-jaguar motif, usually missing on the monuments of the climax region but frequent on smaller representations such as effigy axes, plaques, celts, and "masks" (fig. 43,*a*). Occasionally, as on the headdress of the figure on the Simojovel celt, these scrolls resemble the cleft element. Flame-scroll brows are a characteristic of most later art styles of the Preclassic.

The fangs of the were-jaguar are not pointed, as one would expect, but terminate in a square-ended cleft. This element has a high frequency in Olmec art, appearing by itself or combined with other elements (fig. 43,*b*). On an engraved celt from La Venta, it is united to the U element (see below) to frame a highly stylized face. A similar bracketing of central theme with the fang motif is shown in Petroglyph 1 at Chalcatzingo, in which the central figure is seated within a curvilinear band which has at both ends the cleft fang, probably indicating symbolically the jaws of the were-jaguar. Jaguar paws, with greatly lengthened digits and much stylized, are depicted on certain Tlatilco vessels.

It is apparent that the were-jaguar was depicted at times in a very abstract fashion, with certain elements so reduced that they are hardly recognizable. The brows of the monster can be shown combined as a single or remain as a double geometric element with three pendant bars. Likewise, the face is reduced to four dots and a vertical bar, the two upper dots standing for the eyes, and the two lower ones for the mouth (or the drilled depressions on both sides of the Olmec

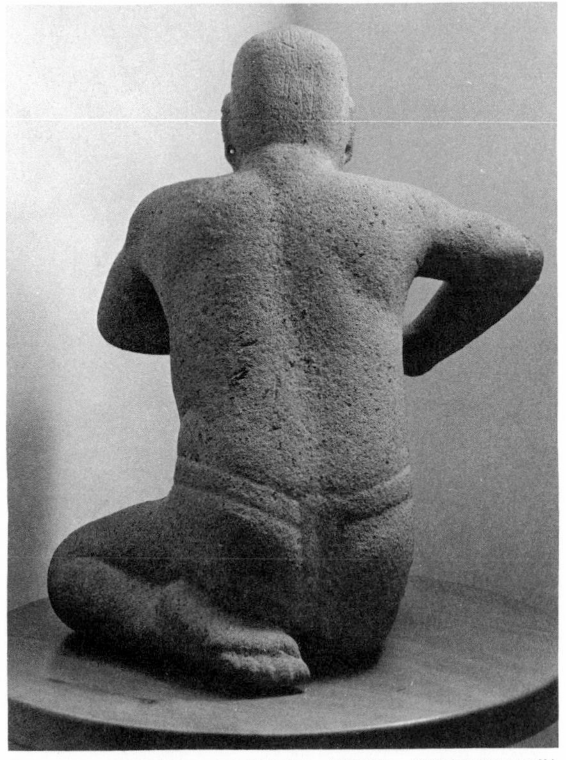

Fig. 36—BASALT FIGURE ("THE WRESTLER") Height 65 cm. Corona Coll., from near Minatitlan, southern Veracruz.

Fig. 37—JADE FIGURE, OLINALA, GUERRERO (From Covarrubias, 1947, figure on p. 98.)

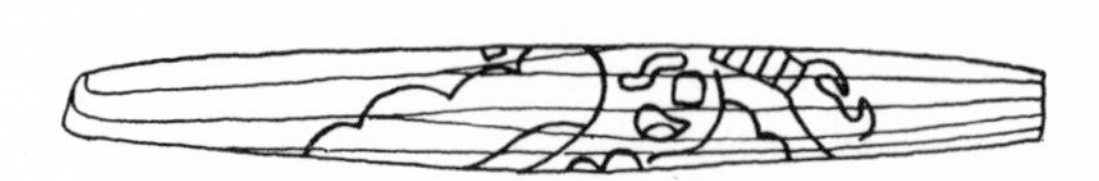

Fig. 38—DESIGN ENGRAVED ON OBSIDIAN CORE, LA VENTA. (From Drucker, 1952a, fig. 48.)

Fig. 39—DESIGN ENGRAVED ON CELT FROM OFFERING NO. 2, LA VENTA. (From Drucker, Heizer, and Squier, 1959, fig. 35,*b*.)

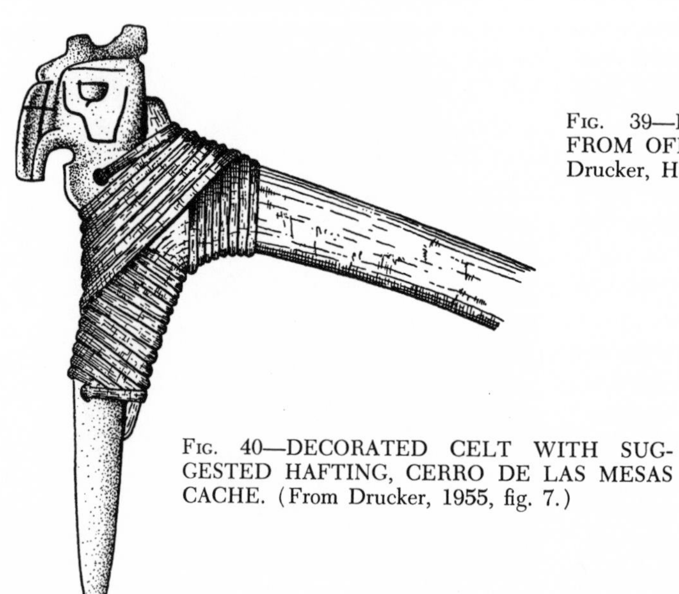

Fig. 40—DECORATED CELT WITH SUGGESTED HAFTING, CERRO DE LAS MESAS CACHE. (From Drucker, 1955, fig. 7.)

Fig. 41—SKY OR CLOUD SYMBOL, PETROGLYPH 1, CHALCATZINGO

mouth) (fig. 43,*c*). The supreme examples of such an abstraction are the famous mosaic pavements at La Venta, formed of serpentine blocks (fig. 45). Drucker, Heizer, and Squier (1959, p. 93, fig. 29) are surely in error in their orientation of this feature and identification of its elements. The cleft should be at the top, not at the jaw, as they indicate. The geometric pendant brow is below the cleft; the four-dot-and-vertical-bar motif stands for the eyes, nose, and mouth; the dots are rectangular in shape and contain the double-step motif (see below). The pendant elements at the bottom of the mask are in the diamond-feather motif and certainly do not represent a headdress. This orientation is confirmed by the same arrangement of elements in abstract were-jaguar faces as seen on an engraved celt from La Venta, Offering No. 2 (fig. 44), in one of the three glyphs on a roller stamp from Tlatilco (fig. 47), and on the lower portion of a votive axe (Covarrubias, 1957, fig. 32, below). The four-dot-and-vertical-bar element appears on several other engraved celts from La Venta, with the cleft always at top. The geometric pendant brow in correct orientation can be seen on the headdress of one of the figures on Petroglyph 2, Chalcatzingo, and so cannot be a mouth, as claimed by the authors above cited.

Some purely geometric elements which have no certain meaning occur very frequently in Olmec art. Most common among these is the St. Andrew's cross, depicted so that one bar crosses over the other (fig. 43,*e*). It appears in the mouth of the were-jaguar face over the niche of Altar 4 at La Venta. It is sometimes worn on the headdresses of figures in Olmec monuments or smaller objects, such as the figure in the niche of Altar 5, La Venta, all figures in Petroglyph 2, Chalcatzingo, or the figure on the Simojovel celt. It can also appear on the fronts of belts as on a figure on a small engraved celt (fig. 52), on the baby were-jaguar from Necaxa, and

FIG. 42—WERE-JAGUAR MASK-PANEL, STELA C, TRES ZAPOTES. (From Covarrubias, 1957, fig. 19, left.)

on a jade figurine from Peto, Yucatan. It can also stand by itself, as on many engraved celts, and obviously is one of the most important elements on the textlike Humboldt celt (fig. 18). Its symbolism is unknown. The St. Andrew's cross is especially characteristic of Izapa art and in its ramifications in the Guatemalan highlands, and appears on the planetary bands of Classic Maya art. Whatever it stood for, it was highly important to the Olmec and other Preclassic peoples.

Another motif with a wide distribution not only in Olmec art but also in that of other Preclassic and Early Classic cultures is the U element (fig. 43,*d*). This may be merely bracket-shaped, rather like an inverted croquet-hoop, or it may have tapering and slightly outflaring ends. Its most notable occurrence is on the front of the headdress of Monument 1, a colossal head, at La Venta. It forms the lowermost element on the Humboldt celt, and appears rather frequently elsewhere. The U element is a characteristic of the Izapa style and of the early monuments of the Maya highlands and lowlands, and may probably correspond to the Maya bracket element, which originally seems to have been the

Fig. 43—SYMBOLIC MOTIFS IN OLMEC ART. *a,* Flame brows. *b,* Fangs. *c,* Four-dots-and-bar. *d,* U element. *e,* St. Andrew's cross. *f,* Kin sign. g, Kan cross. *h,* Step motif.

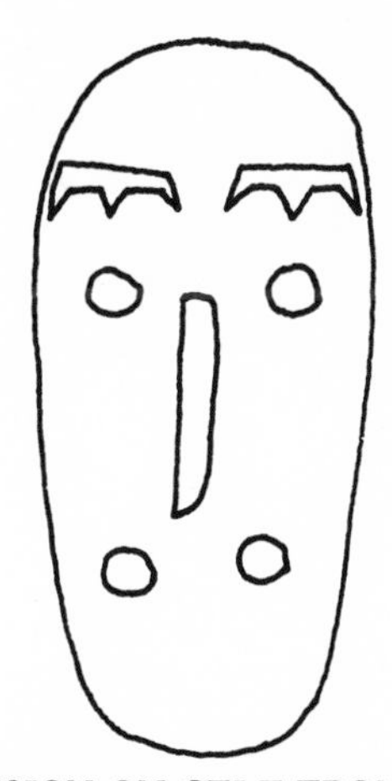

Fig. 44—DESIGN ON CELT FROM OFFERING NO. 2, LA VENTA

Fig. 45—MOSAIC PAVEMENT, LA VENTA

glyph of the moon goddess (Thompson, 1950, p. 232).

The St. Andrew's cross and U element were possibly real Olmec hieroglyphs. Other elements which may have been glyphs occur sporadically. On the pottery stamp from Tlatilco before mentioned, one of the signs is clearly identical to the kin (sun, day) glyph so important in Maya writing and astronomy (fig. 43,*f*); curiously enough, this is its only known occurrence in Olmec art. The Maya kan cross (a cross within a circle) (fig. 43,*g*) is found as the eye of the raptorial bird engraved on the obsidian core from La Venta, as the middle of a complex device engraved on the Humboldt celt, and as one of two glyphs on a jade finial (Covarrubias, 1957, fig. 94). On the forehead of a figurine from Xico, Veracruz (fig. 10), and incised on the skin of a monstrous animal on the pottery figure from Atlihuayan, Morelos (Covarrubias, 1957, fig. 21) is a symbol which may be a reduced version of the kan cross.

The Humboldt celt (fig. 18) has the above-mentioned hieroglyphs and a number of other symbols, arranged in what is apparently a text. At the very top (bit) of the celt are three teardrop-shaped forms. Directly below this device is a curvilinear bundle which closely resembles the glyphs for water in later Mexican codices; three rings appear below this and above the main device. On both sides of this possible water symbol is a total of four Olmec-type war clubs, each a different form of the weapon. Moving down, one encounters a pair of arms; note that the Mesoamerican sign of submission is being made, one hand to the upper part of the other arm. What may be an eye is surrounded on three sides by bracket-shaped elements, below which is a hand stretched out to the triple-circle sign. The lower half of the celt is largely taken up by an extremely elaborate device in the center of which is the kan cross, with four dots in the outer circle. Thompson (1950, p. 275) shows that one meaning of the kan cross in Maya writing is "precious." At the top of the device, below a plumelike element, is what can only be the glyph for the month which the Maya knew as Zip: a St. Andrew's cross underneath the chac (color red) affix (Thompson, 1950, fig. 16, *23–34*). Other glyphs in the device, including the one which is repeated four times, may or may not be present

Fig. 46—STONE EFFIGY AXE, PROVENIENCE UNKNOWN. (From Covarrubias, 1957, fig. 32, lower right.)

Fig. 47—GLYPHS ON ROLLER STAMP FOUND AT TLATILCO. (From Franco C., 1959, fig. 1,*c*.)

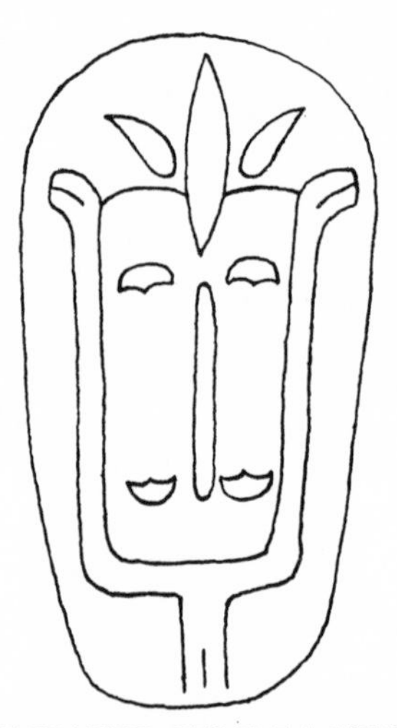

Fig. 48—ENGRAVED CELT, LA VENTA. (From Drucker, 1952a, fig. 47,*b*.)

in Maya writing. One further glyph appears below this, and at the very bottom (poll) of the celt is the U element (the moon?). The entire text may record the downfall of a town (with the water symbol a rebus name?) in the month Zip.

Other cases where we are sure that we are dealing with a glyphic text include the beautiful jade plaque in the British Museum (fig. 22), on which two glyphs are engraved to the left of the youthful face (the lower of these appears at Las Victorias, El Salvador), on the jade finial above mentioned, and on Monument 13 at La Venta. On the latter one of the glyphs is a bird's head; the other two glyphs are now blank but were undoubtedly painted.

Less certainly glyphic are signs which appear by themselves only once or twice in Olmec art. This is the case with the diamond-feather motif, found pendant on the mosaic pavement-masks at La Venta and incised on the figurine from Xico, Veracruz, and the two glyphs on the kilt of a large jade figurine from Puebla (Covarrubias, 1946, pl. 1).

One motif often encountered in Olmec art objects is the step design (fig. 43,*h*): step up two and step down two, with the topmost step split into two equal parts vertically. Its occurrence in the four-dots-and-vertical-bar motif of the La Venta mosaic pavements has already been mentioned. It also presents itself on the Simojovel celt, on a jade plaque from the Mixteca (Covarrubias, 1947, pl. 7), on the top of a "torch" held by a jade figure in the Bliss Collection (fig. 8) and at Las Victorias, El Salvador, as the topmost of two glyphs (?) held by one of the seated figures (fig. 5). Whether it is a symbol or merely a decorative element cannot yet be

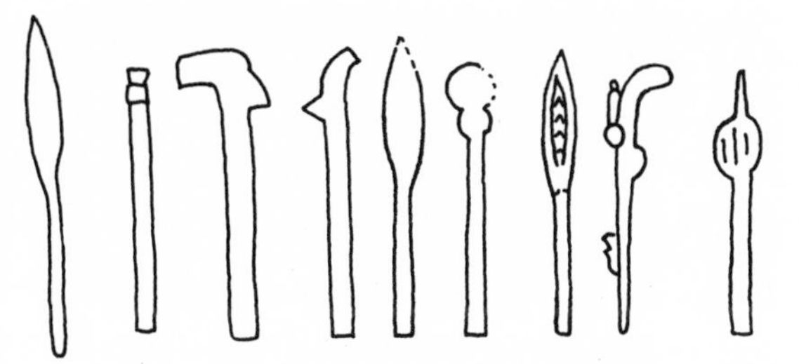

Fig. 49—War clubs in Olmec art

decided. The step design enclosed by diagonal lines which meet at the apex is apparently a marker for very late Preclassic sculpture in the Gulf lowlands, in monuments which are obviously Olmec-derived but which follow in time the Olmec style; these include Stela C at Tres Zapotes (where the motif appears on both sides of the mouth), the Alvarado Stela (Covarrubias, 1957, fig. 29), and the rather un-Olmec stela from Tepatlaxco, Veracruz (Covarrubias, 1957, pl. 18).

Costume, Weapons, and Ceremonial Paraphernalia

The costume worn by the human and were-jaguar figures in Olmec art is as distinctive a feature of the style as the formal features or the iconography. It is true that many items of headdress and sandals become incorporated into later art styles of Mesoamerica, but a piece of Olmec art can often be recognized by the costume alone. Particularly distinctive is the variety of headdresses worn, especially the "football helmet" type with a strap running under the chin or merely down to the cheek on either side. These are largely restricted to the colossal heads of the climax region, but occasionally crop up on figurines. A broad-brimmed headdress can be seen on Altar 4 at San Lorenzo (crowned by an eagle claw) and on Altar 5 at La Venta. A headdress which looks like a mitre is worn by the figure on Altar 3 at La Venta. Rather unusual is the elaboration of the towering, quite Maya-like, headgear of the principal

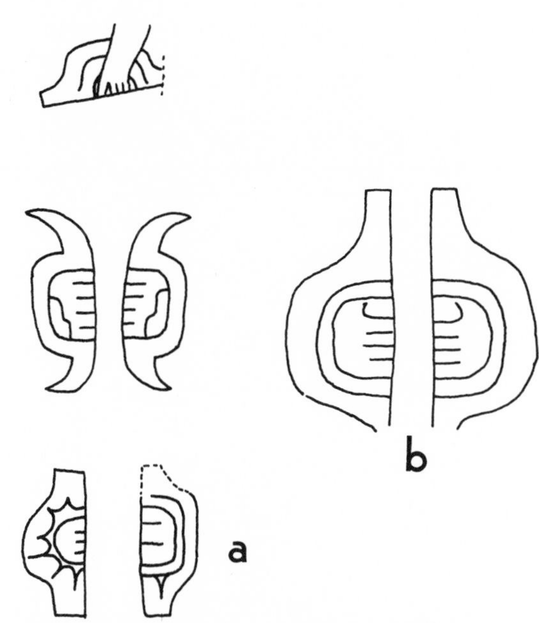

Fig. 50—Olmec "knuckle-dusters"

figures on Stela 3, La Venta. Actually, when one moves away from the Olmec monuments of the climax region, most figures are depicted without any headdress and are apparently bald, as in the Corona "Wrestler." The fancy hairdo of the male figure on Monument 13, La Venta, is quite unusual.

Ear spools and earplugs are commonly depicted, although the former, which have the outline of rounded squares, are more usual. All kinds of pectorals are shown, including what may be mirrors, but necklaces are rare. A few examples of Olmec art depict a nose pendant of some sort, somewhat like those of Early Classic Maya art. Cloaks are sometimes worn over the shoulders, and occasionally the figure appears to be wearing a long-sleeved tailored shirt, although this would be non-adaptive in the tropical lowlands. On the celts, figurines, and other small art objects, the loincloths are mere G-strings, but are more elaborate on the monuments; there the belt portion is wrapped around and knotted with an end hanging down in back (Monu-

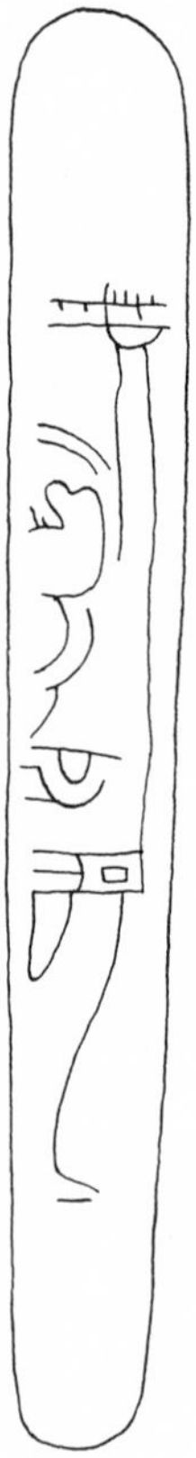

FIG. 51—ENGRAVED CELT FROM OFFERING NO. 4, LA VENTA. (From Drucker, Heizer, and Squier, 1959, fig. 40, no. 3.)

FIG. 52—ENGRAVED CELT, PROVENIENCE UNKNOWN. (Redrawn from Kelemen, 1943, pl. 255,*c*.)

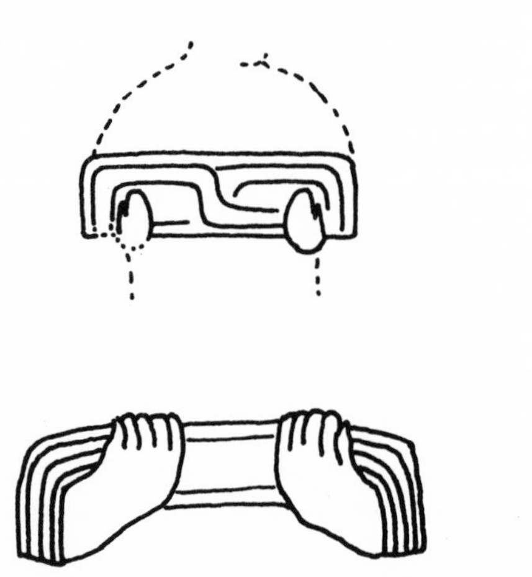

FIG. 53—CEREMONIAL BARS IN OLMEC ART

ment 23, La Venta). The Maya type of loincloth, with an end left hanging in front, is seen on the atlantean dwarfs of Monument 3, Potrero Nuevo. Female figures wear a short wrap-around skirt, a typical feature of the Preclassic, but occasionally males wear a kiltlike garment. Bands are often shown, worn on the upper arms, wrists, just below the knees, and on the ankles; since nothing of the kind has resulted from excavations, these must have been fashioned from some perishable material like bark cloth or leather. Footgear is almost nonexistent, but the Olmec artist was not particularly interested in realistic depiction of feet. The sandals worn by the striding figure of Monument 13, La Venta, are rather like Classic Maya examples, with a large tassel over the toes and a high back, and are unique.

Various objects held by the principal actors also have diagnostic significance. Some of these are definitely weapons or defenses against such. It is curious that on all known monuments and smaller objects in the Olmec style, spears and spearthrowers are absent. Stela D, Tres Zapotes (Stirling, 1943, fig. 4), where both are shown, is not in the *bona fide* style. The Olmec arsenal appears to have been limited to clubs of various shapes, especially paddle-shaped clubs and clubs with a bending out of the business end (fig. 49). In some cases, as on the petroglyphs at Las Victorias, El Salvador, mace heads may be figured. This lack of spears is consonant with the absence of projectile points at La Venta and in many other lowland sites of the Middle Preclassic away from the Valley of Mexico. The famous Olmec "football helmets" may well have been defensive, as could other types of headgear, against such heavy weapons. On the colossal heads these helmets incorporated heavy rope wound in tiers around the head. Another possible defense against club blows, or perhaps an offensive weapon itself, is what Drucker has aptly labeled the "knuckle-duster" (fig. 50); this could easily have been utilized to ward off attacks, but also could have been a fairly effective hand-weapon during close infighting. The stela of Padre Piedra, Chiapas, shows a triumphant figure standing with his knuckle-duster held menacingly over a small, kneeling were-jaguar (fig. 1). Occasionally, as on an engraved celt from La Venta or on Monument 10 at San Lorenzo, a knuckle-duster is held in each hand. Since knuckle-dusters are absent in the archaeological excavations, it is probable that they were of wood.

At times, the knuckle-duster is held as a ceremonial object in one hand, while the other grasps what appears to be a torch. Such a scene is relatively common in Olmec art, especially on small jade figurines and on small engraved celts. A figure holding up a "torch" in one hand and carrying the knuckle-duster close to the waist is found on one of the engraved celts from Offering No. 4 at La Venta (fig. 51) and on a celt of unknown provenience (fig. 52). There are two possible representations of the ceremonial bar, so characteristic of Classic Maya monuments, in Olmec art: one carried by the seated personage of Petroglyph 1, Chalcatzingo, and the other held in the arms of the black stone were-jaguar (fig. 53). In both cases, the "bar" seems to have been somewhat flexible, like those in Early Classic Maya sculpture.

Distribution in Space of the Olmec Style

In presenting a definition of the Olmec style, we have largely restricted it to those features which are characteristic of the climax region during the La Venta phase. As one moves away from the core region and also into later time periods, many objects are encountered which are more or less Olmecoid, but these are not Olmec in our meaning. Nevertheless, the Olmec style *strictu sensu* has a surprisingly extensive distribution, especially in small, portable objects (see fig. 58).

Let us first examine sites with Olmec-style monuments, for with these we are clearly faced with the products of direct Olmec connections, whether through diffusion, migration, or forcible conquest. In the climax area these sites are San Lorenzo, Rio Chiquito, Potrero Nuevo, La Venta, Tres Zapotes, and San Martin Pajapan volcano (the latter consists of a solitary monument). Further reconnaissance will undoubtedly disclose more (since the completion of this article, further sites in the climax area with Olmec monumental art have been reported by Medellín Zenil, 1960c: Estero Rabon, near Sayula, and Laguna de los Cerros, near Corral Nuevo). It is extraordinary that this climax region is little more than 150 km. long and about 50 km. wide. Within this relatively tiny area are the largest and most complex Olmec sites yet known; here, and only here, do the monuments show all the features of what has been termed the "central myth" of Olmec iconography. For these reasons, Drucker, Heizer, and Squier (1959, pp. 253–59) are certainly correct in insisting on the climax region as the birthplace of Olmec civilization; Covarrubias' 1957 claim of Guerrero as the Olmec homeland can hardly be justified.

The dispersal of Olmec culture, as seen in Olmec monuments, is very reminiscent of the distribution of Aztec merchant-warrior groups in Late Postclassic Central America. That is, Olmec monuments appear in widely scattered sites, few and far between, all the way down to El Salvador, apparently the result of migrations by small groups who settled here and there, much like the Aztec enclaves which were found as far as Panama. The subject matter of these colonial Olmec monuments is overwhelmingly military, as opposed to the more mythic content of those in the climax region, implying that these were warrior groups penetrating into foreign territory.

FIG. 54—FRAGMENTARY JADE FIGURINE, EL BAUL, GUATEMALA. (From Shook, 1956a.)

An outstanding colonial Olmec site is Chalcatzingo, Morelos (Piña Chan, 1958); here are two thoroughly Olmec petroglyphs, one showing a seated personage carrying a ceremonial bar (fig. 2), the other exhibiting three were-jaguar figures brandishing war clubs over a bearded, nude captive (fig. 3). The ceramics of the associated mound group are not dissimilar to those of what seems to be the earliest phase at Tres Zapotes, with a good deal of engraved hard, white pottery, as well as to Middle Preclassic pottery at La Venta.

The large, granite stela of Padre Piedra, near Villa Corzo in Chiapas, has already been described (fig. 1). In general features and in detail this is a typically Olmec monument; the details of the costume of the principal figure, the presence of the "knuckle-duster," and the were-jaguar face of the small supplicating figure are all within the range of variation of the style. We have commented on the military aspect of this monument. On the Pacific side of the Sierra Madre de Chiapas lies the large and important site of Tonala (Ferdon, 1953). While there seems to be a long time span represented in the monuments here, most appear to be Late Preclassic to Early Classic in date. Petroglyph 1, however, is a large, quite feline, were-jaguar face in Olmec style; only the roundness of the eyes is at all unusual. The kneeling or running were-jaguar depicted in the petroglyph of San Isidro Piedra Parada, near Colomba on the Pacific slope of Guatemala (Thompson, 1943c, fig. 111,*a*), is in a purely Olmec tradition; in fact, the figure recalls in many details the Chalcatzingo petroglyphs. This figure is brandishing some sort of clublike weapon, but it is difficult to make out the details.

The known limits of Olmec penetration are seen in the petroglyphs (fig. 5), pecked on four sides of a boulder at Las Victorias (Boggs, 1950), 2 km. east of Chalchuapa, El Salvador, 700 air km. southeast of the climax region and a great deal farther overland. The four figures depicted are rudely drawn but still thoroughly Olmec. All wear the typical Olmec costume, including "football helmets" or broad-brimmed headgear and round, concave-mirror-like pectorals. Two are striding along carrying clubs or maces, one carries what appears to be a drum under one arm, and a seated figure holds two hieroglyphs placed vertically. The winglike cloak of one of the figures is of interest, the southernmost Olmec objects known having very definite wings.

Almost all sources are agreed that the majority of Olmec objects in public and private collections come from Guerrero, especially from the Rio Balsas drainage. The absence of Olmec monuments there has been one of the major arguments against Covarrubias' thesis of a Guerrero homeland, but actually he used the same objections to back up his ideas—that is, in Guerrero one encounters a pre-monumental phase of Olmec art. In the present state of our knowledge, it looks as if his opponents are correct. There is no good explanation why there should be so many Olmec art objects (jade figurines, plaques, etc.) in Guerrero unless one assumes either an Olmec-acculturated population eager to obtain objects manufactured in the climax region, which could have been sort of a holy pilgrimage land, or else an actual Olmec population which intruded into the region from the east. Small Olmec objects are found throughout the intervening area, at Tlatilco in the Valley of Mexico, in Morelos, and in Puebla, but not in such quantity; this may be a function of more intense pothunting in Guerrero. Another region where finds are rather frequent is Oaxaca, especially the Mixteca. As a matter of fact, while the "danzante" monuments of Monte Alban I are somewhat outside the pure style, there is no reason to consider the effigy incense burners of the phase, with refined were-jaguar characteristics, as anything but Olmec.

We have discussed the more intense concentration of portable objects. North of the climax region, the Valley of Mexico, and Zihuatanejo, Guerrero, such finds become almost nonexistent. We may be certain that this was the northern boundary of Olmec influence, commercial or otherwise. To the south and east of the Isthmus of Tehuantepec, small Olmec objects are rare, but not absent. In Yucatan, a small jade figurine of a were-jaguar with a "football helmet" (Kidder, 1942, fig. 39,*f*) comes from Peto, but the green stone face found below an altar shrine at Mayapan (A. L. Smith and Ruppert, 1953, fig. 9,*c*) is not Olmec, as claimed, but rather in the Olmecoid style of Puebla. Probably several pieces in collections come from the Pacific slope and coast of Guatemala, but most of these have no provenience, with the exception of the beautiful but fragmentary

FIG. 55—JADE FIGURINE FROM VERAGUAS PROVINCE, PANAMA. (From Lothrop, 1950a, fig. 142.)

jade head of a were-jaguar from El Baul (fig. 54; Shook, 1956a), which is of outstanding size and workmanship and might be from the same hand as the "Kunz" axe. In El Salvador, similar finds have also been made, but often exact data are lacking. A recent repair of the Pan American highway between Chalchuapa and Atiquizaya cut away part of a mound, disclosing two Olmec jade objects, one a fragmentary figure of a ballplayer holding the ball in one hand, the other a plaque with a very abstract were-jaguar engraved on it (information from Carlos Navarrete). Two jade figurines in Olmec style have been found in Guanacaste Province, on the Pacific coast of Costa Rica (fig. 16). Both are winged, recalling the winglike extensions on one of the figures at Las Victorias; this may be a trait of the southern Olmec enclaves. No known pieces in Olmec art style have ever been discovered farther south of these, so that Guanacaste must mark the southern limit of Olmec diffusion. From Veraguas,

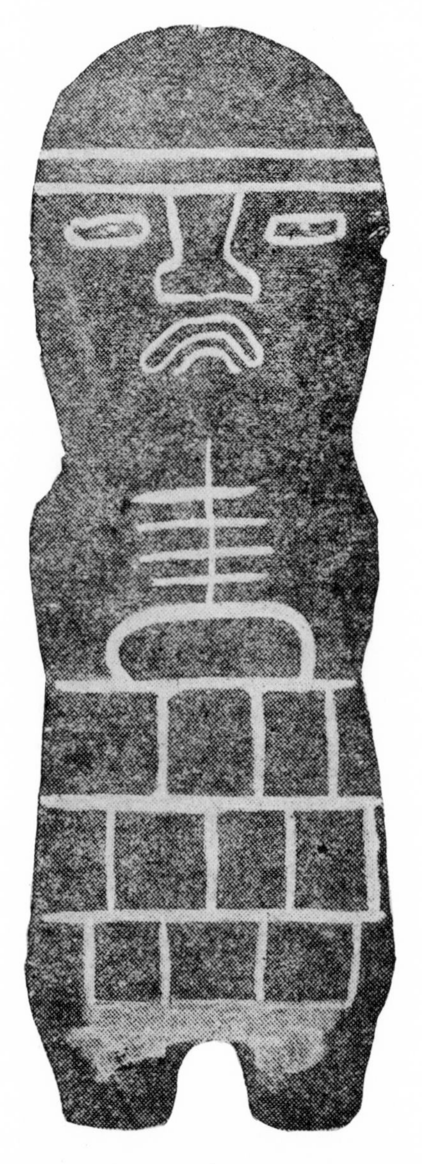

Fig. 56—GREENSTONE PLAQUE, EL OPEÑO, MICHOACAN. (From Noguera, 1946, p. 151.)

Panama, comes a jade dancing figure (fig. 55) which has been identified as "Olmec" (Lothrop, 1950a), but even though the pose of the figurine greatly resembles certain dancing figures in Olmec art, the face is completely outside it stylistically.

In summary, then, we can indicate the climax region of southern Veracruz and adjacent Tabasco as the probable origin of the Olmec style. Olmec groups left this area and penetrated across Morelos, Guerrero, and into Chiapas, thence down the Pacific coast of Guatemala as far as the Chalchuapa zone, leaving large stone monuments on their route and possibly remaining as trading enclaves. Further diffusion of portable objects of Olmec manufacture was most intense in the Puebla-Mixteca-Guerrero region, but continued down the Pacific coast as far as Costa Rica. It is yet uncertain where most of these smaller exports were actually made.

Time Span of the Olmec Style

The real significance of the Olmec style and civilization in the development of Mesoamerican history was obscured for many years by the chronological placement adhered to by most United States archaeologists working in the area. A long series of radiocarbon dates for Complex A, La Venta, published by Drucker, Heizer, and Squier (1959, pp. 264–67), places the single phase represented at this site well back in the Preclassic. Although these dates cover a span of 1154 B.C. ± 300 to 574 B.C. ± 300, the authors interpret the data to indicate that Complex A was constructed and used during approximately the period 800–400 B.C.; presumably the entire phase is confined to these dates, for following this, the site was subjected to extensive destruction. Since La Venta closely correlates archaeologically with other Middle Formative or Preclassic phases of the same time span, such as Chiapa II through III at Chiapa de Corzo and the Conchas phase at La Victoria, the former dated by the radiocarbon method and the latter by typological comparison, it would seem fairly logical to consider these dates as essentially correct.

There is yet no archaeological proof of any art style earlier than that exhibited by the Olmec of La Venta anywhere in Mesoamerica, but it is probable that the antecedents of the style will some day be found in a pre-800 B.C. context. This date may

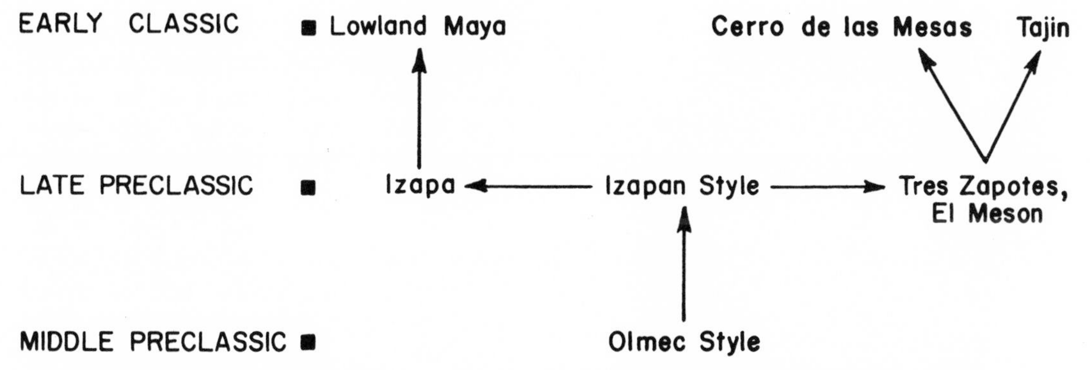

Fig. 57—PROPOSED SEQUENCE OF LOWLAND ART STYLES IN PRECLASSIC AND EARLY CLASSIC PERIODS

therefore be taken as the maximum age of the style as we now know it. With the destruction of La Venta around 400 B.C., the style ends at that site, and presumably throughout the climax region, since truly Olmec monuments elsewhere are almost indistinguishable in style from those of La Venta. At Tres Zapotes, however, one is faced with the problem of Stela C. This monument is dated in the Long Count at 7.16.6.16.18 (Stirling, 1943); there is no valid reason not to consider this a contemporary date (Wauchope, 1950, pp. 237–38; Coe, 1957b), to be read in the Goodman-Thompson correlation as 31 B.C. Now this is more than three-and-a-half centuries after the end of Olmec La Venta; if the face mask on the reverse side is really Olmec, then the style must have persisted long after 400 B.C. at other sites. A careful analysis of this abstract were-jaguar face shows, as Drucker (1952a, pp. 205–09) pointed out, rather evolved characteristics. The presence of the step design within diagonal lines which meet at the apex is a feature of post-Olmec, late Preclassic art of the Veracruz-Tabasco region, as seen in the Alvarado and Tepatlaxco stelae. As will be shown, we have at Tres Zapotes several monuments which are Izapan in style and therefore definitely post-Olmec, belonging to a final Preclassic occupation of the site; Stela C probably is contemporary, but retains more Olmec traits than do the others.

As for the dating of "colonial" art in the Olmec style, it must be admitted that in most cases, in the absence of stratigraphic excavation almost everywhere, it is impossible to be certain that it is contemporaneous with the Olmec monuments of the climax region. Two very good cases of association with stratigraphically known phases suggest that it is on the same time level. The Olmec figurines and pottery at Tlatilco belong to the Transitional phase of Piña Chan (1958), which follows an Early Zacatenco-like phase at the site. This transitional phase is dated by two radiocarbon samples, falling at 983 B.C. ± 250 (M-661) and 568 B.C. ± 250 (M-660), well within the La Venta span (Drucker, Heizer, and Squier, 1959, p. 265). Piña Chan's excavations at Chalcatzingo demonstrated that the bulk of the material from this site belongs to a single phase, assigned by him to his Middle Preclassic; this phase certainly dates the famous Olmec rock carvings above the site. The associated pottery, consisting largely of hard, white, engraved wares, is obviously related to other Mesoamerican ceramic complexes within the time span of 800–400 B.C., such as Conchas, Chiapa II, La Venta, and Mamom (Coe, 1961).

Until we obtain evidence to the con-

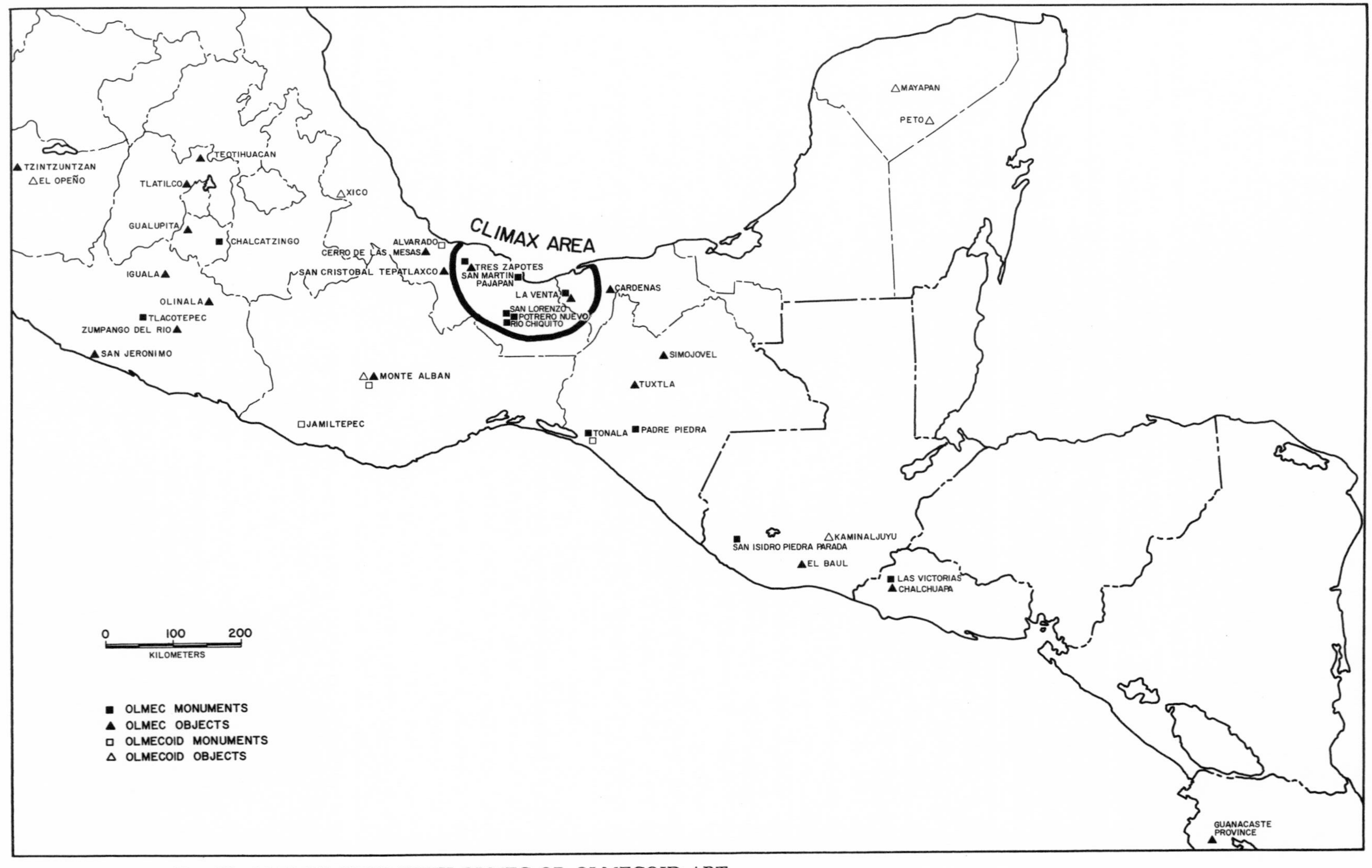

FIG. 58—MAP OF SITES WITH OLMEC OR OLMECOID ART
(Sites reported later than May 1960 not included.)

trary, the Olmec style, then, is confined to the 800–400 B.C. time range, with perhaps a slight extension at each end of the range. As such, it stands at the base of all known Mesoamerican styles.

Olmec Style in Mesoamerican Prehistory

In contrast to the situation in Mesoamerica, Peruvian archaeology, as a study, is singularly fortunate in being able to rely on the broad spread through space of various art styles which are confined to narrow time horizons, a spread which often is presumed to be the result of imperialistic expansion. From these horizon styles, as Kroeber (1948, pp. 108–11) and Willey (1945) have termed them, area-wide integration of Peruvian sequences has been possible. In Mesoamerica, the reverse is true: in practically no case can we see such a broad integration. It might be reasonably asked, in view of the large range over which Olmec monuments and portable objects are scattered, whether the Olmec style is an exception and really does constitute a true horizon style in the meaning set forth by Willey (1948, p. 8):

> This formulation of the horizon is an abstraction based upon the recurrence of specific features of style or manufacture in prehistoric artifacts . . . from one region to another so that the phenomena became pan-Peruvian in scope and coordinate our knowledge of the past in a broad temporal and spatial scheme. This integration is made possible when the same stylistic or technical complex of traits is found in the respective culture sequences of geographically widely separated regions, and by this means the two or more sequences are brought together and equated in time.

As we have here defined the Olmec style, it is fairly certain that we are *not* dealing with a horizon style. We must admit right away that the Preclassic archaeology of Mesoamerica is still very badly known, and not all areas have even been tested. Nevertheless, it is striking that in the Preclassic phases for which we have some knowledge and which seem on the basis of relative or absolute chronology to be contemporaneous with La Venta, objects in the Olmec style are either absent or restricted to a few rare trade pieces. These phases include Chiapa II, Conchas, Mamom, Ponce, Las Charcas, and several others. It is only in and near the Valley of Mexico, at the sites of Tlatilco, Tlapacoya, and Gualupita, where reasonably numerous Olmec objects have been encountered. At all these sites, however, it should be realized that figurines in Olmec style present a minor increment in the total assemblage, for there is nothing particularly Olmec about the bulk of the figurines and vessels from Tlatilco, for instance; to the contrary, they are amazingly un-Olmec. Compare the situation with the coeval Chavin horizon of Peru, with Chavin style designs and forms appearing in pottery, stonework, gold, and even textiles in sites scattered throughout the north and central highlands and almost all along the coast.

That there was expansionism of a military nature out of the Olmec climax region as far south as El Salvador can be reasonably inferred from the evidence of "colonial" monuments, from Chalcatzingo to Las Victorias. Quite probably this military policy opened up trade routes to the commercial spread of portable objects, especially jade, from the original Olmec area to barbaric peoples. Since the range of variation in Olmec art from Guerrero is exactly that of Olmec art in the climax region, it is doubtful if the former was anything more than a particular region which had a strong taste in objects of this sort. Perhaps they were converted to the were-jaguar cult by Olmec missionaries and had a need for the proper ritual paraphernalia; in much the same way, plaster images of the saints are concentrated among those African tribes which have been converted to Catholicism. In other words, Olmec art, whether monumental or portable, was produced by no other culture except that represented by the ceremonial centers of the climax region and so did not constitute a horizon style in the Willey definition. The lack of horizon styles in Mesoamerica throughout its history probably reflects the strong microgeographical differentiation of the area which favored regional development with eventual symbiosis, but not broad cultural integration.

One can detect, it is true, Olmec influence on the art of Monte Alban I, which is probably in part coeval with terminal La Venta. Drucker (1952a, p. 226) sees nothing Olmec about the danzantes incised on slabs of stone at the site, holding that the artists had merely represented the same physical type (heavy-featured, thick-lipped, with prominent forehead and chins) in "a completely different way." He feels that the technique (incising rather than bas-relief), the phallicism, and the "distortion" of pose are all non-Olmec traits, concluding that "Monte Alban culture cannot be reckoned basically Olmecan, nor can it be derived from an Olmec source" (*ibid.*, p. 227). Covarrubias (1957, p. 148) is of the opinion that the danzantes are directly "derived" from Olmec art. It all depends on how one looks at the problem: if one is more concerned with the trees than with the forest, it is correct to say that the danzantes are not Olmec, but if one takes into account the whole artistic feeling of the danzante reliefs, then they must be accounted to be at least under Olmec influence. The heavy, rounded outlines of the bodies, the were-jaguar characteristics, the interest in deformity are all features of the Olmec style. In fact, two purely Olmec figurines are in poses typical of the danzantes. We must conclude that, although the basic features of the Olmec style are not present, the Monte Alban danzantes must be, as Covarrubias always claimed, Olmec-derived. Drucker is right to insist on a rigorous definition of "Olmec," but he obscures the facts by not admitting Olmec influence when present in other cultures.

Many objects exist in collections which unfortunately often lack archaeological context, but which exhibit certain Olmec traits without being specifically Olmec. At some future time it might be possible to decide the geographical and temporal limits of a number of Olmecoid styles, but at present this is possible only for Monte Alban. Most of these objects are infinitely cruder in technique and feeling than *bona fide* Olmec art. The characteristic snarling were-jaguar mouth is often simplified to a mere trapezoid of plain outline, with suppression of the fangs or depiction of them in a non-Olmec fashion. Such Olmecoid objects include the small stone face from Mayapan (Smith and Ruppert, 1953, fig. 9,*c*), a carved jade boulder from Niltepec, Oaxaca (Covarrubias, 1946, fig. 13), the small greenstone plaque found in a Preclassic tomb at El Opeño, Michoacan (Noguera, 1946, p. 151), an axe from Guerrero (Covarrubias, 1957, fig. 32), and the statue at Jamiltepec, Oaxaca (DeCicco and Brockington, 1956, fig. 4).

The real importance of the Olmec style is that it precedes a number of significant artistic developments which appear to be genetically derived from it. The large number of monuments discovered by Stirling at Izapa (Stirling, 1943, pls. 49–62), near the Pacific coast on the Chiapas-Guatemala border, are unfortunately not yet placed in an archaeological context at that site, but there can be little doubt, following the discovery at Kaminaljuyu of an Izapa-style monument below a floor of Miraflores-Arenal date (E. M. Shook, personal information), that the style is Late Preclassic, and therefore post-Olmec. As recognized by Proskouriakoff (1950, p. 177), the Izapan style has a number of features which resemble those in Olmec sculpture, as well as traits which cross-tie with the earliest Maya sculpture known.

One could enumerate Olmec traits in the art as: (1) frequency of the St. Andrew's cross and the U element, (2) scrollwork skies or clouds, (3) scenes contained within stylized jaguar mouths, (4) realistic depiction of well-fed human forms, (5) the flame-scroll brow. There are very significant differences with Olmec art which point to a different direction of development, such as (1) the general absence of the standard were-jaguar and the baby-face, (2) the frequency of representation of a profile face with an upper lip greatly extended below a small, hooked nose with prominent nostril—perhaps the prototype of the Maya "Serpent X," (3) deities descending from the sky, (4) winged figures. Izapan art, in spite of its probable derivation from the Olmec style, is quite opposed to it in most features, with a basically different iconography. It is certainly present in other sites besides Izapa itself, such as Kaminaljuyu in the Guatemalan highlands, at Colomba on the Pacific slope of that country, and appears at Tres Zapotes. Monuments at the latter site which are definitely Izapan are as follows:

Stela D (Stirling, 1943, fig. 4). The front of the monument shows three figures, above which a sky deity is descending. The facial features and stylistic treatment of the figures are Izapan, not Olmec. Two of the figures have plumed headdresses and one carries a spear and spearthrower, all features unknown in Olmec art. A purely Izapan "long-lipped god" is depicted on the north side of Stela D.

Stela A (Stirling, 1943, fig. 3). The monument is badly weathered, but the scene is not Olmec. The two flanking figures carry a knife and a severed head, respectively; head-taking is an Izapan trait.

Monument C (Stirling, 1943, pls. 17, 18). This carved stone box is of great interest, for the style appears to be transitional between Olmec and Izapan. Olmec traits are the "war in heaven" scene, resembling that on Stela 3 at La Venta, and the presence of war clubs, but all other details are Izapan, including the treatment of the face, the use of spears, feathered headdresses, and the general clutter of the design.

There are therefore two Preclassic occupations of Tres Zapotes: one on the level of La Venta, and the other in the Late Preclassic, coeval with Izapa. The great stela of El Meson, central Veracruz (Covarrubias, 1957, fig. 68), likewise exhibits strong Izapan traits such as the plumed headdress and the "long-lipped god." Since Izapan art is probably derivative from the earlier Olmec style, and because there are Izapan-style monuments within and near the Olmec climax region, its genesis may have been there rather than on the Pacific slope.

It is here suggested that all known major art styles of lowland Mesoamerica have a single origin in the Olmec style (fig. 57). The latter is restricted to the culture of the climax zone during the Middle Preclassic, and extensions of that culture. From this was derived the Izapan style of the Late Preclassic, which spread across the Isthmus of Tehuantepec to the Pacific slope and lowlands. In and near the lowlands of southern Veracruz and Tabasco, this Izapan style evolved independently into the Early Classic art of Cerro de las Mesas (Stirling, 1943, pls. 19–31), characterized by dated stelae and other monuments which exhibit markedly conservative Izapan and even Olmec features of pose and detail. From the Pacific slope, Izapan art eventually spread southeast and up across the Valley of Guatemala and down into the Peten lowlands, where it could have given rise to the earliest known Maya art.

The ultimate relation of Classic Maya with Olmec can therefore be traced through the medium of the Izapan style. When all three styles are viewed from a distance, both the Izapan and Maya styles show significant affinities with each other which set them off from Olmec, and which illustrate well the evolution of art in the lowlands of Middle America. Wölfflin (n.d.) has shown that at any one time in the art history of an extensive area such as Europe there are one or more national styles which are mutually contrastive. However, a large area like Europe can also be shown to move through a sequence of periods, in which the national styles of a particular period have more in common with each other than they have with the styles of the preceding or following periods. Although Wölfflin pointed out that the transition from "period type" to "period type" is always gradual, he stressed that in European art and perhaps in the art of all regions, an alternation through time of a "classic" period with a "baroque" period was inevitable. By "classic," he meant styles that emphasized plastic-linear (almost sculptural) forms which stand by themselves as complete entities, as in the paintings of the Italian Renaissance. On the other hand, the term "baroque" he applied to styles which are painterly, that is, where no part is complete in itself but is an inalienable part of a larger composition. The "classic" artist is interested in the relation between discrete forms, the "baroque" in large over-all effects; consequently, "baroque" art is often restless, leading the eye into painterly compositions, and often cluttered with interesting detail.

In terms of this basic contrast, the Olmec style is clearly "classic," Izapan-Maya is "baroque." By the Late Preclassic, the lowland artist had evidently become more interested in an almost overdone application of iconographic detail (see, for instance, Stela 5 at Izapa) to the detriment of the sculptural qualities which we can appreciate in Olmec art. Classic Maya art becomes so complex, with such a profusion of details (especially of costume, an Izapan trait), that it is to the credit of the Maya that any forms are controlled at all. That this is an especially painterly art, in which the forms are sacrificed to over-all effect of richness, is evident in the often-made but unproved assertion that the original Maya monuments must have been painted wooden stelae. Maya art is throughout its history a two-dimensional art, characterized by what Proskouriakoff (1950, p. 181) has termed "order in complexity," a heritage from the Izapan style from which it must be derived.

We have here examined only lowland styles, all of which appear to have their deepest roots in Olmec art. There is no great art in the Mexican highlands, excluding the Olmec objects traded to sites of the Middle Preclassic, until Teotihuacan II, which is presumably very late Preclassic, and Teotihuacan III. The curious interest in almost geometric formalism of life forms which this earliest highland art already exhibits at this date, and maintains throughout its history, is strongly opposed to the curvilinear, naturalistic art of the lowlands, whether "classic" or "baroque." We are here in the realm of macro-styles, traditions which are so broad-scale that we may never know the cultural or psychological factors behind them. At any rate, the highland regions after the Preclassic seem to have gone their own way, having developed independently from the Olmec-derived tradition.

REFERENCES

Blom and LaFarge, 1926–27
Boggs, 1950
Coe, M. D., 1957b, 1961
Covarrubias, 1946, 1947, 1957
DeCicco and Brockington, 1956
Drucker, 1943a, 1943b, 1952a, 1955
——, Heizer, and Squier, 1959
Ferdon, 1953
Franco C., 1959
Greengo, 1952
Groth-Kimball, 1953
Jiménez Moreno, 1959
Kelemen, 1943
Kidder, 1942
Knorosov, 1958a
Kroeber, 1948
Lothrop, 1950a
Medellín Zenil, 1960c
Noguera, 1946
Piña Chan, 1958
Proskouriakoff, 1950
Saville, 1929
Shook, 1956a
Smith, A. L., and Ruppert, 1953
Sociedad Mexicana de Antropología, 1942
Stirling, 1940, 1943, 1955
Thompson, J. E. S., 1943c, 1950
Vaillant, 1932
Vaillant, S. B., and G. C., 1934
Wauchope, 1950, 1954
Willey, 1945, 1948
Wölfflin, n.d.

30. The Olmec Region at Spanish Contact

FRANCE V. SCHOLES and
DAVE WARREN

This paper summarizes available documentary data on some aspects of native society in the "Olmec" region of southern Veracruz, the Tuxtepec district of northeastern Oaxaca, and western Tabasco at the time of Spanish contact. Sixteenth-century sources make reference to three major subdivisions of this region: (a) the Rio Alvarado (Papaloapan) district, (b) the Tuxtla highlands, and (c) the province of Coatzacoalcos. Of these subregions, the province of Coatzacoalcos was the largest and, from the standpoint of events following the coming of the Spaniards, the most important. This province comprised the southern slopes of Sierra San Martin, the drainage basin of the Rio Coatzacoalco, and Gulf coastlands from the Rio Tonala eastward to Laguna Tupilco. The eastern extension of the province, in which lies the archaeological site of La Venta, included native settlements designated in colonial sources as "los Agualulcos," which were in the swampy lowlands below Laguna del Carmen. The boundary between the Spanish provinces of Coatzacoalcos and Tabasco ran a few miles west of Rio Copilco, which emptied into the western end of Laguna Tupilco. The Rio Copilco also marked a linguistic frontier, separating the Chontal Maya district of Tabasco and the settlements in the eastern portion of the province of Coatzacoalcos in which Nahua and Popoluca tongues were spoken (Scholes and Roys, 1948, p. 96).

In his survey of the native peoples of preconquest Mexico, Sahagún (bk. 10, ch. 29) included a section entitled, "De los Olmecas, Uixtotin y Mixtecas." The terms *olmeca* ("the rubber people") and *uixtotin* ("the salt-water people") aptly characterized the inhabitants of the coastlands of southern Veracruz and western Tabasco. The informants of Sahagún described the Olmeca country as a land of riches and abundance, which produced rubber, cacao, and "all manner of food," a source of supply also of the brightly colored feathers and precious stones (jade and turquoise) highly prized by the Aztecs, and of gold. They remarked on the richly wrought cotton fabrics made by women of the region, and the fine clothing and jewelry worn by both men and women. From the same source (bk. 9) we have account of the far-flung trade in luxury goods carried on by way of the Olmeca coastlands between central Mexico and Chiapas and Tabasco.

This picture of the prosperity of the Olmeca country is confirmed by the different kinds of tribute paid to the Aztec rulers by the tributary province of Tochtepec (Tuxtepec), of which the Rio Alvarado and Tuxtla settlements formed a part (Codex Mendoza, ff. 43*v*–44; Barlow, 1949, pp. 97–98). These items included elaborately decorated *mantas*, gold objects (shield, diadem, headband, and beads), lip-plugs of "amber" and crystal with gold settings, liquidamber, large pieces of jade (*chalchihuitl*) and strings of jade beads, rubber, cacao, feather shield and standard, and large quantities of feathers of different colors and sizes.[1]

The Spaniards were quickly attracted to the Olmeca coastlands and adjacent areas, which they brought under fairly effective control during the decade of the 1520's. Soldiers and colonists received *encomienda* grants in the Rio Alvarado district with the right to exact tribute and labor service of the Indians. Cortés reserved to himself the tribute and labor of the Tuxtla highlands. In 1522 Gonzalo de Sandoval established Spanish dominion in the province of Coatzacoalcos and founded the Villa de Espiritu Santo on the right bank of the Rio Coatzacoalco 3 leagues upstream from its mouth. Many of Cortés' veterans, including Bernal Díaz del Castillo, enrolled as citizens of the villa, which became a base of operations for expeditions of conquest into Tabasco and Chiapas. To these settlers grants of encomienda were made in areas under effective or nominal Spanish control.

But the deceptive character of the wealth of the Olmeca region soon became apparent, as Bernal Díaz remarked many years later when he wrote that he and many of his soldier-companions who sought fortune and reward in lands outside the central Mexican highlands were deceived by the gold and luxury products of such areas (Díaz del Castillo, ch. 157). The gold washings in the rivers of the Olmeca region and accumulated stores of gold objects were quickly exhausted, and the Spaniards had little use for the jade, amber, feathers, and rubber. Tribute assessments for the 1540's and 1550's reveal that the principal items of tribute paid by the Indians of the Olmeca coastlands to the Crown or to *encomenderos* were maize, cacao, cotton fabrics, and fowl (turkeys and European hens), and, in some cases, beans, raw cotton, and fish (González de Cossío, 1952). In short, production of staple food products and clothing of ordinary quality had now become the major features of native economy. In the Tuxtla area Cortés and his heirs promoted sugar production, using Negroes for heavy labor in the cane fields and in the sugar mill. In savanna areas scattered through the coastlands a few Spaniards in later decades of the 16th century raised a certain amount of livestock. Trade followed the old routes between the Mexican highlands and the Chiapas-Tabasco areas, but the character of this trade had been altered. Finally, during the half-century following Spanish conquest the native population had sharply declined as the result of epidemic diseases of European origin and the general disorientation of native society under the impact of Spanish domination.

All these factors, plus the debilitating effects of the tropical climate, discouraged the growth and expansion of Spanish settlement within the Olmeca country. The number of Spanish citizens of the Villa de

[1] The Spanish commentary and annotations in the Codex Mendoza for the tributes paid by the towns of the tributary province of Tuxtepec should be compared with Indian testimony on the same subject recorded in 1554 (Scholes and Adams, 1957), which presents a somewhat different picture as to the quantities of the several items of tribute paid to the Aztec rulers.

Espiritu Santo in the Coatzacoalcos province rapidly declined after its founding in 1522. Many disillusioned settlers, among them Bernal Díaz, moved to other areas. The pioneer missionary Orders in New Spain concentrated their evangelizing efforts in the highlands of Mexico. Church reports for the decade 1560–70 indicate that most of the missions in Rio Alvarado–Tuxtla–Coatzacoalcos areas were served by secular clergy.

It is not surprising therefore that 16th-century sources record scant data of specific character relating to native society in the Olmeca region at the time of Spanish contact. The classic colonial chronicles contain little information of value for this area. Tribute documents and reports on missionary foundations provide minimal data concerning the native towns and settlements. For the year 1580 we have *relaciones* for the Tlacotalpa (Rio Alvarado), Tuxtla, and Espiritu Santo (Coatzacoalcos) districts which record a certain amount of useful information on conditions at the time of Spanish conquest, but the total content of such data is unsatisfactory.[2] In 1599–1600 viceregal commissioners were sent to the Agualulcos district in western Tabasco and to the Rio Alvarado region with instructions to congregate the native population of these areas at strategically located sites. Reports of these officials provide some material of value on the location of native settlements at the end of the 16th century, their tributary population, the languages spoken in the several villages, and the general character of native economy.[3]

The paucity of specific information relating to native society in the Olmeca region on the eve of Spanish conquest will be reflected in the succeeding sections of this paper. It may be assumed, in view of the essential unity of many features of native culture in preconquest Mexico, that such features were shared, in varying measure, by the inhabitants of the Olmeca coastlands. This paper, however, will present only the specific data for these areas recorded in the sources to which we have had access.

Population, Settlements, Languages

Sixteenth-century sources record the names of more than a hundred Indian settlements, large and small, in the Rio Alvarado, Tuxtla, and Coatzacoalcos districts. This would suggest a fairly substantial population at the time of Spanish contact. It should be noted, however, that few, if any, of these settlements or clusters of settlements (*cabeceras* and subject villages) had populations equal to those of many towns in the central and southern highlands which would indicate a lesser density of population in the Olmeca coastlands than in other parts of preconquest Mexico. That the native population of Mexico rapidly declined following the Spanish conquest is well established, and there is evidence that the rate of decline was sharper in the Gulf coastlands than in highland areas (Cook and Simpson, 1948; Cook and Borah, 1960). We have not found it possible on the basis of available documentary data to arrive at a satisfactory, reasoned estimate of the total population of the Rio Alvarado, Tuxtla, and Coatzacoalcos areas on the eve of Spanish conquest.[4] With many res-

[2] The Tlacotalpa and Tuxtla reports have been published in Papeles de Nueva España, vol. 5. The original manuscript, with map, of the Espiritu Santo relación, prepared by the alcalde mayor Suero de Cangas y Quiñones, is in the University of Texas Library; a partial text has been published in *Revista mexicana de estudios historicos,* 2: suppl. pp. 176–80.

[3] The report for the Agualulcos district has been published in the *Boletín* of the Mexican National Archive, 16: 195–246, 429–80; the reports on the Rio Alvardo settlements are abstracted in Trens, 1947, pp. 239–51.

[4] In their calculations of preconquest population, Cook, Simpson, and Borah have made use of statistical data for the decade 1560–70 recorded in church reports and tribute assessments. Although data of this kind are available for the Olmeca coastlands, they are incomplete in certain respects and also contradictory. For this reason, and also be-

ervations, we suggest a very tentative estimate of 150,000–200,000.[5]

For the lower drainage basin of the Rio Alvarado we have the names of some 30 Indian towns and villages for the first half-century following the Spanish conquest. Major settlements were located at Tuxtepec, Mixtlan, Cosamaloapan, Amatlan, Puctla, and Tlacotalpa (cf. also the Patiño map of 1580, reproduced in Cline, 1959a). These towns (*cabeceras*) had one or more subsidiary villages (*sujetos, estancias*). This clustering of settlements doubtless reflected preconquest lordships (*señoríos*) which antedated Aztec dominion over the Rio Alvarado area (cf. Espinosa, 1910). Most of the larger towns and their subject villages occupied sites on or near the Rio Alvarado or one of its tributaries. Patterns of settlement were conditioned by local geography and climatic factors. Cosamaloapan, for example, had adequate land suitable for cultivation; Tlacotalpa was located on an island in the lower Rio Alvarado; many of the smaller villages were cramped in by jungle or swamps. Travel by canoe was the principal means of interpueblo communication throughout the entire area. During the 16th century the rapid decline of Indian population brought about the abandonment of some village sites and reduced others to a small fraction of their preconquest inhabitants.

The Tuxtla relación of 1580 (PNE, 5:5) records the names of a half-dozen Indian villages on or near Lake Catemaco and subsidiary to the villa of Tuxtla. These settlements and the pueblo of Tuxtla, where the villa had been established, had constituted an independent señorío prior to imposition of Aztec control over the region.

The Espiritu Santo relación of 1580 states that the province of Coatzacoalcos then comprised more than 70 Indian settlements and lists the names of 67 of these villages. Many of these places are also named in church reports and records of tribute assessments for the period 1550–70. The heaviest concentration of population was in the area extending from the southern slopes of Sierra San Martin southeastward to Rio Coatzacoalco and on the lower course of this stream. Eleven small villages were in the Agualulcos district east of the Rio Tonala.

Documentary sources to which we have had access do not record detailed descriptive accounts of individual pueblos in the Olmeca coastlands. Brief mention is made of religious sanctuaries (cf. Religion and Ritual, *infra*), but these references tell us nothing about the location and orientation of such buildings in relation to pueblo settlement patterns. The relaciones of 1580 state that family dwellings were of the *jacal* type, with roofs of pole and thatch supported by wooden pillars and walls of closely knit reeds (*cañas*) with or without mud plastering. This type of dwelling, characteristic of the tropical lowlands, would suggest loose and dispersed settlement patterns rather than compact villages centered around a ceremonial complex.

Sixteenth-century sources also indicate that mission churches, both large and small, in the Olmeca region reflected jacal structural features. The relaciones of 1580 comment favorably on the strength and moisture-resistant qualities of different kinds of wood available for building purposes. The Espiritu Santo report states that stone was available on the slopes of Sierra San Martin but was not utilized.

Jiménez Moreno (1942, p. 121) has

cause of some doubt concerning the formulae developed by Cook, Simpson, and Borah for estimating population in 1560–70, and for the rate of population decline during the period 1520–70, we do not feel that a carefully reasoned estimate of the preconquest population of the Olmeca coastlands can be made at present.

[5] The Espiritu Santo relación of 1580 records a figure of 50,000 *indios* (heads of families) for the province of Coatzacoalcos prior to Spanish conquest. On this basis we might assume a total population of 150,000 to 175,000 for the region. But the 1580 figure was probably a guess-estimate by the persons who made the report and cannot be accepted at face value (Cangas y Quiñones, 1580).

pointed out that the historic Olmeca of the Gulf coastlands did not constitute a single language group; rather, that they spoke different tongues. Sixteenth-century sources designate these tongues as Mixtec, "Popoluca," and variant forms of the "Mexican" tongue.

The Nahuatl term *popoluca* means "foreigners," "barbarians," "unintelligible," and was applied to peoples who spoke languages "foreign" to that of the Mexican, or Nahuatl, people of central Mexico. Sahagún (bk. 10, ch. 29) described the people of the Olmeca region as *tenimes,* "because they speak a barbarous tongue." Modern students of the native languages of Mexico differentiate two distinct "popoluca" language groups: (a) the Popoloca of Puebla and adjacent areas, whose tongue is classified as part of a Popoloca-Chocho-Mazateca language family, and (b) the Popoluca of southern Veracruz, who speak tongues affiliated with Mixe-Zoquean languages.

After the destruction of Tula in the 12th century Popoloca groups (also designated as Olmeca) in the central highlands migrated, as the result of Tolteca-Chichimeca pressures, southeastward to the Gulf coastlands, where they established petty kingdoms, or señoríos (*Mayas y Olmecas,* 1942; Espinosa, 1910). These lordships were subsequently subjected to Aztec dominion and "nahuatization." The Tlacotalpa relación of 1580 states (PNE, 5:2) that the Indians of this area spoke the "Mexican" language. Church reports for the decade 1560–70 tell us that the native population of missionary districts in the Rio Alvarado area were indoctrinated by Spanish clergy in the Mexican tongue (García Pimentel, 1904). Reports of viceregal commissioners who visited the Rio Alvarado settlements in 1599–1600 also indicate that Mexican was the common tongue spoken in this region, but describe the inhabitants of some of the towns as belonging to the "popoluca nation." Both Mexican and Mixtec were spoken in Cosamaloapan and in Mixtlan (Trens, 1947, pp. 239–51).

The Tuxtla relación of 1580 states (PNE, 5:5) that the Indians of this district spoke an unpolished ("muy tosca") form of the Mexican language, evidence of intrusive Nahua groups in early preconquest times and/or of nahuatization subsequent to the imposition of Aztec dominion over the Tuxtla highlands.

One section of the Espiritu Santo relación of 1580 makes the general statement that different languages were spoken in the province of Coatzacoalcos, but that "in general they speak the Mexican tongue." In another place it specifies the different languages as "corrupt Mexican," Popoluca, Mixtec, and Zapotec. Of the non-Mexican tongues, the most important, of course, was Popoluca.

Foster (1943) has suggested that in early preconquest times Popoluca (Mixe-Zoquean) was spoken in a wide belt of territory extending from Los Tuxtlas across the Gulf coasts of the Isthmus of Tehuantepec, and that subsequently the language picture was changed by intrusive Nahua groups. At present the Popoluca language area comprises an oval-shaped wedge of some 400–500 square miles extending from the southern slopes of the Tuxtla highlands southeastward toward the trans-Isthmian railway. Within this area Foster has identified four mutually unintelligible Popoluca languages. The Espiritu Santo report of 1580 does not identify the towns in which Popoluca, Mixtec, and Zapotec were spoken. The viceregal commissioner who visited the 11 towns of the Agualulco district east of Rio Tonala in 1599 reported that in some of these towns Mexican was spoken by both sexes. In others the men spoke Mexican and Popoluca and the women only Popoluca, which would suggest that for these towns Popoluca was the original and basic tongue.

Political and Social Relationships

The Rio Alvarado and Tuxtla subdivisions of the Olmeca country had been subjected to the dominion of the Aztec confederacy during the reigns of Moctezuma I and his successors. Aztec conquest of these areas had doubtless been facilitated by rivalries of the local señoríos. The most striking evidence of Aztec dominion is provided by the Codex Mendoza (f. 44) which portrays the glyphs of 22 major towns of the tributary province of Tuxtepec. This province comprised a part of eastern Oaxaca and the Rio Alvarado and Tuxtla districts of Southern Veracruz. The list of town-glyphs includes those for Mixtlan, Cosamaloapan, Tuxtla, and Tlacotalpa.

Aztec control over this tributary province was maintained by a large military garrison stationed at Tuxtepec and smaller outposts in other districts. We are also told that an *auditorio*, "or kind of audiencia," of Aztec judges resident in Tuxtepec exercised superior judicial authority over the province, and dealt with cases of rebellion against Aztec supremacy and also those in which the penalty of death might be invoked (Gayangos, 1866, p. 204; Scholes and Roys, 1948, p. 91; PNE, 4:61, 62). In the principal settlements of the province the Aztec rulers had placed officials who were responsible for the collection of tribute and exercised supervisory authority, subject to the superior jurisdiction of the military commander and the judges resident in Tuxtepec.

The pueblo of Tlacotalpa on the lower Rio Alvarado was "governed" by an Aztec official sent by "Motezuma," who collected the tributes, which consisted of decorated cotton fabrics, cacao, parrots, jaguar skins, the teeth of lizards, and jade objects (PNE, 5:2). The Tuxtla area had been ruled by a lord named "Chiconaçen," to whom the Indians gave tribute in the form of white mantas and cacao; later, "in friendship" they gave tribute in mantas and other items of clothing to Moctezuma "who placed in this pueblo a calpisque as governor" (PNE, 5:5).

The pueblos of the province of Coatzacoalcos had not been subjected to Aztec dominion, despite pressures exerted from time to time by Aztec garrisons in neighboring districts. Cortés' Second Letter of Relation and the chronicle of Bernal Díaz mention caciques of towns on the Rio Coatzacoalco who gave assistance to the Spanish expeditions of Diego de Ordaz and Gonzalo de Sandoval to this region in 1520 and 1522 respectively, but these statements provide no evidence of unified or centralized native government in preconquest times (Gayangos, 1866, p. 95; Díaz del Castillo, ch. 160). That the towns of the Coatzacoalcos province enjoyed local independence and autonomy is confirmed by a statement in the Espiritu Santo relación of 1580 that these pueblos had never had a "recognized lord," except for certain caciques who governed them and to whom the Indians gave tribute in the form of cotton fabrics, cacao, maize, birds, copper axes, and gold jewelry (Cangas y Quiñones, 1580).

After the Spanish conquest of Mexico a modified form of Castillian municipal government with elected officials was imposed on the Indian towns and villages, with supervisory authority vested in Spanish *corregidores* or *alcaldes mayores*. At the same time, however, Spanish colonial government accorded special status and privileges to the preconquest native nobility, especially to the descendants of local señores, or caciques. Such privileges included exemption from tributes levied for the benefit of the Crown or of Spanish encomenderos, labor service by the commoners of the caciques' towns, and, in many cases, an annual salary to be paid from the community chests. The post-conquest señores, or caciques, also sought and often obtained recognition of claims for personal use and ownership of lands which, they alleged, had formed part of the patrimony of their noble ancestors in preconquest times and consequently should be set apart from the community holdings of their towns. In some areas these cacique lands had been worked by serfs (*mayeques*) who enjoyed a less favorable status than that of the free commoners (*maceguales*). (Roys, 1943, pp. 129–71; Aguirre Beltrán, 1953; Gibson, 1960; León-Portilla, 1962, pp. 31–36.)

Reference in the 16th-century documents to señores and principales of towns in the Olmeca region constitutes evidence of a recognized native nobility in this area as in other parts of Mexico. To cite a specific case, in 1576 a principal of the pueblo of Tlaliscoya, near the mouth of the Rio Alvarado, filed petition before Viceroy Enríquez requesting formal recognition of status and privileges as cacique on the ground that he was the eldest son and legitimate successor of his father who had been cacique and "señor natural" of the pueblo. On the basis of a favorable report by the corregidor of Tlacotalpa, the viceroy accorded recognition of such status and granted him the labor services of a stated number of Indians (Archivo General de la Nación, Mexico, Ramo de Indios, tomo 1, no. 79). We have no doubt that extended investigation in the archive would reveal similar cases for other towns in the Olmeca coastlands.

Unfortunately the sources to which we have had access do not record adequate data for a more detailed account of the caste or class structure of native society in the Olmeca region. Reference is made to the ritual sacrifice of slaves in the Tuxtla district (cf. Religion and Ritual, *infra*), but it seems likely that these were war captives. The single document cited in the preceding paragraph does not mention lands held or claimed by the cacique of Tlaliscoya. We believe, however, on the basis of some research on native landholdings in other parts of Mexico, that significant documentation on this phase of native society in the Olmeca country will be found in the Tierras and Vínculos ramos of the Mexican National Archive.

Warfare and Weapons

Imposition of Aztec dominion over the Rio Alvarado and Tuxtla districts doubtless served as a deterrent to the rivalries of the local lordships of these areas. Relations of the pueblos of the Tuxtla highlands and those of the province of Coatzacoalcos were characterized by an atmosphere of mutual suspicion and by occasional acts of war (Gayangos, 1866, p. 95; PNE, 5:6), but these conditions do not seem to have posed serious obstacles to the trade carried on by Aztec merchants with the Coatzacoalcos settlements or by way of this area with Tabasco and Chiapas. Within the Coatzacoalcos area inter-pueblo warfare occurred from time to time, but we are told that such hostilities were not prompted by political motives, i.e., to impose lordship over the vanquished towns, but by a cannibalistic custom of eating the bodies of warriors killed in combat or of war captives (Cangas y Quiñones, 1580).

Documents at our disposal do not provide specific data concerning norms of military organization and leadership in the Olmeca region at the time of Spanish contact, except for the fact that within the districts under Aztec dominion the subject pueblos were expected to provide warriors for service under the command of Aztec captains. As in other areas under Aztec control, an important feature of military activity was probably the taking of captives to serve as sacrificial victims in the ritual of native religion.

The principal offensive weapons used by warriors in the Olmeca coastlands were the bow and arrow and the *macana,* or war club edged with obsidian blades. For defensive purposes warriors used cotton armor (ichcahuipilli) and shields of closely knit reeds ("cañas macizas"), which were capable of resisting the bolt of a Spanish crossbow (PNE, 5:6).

Religion and Ritual

The scant data of specific character relating to native religion recorded in 16th-century sources are summarized as follows:

1. The Tlacotalpa relación of 1580 states that in preconquest times the Indians of this town worshipped an idol in the form of a woman which they had carved from a "piedra de esmeralda." Once each year they took this idol to the river (Alvarado), "washed it," and then "returned" it to a *cu* (illustrated by a small triangle in the original manuscript), where a single victim ("una persona") was sacrificed to it. The sacrificial ceremony was not witnessed by the entire pueblo but only by the principales and elders ("viejos") of the town (PNE, 5:2).

2. The Tuxtla relación of 1580 states that the Indians of this district worshipped the god "Ochilobos," or Huitzilopochtli—evidence of Mexican influence resulting from Aztec dominion. Of this deity they had made stone and ceramic representations or effigies—"le tenían pintado en piedras y en bultos de barro." To him they sacrificed slaves. Certain elders, who abstained from carnal relations with women, served as priests and performed the sacrificial rites (PNE, 5:5).

3. As regards native religion in the province of Coatzacoalcos, the Espiritu Santo relación of 1580 records only vague and unsatisfactory data. A brief section on this topic merely states that the Indians worshipped idols of stone and clay for which they had special sanctuaries ("casas diputadas a manera de hermita"), where sacrificial rites were performed. In another place the relación states that each pueblo worshipped a deity for which it had special loyalty ("afición"). Some inference as to religious custom in this region may perhaps be drawn from the meaning of the term Coatzacoalco, which Covarrubias (1947, p. 38) defines as "in the sanctuary of the serpent." And in this connection it should be noted that the Espiritu Santo relación defines "Guazcualco," the name of the pueblo where the Spaniards established their villa in 1522, as "casa de quelebras [culebras] despobladas" (Cangas y Quiñones, 1580).

4. In his account of the Grajalva expedition of 1518 Bernal Díaz related that at a Gulf coast village near the mouth of the Rio Tonala one of his companions "went to a house of idols which was on a hill [*cerro*] which as I have already said are called *cues*," and in that "house" he found many idols, copal, flint knives used by the Indians for sacrifices and "circumcision," and a wooden chest containing many gold articles, including diadems, necklaces, two idols, and hollow beads (Díaz del Castillo, ch. 16). This report, often cited, is suspect, however, because of some doubt that Díaz was actually a member of the Grijalva expedition.[6] Other accounts of the expedition, including the *Itinerario* of the priest Juan Díaz, do not mention a pyramidal structure on the Rio Tonala. They do relate how the Spaniards uncovered a recent burial containing bodies of young sacrificial victims whose hearts had been excised and heads cut off. With these bodies, covered by cotton mantas, they found gold necklaces and an idol ("cemi") of gold. These accounts also mention the ceremonial drawing of blood from the tongue and ears practiced by the Indians of this area (Wagner, 1942).

The references to pyramidal religious structures cited above have considerable interest. Unfortunately such accounts do not describe other structural details of

[6] Wagner (1942) has called attention to the fact that in a *probanza* of merits and services formulated by Díaz in 1539 no claim is made that he accompanied Grijalva in 1518, although specific reference is made to his participation in the expeditions of Córdoba (1517) and Cortés (1519).

these sanctuaries or the materials of which they were built.

Native Economy

Staple cultivated food products of the Olmeca coastlands were maize, beans, chiles, calabashes, and camotes. Postconquest tribute assessments for the period 1530–60 suggest a greater volume of maize production in the province of Coatzacoalcos than in the Rio Alvarado district. Both of these areas produced large quantities of cacao, which was an important item of local food supply and of export, and also served as a medium of exchange in business transactions. Sixteenth-century sources record scant information of specific character concerning native methods for the preparation and cultivation of maize, or for the care and harvesting of the cacao groves (*cacaguatales*). In addition to the food products already mentioned, the Indians of the Olmeca region made use of a variety of tropical plants and fruits, including aguacates, yuca, red tunas, chicozapotes, anonas, mameyes, and wild plums and grapes. Plant foods were supplemented by the flesh of turkeys, birds, waterfowl, deer, rabbits, small dogs, and reptiles, and by fresh- and salt-water fish, oysters, and shrimp. Specific reference is made in one source to oyster beds in the coastal lagoons of the Agualulcos district. (González de Cossío, 1952; PNE, 5:3–8, *passim;* Cangas y Quiñones, 1580.)

Backwash lagoons along the Gulf coast were utilized as a limited source of salt supply of poor quality. We also have a reference to a hot mineral spring at a site named Acalapa 5 leagues east of Espiritu Santo which overflowed into adjacent depressions where salt was gathered. In the 16th century salt was imported from western Yucatan, and we may assume that this was also true for preconquest times. The Olmeca region produced a native pepper, or spice ("pimienta"), which was used for medicinal purposes and in the preparation of food and cacao beverages (PNE, 5:3–8, *passim;* Cangas y Quiñones, 1580).

The production, on a rather extensive scale, of cotton and manufactured cotton fabrics in the Olmeca area is attested by both native and Spanish sources. Elaborately decorated cotton mantas were an important item of tribute paid to local señores and to Aztec rulers by the tributary province of Tuxtepec. As we have already noted, Sahagún's informants remarked on the rich apparel worn by the Olmeca men and women. Cotton mantas, white and colored, and the *maxtlatl,* or breechcloth, were the principal items of male attire, but we also find references to mantas made of feathers, and to "paper" clothing made of the bark of the ceiba tree. Women wore cotton *naguas* and *huipiles,* which, in view of the skill of Olmeca women in embroidery, attested by Sahagún, were probably of rather elaborate design. (Codex Mendoza, f.44; Sahagún, bk. 10, ch. 29; PNE, 5:3–8, *passim*; Cangas y Quiñones, 1580).

Sahagún states that both men and women in the Olmeca area wore sandals, "but those worn by the men are better made, and they also use sandals made of rubber." This reference to rubber produced in the Olmeca coastlands calls to mind the large quantities of rubber pellets paid as tribute to the Aztec state by the province of Tuxtepec (Sahagún, bk. 10, ch. 29; Codex Mendoza, f. 44).

Luxury goods produced in or derived from the Olmeca region included gold objects, jade, turquoise, and "amber," coral and articles of tortoiseshell, rich feather pieces, and large quantities of feathers utilized by Aztec artisans. The rivers of the Olmeca region produced a certain amount of gold, but it would appear that some of the gold objects paid as tribute to local señores or to the Aztec rulers by the tributary province of Tuxtepec were acquired in trade with other areas. References to jade as items of tribute and to the

Tlacotalpa idol carved from a "piedra de esmeralda" have considerable interest in view of the numerous jade artifacts found in Olmec archaeological sites. Jade objects of different kinds, forms, and colors were major items of export acquired by Aztec merchants, including the "precious green stone which today we call the finest emerald-green jade" (Anderson and Dibble, 1959, p. 19); Garibay K. (1961, p. 65) translates the equivalent Nahuatl text in the Madrid Codex as "jades de quetzal—hoy día los llamamos esmeraldas." The geographical provenience of jade in Middle America has been the subject of considerable discussion, and we do not wish to offer any conjecture as to the source of the jade derived from the Olmeca area. The "amber" used in the manufacture of lip-plugs which figured as an item of tribute paid by the province of Tuxtepec was evidently yellow topaz derived in trade with the Chiapas highlands (Scholes and Roys, 1948, p. 29). The export of manufactured feather pieces, the skins of tropical birds, and colored feathers from the Olmeca area require no comment, except that the large green quetzal feathers derived from this region were probably trade items from the Chiapas area.

Reference has been made to copper axes as items of tribute paid by Indians of the Coatzacoalcos province to their native lords. Sahagún (bk. 10, ch. 29) mentioned the use of copper axes by the Olmeca as a defensive weapon against wild animals. In this connection reference should also be made to accounts, recorded in the chronicles of the Grijalva expedition of 1518, of the barter carried on by the Spaniards at the Rio Tonala for similar artifacts which they believed were made of gold, but to their discomfiture found were only of copper (Díaz del Castillo, ch. 16; Wagner, 1942).

It is not surprising, in view of the luxury products of the Olmeca coastlands, that Aztec merchants carried on an active trade with this area and the neighboring districts of Tabasco and Chiapas. Sahagún and his informants (Sahagún, bk. 9; Garibay K., 1961) have given us rather extensive and illuminating accounts of this commerce, of which only a few details can be mentioned in this paper. A significant feature of this commerce was its active sponsorship by the Aztec rulers, who supplied capital in the form of goods to be traded in the Olmeca country. These accounts also tell how the Aztec merchants served as a kind of intelligence corps for their sponsors, and record the manner in which they sought to conceal their identity, or prepared themselves against the possibility of a hostile reception in the areas visited. It would appear that in the time of Moctezuma I, Aztec merchants received a friendly reception in the province of Coatzacoalcos, and that the caciques of this area "willingly" supplied gold and tortoiseshells requested on behalf of the Aztec ruler (cf. Durán, 1951, 1:230). Subsequently, after the Aztec conquest of the Rio Alvarado and Tuxtla districts, an atmosphere of suspicion and occasional acts of war characterized the relations of the Coatzacoalcos pueblos with their neighbors under Aztec dominion, but these conditions did not constitute a serious obstacle to the trade of Aztec merchants with the Coatzacoalcos area, or by way of this region with Tabasco and Chiapas.

The status of the Aztec merchants as a privileged class and the increasing influence which they enjoyed within the Aztec state have been the subject of significant commentary by students of the preconquest history of Mexico. León-Portilla (1962) has suggested that the merchant class on the eve of Spanish conquest had achieved a position of influence equal to, or more potent than, that of the military caste, and that they might have superseded the military as the directing force in Aztec affairs if the coming of the Spaniards had not intervened to interrupt this political trend. The role of merchants in the Olmeca region, and especially within the province of Coatzacoalcos which had escaped Aztec dominion, would have particular interest for students of Middle American history, but unfortunately available documentary sources do not provide any basis for a reasoned conjecture as to their role, actual or potential, in native society on the eve of Spanish contact.

Other Features of Olmeca Culture

Kirchhoff has listed as typical Olmeca traits: flattened and shaved heads, the filing, inlay, and blackening of teeth, and tattooing (*Mayas y Olmecas,* 1942, p. 40). Evidence of head deformation by historic Olmeca is recorded in the Tuxtla relación of 1580 which incorrectly defines the meaning of the place name Tuxtla as "cabeza ancha,"[7] and relates that in "heathen times" mothers and midwives flattened ("apretaban") the heads of infants at birth (PNE, 5:5). That Olmeca men shaved their heads only to the crown is suggested by a statement in the Tlacotalpa relación of 1580 (PNE, 5:2) that males in this area wore their hair long like women ("con los cabellos largos como mujeres"). We have not found reference to dental deformation and inlay in the 16th-century documents at our disposal. Nor have we found specific mention of tattooing, although this form of body decoration may be implied in a statement in the Tlacotalpa report that men painted (the Spanish verb is "embijar") their bodies (PNE, 5:2).

The relaciones of 1580 give some attention to health and disease in the Olmeca region and take note of the effects of epidemic diseases of European origin in post-conquest times. An interesting feature of these reports is the statement that in "heathen times" men lived to a more advanced age than after the Spanish conquest. This greater longevity was ascribed to the fact that in earlier times men did not marry or have sexual relations with women until they had achieved "mucha edad" (PNE, 5:6; Cangas y Quiñones, 1580). If these reports have any validity, they may reflect the influence of some feature of native religion.

The Tuxtla and Espiritu Santo relaciones also record some information concerning medical plants used in the Olmeca area for the alleviation and cure of physical ailments. One of these plants was *cececpatli,* of which Francisco Hernández, the famous *protomédico* of New Spain, described several varieties in his celebrated treatise on the medicinal flora of Mexico (Hernández, 1959–60, vols. 2, 3). Other medicinal plants named in the reports of 1580 are: *suchimecatle,* the juice of which was used for ailments of the eyes; *mimizpatle,* used as a purge and for the treatment of dropsy, which seems to have been a fairly common form of illness; and a species of camomile that was also used as a purge (PNE, 5:6; Cangas y Quiñones, 1580).

The Espiritu Santo report also mentions tobacco as a medicinal plant utilized in the Coatzacoalcos area. Mixed with lime, it was chewed to deaden hunger. Powdered tobacco, without lime, was smoked for the alleviation of asthma, colds, catarrh, coughs, and "bubas," and "for many other illnesses" (Cangas y Quiñones, 1580).

[7] The name Tuxtla, or Toztlan, is derived from the Nahuatl term *toztli,* "yellow macaw."

REFERENCES

Aguirre Beltrán, 1953
Anderson and Dibble, 1959
Barlow, 1949
Cangas y Quiñones, 1580
Cline, 1959a
Codex Mendoza
Cook and Borah, 1960
—— and Simpson, 1948
Covarrubias, 1947
Díaz del Castillo, 1939
Durán, 1951
Espinosa, 1910
Estado . . . Coatzacoalcos, 1945
Foster, 1943
García Pimentel, 1904
Garibay K., 1961
Gayangos, 1866
Gibson, 1960
González de Cossío, 1952
Hernández, 1959–60
Jiménez Moreno, 1942
León-Portilla, 1962
Mayas y Olmecas, 1942
Papeles de Nueva España, 1905
Paso y Troncoso, 1939–42
Roys, R. L., 1943
Scholes and Adams, 1957
—— and Roys, 1948
Trens, 1947
Wagner, H. R., 1942

31. Archaeological Synthesis of Oaxaca

IGNACIO BERNAL

Of the archaeology of the present state of Oaxaca (94,211 sq. km.) we know about only the valley of Oaxaca and the Mixteca Alta. These two regions form the basis of our study, to which will be added the few data available from elsewhere in the state.

In an area marked by diversity of natural environment and ethnic and linguistic composition, Oaxaca is one of the zones most characteristically Mesoamerican. Here are tropical coastlands, the hot and humid Papaloapan region, a great temperate valley, and high mountains cut by small valleys with much colder climates. In these variable habitats live, and have lived, numerous indigenous groups with distinct characteristics and cultures. Today, 14 languages are spoken, without counting the dialects which, at times, are almost unintelligible among themselves.

The mosaic formed by these 14 groups has an exclusively linguistic basis; more recent studies have provided ethnographic subdivisions. The distinct regions, such as appear on the maps based on 16th-century documents, correspond in general to archaeological regions of that epoch but not to those of a more remote past. The known data demonstrate that the geographical distribution of cultures was different in prehistoric times from what it was in historic times. It is obvious that more than a dozen human groups evidently changed, in three millennia, the map of their territory. But as we do not know the archaeology of all these groups, it is impossible to indicate their more ancient distributions, the formation of those historically known, and the distinct regions occupied by each people in their long history. Possibly those groups of seemingly secondary importance played a major role in the past, a role that, when clear, could change our conception of the archaeological history of their more powerful neighbors. The complexity of all this increases not only because the groups were numerous but because they were frequently mixed with each other. Already we can see (and shall discuss later) some of the movements and territorial changes which occurred between the Mixtecs and Zapotecs or their predecessors.

Many people are much concerned with

CHART 1—CHRONOLOGICAL CHART OF THE CULTURES OF OAXACA
(Only the Principal Sites Explored)

PERIODS	MONTE ALBAN	VALLEY OF OAXACA	MIXTECA	OTHER REGIONS	DATES
V	V	Mitla Yagul Cuilapan	Coixtlahuaca Tilantongo Nativitas Tututepec and other sites in the Mixteca Baja	Tuxtepec Monte Flor and various sites in the Chinantla Quiotepec Istmo	1521
IV	IV	Mitla Yagul Cuilapan San Luis Beltran Noriega Etla			1000
IIIB	IIIB	Cuilapan	Yatachio	Yagila? Quiotepec?	650
Transition IIIA–IIIB	Transition IIIA–IIIB		Yucuñudahui Yatachio		550
IIIA	IIIA		Yatachio		A.D. 200
Transition II–IIIA	Transition II–IIIA	Loma Larga			B.C. 100
II	II	Caballito Blanco	Tliltepec Huamelulpan		300
I	I	Yagul	Monte Negro	Istmo Monte Flor Honduras Cocuyo	900
Preceramic			Yuzanu		

the "ethnic baptism" of archaeological remains. Here we shall give ethnic names only to those antiquities which in all probability were produced by the historic peoples to which we link them; we shall not do this with cultures of early periods or with those whose connection with the historic horizon is not evident. Thus, we shall apply the name Zapotec only to those cultures of Monte Alban IIIA and later, whose descendants, physically and culturally, are undoubtedly the Zapotecs of the 16th century and today. We shall not consider a culture as Mixtec unless it has traits characteristic of the Mixtecs of the 16th century. Thus, we hope to free ourselves from the danger of false ethnic attributions without falling into the opposite extreme of making no linkages whatsoever between archaeological cultures and those of the historical or ethnographic horizon.

Recently Nicholson (1961) has criticized the indiscriminate use of the term Mixtec when it refers to the cultural complex of "Mixteca-Puebla," which naturally also includes Tlaxcala. In this article, if we employ the term Mixtec style or culture we refer only to that much-reduced area of the Mixteca-Puebla culture, the Mixteca, as this is understood today in its geographic sense. Of course, the Mixteca territory of today includes some small ethnolinguistic islands (Chocho, Trique, etc.) which archaeologically, as of now, are indistinguishable. Thus, one of the most characteristic sites of the Mixteca-Puebla style is Coixtlahuaca where Chocho is spoken, a language of the Popoloca family. I do not believe it risky to affirm that the historic Mixtecs were the bearers of Mixteca-Puebla culture *in the Oaxaca region,* although this does not signify that they were its initiators or principal bearers. In fact, the same style is also encountered in the final phase of the Chinantla and of the Cuicateca area. This recalls the prob-

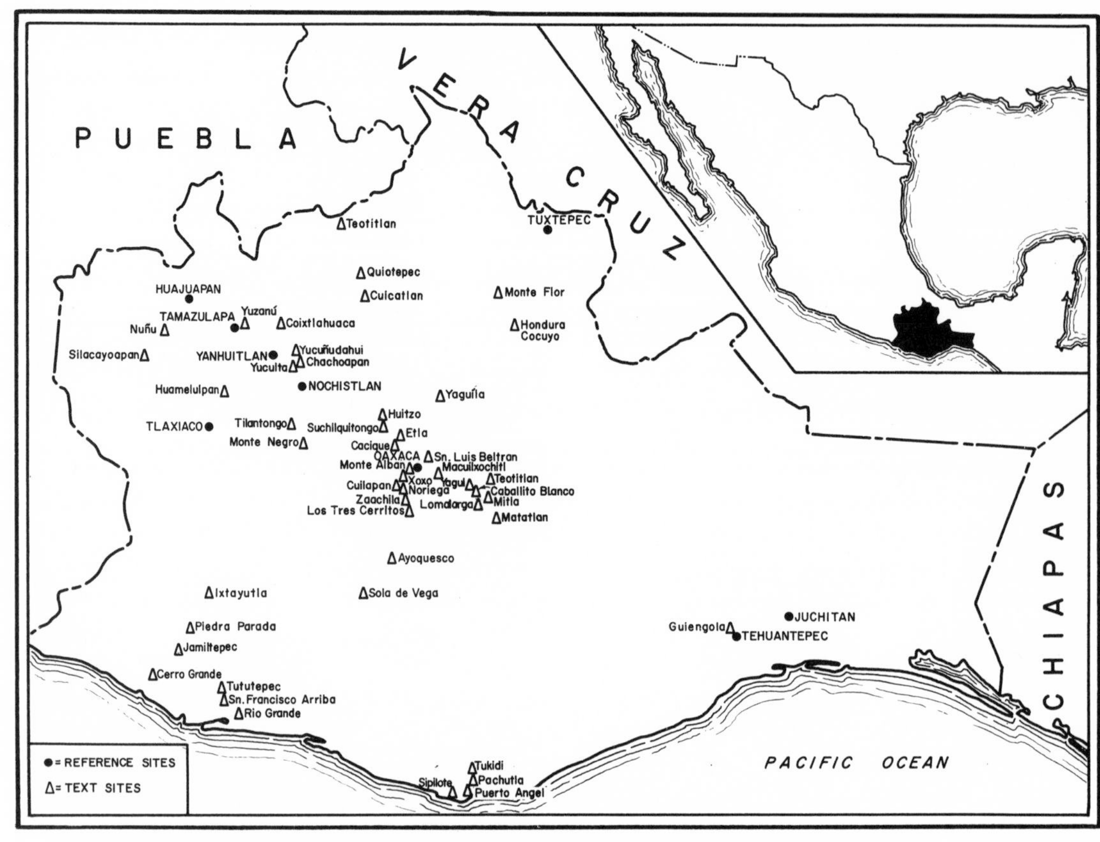

Fig. 1—MAP SHOWING ARCHAEOLOGICAL SITES IN OAXACA

lem, of which we have already spoken, about the possible role played by other peoples in the development of the ancient cultures of Oaxaca. Because such a role, or roles, are unknown to us we may very well attribute the accomplishments of secondary or unknown peoples to those groups that are today most important because they have survived the hazards of history.

History of Archaeological Studies in Oaxaca

The Oaxacan region is one of the poorest in Mesoamerica in colonial publications about its pre-Spanish past. Except for general works like Herrera, we have neither accounts of the time of the conquest nor chroniclers who interested themselves in collecting its history and traditions during the 16th century. It is difficult to explain this state of affairs because it is just this area, so lacking in documents in European script, which is the richest in native picture writings. Why is it that the conquistadores, missionaries, and friars apparently took the least interest in collecting data in the place where the most codices have survived? Why in view of the strong historiographic tradition of the Mixteca did no Ixtlilxochitl or Tezozomoc arise in that region? The fact is that the only important sources which we know from the 16th century are the Relaciones Geográficas (Paso y Troncoso, 1905; Gómez de Orozco, 1928; and Vargas Rea in recent years). There are others unpublished. Some friars, whose interests were chiefly linguistic, have left other important data in their "Artes." Among these Fr. Juan de Córdova

(1578a,b), for Zapotec, and Fr. Francisco de Alvarado (1593) and Fr. Antonio de los Reyes (1593), for Mixtec are outstanding.

All things considered, Fr. Francisco de Burgoa is the most valuable chronicler of Oaxaca, in spite of his many faults. He has left two works: the Palestra Historial . . . (1670) and the Geográfica Descripción . . . (1674), both republished in 1934. Amidst a welter of biblical quotations and unimportant data, there is a considerable volume of useful information collected by one who knew the region at first hand. Unfortunately, when he wrote, in the second half of the 17th century, the upper-class native culture had almost entirely disappeared and history had become a jumble of disconnected legends, frequently unintelligible.

Burgoa was born in the city of Oaxaca about 1600. At the age of 18 he entered the convent of Santo Domingo as a novice and was ordained there in 1625. At different times he traveled over the whole region, taking advantage of these journeys to collect historical data, much helped by his thorough knowledge of both Zapotec and Mixtec tongues. He held many offices in his Order and died in Zaachila in 1681. The work of Balsalobre (1892), first published in 1656, is a little older and, though important, is of less interest. His information about Zapotec religion has recently been confirmed and amplified by Berlin (1957).

In the last century of colonial government we find no author in Oaxaca comparable to Clavijero, Alzate, Marquez, or León y Gama, the first Mexican archaeologist.

With the 19th century begins the long series of amateurs, more tourists than archaeologists, who sometimes paid attention to ruins and later did excavations. Mitla had been the only ruin in Oaxaca to be described in the 16th century, by Motolinía (1858), as well as in the Relación de Tlacolula y Mitla (Canseco, 1905), and in the 17th century by Burgoa (1674, 2:121–25). In the 19th century it was the most visited and studied town in all Mesoamerica. It was popularized by Humboldt, who published (1810, pls. 49, 50) the plans made in 1802 by Luis Martín and Pedro de Laguna. These were given to Humboldt by the viceroy, the Marquis of Branciforte. Although Humboldt never went to Oaxaca, he preserved in this way the first-known plans of a ruin in that region, and the publication is important because the originals have been lost.

Among the first travelers and archaeologists who saw Mitla, we mention the best known, Dupaix, who was there in 1806 (but did not publish until 1834), and Mühlenpfordt, who went there with Carriedo in 1830 and made the first general plan as well as ones of individual buildings. Carriedo published part of the work in 1851, but not until much later did Peñafiel (1890, pls. 46–55) complete it by publishing all Mühlenpfordt's plates.[1] The first description of Monte Alban of which I know was published as an appendix to the Estadística de Oaxaca by Murguía (García, 1859); it includes a sketch of the great plaza and imaginative drawings of certain details.

With Bandelier, who arrived in Oaxaca in June 1881, begins the stage of the great explorers. He went to Monte Alban, was the first to mention Yagul (Gui-y-Baa) (Bandelier, 1884, p. 315), and visited Mitla and several other places.

Charnay had been in Oaxaca at least twice since 1858 (Charnay, 1863) and returned a little before Bandelier (they went together to explore the "Ville Lorillard"); but he paid little attention to Mitla and, as he himself said of the ruins, "nous ne les

[1] I do not include travelers of secondary importance, who contribute little, such as Mayer (1857), Tempsky (1858) who calls his book Mitla but scarcely pays any attention to it, Doutrelaine (1867), Helbrüger (1874), Aymé (1882), Ober (1884).

avons pas etudiées avec autant de soin que les autres" (Charnay, 1885, p. 458). He was a pioneer of archaeological photography in Mexico and obtained excellent results.

Seler's first journey to Mexico, in 1888, resulted in a large number of publications. The most important on Oaxaca (Seler, 1888, 1890a, 1891, 1894, 1895, 1896)[2] cover various subjects and are not merely descriptive but introduce a new and particularly important way of studying its antiquities. The chief thing he did was to copy and publish the paintings at Mitla, which have almost disappeared. The passage of time and changes in our archaeological interests have not taken away the value of Seler's work. The same can be said of another great scholar, William H. Holmes, who arrived in February 1895. He studied Monte Alban superficially and Mitla thoroughly, and left splendid panoramas of both places. His description of Mitla is particularly complete and is still valuable (Holmes, 1895–97). Alvarez visited Mitla in 1895 and 1898, and published his work in 1900. The following year appeared Nicolas León's guide to Mitla, an enlargement of the first edition of 1893.

None of the authors mentioned had so far done any excavations in Oaxaca, although they sometimes quote data obtained by amateurs who had excavated or collected antiquities. Thus, Martínez Gracida has left interesting albums (unpublished) of drawings of many specimens, frequently with their exact localities and sometimes with details about their discovery. He was an historian with a touch of the novelist who followed the tradition of Murguía y Galardi (1861), Carriedo (1846), and Gay (1881).

Except for Burgoa, whom Murguía calls "my teacher," the Oaxacan historical writers of the 19th century appear to have had only verbal sources of information. Gay, the most explicit, cites—in addition to Burgoa—only general sources like Herrera or Torquemada, legends, and oral traditions.

I myself have sometimes heard stories similar to those given by Gay or Martínez Gracida from countrymen in the region, but have not been able to discover whether they were these historians' original sources or were a result of the considerable local vogue that their writings have had.

Sporadic works of conservation were begun on the palaces of Mitla in 1888, but they made no real progress until 1901 when Leopoldo Batres carried out the existing restorations. These, though defective, have resulted in the preservation of the monuments, which were much damaged at the time. The following year Batres undertook the first exploration of Monte Alban (Batres, 1902).

In 1898 Marshall Saville began his explorations in various places in the valley of Oaxaca: Xoxo in 1898, Mitla in 1900 and 1901 (Saville, 1899, 1900, 1909). His work in Cuilapan, done in 1902, was not published until much later (Bernal, 1958c).

These pioneer efforts showed clearly the richness of the archaeology of the region and opened the door to more important later studies.

Besides other workers in Oaxaca in subsequent years was Manuel Gamio, who attempted, in the second decade of this century, to carry out in the valley of Oaxaca a study like that which he had accomplished in the valley of Teotihuacan. Nothing of this remains except some manuscript reports of his surveys, mostly in the Etla valley, but he did no excavating (Archives of the Instituto Nacional de Antropología e Historia).

Up to now, information on the archaeology of the Mixteca and some other parts of Oaxaca is not worth mention.

[2] All these articles were republished in his "Gesammelte Abhandlungen" (1902–13). The five volumes are being reprinted in Graz, 1960—. See also Smithsonian Institution, Bureau of American Ethnology, Bull. 28, Washington, 1904.

Modern archaeological work in Oaxaca began at the end of 1931 when Alfonso Caso and his collaborators began exploration of Monte Alban, where 18 seasons have been spent (Caso, 1932a, 1935, 1938, 1939b; Acosta, 1958–59); the first series of explorations in the Mixteca were carried out by the same scholars starting in 1933 (Caso, 1938, pp. 41, 42). The first great work of Caso (1928) on Oaxaca, as well as his numerous publications on the calendar, glyphs, and codices, pertains to Articles 37 and 38, as do sections on the Mixtec codices and the history of their interpretation.

To widen knowledge of Monte Alban, Acosta explored in Etla and Xoxo, and Caso and Rubín de la Borbolla in Mitla (1936). In the Mixteca Alta, Guzmán (1934) made a reconnaissance; Caso and some collaborators explored in Yucuñudahui, Tilantongo (Caso, 1938), and Montenegro. Many of the results are still unpublished.

These explorations uncovered definite stratification, at least in outline, for the valley of Oaxaca as a whole, as well as fundamental knowledge of the architecture, sculpture, paintings, and tombs of the Zapotecs of the valley. The oldest-known period of the Mixteca Alta was established, as well as some relations between the two areas.

In 1948 I explored the hill of Inguiteria in Coixtlahuaca (Bernal, 1949a) and from this published the first representative study of the Mixtec ceramic complex. In the winter of 1952 I directed the exploration of the hill of Yatachio near Tamazulapan, published in part (1953). Similarly I investigated Cuilapan (Bernal, 1958c) and Yagul, starting in 1954 (1955). Because this site has proved particularly interesting, work there has been continued both by myself and by students of Mexico City College under John Paddock and Charles Wicke. These explorations, discussed below, followed a joint plan which produced very satisfactory results although they were carried out by two independent groups (Paddock, 1957, 1960; Wicke, 1957; Bernal, 1960b). Important discoveries have been made by the same groups in Caballito Blanco (unpublished) in the last few years. Also in the valley of Oaxaca, Bernal, Lorenzo Gamio, and others have explored Noriega (Bernal, 1960a) and San Luis Beltran (manuscript in preparation). These archaeologists have made an almost complete survey of the valley of Oaxaca, locating the ruins and classifying them by periods, sizes, and settlement patterns.

In the Mixteca Alta, Lorenzo Gamio worked for one season in Huamelulpan (Gamio, 1957) and with Alfonso Caso for a second in 1961 (Caso and Gamio, 1961), making the only excavation in this area since that of Tamazulapan. The highland Zapotec region has not been explored archaeologically but useful information can be found in De la Fuente (1942a) and Pérez García (1956).

In Chinantla, Cline worked for a season in Monte Flor in 1951 (Cline, 1959b) and Delgado worked in various places (Delgado, 1960a,b). Gamio (MS in the archives of I.N.A.H., 1950) and Pareyón (1960) worked in Quiotepec, with useful, though incomplete, results.

Part of the Mixteca Baja was reconnoitered at the beginning of 1956 (DeCicco and Brockington, 1956); in 1957 Sáenz made another reconnaissance in the region adjoining Guerrero (Sáenz, 1957; Piña Chan, 1960b).

The isthmian region of Oaxaca has been little explored archaeologically although it has been visited frequently since the colonial period. Apart from some studies on Quiengola (Guengola) (Seler, 1896) and disconnected information supplied by travelers, scarcely anything is known of either the Zapotec or the Huave area. Forster made an attempt to study it (1955), and Delgado found an interesting stratigraphic sequence (1961). Recent work of the Institute of Andean Research is not yet published.

A subject of continuous interest is the study of the celebrated urns which are one of the best-known characteristics of Zapotec culture. Although by no means confined to the valley of Oaxaca, most of them have been found in and around it. Of the projected volumes on Monte Alban and the Zapotec culture only that on the urns has appeared so far (Caso and Bernal, 1952). Among the many earlier studies on the subject that of Linné (1938) is outstanding.

Apart from those already mentioned, there are many works which treat of some aspect of Oaxacan culture, or some element or individual find, but it is not possible to discuss them here (Acosta, 1949; Beals, 1934; Berlin, 1957; Bernal, 1946, 1949b,c,d; Caso, 1927a, 1932a,b,c, 1933, 1936, 1942, 1949b; Covarrubias, 1947; Dahlgren, 1954; Séjourné, 1956).

Long after an attempt by Lejeal (1903), Caso (1936, 1942) published a synthesis of Mixtec and Zapotec archaeology which appears to have been the first attempt at a general view of the archaeology of the state of Oaxaca. The results of these latter investigations will be found in the main body of this article, and the results of other explorations in the region appear elsewhere in this *Handbook*. This brief history of research shows how many areas have not even been touched, whereas others are in only the first stages of exploration.[3]

Zapotec Area

Lack of exploration makes it impossible to delimit this area precisely. Maps compiled from linguistic information of the 16th century, chiefly from the Relaciones de Nueva España (García Granados, 1935) and from other colonial or recent data, do not agree exactly with archaeological ones. These discrepancies apply to the total areas of the Zapotec and Mixtec at different stages and to the boundaries between them. For example, historical sources indicate that the occupation of Tehuantepec and a large part of the isthmus by the Zapotecs took place shortly before the conquest, but objects found there are very like those in the valley of Oaxaca. Although they do not come from stratigraphic excavations, they at least suggest Zapotec establishments in the isthmus from the Classic period of Monte Alban onwards (Forster, 1955; Delgado, 1961). On the other hand, the extreme northern and some of the western parts of the valley of Oaxaca are considered Mixtec; but the pottery collected in places like Suchilquitongo or Cuilapan is fundamentally Zapotec or earlier. Only a thin stratum on the surface belongs to a Mixtec invasion, very near to the time of the Spanish conquest. In this case, historical data (e.g., Relación de Cuilapan) agree.

Even within the area now occupied by the Zapotecs we can distinguish various subdivisions which correspond only in the most general way with those suggested by 16th-century documents or by modern ethnography (De la Fuente, 1942a,b). I mention this point to show how much greater these differences will be if we go further back in time, but as we are dealing here with only part of the Zapotec area, the boundaries of the whole will not affect the results. This part is the central region of the three great valleys of Oaxaca here called simply the valley of Oaxaca. Although its vegetation varies, it forms a geographical unit.

Although not yet proved geologically, indications point to the former existence of a lake, or at least large swamps, in the valley. Today there are swamps, now largely dried up, which were doubtless bigger at one time. It is also probable that the Peñon de Zaachila was on an island.

[3] I am particularly grateful to Dr. Alfonso Caso and to Prof. John Paddock for valuable additions and corrections to the present work.

Representation of aquatic animals and swimmers appears persistently on Monte Alban I pottery; deeply rooted legends tell that lakes or swamps once existed here. Not only do ancient writers speak of projects by Zapotec sovereigns to drain the valley, but the belief persists in the folklore of today. I have collected legends to this effect in a number of places, for example at Los Cerritos, a ruin some 3 km. south of Zaachila.

From the upper Preclassic period onward the valley of Oaxaca has proved particularly rich in finds, Monte Alban being much the most important site. Placed on a hill 2000 m. above sea level, at the junction of three valleys which form the valley of Oaxaca, this vast and spectacular ruin is one of the masterworks of the American continent. Besides this, it is not only the best-studied site in Oaxaca but the one which has provided the basic chronology for the region from the Protoclassic period onwards.

Further, the valley of Oaxaca provides all the conditions which suggest close correlation between geographical features and distribution of cultures. Although a complete reconnaissance of the valley proved too great an undertaking for one person, it has been possible to discover and visit many sites and to obtain valuable results.

In collaboration with Lorenzo Gamio, I began the work by trying in all innocence to collect pottery wherever it lay and to mark the sites on the map. I soon found that it was easier to mark places where there was nothing, since the valley is literally covered with remains of all sorts, especially potsherds. It was then decided not to list any site which did not include a mound, a tomb, or such an agglomeration of pottery as to be clearly distinguishable from other locations (only two cases of this last). Of the 251 sites thus visited, I shall limit discussion to the 164 of which the pottery has so far been studied.

All these sites appear in figure 1, which needs some explanation. Primarily, it lays no claim to geographical accuracy because the mapping of the area is disgraceful. This increased the difficulties so much that it is possible to locate many sites, marked approximately on the map, only by a series of explanatory notes, which will appear in the final publication but can not be included here.

The sites vary greatly in size. Some (Cacique, Huitzo-Suchilquitongo, Ayoquezco, Macuilxochitl) are nearly as large as Monte Alban, with great plazas, many buildings, ball courts, and remains of houses; others are no more than a hillock. Their most usual characteristics seem to be: mounds arranged around square or rectangular courts; mounds made of stone and mud, or adobe (in high places some are of stone alone); walls, mound slopes, and floors covered with plaster; shrines in the center of courts in at least 21 places; ball courts in 15; fortifications I noted in only seven places (Las Relaciones de Nueva España mention them also in Zaachila and Santa Cruz Ixtepec); and agricultural terraces very commonly on the hillslopes.

Superficial inspection showed no architectural remains different from those already known in Monte Alban, Mitla, or Yagul; and I did not collect any stone objects of unknown types. It is the same with the pottery. Instead of long tables, for which there is no space, I give the somewhat subjective impression that nearly 90 per cent of the sherds collected on all the sites were easily classified into Monte Alban types. The remaining 10 per cent were mainly of types from outside the valley, which are usually found at Monte Alban also. On the other hand, on the few sites visited outside the valley, the percentage of sherds which did not fall into Monte Alban types rose rapidly to about 60 per cent. Since this applies to all periods, we can make an important deduction: the whole valley of Oaxaca has had a common history and is an ecological unit in which the same cultures have succeeded one another throughout in the same order. I have noted only two exceptions. First, many sites, especially the small ones, were apparently not occupied by the users of Monte Alban II pottery; it appears from surface collections that they pass straight from Period I to IIIA, but until all the sites have been excavated we shall not be sure of that. Second, the Mixtecs, the bearers of the culture which is called Period V in Monte Alban, did not occupy the whole valley, so that some sites finish their pre-Spanish history in Period IV. This is not to say that they were abandoned—many of them are still occupied today—but that the Mixtecs did not occupy them, as we already know from historical sources. There remains a small problem affecting Yagul, Mitla, and at least one other site (Matatlan) at the extreme east end of the valley. Here is a series of very late remains which are mostly Mixtec with an admixture of another undefined culture. This variation is found only at this end of the valley and will be discussed later.

The classification of sites by periods is still provisional, since the presence of sherds belonging to a particular period in the surface collections can be taken to show that the site was occupied at that time, but their absence does not necessarily prove that it was not. In the final publication of this work there will be maps of each period and a study of the pottery of each site.

Finally, the number of ruins, the abundance of material in them, and the large size of some, suggest a very dense population for the valley of Oaxaca. Rough calculations have suggested to me that the population from Period IIIB onwards was very near that of the present time, but this is only an estimate.

Mixtec Area

The Mixtec region occupies a large area including not only all the western state of Oaxaca but also parts of Guerrero and Puebla. Within it are linguistic islets. It is divided into two very different areas commonly called Mixteca Alta and Baja. As in the case of the Zapotec area we are concerned only with part: that of the Mixteca Alta which forms a square contained approximately by Huajuapan, Coixtlahuaca, Nochixtlan, and Tlaxiaco. It consists of high, cold, fertile valleys surrounded by eroded mountains. Only Coixtlahuaca lies lower and has scarcely any cultivable valley. Soil erosion is very ancient and is caused mainly by natural agencies, although these have been accentuated by man in more recent times (López de Llergo, 1960, pl. 28).[4] Thus, it is probable that the situation was but little better at the time of the great expansion of Mixtec culture which started in the 10th century than it is now. We must, for that time, imagine the Mixtec habitat as a series of small and fertile valleys separated by practically desert hills. Later we will consider the cultural implications of these physical surroundings.

Preceramic Cultures

It seems extraordinary that such a favorable area for human development as the valley of Oaxaca was apparently not inhabited until so late. We have no reliable data which could allow us to speak of preceramic cultures there.

Holmes (1895–97, pp. 284–87) illustrates stone implements found in Mitla and its surroundings, and believes that they were used to work the stones for the palace façades. For this reason they would belong to a very late horizon although, in a sense, they are of Paleolithic type. Adán (1927) described 23 worked stones "of Paleolithic aspect" also found unstratified at Mitla, which look similar to those pub-

[4] Cook (1949) comes to similar conclusions in that he thinks that erosion began at least 4000–5000 years ago.

lished by Holmes although he does not say so. Similarly, De Terra (1947, p. 72) refers to stone implements which appear similar; he mentions neither Holmes nor Adán and includes these implements in his "Chalco Culture." There are doubts both about these finds and about the "Chalco Culture" itself (Aveleyra, 1950, pp. 41, 96). To sum up, no conclusion can at present be drawn from them; nevertheless, MacNeish thinks that some flints collected near Mitla belong to late preceramic horizons. It is quite possible that the same applies to implements collected in Caballito Blanco and Yagul.

More interesting is the site explored at Yuzanu, north of Yanhuitlan, in the middle of the Mixteca Alta. It is the oldest site so far published in Oaxaca (Lorenzo, 1958) since it has yielded two radiocarbon dates of 4050 and 3950 ± 200 B.P. (ca. 2100 and 2000 B.C.). A hearth containing charcoal was found associated with various atypical stone implements.

Basing his conclusions chiefly on geological evidence and the absence of animal bones, Lorenzo thinks that this is a preceramic agricultural culture. It is clear that the date is not too old for this, but we have no adequate local information to say that it is so; neither is it possible yet to correlate it with similar cultures, like those of Coxcatlan Cave whose early horizon is dated 3600 ± 250 B.C. (MacNeish, 1961, p. 24).

Other stone implements from Yatachio are probably very old also, as are probably the lower horizons, not yet properly explored, of some caves between Tamazulapan and Huajuapan.

Even more extraordinary than the paucity of information about preceramic man in Oaxaca is the lack of it for the earlier Preclassic subperiods. Of all the sites so far known in the state, none has yielded pottery of an age comparable with the period of Zacatenco-Copilco in the Valley of Mexico or its contemporaries elsewhere in Mesoamerica. The oldest ceramic culture which we know in the state, Monte Alban I, belongs to a very well developed phase of the upper Preclassic. Although Monte Negro is possibly older than Monte Alban I, this does not alter the situation since Monte Negro is also upper Preclassic.[5]

Monte Alban I

This is unquestionably the oldest culture at Monte Alban, since it has been found on virgin soil—the chernozem characteristic of Oaxaca—in all stratigraphic excavations.

It has been divided into phases IA, IB, and IC, but it is not possible to extend these divisions to aspects of the culture other than pottery. We can thus consider the three phases as a unity, without trying to point out here the small differences, exclusively ceramic, between them.

In Yagul, too, Monte Alban I remains are always on natural rock, as is true in Cuilapan. There is a stratigraphic sequence in Etla and Xoxo, but the occupation is later than this period. We have found Monte Alban I occupation in 39 sites in the valley of Oaxaca; and although we have no stratigraphy in them, we have found nothing older. We know only one site of this period in the Mixteca–Monte Negro—and it appears to be the only place where this period alone is found, since it was probably abandoned at the end of it. Objects which undoubtedly belong to this horizon come from various places in the Mixteca. None of them were found in excavations so their origin remains in doubt; nevertheless, as they belong to the older collections in the National Museum of Mexico, their proveniences are probably correct since there would have been no commercial advantage to the ama-

[5] Ed. note: By "upper Preclassic" the author apparently refers to what is elsewhere called Late Preclassic and, probably, the latter part of Middle Preclassic. See Willey, Ekholm, and Millon, Article 14, volume 1. See also Wauchope, 1950, p. 241; 1954, p. 28.

teur collectors at that time in falsifying these proveniences. Two cases are quite certain. One is a whistling jar (Monte Alban IC) decorated with stucco from Coixtlahuaca, which is identical with one from Monte Alban; the other consists of vessels and sherds found in holes cut in the rock (they do not appear to have been tombs) immediately under the hill of Pueblo Viejo in Tamazulapam. Also, sherds and figurines of Monte Alban I were found in other parts of the excavation (Bernal, 1953, pp. 19, 47, 48). Sherds of Monte Alban I were found also in Yucuñudahui (Caso, 1938, p. 50) and in Tehuacan (Noguera, 1940, p. 18).

In the Mixteca Baja, Piedra Parada, Cerro Grande, San Francisco Arriba, and Zipilote (DeCicco and Brockington, 1956; Piña Chan, 1960b) show that the Monte Alban I culture was present there. Similar pottery and figurines come from Juchitan and Tehuantepec; in Laguna Zope, Delgado (1961) found two periods which are probably contemporary with it. In Monte Flor (Cline, 1959b), in Honduras Cocuyo (Delgado, 1960a,b), and in Chinantla, the relationship is not with Monte Alban but rather with the great Olmec sites of Veracruz and Tabasco.

It could be supposed that these objects found on different sites were brought by trade from the valley of Oaxaca; but I do not believe that they were, because they are found in so many places and are of types not generally exported. Similarly, not a vestige of any other culture has so far been found in the whole area, and we can not imagine that the region was uninhabited. Above all, in Monte Negro the whole culture is certainly linked to that of Monte Alban I, but that does not necessarily imply that it was imported from there. On the contrary, most of the pieces are of local manufacture and show local variations, although some were probably brought from the valley of Oaxaca. Some appear to be imitations of Monte Alban; for example, the braziers showing the Young God are almost identical (Caso and Bernal, 1952, pp. 326, 336). Another example of this deity was recently found in a Period I tomb in Yagul.

The Monte Negro culture which is related to Monte Alban I appears to be less complete and less developed. Although some architectural features, such as streets and drains, are more advanced in Monte Negro, there are neither glyphs, calendar, nor carved stones; fine pottery is scarcer. Unfortunately, we can not decide whether Monte Negro represents a culture slightly older than Monte Alban, slightly newer (but with some overlap in each case), or entirely contemporary but more provincial and, in general, less urbanized and "professionalized" in its manufactures than Monte Alban.

Study of the skeletons in Monte Negro poses an interesting problem, whose meaning I do not fully understand. All the skeletal material so far found in Oaxaca, both in the Mixtec and the Zapotec zones, shows identical racial characteristics, and these still predominate in the region. On the other hand, we find different characteristics in Monte Negro; there is a tendency to dolichocephaly and probably greater head height (Romero, 1951, p. 328).

As early as the first period many different glyphs were used in Monte Alban, 11 of them being calendrical. We know 10 gods, all masculine if we do not include the figurines of naked women. The men wear cloaks, breech clouts, bracelets, and, perhaps, sandals; on their heads, scarves, helmets, and hats. Nearly all the objects of personal adornment which are characteristic of Mesoamerica are represented, as well as the customs of painting face and body, tattooing, masks, and false beards. Dental mutilation and inlay with pyrites are already present (Romero, 1958, p. 100).

Towards the end of the period, in Monte Alban IC, we begin to find features characteristic of Period II: a sort of false potstand like a reel, pottery decorated with stucco, whistling jars, gourd-shaped jars, and other ceramic types.

The style which predominates in Monte Alban at this time could be considered a variant of the Olmec of Veracruz-Tabasco, which we could call "danzante" since this very characteristic motif is found not only in stone but also in pottery and minor objects.[6] It is not so apparent in Monte Negro or in the other sites of the same period. The predominance of the Olmec style in Period I does not appear to have come directly from the Tabasco region, but possibly via two main routes, one across the Sierra de Oaxaca and the other, perhaps more important, by the Isthmus of Tehuantepec, along the coastal plain and up the valley. We do not for a moment suggest that Monte Alban I culture was a simple copy or product of the archaeological Olmecs, but rather that the fundamental elements were the same and that there was some acculturation between the two during their development, although each people produced some elements of its own. As time went on each developed its own individuality until they separated entirely in the subsequent stages.

These data suggest strongly that there were no basic differences in Monte Alban I between the two main areas of Oaxaca, which later became Zapotec and Mixtec, nor, indeed, between any of the others. This is to say that a single culture covered Oaxaca, though at different degrees of intensity. On the other hand, the general characteristics of this culture relate it to the Olmec culture which we know to have been at its climax on the Atlantic coast. This Olmec culture of the Atlantic coastal plain left many contemporary traces in Guerrero, Morelos, and the Valley of Mexico, although it had many specific features of its own in Veracruz-Tabasco. Oaxaca formed part of this general Olmec-influenced area, and I believe that we can say that Oaxacan cultures are rooted in this Olmec tradition and are Olmecoid. The division into various separate and definable cultural entities had not yet appeared.

The radiocarbon dates for Period I are two from Monte Negro (C-424) which give a mean of 649 ± 170 years B.C., and another from Yagul which gives 390 ± 275 B.C.[7] For the beginning of the Monte Alban I period I prefer to postulate an earlier date, not only for the general reason that it is improbable that the samples give the earliest possible date, but that in both cases we are dealing with dates late in Period I. The samples from Monte Negro come from the beams of Temple X which was burned and had nothing built on top of it, so that it appears to belong to the final occupation of that town. In Yagul the date comes from material associated with Period IC. We can thus estimate that Monte Alban I begins about 900 B.C. (cf. Wauchope, 1954, pp. 32–33).

Monte Alban II

In Monte Alban this period begins immediately after Period IC. As we have already seen, it is found in fewer places than the cultures of Period I or of the later periods. In the valley of Oaxaca Period II materials occur only at Caballito Blanco and at 23 other sites, almost all large. The most important site at this period in the Mixteca Alta seems to be Huamelulpar (Caso and Gamio, 1961). The archaeological zone there is relatively large, and the partly excavated mound has revealed a

[6] It is within the Olmec tradition but not in the same way as Morelos or Tlatilco; these are examples of poor sites of a culture identical with that of La Venta, whereas Monte Alban I is a related but distinctive site, not identical.

[7] Humble Oil and Refining Company.

stairway bounded by enormous rectangular stones on whose outer faces are hieroglyphs and numerals in the Monte Alban II style. The pottery of this building appears to belong to the same period or to the end of Period I.

A tomb found accidentally at Tliltepec (Cerro del Jasmin), near Yanhuitlan, produced a good number of vessels which resemble those of Monte Alban II in some respects, although they differ from them in others. With these, we practically come to the end of the occupation of this period, and even these are so scarce and incomplete that if it were not for the excavations in Monte Alban proper, we would not have believed that this period existed. I have the impression, not yet proved, that many sites in the valley show a direct passage from Period IC to the transitional Period II–IIIA, so that in these sites a Period I type of culture continued while Period II developed in Monte Alban and a few other places in the valley. It is clear that this point can be settled only by careful excavations in places where Period II appears to be absent from the surface collections. For the present the period must be defined by what is found at Monte Alban.

Period IC leads up to Period II because some of the elements which constitute the former continue in the latter phase. As can be seen from the list of traits, the bearers of Period II culture brought or invented many elements of their own but went on using others which were characteristic of the previous period. In other words, we are dealing with a new and different culture which retains many of its predecessor's traits. Study of the list of traits tends to show that the bearers of Period II culture (at least in Monte Alban) were an aristocracy of rulers or priests who imposed their own ideas but did not constitute a majority capable of obliterating the old culture, which survived among the bulk of the population. The relatively few sites in the valley where Period II appears to have flourished (there were hardly any outside it) are important ceremonial centers. This is exactly where an aristocratic minority would have settled, without immediately influencing the smaller sites, which would have acquired some of the new traits only gradually. So slow was this process that there was time for the first influences from Teotihuacan to arrive before they had been assimilated. I believe, indeed, that Period IIIA consists of the final fusion of Periods I and II, combined with ideas from Teotihuacan.

Another clue in the same direction is that the changes occurred chiefly in ceremonial life, whereas many of the more popular traits remained unaltered. Thus, for example, the figurines of Period II are identical with those of Period I. Working techniques remained almost unchanged, as though the workmen were the same although the authorities were different. The same impression is gained by noticing that it is the most sophisticated traits of Period I which disappear, whereas the simpler ones survive. Thus the danzante style vanished, but the custom of decorating the large stones forming the façades of certain buildings, such as Mound J, with incised designs survived (see Acosta, Article 32, fig. 10). With reference to writing in this period, Caso (1947, p. 19) says: "There is no sudden interruption in passing from Period I to II; on the contrary many glyphs continue to be used in almost the same form, and if new signs appear it may be because they have not been found before, owing to the scarcity of material and not because they were not used in Period I. It is clear that new ideas arise and that old sculptural forms fall into disuse. . . ."

Very important is the discovery of a building similar to Mound J at Monte Alban at Caballito Blanco, near Yagul. The Caballito Blanco building is smaller and simpler and lacks carved stones, but the form is the same and the associated pottery is also of Period II (Paddock, personal communication). A radiocarbon reading from this building gave the date of 264 ± 120 B.C.[8]

Although few monuments of Period II remain in Monte Alban, the whole of the Great Plaza was built and plastered at the time. Abundant offerings of that period have been found below the floor, among which is the famous jade mask of a bat. We know representations of 15 gods, of which one is feminine; there may have been another goddess (8Z). They are clothed by this time. Male attire gets more elaborate, and the headdresses are more complicated with chinstraps, plumes, topknots, and ribbons which fall to the neck.

The magnificent modeled pottery of Period I disappears and gives place to the more geometrical and impersonal style of Period II. For this first time we have the *xicalcoliuhqui*, one of the most characteristic symbolic and decorative motifs not only of Oaxaca but of all Mesoamerica. There are other more elaborate motifs such as flowers and human bones. The trefoil ornament, so characteristic of Zapotec art and generally used as a terminal element, becomes common.

To this period belongs the only radiocarbon date obtained from Monte Alban (C-425), 272 ± 145 B.C. It is in close agreement with that of Caballito Blanco.

We believe that the most probable homeland of the bearers of the Monte Alman II culture was Chiapas or the Guatemalan highlands; or the bearers may have come from the latter by way of the former. Tombs 2 and 3 of Chiapa de Corzo contain several vessels very like those of Monte Alban II.

Monte Alban II still preserves an Olmecoid substratum, perhaps a simple inheritance from Monte Alban I, or possibly derived from neighboring regions where that style had survived. Indeed, this seems to have happened in the Mixteca area, although the evidence is too thin to reach even a provisional conclusion about it.

[8] Humble Oil and Refining Company, by courtesy of Mrs. Bullington.

Transition from Monte Alban II to IIIA

We can define this phase as that in which Monte Alban II elements exist alongside Teotihuacan ones. It has been found so far only in Monte Alban tombs and in Loma Larga, in the valley of Oaxaca. This is not surprising since the phase can not be recognized from surface collections or from soundings unless these are made in a rubbish dump, which has not yet been done. Indeed, we must not forget that, since the whole stratigraphy of the valley is artificial, a horizon must be considered to be Period IIIA when sherds of that period appear, even though there are many older ones not necessarily contemporary. This adds to the difficulty of defining the transition we are considering. On the other hand, it is easy to recognize this transition in tombs, because we find objects of two periods together, buried at the same time. As it is not a very long period we know few tombs from it; nevertheless, we can divide it typologically into three phases which contain, progressively, more and more Teotihuacan features although a percentage of Period II ones is always retained. It is dangerous, however, to base conclusions on typological stages, and better not to do so for the present.

This grouping of elements of two cultures to form a transition without any fusion between them seems to apply to everything found so far except one class: the urns. We find not only urns like those of Period II but others of a type peculiar to the transition and, finally, a third group (very rare) which could be regarded as belonging to Period IIIA. This important and useful exception to the rule can be explained if we consider that Teotihuacan influence did not affect the manufacture of these typical Oaxacan objects. This implies that the evolution of the urn style was in this case internal and that the outside ideas, mainly Teotihuacan, which were affecting the valley of Oaxaca, merely influenced the style of the urns. The local Oaxacan pottery did not make direct copies of any model coming from outside. The arms of the urn figures of this transitional type are usually separated from the body; the legs are crossed, leaving a space between them. Headdresses with a visor are common, and other more complicated headdresses are reminiscent of Teotihuacan. They are also like some of those carved on the stones of Mound J at Monte Alban. The eyes are still slanting and elongated, a Preclassic feature which disappears in the next period. Eighteen gods have been found, four of them feminine.

The great importance of this short phase seems to lie in the fact that it marks the completion of the appearance of the elements which make up the style we call Zapotec.

Monte Alban IIIA

The fusion we have spoken of between the elements of Periods I and II and those coming from Teotihuacan produced a new culture with characteristics of its own, which is, in Monte Alban, Period IIIA. Historically, it is the moment when we can begin to speak of Zapotecs, since it is possible to demonstrate that there was a continuous cultural tradition in the valley of Oaxaca from that time until the Spanish conquest and, consequently, to the present day. Indeed, the later Zapotec periods make no change in the basic elements or fundamental style of the culture of Period IIIA. Period IIIB, as we shall see, is simply a modification of IIIA brought about by an event outside the Zapotec culture, namely the disappearance of Teotihuacan. Period IV is exactly the same culturally as Period IIIB, and is distinguishable from it only in minor details; its historic importance is that Monte Alban disappears as the main center of the valley of Oaxaca. We shall return to these points later.

The only outside influence to be seen in Period IIIA comes from Teotihuacan; for the first time Monte Alban is connected with central Mexico rather than with regions to the south and southeast. We do not believe that Oaxaca was part of a possible Teotihuacan empire, because we are dealing with cultural influences which did not produce the Zapotec culture but merely modified it. Indeed most of the basic traits and those which endured were of local origin.

We have found remains of Period IIIA in 30 sites in the valley of Oaxaca. It should be possible to find them in many more, but it is not easy to identify this horizon from unstratified sherds because few ceramic types are diagnostic of IIIA; most types are also common to the next period. Further, in a surface survey we lack the data given by other cultural features like architecture.

Only one site in the Mixteca which belongs partly to this period has been studied, namely Yatachio. Tomb I at that site yielded some vessels closely linked to Monte Alban IIIA and not a little to Teotihuacan. The best examples are cups with annular bases made of Thin Orange ware and with incised decoration typical of Teotihuacan III (Bernal, 1953, p. 17, fig. 41). We must not forget, however, that it is their common Teotihuacan traits which allow us to correlate the Yatachio tomb with Monte Alban IIIA. In truth, if it were not that we again find Zapotec influences in the Mixteca in the next period, IIIB, we might think that the cultures of the two areas were entirely separate from the beginning of Period IIIA, and that their only common feature was Teotihuacan pottery. A few Zapotec vessels or urns of this period which are ascribed to Mixtec sites are in the National Museum of Mexico.

Outside Monte Alban we do not know a single monument, sculpture, or mural painting belonging to this period, so its definition in these features is based solely on that place.[9] Here was great activity, and many buildings were constructed during the period. The most characteristic architectural element appears to be the scapular-shaped panel, which continues in use in the succeeding period. Although the main outlines of the platforms are surely influenced by Teotihuacan, they have special features which enable us to speak henceforward of a Zapotec architecture. Exactly the same appears to apply to the mural paintings, which, at Monte Alban, have been found only in tombs.

On the other hand, writing and the calendar continue on their own lines. It is not that they lack elements common to other regions since the Mesoamerican calendrical system was generally the same, and there are widespread resemblances to some of the glyphs; but the Zapotec calendar and system of writing have features of their own. In some traits the valley of Oaxaca maintained ideas which were rather southern—we generally call them "Mayoid"—such as the erection of stelae and the use of bars in numerals. Presumably these are elements which had survived from earlier Monte Alban periods and had fused with more recent influences and developments.

The pottery of Monte Alban IIIA provides the best illustration of this interesting state of affairs. Thus, we have several shapes which pass with slight changes from Period II to IIIA, such as the spout-handle, the spider-foot vessel, the perforated incense burner, and the bird-shaped bowls. The small changes in these forms were brought about by Teotihuacan influence. Together with this group of survivals, we have the whole Teotihuacan complex in Monte Alban: Thin Orange ware, cooking pots, *floreros*, low tripods with covers, ring bases, double cups (*candeleros*), stucco-coating, cups, the reptilian eye motif. Very soon these elements (some of them actually brought from Teotihuacan as objects) underwent local changes which turned them into the characteristic Zapotec pottery of Period IIIB. Nevertheless, there are at least two pottery types, apart from many others of less importance, which are characteristic of the valley and neither old survivals nor products of Teotihuacan culture, namely the serpentine motif as a basic element of vessels with carved or incised ornament and the urns in their developed form. Both have been fully studied (Caso and Bernal, 1952; Bernal, 1949c).

A greater variety of gods is represented on the Period IIIA urns, 30 or possibly 31, of whom 7 are feminine. The style is sober, with clean lines, somewhat conventional and with little creative imagination. Identical motifs are repeated, but they are always carried out elegantly and are technically perfect. It is a highly professional art. On the urns the faces, which are very regular, serene, and sometimes very beautiful, are balanced; the ornaments are not excessive.

Between the end of Period IIIA and the beginning of the next period there may be a short transitional period, represented in Monte Alban by Tombs 103 and 104; but these tombs may also be considered to be typologically the last of the one period or the first of the other. However that may be, the tomb at Yucuñudahui, the most important so far studied in Mixteca, seems to be contemporary with them. Although there are many elements which differ, many pieces of pottery are very similar (Caso, 1938, fig. 73). Other vessels from this tomb are similar to those of Teotihuacan style. The three carved stones found in the tomb are undoubtedly Zapotec in style and bear Zapotec glyphs; the stairway which gives access to it is very like that of Tomb 1 at

[9] There are some monuments on the coasts of Oaxaca and Guerrero which are unquestionably related to the Zapotec style. Especially notable are those of Rio Grande and the stelae of Piedra Parada (Piña Chan, 1960b, photos 4, 12, 13, 14), but we do not know if they belong to this period.

Yatachio. The large tomb at Cuilapan (Bernal, 1958c) has the same arrangement but on a far larger scale. Although steps giving access to a tomb are not a new feature, it seems that the true staircase begins in Period IIIA and goes on until the end of the Classic period; but I know of no later tomb which has it. The tomb at Chila (Dupaix, 1834, pl. 18), whose age is unknown, is very similar to those mentioned above.

The small urn found in the very complex offertory box at Yatachio seems to belong to Period IIIA, as do other vessels from the same site (Bernal, 1953, figs. 10, 11). It is clear, here, that we are dealing not with influences coming from Monte Alban but with people of the same culture living in the area which was later the Mixteca. Tomb 1 at Yucuñudahui (see Acosta, Article 32, fig. 29) was roofed with juniper beams (the only instance which we know in Oaxaca), and a radiocarbon reading on one of them gave a date of A.D. 299 ± 185 (C-426). According to Frederick Johnson (1951, p. 12), however, this date needs further verification. From the dates accepted for other Mesoamerican regions, Period IIIA in Oaxaca probably began about the year A.D. 200 and finished about 600.

On the Isthmus of Tehuantepec the Ladrillera phase appears to belong to this horizon (Delgado, 1961).

Monte Alban IIIB

This period is the climax and the end of Monte Alban. The whole city appears to have been rebuilt; nearly all the monuments which can be seen today, as well as many glyphic inscriptions and tombs, belong to this period (see Acosta, Article 32, fig. 13). Its definition and above all its differentiation from Period IV are nevertheless difficult, because the culture of both is practically the same and what separates them is an important but purely local event —the end of Monte Alban. Thus, nearly all the sites in the valley have pottery which could be Period IIIB but equally well Period IV; thus, they can not be classified separately. In Monte Alban it has not been possible to distinguish these ceramics properly, in spite of extensive explorations and numerous tombs. There are some objects from the valley of Oaxaca, however, which have not so far been found in Monte Alban, and which are doubtless late. This suggests that study of late sites in the valley might help to solve the problem. I have made two attempts so far: at Noriega (Bernal, 1960a), which turned out to be an unimportant site, and at San Luis Beltran (unpublished), where study of the material is not yet finished. Although the finds at the latter site will not solve the problem completely, I believe that they will be a great help because it appears that Period IV is well represented and that San Luis Beltran did not exist before IIIB. Various ceramic features and some elements are not identical with those of Monte Alban. Another attempt was made at Etla (Acosta, unpublished), but the result was inconclusive here, too.

One thing is clear both in Monte Alban and in other sites in the valley, namely, that any changes between Periods IIIB and IV were only slight, so that we are dealing rather with one long period with two subphases than with two periods. The distinction was made because it was marked in Monte Alban by its fall. This does not mean that all its inhabitants left it, but that the ceremonial part was abandoned; its buildings were not repaired, and no new ones were built. Instead, houses must have been put up, and many new tombs made and used. Monte Alban became an inhabited graveyard.

We have referred several times to Monte Alban as a city, and have not used the term "ceremonial center," which is frequently preferred. We believe that we are dealing with a true city in the sense that a considerable number of people lived there, people of various social classes and professions. Since we have hardly touched the slopes of the hill or the places where there are no large ceremonial monuments, we know little of any inhabitants who did not belong to the upper class, which was probably priestly. The belief that Monte Alban was a true city is based on the extraordinary abundance of pottery, mostly of daily use, found there; the many evidently poor burials alongside the rich tombs; the presence of terraces for agriculture or platforms which cover the hillsides below the principal buildings on the summit of the hill; and the large quantity of implements, figurines, and other objects not really ceremonial. With the possible exception of Teotihuacan, I recall no other site in Mesoamerica where excavation has yielded such a large number of sherds. It must be remembered, too, that the Great Plaza on top of the hill is but a fraction of the 40 sq. km. which constitute the site. It is true that in Yagul a great many more metates, manos, and other kitchen utensils have been reported, but this may be because a much greater proportion of that site has been excavated.

Another reason for calling Monte Alban a city is that most of the sites of this period in the valley are very rich in cultural remains, and have a ceremonial arrangement (or grouping) very similar to Monte Alban. If we consider Monte Alban to be a nonurban ceremonial center, we must assume the same to be true of all the large sites in the valley, of which there are at least 18, and of the approximately 90 medium-sized ones. It seems impossible to believe this, because the whole enormous population necessary to feed this large number of ceremonial centers could not have lived in the modest number of small hamlets or isolated farms which are reported from the valley.[10] Instead, I believe that the modern settlement pattern in the valley of Oaxaca is very like the pre-Spanish one, with a great many occupied towns. In fact, many of the archaeological sites are still inhabited. The chief difference now is that a Christian church has been built on the foundations of the native temple.

A characteristic of Period IIIB which is negative and therefore, perhaps, deceptive seems to be the cultural isolation of the Zapotec world. In contrast with the older periods, we have found nothing at this time which comes from outside. It appears that Zapotec culture turns in on itself and becomes detached from the stream of events in Mesoamerica. I believe that this complete introversion was responsible for the marked aesthetic and technical decadence in Period IV.

A result or perhaps a cause of this situation is to be found in the Mixteca, which begins, for the first time, to be separate from the valley of Oaxaca. At the beginning of the period we still find strong resemblances, like those already mentioned for Yucuñudahui, or the tombs at Quiotepec. The same is true of a number of isolated finds; in Yatachio the relations with the valley are obvious. These relationships diminish steadily so that by the end of the period they have vanished completely. Although I, myself, believe that it began a little later, it is possible that the style historically attributed to the Mixtecs began about the end of the Monte Alban IIIB period. One reason for believing this is that the subject matter of the Mixtec codices starts exactly in that period, about the 8th century A.D. Of course, it is unlikely that the codices we know are "first editions," and it may be that the older ones were painted in a different style, although they may have depicted the same events. This is to say that the later editions were not simple copies but were modified to show contemporary fashions in dress, pottery, and architecture.

[10] It is possible, however, that there are many more such small hamlet or farm sites which we have not recognized or found.

It is difficult to believe that there were no changes in the culture which can properly be called Mixtec between the 8th and the 16th centuries A.D., but the present archaeological information in the area we are describing shows neither changes nor phases but a single stage, a stable one indeed.

It seems to me that it is more prudent, to judge from the archaeological record alone, not to speak of Mixtecs during Period IIIB although one can in the periods immediately following. Mixtec cultural remains can not be dated before the beginning of Period IV or about the beginning of the 10th century.

Very generally, glottochronology favors the idea that the Zapotecs existed as an entity before the Mixtecs (Fernández de Miranda, Swadesh, and Weitlaner, 1960) because the differences between Mixtec dialects are not so great as among Zapotec dialects. Chatino is a very near relation of Zapotec, and the archaeology of that area is indistinguishable from that of the Zapotec; but even if it is excluded, the differences between the various Zapotec dialects are greater than between the Mixtec ones, even if we include the more remote Mixtec groups in the modern state of Puebla.

In Monte Alban, where alone Periods IIIB and IV can be distinguished, it can be seen that the style of Period IIIA became more baroque in IIIB. The buildings have more decoration without losing their characteristic sobriety. The funerary urns became exuberant in decoration, which is sometimes more prominent than the god himself; the faces of the gods became stereotyped; and all the pottery began to show the characteristics of mass production so clear in Period IV. The process of "industrialization" is seen not only in lack of individuality but also in quantity.

Thirty-nine gods are represented in Monte Alban IIIB, eleven being feminine. Their faces are heavy, impassive, and with no feeling of movement. The noses are frequently aquiline; the upper eyelids are heavy. Almost the only decorative technique used on pottery is that of stick polishing, done rather carelessly. Teotihuacan influence vanished, not surprising in view of the fact that the great city of the highlands had disappeared by this time or was in a profound state of decay. What is more curious is that no influences whatever from outside can be detected; the valley of Oaxaca appears to turn in on itself and to forget its neighbors. This, of course, was theoretically impossible as it was not surrounded by a "Great Wall of China." We have no radiocarbon dates for this period, but I believe that Monte Alban must have been abandoned about 1000.

From the little that we know about the antiquities of the Zapotec-Serrana region it appears that there are many archaeological sites here (De la Fuente, 1942a) and that the objects are generally similar to those of the valley of Oaxaca at this period, but it is impossible to say more for the present. There is a fine stela covered with glyphs at Yagila (Pérez García, 1956, 1:53).

Monte Alban IV

This period is represented at Monte Alban only by tombs and some burials and offerings deposited in the ruins of destroyed temples. We have found evidences of this period in nearly all the sites in the valley, but it is difficult to describe them in detail in these outlying sites because they can not be clearly distinguished from IIIB. In many places this culture, identified with Period IV at Monte Alban, seems to have survived until the Spanish conquest, though becoming more and more mixed or associated with the Mixtec culture.

Period IV begins with the appearance of Toltec elements, in the broadest sense, and by the time of the Spanish conquest it was much influenced by the Mixtec culture. This Mixtec influence was felt in varying degrees in different sites in the valley, differences in which the time factor was probably involved. At the risk of confusion, we shall deal first with the Monte Alban IV culture and then with the Mixtec, on the understanding that they may have been partly contemporary in the valley of Oaxaca. They were certainly partly, or fully, coeval in the Mixteca area itself.

There does not appear to be any difference between the architecture of Periods IIIB and IV, but we can not be sure of this because no indubitable Zapotec structure of Period IV has been completely excavated. Thus, the main plaza and the ball court of San Luis Beltran, as far as we know, show no essential differences from Monte Alban, and the same applies to Mound III at Cuilapan (Bernal, 1958c, pp. 78–81). Buildings of Period IV must be common in the valley, so we can hope soon to know more about this. It may be that rather a common type of stone monument, whose main design consists of two personages sitting face to face, belongs to this period; but we know of no sculptures showing obvious Toltec influence in the valley. The tigers of Monte Alban appear to be older, and we know of no chac mools, atlantean figures, or ball courts with rings in the region.

Ball courts are common in the valley of Oaxaca. None have stone rings, whether of Classic or Postclassic date. This is largely true also of the Mixteca. There were no stone rings at Monte Negro and Yucuñudahui, although this can be explained by the antiquity of these examples. Ball courts were either lacking at Coixtlahuaca, Yatachio, and Tilantongo or have not been found. If we examine the many representations of ball-court buildings in the Mixtec codices, we find that they do not have rings. This applies to the several examples appearing in the Vindobonensis, Bologna, Bodley, and the two Seldens. In the Nuttall there are at least 10 courts, and only one has rings (p. 74). The gold breast-ornament from Tomb 7, Monte Alban, which shows a ball court, has no rings, but on this object it is possible that snakes take their place. On the other hand, nearly all those courts in Nahua codices clearly show rings on either side of the court, as in the Borbonicus, the Florentine, the Atlas of Durán, and even the Borgia. I think that we can conclude that this feature is certainly very rare in both the Zapotec and Mixtec regions.

Other objects common in other parts of Mesoamerica but rare or missing in the valley of Oaxaca are spindle whorls, pipes, circular platforms alone or combined with rectangular ones, eagle vases (*cuauhxicallis*), the whole complex of Tezcatlipoca, *tzontemocs,* pepper grinders, polished obsidian, pottery flutes and whistles, and the *omichicahuaztli.* The following traits are uncommon in the valley of Oaxaca: stone knives, arrow- or spearheads, sculpture in the round, griddles, lip-plugs, and the phallic cult.

It is difficult to be sure what traits are lacking in the Mixteca Alta because of the sparsity of excavations, but some of those listed above are common, such as spindle whorls and polished obsidian.

In the Mixteca Baja things are different, since we know some carvings which are obviously Toltec, the most important being at Tututepec (Piña Chan, 1960b, photo 5).

On the other hand, relationships between Mixtecs and Nahuas are shown clearly not only by a series of material traits but by features such as land tenure, divine kings, nobility, and the similarity between tenants and *mayeques.* Although we know these similarities only in Aztec times, it is most likely that they date from the time of Tula. It must not be forgotten that this town (Tula) was mentioned in the codices in the time of 8 Deer.

Pottery of Period IV is abundant although of indifferent quality, as though carelessly mass-produced. Urns, more standardized than ever, are often found in groups of five identical examples, or four identical and one different. This is not confined to this period, but appears more frequently than in Period IIIB. On the other hand, there is a whole series of vessels, new to Oaxaca, which show Toltec influence, possibly indirect. I say indirect because we are dealing not with vessels coming from central Mexico but rather with general ideas and fashions, copied locally. The best example is the group of vessels which copy the paste, color, and shapes of Fine Orange ware, which is so characteristic of this general period in Mesoamerica. In Monte Alban alone, 36 examples of this style have been recovered, and sherds are common at many sites in the valley. On the other hand, we have two plumbate vessels of Tohil type found at Monte Alban as well as some sherds obtained at Chachuapan in the Mixteca (Caso, 1938, p. 54). Metals seem to be rare in the valley. Of all the tombs and offerings at Monte Alban, there was only one fragment of a copper pellet-bell in Tomb 50; 35 of such bells associated with a mosaic of Zapotec style, together with five "money axes," were in the mound over Tomb 21. All other metal objects belong to Period V.

To sum up, it seems that outside influences were as slight in Period IV as in IIIB. The Zapotec world was shrinking, for it had lost the whole of the Mixteca and was soon to lose part of the great valley of Oaxaca as well.

Mixtec Culture

The immediate archaeological problem is to inquire when, how, and whence developed the culture we call Mixtec, so filling the gap between the finds at Yucuñudahui and Yatachio and the appearance of objects unquestionably Mixtec in style.

The scarcity of objects clearly recognizable as Toltec in the valley of Oaxaca, and the cultural difference between the Mixtec and Zapotec areas, can, I believe, be explained by assuming that the Mixtec culture as we know it, which lasted until the Spanish conquest and even some decades later, had arisen by the 10th century. This culture of obvious Toltec affinities would then have served as a barrier between Tula and the valley of Oaxaca. Unfortunately, I can not offer supporting evidence for this hypothesis.

As we have seen, it is still hard to define exactly when Mixtec culture began, as well as when it began to flourish in the Mixtec area itself. Nowhere in the Mixteca has it been possible to find the characteristic features of the Mixtec culture lying directly over those of the end of Monte Alban IIIB. Neither has it been possible, from excavations so far made, to determine the length of time between the earliest stratum containing Mixtec cultural remains and the Spanish conquest.

In the absence of such stratigraphic evidence, we have to resort to indirect indications, such as: (1) In Cholula the first Choluteca period was identified by "lacquered" polychrome ware among other features. This is one of the characteristic wares of the Mixtec culture, and, as Noguera has pointed out, it seems to have continued in the Mixteca after it almost ceased to be used in Cholula. (2) Another characteristic Mixtec pottery type is a cream ware with red decoration which vaguely recalls Coyotlatelco ware. I believe it to be a direct derivative of Coyotlatelco and, further, I feel that the two wares were partly contemporaneous. (3) Many of the Mixtec figurines closely resemble Mazapan ones, as well as Aztec ones.

According to Noguera (1954, p. 300) all these elements are early in Cholula, inasmuch as they seem to come immediately after the Teotihuacan horizon. It is therefore likely that the style developed in the Puebla-Tlaxcala region. It diffused from there to the Mixteca, where it formed a separate branch, giving rise to the culture found later in Monte Alban V. We suggest that it began in the 10th century *in the Mixteca,* although its main development was later. At the same time, I believe that the fall of Monte Alban was in some way directly connected with these changes in the Mixteca and, indirectly, with the formation of the Toltec Empire.

We are concerned here only with that branch of the great Mixteca-Puebla culture that occupied the Mixtec country. Its center of development seems to be the Mixteca Alta, whence it spread to the whole more southerly region we call the Mixteca Baja. Whenever it began in the region, it is very different in character, almost the opposite, from the Zapotec culture. Obviously, both spring from the same Mesoamerican base and have a long list of elements in common, but their differences go deeper than style alone.

Perhaps the chief difference between them is that the Zapotec culture, even in its final stages, has all the feeling of the Classic, whereas the Mixtec is a "modern" culture with all the qualities of the Postclassic. Its Toltec and Nahua connections, its aesthetic expression, its fundamental interests, and the lessening theocratic emphasis all impart these qualities. Let us look at some aspects of it which seem especially illuminating.

In contrast with the excellence of the Zapotecs as architects, it seems that Mixtec culture lacked major monuments. Although we know many Mixtec ruins—most of them unexplored, it is true–none have ceremonial and monumental groupings which compare with the great plaza of Monte Alban. On the other hand, when the Mixtecs occupied parts of the great valley and came in contact with the Zapotecs directly, the interaction between the two cultures produced great buildings like the palaces of Mitla and Yagul, whose socio-political difference from Monte Alban we shall discuss below.

Few of the comparatively great number of large stone sculptures in the Mixteca Baja appear to be Mixtec. Most are Toltec or Zapotec, as we have seen. In the Mixteca Alta there is a notable absence of such large stone sculptures so characteristic of other native cultures. To be sure, this art did not rise to great heights among the Zapotecs, but in spite of this there are more carved stones in the valley of Oaxaca alone than in the whole of the Mixteca.

In the production of small and very fine objects, the Mixteca is, however, a great center. There are mosaics of turquoise and jade, goldwork, small carvings in hard stone, and handsome polychrome pottery. This does not imply that they are not found elsewhere in Oaxaca, but it seems that most of them, at least of those so far known, come from the Mixteca or are inspired by its style. For example, it is almost certain that most of the known examples of turquoise mosaics come from that region. I am not referring, of course, to the earlier mosaics, like those from Monte Alban, which are of a very different technique. Similarly, nearly all the goldwork of which we know is Mixtec or derived from the Mixtec style. A notable exception is the Tarascan metalwork.

The polychrome pottery which is so abundant at sites like Coixtlahuaca or Nativitas (Chachuapan) (Caso, 1938) is very like that of Cholula, although a deeper study would probably bring out certain differences. These wares were, indeed, produced locally, in the valley of Puebla-Tlaxcala as well as in the Mixteca and in those areas which I call Mixtecoid.

Finally, the most important feature of Mixtec culture, its pictographic books, contain essentially historical matter and suggest a fundamental interest in the dynastic and military chronicles of local chiefs. They are of great artistic merit, and much care was lavished on their innumerable details. They deal with the doings of men rather than the worship of the gods. These manuscripts are studied elsewhere in this volume, and I call attention here only to the closeness of the connection between them and the culture which produced them. In sum, the traits we have mentioned show that the Mixtec culture was one of exquisite refinement, more interested in perfection of finish than in art on a grand scale. It began a trend in Oaxaca towards a concern with human affairs without losing, at the same time, its deep religious feeling.

Owing probably to its geographical character, the Mixteca, unlike the valley of Oaxaca, appears nearly always, except perhaps in the reign of 8 Deer, to have been divided into a series of small independent states. These shared to a considerable degree a common culture and a common language. Perhaps when we know more we shall find that the different valleys of the Mixteca Alta have minor individual characteristics, although they belong to the same culture as a whole. This is a very different state of affairs from that in the central valley of Oaxaca where all the sites are culturally the same and pass through the same stages, varying only in size and importance.

The chief sites of the Mixtec culture which have been excavated are Tilantongo and Coixtlahuaca in the Mixteca; Monte Alban V, Mitla, Yagul, and Cuilapan in the valley of Oaxaca; and some in Chinantla. We have isolated data from the Mixteca Baja and the isthmus, and from other sites in nearly all parts of Oaxaca.

No site in the Mixteca Alta is so rich as Coixtlahuaca, where the monuments (in Inguiteria, the site excavated) are not important, although the platform of the main temple, where the magnificent 16th-century church now stands, must have been so. The same applies to Yanhuitlan.

During the first season at Coixtlahuaca (unpublished) gold objects were found in a triple tomb, or rather a group of three tombs with a common antechamber, very like another found in Yagul. In the second season (Bernal, 1949a) we found many separate tombs, not constructed in the old style but cut out of natural *tepetate*. These are very small, and will scarcely take a seated burial. They are entirely different from all their predecessors, and they resemble in shape those of western Mexico in that they have a shaft leading down to one side of a chamber. Locally called *sótanos* (cellars), they have been found in several parts of Mixteca Alta and appear to have been the only sort of tomb used by the Mixtecs of that area.

The commonest type of decorated pottery at Coixtlahuaca has motifs painted in brown on the natural color of the ware, and chiefly takes the form of open bowls. This seems to be the principal Mixtec ceramic type, but it is not found in the valley of Oaxaca. The outstanding Mixtec type is naturally the polychrome; it is not common in tombs but has been found in sufficient quantity in stratigraphic soundings and in the excavation of buildings. Techniques, shapes, motifs, and colors are the same as those found at other sites in the Mixteca Alta such as Nativitas, and in some places in the western part of the valley of Oaxaca, especially in the Cuilapan region though not at that site. With the possible variations already suggested, it is the same as that of Cholula.

Curiously enough, it seems that the culmination of the Mixtec style, at least in architecture, was in the valley of Oaxaca, outside the homeland of these people. It was there also, in Tomb 7 at Monte Alban, that the richest burial of this culture was found (Caso, 1932c). It appears that the Mixtecs gained a new vigor and a greater development when they left their own country and exported their culture. Perhaps this can be ascribed to the difference between the rich surroundings of the valley of Oaxaca and the poverty of the Mixteca.

It appears that by the 16th century the north, west, and the extreme east of the valley were Mixtec territory, and that all the rest, although inhabited by Zapotecs (who also lived more or less under Mixtec rule in the "Mixtec" parts of the valley), was influenced to various extents by the Mixtec culture. Thus, we know of no less than 70 sites in the valley where Mixtec pottery has been found, and it is probably present in smaller proportions in almost all parts of the valley. We can speak only of the most important sites known up to now, Mitla and Yagul at the eastern end, Monte Alban in the center, and Cuilapan in the west.

Although Mitla and Yagul were both occupied from Period I, their importance dates from Period IV. With the arrival of Mixtec influence, or Mixtecoid as I prefer to call it for reasons which appear below, they built those extraordinary palaces which are remarkable not only for their differences from the older buildings in the area, their size and their architectural merit, but also because they belong to a way of life apparently unknown previously in the valley.

The five main groups of buildings at Mitla are made up of 11 rectangular courts, of which nine have a dwelling on all sides. The other two (Southern Group and Adobe Group) appear rather to be pyramidal platforms surmounted by temples, although at least in the only case which has been partly excavated (Bernal, unpublished) the temple was later and was built on the ruins of a building like the other nine. Also, the remains of a large cruciform tomb, like the two well-known ones in the Group of the Columns, were found underneath this last. In most cases, therefore, we are dealing with buildings designed for living in or for meetings, but not for religious purposes. Apart from these, there are a few isolated platforms which supported temples.

Each living-group consists of three courts with rooms around them, sometimes separate, sometimes joined at the corners.

The palace of the six courts at Yagul (see Bernal, Article 33, fig. 12) is fundamentally similar to Mitla in all respects. The main difference springs from the fact that we are dealing with a unit and not with several as at Mitla. It has a single entrance, and the six courts are surrounded by rooms, one on each side. Subsequent changes divided, closed, or added rooms, but even then the basic plan was not affected. The method of construction, as in Mitla, is a wall of stone and mud, covered with stucco or with a veneer of small stones skillfully cut to form the famous mosaics. The roofs were flat in both cases. The whole building stands on a platform which backs on a hill sloping from north to south, whence the north side is at the level of natural rock whereas the south has been built up artificially to the level of the north. This great platform was built up by stages, and there are three or perhaps four Zapotec buildings of Period IV (the earliest might be of IIIB), one on top of the other. The last of them was razed, and on the ruins three palaces, very like the last, were superimposed. Mixtec pottery appears at the same time as the first palace, or slightly before, and polychrome only in the last building stage.

Although the ruins of Yagul are relatively large, since it includes temples, a very large ball court and many remains of ceremonial and domestic buildings, the palace of the six courts is enormous in proportion. Apparently it is the same at Mitla; in other words the emphasis is on the dwelling of the chief or chiefs rather than on that of the gods, in violent contrast with Monte Alban. Mixtec influence appears, and not for this reason only, to have brought a considerable degree of secularization to Oaxacan culture, though it would be absurd to think that priestly power had disappeared or the worship of the gods diminished.

We know so little of the architecture of the Mixteca Alta that we can not compare the buildings of Yagul or Mitla with it, but up to now no prototype is known for them there. On the other hand, they have many clearly Zapotec features which are found at Monte Alban, like the covering of walls with small stones well cut to form fret patterns. A tomb at Zoochina has niches and the same decoration (De la Fuente, 1942a). Doubtless they arose from the fusion of Zapotec and another style which might be Mixtec, but which for the present I think it safer to call Mixtecoid. More or less the same thing happens with pottery. Although some types are identical with ones found in the Mixteca, some are different, and some Mixtec types are absent from Yagul, for example that with brown or red decoration on the natural color of the ware, which is so characteristic and common in the whole of the Mixteca Alta and missing from Yagul and Mitla. The polychrome is the same in shapes and techniques in both areas, but the decoration, of the same general style, seems to show slight variations, perhaps nearer to what is found in the Cuicateca or Chinanteca without being identical with them. On the other hand, these two towns and Matatlan, very near them but not excavated, are in the eastern extremity of the valley, without direct access to the Mixteca, a very different position from that of the Mixtec sites at the western end, which not only adjoin the Mixtec area but are tied to it historically, as is shown, for example, by the Relación de Cuilapan. It seems, then, that we are dealing with two different but closely similar groups living at the eastern and western ends of the great valley, the one really Mixtec and the other related to the Mixtec culture by many of its characteristics.

Monte Alban belongs by its western position to the true Mixtec occupation in Period V, and we do indeed find the characteristic features there. The Mixtecs did not build much there, but they did build enough to prove their presence and their typical architectural style in what little we know of it. The tombs contain Mixtec objects and the golden jewels from the famous Tomb 7 are of the same style as those known at Coixtlahuaca and Yanhuitlan. Further, it is the style of the codices produced by this culture. Archaeologically, then, the late arrival of the Mixtecs in the valley is proved, and the few historical data suggest the same thing, since the Relación de Cuilapan gives a date of about 1350 for their arrival. Glottochronology also indicates that the Mixtec spoken in Cuilapan separated from that of the Mixteca Alta about 500 years ago (E. Arana Osnaya, personal communication). All lines of evidence are therefore more or less in agreement.

Variations of the Mixtec style spread during this period over almost the whole of modern Oaxaca. In the Chinanteca area several burials and tombs containing characteristic objects, such as goldwork and polychrome pottery of Mixtec type, have been found; and in addition there are tombs which attempt to reproduce in paint the characteristic stone frets of the tombs at Mitla, Xaaga, and Guiaro (Delgado, 1957, 1960b; see also Bernal, Article 33, fig. 4). Just as in Chachuapan (Caso, 1938, p. 53) these late objects in Chinantla are sometimes associated with glass beads, arms, or assorted objects of Spanish origin (Delgado, 1960a,b), showing that we are dealing not only with the last native culture in the district but with its survival for a few years after the conquest. We find the same style in the last phase of Monte Flor (Cline, 1959b) and in Quiotepec (Pareyón, 1960).

The same is true of the Tuxtepec area. This district was always related to the Atlantic cultures, even after the Olmec period. A palmate stone has been found at Tolome and a figurine vaguely resembling the smiling type near Acatlan, but in the latest period its culture is essentially Mixteco-Aztec, with metals and polychrome pottery of Mixtec style, and spindle whorls and other objects associated with Aztec remains (Henning, 1912; Valenzuela, 1942). Similar pottery comes from the isthmus, where the Xadaui and Lidchi Bigu phases are contemporary with Monte Alban V (Delgado, 1961), and metal objects are also found (Maler, 1942). In the Mixteca Baja, as far as we know, there is a culture very similar to that of the Mixteca Alta, which is spread all over the area and not confined to its capital Tututepec (Berlin, 1947a; Gamio, 1954; Piña Chan, 1960b). To sum up, varieties of the Mixtec culture can be found in almost the whole of Oaxaca in the latest stage. This does not in any way imply that the other ethnic groups had disappeared, but it does show the success and the dispersion achieved by the Mixtec culture, which was not confined to this region but was also one of the dominant strains in the territory of the Aztecs.

REFERENCES

Acosta, 1949, 1958–59
Adán, 1927
Alvarado, 1593
Alvarez, 1900
Aveleyra, 1950
Aymé, 1882
Balsalobre, 1892
Bandelier, 1884
Batres, 1902
Beals, 1934
Berlin, 1947a, 1957
Bernal, 1946, 1949a, 1949b, 1949c, 1949d, 1953, 1955, 1958c, 1960a, 1960b
Burgoa, 1670, 1674
Canseco, 1905
Carriedo, 1846, 1851
Caso, 1927a, 1928, 1932a, 1932b, 1932c, 1933, 1935, 1936, 1938, 1939b, 1942, 1947, 1949b
—— and Bernal, 1952
—— and Gamio, 1961
—— and Rubín de la Borbolla, 1936
Charnay, 1863, 1885
Cline, 1959b
Cook, 1949
Córdova, 1578a, 1578b
Covarrubias, 1947
Dahlgren de Jordan, 1954
DeCicco and Brockington, 1956
De la Fuente, 1942a, 1942b
Delgado, 1957, 1960a, 1960b, 1961
De Terra, 1949
Doutrelaine, 1867
Dupaix, 1834
Fernández de Miranda, Swadesh, and Weitlaner, 1960
Forster, 1955
Gamio, L., 1950, 1954, 1957
García, 1859
García Granados, 1935
Gay, 1881
Gómez de Orozco, 1928
Guzmán, 1934
Helbrüger, 1874
Henning, 1912
Holmes, 1895–97
Humboldt, 1810
Johnson, F., 1951
Lejeal, 1903
León, 1901
Linné, 1938
López de Llergo, 1960
Lorenzo, 1958
MacNeish, 1961
Maler, 1942
Mayer, 1857
Motolinía, 1858
Murguía y Galardi, 1861
Nicholson, 1961
Noguera, 1940, 1954
Ober, 1884
Paddock, 1957, 1960
Pareyón Moreno, 1960
Paso y Troncoso, 1905–06
Peñafiel, 1890
Pérez García, 1956
Piña Chan, 1960b
Reyes, 1593
Romero, 1951, 1958
Sáenz, 1957
Saville, 1899, 1900, 1909
Séjourné, 1956
Seler, 1888, 1890a, 1891, 1894, 1895, 1896
Tempsky, 1858
Valenzuela, 1942
Wauchope, 1950, 1954
Wicke, 1957

32. Preclassic and Classic Architecture of Oaxaca

JORGE R. ACOSTA

To understand Zapotec architecture, which covers the greater part of the area now known as Oaxaca, one has to know something of the occupations by different ethnic groups which occurred in the ancient city of Monte Alban.

The hill of Monte Alban is a series of high ridges about 400 m. above the floor of the valley of Oaxaca and about 1,540 m. above sea level. On the highest part are several platforms on which stand the remains of the great monuments that were constructed over a period of about 2000 years. Many of them have been excavated and are taken as the basis of this study (figs. 1, 2).

The cultural history of Monte Alban has been divided into five great stages—Periods I, II, IIIA, IIIB-IV, V—based principally on the changes in the pottery of the site. We are not taking into account here the short transitions between Periods I and II, between II and IIIA, and between IIIA and IIIB; nor do we discuss Period V, which corresponds with the conquest of the place by the Mixtecs whose occupation left no structure of any importance. This last period forms part of another study.

Monte Alban

Period I

We shall look now at the nature of these occupations, at the first inhabitants and when they arrived. We can say, tentatively, that by the middle of the 7th century B.C. the central platform of Monte Alban and the surrounding valleys were already inhabited. As much from pottery as from other artistic products, it is clear that we are dealing with people closely related to the "Olmecs" of Veracruz–Tabasco.

There are few architectural remains. Many of the buildings were destroyed; others are still buried at great depths or covered by series of later buildings. Enough does exist, though, to provide a general idea of the principal characteristics.

We cannot speak of a site plan, but the buildings evidently are oriented to the four cardinal points. All later structures also have the same orientation, which seems to be a peculiarity of the region of Oaxaca.

Most of our data come from the building known as the Mound of the Danzantes in the southwest corner of the central square

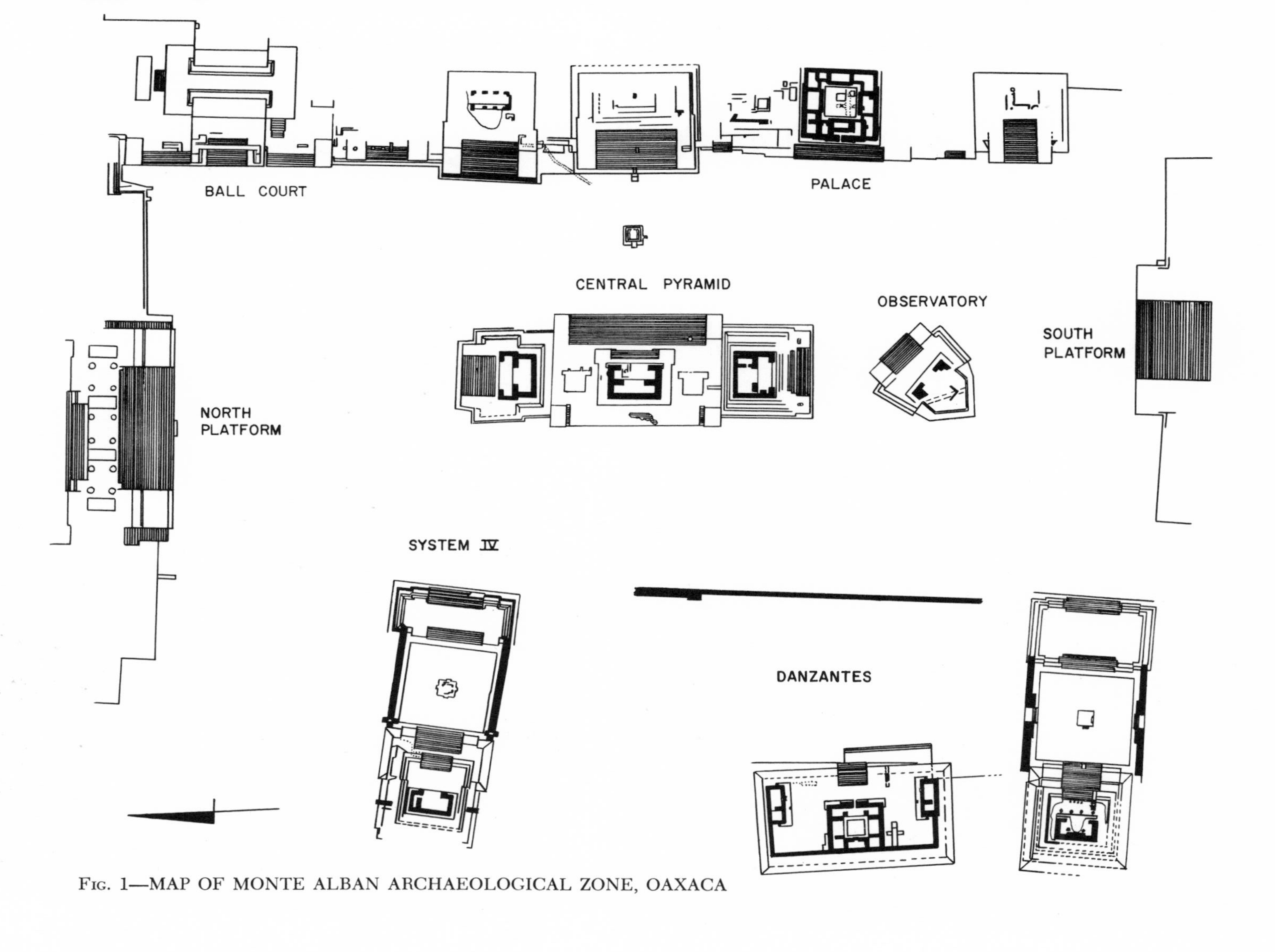

FIG. 1—MAP OF MONTE ALBAN ARCHAEOLOGICAL ZONE, OAXACA

FIG. 2—AERIAL VIEW OF MONTE ALBAN ARCHAEOLOGICAL ZONE

of the site. Although this was covered by a later building, constant collapses revealed part of the inner structure and archaeological excavations finally disclosed its shape. It was perhaps one of the first to be built in the locality.

This structure is a pyramidal platform of huge irregular rectangular stones, varying in size and set in rows. Most of the stones display bas-relief sculptures of nudes in grotesque positions which suggest dancing (fig. 3). It is these that have provoked most attention and given the name to the building. At the central axis is a raised platform, with a stairway of enormous stone blocks, also decorated with "danzantes," except that here they are in a horizontal position as if swimming. The base of another stairway leading to the upper part of the pyramid is on this platform.

This building indicates that already in this primitive period constructions were profusely decorated with human figures in bas-relief, which were, moreover, associated with hieroglyphics and numerals.

The stairways stand out from the body of the building and are entirely without balustrades. We have no information on the upper temples, though very probably they consisted of one or two rooms thatched with straw.

The rubble column also existed and, in exceptional cases, is not entirely round, but flat at the back and with a small recess. Lime mortar for floors was already in use; in the interior structure of the North Platform was a building covered with serpentine motifs modeled in stucco. It vaguely reminds us of the famous Str. E-VIIsub of Uaxactun in Guatemala, which more or less corresponds to the same period (fig. 4).[1]

Funerary architecture is very simple, be-

[1] Ed. note: This chronological correlation is at variance with other interpretations in the *Handbook* which would place Monte Alban I as considerably earlier than Str. E-VIIsub at Uaxactun.

FIG. 3—"LOS DANZANTES," MONTE ALBAN

cause only one type of tomb exists: a plain rectangular construction, doorless and roofed with slabs of stone laid horizontally. It is popularly known as a "cajón" (fig. 5,*d,i*).

In general the buildings of this Preclassic period were more solid and better constructed than later ones. The stones of the great platforms are bonded with mud and lie on deep foundations, a feature not seen in later buildings. The builders were still in an experimental stage. A freedom of expression shows they were not subject to the rules and ritual canons which later dominate Mesoamerican architecture.

Period II

Around the end of the 3d century B.C. new people arrived and settled in Monte Alban. Pottery and certain architectural characteristics proclaim that they came from the south, from Chiapas or Guatemala. Nevertheless, some earlier traits persist in the new buildings: for example, the solid

Fig. 4—ANCIENT STRUCTURE WITH SERPENT MOTIFS MODELED IN STUCCO, MONTE ALBAN

walls made with huge stones (Mound J or the inner building of Mound IV [fig. 6]) and the raised stairways without balustrades. At the same time we encounter a multitude of innovations which did not evolve from the previous resident culture.

During Period II the leveling of the Central Plaza of the city was begun, a titanic feat which required the leveling of enormous rock outcrops and the filling of deep concavities. Intelligent advantage was taken of some of the outcrops by using them as nuclei for the great stone constructions which border the plaza on the north and south sides.

It is very probable that they also began to put into practice a well-designed planning scheme which served as a foundation for the works of Periods IIIA and IIIB-IV (to be discussed later).

Among the new architectural characteristics are the stairways bordered with balustrades which follow the same slope as the steps. Also a form of "tablero" or sunken panel, decorated with a series of white discs aligned so that their edges touch one another, appears for the first time (fig. 7,*b*).

The temple platforms were not very high; they generally consisted of a single vertical body, topped with a plaster-coated inclined cornice (fig. 7,*a*).

The surmounting temple usually had two rooms with rubble columns on both sides of the entrance to form three openings. The adobe walls were set on a stone base for greater stability (fig. 8). Although no roofs now exist, they were almost certainly still built of thatch.

A new construction technique subsequently used in all later buildings now appears for the first time: a building up of "taludes" or sloping planes by covering small stone steps with a thick layer of plaster (fig. 7,*c*). This method was also applied to the steps of the stairways. These were no longer made of large blocks but of medium-sized stones on which were placed smaller stones to support the thick layer of plaster partially or completely covering them (figs. 7,*d*,*e*; 9).

There is a change in the style and type of funerary architecture in Period II. Although the "cajón" type continued in use, the majority of the tombs now have simple entrances as well as façades. There may be a small antechamber and, occasionally, recesses in the walls of the tomb (fig. 5,*d*-*g*). The flat roof continued in use, but the type of roof known as the "angular vault" (two inclined slabs leaning against each other) appears for the first time (fig. 5,*k*,*l*). Sometimes the two types occur in the same tomb. It was in this period that the inhabitants began to plaster the chamber walls and decorate them with multicolored frescoes. Although not invariably, many of the

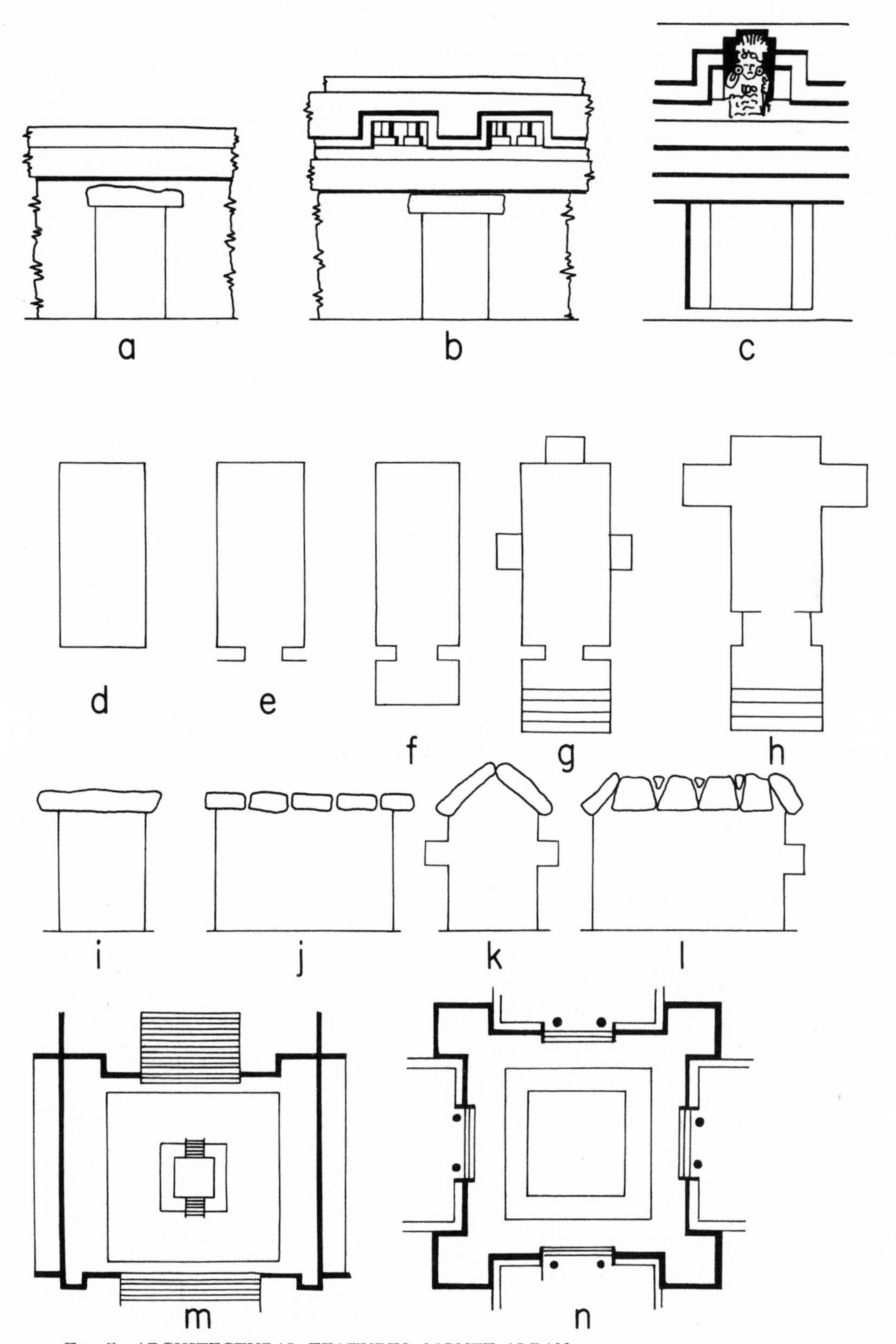

FIG. 5—ARCHITECTURAL FEATURES, MONTE ALBAN

Fig. 6—GREAT SLOPING WALL OF PERIOD II, WHICH STILL RETAINS SOME ARCHITECTURAL FEATURES OF PREVIOUS PERIOD, MONTE ALBAN

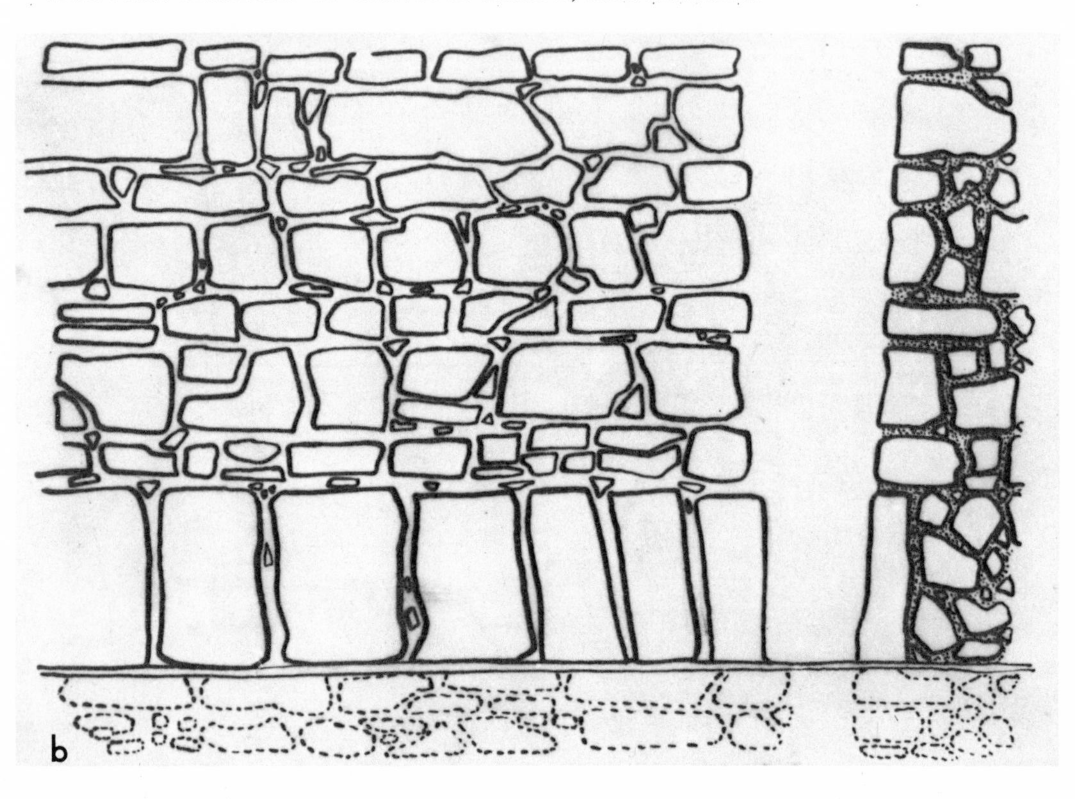

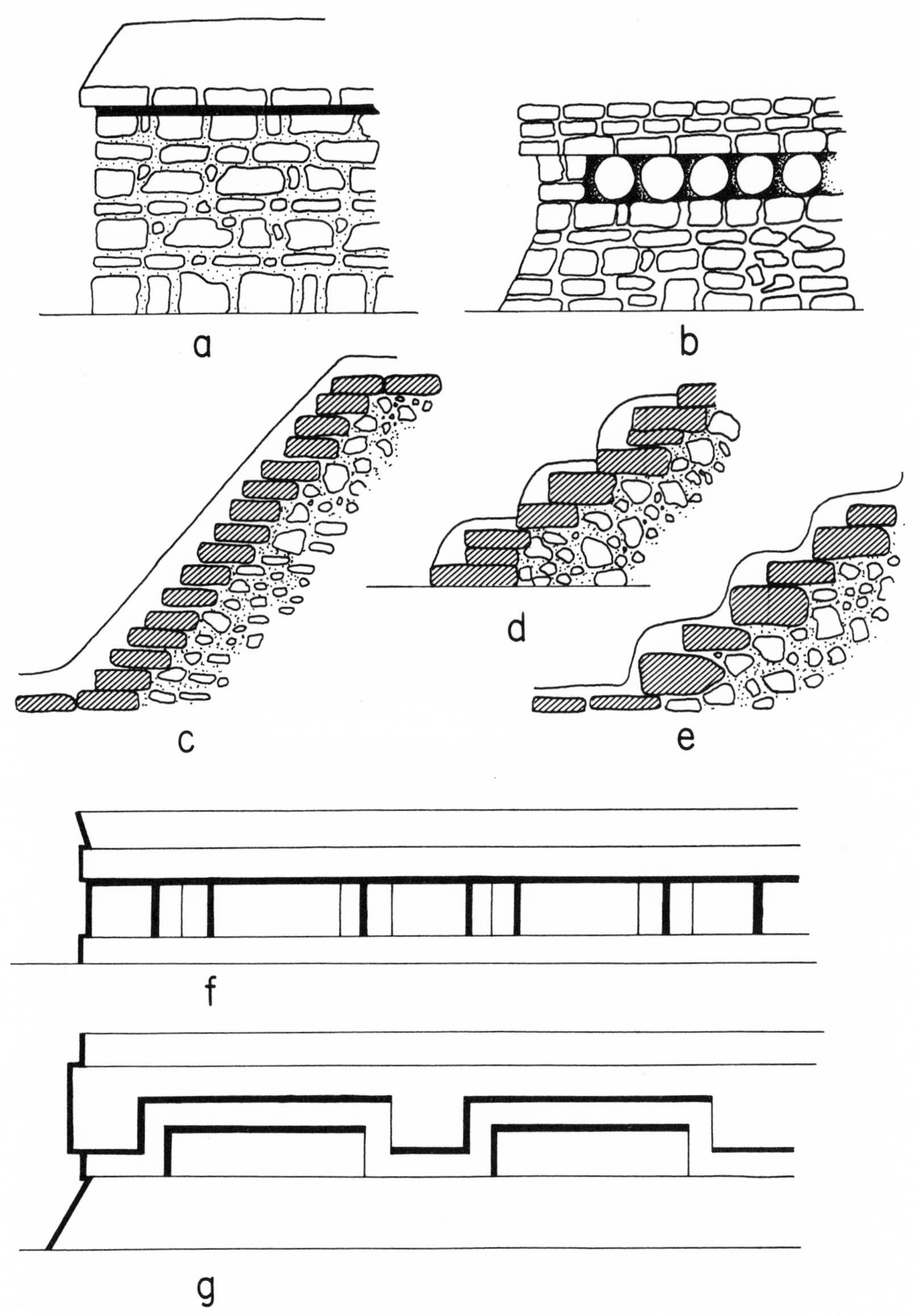

Fig. 7—ARCHITECTURAL FEATURES, MONTE ALBAN

Fig. 8—TEMPLE OF MOUND X, MONTE ALBAN, SHOWING RUBBLE MASONRY COLUMNS LOCATED IN ENTRANCES

Fig. 9—STAIRWAY STEPS OF PERIOD II COVERED WITH STUCCO ON UPPER PARTS, MONTE ALBAN

FIG. 10—GENERAL VIEW OF MOUND J, MONTE ALBAN

FIG. 11—DETAIL OF SOUTH SIDE OF MOUND J, MONTE ALBAN, SHOWING METHOD OF CONSTRUCTION AND LARGE STONES WITH BAS-RELIEF SCULPTURES

Fig. 12—REMAINS OF A PERIOD II STELA, MONTE ALBAN

tombs were located in the fill of temple platforms.

A very unusual building constructed in this period is Mound J at the south edge of the Central Plaza. Its plan is like the point of an arrow (fig. 10). There is a stairway on the widest side and a type of covered gallery running northwest-southeast through the structure. The back of the building is built on a foundation of large stones, placed in the same way as those of the Mound of the Danzantes but differently decorated (fig. 11). Because of its strange plan and orientation, this building is tentatively thought to have been an observatory. Recently a similar structure has been found in the region of Caballito Blanco, near Yagul.

The ball-court type of structure appears for the first time in Period II, but the remains are too incomplete to indicate whether or not its characteristics resembled those of later courts.

Another feature which came from either the Olmec or the Maya region is the stela, engraved with hieroglyphics and numerals commemorating important mythical or historical events (fig. 12). The stela appears during the earlier period, for some of the danzante type of stones were never set into a building but were freestanding, displaying all four faces (Caso, 1928).

Period IIIA

With the beginning of the 5th century A.D. comes a radical change, caused by the arrival of powerful groups of people of a different culture who, after invading the valleys, settled in Monte Alban.

Their culture shows a strong Teotihuacan influence, although they did not actually come from that city. They must have come from the north, perhaps from the Mixtec region, or from south of Puebla.

With their arrival begins what we can call the true Zapotec period, because in earlier times Monte Alban was inhabited by people related to the Olmecs of Veracruz, and then later by Mayoid races from the south. From this migration from the northeast, the descendants still live in the valley of Oaxaca.

Although the following nine centuries of Monte Alban have been divided into Periods IIIA and IIIB-IV on the basis of the pottery, this division cannot be clearly distinguished in the architecture. For purposes of organization, however, we shall recognize these periods in this presentation.

Most of the buildings of the Great Plaza now visible belong to these periods. The only exceptions are the Mound of the Danzantes and Mound J or the Observatory (both already discussed) which, although built in Period II, continued in use with very few changes (fig. 13).

Period IIIA retains many elements of the preceding period. These are not just surviv-

Fig. 13—PANORAMIC VIEW OF GREAT PLAZA, MONTE ALBAN, SHOWING BUILDINGS OF LAST OCCUPATION PHASE

Fig. 14—MOUND M, MONTE ALBAN, SHOWING COMBINATION OF INCLINED AND VERTICAL PLANES

Fig. 15—MOUND O, MONTE ALBAN, ANOTHER EXAMPLE OF COMBINATION OF VERTICAL WALLS AND SLOPING SURFACES

Fig. 16—NORTH FACE OF MOUND II, MONTE ALBAN, WITH PANELS AT BASE AS WELL AS AT TOP

als of the past but, rather, common characteristics of all Mesoamerican cultures. But one very important change has occured: the vertical terrace with broad, slightly sloping top, typical of Period II, has completely disappeared. The presence of this architectural form establishes a date and a culture, two of the most difficult tasks in archaeology.

Although many previously known elements occur in the buildings of Period IIIA, a host of new things form the basis of what we can call the true Zapotec architecture. We shall now see what these new characteristics were.

What commands most attention are the great pyramid-temple mounds of several terraces, which break the monotony of the previous period and provide a more harmonious combination of vertical and horizontal planes, cut by the diagonal lines of the taludes (figs. 14, 15). An extremely important element of decoration, one of the basic characteristics of Zapotec architecture, now makes its appearance. This is the "tablero" or panel known as the "doble escapulario" which is present in 90 per cent of the buildings of Monte Alban (fig. 7,*f*). It is not the closed Teotihuacan type but the open kind, formed from a series of rectangular tableros in two planes. These alternate with sunken spaces which are crowned with vertical or inclined cornices. We believe that this evolved from another type of tablero (fig. 7,*g*) first used at the beginning of this period and now seen decorating the lower part of the temples of the Mound of the Danzantes. We have called this primitive tablero Type A, and the other, Type B. Alfonso Caso believes that the first type depicts the entrance of a temple with two columns dividing a doorway.

The stairways undergo changes in the balustrades. Although these follow the same gradient as the steps, as in the previous period, they are now ornamented on the base, as well as on the upper part, with panels of Type B (fig. 16). Another important modification is that some of the stairways are no longer added to the body of temple platforms but are set into the structures. In some cases, when the pyramid is composed of several terraces, the stairway is divided into two flights, the upper one being narrower than the lower. This is done for two reasons: first, to accommodate the terraces, which become narrower as they ascend, and second, to create a perspective of height by means of converging lines (fig. 14).

Fig. 17—STELA SITUATED AT AXIS OF NORTH PLATFORM, MONTE ALBAN

Another characteristic of Period IIIA is the careful working of the masonry stones, which fit perfectly when placed in the walls, rather like those at Mitla. Almost all temple platforms, balustrades, and panels terminate on the top with a series of cornices, of which the uppermost one at times sloped outwards. This is an architectural feature which does not appear earlier (fig. 23).

The engraving and erection of stelae con-

FIG. 18—ARCHITECTURAL UNIT CALLED SYSTEM IV, MONTE ALBAN

FIG. 19—BALL COURT, MONTE ALBAN, SHOWING LARGE SLOPING SURFACES BORDERING CENTRAL COURT

tinue in this period (fig. 17), and there are many stones beautifully carved in bas-relief with representations of gods and chiefs (Caso, 1928). It seems that from this period on, the most important buildings were plastered and painted, generally red.

Another important trait is the great quadrangular patio surrounded by buildings (fig. 18). The patios are either ceremonial or residential. The difference lies in the size and in the nature of the surrounding buildings. In the center of the ceremonial patio there is invariably an altar or a rectangular adoratorio. The patios can also be divided into those with rectangular plan (fig. 5,*m*) and those with a ground plan in the form of a spool (fig. 5,*n*). The former are no more than simple squared patios with or without a low surrounding banquette. The latter are much more complicated and, although they are also square, display a special characteristic: the corners are open and lead to other small patios built in each angle. This architectural feature is very common in Teotihuacan, but we do not believe it originated there, for it is very common in Monte Negro, an archaeological site in the Mixteca which dates from at least six centuries B.C., contemporary with Period I of Monte Alban.

Although the type of building called Juego de Pelota or ball court was known from Period II, it is only now that its characteristics are clear. The plan is shaped like an I. The transverse sides are bordered by low inclined platforms from which rise great sloping taludes, 7 m. high. On the summits, above the taludes, are temples which provided the ideal places from which to watch the game (fig. 19). It is important to point out that the Zapotec ball courts never had stone rings, and are peculiar in having two niches in opposite diagonal interior angles of the court (fig. 20). Another interesting feature is the presence of a circular stone, set in the floor of the court at the line of its central axis.

There are almost no changes in the architecture of Period IIIA tombs. However, there is one new type of structure, with a cruciform ground plan, which probably evolved from the tomb with large recesses which appeared in the previous period. These structures seem to have served as charnel houses; they are few in number and occur only in this period (fig. 5,*h*). The great majority of tombs of this period are below the rooms which surround open patios.

FIG. 20—NICHE IN INTERIOR SOUTHWEST CORNER OF BALL COURT, MONTE ALBAN

Finally, the leveling of the Central Plaza of Monte Alban continued in IIIA, but was not yet finished.

In sum, architecture in this period advanced a long way technically, but lost freedom of expression and became rigidly sub-

Fig. 21—MONOLITHIC COLUMN WITH BAS-RELIEF SCULPTURES ON UPPER PART, MONTE ALBAN

Fig. 22—SOUTHEAST CORNER OF SOUTH PLATFORM, MONTE ALBAN, BUILT OF GREAT STONES DECORATED WITH BAS-RELIEF SCULPTURES

ject to the rules and canons of religious necessity which were then fashionable.

Period IIIB-IV

Architecturally the period called Monte Alban IIIB-IV is a continuation of IIIA, although the typical features of Period IIIA pottery suddenly disappear. Perhaps, we treat of a change in artistic taste among the potters which had no influence on the architects, who continued with their old models.

At this time the inhabitants began to decorate the sunken spaces of tableros or panels with serpentine motifs, zoomorphic figures, simple fret patterns, or with a motif like an inverted capital T (fig. 5,*b*). Here may be the antecedent of the patterns which decorate the walls of the temples of Mitla. They are present also in paintings in the tombs of this period (Tomb 125).

The builders continued to use isolated rubble column supports but also erected enormous monolithic columns, sometimes decorated in bas-relief (fig. 21). A new trend was the use of huge, beautifully worked stones to form the lower angles of the principal monuments (fig. 22).

The North Platform has unique rounded corners not yet found elsewhere in Oaxaca (fig. 23).

The plan of the temples is the same as that in Period II, with two rooms each with rubble columns at the entrances (fig. 24). However, the discovery of several earthenware or stone models shows us the type of roofing in use. They depict a flat roof constructed on a center-beam base supported by large transverse timbers or rafters of wood. The front side was decorated with Type B panels (fig. 25). It is almost certain that this type of roof began to be used in the preceding period, but we cannot be sure.

This cultural continuity can also be seen in the funerary architecture. Now, however, some of the tomb façades become more complex and, for the first time, are decorated with multiple cornices and panels. In some cases there is an adornment which could represent a pottery urn or a zoomorphic head modeled in plaster or worked in stone (fig. 5,*c*). Although the painting of the tomb interiors began in Period II, it is now that this form of art reaches its peak. Most of the tomb murals so far found belong to this period.

During the first half of this period (IIIB) building activity reached its zenith, with the termination of work on the imposing Central Plaza, which is 700 m. long and 250 m. wide, and bordered on all four sides with great pyramidal structures, linked to one another by broad platforms on which there are palaces and dwelling houses (fig. 26).

The city must have been magnificent, with its monuments placed symmetrically and at different levels. Within its limitations, Zapotec architecture sought a perspective based on horizontal lines combined with chiaroscuro, accenting the contrasts in flat and relief.

When the Zapotecs reached their apogee, around the 10th and 11th centuries A.D., an enemy was already penetrating the valleys of Oaxaca. Monte Alban, under pressure from the Mixtec invaders, slowly began to lose its population, until the ceremonial precincts became deserted and little by little the monuments began to crumble and turn to rubble.

During the last phase (Period IV), buildings were constructed only on the north slope of the hill where a small nucleus of Zapotecs remained. They lived in simple houses built around patios, below which have been found tombs, identical to earlier ones except that the cajón type has entirely disappeared.

Monte Negro

Outside the valley of Oaxaca and Monte Alban little is known of architecture except in one Preclassic site extensively excavated: Monte Negro, near the town of Tilantongo and more than 2000 m. above sea level.

There are two groups of monuments, the more important stretching from north to

Fig. 23—ROUNDED CORNER OF NORTH PLATFORM, MONTE ALBAN

Fig. 24—TEMPLE ON TOP OF TOMB 7, MONTE ALBAN

Fig. 25—ANCIENT STONE MODEL OF A MONTE ALBAN TEMPLE, WITH PANELS ON UPPER PART

FIG. 26—EAST SIDE OF GREAT PLAZA, MONTE ALBAN, SHOWING CEREMONIAL PYRAMIDS CONNECTED WITH RESIDENTIAL PLATFORMS

south and the smaller facing east. The area is very small, covering about half a square kilometer (fig. 27).

All the buildings are of single terraces and are no more than 2 m. high. The walls are always vertical, extremely simple in line, and without cornices or finishing touches. They are built of white stones placed more or less in rows and bonded with the characteristic red clay of the area. Most of the buildings are rectangular in plan and arranged symmetrically around patios, but others are irregularly shaped with many haphazard entrances. The monuments are oriented to astronomical points with precision.

A characteristic building not yet found elsewhere is a rectangular structure with two stairways, each on opposite sides. On the summit a peculiar construction had no proper rooms but only two little roofed vestibules. These buildings could not have been dwellings nor do they seem to have served as sanctuaries, but rather as monuments used exclusively during festivals to pass from one patio to another (fig. 28).

The stairways have no balustrades and are built onto the body of the building, seldom with more than five or six steps of long stones. In Temple T are almost imperceptible geometrical motifs on the risers of some of the steps. In another case, at each end of the first step there is a stone forming a small "talud" or slope, the only example in Monte Negro of an inclined plane.

Dwelling houses are found near and sometimes joined to the ceremonial buildings. These are generally of three or four rooms built around an open patio, rather similar to the Roman impluvium. This type of inner patio is found later at Monte Alban and at Teotihuacan.

One of the most characteristic features of the architecture of Monte Negro is the multiple columns. They are of rubble with a core of irregular circular stones, faced with smaller stones to form a cylinder. They are very tall, in some cases more than 4 m.

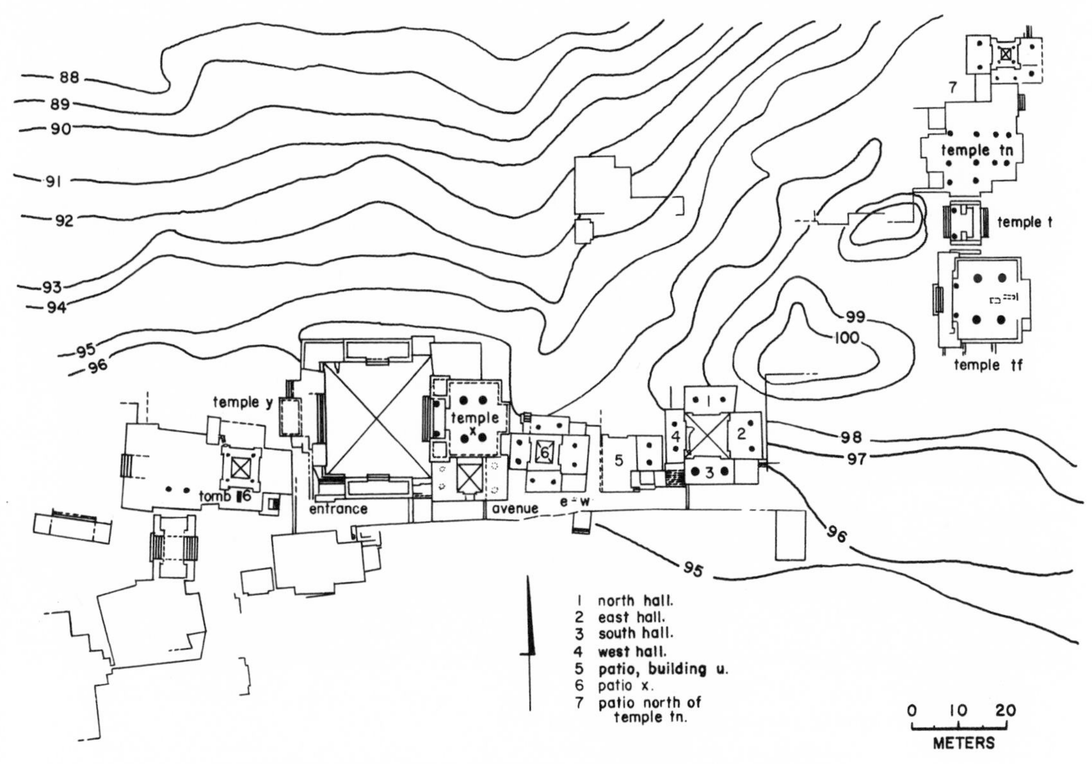

FIG. 27—MAP OF MONTE NEGRO ARCHAEOLOGICAL ZONE, OAXACA

high. In the most important temples there are about ten columns placed in rows.

Although the substructures are of stone, the upper buildings were of adobe or mud and timber. There are several sizes of adobe bricks, but the differences are not great; the width is normally about half the length, which varies between 32 and 36 cm. Roofs have not survived, but remains indicate that they were of thatch on a wooden framework. This must have been very complicated, probably with several different slopes, in the large temples.

A drainage system ran through the city, passing beneath buildings. The channels are rectangular, made of stone slabs. In the floor of the open patios a hole connects with the conduit which passes below. Sometimes the drain is reached by a clay pipe (11 cm. in diameter).

The dead were placed either in tombs or in simple graves dug in the ground. The tombs are box-shaped, without entrance, and are roofed with stone slabs or wooden beams. The most important tombs are walled with adobe and were built inside the substructures, some at the foot of the platforms.

A road about 100 m. long and 4–6 m. wide crosses the city from east to west, bordered on both sides by buildings. It does not follow a uniform gradient but is on several levels connected by one or two steps at varying intervals. In this last feature it is similar to the later "Street of the Dead" in Teotihuacan.

The pottery of Monte Negro is closely related to that of Monte Alban I. A carbon-14 specimen of wood and carbonized thatch from a tomb provides our only date for the Monte Alban I period, 649 B.C. ± 170 years.

YUCUNUDAHUI

In the same Mixteca region as Monte Negro another important site lies on the summit of a hill of Yucuñudahui, near the town of

Fig. 28—MOUND T, MONTE NEGRO

Fig. 29—WOODEN ROOF OF TOMB AT YUCUÑUDAHUI, OAXACA

Chachoapan. Among the remains is one known as the Temple of the Rain God and another called Mogote Grande, both destroyed by treasure-hunters. There is also a ball court, partly excavated, on a north-south axis. It is 68.5 m. long, its ground plan in the shape of a capital I. The great benches bordering the central playing alley have a slope of 8 degrees. It is not known if recesses lay in the inner angles as at Monte Alban.

On a spur of the same hill of Yucuñudahui an isolated mound contains an enormous tomb with an intact roof of wood. Seventeen tree trunks rest on a beam and on top of the north and south side walls (fig. 29). The tomb is entered by five steps leading down into two antechambers which open into a huge burial vault. On the walls are the remains of plaster painted red. Two stone slabs have been sunk into the walls; one shows two seated figures, the other, hieroglyphics with numerals.

The pottery inside the tomb displays a strong Teotihuacan influence and is similar to that of Tombs 103 and 104 of Monte Alban. This leads one to suppose that the building is contemporary with the transition Period IIIA-IIIB at that site.

Huamelulpan

Another important archaeological site is in the town of Haumelulpan, District of Tlaxiaco. Several huge mounds are still covered with vegetation, but one, partially cleared, is a platform built of enormous stone blocks, weighing between 3 and 4 tons each and lying horizontally. The stones at the corners display calendric hieroglyphics and numerals, beautifully sculptured in bas-relief. The steps of this structure are made of both large and small stones set in three rows for each step, which is 30–37 cm. high and 42–49 cm. deep.

Excavations show that the site corresponds to the transition between Periods I and II at Monte Alban.

Quiotepec

Some of the monuments in the zone of Quiotepec are related to Period III-IV at Monte Alban. The majority of the buildings are in the high part of a series of hills. They are grouped around patios. Each unit is usually composed of two large structures, one each at the north and south ends, with small platforms on the other sides. The principal plaza of the site, about 100 m. long and 60 m. wide, is, logically, where the largest monuments are grouped. Among them is one which appears to be a ball court.

Some of the buildings not covered with vegetation reveal a rectangular plan, with three stepped terraces and staircases without balustrades. A thick plaster coating originally covered the monuments.

The most spectacular feature of the site is the tombs which, though basically similar to those of Monte Alban, are much more elaborate. A small stairway leads into an antechamber, at the inner end of which is a façade, decorated profusely with cornices and panels of Monte Alban Type B. The tomb itself is a single chamber roofed with large stone slabs placed horizontally. Inside, there are two niches in the side walls and one at the other end. The latter simulates a façade with a door, formed by two jambs, a lintel, and, above, cornices and panels similar to those that decorated the outer façade of the tomb.

Guiengola

Guiengola, on the isthmus of Tehuantepec, is far from the sites we have been discussing. Although no excavation has been done on these monuments, lack of debris has made it possible to establish that the central plaza is 150 m. long and that there is a mound in a very good state of preservation. This is a rectangular pyramid with four terraces, the lowest of which is vertical and the others are sloping. There is a main stairway on the east side as well as two lateral stairways.

Among the buildings forming other architectural complexes are some of circular plan, about 10 m. in diameter.

The usual type of building is based on slabs, placed one above the other without mortar. Plaster is used only for exterior finishing.

What commands most attention is that many of the platform terraces are decorated at intervals with projecting stones as in Aztec buildings. This leads us to think that the site could be very late, dating probably to the time when the Mixtecs were already masters of the Zapotec lands.

In addition to those sites described there are many others in Oaxaca so shrouded by forest that we have no idea of their features or their age.

REFERENCES

Acosta, 1958–59, 1959
Batres, 1902
Bernal, 1958c
Caso, 1928, 1932a, 1935, 1938, 1939b
Marquina, 1951
Villagra, 1939

33. Architecture in Oaxaca after the End of Monte Alban

IGNACIO BERNAL

There are very few excavated sites in Oaxaca later than the last major building period at Monte Alban—Period IIIB. Except for one or two isolated details all our information comes from Mitla, Yagul, Cuilapan, and San Luis Beltran, in the valley of Oaxaca; Coixtlahuaca, in the Mixteca Alta; and some unconnected data from sites in the rest of the state. Even these few sources are optimistic, for only the first two places yield any important architectural data.

The architecture which corresponds to Monte Alban IV, at least in the valley of Oaxaca, does not seem to differ from that of Period IIIB. This is true also of the pottery: Periods IIIB and IV are identical and are distinguished at Monte Alban only by the disappearance of the ceremonial center of that city. The excavations of Period IV material in the valley are very limited, but from the little we know at Cuilapan, from San Luis Beltran and Noriega, and the corresponding phase at Yagul and Mitla we cannot speak of a different architecture. As we understand it, what we call Period IV at Monte Alban is the same as the Zapotec style from the 10th to the 16th centuries in the valley of Oaxaca. There was, indeed, a deterioration in the style of Period IIIB, but there were no changes. This continuity results seemingly from lack of Toltec influence on the area. We shall therefore consider only the architecture which corresponds to the pottery, called at Monte Alban Period V but, as we know, partly contemporaneous with Period IV. That style, although of Zapotec origin, has incorporated ideas which are probably Mixtec. We have no knowledge of this architceture except in Mitla and Yagul.

Mitla

From pottery finds, it is evident that this city at the east end of the valley of Oaxaca was inhabited from the equivalent of Period I at Monte Alban, but we have found buildings only of the later periods. In the South Group, Burial 1 corresponds to Period IIIA (Caso and Borbolla, 1936, pp. 13–15). Tomb 7 in the same group has a roof which is partly sloped in typical Zapotec style.

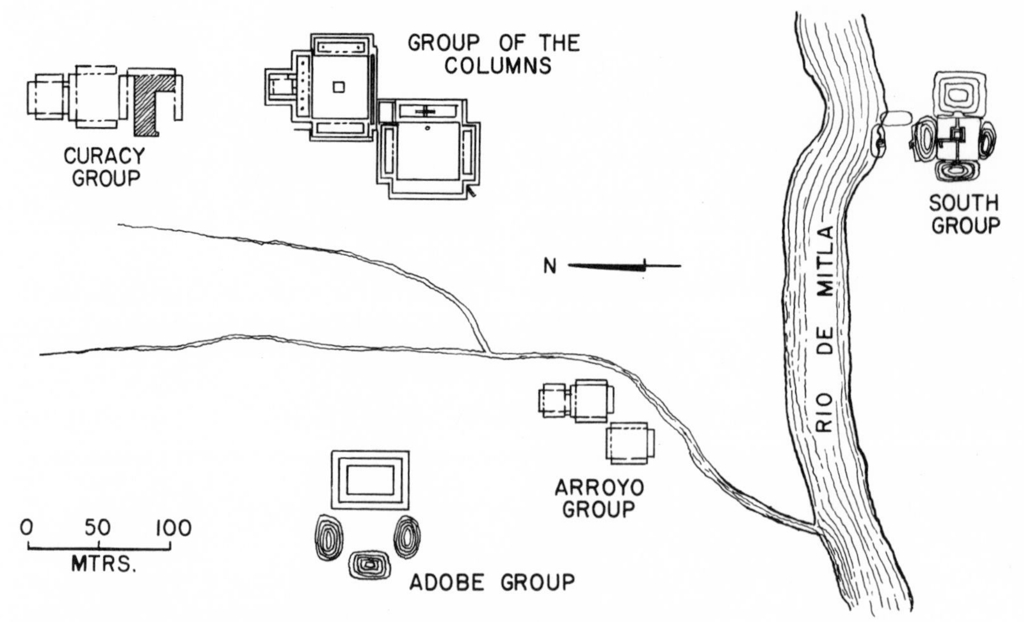

FIG. 1—MAP OF ARCHAEOLOGICAL ZONE, MITLA, OAXACA

From the objects in it, it cannot be from IIIB but must date from Period IV. Tomb 3 also seems to be of Period IV; all the other tombs are of Period V. Burial 22 was also probably IIIB, but none of the other burials contained objects from which it was possible to determine their period.

The present ruins of Mitla constitute five groups (fig. 1). Probably the spaces within the groups were once filled with dwellings or other buildings which have now disintegrated or are underneath the buildings of the modern town. Without detailed investigation we cannot picture the general plan of the city and so we must confine our discussion to isolated buildings. These have been often studied from the beginning of the 19th century; even today Holmes' plan (1895–97, pl. 39) remains, for the most part, valid. It served as the basis of the plan by Caso and Borbolla (1936), which we are using here.

The Group of the Adobe, in a poor state of preservation, has not been excavated. It is noteworthy because the quadrangle which it forms is bordered on the east by a pyramid and not by the platform with apartments. In this it resembles the South Group, with which it may be contemporaneous. The South Group, only partially studied, also has a pyramid on the east, as well as on the north. The west side is badly destroyed, the south has almost disappeared. In the center is an adoratorio of two terraces such as probably also existed in the Adobe Group. Below the east pyramid was Tomb 7. Below the north pyramid I recently found another tomb (not yet published), which presents interesting problems of chronology.

The three remaining groups are typical and have many common features. In all cases the rectangular patios are bordered on each side by an apartment. The Group of the Columns is on a platform; the others are only slightly raised above the level of the patio. These patios are sometimes connected to one another or, as in the Group of Columns, are separate. Only in one case is there a small adoratorio in the center. The rooms are long and narrow; when two patios are connected, it is by a winding passage from a room to its adjacent patio. The rooms have either one or three doors. In some cases the outside corners of the apartments meet in a right angle; in others there is an empty space between them.

The method of construction seems to be always the same: a core of mud and stone covered with plaster or well-cut trachite. Although the stones are not of the same size, they are perfectly fitted; a little bit of mortar, however, almost always joins them. In smoothed parts the facing is only superficial but on uneven surfaces the stones penetrate deep into the rubble, which is one of the main reasons for the stability of these buildings (Marquina, 1951, p. 380). The door frames are decorated with a mosaic of perfectly worked and fitted small stones forming stepped fret patterns with a wide variety of designs. In some cases the patterns are not formed by the juxtaposition of several stones but are carved from a single larger one—a false mosaic (figs. 3, 4).

Caso (1947) has drawn reconstructions of the roofs. They consisted of beams supported from wall to wall on which large slabs

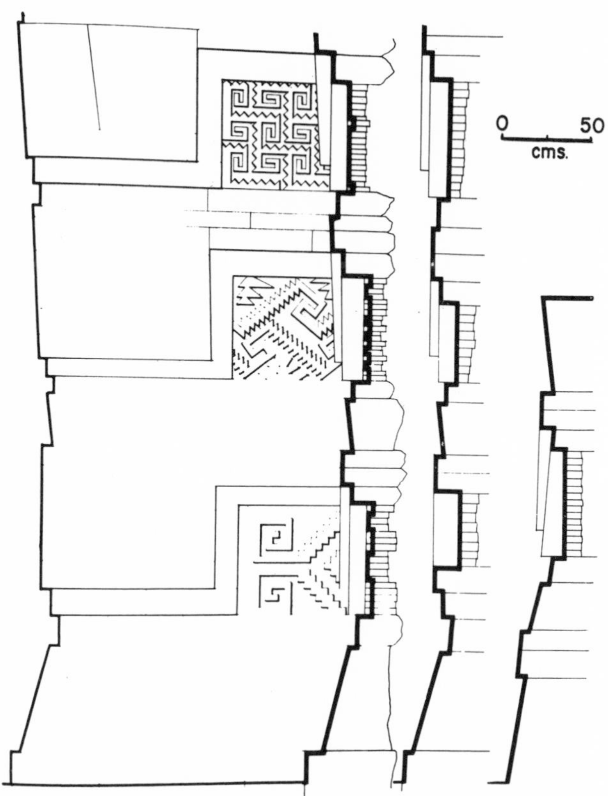

FIG. 2—DETAIL OF MOLDINGS AND CORNICE, BUILDING OF THE COLUMNS, MITLA, OAXACA (Drawing by L. MacGregor K.)

FIG. 3—BUILDING OF THE COLUMNS, MITLA, OAXACA

Fig. 4—STEPPED-FRET STONE MOSAICS, INTERIOR OF ROOM, MITLA, OAXACA

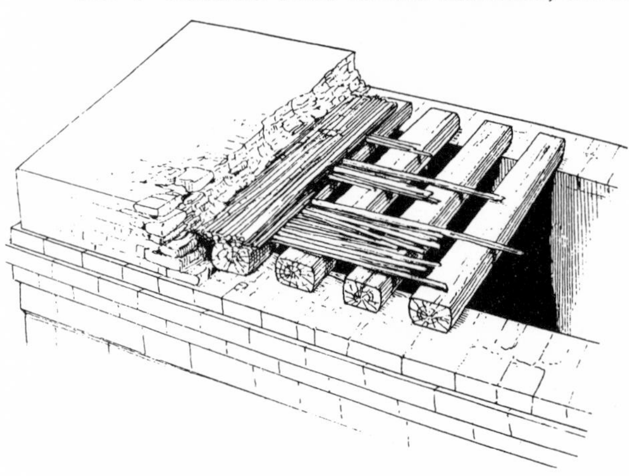

Fig. 5—ROOF CONSTRUCTION, MITLA, OAXACA. (After Holmes, 1895, fig. 82.)

Fig. 6—SECTION THROUGH BUILDING OF DOUBLE BEAM SPAN, MITLA, OAXACA. (After Holmes, 1895, fig. 77.)

Fig. 7—HALL OF THE COLUMNS, MITLA, OAXACA

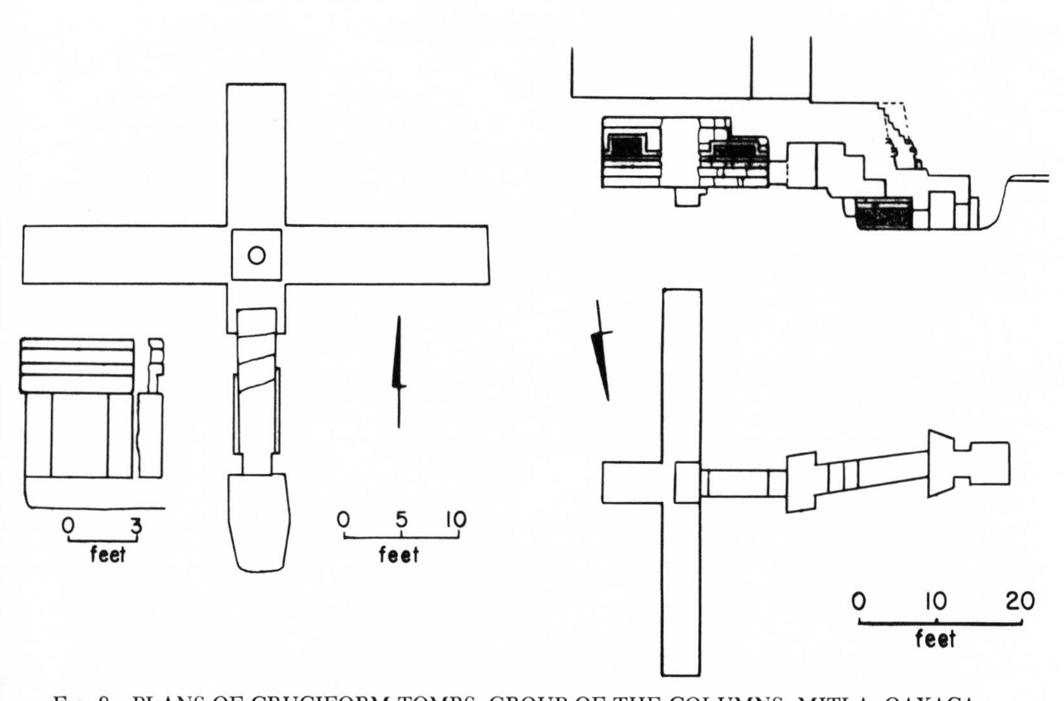

Fig. 8—PLANS OF CRUCIFORM TOMBS, GROUP OF THE COLUMNS, MITLA, OAXACA

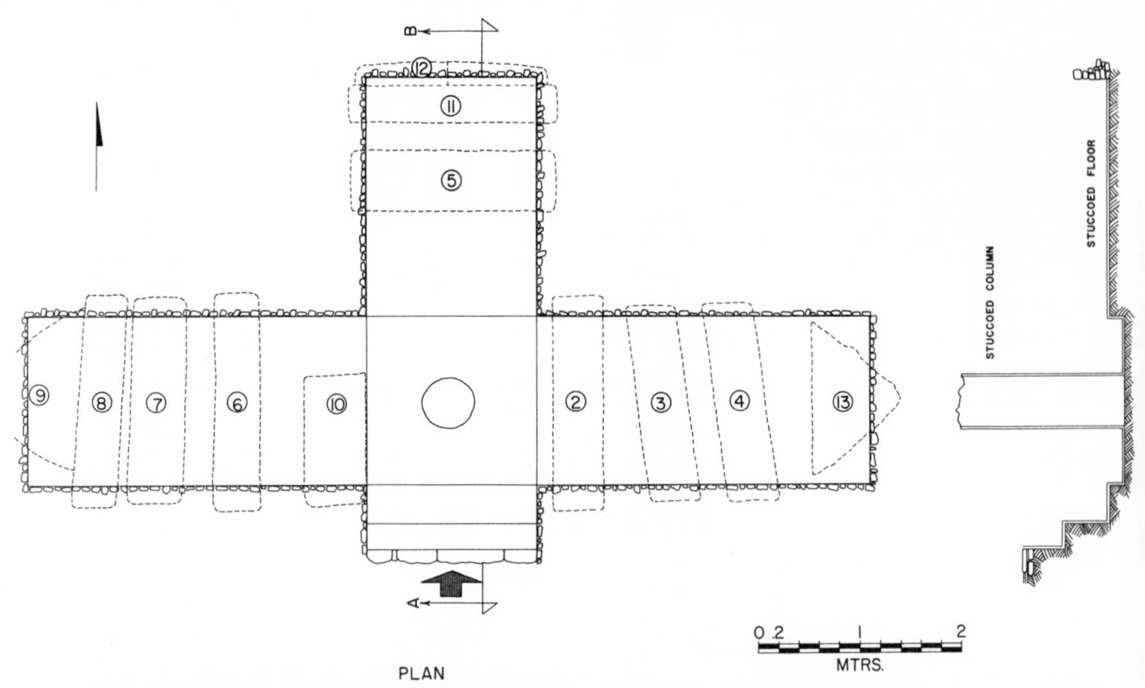

Fig. 9—PLAN OF CRUCIFORM TOMB, SOUTH GROUP, MITLA, OAXACA

Fig. 10—VIEW OF YAGUL, OAXACA

were placed perpendicularly, and these probably were covered with small slabs over which was placed a thick layer of gravel (fig. 5). Finally the flat roof was plastered, with a slope towards the interior of the patio to take off the rainwater. In the larger room of the columns, the beams rested with one end on the outside wall and the other on a wooden cross-member which ran along the tops of the columns (fig. 6). The latter are monoliths without base or capital; they are very slightly tapered towards the top (fig. 7).

The lintels are frequently formed of large rectangular monoliths of extraordinary size and weight, very similar to those used for roofing tombs. There are three such tombs of particular importance: two are in the Group of the Columns and are cruciform (fig. 8); the third, recently discovered in the South Group, is smaller (fig. 9). The last was decorated with a mosaic of fret patterns identical with those of the other tombs, and was roofed with enormous rectangular stones. At the ends of these stones were cut small holes to accommodate a rope for moving them into their final positions, a method always used at Mitla. This tomb, like Tombs 1 and 2, was below an apartment. Later a pyramidal temple mound was built, destroying both the apartment and the tomb.

Yagul

Yagul is more dilapidated and less sumptuous than Mitla but it stands in infinitely more beautiful surroundings. The city is built on the south and west slopes of a hill, northeast of Tlacolula. The summit forms a wide and very inaccessible platform for a fortress reinforced by stone and mud walls. Only part of the south slope, where the ceremonial and municipal center of the ancient city stood, has been excavated. As well as some pyramidal mounds, evidently bases for temples, which are of no particular interest, we can recognize the palace, the

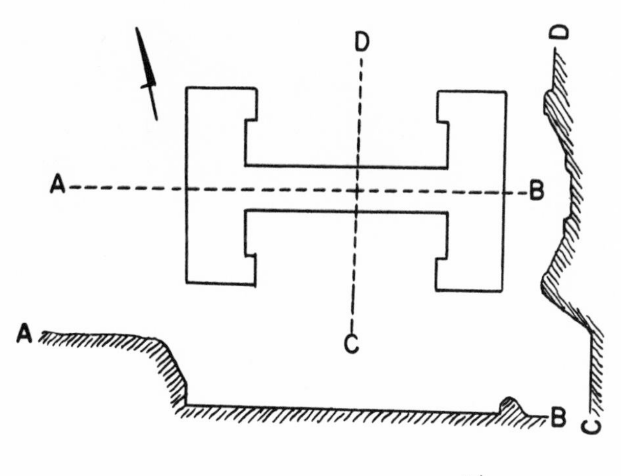

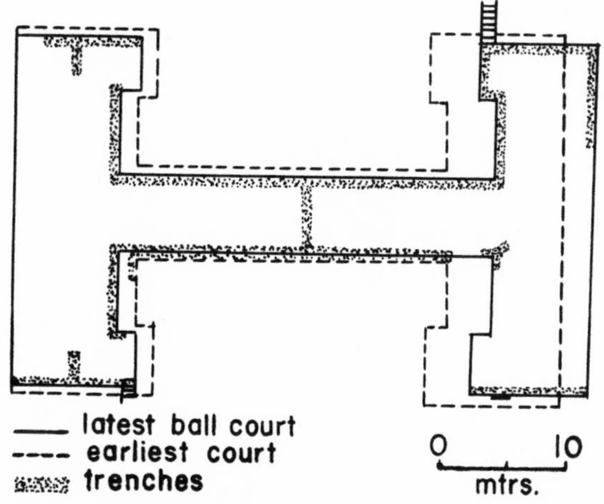

Fig. 11—PLAN OF BALL COURT, YAGUL, OAXACA

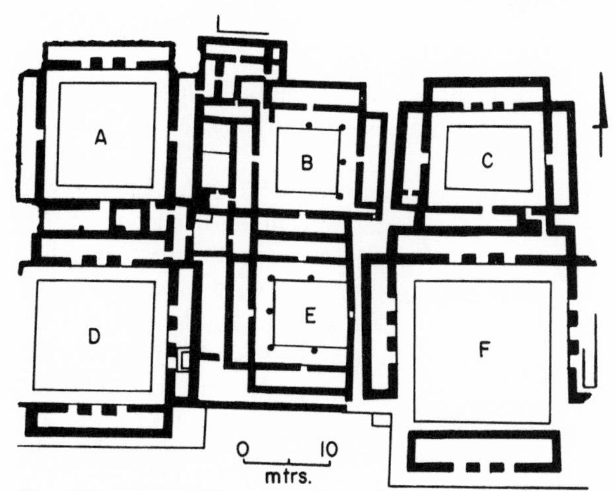

Fig. 12—PLAN OF PALACE OF THE SIX PATIOS, YAGUL, OAXACA

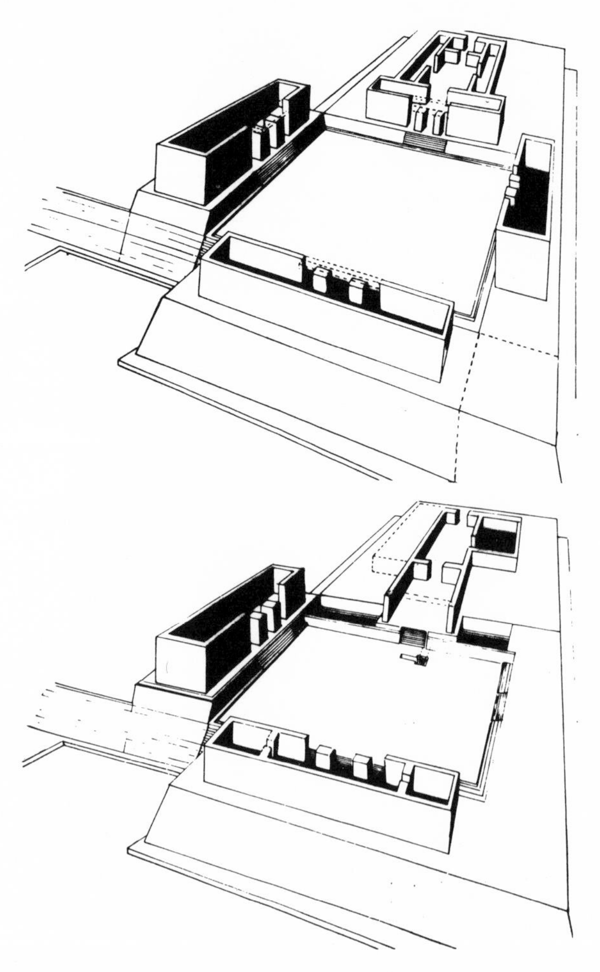

FIG. 13—RECONSTRUCTIONS OF BUILDING PHASES OF PALACE PATIO, YAGUL, OAXACA. (After J. Oliver.)

"council chamber," the ball court, and some patios and lesser buildings, as well as 35 tombs.

As there is no map of Yagul, I have made use of a photograph taken from one of the huge rocks which form the fortress (fig. 10). The center is a very close group of buildings, some adjoining, others separated by streets running east-west. The principal streets are to the north and south of the palace and separate it from other buildings to the north and from the ball court on the south.

The ball court (Wicke, 1957) differs appreciably from the one at Monte Alban. The stairways are different; there are no niches or central marker stone; and the whole court is somewhat larger (fig. 11). It must be considered, however, as of Zapotec style and as one of the buildings showing most clearly that Yagul is a city which has used many of the elements of the usual architecture of the valley of Oaxaca. There are at least two quite similar building periods. At least one part of the west "end field" had walls covered with stone mosaic after the style of Mitla. Although this form of decoration may be very old and is found occasionally at Monte Alban, its large-scale use at Yagul and Mitla is late and it may belong, at least in part, to a style not characteristic of the valley. More similar to Monte Alban is the ball court of San Luis Beltran; without doubt it is from Period IV and so is much later than that of Monte Alban and is purely Zapotec. It is an intermediate stage between Monte Alban and Yagul because it is probably earlier than the last reconstruction there.

Across the street towards the north is the Palace of Six Patios, built on an artificial platform made from the remains of at least three earlier buildings of Zapotec type and of three similar to the latest building (fig. 12). I consider these three periods to be Mixtec from the pottery, but polychrome is associated only with the latest building. This building has its only entrance on the north side. Passages and doorways allow movement between the different patios and rooms. At one time the structure was a single unit with interior communication to all parts, but later a wall separated the present Rooms 4 and 5, thus dividing the whole building into two sections. Moreover, walls were built to close off some rooms like that on the south side of Patio C and that which divides Rooms 8 and 8′ and Rooms 2 and 3. Room 15 is the only one which was originally closed; it was probably entered from above by the small stairway still partly

Fig. 14—SLAB DOOR OF TOMB, CARVED AS "FALSE MOSAIC," YAGUL, OAXACA

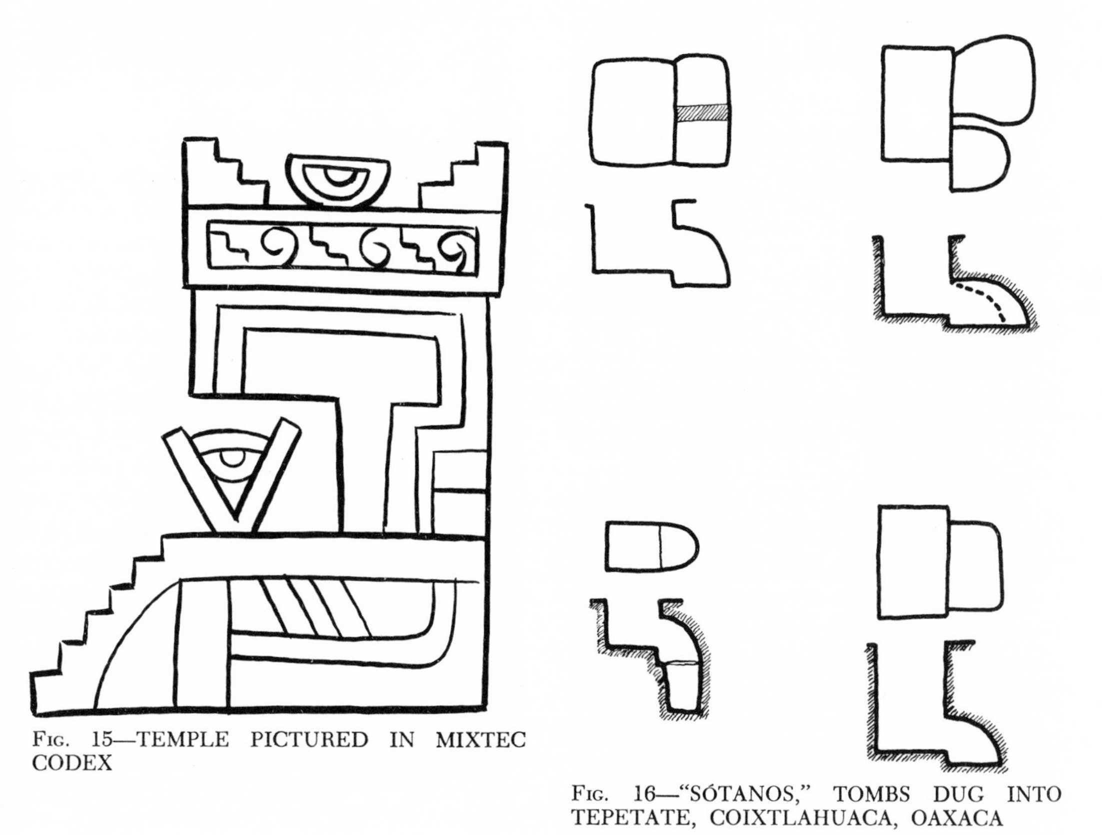

Fig. 15—TEMPLE PICTURED IN MIXTEC CODEX

Fig. 16—"SÓTANOS," TOMBS DUG INTO TEPETATE, COIXTLAHUACA, OAXACA

Fig. 17—INTERIOR OF TOMB 6, CERRO GUACAMAYA EL CARRIZAL, YOLOX, OAXACA. *b (opposite)* is a detail of wall at right in *a (above).*

standing. The method of construction is the same as at Mitla, although stone mosaic is much less abundant on outside walls and unknown on interior walls, which are surfaced with red plaster. I do not think that there can have been large stone lintels as at Mitla, but the roofs were probably similar.

The "council chamber," running along the north side of one of the large patios, is very similar in size to the columned room at Mitla but has no columns. Its façade was also decorated with stone mosaic although the interior was only plastered. This, however, is an isolated room, its only entrance giving onto the patio and not to other rooms. This building is on the north side of a patio bordered on the west by another apartment which was later divided into three, and on the east by one which was altered several times (fig. 13). All this reminds one strongly of the buildings at Mitla.

The tombs at Yagul are rectangular in plan, usually with a fairly wide antechamber. Most of the roofs are flat as is characteristic of the Mixtec tombs of Monte Alban V, but some are sloped or a combination of the two types. They may or may not have niches; the door is not oriented in any particular direction, although the few tombs with exclusively Period IV pottery face west. In many cases the façade is decorated with stone fret patterns.

All this shows that the tombs are essentially in Zapotec tradition although most contain Period V pottery. There are groups of two (two examples) and of three tombs (two examples) linked by a common antechamber, whereas each tomb may have its own antechamber. The most important of these groups is in Patio 4 and consists of three tombs facing south, west, and north, all of which share an antechamber. A magnificent slab worked with false mosaic on its two principal faces served as a door (fig. 14). The panels or jambs are decorated with two heads of inlaid stone; the sides of the long façade are ornamented with fret patterns shamming mosaic, as in the interior of tombs at Mitla or Guiaroo. These joined triple tombs are unknown in other parts of the valley, but one example, now lost, occurred at Coixtlahuaca. This suggests that the idea is Mixtec.

The similarity between the palaces at Mitla and Yagul is remarkable. Patios C and F at Yagul and A and B in the Church Group at Mitla are almost identical. Their placement, the relative size of each, the number of doors in each apartment, and the passage with two bends which joins them are all identical. At Yagul the room south of the patio which faces outward in an unusual way seems to correspond to the north room of Patio C at Mitla, except that at Yagul the third patio, which encloses the outer doors of this room, is not complete because of lack of space on the platform. This detail seems to suggest that Yagul is copying Mitla and the latest building of the Palace, but at a slightly later date.

Apart from differences of style, the most noteworthy point at Yagul and Mitla is a preponderance of palaces and civic buildings. This is exactly opposite to Monte Alban, where temples predominate. This, of course, must not be taken to mean that temples did not exist in the first two cities, or that dwelling houses were few at Monte Alban.

Mixtec Architecture

In the excavations at Coixtlahuaca (Bernal, 1949a) very little effort was devoted, because of the special conditions, to studying monuments. One can only say that without doubt they show a refined character with walls of worked stone or brick decorated with sculptured stones and spikes. This comes closest to the style of architecture often pictured in the Mixtec codices. These show temples, palaces, adoratorios, ball courts, sweat baths, all with elaborate sculptured or painted façades, flat roofs surrounded by crenellations, mound platforms, stairways, and balustrades (fig. 15).

With the exception of the triple tomb at

Coixtlahuaca, already mentioned, we know of no Mixtec tomb of this final period built like those of the valley of Oaxaca. The characteristic Mixtec type are those called "sótanos," small in size and not built but dug into the tepetate. Several variations of this type appear in figure 16. In the Chinantec region there are Zapotec-style tombs we would think were earlier if it were not for the contents which are evidently late and for the fact that one of them is painted with stepped-fret patterns of Mitla style (fig. 17,*b*).

REFERENCES

Bernal, 1949a, 1958c
Brockington, 1955
Caso, 1935, 1947
—— and Rubín de la Borbolla, 1936
Holmes, 1895–97
Marquina, 1951
Oliver, 1955
Saville, 1909
Wicke, 1957

34. Sculpture and Mural Painting of Oaxaca

ALFONSO CASO

WE CAN DISTINGUISH in the sculpture of Oaxaca the same periods that are recognized in its pottery and its writing. Since the earliest human traces in the valley are found just above the black earth which covers the original rocks of Monte Alban and which has always been found sterile of cultural remains, the sculpture appears already linked to a fully developed calendar and system of writing. For that reason this first Monte Alban culture is in no sense "primitive." On the contrary, it is a culture with technically perfect ceramics and deep aesthetic feeling; the system of writing is no mere iconographic representation of objects; and, above all, the calendar (as emphasized in Article 37) must bear witness to a long period of development as well as to a continuous observation of the stars.

The connection of this Monte Alban culture, the oldest we have found in the valley of Oaxaca, with the very similar culture of Monte Negro in the Mixteca region and the carbon-14 date obtained for that site (Libby, 1952, p. 92, Sample 424), confirms an antiquity of several centuries B.C. which we had already attributed to it on a stylistic basis (Caso, 1947, p. 32). Moreover, the C14 date obtained for the second Monte Alban phase, Monte Alban II, from materials in that site zone, indicates that the first phase could not have come to an end after 223 ± 145 years B.C. (Libby, 1952, p. 92, Sample 425).

We are not yet able to identify the people who built up this ancient culture. During the first millennium B.C., however, there was a strong similarity between the cultures of the valley of Oaxaca and those in the mountains of the west, which later can be classified as a Mixtec zone. In Monte Alban the style of writing which is contemporaneous with the first period corresponds to the figures which are popularly named "danzantes." In a temple built during this period these danzantes are *in situ* or have fallen from the wall; the interior of this temple yielded pottery which corresponds to only the oldest types of Monte Alban I.

As many of these danzantes have hieroglyphic names and as there are stelae with glyphs which were in a wall decorated with danzantes, we have been able to establish

Fig. 1—DANZANTE 2, MONTE ALBAN

Fig. 2—DANZANTE 11, MONTE ALBAN

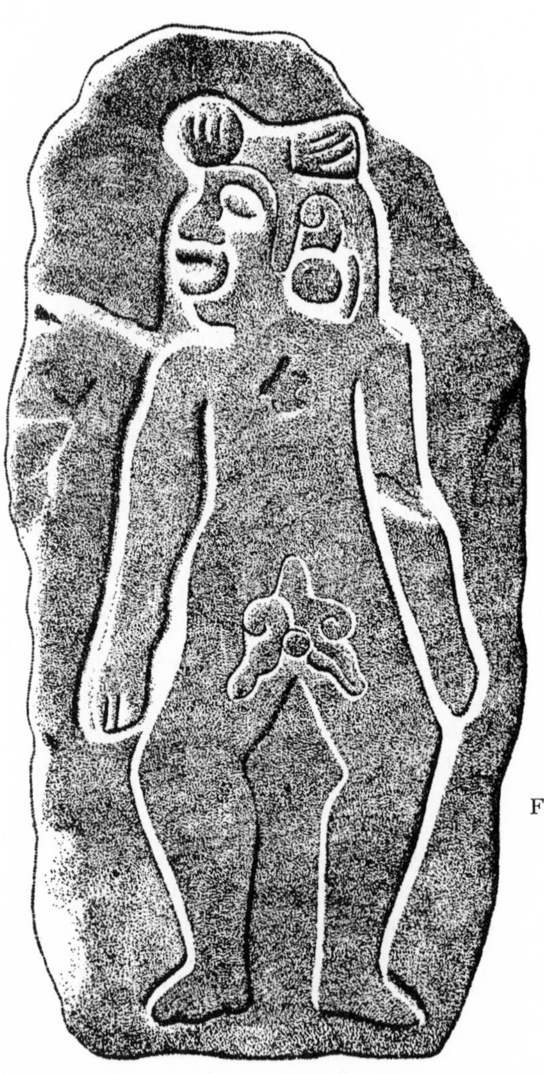

Fig. 3—DANZANTE 12, MONTE ALBAN

the contemporaneity of (a) the sculpture of the danzante type, (b) the pottery of Monte Alban I, and (c) the system of writing associated with the sculpture of the danzante type.

Monte Alban I or Danzante Style

Several characteristics distinguish this type from later human representations. The stones on which these danzantes were engraved were almost never perfectly squared. They were commonly left, especially the large ones, with one or two sides uncut (figs. 1-4).

The danzantes should be considered not as sculpture but as figures engraved in stone; in all periods it is extremely rare to find full-round sculpture in the cultures of Oaxaca. High relief is also rare; engraving or bas-relief is the rule. Let us repeat briefly the style as we have described it elsewhere (Caso, 1947, pp. 17–19). Although we can speak generally about danzante sculptures, not all belong to the same style.

Great movement characterizes all the sculptures, even those depicting seated or prostrate figures. Heads are always in profile; bodies are either in profile or in front view. The stone on which the figure was to be chiseled was cut out and then arranged so that the figure filled the maximum space. This perhaps explains the movement evident in the figures.

In the standing figures the legs are never straight but somewhat bent; when the body is in front view, the arms extend from the body, just as in the little jade Olmec figures which represent standing men.

The mouth is always open. The chin, differing from that on the Olmec figures, never protrudes from the plane of the lips. The nose is broad and aquiline; eyes are always an ellipse with a horizontal line through the center. The brow is rounded and not deformed. The neck is so short that it scarcely exists. The ears are in front view, just as are the disc-shaped ear pendants which generally decorate them.

Fig. 4—DANZANTE, MONTE ALBAN

The body is muscular, almost squat. The soles of the feet are represented by a curious curve which can also be seen on the stela at Alvarado, Veracruz, and on other ancient sculptures discovered by Shook in Kaminaljuyu, corresponding to Preclassic levels.

First Danzante Type

The type which seems classic and oldest does not depict the smaller toes and very seldom the big toe. Fingers are sometimes not apparent although the thumb is always distinguished from the other fingers (figs. 1–4).

The figures have more motion than those of the second type (described below), and the postures have more variety: standing; seated with one leg stretched out; lying supine with one or both legs bent; lying

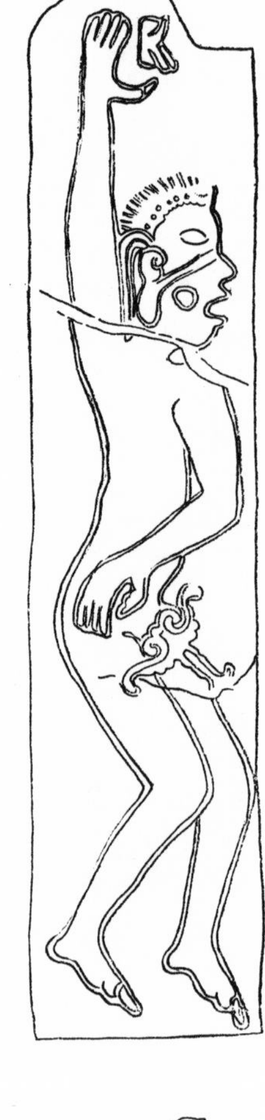

Fig. 5—DANZANTE, SOUTH PLATFORM 10, MONTE ALBAN

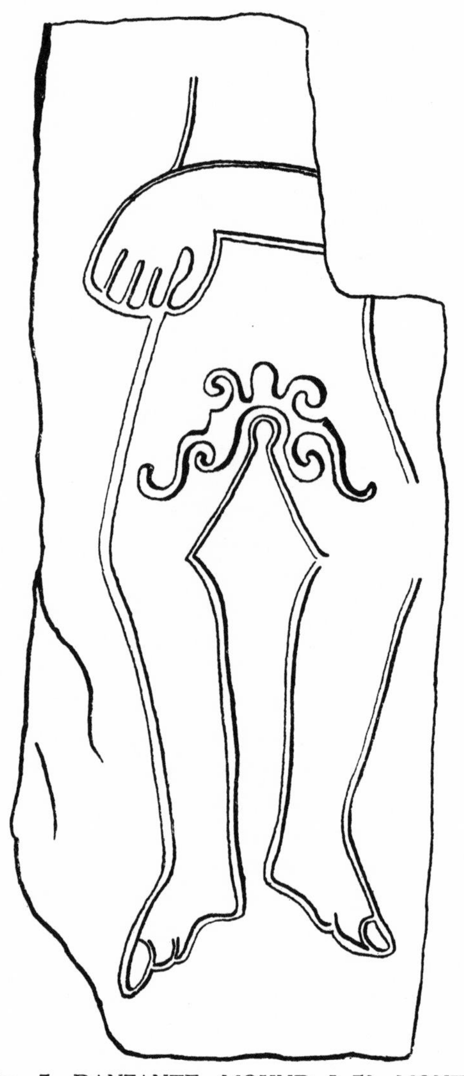

Fig. 7—DANZANTE, MOUND J 70, MONTE ALBAN

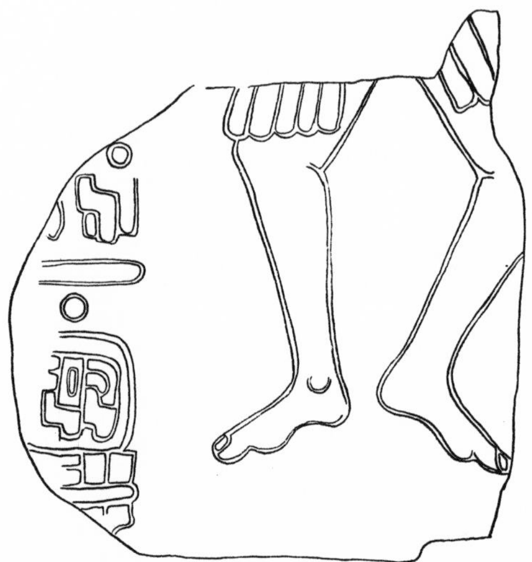

Fig. 6—DANZANTE, SOUTH PLATFORM 11, MONTE ALBAN

prone with hands open as if swimming; squatting with legs apart; crouching, running, or jumping; kneeling with one knee on the ground; seated on the floor in oriental fashion but with one leg drawn up. Hands sometimes look as if hanging limp, feet as if twisted. In one figure the head is deformed at the back (similar to the deformation found in La Venta and in Tlatilco). Old men are frequently depicted.

The outline of the body is traced by a broad deep line, giving the figure a little relief. Generally relief also marks cheek bones, eyes, nose, and open mouth showing two teeth. Lips are thick and commissures turn down.

Second Danzante Type

In the second type of danzantes, which we consider to be later than, or evolved from, the first, the lines are engraved deeper and better chiseled at the edges, but the exterior border of the cutting has not been reduced and consequently there is no relief. The figures are more slender and limbs longer, perhaps excessively long. The curve which appeared on the soles of the feet in the first style is doubled and drawn clearly to show the softness of the big toe and the sole. Similarly, in the hands the thumb is represented by two curves. The nails on the thumb and the big toe are enormous and are always evident. In one figure even the lump caused by malleolus of the tibia is shown. The principal difference, however, lies in the face, of which we have only two examples on the five fragments of this style so far found (figs. 5–7.)

The lips are not prominent and are very fine. The mouth is open but does not disclose teeth. Facial painting or tattooing consists of a line running from ears to nose, dividing the face in two, the lower part being decorated with discs, tattooing, or facial painting like that found on small pottery figurine heads from Guerrero. A similar tattoo is on the hand of Stela 15. The brow is

Fig. 8—DANZANTE, MOUND J 41, MONTE ALBAN

Fig. 9—IDOL AT HUAMELULPAN

Fig. 10—HEADS, MOUND J, MONTE ALBAN

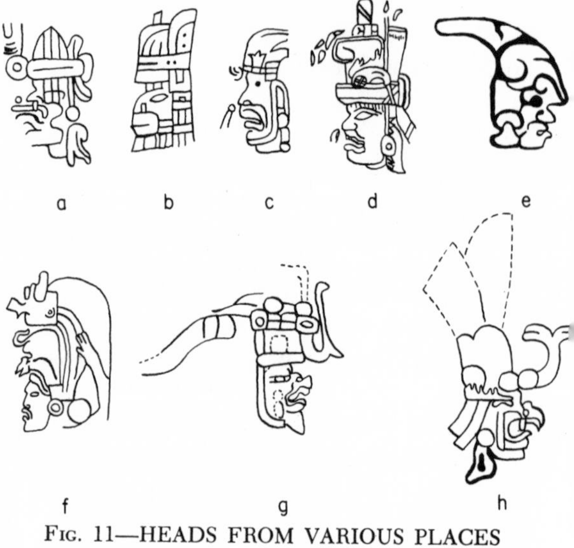

Fig. 11—HEADS FROM VARIOUS PLACES

furrowed. One clear representation of an ear shows no ear ornament, but the hole pierced through the lobe shows where it would hang. In two instances, and only in this second type of danzante, what we have called sexual tattooing appears out of place. In one of these examples it is outside the body, as if a symbol of the male sex and not a tattoo, as we had considered.

Everywhere that we found fragments of this type of danzante they were being used as building material and so it has not been possible to relate them to the pottery. But it may be that, just as the little pottery figurines of Period I continue into Period II in the same style, the second, more developed danzante style may be a continuation of danzante sculpture during Period II. In any event, Danzante 41, in Mound J (fig. 8) already exhibits certain characteristics, such as the glyph for hill, mantle, and other glyphs which decorate its body and clothing, which are perhaps closer to the sculpture of Period II than that of Period I.

In Article 36 we note Olmec jade figures found in Veracruz, Puebla, and Guerrero which strongly resemble this danzante style. We have also found this similarity in the carved gray pottery which is one of the most beautiful products to be found in Oaxaca or elsewhere (Caso and Bernal, 1952, figs. 245, 250; Caso, 1947, pls. 4–7).

Without doubt the sculpture of this first Monte Alban period has close connections with the Olmec style of La Venta and Tres Zapotes, but it is still an individual and

Fig. 12—BRAZIER (HEAD-SHAPED), TOMB 111, MONTE ALBAN

Fig. 13—LÁPIDA DE BAZÁN

characteristic style which should not be confused with the southern style of Veracruz and Tabasco.

This Olmecoid style also exists in the Mixteca region, one example being in the great idol of Huamelulpan (fig. 9). Both earlier and in Article 38 I have described a beautiful engraved stone from the same place (Caso, 1956, pl. 1).

Lastly, from Period I, large serpentine motifs of this Olmecoid style modeled in stucco and high relief decorate a panel on building P.S.A. Sub.

Period II

In Monte Alban and Zimatlan we have found stone heads that are not fragments but complete sculptures and that recall the colossal Olmec heads, even though they are little larger than twice natural size. They were probably carved during Period II. Although we have no other complete sculptures of that period, except possibly those of the second danzante type which may belong to it, these many sculptured heads of Mound J of Monte Alban remind us of the Olmec style. This can be seen by comparing the heads in figure 10 with those in figure 11. These last show examples of varied provenance from Tabasco, Veracruz, Morelos, Oaxaca, and Guatemala, all dating to the Preclassic horizons. In addition to those already published (Caso, 1947, fig. 58), are others from Chiapas (Agrinier, 1960, figs. 3, 7, 11).

There is also a remarkable similarity be-

Fig. 14—STELA 7, DUPAIX, RIGHT SIDE

tween these heads and the great incensarios in the form of human heads from Period I in Monte Alban and Monte Negro (fig. 12) published elsewhere (Caso and Bernal, 1952, figs. 480–91).

The Olmecoid traits in the carved stones of Mound J are even more evident in the pottery sculptures found in Tomb 113 in association with Monte Alban II pottery (Caso, 1947, pls. 17, 18; Caso and Bernal, 1952, figs. 498–500). Such characteristics are also visible in the famous idol of Cuilapan which belongs to this period. But the pottery sculpture closest to realistic human form is the urn found in Tomb 77 (Caso and Bernal, 1952, figs. 341, 341 bis).

Period IIIA

We have no sculpture attributable with certainty to the transition period between Periods II and IIIA in Monte Alban. This corresponds to Teotihuacan II and is the time when the influence of the latter city begins to be felt in the valley of Oaxaca. But of the following period, IIIA, we have examples showing that the fundamental forms of the Zapotec style had already become predominant.

A characteristic example of this type of sculpture is the beautiful *tecali* plaque, to which we have given the name "Lápida de Bazán" (Caso, 1938, p. 38, fig. 25), found in the debris of Temple X (fig. 13). The strong influence of the Classic period of Teotihuacan is marked in this stone; the priest known as 8 Turquoise, who stands on the left of the god of Monte Alban (Tiger 3 Turquoise), bears a close resemblance to those figures which appear in Tombs 104 and 105 (described later). He is also similar to the *tlaloques* which appear in the frescoes of Tepantitla in Teotihuacan and which have surely influenced this style of representation. Here again we see that Zapotec sculpture restricted itself to engravings rather than high relief or full-round figures, the latter technique being almost exclusively reserved for jades. It would therefore be more exact to call such stones not sculptures but stone engravings.

A good many of the stelae which we published some years ago (Caso, 1928) are undoubtedly from this period. The work done recently by Acosta (1958–59) clearly shows that Stelae 1–6 and 8 were erected in their respective locations *after* offerings of handle-spout vessels, which are characteristic of Period IIIA, had been made in these

Fig. 15—THE "PLAIN" STELA

FIG. 16—ZAACHILA LÁPIDA 1, NATIONAL MUSEUM OF MEXICO

FIG. 17—STONE FROM MOUND II, MONTE ALBAN

FIG. 18—SERPENT HEAD, ZAACHILA

places. But because Stela 7 shows a person who has been made prisoner (a scene also represented on Stelae 2, 3, 5, 6, and 8) and because it also depicts, as do Stela 1 and the one known as the "Plain Stela," a procession of priests, I consider that these nine stelae located in the angles of the southern platform of Monte Alban were set up in Period IIIA, which corresponds fully to the Classic horizon (figs. 14, 15).

I believe that Stela 11, perhaps also Lápida 1 of the Museo Nacional (fig. 16) which we have catalogued as no. 13 (Caso, 1928, fig. 93), and the tablet from Mound II (fig. 17) belong to the same period.

We owe to Berlin (1946, p. 36) the description of three stones found in San Juan Sola. Two of them, as Berlin had supposed, seem to be the markers and were in the upper part of the ball court. At Monte Alban, precisely in the building west of the ball court, we found a similar stone (Caso, 1935, fig. 26); another which we believe served the same function comes from Tututepec (Piña Chan, 1960b, photo 9). These stones, being worked in the full round, are exceptions in Zapotec sculpture. There was another similar stone in Zaachila (fig. 18). I believe that the other stone published by Berlin, bearing a hieroglyphic inscription, also belongs to the same period.

But Monte Alban is not where the most

Fig. 19—MONUMENT AT YAGUILA

Fig. 20—STELA AT GUADALUPE SANTA ANA

Fig. 21—COAT-OF-ARMS OF TILANTONGO

beautiful sculptures of this period are found; we know of other places with magnificent stelae as yet unpublished. One is in Yaguila, ex-district of Ixtlan, and I was informed of it by Frans Blom. Two of its faces are covered with very deep reliefs. The photograph here published (fig. 19) was taken by Dr. Francisco Ruiz Reyes. Although this stela is broken, in Blom's drawing one can see on the main face a glyph within a frame; it appears to be a head with a small feather headdress. This engraving cannot be seen in figure 19. Further, there is a glyph of a tree which appears to emerge from a volute and is above the symbol of year 10N.

Higher (fig. 19) one can see mouths displaying teeth and fangs and, above them, five glyphs: 5 Monkey, 5A, 1 Death, 10P, and 5 Arrow (?). Of the glyphs on the back of the stone, only one has numerals, 4 Turquoise. The others appear to represent the

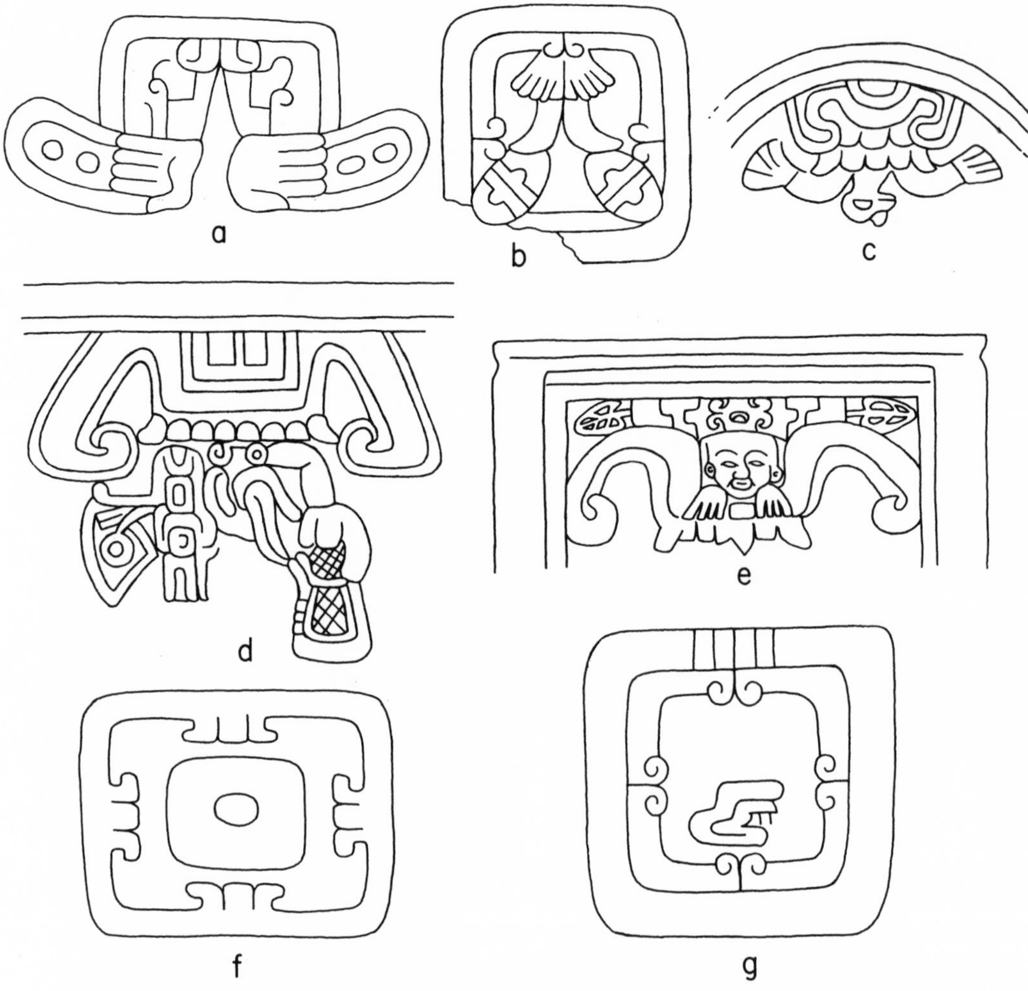

Fig. 22—GLYPHS OF THE DESCENDING GOD AND OTHERS

head of a deer and a hand, but without photographs of this side I cannot be sure of this interpretation.

In the Rio Grande, Oaxaca, is a magnificent stela depicting a man with crossed arms and cloaked with a tiger skin. Opposite are two glyphs, 7(?) and 3 Tiger. A similar figure with the same glyph, which we cannot interpret, was found in Tututepec; this same glyph again appears on a small stone recently found in Xochicalco (Piña Chan, 1960b, fig. 9).

Lastly, we have two examples of stone panels decorated with high relief, corresponding to this third period (Caso, 1939b, 2:176, fig. 16). There are also other stones, found during excavation in stratified situations, which give us reliable proof that they were carved in Period IIIA.

Work done in the Mixteca has also provided examples of the high-quality sculpture of the Classic period. Here, too, symbolic representations are more common than human figures. I have already published several of these stones (Caso, 1956, figs. 3, 5; pls. 3, 4), but I was told of a magnificent stela in Guadalupe Santa Ana by Berlin, who sent me a photograph taken by Dr. Erardo Weihmann C. of Mexico City. Thanks to the latter I am able to publish this (fig. 20). The front of the stela shows a Mixtec year symbol, within which a thatched-roof house stands on a double platform. Below are what seem to be two bars and one or three dots. They would read: Year 11 or 13 House. The other side of the stone has a representation of a tiger skin crossed by an arrow with a numeral dot, perhaps the day 1 Reed.

In the same locality are other stones; one is important because it depicts a serpent-man, probably Quetzalcoatl. It probably dates from the Postclassic period, as do the stones I have published (Caso, 1950, pl. 5, fig. 8; pls. 10, 11), as well as many of the surviving objects of wood and bone which are proof of the exquisite ability of the Mixtec sculptors of that period.

There exist in Teotitlan del Camino several stones of this Mixtec style whose similarity to the paintings of Mitla has already been noted by Seler (1902–15, 2:349). Also of the same style are the stones in the foundations of the Municipal Palace of Mitla which we have previously catalogued as Mixtec. They are very different from the stone found as building material in Tomb 7 at Mitla which is definitely of Zapotec style (Caso and Rubín de la Borbolla, 1936, pp. 6, 7, 11, and pertinent plates).

This Mixtec style persisted until the end of the historical period, as the stone of Cuilapan (which we published in 1928) shows, and even into the colonial period, as can be seen in the beautiful shield of Tilantongo (fig. 21).

FIG. 23—STONE AT ETLA

PERIODS IIIB AND IV

Of the final period of Monte Alban, Period IIIB, and the one which followed after the metropolis had been abandoned during the historical period, we have many examples.

We believe that Stelae 9 and 10 and all the stones which formed the adoratorio at the northeast angle of the north platform (Stela 15, Door Jambs 1, 2, 3, and Lintel 1) belong to Period IIIB. Acosta found in this adoratorio an offering which contained a vessel typical of this last pottery period. Jambs 4 and 5 of the adoratorio at the center of the stairway on the north platform, opposite Stela 9 (Caso, 1928; Acosta, 1958) must also belong to this period. We believe that Lintels 1 of Zaachila and Cuilapan must be assigned to the same period, for the similarity between the central part of the Zaachila lintel and the glyph in B5 position on the north side of Stela 9 is remarkable. This glyph (fig. 22) shows a god descending from the sky and throwing something over the earth (fig. 22,*a–e*). But the glyph is enclosed in a border, the inner side of which is decorated with volutes.

FIG. 24—"EL CABALLITO BLANCO" MURAL

These elements, although appearing in the previous period (fig. 22,*f*), again become characteristic of the last sculptures of Monte Alban and of many other Oaxaca sites (fig. 22,*g*).

Characteristic of this period are stones on which the figure of a person appears on a hand-barrow or on a hill which signifies a place name (fig. 23). On other stones a god descends from the sky (fig. 22).

Also of the same period is the tomb of Xoxo explored by Sologuren and of which a drawing is published by Seler (1902–23, 2:335, fig. 60,*c*) showing in combined carved sculpture and stucco modeling a tiger or a bat and the date: year 1 E (Turquoise), day 5 F (Owl). In this tomb there appears a painting of red frets which we shall mention later.

MURAL PAINTING IN OAXACA

Our knowledge of murals in Oaxaca is almost exclusively of funerary paintings. Not one of the surviving temples, with the exception of Mitla, still boasts paintings, although it is clear from a few fragments of stucco in Mound H at Monte Alban that the walls of Zapotec buildings were also decorated with paintings. As a rule, however, the extant stuccos lack this form of decoration.

If, on the other hand, we accept what the Mixtec codices tell us, temples and palaces were painted very colorfully, although paintings of scenes, people, or animals, common in the art of the Mayas and Teotihuacan, are rare. Instead, decoration is geometric and consists, almost always, in the motif which the Mexicans called *xicalcoliuhqui*.

Stylistically, mural painting in Oaxaca must be considered as part of Mesoamerican wall painting (Caso, 1962). Its characteristics are: the utilization of mineral colors, excepting, perhaps, black, which is made with charcoal; the application of the colors *al fresco* in almost all cases, except for blue and green which seem to have been applied in tempera; the use of one or two reds which were sometimes diluted to pinks; and the use of yellow ochre, green, or turquoise blue and black. White was used as a base color. Neither brown nor purple appears in the paintings of Oaxaca. The colors were applied "flat" without any shading to suggest highlight or shadow or perspective although occasionally foreshortening was used.

People and animals are never shown in front view. For profile representation half the object is seen from the front; many details, to make them clearer, were put in front view even when the person was in profile.

As clearly seen in Tomb 104, the painter began by making an outline on the wall, using a dilute red paint. Afterwards, he filled the various areas with colors and finished by applying black lines to separate these areas. Sometimes the final delineation and the original outline do not coincide because the painter has made some changes.

The painting of Oaxaca has a religious motif, as seems usual with Mesoamerican paintings. It is thus very rigid and hieratic; its purpose is to represent symbols, not to suggest reality. The rarity of mural paint-

Fig. 25—MURALS OF TOMB 72, MONTE ALBAN

Fig. 26—MURALS OF TOMB 105, MONTE ALBAN

Fig. 27—MURALS OF TOMB 104, MONTE ALBAN

ings prevents our following its evolution as we have done with pottery, architecture, sculpture, stonework, and writing. Although we cannot assign them to a precise period, probably the oldest-known paintings in Oaxaca are the pictographs on rocks in the Tlacolula region, found in the site called "El Caballito Blanco" (fig. 24). Like the greater part of rock paintings of this type, they are difficult to interpret. Some would like to see in them an insect skimming across the water, perhaps the one which the Mexicans called *axayacatl.*

We have no mural paintings which surely belong to Period I. We have found in several tombs of this era a red paint smeared on the walls and roof, but this is a funerary custom rather than a decoration—it may even have been done for magical reasons. It was continued until the end of the occupation of Monte Alban in the form of three large red patches on the stones and walls of the tombs. Nor can we be sure that there were paintings in tombs at the end of the Preclassic, in Period II, for we have found none definitely attributable to this period.

Tomb 72, however, which is earlier than Period III, was robbed and refilled by the makers of Tomb 58. It is of great size and lacks a façade, as do those of Period II, and the style of the paintings is very different from those of the Classic period. These paintings (fig. 25) are done in red paint only. The decoration, on the two walls and the inner end, consisted of a broad red band bordering the walls to form a massive frame. On the north wall the glyphs of the day 7G and 3L were painted on a large scale. They were indicated with the head of the god of Glyph L, or Pitao Cozobi, god of maize; and, as we know, the rain god Cocijo used to be called calendrically 3L (Caso and Bernal, 1952, pp. 34, 94–101). On the south wall are the glyphs 8L and 10E or Turquoise. The figures on the end wall are destroyed, but the numeral 13 can be seen on the right and the numeral 7, accompanied by the element which ends the inscription, is on the left (Caso, 1928). All these glyphs are inside frames; the point at the top and sides is finished with the trilobed or crenelated element which always accompanied points in Zapotec art.

We do, however, possess some examples from Period III, or Classic Zapotec, which allow us to study the mural paintings of this period in detail. The strong influence which Teotihuacan then exerted on the whole culture of this period can be seen clearly in the paintings.

The two tombs (105 and 112) which we can place in this period show this to be so. Both tombs were empty. The first is cruciform and was probably an ossuary, for, although it had not been robbed, we found only bones in it; the second was not only sacked by the builders of Tomb 103 (referred to later) but also the wall of the tomb had been crisscrossed with a sharp tool as a sign of hate or at least contempt for its original builders.

Elsewhere (Caso, 1938) we reproduced pictures of the tomb in color; photographs, also in color, were published by UNESCO (Bernal, 1958d, pls. 8, 9). For this reason we have reproduced here only parts of the north wall (fig. 26). The tomb was painted twice, a fact which may explain why, although it has not been robbed, we found nothing in it; it is very probable that anything in it was taken out by those who did the second painting. Painted on the interior was a scene showing nine gods and nine goddesses paired in a procession. Three gods and three goddesses face the inner end of the tomb, on which can be seen the large Glyph 13 Death. Four gods and four goddesses, arranged in four pairs, are on the north and south walls. On the door panels or jambs are two seated pairs, one on each side, but the paint is almost destroyed. The nine pairs of deities seem to suggest the pairs of infernal gods which the Popol Vuh (Recinos, 1947) mentions, and which are also referred to in the Codex Rios.

In the section reproduced here the glyph for the sky can be seen; it is formed by the duplication of the face of the god with helmet crest of a broad-beaked bird (Caso, 1928, fig. 12), from which hang three starlike eyes. At each side of this glyph is a stylized pouch.

The four deities, like all others in this tomb, are shown as old people with toothless mouths. The first is a goddess called 7 Turquoise, who stands with arms crossed. She is richly clothed with huipil and skirt and adorned with a necklace and strings of jade beads around her ankles. She wears a great headdress decorated with the mask of the sky gods and with flowers; like her companions, she is singing. We cannot interpret the other glyphs in front of her. Behind comes her partner, called 1,I (?)

Fig. 28—MURAL ON NORTH WALL OF TOMB 104, MONTE ALBAN. Figure probably represents the maize god.

Fig. 29—MURAL OF TOMB 10, MONTE ALBAN

(Caso, 1938), before him is a flower glyph. His eye is surrounded by a blue ring as if he were a rain god. He clutches a lance and wears a large headdress of feathers. Behind him is a goddess whose name seems to be 1 Water (?) and higher up is a glyph of the "hill" with three numeral dots. Like the other goddess, she is richly dressed; her headdress has a mask at the front and many tassels. She probably represents the water goddess, whom the Aztecs called Chalchihuitlicue (Caso and Bernal, 1952, pp. 280–82). Her companion, who is walking behind her, is the god called 8 Turquoise, who also appears on the Lápida de Bazán (Caso, 1938, p. 18) in association with the god of Monte Alban, 3 Turquoise. His *maxtlatl* is decorated in the same way and he carries a bag in his hand; but here he is holding a bone-tipped lance, and we do not know if his very complicated headdress corresponds with that of the Lápida de Bazán, for a piece is missing from this.

The paintings decorating Tomb 112 may be earlier than those of Tomb 105. The painting of Tomb 112 was defaced by the people who robbed it in pre-Hispanic times, for it was below an intact layer of stucco which would correspond to the period of Tombs 103 and 104. As descriptions and pictures of Tomb 112 have never been published, we shall discuss this more fully.

The two walls of the tomb represent panels decorated above and below by bands which stand out, against a red background, as green volutes between two yellow lines, similar to those mentioned in the tomb of Xoxo. These bands of color continue along both sides and on the inner end of the tomb. Below the lower band is a decoration which seems to consist of a border of jade pendants. The door jambs are decorated with complicated glyphs which we cannot read, but the principal one suggests the glyph of the planet Venus. It is cruciform, picked out in red, bordered with yellow on the green background.

On each of the side walls are two niches separated by a single stone and placed near the roof. The ground color on these walls was red as far in as the line of the niches and white towards the far end of the tomb. The decoration, as in Tomb 105, consisted of a procession of old men and women richly attired. The red outline of some of these figures is still visible and two are relatively well preserved, one of a woman called 10 Serpent and the other of a man called 4P, over whose glyph two human footprints are painted in yellow in an ascending position. It is this figure that appears to have been mutilated by the crisscross lines.

Like the persons of Tomb 105 he has in one hand a lance with a bone tip and in the other a large bag. An eagle's head can be seen in his headdress. At one side above his glyph a god is descending (a theme common in the stone carvings of the last period), and the rattles of a snake are visible. The other surviving glyphs cannot be read with certainty.

The style of drawing in Period IIIA seems very much finer than that of the transition period between IIIA and IIIB to which Tombs 103 and 104 belong; they are contemporaneous with the tomb of Yucuñudahui in the Mixteca.

As Tomb 104 has been published in color (Caso, 1938) we illustrate only a detail here, as well as a detail from the poorly preserved paintings of Tomb 103. Tomb 103 had a painted façade on which there were bands of green waves on a red background. On the lintel the numeral 3 is still clear, joined to what looks like a snake's head. Only the glyph of the "tied bundle" is preserved on the end wall, in which there are three niches. On the side walls, however, the motif of the green wavy lines is repeated at top and bottom; several day glyphs are clear. These, being painted and not carved, are valuable additions to our knowledge of Zapotec writing: 1J, 4 or 9F, 3G (Deer) and 3N are on one wall and 1B (Tiger) and 2D, as well as others too difficult to read, are on the other.

FIG. 30—MURALS OF TOMB 123, MONTE ALBAN

The façade of Tomb 104 was also painted and was decorated, moreover, with an urn of the god who bears a Cocijo head in his headdress (Caso and Bernal, 1952, fig. 72). Without doubt it is the best preserved of all the painted tombs in Monte Alban and, although the paint was sometimes applied direct to the clay which cemented the stones, we still have all the details of the fresco. The detail published here (fig. 28), from the north wall, shows a god or priest who has as a headdress the head of a serpent whose nose is pointed upward. One hand holds a bag; the other is outstretched in the same way as the figure on the urn of the façade, and as with the priests in Casa de Barrios at Tepantitla, in Teotihuacan. The toothless mouth, the protruding chin, and the eye in the form of a crescent show that here, as in Tombs 105 and 112, the paintings are of old people. The stone which covered the entrance to the tomb also shows this kind of representation. In front and exactly above the niche is a picture of a box and on it a yellow bird, probably a parrot (*toztli*) carrying perhaps a grain of maize

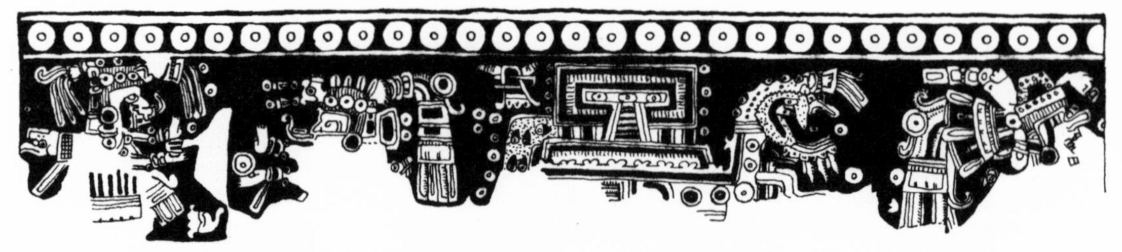

Fig. 31—PALACE MURAL, MITLA, OAXACA

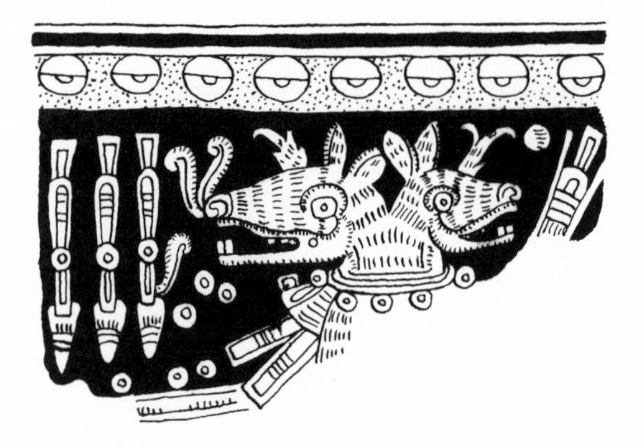

Fig. 32—PALACE MURAL, MITLA, OAXACA

in its beak. On the other side of the niche is a similar box decorated with the numerals 10 and 3. Above this is the day 5 Serpent or Tiger; higher up still are two other numeral dots and what seems to be a serpent mask.

The paintings of Tombs 105, 112, 103, and 104 show the strong influence which Teotihuacan exerted over Zapotec painting during Period IIIA and the transition between IIIA and IIIB. Of this last period of the occupation of Monte Alban we know of several tombs containing some remains of paintings. They are numbers 10, 50, and 123 (figs. 29, 30). The simplest painting is in Tomb 10, already published (Caso, 1936, p. 234). It consists of three glyphs which decorate the outer face of the lintel: on the right 7E (Turquoise); in the center the most important is 12D (Water?); and on the left is a serpent mask accompanied by the numeral 5 which could be the glyph of the year.

On the façade of Tomb 50, situated on the south slope of Monte Alban, sculpture and painting are combined. The lintel is painted with green volutes on a red background, a pattern like those in the tombs of Period IIIA. But above the lintel is the head of a bat modeled with stones and stucco and painted. On both sides of this head are two square projecting constructions of stucco, decorated with the green-on-red sign of the *ilhuitl* (day or fiesta), and two squared on both sides (Caso and Bernal, 1952, fig. 122). The head of the bat and its large plumed crest are also painted in red and green. In the paintings within the tomb we discern yellow in addition to the other two colors, but the glyphs which once decorated the walls are in a very bad state of preservation and we can identify only Glyph E (Turquoise) with any certainty. In this tomb we found Plumbate and Fine Orange pottery, which places it in the Toltec horizon.

In Tomb 123 it seems that only the façade was painted (fig. 30); and, at least above the lintel, it appears to have been done twice. Here, too, there is a combination of sculpture and painting, for at the center of this part of the façade a carved serpent's head protrudes and at both sides two jaguars are walking in the same direction, a theme which is very Toltec and one which we find in Tula and Chichen. The lintel is decorated with two intertwined snakes, one green and the other tiger-striped. The cornice, which is above and larger than the lintel, bears a fret formed by T-shaped motifs either in normal or inverted position, alternately painted red and yellow on a green background. The most important decoration, however, is on the jambs. On the left jamb a man with a headdress of tiger skin with quetzal feathers uses both hands to grip the long handle of a green circular ornament from which feathers emerge. The painting on the right jamb is more complicated. On the lower part is the symbol of the hill decorated with the *ihuitl* sign. Above this glyph is painted a deer with a long crest which falls over its body, and above this is a scene in which a man with a tiger helmet is carrying a headdress in his hand while a lady with green *quechquemitl* is seated behind him. There is also a plant in flower. The scene of a couple or of a man seated above the symbol of the hill is, as we have seen, characteristic of the last period of Monte Alban sculpture.

Recently Delgado (1960a) provided information about the discovery of a tomb at Yolox in the Chinantla section of Oaxaca and has kindly permitted use of his photographs (see Bernal, Article 33, fig. 17). It shows a decoration of red frets on a yellow background and other pictures such as squared human heads, serpents, and suns, all very badly executed. It is even possible that this tomb was made and painted in the colonial period.

From the period in which part of the valley of Oaxaca was occupied by the Mixtecs we have the wall paintings of Mitla. These paintings have been reproduced in

Fig. 33—TOMB MURAL, YUCUÑUDAHUI

full by Seler (1895) and by León (1901) and so we reproduce here only a few details: one of the Temple of Guajolote with the symbol of the Mixtec year 4 Flint (fig. 31) and one of the deer with two heads which, according to the legend preserved by the Mexicans, was the god Mixcoatl (fig. 32). I found a painting of the same style in Tomb 2, explored by Saville (1909), and have published it elsewhere (Caso, 1927a).

These paintings are not definitely Zapotec. By their style they belong to the Mixtecs and probably date from the Mixtec occupation of the valley of Oaxaca. The classic Mixtec year symbols can be seen. They appear consistently in the Mixtec codices but never in true Zapotec paintings.

From this Mixtec zone there are several surviving manuscripts on which we have commented elsewhere in this *Handbook*, but mural painting is represented by only two stones found in the tomb of Yucuñudahui (fig. 33) (Caso, 1938, fig. 65).

At Quiotepec, in the Cuicateca region, Pareyón (1960) found remains of stucco painted with religious motifs, perhaps a sun and other symbols.

REFERENCES

Acosta, 1958–59
Agrinier, 1960
Arnold and Libby, 1951
Berlin, 1946b
Bernal, 1958d
Caso, 1927a, 1928, 1935, 1936, 1938, 1939b, 1947, 1950, 1956, 1962
—— and Bernal, 1952
—— and Rubín de la Borbolla, 1936
Delgado, 1960a
Johnson, F., 1951
León, 1901
Libby, 1952
Mahoney, 1961
Mexico City Collegian, 1960
Pareyón, 1960
Piña Chan, 1960b
Recinos, 1947
Saville, 1909
Seler, 1895, 1902–23
Vincent, 1960

35. Ceramics of Oaxaca

ALFONSO CASO and
IGNACIO BERNAL

In an extensive work devoted to the study of Monte Alban ceramics, we have published in detail the results of 17 seasons of exploration (Caso, Bernal, and Acosta, 1965). A preliminary classification by Caso and Acosta has been recognized since 1938 (Caso, 1938) and publications on certain ceramics were made by Bernal (1949b,c) and by Caso and Bernal (1952). On the basis of stratigraphy, offerings, tombs, and burials, it has been possible to divide the pottery at the site into the following periods.

Period I, upper Preclassic horizon.[1] Contemporaneous with Monte Negro in the Mixtec area, with Ticoman-Cuicuilco and Tlatilco in the Valley of Mexico, with Panuco I in the Huaxtec area, with lower Tres Zapotes in Veracruz, with La Venta near Coatzacoalcos, with Mamom-Chicanel in the Peten, and with Providencia in Guatemala. Carbon-14 dates average about 650 B.C. (Libby, 1952).

Period II, end of the Preclassic horizon or Formative period.[2] Contemporaneous with Tliltepec and Huamelulpan (?) in the Mixtec area; with Panuco II, Middle Tres Zapotes, Lower Remojadas, Teotihuacan I in Chiapa de Corzo; with Holmul and Arenal in Guatemala; and with various sites of British Honduras. C14 date is approximately 273 B.C.

Transitional between Periods II and III, beginning of the Classic horizon. Contemporaneous with Teotihuacan II, Panuco III, Upper Remojadas I. There is no C14 date.

Period IIIA, Classic horizon. Contemporaneous with Yatachio in the Mixtec area; with Panuco III, El Tajin, Upper Remojadas II, Lower Cerro de Las Mesas II, Upper Tres Zapotes, Tzakol, and Esperanza in Guatemala. There is no C14 date.

Transitional between Periods IIIA and IIIB. Appears to be a very short period, contemporaneous with Yucuñudahui in Chachoapan in the Mixtec area. C14 date

[1] Ed. note: This corresponds to the Mesoamerican Middle Preclassic period as defined by other writers.

[2] Ed. note: Essentially corresponds to Late Preclassic and Protoclassic periods.

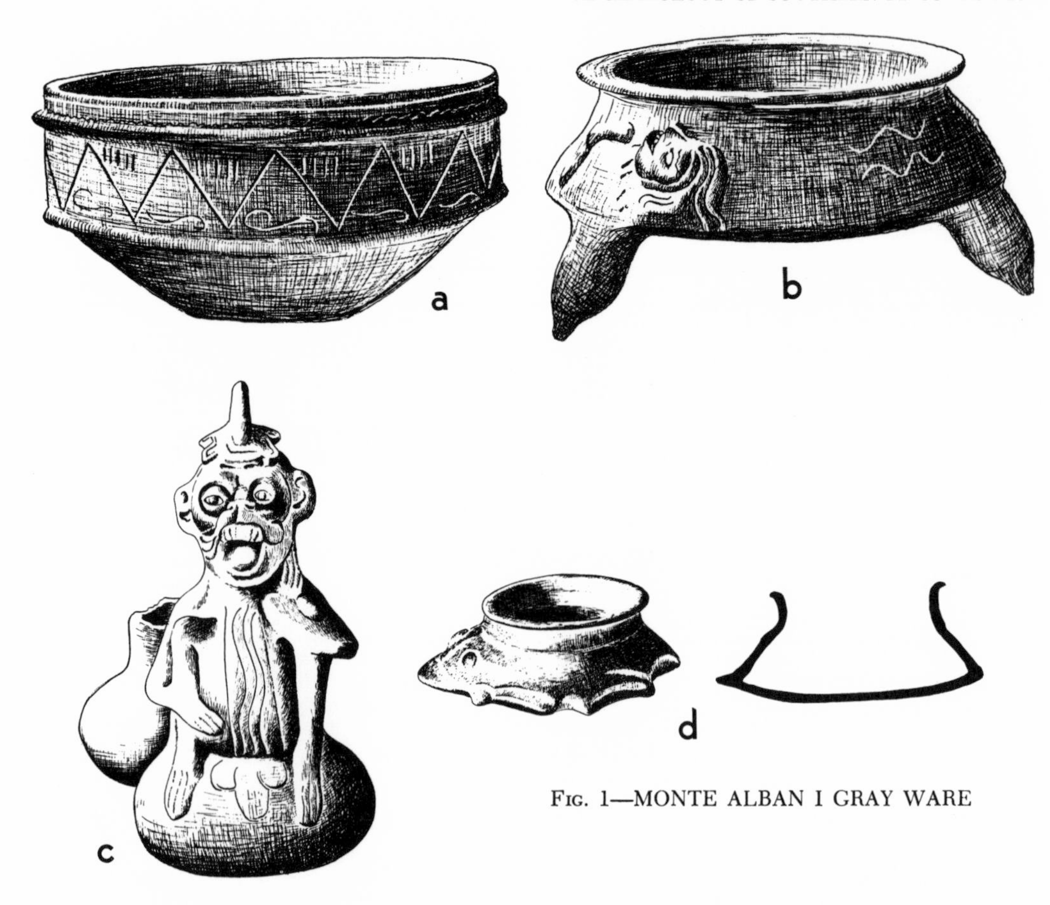

FIG. 1—MONTE ALBAN I GRAY WARE

is estimated to be about A.D. 500. It may be contemporaneous with Teotihuacan IV and with Xochicalco III.

Period IIIB, end of the Classic horizon. It may correspond with Panuco IV, El Tajin II, Tepeu, and Amatle in Guatemala. We have no C14 dates from here on.

Period IV, historic horizon, in the Toltec period. Monte Alban was already abandoned, but still offered a place for burials and offerings in the debris of its temples and palaces. The ceramics are almost the same as in the previous period.

Period V. Seems to be partly contemporaneous with the previous period. Because of its characteristics it is designated as Mixtec. During this period only the surrounding slopes of Monte Alban were occupied.

Our classification of the pottery of these periods is based principally on color, temper, finish (polished or not), thickness, slip, form, and occasionally decoration (painted, incised, modeled, or sculptured), for the pottery of Monte Alban as a whole is not generally decorated.

According to Anna O. Shepard (1965), differences in color of paste are caused by composition of the clays and methods of firing. The wares are divided into grays (G), creams (C), browns (K), and yellows (A). Of the two fundamental kinds of clay, according to Shepard, one has quartz sand as temper and the other diorite sand. In the quartz-sand clay are almost all the gray types, all the yellow types, and eight of the brown; the cream types, six of the brown types, and four of the gray are composed of the clay with diorite. This diversity of tem-

FIG. 2—MONTE ALBAN I GRAY WARE

FIG. 3—MONTE ALBAN I GRAY WARE

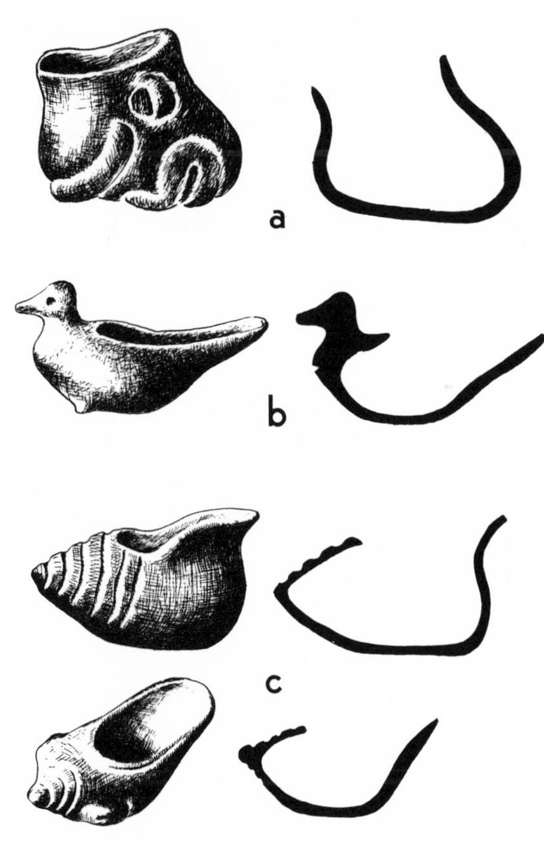

FIG. 4—MONTE ALBAN I GRAY WARE

per, she believes, probably indicates that there were different ceramic production centers.

In our study (Caso, Bernal, and Acosta, 1965) we itemized the types according to period, composition, color, thickness, and texture, as well as by decoration when this was present.

CERAMICS OF PERIOD I

After our numerous excavations reaching down to rock or sterile earth in Monte Alban and elsewhere in the valley, the pottery of Period I is found to be the oldest in the Oaxaca Valley. Nevertheless, it is far from being crude or "primitive"; it reveals a very complex culture, which is consonant with what we know of the inhabitants of Monte Alban, who had a well-developed architecture and knowledge of writing and the calendar. The first inhabitants must therefore have arrived at Monte Alban already having ceramics of high artistic and technical quality.

Period I seems to have been of great duration. We find this style of ceramics not only in the Great Plaza, but in practically all the sites of Monte Alban and in others in the valley. In the stratigraphic explorations we have been able to place three levels in this

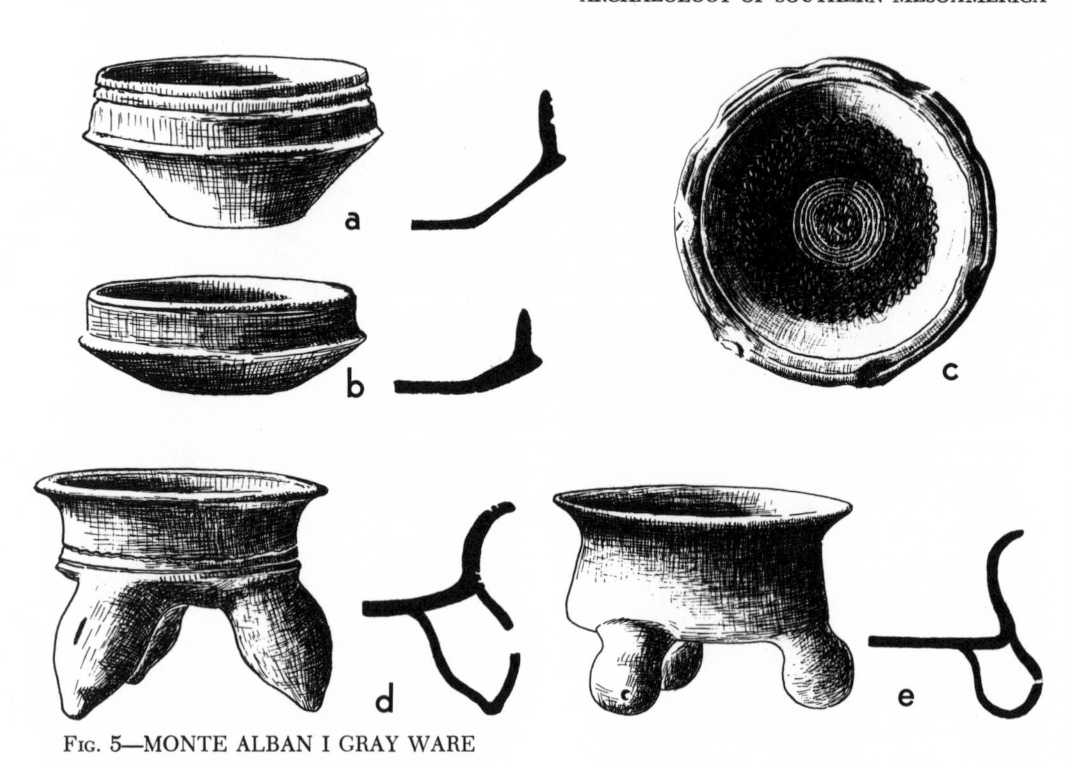

Fig. 5—MONTE ALBAN I GRAY WARE

period. The predominant types in the pottery of daily use were the cream and probably also the brown. On the other hand, the luxury or ceremonial pottery, found in tombs, burials, and offerings, was predominately gray. The stratigraphy, the contents of eight tombs and of Burial VI-12 which was particularly rich, and some offerings give an accurate idea of the ceramics of this period.

Gray Ware

Among the gray ware is a type, simply polished on one or both surfaces, that is characteristic of the valley in all periods, and for this reason it cannot be used as diagnostic of any of them. Sometimes the vessels made of this ware are incised with angles or crossed lines and sometimes painted with cinnabar (fig. 1,*a*). At times the vessels are covered with a dark gray or black slip and incised or engraved after firing. The most beautiful pieces are of modeled men and animals, sometimes sculptured in the full round, (fig. 1,*b-d*).

Already in this period gray ware are bottles decorated with the rain god, known by the Zapotecs as Cocijo. In addition are high-necked jars with spout handles decorated in low or high relief (fig. 2) and also modeled in the round with anthropomorphic figures.

A type of dish with thickened and everted lip is characteristic of this period. It is decorated with engraved or incised lines which often outline fish or birds with the head, wings, and tail on the lip. Human heads are also similarly used as decorative elements. In general, this is a form characteristic of Preclassic ceramics (fig. 3).

There are many examples of gray ware or ware covered with a black slip. These are animal-effigy vessels, principally aquatic ones: herons, ducks, frogs, and snails, all generally small (fig. 4). There are also whistling jars of gray ware.

Undoubtedly the objects of gray ware often found in Period I are the composite-silhouette dishes and bowls (fig. 5,*a,b*) adorned with a lip or basal flange and the conical vessels frequently decorated on the lip with two engraved or incised lines (fig. 5,*c*) and on the base with concentric circles. There are also certain other forms such as hemispherical or cylindrical bowls, usually with hollow feet of mammiform shape or in the form of fruits (fig. 5,*d,e*).

Although very rare, the bowls decorated with fresco painting, such as those mentioned in Period II, were first used at the end of Period I. This holds true also for the pot stands that, although much more frequent in Period II and with a distinctive form, were first known in Period I. In both periods we find them used to support vessels with spherical bases (*tecomates*). Other objects of gray ware are vases and incense burners which have handles modeled in the form of serpents (fig. 7,*c*).

Cream Ware

This ware was primarily used for domestic pottery but also for ceremonial purposes. Braziers, in the form of human heads and with Olmec elements, were made of both this and brown ware (Caso and Bernal, 1952, figs. 480–95).

The type we call C2 has wide painted red bands and the surface is not polished. We have an eagle and a dog or tiger in this ware.

The ceremonial cream wares were covered with slips of cherry-red, white, and dark brown or black. They were very brilliantly polished, with a waxy appearance, and today have a "crackled" surface. The cream wares are finely finished and their shapes are, in general, similar to those of the gray wares.

Type C5, with a white slip, is similar in its finish to the Chila White of the Huaxtec area (Shepard, 1962) or to the white of Zacatenco; Type C20, with a black slip, is similar to the type of the same class from the earliest levels at Teotihuacan.

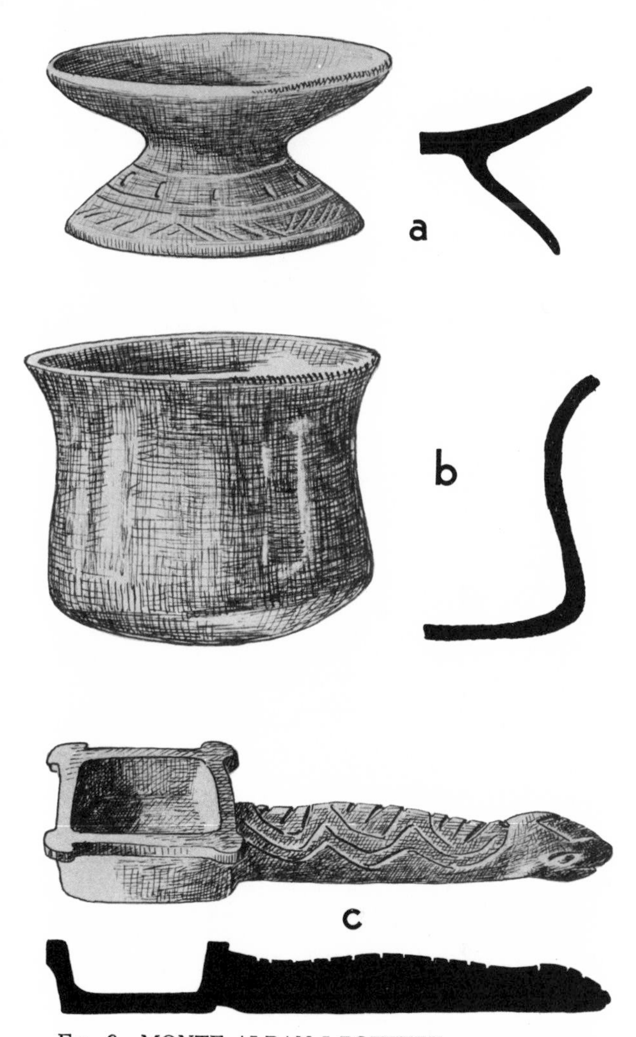

FIG. 6—MONTE ALBAN I POTTERY

Brown and Yellow Wares

Very coarse brown clay was used in the manufacture of ordinary pieces, such as great conical vases in the shape of flowerpots, comales, ollas, and also large boot-shaped vessels (fig. 7,*b*).

We have only a few examples of yellow

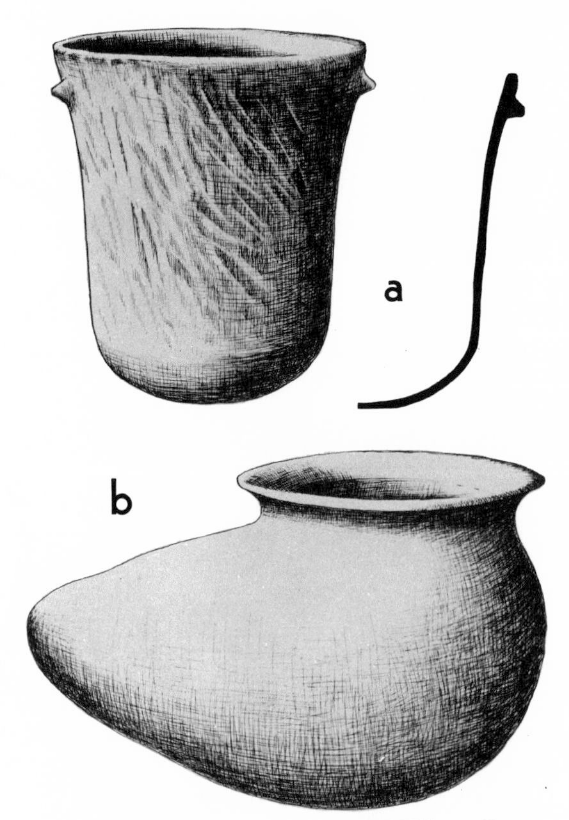

Fig. 7—MONTE ALBAN I POTTERY. *a*, Cream ware. *b*, Brown ware.

ware. These are finely worked and include a flat-bottomed vase, a tripod bowl, and an incensario as well as a human head that formed part of a whistling vase.

Period II

The change from Period I to Period II is marked not by cultural evolution but rather by new contributions coming in from a distance, probably from the highlands of Guatemala via Chiapas. These innovations manifest themselves in architecture, sculpture, writing, calendar, and religion, which shows that new people had arrived, with new ideas. In spite of certain traits that carry over from Period I to Period II—and even assert themselves more strongly in the latter period—it is certain that, as a whole, Period II represents a new culture distinct from the old.

The elements that carry over from I to II are those that could be called "popular" —small identical figurines, and similar ways of firing cream wares. On the other hand, the ceremonial pottery has a large number of new elements that do not appear in Period I. One of these new traits is the tetrapod vessel frequently encountered in Period II.

We can say that 22 of the 49 pottery types used in Period I carry over to Period II and that in the latter epoch 17 new types appear. In effect, the ceremonial types used in Period I disappear whereas the common types remain. Some types that begin at the end of Period I and are conserved in II show outside influences, but foreign influences are much more common in Period II, for example, the fresco painting and the cream ware with a black slip.

Some 21 tombs, 14 burials, and 72 offerings have been found at Monte Alban. This has provided a large quantity of entire pieces that, together with the stratigraphic explorations, allows us to assemble sufficiently complete information on the ceramics of this period.

Anthropomorphic vases and urns (described in Caso and Bernal, 1952) are the most interesting forms, including the large anthropomorphic figures which are not attached to a vessel (fig. 8). Important also are the vases with figures of animals, especially the little plates with a cylindrical low edge decorated with the head, wings, and tail of a bird; attached by a pastillage technique (fig. 9,*a*).

The characteristic ollas of this period are similar to those found by Shook in Mound C-III-6 at Kaminaljuyu and to others which have appeared at Teotihuacan and are distinguished by having a composite-silhouette body and divided in lobes with depressions or rather spherical bosses in relief (fig. 9,*b*).

The large bottles and spout-handled jars follow the tradition of Period I, but none have been found that are decorated with

FIG. 8—MONTE ALBAN II ANTHROPOMORPHIC FIGURES

human figures like those of that period (fig. 9,*c*).

The most common bowls of Period II have sides more vertical and higher than those of Period I. Often they are decorated with fresco painting in red, yellow, green and black, on white stucco background. Other forms of bowls, also characteristic of this period, have a rudimentary annular base and finger grooves in this base; others have one or more lines grooved in the rim (fig. 9,*d*). Also, their grooving is seen on spherical-based bowls on the interior surface near the rim (fig. 9,*e*).

Although the tripod bowl continues with globular or mammiform feet, the tetrapod bowl is more characteristic, especially those of large dimensions and with huge globular feet. The decoration may consist simply of a red or orange slip or both, and often incised lines that reproduce the *xicalcoliuhqui* or parts of the body of a serpent. Often these incised lines are painted with cinnabar.

Beginning at this time, although found most frequently in Period IIIA, are bowls with three divergent curved legs and a spout in the form of a duck's bill, a form which

Fig. 9—MONTE ALBAN II POTTERY

Fig. 10—MONTE ALBAN II POTTERY

we have called "spider feet"; but these are always in cream ware, not in gray ware as in Period IIIA (fig. 9,*f*).

The great cone-shaped bowls, called *apaztlis* or tubs, are also notable. These are used still in Oaxaca for washing clothes or dishes (fig. 9,*g*).

The vases are usually cylindrical; generally their heights are double the diameters but this relationship is variable. They are made of cream ware with a cream or black slip, but there are also some in a polished gray ware, with or without a black slip, and even some in the brown wares. Often these vases have lids topped with knobs modeled in the shape of animals. Sometimes the lid is cylindrical and fits onto a tapered part that forms the rim of the vase (fig. 10,*a*).

Forms similar to those of Period I include the *tecomates,* which at times appear together with spool-shaped pot stands or at times form one piece with the pot stand (fig. 10,*b*). Also the boot-shaped vessels continue from Period I, although in smaller proportions (fig. 10,*c*).

The incense burners of Period II are in the form of a round, perforated dipper, to which was attached a cylindrical hollow handle. The handle, however, is no longer in the form of a serpent (fig. 10,*d*).

Among the rarer pieces that have appeared are some like small, edged, elliptical trays (fig. 10,*e*); some pottery tubes that were not used for drainage but probably had, as at Palenque (Ruz, 1955a), a magical function; little spherical, perforated jars

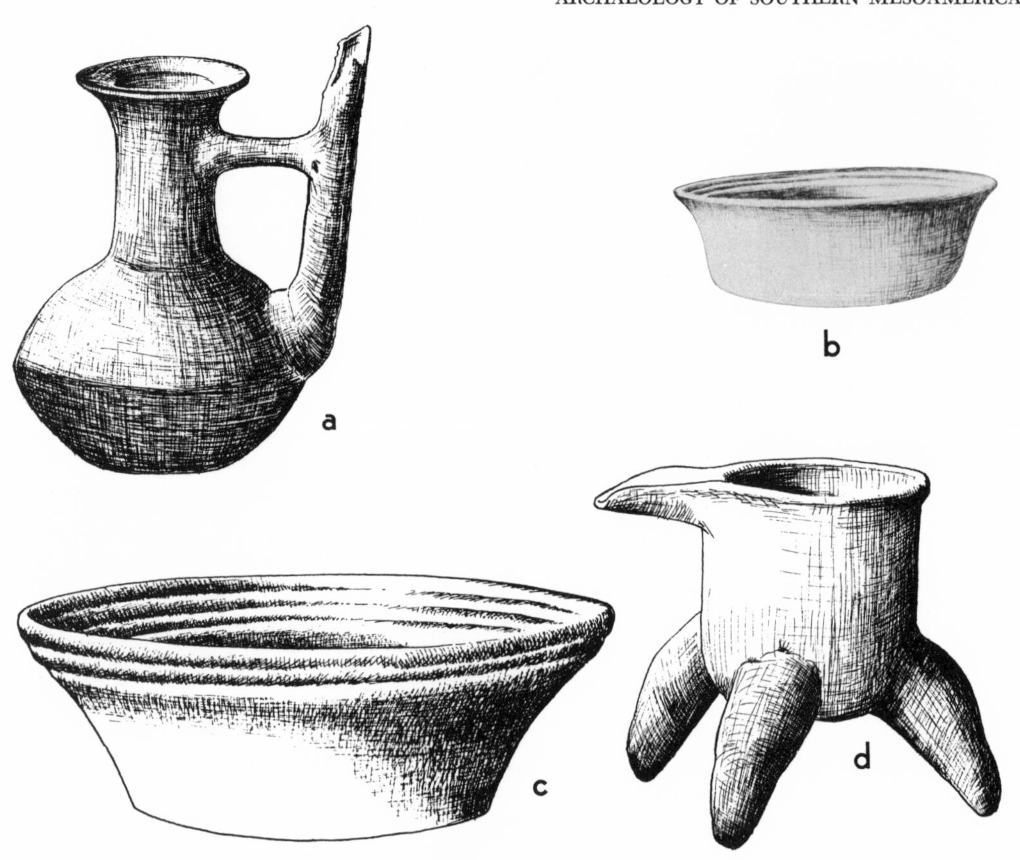

FIG. 11—MONTE ALBAN TRANSITION II–IIIA POTTERY

used for straining cooked corn, and which are used today and called *pichanchas* (fig. 10,*f*); and great boxes with covers, decorated with glyphs referring to water and with those called "the eye of the reptile" (Beyer, 1922) (fig. 10,*g*).

One type of pottery, completely different from the types of Period I and pertaining only to this period, is that designated as A9. It is a yellow or orange ware, very well fired, and decorated with figures painted in red. This type of ceramics is a very important characteristic of Period II, as it was used only during this period.

COMPARISON WITH OTHER PRECLASSIC CERAMICS OF MESOAMERICA

It has already been said that during the Preclassic periods Monte Alban appears to be related through its ceramics with other localities in Mesoamerica. In Period I, it is related especially to Monte Negro, Tlatilco, Morelos, Chiapas, the highlands of Guatemala, British Honduras, Tabasco, Veracruz, and, less closely, with Honduras, Campeche, and Panuco. It is also related to archaic sites of the Valley of Mexico, with El Salvador, El Opeño in Michoacan, Yucatan, and with Veraguas in Panama.

In Period II the principal connection is with Tliltepec, in the Mixteca. Connections also exist with Guatemala and British Honduras, with Chiapas, Honduras, Veracruz, El Salvador, Teotihuacan, Panuco, and Veraguas. These facts seem to indicate that in Period I there was a close connection with the "Olmec" sites in Tlatilco, Morelos, and Guatemala; in Period II, evidently Guate-

Fig. 12—MONTE ALBAN TRANSITION II–IIIA POTTERY

mala, British Honduras, Honduras, and Chiapas occupy first place.

The strong influence of Teotihuacan culture of central Mexico had not yet made itself felt and for this reason its appearance is notable in the following period.

Transitional Period between II-IIIA

Between Periods II and IIIA there is a short period which we call Transition II-IIIA. Its main characteristic is the association in tombs and burials of the vessels of Period II with those of Period IIIA; the former represent a conservatism and the latter the new fashions of the Teotihuacan culture. The definition of the period is based on the tomb of Loma Larga (Caso and Rubín de la Borbolla, 1936) and six tombs, three burials, and eight offerings at Monte Alban. At Monte Alban this period is known not only typologically but also stratigraphically.

Of the characteristic types of Period II that are retained we mention the jar with a spout of the type used during that period

FIG. 13—MONTE ALBAN TRANSITION II–IIIA POTTERY URNS

FIG. 14—MONTE ALBAN IIIA POTTERY

(fig. 11,*a*), gray ware bowls with incised decorations on the base (fig. 11,*b*,*c*) (G12 and G21) and vessels with the "spider foot" of type 1 (fig. 11,*d*). It is important to note that wares very popular in Period II were rendered at times in the shapes of Period IIIA. On the other hand, some of the most characteristic elements of Period II, such as the tetrapod, the red-on-orange type (A9), and the tripod bowls with the scored decoration (C11 and C12), disappeared.

For the first time there appears, associated with earlier objects, the following forms characteristic of Period IIIA: the Teotihuacan jar with spout (fig. 12,*a*), Tlaloc jars (fig. 12,*b*), tripod bowls identical to those of Teotihuacan II (fig. 12,*c*), negative decoration (fig. 12,*d*), vases with "spider feet" of type 2 (fig. 17,*b*), Teotihuacanoid vases (fig. 12,*e*), and the florero type (fig. 12,*f*). Besides these are vessels imported into Monte Alban with clear Teotihuacan characteristics like those of figures 12,*g*,*h*.

The urns represent at least nine different gods. The faces are rather in the style of Period II with elongated eyes; the legs, although crossed in the usual way, leave the natural space between them open and not forming a solid block as in the following epochs. Frequently the arms are crossed on the breast instead of the hands resting on the knees.

The headdress is notable for almost al-

Fig. 15—MONTE ALBAN IIIA POTTERY

ways having a type of visor. In the back are something like wings finished off with a glyph. From both sides of the head descend bands that reach to the shoulders. The shoulders are covered with a cape with a collar pleated like a ruff. Frequently there is no breechclout. These details show the connection between these urns and the Teotihuacan II figurines (fig. 13,*a-d*). In fact, the urns are the only isolated trait that can be identified with this transitional period.

The fundamental importance of this transition period, which probably started around the beginning of the Christian Era and ended a century later, lies in the fact that Monte Alban is for the first time oriented toward central Mexico and not, as previously, toward Veracruz or the Maya

Fig. 16—MONTE ALBAN IIIA POTTERY

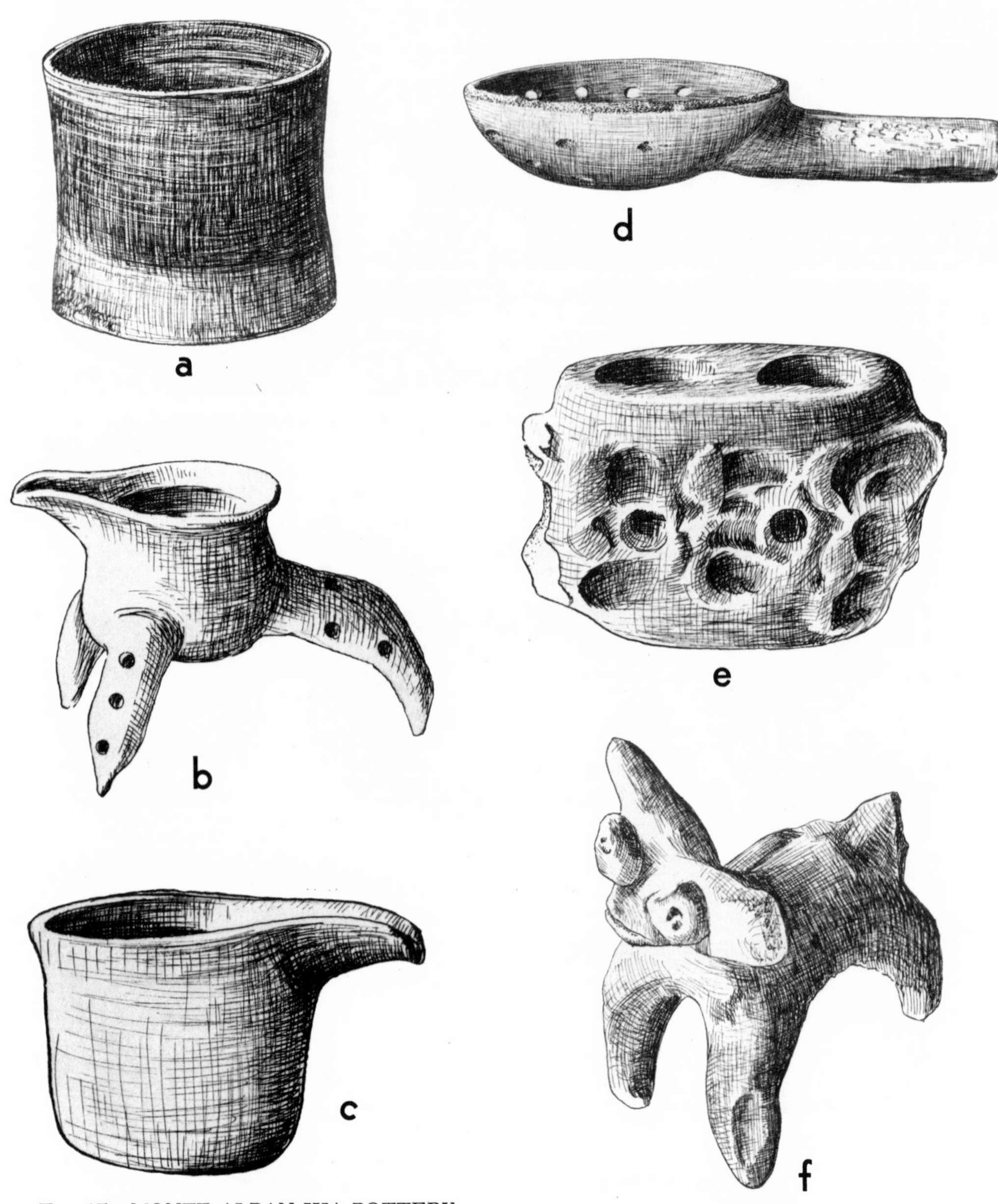

FIG. 17—MONTE ALBAN IIIA POTTERY

area. The Zapotec culture which now seems to begin has its own style, the development of which corresponds to Period IIIA.

PERIOD IIIA

The new influence of Teotihuacan that begins with the transition period is the external factor that dominates Period IIIA, for which in Monte Alban we have 22 tombs, 12 burials, and 51 offerings. Besides this, Period IIIA has been localized in many sites in the Oaxaca Valley.

The most characteristic type, which we call G23, consists of polished gray vessels with engraved or incised decoration. Both types have been amply discussed by Bernal

(1949b), in whose Table 1 appear all the known variants. The engraved decoration was used on gray or yellow ware vessels (Types G23 and A8); the incised decoration was only used on the gray ware. The motifs are generally serpentine, although they occasionally appear as glyphs; they also include parallel lines and triangles and, in one case, a human figure. These are arranged in horizontal bands, in panels, or, more rarely, in ascending bands (fig. 14,*a-c*).

The other most important types of Period IIIA are Teotihuacanoid globular (fig. 14,*d*) or spouted jars (fig. 14,*f*), hemispherical bowls (fig. 14,*g*), conical vessels (fig. 14,*h*), bowls with supports (fig. 15,*a*) cylindrical vases (fig. 15,*b*), vases in Teotihuacan form with cylindrical supports (fig. 15,*c*), and *tecomates* (fig. 15,*d*).

Less frequently but continually present in this period in Monte Alban, is the thin orange ware in which we have Teotihuacan jars (fig. 16,*e*), cups (fig. 15,*f*), conical bowls (fig. 15,*g*), bowls with rounded bases (fig. 15,*h*), and reclining dog effigies (fig. 15,*i*). Sometimes incised, these vessels have decoration of straight, curved, or parallel lines. Some of the coarser specimens are of local origin, whereas the delicate ones come from the Teotihuacan culture.

Negative decoration is extremely rare and is always found on hemispherical or cylindrical bowls (fig. 15,*k*). All are imported pieces, also from the Teotihuacan culture, where they are abundant.

Even more rare is the stucco-and-painted decoration characteristic of Period II. The colors are separated by fine black lines, which never occurred before and which appear also to be a trait of Teotihuacan origin, where it is common.

Although some of the old wares continue in use, they are slightly modified, so slightly that it is not possible to consider them as new types but nevertheless to be noted.

Aside from jars of Teotihuacan form

FIG. 18—MONTE ALBAN IIIA FIGURINES

made in local wares, we have in this period jars with two spout handles decorated with nodes attached around the neck (fig. 16,*a*), other biconical jars (fig. 16,*b*), rounded ones with flat rims (fig. 16,*c*), and globular ones with or without handles (fig. 16,*d*,*e*).

The florero that also reflects Teotihuacan influence is very common (fig. 16,*f*). This shape, little by little, came to be combined with the traditional globular jars of the Oaxaca Valley to form, in Period IIIB, what we call the "florero-olla" (fig. 21,*e*).

Among the numerous bowls of this period, aside from those already mentioned, the most abundant are the hemispherical ones without decoration (fig. 16,*g*), conical ones without feet (a type which has many varia-

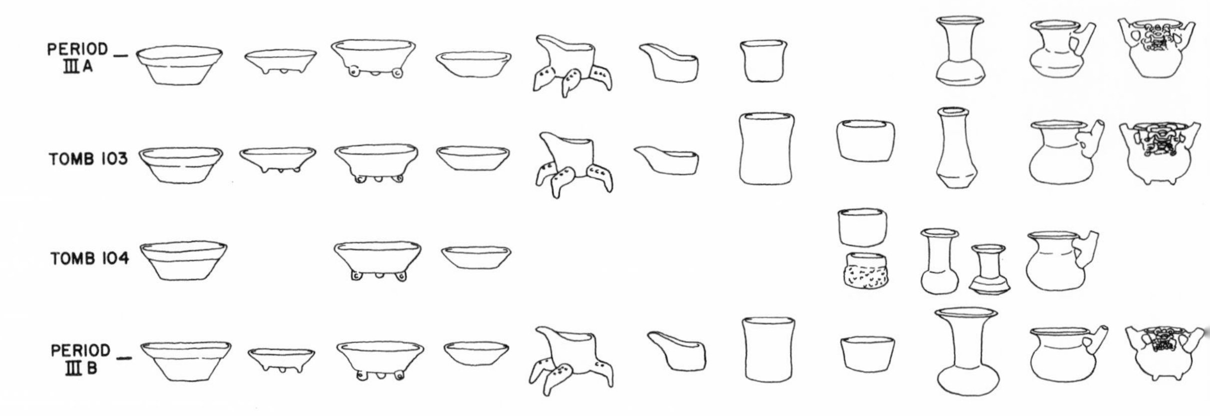

FIG. 19—MONTE ALBAN TRANSITION IIIA–IIIB POTTERY. Shapes in the two middle

tions), and those of the G35 type. The latter, common now, will become the characteristic object of Periods IIIB and IV; they are large, conical, and have a flat base with a smooth interior and a rough exterior. They sometimes have a reinforced rim and either solid and conical or globular and hollow feet. The bowl interior frequently had, throughout Period IIIB, a simple stick-made design. Most of the examples are made of gray ware but there are some of brown (fig. 16,*h*).

We have discovered some cylindrical bowls with a little vase inside which, by their form, resemble the chocolate-cup saucers of the colonial epoch (fig. 16,*i*). Very distinct but characteristic of this period are the groups of little jars that are sometimes associated with a figure or urn.

Evidently important are vessels of Teotihuacan style. These are rare but we have found six in Monte Alban; the only complete one is that shown in figure 16,*j*.

Most abundant are vases of the traditional style of Oaxaca. Some of these are tubular; others are more or less cylindrical and in some cases show the girdle or belt characteristic of Teotihuacan vases (fig. 17,*a*).

The bases with "spider feet" are made now in gray ware; they are smaller and have perforations in the supports (fig. 17,*b*). There are simple little vases that, like those with "spider feet," have a spout on the rim (fig. 17,*c*). These types of vessels do not carry over into Period IIIB; they are found for the last time in the transition between Period IIIA and IIIB.

The incense burners are similar to those of Period II, but, along with them, others begin to appear; these are smaller, gray, and more coarsely made and will continue to be characteristic of the last periods (fig. 17,*d*).

In some of the tombs fragments of tubes are found. Of gray or brown ware and always very rough, these had been used since Period II.

Contrary to expectations, vessel lids, so characteristic of Teotihuacan III, are rare in Monte Alban. On the other hand, there are some *candeleros* identical to those of the latter city and surely imported (fig. 17,*e*).

Dog effigies (perhaps toys), very simply made in grayish unpolished clay, are common (fig. 17,*f*).

Although we have only nine complete urns from this period in Monte Alban, they show the characteristics of these effigies that are to change very little until the end of Period IV, that is, until the Spanish conquest. They are one of the most purely Zapotec features that we know, although

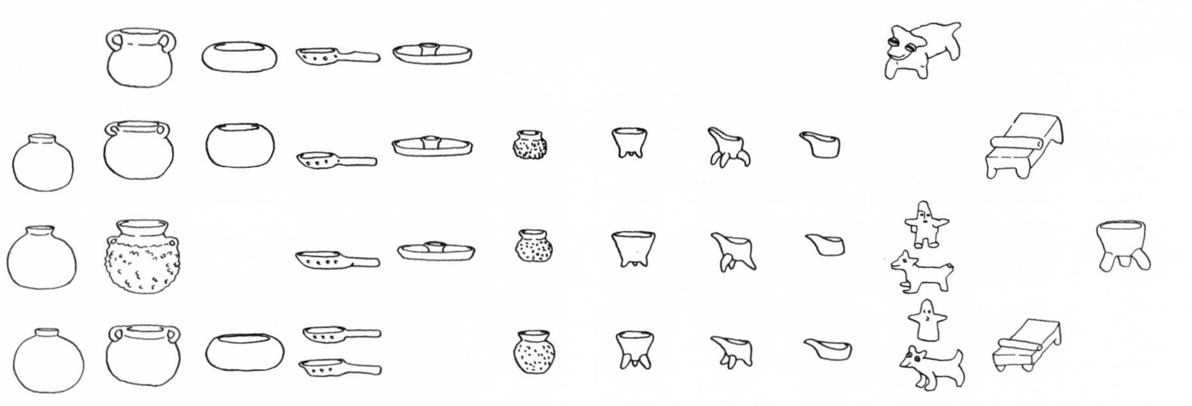

lines are from Tombs 103 and 104, respectively.

their origin dates back to an epoch that ought to be considered pre-Zapotec. There appear flat, wide figurines, representing gods (fig. 18,*a*), and a series of human figurine whistles. All are made of a gray unpolished clay. It is interesting to note that both whistles and figurines in no way resemble the numerous Teotihuacan figurines (figs. 18,*a-c*).

As a whole it can be asserted that although there remain at this time leftovers from the old cultures, and even some Mayan influences, the great influence in Period IIIA arises from Teotihuacan; to it belong a series of forms and local wares that, by their resemblance to the subsequent ones, we can call Zapotec.

Transitional Period Between IIIA and IIIB

Between Period IIIA and the beginning of the next one there is another short transition represented in Monte Alban by Tombs 103 and 104 and by some offerings. It is characterized by the simultaneous existence of the forms of Period IIIA and some new ones that come to characterize Period IIIB-IV. The types characteristic of Period IIIA have disappeared, since there are no engraved ceramics or Thin Orange although others are conserved; however, all types of Period IIIB-IV are not yet present. This period is distinguished not only by the concurrence of ceramic types of the two periods but by the proportions of each one, very different from those in the previous period or in the following. In the upper row of figure 19 are some types of Period IIIA that lasted into the transition or into IIIB-IV; in the two intermediate rows are vessels that principally characterize this transition; and in the lower rows are forms of Period IIIB that resemble those of the three upper rows. However, neither does the upper row show all the features of Period IIIA, nor does the lower all those of Period IIIB-IV but only those encountered in Tombs 103 and 104.

Period IIIB-IV

Ceramically, we cannot speak of two periods, for they are almost indistinguishable. We have established two periods, however, because in Monte Alban the end of Period IIIB marks the termination of the construction of the city whereas Period IV is a time when Monte Alban was no longer a great center but when dominance had passed to several other cities in the valley. That is to say, if we are studying not Monte Alban but the valley as a whole, this division into two periods does not seem to exist. Only with

Fig. 20—MONTE ALBAN IIIB–IV POTTERY

the arrival of Mixtec ceramics, or Period V in Monte Alban, are there sufficient ceramic elements for a distinction of an epochal kind.

The most important type of this period is a conical bowl of gray ware (G35), polished inside and rough on the exterior with a reinforced lip made by the coiling technique. Many examples have a simple stick-made decoration in the interior. We have found 514 of these bowls in Monte Alban, and there are many more from other sites. At Monte Alban many show other associated traits; 166 have an incipient annular base (fig. 20,*a*), 64 have hemispherical supports (fig. 20,*b*), and 33 have little solid conical feet (fig. 20,*c*). The same form appears in brown ware but much less frequently (K14); there are only 36 examples. None have supports. It has not been possible to establish a chronological sequence with these variations, except that the brown bowls are more abundant towards the end of the period, corresponding to Period IV.

The hemispherical bowls that recall the predominant forms in Period IIIA continue in importance, but none have engraved decoration (fig. 20,*d*).

At the end of the period appear the Mixtec spherical bowls that can, or rather do, appear with Mixtec ceramics and with Zapotec ceramics. This, among other data, demonstrates the contemporaneity of both styles during the final horizon.

To conclude the discussion of bowls, we

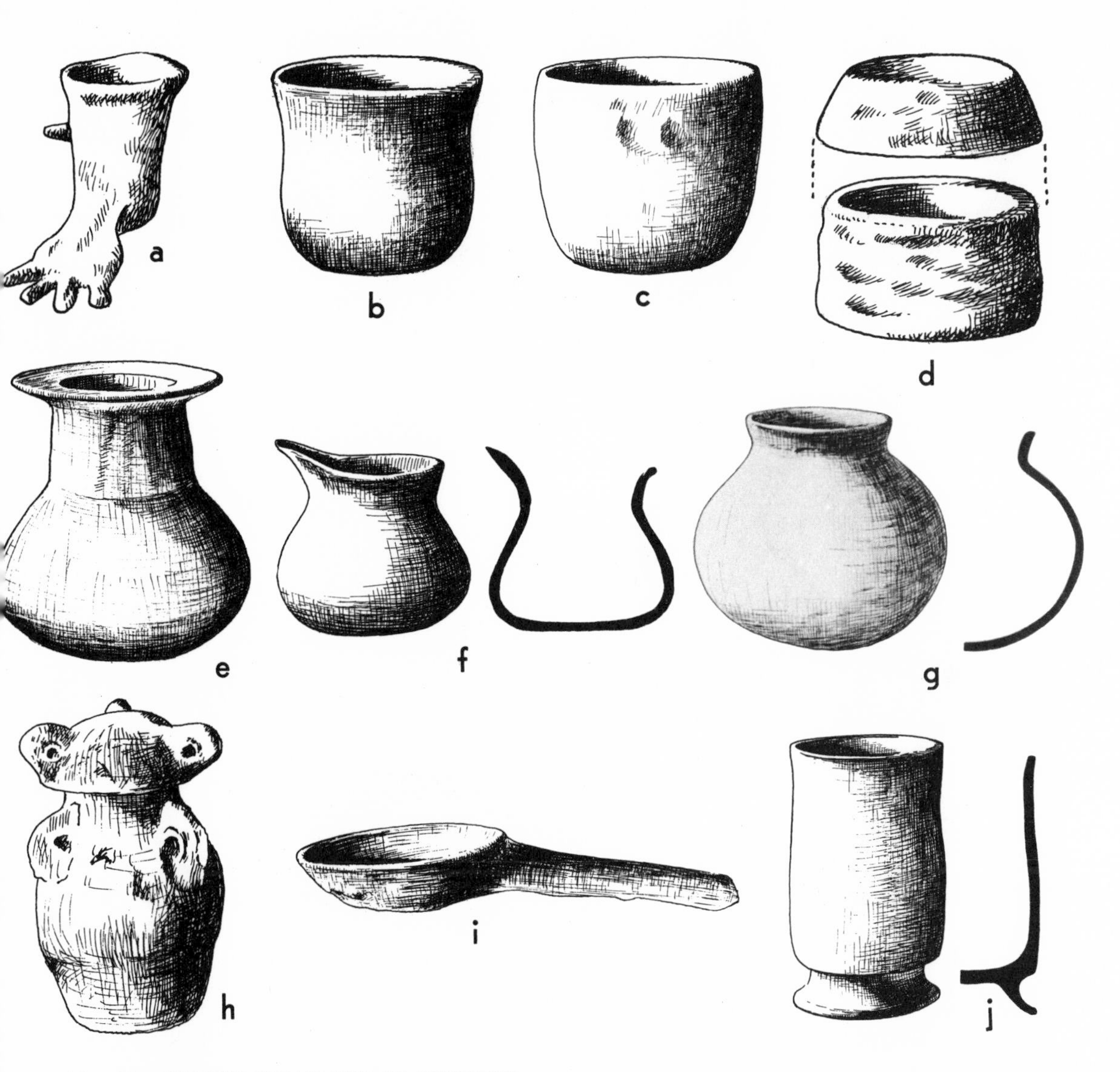

FIG. 21—MONTE ALBAN IIIB–IV POTTERY

mention the "miniatures" that may have three solid conical supports or finger-made grooves around the base (fig. 20,*e-g*). Some are a little larger with a miniature spout but are not distinguished by any other trait.

Characteristics of this period are the "tiger claw" vases, both in gray and yellow ware and similar to Fine Orange ware (fig. 21,*a*). Their silhouettes suggest that of a half-filled *tompeate*. They are made of gray ware, polished and generally fine (fig. 21,*b*); some have walls that are slightly conical (fig. 21,*c*). The cylindrical vase appears less frequently than in the previous periods. There are small vases with lids (fig. 21,*d*) always in gray ware.

The "florero-olla" mentioned before is characteristic of this period (fig. 21,*e*). It is always in gray ware and generally only smoothed. Some jars continue to appear with tubular spouts, but the open spout is also present (fig. 21,*f*). Without doubt, the most characteristic jar is small, always polished and gray, with spherical body, flat

Fig. 22—PERIOD V MIXTEC POTTERY. *a–c,* Monte Alban. *d,* Coixtlahuaca.

bottom, and open neck (fig. 21,*g*). There are also little jars with three handles and, sometimes, a cover.

Almost as abundant as the bowls of the G35 type that we mentioned at the beginning are the incense burners. These are almost always of gray ware, coarse and with conical or hemispherical body. The perforations are, at times, only indicated. The cylindrical handle is manufactured separately, being attached to the bowl before firing (fig. 21,*i*).

Undoubtedly all these vessels are local forms and made of local clays. We cannot demonstrate definite influences or connections with any other Mesoamerican area. Nevertheless, there are two types of ware that require a separate discussion.

The first is the characteristic Plumbate, of which only two jars have been found in Monte Alban and some fragments in other sites in the valley. This indicates its rarity in the region and the few relations that existed with the producers of that pottery.

The second is a local copy of Fine Orange, which is fairly frequent. In Monte Alban, 35 such specimens have been found, more in Yagul and other sites. This type is undoubtedly associated with the Plumbate, for they have been found together. The forms of this pseudo-Fine Orange are of local inspiration ("tiger claw" vases and spherical bowls) or they are copied from forms from the Atlantic coast (cylindrical vases with open annular bases; fig. 21,*j*).

The figurines and whistles with human figures are directly connected to those of Period IIIA. In general this is true of the urns, although these are abundant now and reveal certain characteristic modes.

As already indicated, Period IV did not end until the Spanish conquest and, therefore, in its final times, was contemporaneous with Period V of Monte Alban that we call Mixtec. Each day more data appear to indicate that this Mixtec culture spread through nearly all the Oaxaca Valley.

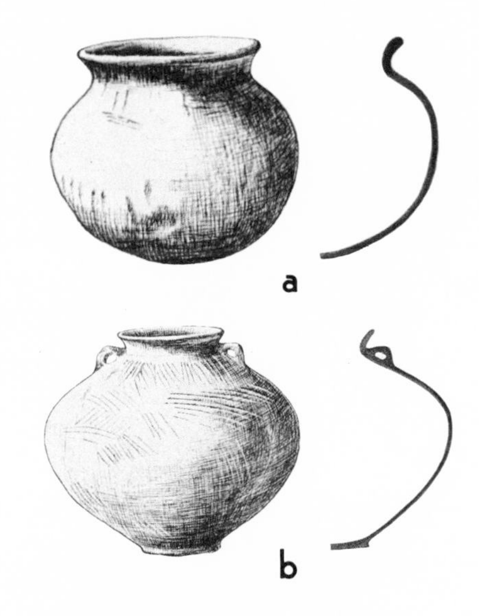

Fig. 23—PERIOD V MIXTEC POTTERY. *a,b,* Monte Alban.

Period V Mixtec Ceramics

We are concerned here only with the principal types known both in the Mixtec area itself and in the valley or in the other regions of Oaxaca.

The few explorations conducted in the Mixteca Alta have brought to light there certain characteristic and predominant types. The most is polished, gray, fine, and well fired. It ranges from the very light to very dark gray, sometimes with a black slip. A band around the neck of the vessels undoubtedly is often intentionally made. This band may be darker or lighter than the rest of the vessel. In this ware bowls appear that in Coixtlahuaca often have a stamped base and long animal-head feet which are made separately and attached (fig. 22,*a*). Globular tripod jars with cylindrical necks (fig. 22,*b*), jars with handles and open spouts (fig. 22,*c*), and goblets with wide annular supports (fig. 22,*d*) also occur in the ware. In the same group of pottery are two types of bowls: those with a simple spherical base, and those with a composite silhouette (figs. 22,*e-f*). These are much more characteristic of the valley than of the Mixteca itself. Like the previous types, they present a good number of variations.

Fig. 24—PERIOD V MIXTEC INCENSE BURNER, COIXTLAHUACA, OAXACA

The decorated type that seems basic for the Mixteca (more than half the total number of specimens come from Coixtlahuaca) but is not generally found outside it is the unpolished cream ware with a red decoration (sometimes almost black on an almost white background). Its most frequent form is that of conical or a hemispherical bowl. The painted motifs are always geometric and show little variation. In this ware they

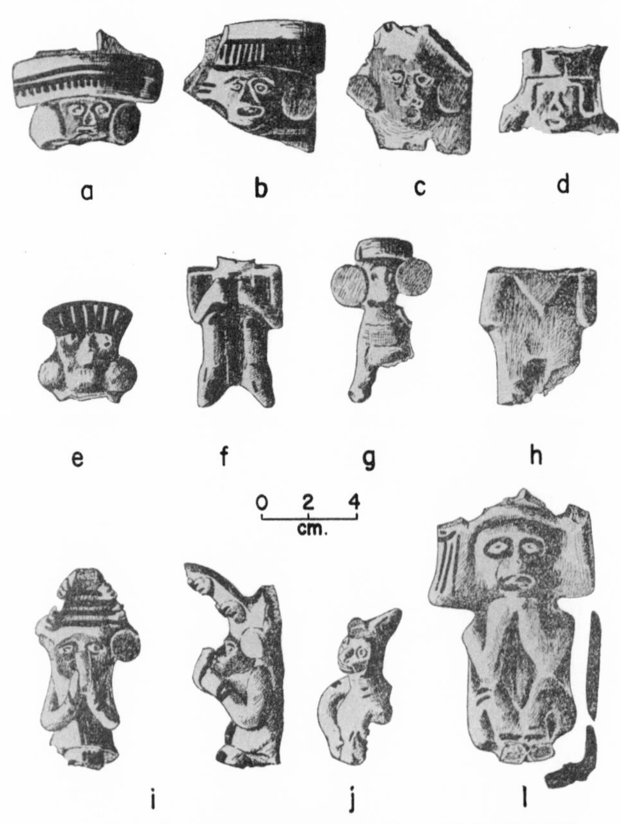

FIG. 25—PERIOD V MIXTEC FIGURINES, MIXTECA.

made little jars with or without lids, big pots, and bowls with stepped feet.

Especially characteristic is the most sumptuous pottery of the Mixtec, the polychrome that with variations and differences in quality is found in the whole area. Proportionately abundant in the Mixteca Alta, it is rarer but still frequently found in the Valley of Oaxaca. It is also distributed through the Mixtec lowlands and the Cuicateca region. Its similarities with the Cholula polychrome are evident. Many of the forms are the same as those of the fine gray pottery (long tripod bowls finished with animal feet or with stepped ends, globular jars also tripod, and goblets), but there is much more variety in the forms. Over the polished brown ware they painted colors that on firing acquired luster. The most common colors are black, white, yellow, ochre, pink, red, and orange. As for motifs, these are geometrical (frets, meanders) and ceremonial. These last, in a style similar to those of the Mixtec codices, include *xicalcoliuhquis,* feather plumes, ritual animals, day glyphs with numerals, *tonallo,* ceremonial objects (flint knives, sacrificial spines), gods, symbols of war (darts, atlatls, shields), flowers, clouds, crossed bones. A different style, the "Peruvian style" has been referred to by Seler (1908, pp. 530–31).

At least in Yagul the polychrome is the last Mixtec type to appear in the Oaxaca Valley; although older in the Mixtec Alta, it also continued in use there until conquest times.

Abundant in all the areas (particularly in Coixtlahuaca and Yagul) are large gray pottery jars which are very thin and fine, globular, and with a simple neck (fig. 23,*a*). Others have a wide flat handle and open spout. Great jars of a brown coarse ware, with a striated decoration, are found in the valley (Cuilapan, for example) and the Mixteca (fig. 23,*b*). Very abundant in Coixtlahuaca and frequently found in Yagul, but absent in Monte Alban, are the thin comales, polished on the upper side and rough on the under. They range from cream color to dark brown. They are very thin with a simple rim, sometimes with handles. The characteristic incense burners are very different from the previous ones in the Oaxaca Valley. Much finer, of polished brown-red ware, they have a long handle often ending in the head of a serpent. The pan or body of the burner, with two supports, is sometimes perforated with triangles (fig. 24). In some cases there is a decoration of black lines made with graphite.

Miniature vessels are very abundant over all the Valley of Oaxaca but are not unknown in the Mixteca. As opposed to this, whereas spindle whorls are normally abundant in the Mixteca they turn out to be extraordinarily rare in the valley. We know only of those encountered in Tomb 7 of Monte Alban and one or two from Yagul. The figurines of the Mixteca in no way resemble the Zapotec figurines of the valley, but belong to the central Mexican tradition, Toltec or Aztec (fig. 25). In Yagul they are quite different. There are no urns in Period V.

REFERENCES

Bernal, 1949b, 1949c
Beyer, 1922
Caso, 1938
—— and Bernal, 1952
——, Bernal, and Acosta, 1965
——, and Rubín de la Borbolla, 1936
Libby, 1952
Ruz, 1955a
Seler, 1908
Shepard, 1965

36. Lapidary Work, Goldwork, and Copperwork from Oaxaca

ALFONSO CASO

Lapidary Work

The jade and other green stones which the Aztecs called *chalchihuitl* were highly prized by all Mesoamerican peoples from the earliest times. Deposits of the two varieties of stone known commercially as jade have not so far been found in Mexico. Kunz wrote in 1907:

> Under the name of jade, however, are included two minerals, nephrite and jadeite, closely similar in appearance and properties, which were separated by Damour in 1865. Jadeite is a silica of alumina and soda, classed in the pyroxene group by mineralogists, while nephrite is a variety of amphibole or hornblende, a silica of alumina, lime and magnesia.
>
> In Mexico and Central America only jadeite is found, not nephrite, while among the jades of the Northwest Coast of America and Siberia, in New Zealand and Oceania, jadeite has not yet been recognized.

Since then, nephrite has been found in Mexico and Central America, and jadeite in Alaska and British Columbia (Skinner, 1920; Emmons, 1923). Foshag (1957) has contributed to the mineralogical study of the jade and other green stones worked by the Indians, and to a study of their techniques in carving and polishing.

Zelia Nuttall (1901) tried to discover the sites where jade was extracted by examining the tribute roll in which are listed the localities which were required to send tribute to Tenochtitlan in the form of strings or large beads of jade. No mention is made, however, of other objects, like figurines, lipplugs, ear ornaments, and rings, which we know were made of jade.

Jade, turquoise, rock crystal, and amber all come from a belt of country running through northern Guerrero, from the river Alahuiztan and the north bank of the Balsas, down to the frontier between Guerrero and Oaxaca in the region of Olinala, Totomixtlahuaca, Zilacayoapan, and Tlaxiaco. It includes all the northern Mixteca and extends into Veracruz, through Cosamaloapan and Cotaxtla, as far as Tuxpan and Papantla; to the south it continues across the valley of Oaxaca to the coast of Chiapas near Soconusco and Ayotlan.

In 16th-century accounts Nejapa is expressly mentioned as a place where jade occurs (Paso y Troncoso, 1905), but as a mineral jade seems to have been very scarce and therefore highly valued from the earliest times. Certain varieties—for example, the dark bluish-green type so much in vogue in the Olmec culture—seem to have disappeared or to have soon become worked out since there are no later objects of this type of jade apart from those made by refashioning the material from broken pieces into new forms.

Besides jade and various green stones, the Zapotecs and Mixtecs worked other hard stones like rock crystal, agate, and amethyst. Perhaps they also knew sapphire (Sahagún, 1938, bk. 11, ch. 9), heliotrope, and topaz, although our only evidence for these and for emeralds comes from references in the chronicles. No archaeological object made from or decorated with these materials has come down to us. Emeralds, garnets, and topaz certainly occur in Mexico, but there is no proof that they were known to the ancient Mexicans.

On the other hand, the stones mentioned above, together with other materials easier to work, like opal, *tecali* (Mexican onyx), turquoise, amber, jet, and, of course, obsidian, are found among the archaeological objects. Obsidian was used not only to make knives, razors, arrows, and lance heads but was also polished to produce ornaments like pendants in the form of ducks' heads, lipplugs, and beads for necklaces and earrings.

We still lack a good mineralogical study of Mexican jades comparable to that made by Foshag of the Guatemalan examples. Although many beautiful jade pieces come from Oaxaca, only the investigations made at Monte Alban allow us to classify them by periods on the basis of their relationship with the pottery of the tombs, burials, and votive deposits.

We owe the first chronological classification of Mesoamerican jades to Kidder, who in his publication of the investigations at Nebaj, Guatemala, managed to establish the sequence of various styles of Maya jades

Fig. 1—JADE EARPLUGS WITH JADE MOSAIC. Tomb 43, Monte Alban, Oaxaca.

Fig. 2—JADE BREAST PLAQUE REPRESENTING OLMEC JAGUAR HEAD. 10.2 by 12.6 cm. La Mixteca, Oaxaca.

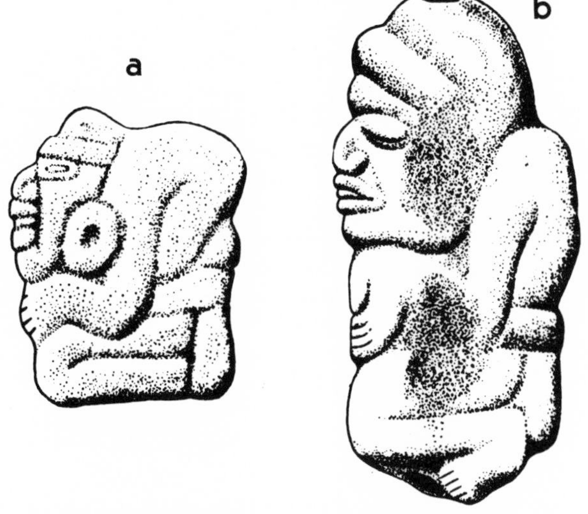

Fig. 3—JADE FIGURES. *a*, San Miguel Amuco, Guerrero. *b*, Zacatlan, Puebla. (Drawings by M. Covarrubias.)

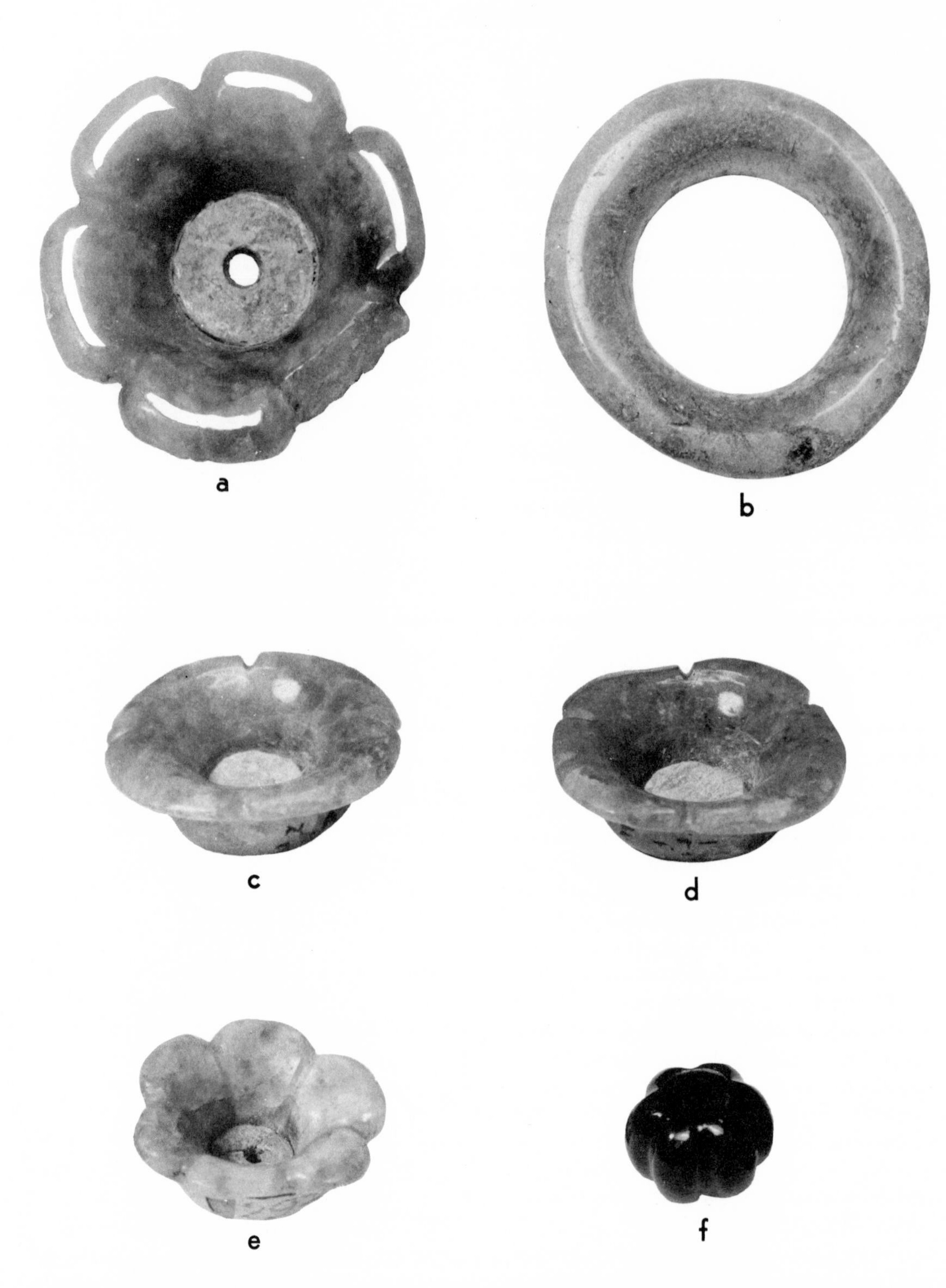

Fig. 4—MONTE ALBAN II EARPLUGS AND JADE ARTIFACTS. *a,* Mound II. *b,* Tomb 78, no. 5. *c,d,* Multiple burial XIV-10, E-2. *e,* Multiple burial XIV, 10-B. *f,* Tomb 96, no. 54.

during two phases of the Classic horizon (Early and Late), as well as during the Postclassic. The latter would correspond in Guatemala with the Tohil phase, in which there are already elements like gold and copper objects, plumbate ware, and alabaster vases. According to Kidder, these styles developed more or less during the five centuries between A.D. 600 and 1100 (A. L. Smith and Kidder, 1951, p. 78).

Kidder notes that the study of Mesoamerican jades falls into serious difficulties because the greater part of those known to us have no definite proveniences. Other examples may have been kept in store by the Indians to reappear later associated with more recent pottery. Further, we almost always lack a technological study of the material which would allow us to relate the various classes of jade to the sites where the raw material was obtained and to study the relations between those who produced the objects and those who used them.

As we shall see, Maya influence is apparent in the jade carving at Monte Alban during Period IIIB. Furthermore, fragments of examples from the Maya region—and even complete offerings including the vessel which contained them—came from Chiapas or from Yucatan. We shall here discuss the jades found at Monte Alban, and establish as far as possible the relationship between this and other sites in Mesoamerica.

FIG. 5—MOUND X, OFFERING 1

Monte Alban I

This period corresponds with the sculpture of the "danzantes" and also seems to be linked with the Olmec style of southern Veracruz. At Monte Alban we have found no jade figurines belonging to this period. The finds in tombs, burials, and votive offerings are of spherical or cylindrical beads, together with little earplugs mounted in bone cylinders or decorated with jade mosaic (fig. 1). At another site the mosaic was mounted on a bone plaque formed by small plates of jade, shell, and obsidian. A bluish-green bead showed the favorite color of the Olmecs. In Burial VI-12 were drill-cores of green stone and *tecali* which show that the cylindrical drill was already in use.

Obviously the production of Monte Alban during this first period cannot be compared with that of other sites in Oaxaca, Veracruz, and Tabasco, which were of the same date and have yielded masterpieces. In general, "jade carving was not one of the specialties

FIG. 6—MASK OF BAT GOD, MONTE ALBAN II

of the Monte Alban artists, and the finest jades [found at this site] were all imported" (Covarrubias, 1957, p. 151).

Many very beautiful jades in museums of Mexico, the United States, and Europe are labeled as coming from Oaxaca, but by their technique are indubitably connected with the Olmec style of Veracruz and Tabasco. Some of these pieces, like the Kunz axe, are thought to come from Oaxaca, but others, like the idol published by Saville (1929, fig. 92) and the jadeite pendants (*ibid.*, figs. 93, 94), undoubtedly come from Oaxaca and other nearby sites in Puebla and Veracruz (Saville, 1929, pp. 269, 336–37, 342). Also from Oaxaca comes the magnificent plaque with a jaguar's head, now in the Museo Nacional de Mexico (fig. 2).

One type of jade carving which comes from various sites close to Oaxaca is notable for its similarity to the danzantes and to pottery from Monte Alban I. Perhaps this was the style of the jadework in the first period of Monte Alban (fig. 3).

Monte Alban II

During this period jade served in even greater profusion for ornaments like earplugs and necklaces, in which the beads of jade sometimes alternated with others made of conch shells or snail shells. The noseplug made from a long cylinder of jade was already in use, both in the dark green material like that which we have called "Olmec," and in an apple-green variety. Some beads already show the gourd shape so frequent later on (fig. 4,*f*), and mosaic began to be used to decorate the inside of the ear ornaments, many of which were in the form of flowers with central discs (fig. 4,*a,c-e*). Besides obsidian and jade, fragments of quartz made up the mosaic; a small block of this material was discovered.

For the first time at Monte Alban we have jades with representations of human beings. The best is the one discovered in Mound X, Offering 1, no. 1 (fig. 5). It retains definite Olmecoid features like the wide flat nose, thick mouth and lips, and slanting eyes, but it belongs to a different and distinct style. The neck is thick and short, the shoulders hunched, the arms crossed over the chest. As the figure, carved from a greenish stone and of crude manufacture, appears to be wearing a skirt, it may represent a woman, as in the example from El Opeño, Michoacan (Noguera, 1939, fig. 13), with which it has a certain similarity.

Fig. 7—MOUND I, MONTE ALBAN

Fig. 9—GREEN STONE FIGURINE, MONTE ALBAN IIIA. Mound P, Offering 1.

a

Fig. 8—MONTE ALBAN FIGURINES. *a,* Mound P, Offering 1, no. 7. *b,* Mound I.

Fig. 10—GREEN STONE FIGURINES, MONTE ALBAN IIIA

Fig. 11—FEMALE FIGURE CARVED IN GREEN STONE, MONTE ALBAN IIIA

Very different is the mask found with Burial XIV-10. Made of pieces of jade, it is one of the most beautiful jades discovered in Mesoamerica. It represents a bat god, an important deity of Monte Alban II whose cult was imported from the south, from the region in which the Maya culture was to spread at a later date, and where the Zotziles and Tzinacantecos are called "Gentes del murcielago," the Bat Peoples (fig. 6) (Caso, 1938, figs. 4–13).

In the same burial, but with another skeleton, was a carved jade head and a concave object of pure Olmec style. Tubular and prismatic beads, alternating with others of gastropod shells and little snails, composed the necklaces. There was also a small bead shaped like the head of a dog or coyote.

Very characteristic of this period are certain large stone balls, about 15 cm. in diameter, which appear to have been offerings.

A jade piece which, although found in a votive deposit of the beginning of Period IIIA, we believe to correspond with the

Fig. 12—FEMALE FIGURE CARVED IN GREEN STONE, MONTE ALBAN IIIA

FIG. 13—MEXICAN ONYX OBJECTS, MONTE ALBAN IIIA. *a,* Above roof, Tomb 62. *b,* Tomb 9, no. 37. *c,* Mound V-G, Offering 3, no. 5.

transitional period between II and IIIA and to have been preserved into the succeeding phase (fig. 7), came from an offering in Mound I in the Great Plaza of Monte Alban. The pieces making up this votive deposit, together with the vessel and the urn in which they were found, have been published (Acosta, 1949). The little figure referred to is the only one made of jade and was found by itself inside a pot. The other 24 pieces are of a green stone and were found together in an urn (fig. 8).

In the shape of the head and in the treatment of the cleft at the back, some of the green stone figures mentioned above resemble the little Olmecoid sculptures and the style of Period II, but all the others are of a style clearly inspired by Teotihuacan (see for example fig. 8). This shows that in the transitional period and the beginning of IIIA many characteristics of Period II are still retained, not only in the pottery but also in the carving of jade and other green stones. Elements inspired by the culture of Teotihuacan, however, have already made their appearance.

FIG. 14—BIRD HEAD CARVED IN JADE. Tomb 103, Monte Alban.

Monte Alban IIIA

In this period, entirely within the Classic horizon, the figurines are already of a style very like that of Teotihuacan (figs. 9-13). Some of these pieces could be imports from Teotihuacan, and they are all similar to those discovered among the offerings in the Temple of Quetzalcoatl in that city (Rubín

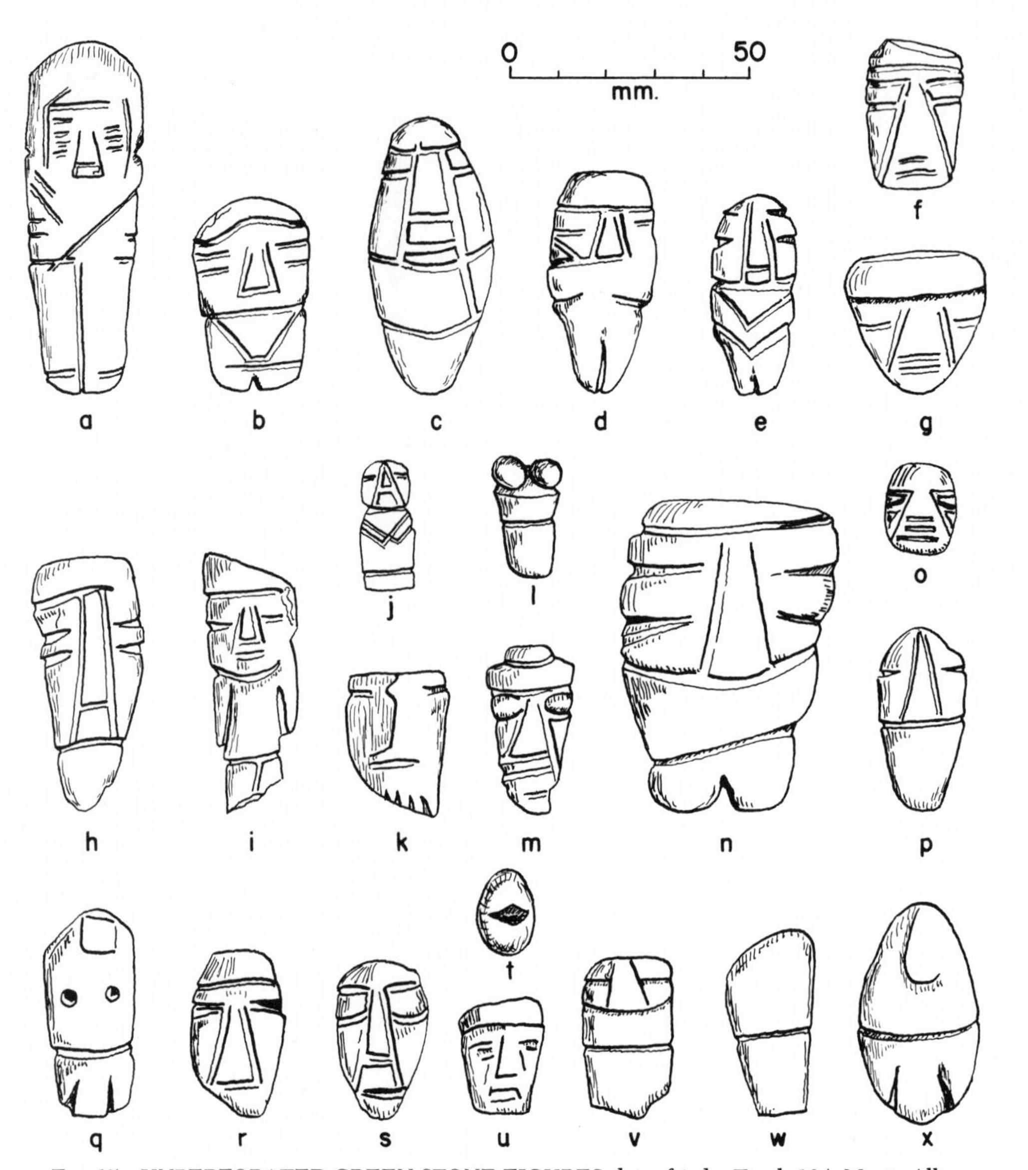

FIG. 15—UNPERFORATED GREEN STONE FIGURES. *k* is of jade. Tomb 104, Monte Alban.

de la Borbolla, 1947), although we never find in Oaxaca the "*resplandor*" or composite ear ornaments. Some figurines are female (figs. 11, 12), both carved in jade and other green stones and worked in tecali, like the example from Tomb 9 (fig. 13).

In the transitional period between IIIA and IIIB, to which belong Tombs 103 and 104, there are two completely different styles of jades. The first style is represented in Tomb 103 by a large plaque of dark-green jade on which is carved the head of a bird, perhaps the one representing Glyph F. The beak is openwork; the creature wears ear ornaments and headdress, which show that it is a deity. Behind, it wears what seems to be a monkey's head. The object has two lateral perforations and a single vertical one which passes through the whole piece (fig. 14). In this tomb were beads and polished plaques of jade and other green stones, ear ornaments made of jade and tecali, and a mosaic of little jade plaques set into a matrix of stucco. There were, however, no anthropomorphic carvings of the style encountered in the other burial belonging to this period (Tomb 104).

In Tomb 104 were also found ear ornaments of tecali, mosaics with plaques of jade or green stone, quartz, obsidian, tecali, mica, and shell set in a stucco matrix, but very abundant here were figurines and little human heads roughly carved from pebbles, and plaques (figs. 15, 16). The technique employed in carving these crude figures involved the cutting of lines (generally straight) with a knife made probably of flint, although we can be certain that use was also made of the hollow cylindrical drill held in a vertical or inclined position. This cylindrical drill, as Foshag (1957) suggests, could at first have been made of bone, bamboo, or reed, and been transformed later into the tubular drill made of copper.

As the pottery of these two tombs is practically identical, the great difference between the two styles of jade carving cannot be attributed to a difference in period. It is our opinion that the jade in the form of a bird's head from Tomb 103 is an object imported into Monte Alban, whereas the figurines and heads of Tomb 104 represent a local style still remotely inspired by the Teotihuacanoid style of Period IIIA.

By the end of this transition between IIIA and IIIB, or at the beginning of the latter, are offerings in which Teotihuacanoid figurines still appear together with figures carved with simple lines. These figurines are frequently worked in tecali and are sometimes found joined together like the so-called "twins" of the offering in the Patio Hundido (fig. 17) or those known as "quintuplets" in a votive deposit on the Vertice Geodésico (fig. 18). Both groups were discovered with pottery of Period IIIB.

Ever since Period I we have noted the use

Fig. 16—GREEN STONE FIGURINE. Tomb 104, Monte Alban.

Fig. 17—WHITE ALABASTER TWINS, MONTE ALBAN IIIB. Sunken Patio, North Entrance, in offertory box under Floor 12.

Fig. 18—JOINED FIGURINES IN ALABASTER, MONTE ALBAN. Vértice Geodésico, Offering 3, no. 15.

Fig. 19—JADE MOSAIC MOUNTED ON STUCCO. Patio of Tomb 119, Monte Alban.

at Monte Alban of mosaic made with little plaques of jade (see in fig. 19 the Period IIIA example which we found in the patio of Tomb 119, and which was mounted on a stucco matrix). Other materials like quartz, obsidian, and red and white shell were used to produce different colors.

Monte Alban IIIB

After the degeneration of the Teotihuacan styles, a revival in jade carving seems to have taken place at Monte Alban contemporaneously with or a little later than that of the Late Classic Maya style, since pieces which undoubtedly came from this region are found together with pieces which are Zapotec or perhaps Chiapanec.

For example, in what is called the Temple of the Jaguar was a votive deposit with magnificent jades (fig. 20), among which was a fragment from a plaque of an intense green which closely resembles the famous example from Nebaj (fig. 21) (A. L. Smith and Kidder, 1951, fig. 596). This is not the only case in which Maya jades appear at Monte Alban during this period. Batres (1902, pls. 20, 22) found a plaque similar in style to the one from Nebaj, together with other Maya jades which will be described later (fig. 22). The whole offering lay inside a pot of carved slate type. Another fragment of a plaque in the same style was found in an offering.

The second type mentioned by Kidder as contemporary with these plaques is a head with compressed lips, slanting eyes, and as a headdress a crown or helmet with an arc-shaped element over the forehead which probably represents the palate of a snake. Jade figures with serpent helmets and hands turned palm outward were discovered at Copan with a stela dated 9.9.0.0.0 (A.D. 613; Gann, 1925b; date given in Goodman-Martínez-Thompson correlation). In the votive deposit discovered by Batres were three heads in this style, and we have found others at Monte Alban, all in this level. In some examples we believe the sign Ahau can be discerned (fig. 22). Other similar heads have been published by Kidder (1949a, fig. 2,*a*) and Lothrop (1936, pl. 65; Lothrop, Foshag, and Mahler, 1957, pls. 105, 106, 112).

In Offering 3 at the Temple of the Jaguar (figs. 20 and 24), some other jades of Maya inspiration (fig. 20, upper line) appeared

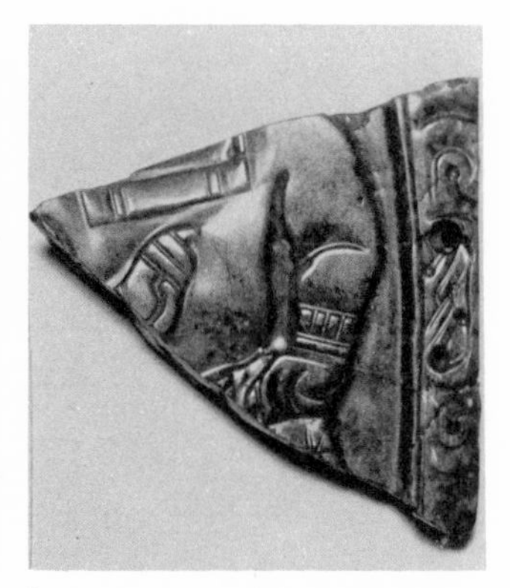

FIG. 20—MONTE ALBAN IIIB JADES. Temple of the Jaguar, Offering 3.

FIG. 21—JADE PLAQUE, NEBAJ, GUATEMALA. (After A. L. Smith and Kidder, 1951, fig. 59*b*.)

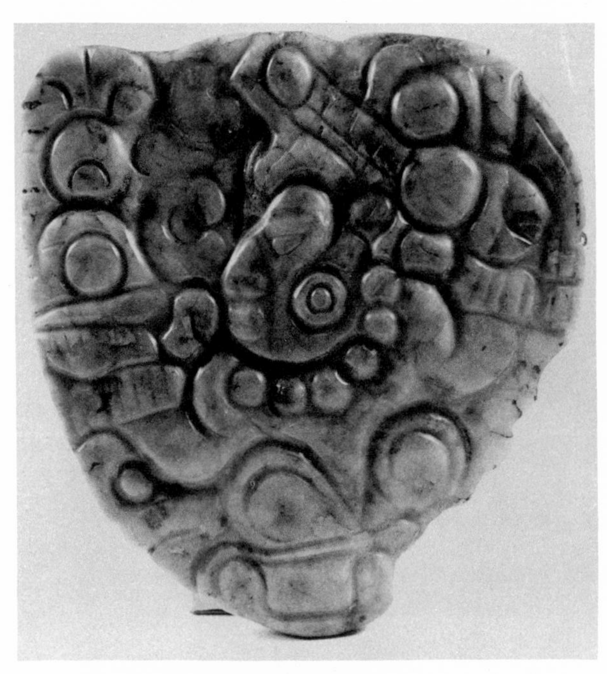

FIG. 22—MAYA JADE PLAQUE FOUND AT MONTE ALBAN. Batres exploration.

together with the fragment of a plaque of pure Nebaj style, but side by side with these two types of jade imported from the Maya zone were certain local kinds which we believe were characteristic of Monte Alban IIIB. Sculptured in the round, they represent either a subject with a jaguar helmet or else the head of the bird god with a broad beak. I believe that the beautiful jade idol found at Quiengola (sometimes spelled Guengola or Giengola), in the Isthmus of Tehuantepec (fig. 26) belongs to this style. I believe, too, that within this period must also be placed one of the most beautiful jades found at Monte Alban, perhaps representing a man with the attributes of a feathered serpent (i.e. Quetzalcoatl) already known in a similar style in the Toltec region (fig. 27).

After the end of Period IIIB, during which Plumbate and Fine Orange wares had already appeared at Monte Alban (see, for example, the find in Tomb 47), there is a type of plaque which still recalls the Maya examples (Kidder, 1949a, figs. 1,*b*,*c*; 6,*d*,*f*) and in which great use is made of the cylindrical drill (fig. 28).

Monte Alban IV

To this period belong certain plaques like the one found by Acosta (1956, pl. 28) at Tula (fig. 29) and one of those discovered by us in the rich Third Offering of Mound B (fig. 30). But perhaps this object belongs to a time earlier than that at which the offering was deposited very near the surface. With it were the other objects shown in figure 30, which already seem to show Mixtec influence in the caricatured figures of certain prismatic household gods or penates and in plaques shaped by a cylindrical drill.

Monte Alban V

In the last, or Mixtec, period at Monte Alban are the magnificent objects from Tomb 7 as well as others from tombs, burials, and votive deposits of this period. Common in the Mixteca and well represented in private and museum collections are the objects known as penates. These are human figurines, standing or seated, of prismatic or cuboid form, and generally made of green stone with only a slight polish, although sometimes they may be carved from jade or other hard stones (fig. 31). The technique, generally very poor, consists both of straight incised lines and of circles made with a cylindrical drill. These human figures sometimes achieve an almost abstract quality—see the parallelepiped block of gray stone which served as a pendant (fig. 32).

Not a single human figure carved in stone was found in Tomb 7. We have a quetzal head set in gold to form a lip-plug, one of the few pieces that survived complete with its setting (fig. 33), and a bead of brilliant green jade which represents a quetzal with wings and tail, the eyes formed by two thin cappings of gold (fig. 34,*a*). There is also another bead in the shape of a tortoiseshell (fig. 34,*b*), and a fan handle which represents a serpent and was perhaps partially

Fig. 23—MONTE ALBAN STONE CARVING. *a*, Offering found by Batres exploration. *b*, Polished white jade plaque, Mound M. *c*, In National Museum, from Oaxaca. *d*, Mound MM-3. *e*, Mound M.

covered with gold leaf (fig. 35). Besides these are ear ornaments, rings, nose ornaments, discs, and spherical, cylindrical, and prismatic beads. Outstanding among this material is an extraordinary pale-green necklace made up of three large prismatic beads, four little round ones, and two large spherical ones (fig. 36). Several of these beads were combined with others of different materials, including gold, turquoise, rock crystal, shell, coral, and pearl. The quality of jade in all these objects is outstanding. Also in Tomb 7 were the work of craftsmen in rock crystal (fig. 37) (a cup, earrings, and beads), in turquoise (beads and plaques for mosaics), in amber (earrings, beads, and a duck's head), in jet (plaques and beads), and in obsidian (ear ornaments and beads).

Eight vessels of tecali were found in

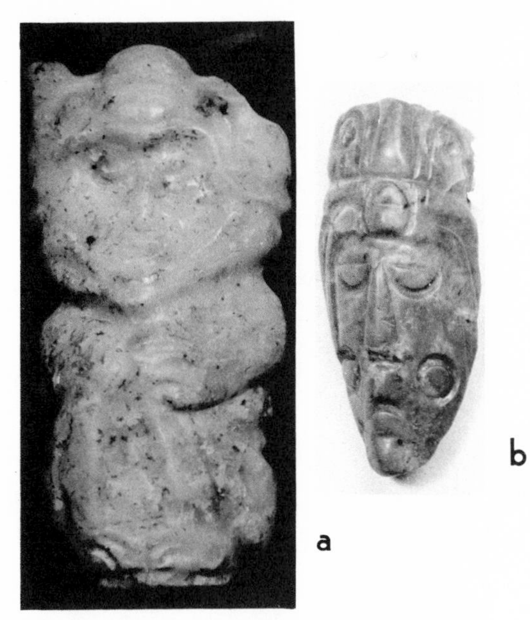

Fig. 24—ZAPOTEC JADES, MONTE ALBAN IIIB. Temple of the Jaguar.

Fig. 25—MONTE ALBAN STONE CARVING. Mound B, Stairway offering.

Fig. 26—LITTLE JADE IDOL, QUIENGOLA, OAXACA

Fig. 27—JADE PLAQUE, MONTE ALBAN. In the first offering of the stairway of Mound B (Sunken Patio).

Fig. 28—STONE CARVING, MONTE ALBAN. Mound Burial 28; museum cat. no. 26–584.

Fig. 29—JADE PLAQUE, TULA, HIDALGO. In offering of Room 2, Building 3. (After Acosta, 1957, pl. 28-1.)

Fig. 30—STONE CARVING, MONTE ALBAN. Third offering, Mound B.
Scales are different.

Fig. 31—MIXTEC JADES

Fig. 32—PENDANT WITH STYLIZED HUMAN FIGURE. Tomb 75, no. 30, Monte Alban.

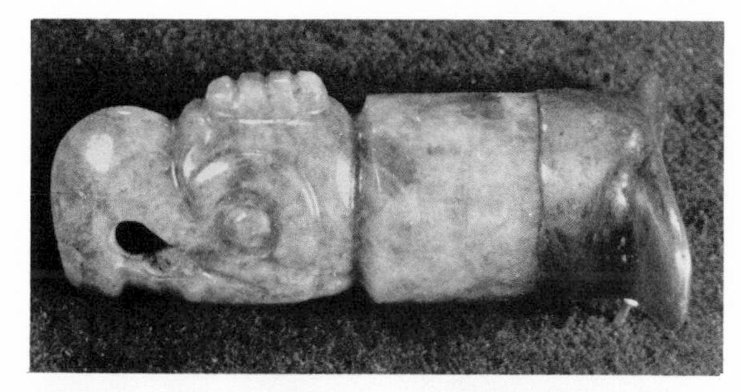

Fig. 33—JADE LIP-PLUG IN FORM OF QUETZAL, SET IN GOLD. Tomb 7, Monte Alban.

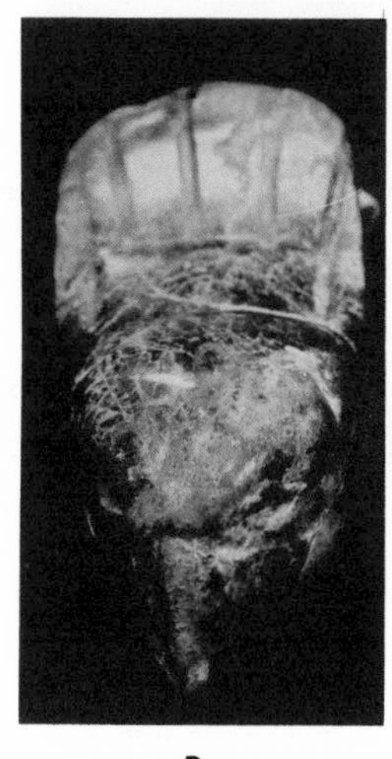

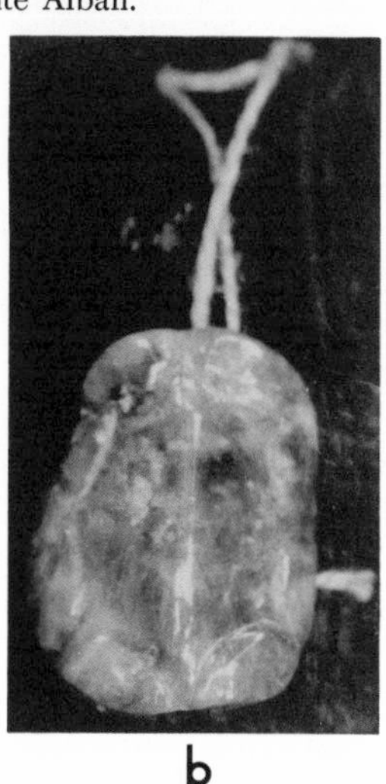

a b

Fig. 34—MONTE ALBAN, TOMB 7, JADE CARVING. *a,* Quetzal. *b,* Turtle shell.

Tomb 7, some incised and all with thin walls.

The mastery shown by these Mixtec stoneworkers proves that the crude penates are nothing but the manifestation of a wholesale and mass-produced art, made perhaps by artisans to satisfy popular needs if, as we believe, these figures represent dead ancestors. It cannot be credited that those who carved the jade lip-plug set in gold also produced such a poor representation of the human figure.

Perhaps the supreme demonstration of the technical virtuosity attained by Mixtec lapidaries is provided by the obsidian ear ornaments, with a thickness of less than a millimeter, which as works of art achieve a standard very hard to surpass (fig. 38).

It is curious to note the great importance given in this phase to turquoise, which was hardly known or used before, but which among the Mixtecs came to rival jade for use in mosaics and beads (Saville, 1922). A breast ornament reconstructed from materials found in Tomb 7 shows the actual appearance of these objects which are figured in the codices, for example Codex Borboni-

Fig. 35—FAN HANDLE. Perhaps partly covered with a thin layer of gold. Tomb 7, Monte Alban.

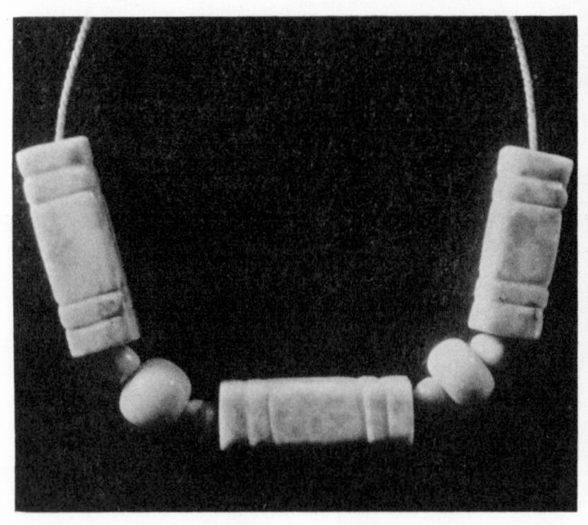

Fig. 36—JADE NECKLACE. Tomb 7, Monte Alban.

Fig. 37—ROCK CRYSTAL CUP. Tomb 7, Monte Alban.

cus and Codex Vindobonensis. It was made chiefly of turquoise, with rows of pearls, red shells, and coral. These rows were joined by gold plaques; of the same material were the beads and the little bells which finish off the jewel (fig. 39).

Prehispanic Techniques

In a chapter of Sahagún's work translated by Seler (1890b), and later published in Spanish (Sahagún, 1938, 5: 209–10; 1956, 3: 72) and in English (Anderson and Dibble, 1959, 10:80) are mentioned the techniques used by Aztec lapidaries in the working of jade, rock crystal, amethyst, and other stones including opals and turquoise.

It can be seen that these stoneworkers used flint for cutting, knew the tubular copper drill, and used special sands as abrasives, and that wood, bone, and bamboo (*quetzalcoatl*) were employed for polishing.

An interesting analysis of these native techniques brought together by Sahagún has recently been made by the Easbys (1953).

Goldwork

General Description and Techniques

Perhaps what most distinguished the indigenous peoples of Oaxaca, and the Mixtecs above all, was their extraordinary ability as goldsmiths. It is very probable that the Texcocans and the Mexicans learned from them the art of working metals.

Ixtlilxochitl (1892, 1: 123, 289; 2: 69 and note), accepting the account in the Mapa Quinatzin, says that during the reign of this king of Texcoco the Tlailotlacas and the Chimalpanecas arrived from the Mixteca. The former were excellent painters, "they painted and wrote histories," and had lived for a long time in Chalco before coming to Texcoco in 4 Acatl 1170 (Chimalpahin, 1889).

In Saville's study of Mexican goldwork

(1920) abundant objects are listed as coming from Oaxaca. Our find in Tomb 7 at Monte Alban shows that the accounts given by the conquistadores of the magnificent work of the Mexican goldsmiths and of the profusion of gold and silver jewels were not exaggerated (Caso, 1932 d,e). The list of gold objects sent to Spain by the conquistadores and obtained by barter, pillage, and tribute, demonstrates this abundance (Saville, 1920; García Granados, 1942). Hernán Cortés (1922, 3: 31) relates his finding a tomb in the Great Temple of Tenochtitlan containing gold objects to the value of 1,500 *castellanos* (about $400).

But the richness of gold objects in the tombs of Oaxaca had been known ever since the 16th century. Bernal Díaz (1939, ch. 194, pp. 126–27) tells us that the conquest of the Zapotecs was entrusted to Captain Diego de Figueroa, friend of the treasurer Alonso de Estrada, and founder of Villa Alta (San Ildefonso) in 1526 (Paso y Troncoso, 1905, 3: 11, 14, 15; 15: 83). He set out with 100 soldiers to put it into effect but had trouble over the question of command with another captain, Alonso de Herrera, who left him shorthanded. Because of this, and hearing news that there were many treasures in the Zapotec tombs, he abandoned the conquest and instead of going into the mountains where the Zapotecs and Mixtecs were he "decided to set about excavating burials." This activity brought him excellent rewards, and he made up his mind to leave for Spain with the spoil he had collected. He took a boat but was shipwrecked off the coast of Veracruz, where he lost not only his booty but his life.

Unlike the lapidary work practiced since the beginning of the archaic horizon, metalworking is seen in Mesoamerica only in the Toltec horizon and after. It is precisely to the Toltecs that Sahagún attributes the invention of metallurgy (1938, 3: 113). In the archaeological explorations carried out in different parts of Mesoamerica, metal objects have never been discovered from a period earlier than Late Classic or Postclassic. They have been found, that is to say, precisely during Toltec times and accompanied (at Texmilincan, Guerrero, for example) by pottery which belongs in this horizon (Caso, 1941).

FIG. 38—OBSIDIAN EARPLUGS. Tomb 7, Monte Alban.

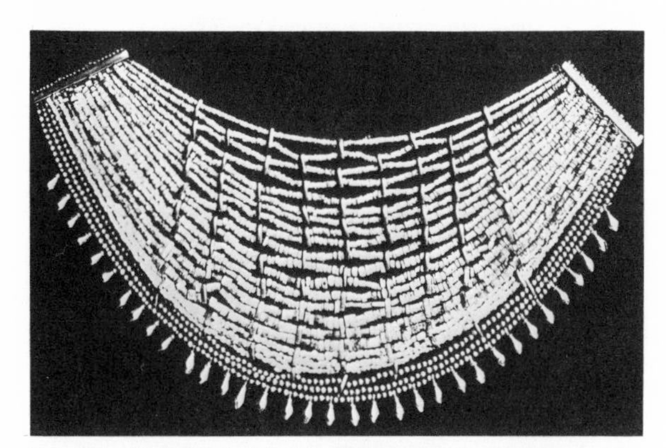

FIG. 39—NECKLACE OF TURQUOISE, CORAL, RED SHELL, GOLD, AND PEARLS. Gold rattles and plaques.

It seems most probable that metallurgical techniques were introduced into Mesoamerica from Costa Rica and Panama. One type of pectoral so characteristic that it came to have the general meaning of "gold" in the Mixtec codices (fig. 40) and in Codex Laud (pl. 10), and found frequently among the gold treasures preserved in Oaxaca, Veracruz, and the Valley of Mexico, is inspired by frog figures with the hind feet transformed into plaques. This type of frog (fig. 41) is very common in the art of Costa Rica and Panama (Veraguas and Chiriqui)

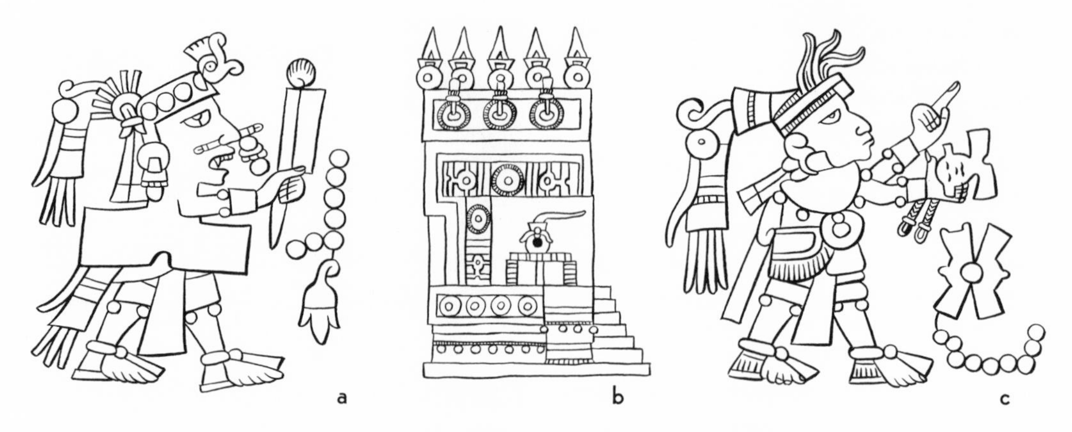

FIG. 40—GOLD PECTORALS. *a,* Personage pectoral (Codex Nuttall). *b,* Pectoral as symbol of gold (Codex Becker). *c,* Personage offering a pectoral (Codex Nuttall).

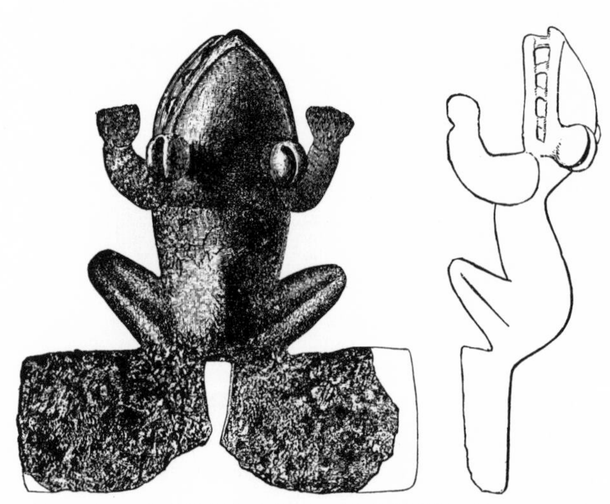

FIG. 41—CHIRIQUI FROG FIGURINE. Base metal plated with gold. (After Holmes, 1888, fig. 37.)

(Holmes, 1888, fig. 37; Lothrop, 1937, figs. 44,*a*; 86,*a*,*c*; Lothrop, 1950a, figs. 1,*e*; 96–98; Lothrop, Foshag, and Mahler, 1957, pls. 103, 104; Joyce, 1916, pl. 13,*l*; Stone and Balser, 1958, figs. 3,*c*,*e*; 6,*k*).

In contrast, Rivet and Arsandaux (1946, p. 179) believe that Mexican metallurgy has its origin in the Peruvian coastal region by reason of its late appearance and lack of antecedents in Mesoamerica and because it already shows great technical and artistic maturity with no signs of an experimental stage. The similarity which they list between the techniques known in both areas is noteworthy: hammering, cold-hammered hardening, simple and *cire-perdue* casting, *mise-en-couleur*, gilding on a base of silver or copper, fusing and ordinary soldering, filigree, repoussé work, overlaying with metals and cutout openwork. On the other hand, arguments based on certain opinions of Lothrop (1936) are invalid, since, as we have shown, the gold disc which this author cites as Peruvian was wrongly interpreted and is more correctly seen as a representation of Tlaloc. The gold plume which he considers to be produced by a Peruvian technique is no more than the *cuauhpilloni* or feather tassel of the Mexican captains, and the object which he considers a bivalve shell cannot be one since it is cylindrical. It was probably a posterior belt clasp or *tezcacuitlapilli,* as can be seen from figure 57.

If from the point of view of technology it seems probable that Mexican metallurgy had its origin in Costa Rica or Panama, it is equally certain that a native style developed, based on the religious and aesthetic concepts held by the various peoples of Mesoamerica (Mayas, Zapotecs, Mixtecs, Mexicans, and Tarascans). All of them, however, seem to have been inspired by characteristically Toltec ideas found in the culture of Mixteca-Puebla.

We know that the Mixtecs and Zapotecs made ornaments and implements from gold, silver, and copper. They were also acquainted with tin and lead (Rivet and Arsandaux, 1946, p. 18 ff., 109–110; Bergsøe, 1938, p. 21; Arsandaux and Rivet, 1921, p. 264 ff.). Cortés says that he had dishes and vessels of tin, a metal used for making native money in the form of axes, and he says that it came from Taxco. In contradiction to general belief, metal was used not only for jewels but also for implements. The following list, published elsewhere (Caso, 1946), gives an idea of the range of objects: hoes, axes, spades, adzes, chisels, fishhooks, blowpipes, awls, punches, tweezers, nails and gauntlets, nets, needles, pins, lance- and arrowheads, "money-axes," mirrors, vessels, pipes, mouthpieces and sights for blowpipes, bows, belt-clasps, batons, fan handles, human and animal statues, masks, helmets, crests, shields, diadems, belts, ornaments for clothes, the soles of sandals, as well as such trinkets as bells, beads, earrings and earplugs, pendants, brooches, pectorals, nose-ornaments, lip-plugs, bracelets, arm-rings, anklets, finger-rings, and artificial fingernails.

It can be said that all the techniques known in antiquity for working precious metals were employed in Mexico, and especially in Oaxaca. The great difference between the Old and New Worlds lies in the date at which these processes were discovered (Forbes, 1950, chronological chart).

A good description of the methods employed by the native goldsmiths has been recorded by Sahagún (1938, 5: 197) and translated several times into French, English, and Spanish (Seler, 1890b; Saville, 1920; Anderson and Dibble, 1959; Sahagún, 1938, 1956). Easby (1957) has recently concerned himself with interpreting the data which appear obscure in Sahagún's reports.

The Mixtecs, like the Aztecs, had two basic techniques of metalworking. The

Fig. 42—DIADEM AND PLUME IN GOLD LEAF. Tomb 7, Monte Alban.

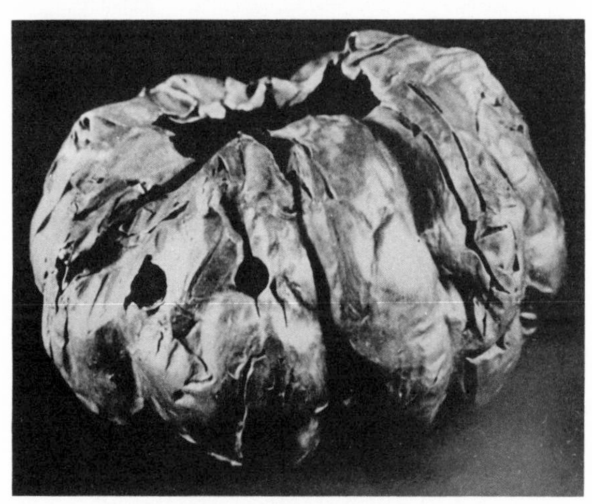

Fig. 43—GOLD LEAF COVERING A LITTLE GOURD FOR CARRYING TOBACCO (YETECOMATL). Tomb 7, Monte Alban. (Photo by D. T. Easby.)

simpler method consists of hammering an ingot of gold or silver—either in a cold or a hot state, or sometimes in both conditions—and of using the sheet metal thus obtained to make vessels, bracelets, diadems, and plaques which were then decorated with incised or repoussé patterns. By this process were made some of the pieces of jewelry from Tomb 7, like the diadem and the plume (fig. 42), the bracelets and certain plaques (fig. 44).

The second method, much more complicated, consists of *cire-perdue* casting. This is

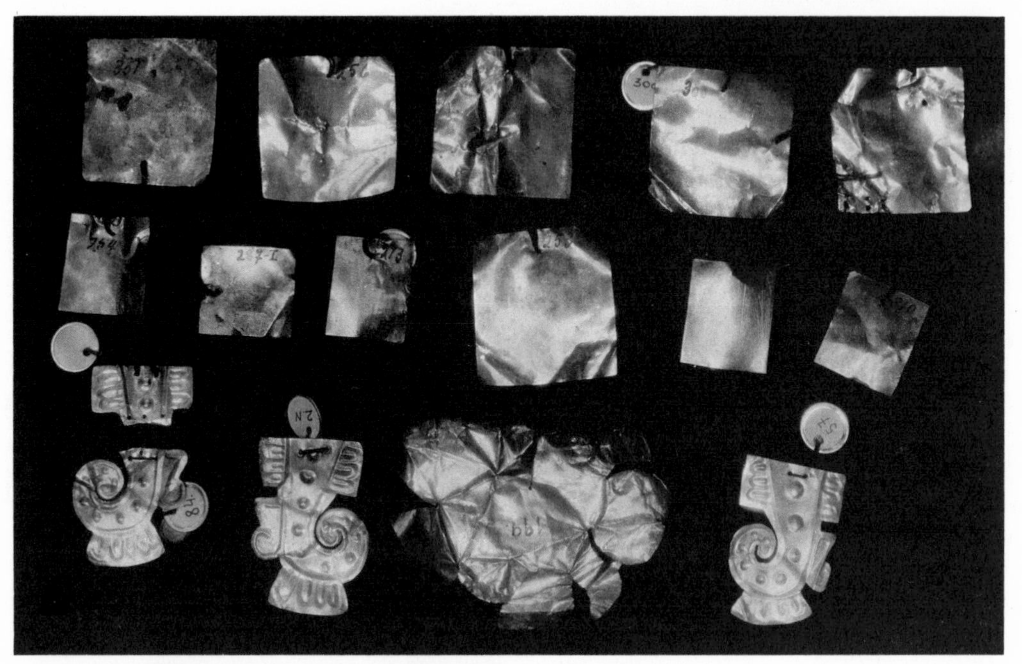

Fig. 44—GOLD-LEAF OBJECTS, TOMB 7, MONTE ALBAN

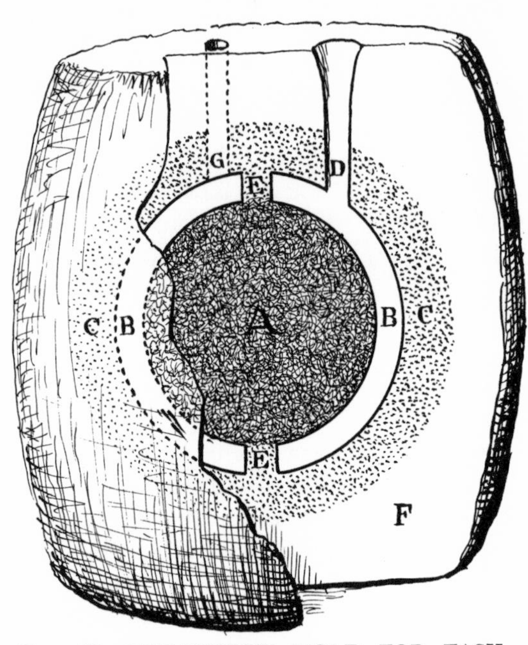

Fig. 45—*CIRE-PERDUE* MOLD FOR FASHIONING GOLD OBJECT. A, Core of clay and finely powdered charcoal shaped into a sphere. B, B, Wax covering the core. C, Mixture of charcoal, clay, and water to be placed over the wax. D, Tube through which the gold enters. E, E, Supports for the core. F, Case or shell made of charcoal and less fine clay. G, Tube allowing air to escape.

the one described in detail by Sahagún and recently explained by Easby. First, a paste of clay mixed with finely powdered charcoal was made. This was allowed to dry very slowly to prevent cracking and was given the general form to be taken by the finished object. This core was engraved with all the details intended to appear on the final product, and it is possible that besides metal instruments, certain sharp strong thorns were used to achieve a high degree of delicacy.

After the core had been sculpted and had become perfectly dry, it was covered with a mixture of wax and *copal*; certain parts of the piece were modeled and carved in the same wax. But before covering the object with the coating of clay and charcoal which made up the final part of the mold, little clay supports or props were put in place to hold the core in a fixed position within the mold when the wax which originally covered it had melted. Cylinders of wax were also attached to the piece and, after the wax had melted, these formed tubular holes through which the metal could be introduced and the air allowed to escape.

Then the whole thing was covered with a layer of charcoal and clay which had been finely powdered and mixed with water to produce a semiliquid paste. Probably several coats were applied and the object then allowed to dry.

Lastly it was covered with a less fine mixture of clay and charcoal and left for two days so that it could dry slowly and without cracking. The mold was then heated to melt the wax, and was afterwards placed in sand where it could cool slowly with no danger of splitting.

At this stage the core inside the mold was held in place only by the clay supports, for the wax which covered it had by now melted to leave a space between the core and the covering of charcoal and less fine clay.

When the gold was ready to be cast, the mold was heated again to prevent the gold from solidifying as it entered and to avoid the formation of bubbles by allowing the maximum amount of air to make its way out through the tubes. The gold, which had been melted with the aid of charcoal and a blowpipe to attain a high temperature, ran into the mold through a tube which had been left for the purpose and there took the place previously occupied by the wax, reproducing every detail and driving out the air through the escape holes.

The exterior shell of the mold was then broken, the gold remaining in the entrance tube and the air escape holes was filed off, the clay supports were removed and the core broken up.

Then the object was polished with a hard stone, probably agate or quartz since pottery-burnishers made of these stones have been discovered. Next it was given an alum wash and heated again in the fire, then given a coating with *teocuitlapatli*, "gold-medicine," which by dissolving the excess copper (when the gold contained copper or when the metal used was a gold-copper

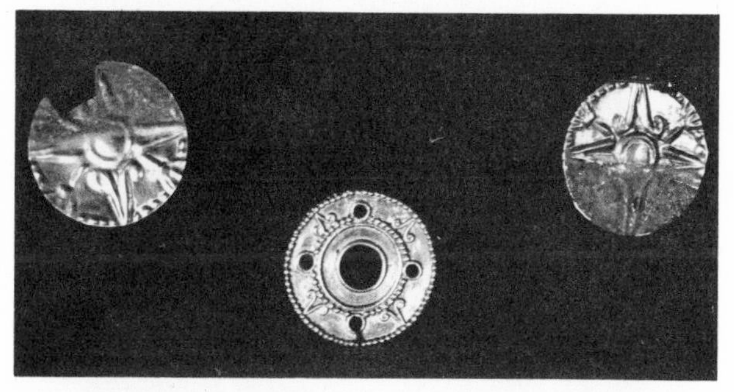

FIG. 46—GOLD DISCS, TOMB 7, MONTE ALBAN. At sides, gold and silver; center, cast gold.

FIG. 47—GOLD BROOCH, YANHUITLAN

FIG. 48—SILVER OBJECTS, TOMB 7, MONTE ALBAN

Fig. 49—ORNAMENTAL FINGERNAILS, TOMB 7, MONTE ALBAN. *a,* Gold. *b,* Silver. (Photo by D. T. Easby.)

Fig. 50—GOLD PECTORALS REPRESENTING THE GOD OF SUMMER, XOCHIPILLI. Tomb 7, Monte Alban.

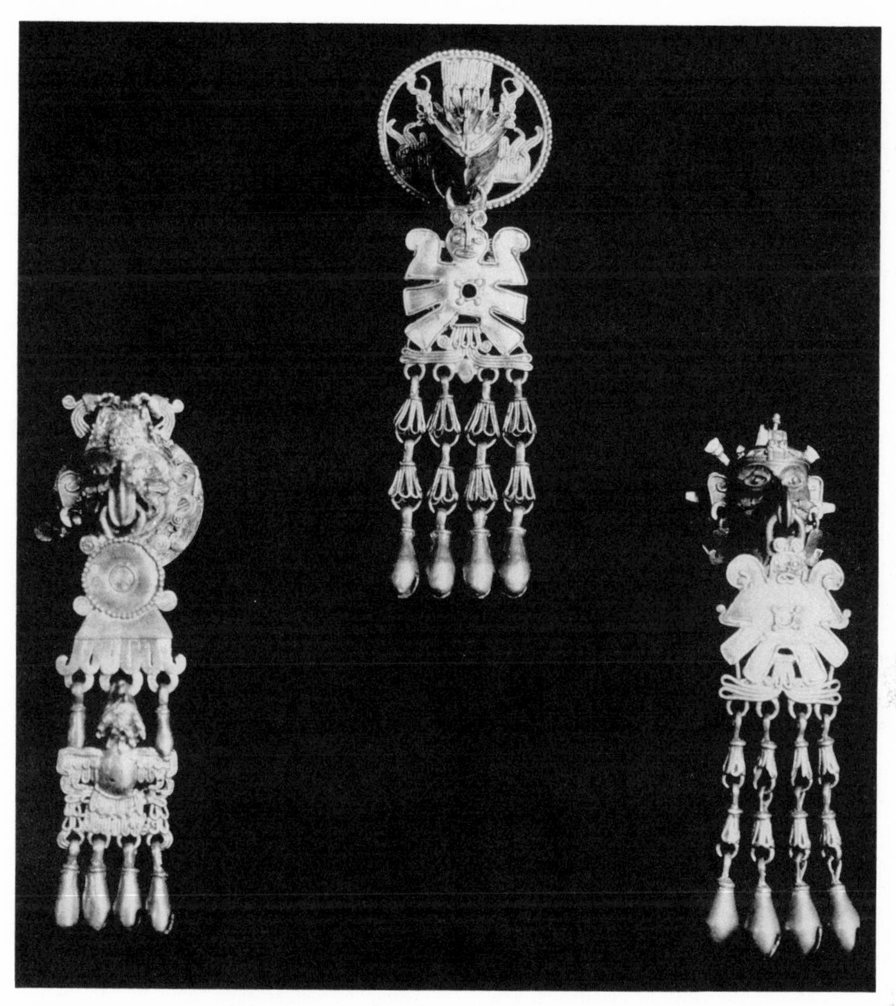

FIG. 51—GOLD BROOCHES, TOMB 7, MONTE ALBAN. Center, falling eagle; sides, the god Quetzalcoatl.

alloy) in acid leaves the object the color of purest gold. It was also treated with a mixture of clay and salt and polished a second time before the piece of jewelry was completed.

Figure 45 shows the plan of the mold for a bead made by the method just described. The wax occupies the areas B, G, and D. Once it has melted, these spaces remain empty and the core A is held in position only by the clay supports E, E, or by little sticks sometimes used instead.

Although it appears that the Mixtecs also knew the technique of filigree and twisted gold wire, all the objects we have examined so far are cast in the style called "false filigree."

Solder was used to join the parts of very complicated pieces or else they were linked by rings. Both processes were employed in the jewelry found at Monte Alban.

Two of these objects in which the solder is unusual are discs, half gold and half silver, which represent the sun and the moon (fig. 46). Descriptions of these pieces of jewelry made of two metals are already well known; the object found at Teotitlan and now in the Museo Nacional de Mexico has been described before.

As for sheet metalwork, the join can be

FIG. 52—GOLD RING WITH FALLING EAGLE. Tomb 7, Monte Alban.

FIG. 53—GOLD RING WITH EAGLE. Tomb 7, Alban.

made by hammering the metal in either a cold or a hot state (annealing). The chief method used to decorate these sheets is repoussé, in which the sheet is placed on an object which is not too hard (on wood, for example) and, with a stone or copper punch, lines or dots are produced which appear in relief on the obverse.

In the military insignia, these gold plaques are cut out and mounted on a background of feather mosaic which can be seen through the areas of openwork.

To sum up, from the point of view of technology, the goldwork of Oaxaca seems a derivation from the goldwork of Panama and Costa Rica, or perhaps from that of the Peruvian coast; from the point of view of its exquisite fineness of workmanship, however, we consider that it is far superior to that of other regions of the American continent, and that it has a taste of its own which belongs within the style of the codices and the sculptures in stone, bone, and wood of what we have called the Mixteca-Puebla culture.

Jewelry of Tomb 7 at Monte Alban

Gold objects known and preserved in European and American museums, including the Museo Nacional de Mexico and private collections, used to be very rare. Even more so were pre-Hispanic silver objects. Some of these objects, like the brooch from Yanhuitlan made of gold with turquoise mosaic (fig. 47), the pectoral of gold and silver from Teotitlan already mentioned, or the pectoral from Papantla, demonstrate the exquisite art of Mixtec goldsmiths and confirm the reports which the conquistadores and the chroniclers give of Mixtec and Mexican craftsmen. But the great abundance of gold and silver objects which once existed in the royal treasury of Mexico, which Bernal Díaz writes about (1939, 1: 339) and which can be verified by examination of the distributions made among the conquistadores, as well as by the remittances made to Charles V of which inventories still exist, had not yet been archaeologically encountered, apart from a few rare and sporadic discoveries.

The discovery of Tomb 7 at Monte Alban, made with the help of my wife María L. de Caso and Srs. Juan Valenzuela and Martín Bazán, has quadrupled the number of gold objects known to us; the silver ones found in the tomb are practically the only ones recorded, if one excepts the gold and silver pectoral from Teotitlan del Camino, two beads in the form of tortoises found in the same place (Saville, 1920, p. 165), a mask which we found in the Mixteca (Caso, 1938, p. 54), and the one mentioned by Lothrop (Lothrop, Foshag, and Mahler, 1957, no. 66).

In Tomb 7 we found 24 silver objects with a total weight of 325 grams. The scarcity of silver objects is explained by the fact that in its native state silver is much rarer than gold and is more easily destroyed. In some of these pieces the silver was mixed with copper, which, according to the native informants of Sahagún, made it easier to work, but it is also possible that the ore contained a high proportion of copper. Analysis of a gold bead by the Instituto de Geología de México revealed 62 per cent gold and 38 per cent silver, an alloy called "oroche" (electrum). These objects were made by two techniques: by working sheet metal and by casting (fig. 48). The vessel (which is the largest known silver object from Mexico), the bracelets, tweezers, the eyes of the mask, and the plaques, are made of sheet metal, whereas the rings and the perforated bells were, like the gold objects, made by *cire-perdue* casting. The design of the rings, decorated with an eagle or a quetzal, was the same in both metals. On the other hand, the artificial fingernail made of silver had nocturnal symbols, whereas those on the gold example were diurnal (fig. 49).

FIG. 54—GOLD PECTORAL. Tomb 7, Monte Alban.

In Tomb 7 were found also 121 gold objects which had a total weight of 3 kilos 598.7 grams. (The total number of gold objects illustrated by Saville is 32.) These included pectorals of various shapes and sizes (fig. 50), ornaments in the form of heads of deities which surely served as decoration on garments or as pendants in necklaces (fig. 51), rings which ranged from the simplest types, plain or very simply decorated, to those decorated with eagles,

Fig. 55—GOLD PECTORAL. Tomb 7, Monte Alban.

Fig. 56—GOLD PECTORAL. Tomb 7, Monte Alban.

pheasants, and quetzals (figs. 52, 53), necklaces with beads in the form of jaguar molars, tortoiseshells, or made of openwork, bells of various forms, depilatory tweezers, a diadem with the plume which decorated it (fig. 42), a piece of gold leaf which covered a gourd for carrying tobacco (*yetecomatl*) (fig. 43). Other more delicate pieces include those which perhaps covered the jade handle of a fan, sheets of gold cut into the shape of butterflies, and still more which keep the shapes of the various perishable objects they originally covered. Another object with a perforation in the center could have served to cover the mouth of a corpse. Very delicate and undecorated gold sheets, with perforations, were probably sewn onto cloth. Other very fine sheets were used, for example, in the mosaic which covered the cup made out of a human skull.

We have already published preliminary descriptions and photographs of these objects, so we shall mention below only some of the most important ones.

Perhaps the most notable is a pectoral with a personage wearing a crown in the form of a jaguar (or serpent?) head and with a cheek mask shaped like a fleshless jaw (fig. 54). In the tomb were human jaws which served this purpose, since they had holes through which passed the cords which held them in place against the chin of the wearer, just as we have seen on the pectoral.

Personages wearing this macabre mask are frequently found in Mixtec codices (Vindobonensis 1, 14, 15, 25, 36; Nuttall 20, 23, 25, 29, 68; Bodley 4, 6, 7, 10, 15, 17, 19). One such person is ♂ 5 Lizard, "Sol Comido," who also wears a serpent cap (Nuttall 25) and who founded the second dynasty of Tilantongo and reformed the calendar. The crest of this individual, which in reality must have been made of mosaic mounted on wood, paper, and feathers, was represented by fine gold lines which seem to be of filigree but were, in fact, made, like the whole object, by the process of *cire-perdue* casting described above.

The round ear ornaments of the personage, on this above-mentioned pectoral, have serpent heads at their centers from which hang strips. His necklace is made up of three strands. The lower of these strands is decorated with amygdaloid bells, like those found in the tomb; it also has a pendant in the form of a little bird flying downwards.

To add to the interest of one of the most masterly pieces of casting by the Mixtecs, the two plaques which form the body of the figure are decorated with glyphs of unusual historical and scientific interest. On the left is a year symbol; in the center is the head of Quetzalcoatl as god of the wind, and surrounding this figure are 10 numeral dots. Opposite this head is the flint knife symbol and two numeral dots. The inscription on the plaque may therefore be read as year 10 Wind, day 2 Flint. In the right-hand plaque is another year symbol and inside it the glyph for "house." Outside are 11 numeral dots; there is no day sign. This plaque may be read as year 11 House.

As explained elsewhere (Caso, 1932d,e; 1950; 1960), we believe that this pectoral establishes a synchronism and tells us that the day 2 Flint of the year 10 Wind of the old (Zapotec style) calendar is *the same day* as 2 Flint of the year 11 House in the new (Mixtec style) calendar. In other words, the reform of the calendar mentioned by Codex Nuttall and carried out by ♂ 5 Lizard, "Sol Comido," is probably commemorated on this jewel, and the personage represented could

FIG. 57—GOLD BELT BROOCH. Tomb 7, Monte Alban. (Photo by D. T. Easby.)

FIG. 58—GOLD RATTLE. Tomb 1, Coixtlahuaca. Apparently an import from Panama. Represents a bat god, with a thunderbolt in one hand and throwing stick in the other.

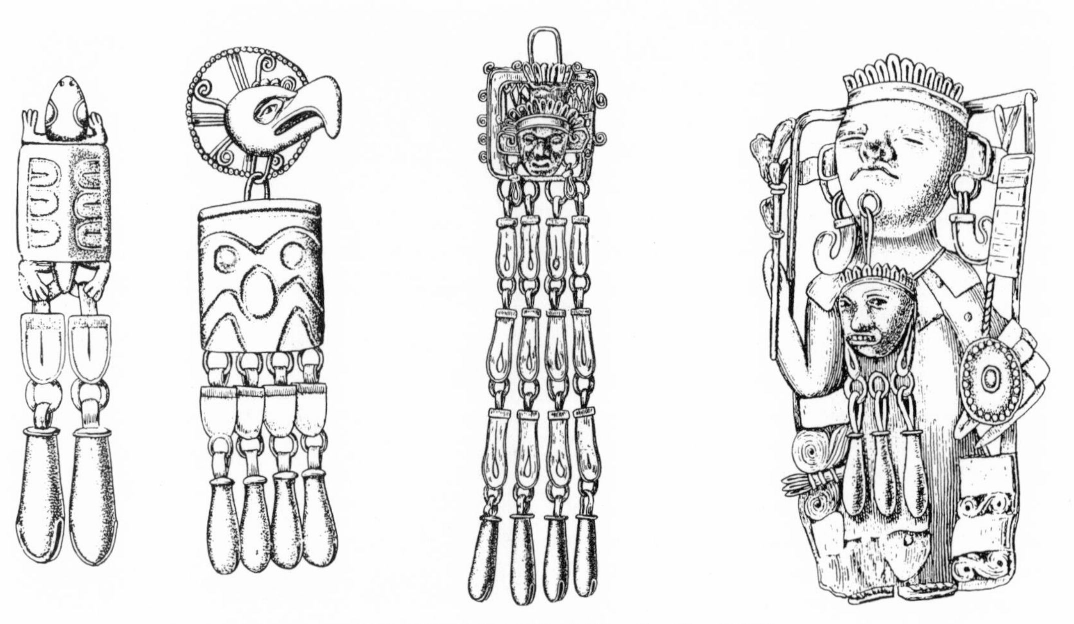

Fig. 59—GOLD OBJECTS, PROBABLY ZAPOTEC. (After Saville, 1920)

well be this same ♂ 5 Lizard. One can thus see that this beautiful pectoral is not only a work of art and a triumph of goldsmith's technique, but also a historical and scientific document.

Another item of goldwork which is also a document dealing with Mixtec ideas of cosmogony is another pectoral which represents the universe as it was known to the natives of Mesoamerica (fig. 55). It is made of four sections which are joined by rings and finished off by ornaments representing feathers from which hang both round and long bells. On the upper part of the object is a hook for suspension, and the great mobility of the four hanging pieces which finish it off must have produced a pleasant jingle. On the upper part is the well-known *tlachtli* (ball-court) symbol, decorated with a skull in the center, and the intimate connection between the ball game and the head of the decapitated victim is already fully realized. From each side projects a snake head which indicates the ring through which ball was passed, and on either side of the skull are two personages carrying balls in their hands. One is a sun god, for he holds the string of *chalchihuites* ending in a bird or a butterfly; the other seems to be a god of the night since he has a fleshless jaw. The ball game represented for the natives the motion (and the eclipse) of a heavenly body like the sun or the moon, or more precisely the movement of the whole vault of the heavens. I think that in this case the glyph represents the sky. The *tlachtli* or ball game also represents the succession of and the struggle between the two cosmic powers—day and night, life and death—as we can clearly see from Codex Borgia.

The second part of this pectoral is formed by a plaque which represents the sun disc surrounded with blood and with a skull in the center.

On the third plaque, within a square frame, is a flint knife which seems to have eyes and a wide-open mouth from which issues the symbol for "word." From behind the knife come smoke and fire. In various representations in Codex Borgia, as well as in other manuscripts and in the frescoes at

Cempoala, the moon is shown with a flint knife at its center. This is a constant attribute of the black Tezcatlipoca, the night god par excellence.

Lastly, the fourth plaque also consists of a square frame in which appears the earth monster whom the Mexicans called Tlaltecuhtli.

We have, therefore, from top to bottom, the sky, the sun, the moon, and the earth—a sort of cross section of the universe.

Another of the important objects found in Tomb 7 was a little mask of the god Xipe Totec, "our lord the flayed one" (fig. 56). This undoubtedly formed the centerpiece of a necklace made up of two rows of beads. Below the chin of the mask must have hung an ornament, perhaps of jade. The upper part is shaped like the neck of a jar and could have served for the insertion of feathers. The god ♂ 7 Flower in Codex Vindobonensis 18 wears a similar mask as a necklace pendant.

The god Xipe, whose cult comes from the neighboring region between the states of Guerrero and Oaxaca, is the god of springtime, for the flayed human skin which covers his priest symbolizes the old covering of vegetation which is replaced by the new at this time of year; but he is also the god of the goldsmiths who cover objects of clay, wood, or stone with a shining yellow skin made of gold leaf. Among the objects sent to Spain are several of these gold "skins" of both men and women (García Granados, 1942, p. 61).

To return to the Tomb 7 object, the mask portion representing the facial skin has a step-shaped tattoo-mark, very common among Mixtec women. Behind the mask are representations of the cords and tassels which bound it to the head of whoever wore it. The hair of the warrior-priest, which would have been covered by this mask, overlaps above it and is represented by cast gold wires of two different lengths, just as the hair would have been worn by living warriors. A nose ornament with central cone and the tips in the form of a swallow's tail, corresponding to the god Xipe, hangs from the nose by a ring. From the artistic point of view this object is remarkable for its realism and for the funereal expression of the face, while technically it is noteworthy for the magnificent polish which the goldsmith managed to give it.

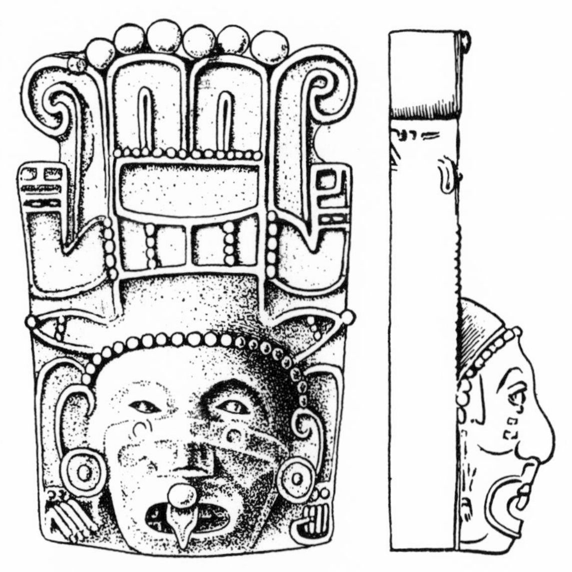

Fig. 60—THE GODDESS OF EARTH. (After Saville, 1920)

The last of these cast pieces to be considered is the heaviest of those found in the tomb and has a weight of 305.7 grams (fig. 57). It is not a bivalve shell, as Lothrop believed, obviously basing his judgment on a drawing or a photograph (1936, fig. 71,*a*), but is a cylinder 84 mm. in diameter and 30 mm. high, and having on one of its faces the figure of what seems to be a spider with a heart for its body. The hollow walls of this cylinder are 11 mm. thick. The entire jewel was cast and is covered with what appears to have been resin. At the sides it has two holes of markedly rectangular section. It seems to us that this jewel could have been used as the back clasp of a belt (*tezcacuitlapilli*) or as a necklace pendant, although its weight makes the former interpretation more probable.

Fig. 61—GOLD RING, ZAPOTEC (?)

Among the objects of repoussé work we mention only the diadem and the crest which adorned it (fig. 42). The first of these is oval; its wall is concave. It is not soldered and must therefore have been made by hammering out a sheet of gold over a stone or wooden cone and then cutting out the upper part. The semicylindrical shape must have been given to it later by beating it out on a convex wooden mold. It was probably lined with leather or cloth. The ornament which completes it was made from a thin sheet of gold; the decoration is of repoussé lines and dots. It has a peg by which it could have been attached to the hair or fitted into the socket of the diadem. The decoration consists of a volute surrounded by 11 dots and represents a ball of feathers. From this rises an ornament consisting of a wide plume bordered with little dots; two further plumes project from this construction. This ornament was called *cuauhpilloni* by the Aztecs and was characteristic of the god of the north and of hunting, Mixcoatl, the mythical father of Quetzalcoatl.

Gold Jewelry from Other Sites in Oaxaca

Since the discovery of Tomb 7 at Monte Alban, other sites have been found in the Mixteca and the neighboring zones of the state of Veracruz.

The most important find was the one from Coixtlahuaca which yielded a necklace with beads in the form of human skulls, and where, in 1940, Alfonso Ortega recovered the objects from a plundered tomb (Tomb 1). Jewels of cast and of sheet gold were found. Among the pieces of cast jewelry was a necklace with both plain and incised beads, some little bells, a fine pendant representing the "Old God" (Toscano, 1944), and a large bell decorated with the figure of a bat god which seems to be a piece imported from Panama (fig. 58). The objects made of sheet metal included two ear ornaments, a fragment from a disc on which butterfly elements could still be made out, and another plaque with a volute decoration which seems to represent a headdress.

Another very important discovery was made recently in Zaachila by Gallegos.

Zapotec Goldwork

The provenience of a piece of gold or silver jewelry does not necessarily indicate that it was made at that site. Precious objects pass from one place to another by trade, tribute, or pillage, so that the provenience by itself can be only a very uncertain indication that the object was a local product. Gold objects of Mixtec technique have been found in Veracruz, the Valley of Mexico, and in Guatemala. For this reason the style of an object is more important for deciding who were its possible makers. We have already mentioned that the large bell found at Coixtlahuaca may perhaps have come from Panama.

Certain pieces of gold jewelry, which by their style seem to me to have been made by the Zapotecs (fig. 59), were published by Saville (1920, pls. 4–6). They were found in Tehuantepec, and their style is different from, but related to, that of other jewels from Oaxaca, especially the figure of Xipe.

Another object from Oaxaca, although not exactly in the Mixtec style, is the piece published by Peñafiel and Saville (*ibid.*, pl. 13) (fig. 60). It is evidently a representation of the earth goddess. What Saville interprets as a headdress is the goddess' skirt, and one can see the bare breasts on either side when the figure is arranged as we have illustrated it.

Lastly, the ring reproduced in figure 61 is much more Zapotec in style because the figure has a cap similar to that worn by the kings of Zaachila in the *lienzo* of that city. Although it is doubtful if we can attribute it to the Zapotecs, we have mentioned it here to complete the list of gold objects which possibly could be credited to this people.

Fig. 62—COPPER RATTLES. Patio of Tomb 105, Monte Alban.

Fig. 63—COPPER AX. Tomb 7, Monte Alban.

Copperwork

Copper objects have been discovered as surface finds at Monte Alban. The most spectacular was a find of rattles (fig. 62) which appeared together with the remains of a mosaic of jades and green stones already published (Caso, 1938, fig. 103).

Also found together, as if forming a treasure cache, were five money-axes (mound of Tomb 21). These two finds belong to Period IV at Monte Alban, a time when the city had already been abandoned and when offerings were made in the debris. They certainly belong to the Zapotec culture, however.

On the other hand, we find Mixtec objects like the chisels and awls which were discovered in the burial (V-20) of a craftsman who carved bone pieces like the ones in Tomb 7. We have already published these instruments and the polychrome jar which contained them (Caso, 1938, figs. 52–54).

The most important copper object discovered, however, was an axe found in Tomb 7 (fig. 63). We believe this object was not used as an axe for cutting wood but rather as a ceremonial weapon; it still shows traces of the mark left by the handle.

Metals: Summary Comment

We can say that the use of metals for implements and jewels was known by the Zapotecs and Mixtecs from the time of

Monte Alban IV, which we would date as contemporaneous with Tula. Objects of gold and silver—even if those from Tomb 7 are omitted—have not been found in such abundance at any other site in Mexico. It seems, too, that the goldsmiths of Oaxaca attained the highest perfection in goldworking and that they taught it to the Texcocans and Mexicans. This art reached such perfection that Durero (in Westheim, 1957), on seeing the jewels which the Spaniards sent to Charles V, said:

> I also saw the things which were brought to the king from the new land of gold: a sun six feet in diameter and made entirely of gold, likewise a moon, all of silver and equally large. . . . So precious were all these objects that they were valued at a hundred thousand florins. As for myself, in all the days of my life I never saw things which delighted my heart so much as these, for I saw among them marvellous works of art and I remained astounded at the subtle skill of the men of those distant lands. I really cannot say enough about the things which were before my eyes.

REFERENCES

Acosta, 1949, 1956, 1957
Anderson and Dibble, 1959
Arsandaux and Rivet, 1921
Batres, 1902
Bergsøe, 1937, 1938
Caso, 1932d, 1932e, 1938, 1939b, 1941, 1946, 1950, 1955c, 1960
—— and Rubín de la Borbolla, 1936
Chimalpahin Quauhtlehuanitzin, 1889
Coghlan, 1951
Cortés, 1922
Covarrubias, 1957
Díaz del Castillo, 1939
Easby and Easby, 1953
Easby, 1956, 1957
Emmons, 1923
Forbes, 1950
Foshag, 1957
Gann, 1925b
García Granados, 1942
Holmes, 1888
Icaza, 1928
Ixtlilxochitl, 1892
Joyce, 1916
Kelemen, 1943
Kidder, 1949a
Kunz, 1907
Lothrop, 1936, 1937, 1950a
——, Foshag, and Mahler, 1957
Martínez Gracida, 1895
Medina, 1910
Noguera, 1939
Nuttall, 1901
Orchard, 1925
Paso y Troncoso, 1905
Rivet and Arsandaux, 1946
Root, 1951
Rubín de la Borbolla, 1944, 1947
Sahagún, 1938, 1956
Saville, 1920, 1922, 1929
Seler, 1890b
Skinner, 1920
Smith and Kidder, 1951
Stone and Balser, 1958
Toscano, 1944
Westheim, 1957

37. Zapotec Writing and Calendar

ALFONSO CASO

Writing and the Calendar in Monte Alban I

Writing and the calendar in the Zapotec region are the most ancient that have been found in Mesoamerica.

Archaeological explorations have revealed a very ancient level in ceramics that we have called Monte Alban I, contemporaneous with a Mixtec city called Yuconoo or Monte Negro, near Tilantongo; from the latter city we have obtained a radiocarbon date which places it about 600 B.C. (Arnold and Libby, 1950, p. 14). This ancient Monte Alban I culture, characterized by sculptures in a special style designated "danzante," the term by which it is commonly known, exhibited writing and a perfectly formalized calendar, which are the earliest yet discovered in Mesoamerica (see Article 34 and Caso, 1947).

Ceramic similarities demonstrate that the danzante culture, or Monte Alban I, may be placed chronologically between Mamon and Chicanel in the Maya region; and, as no writing or calendar has been reported from these phases in the Maya area, we believe that the Maya calendar originated outside the zone where this culture attained its classic manifestation. As this seems corroborated by sculptured inscriptions dated in Baktun 7 of the Long Count system found in the Olmec zone, Veracruz, we believe that what has been called the Maya calendar was an earlier invention which already existed, with its basic characteristics, in Olmec culture as well as in that of Monte Alban I.

It may be argued, however, that Olmecs and danzantes were Maya people, but this does not seem likely. At least they differ considerably in physical type evident from the human representations in jade and sculpture. For the same reason we would not apply the term Zapotec to this early writing and calendar which we find in Oaxaca in Monte Alban I; however, the similarity between the danzante physical type and the Olmec physical type is noticeable. Compare, for example, the profiles of typical Olmec heads from Veracruz and Puebla with a danzante head (fig. 1); and compare the

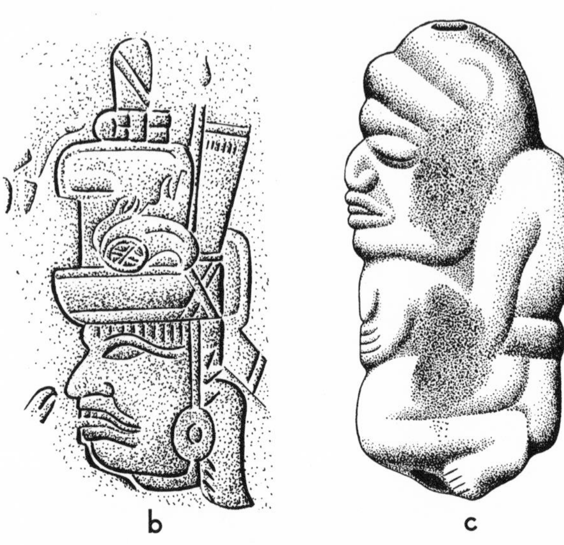

Fig. 1—EARLY STONE SCULPTURE, OAXACA. *a*, "Danzante." *b*, Olmec head. Ax from Tapijulapa. *c*, Jade from Zacatlan.

latter with heads, undoubtedly of the same type, from other areas of Veracruz like those seen on the slabs of Matisse and Tepatlaxco (Covarrubias, 1957, pl. 17). Consequently, it seems that what has been called the Maya calendar, including its Initial Series or Long Count and its positional numeration, is characteristic of Olmec culture, for it is found in Veracruz in very early times, corresponding to the Maya Baktun 7 as on Stela C of Tres Zapotes. (See the photographs of this monolith taken at the National Museum of Mexico in Stirling, 1940).

The date on Tres Zapotes Stela C, (7). 16.6.16.18, following Spinden's correlation, takes us back only to the third century B.C., whereas the danzante inscriptions take us back 300 years before, when perhaps neither the Initial Series nor the positional numeration were used but when the *tonalpohualli*, the division of the year and its symbol, was already invented. And this writing and calendar of the danzantes were already fully developed, thus causing us to ignore the origins of writing and calendrical systems in Mesoamerica.

In Oaxaca, the Monte Alban I or danzante culture seems more closely connected with Veracruz and Chiapas than with the archaic cultures then flourishing in the Valley of Mexico.

We have found that the Monte Alban I culture exhibits, in spite of its antiquity, the essential elements of the Mesoamerican calendar, such as, the *tonalpohualli*, the year, the four year bearers, and probably the division of the year of 365 days into units of twenty or "months." Stelae 12 and 13 undoubtedly belong to this epoch (figs. 2, 3).

The glyphs for the days, with numerals, are shown in figure 4, but there are others that are surely signs for days and do not appear accompanied by numbers (fig. 5). Those that do not look like day signs may be seen in figures 6, 7, and 8. These glyphs have been described in detail (Caso, 1947) and classified according to the scheme estab-

Fig. 2—STELA 12, MONTE ALBAN

Fig. 3—STELA 13, MONTE ALBAN

lished in 1928, when glyph names were given them at that time (Caso, 1928, fig. 8).

Glyph B, the tiger head, is found with two numeral bars (10 Tiger) (fig. 4).

The next three are Glyph E, turquoise or jade. The first appears with the year symbol and two numeral bars (year 10 Turquoise); the second, also with the year symbol and two number dots (year 2 Turquoise); the third does not exhibit numerals.

The following sign, marked with M and the year symbol, is the serpent mask, perhaps corresponding to the day Ehecatl of the Mexicans represented by the mask of Quetzacoatl; it has four number dots (year 4 M).

The two following glyphs possibly represent water, and although I mistook them for the serpent in my first publication, I believe it best to distinguish them from those I have called M. The first would be 6 Water and the second 10 Water. The following are the monkey's head, Glyph O, and in both cases the numbers are not indicated by dots, as normally, but by fingers.

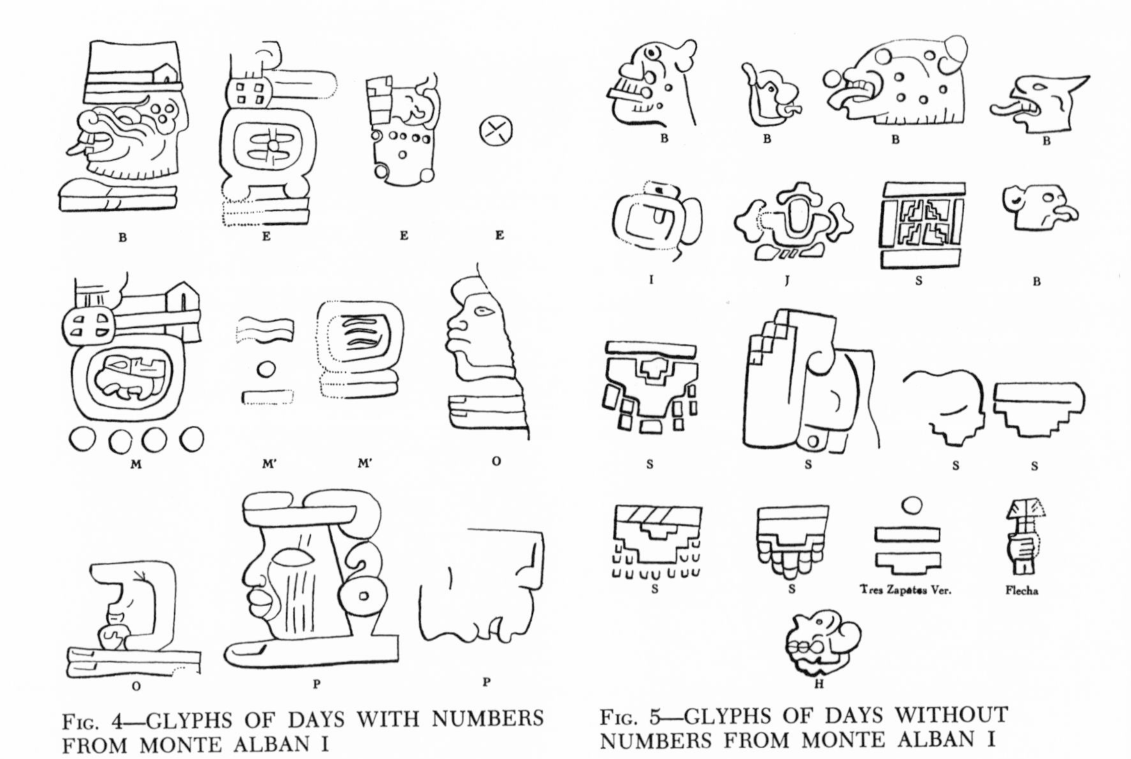

Fig. 4—GLYPHS OF DAYS WITH NUMBERS FROM MONTE ALBAN I

Fig. 5—GLYPHS OF DAYS WITHOUT NUMBERS FROM MONTE ALBAN I

Fig. 6—SEVERAL GLYPHS

Fig. 7—SEVERAL GLYPHS

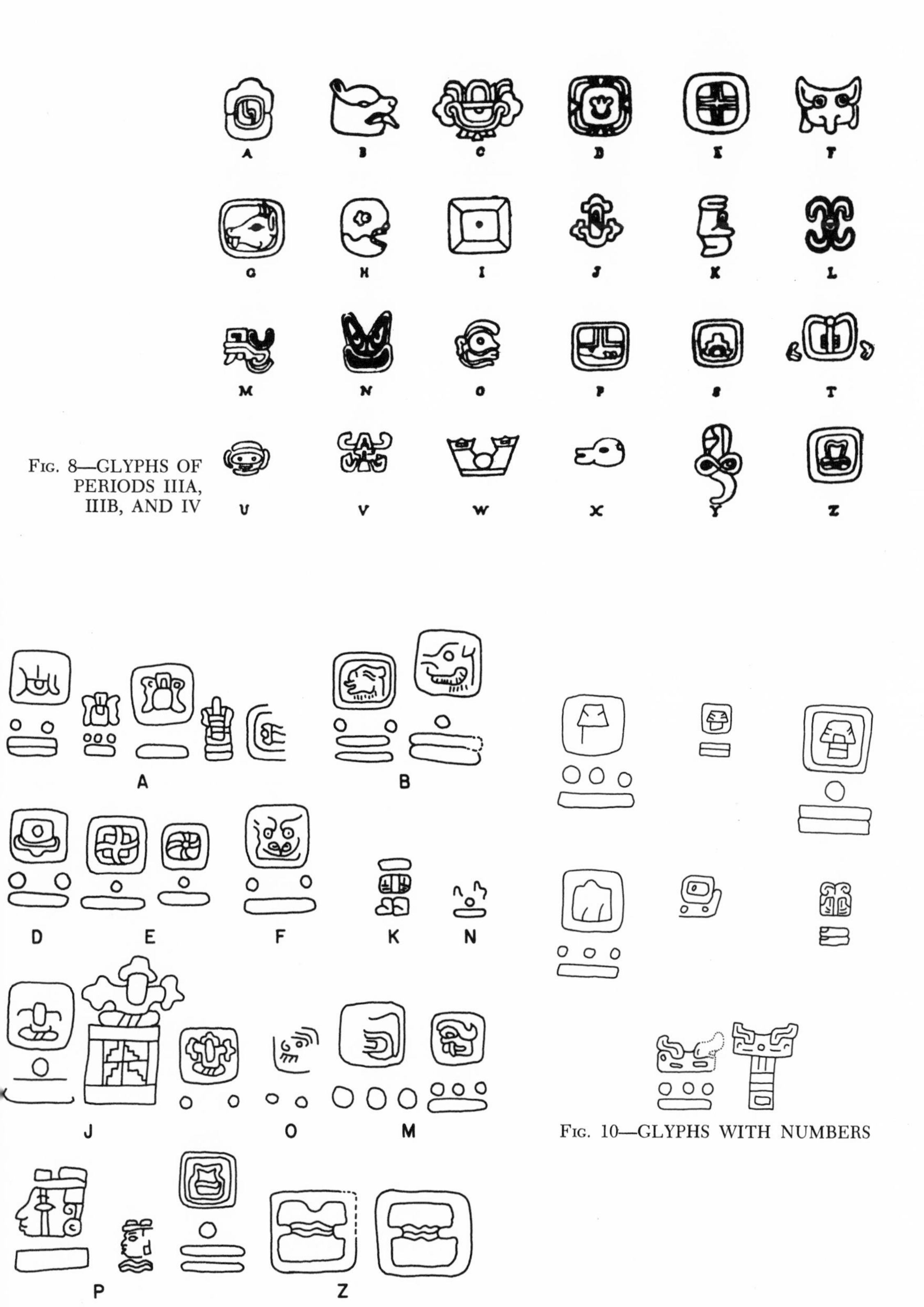

Fig. 8—Glyphs of Periods IIIA, IIIB, and IV

Fig. 9—Day Glyphs, Monte Alban II

Fig. 10—Glyphs with Numbers

FIG. 11—YEAR GLYPH, MONTE ALBAN II

In the next case the number is also a finger, and the glyph is a human head with vertical strips or lines on its face, perhaps a head of the god Xipe. We have called this Glyph P.

In figure 5 there are other glyphs that look like day signs though they have no numbers. The tiger head makes its appearance again, Glyph B; the flower (perhaps 5 Flower) or Glyph J, a very doubtful example of Glyph I, and various examples of the "stepped pectoral," Glyph S, of which the inscription discovered on a rock in an arroyo at Tres Zapotes may be a variant (Stirling, 1943, p. 21, fig. 5).

The glyph we have considered as representing an arrow, even if it does not have a point, appears with numerals in Period II (fig. 11).

Lastly, a glyph which is a skull, Glyph H, later appears as a definite day sign.

Notable because, perhaps, they indicate actions or verbs, are human hands in different positions or holding objects (fig. 6); the atlatl, similar to that in the Maya codices (fig. 7,*k-p*); and the element we have called the "tied bow" which, perhaps, is a net or *chita* for carrying game and which appears in Maya writing (fig. 7,*a-c*).

One trait that begins in Monte Alban I and continues into the artistic style of the historic Zapotecs is the trilobate decorative element seen, for example, in Glyph J (fig. 5) or in the figure for "cerro" or hill (fig. 15).

WRITING AND THE CALENDAR IN MONTE ALBAN II

Although many of the glyphs which first appeared in Period I continue in Period II, new ones are established; those for the days and the year remain essentially the same (figs. 9, 10, 11). The main source of Period II writing is the engraved slabs or lápidas found in the walls of what we have called the "Observatory" or Mound J. But there are also glyphs on Stela 18, on some clay boxes (Caso and Bernal, 1952, p. 30), and, perhaps also belonging to this time, in the painted murals which decorate Tomb 72 (Caso, 1935) and on the idol of Cuilapan (Caso and Bernal, 1952, p. 337; Kelemen, 1943, pl. 123,*d*).

On the stones set in the walls of Mound J of Monte Alban are long inscriptions that bring us closer to the long inscriptions that later appear on the Maya stelae. An example is Lápida 14 (fig. 12). The central motif of this slab is formed by the same glyphs that are carved on other slabs of

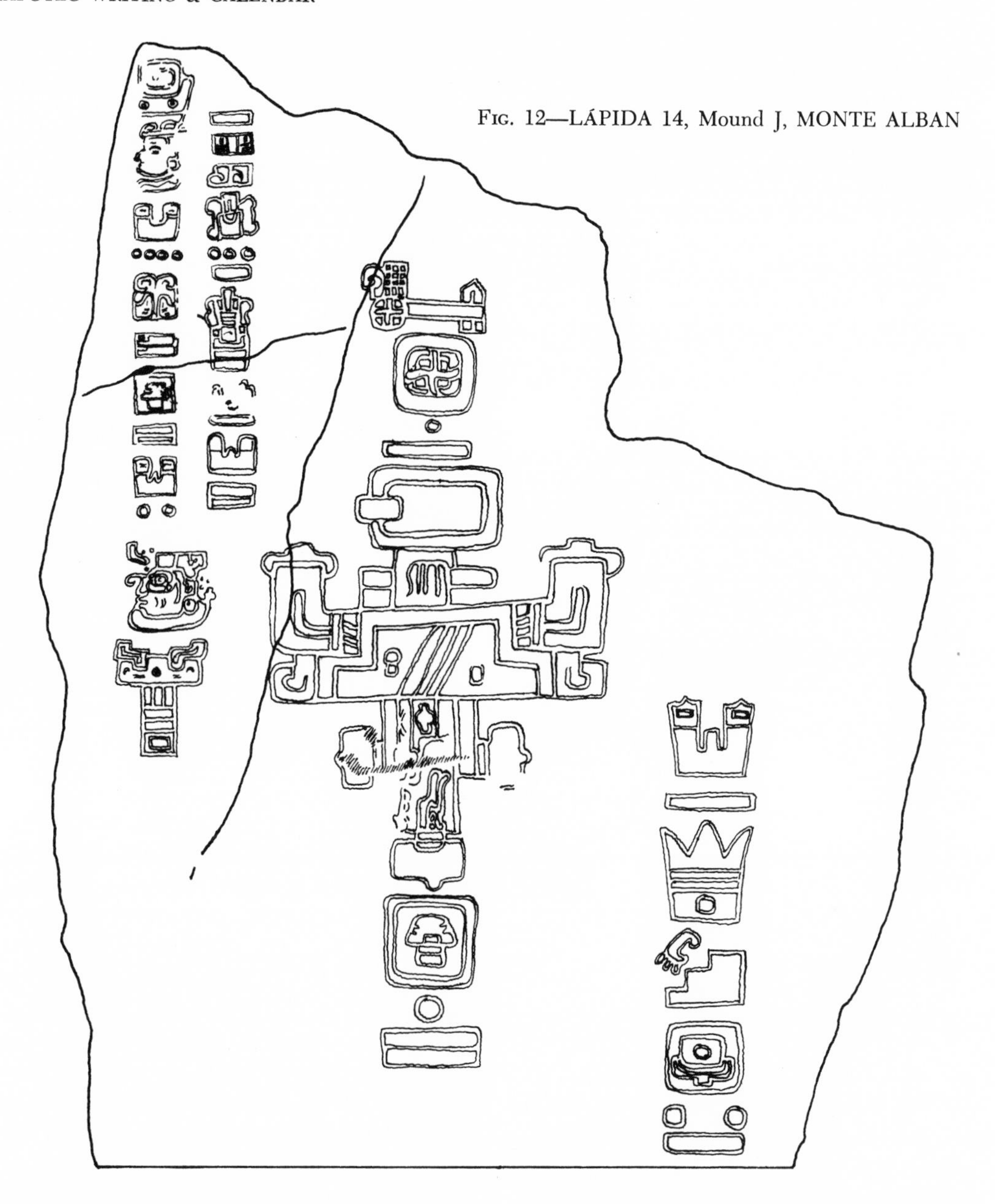

FIG. 12—LÁPIDA 14, Mound J, MONTE ALBAN

the same building, but here they are in their most complete form. Above is the symbol for the year 6 Turquoise; below it a glyph I have been unable to interpret; and farther below, a hand grasping an object placed directly above the glyph for "cerro" or hill, which already in this period had acquired a definitive form. Below the hill is an inverted glyph which substitutes for the inverted heads which appear on most of these stones, as in Lápida 10 (fig. 13) and, I believe, which represent the lords or gods conquered by Monte Alban. Still farther below is a sign for a day that we have called "flecha" or arrow with the number 11. Probably this central inscription says that the

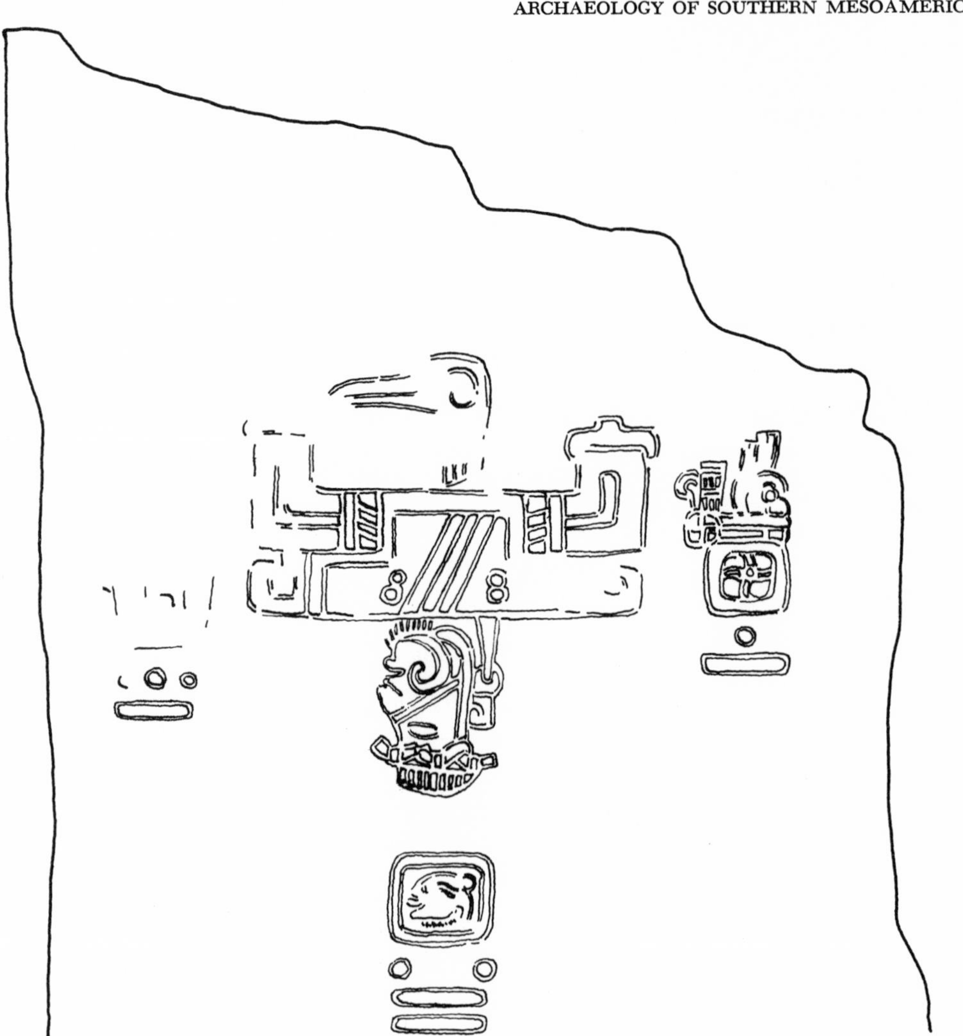

Fig. 13—LÁPIDA 10, MOUND J, MONTE ALBAN

place was conquered on the day 11 flecha (?) of the year 6 Turquoise.

On both sides of this central inscription are rows of glyphs, some with numerals, sometimes formed by fingers; and in the inscription to the right is a stairway with the print of a foot descending it, possibly indicating the verb "to descend."

In this inscription there is also a glyph which is first accompanied by the number 5 formed by a bar or dash, but in Lápida 13 is accompanied by number 15 and on Lápida 16 is inverted and without a numeral. Since the number 15 is not possible in a day of the *tonalpohualli* and since we also have another glyph with number 18, I believe that in such cases these are the glyphs for months (fig. 14).

On these slabs there are usually represented human heads in an inverted position below the glyphs for "cerros" or hills, which in this period are characterized by very long pointed ends (fig. 15). There is also a variety of toponymic glyphs which give some interesting ethnographic data. For example, we see a brush and the liquid with which it is used to paint, a house, a plant with chili peppers, and some other figures, which indicate by their complexity the use of perhaps a phonetic system similar to that employed by the Mexicans and the Mixtecs (fig. 16).

We have the following day glyphs that appear later on the stelae, urns, and murals (fig. 9):

A, a knotted object
B, tiger (jaguar)
D, water (?)
E, turquoise or jade
F, owl
J, flower
K, foot (?)
L, similar to the *ollin* of the Nahua (Tomb 72)
M, mask of the serpent
N, bat
O, monkey
P, human head
W, probably a month
Z, vessel with water (?)

But there are other glyphs not considered in my previous publication (Caso, 1928) and here reproduced in figure 10. The one I have called "arrow" is quite frequent.

In short, then, during Preclassic times,

Fig. 14—MONTH GLYPHS

Fig. 15—GLYPH FOR "CERRO" OR HILL FROM SEVERAL PERIODS

FIG. 16—TOPONYMIC GLYPHS, MONTE ALBAN II

in Monte Alban I and II, a writing with glyphs is already evident, and these glyphs have a more symbolic and ideographic character than a realistic or representative one. Furthermore, the complexity of the elements that make up the place names suggests that a phonetic system was employed similar to the rebus system of the later Mexicans and the Mixtecs.

There is no doubt, as we see in several danzante sculptures, that this system of writing also served to express names of people; and that these names were taken from the day names of the *tonalpohualli,* most probably that of the birthday of the individual, and were also expressed by other symbols that we have called the surnames, a system also used by the Mexicans and the Mixtecs. For example, the famous king of Texcoco who was named after the day of his birth—1 Deer—was better known by his surname, "Fasting Coyote" or *Nezahual coyotl.*

The fundamental elements of this writing —glyphs for days, dot-and-bar numbers, a glyph for the year, year bearers among whom are the turquoise, the jade, and the mask of the serpent, glyph of the "cerro" or hill, and so on—are all found subsequently in Zapotec writing of the periods of Transition, IIIA, IIIB, and IV, and are not known in other parts of Mesoamerica. On the other hand, this type of writing seems to have spread extensively in Preclassic times; it is found in southern Veracruz, in Puebla (as far as the Tepeaca region and Tehuacan), and in the Mixtec district.

The calendar of this early time is already formalized with the days of the *tonalpohualli,* the year, the year bearers, and perhaps the 20-day periods or months. But there is no indication of position enumeration, as it exists on Stela C of Tres Zapotes, or of any other trait that later appears in the Maya Long Count, nor do we find these traits in the Zapotec calendar proper of the Monte Alban III and IV periods.

In spite of the extensive explorations carried out at Monte Alban and in other sites of Oaxaca I have been unable to find an earlier writing, although there is another calendrical system to which I shall later refer. It was discovered by Carrasco (1951) and studied by Weitlaner (1958, 1961).

The Zapotec system of writing and calendar that I have described existed in the Mixteca until A.D. 973, when o 5 Crocodile —Tlachitonatiuh, king of Tilantongo—introduced the Toltec type of calendar (Caso, 1956; see also Article 38 in this volume).

WRITING AND THE CALENDAR IN LATER TIMES

Transition II–IIIA and Period IIIA

From information based on the ceramics of Monte Alban we can say that the characteristics of Zapotec culture may be found in a Transition epoch between Periods II and III, contemporaneous with Teotihuacan II and, we believe, the beginning of the second century A.D. It is in this Transition epoch that the culture of Monte Alban apparently turns its back to the south, stops receiving influences from Chiapas and Guatemala, and begins to take its inspiration from the great metropolis in central Mexico upon establishing contact with Teotihuacan. Unfortunately, this period is poorly represented in the carved slabs, stelae, and frescoes, and we have been unable to distinguish it from the following period, Monte Alban IIIA, which belongs to the Classic horizon of Mesoamerica. However, if we limit ourselves to pottery urns, we can say that in the Transition period there appears, for the first time, what we have called Glyph C. This glyph is the head of a jaguar when seen from the front as in the brooch on the headdress of the rain god, Cocijo, although it is still seen sometimes in the form of a vessel with wavy lines.

In this same Transition period appear the old god 5F (5 Owl) and the goddesses 8Z, 11H (11 Death), and 13N (13 Serpent).

Period IIIA may be already considered as Classic Zapotec, corresponding with Teotihuacan III and with Tzakol of the Maya area. For example, influences of Teotihuacan and of Monte Alban are noted in Kaminaljuyu in the Guatemalan highlands (Kidder, Jennings, and Shook, 1946). From this time until the 16th century Zapotec writing and calendar exhibit few important changes.

The main characteristic of the Classic period is the fineness of the inscriptions. Important examples of this are the Lápida of Bazán (see Article 34, fig. 13) and the stelae recently discovered in Monte Alban by Acosta (1958–59) which were accompanied by ceramic offerings of this period. Two personages are on the Lápida of Bazán: the Jaguar, god of Monte Alban, called 3 Turquoise; and another figure, very similar to the priests of Teotihuacan, called 8 Turquoise. Above them is a glyph representing the sky, which is nothing more than the face of a god wearing as a helmet the *cozcacuauhtli* (*Sarcorhampus papa* Dum.) (Caso and Bernal, 1952, p. 199 et seq.).

Fig. 17—GLYPHS FOR YEAR, MONTE ALBAN IIIB AND IV

Each of the two deities is flanked by a column of glyphs without numbers. Some of these may, perhaps, be months or 20-day periods; they appear in other inscriptions. The certainty that Acosta's stelae belong to Period IIIA allows us to classify other undoubtedly contemporaneous monuments such as Stela 1 (which also has two rows of glyphs), Stelae 2, 3, 4, 5, and probably Stelae 6, 7, 8, and 11.

By Classic times there appear on the stelae all the day glyphs that we have classified with the letters A through Z (Caso, 1928) (fig. 8), except Glyphs Q and R, which are Mixtec; Glyph W, which disappears at the end of Period II; and Glyphs U, V, X, and Y, which show up only once and on very late monuments.

The older inscription on the lápida of Tomb 104 (Caso, 1938, fig. 95) belongs to Period IIIA although the ceramics from the tomb are of a slightly later period, the transition between Periods IIIA and IIIB. The lápida was re-used as a door for the tomb and given a new inscription.

I also believe that the stucco reliefs on Building B of the Vértice Geodésico, a building covered by another, date from Period IIIA. The serpentine reliefs, as well as those of flowers, are quite similar to the engraved pottery of the time (Caso, 1939b, 2: 176). I also believe that the paintings of Tombs 105 and 112, although ceramics are

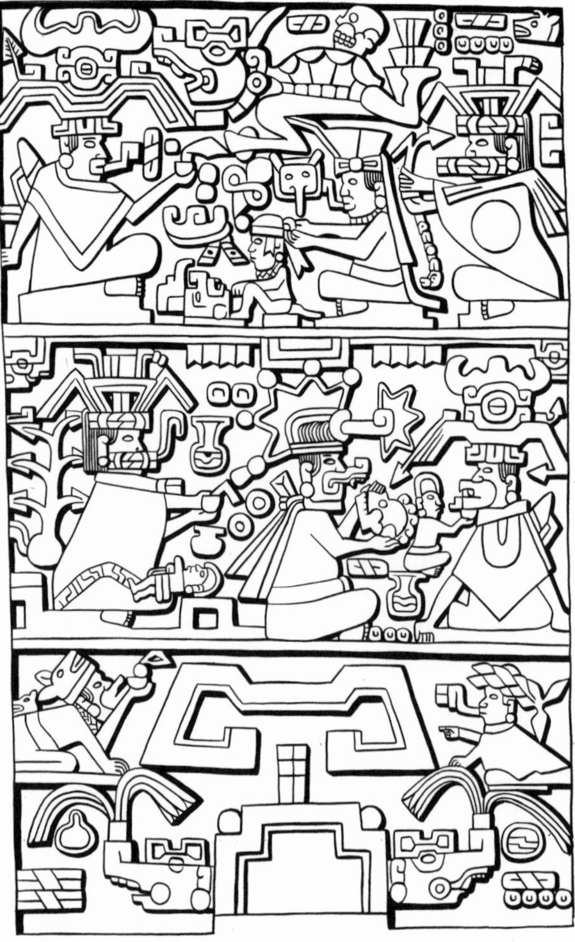

Fig. 18—LÁPIDA FROM A TOMB BETWEEN ZAACHILA AND CUILAPAN

lacking, are contemporaneous (Caso, 1938, figs. 2–5).

Periods IIIB–IV

The glyphs of these later periods of Monte Alban are rather difficult to distinguish from those of Period IIIA or from those carved or painted on Tombs 103 and 104, which belong to a transition period between IIIA and IIIB and which are very rich, incidentally, in graphic material.

In figure 8 we see the glyphs for days which exhibit practically no change from Period IIIA and great similarity with those from Period I. In figure 17 are the year glyphs from Periods IIIB and IV.

What does seem characteristic of later Zapotec culture is the use of lápida slabs, generally small, which in these periods seem to replace the great stelae of earlier times. In addition, they suggest that the dates on them are historic.

From these periods are Lápida 1, in the National Museum of Mexico, which was found in Zaachila, the Zapotec capital of historic times, and other monuments that I have published (Caso, 1928, figs. 81–84, 93, 94). There are also others in the same style, such as the one in the floor of the church at Zaachila and one (fig. 18) in the roof of a tomb between this city and Cuilapan. It seems likely that Zaachila was the main origin of these we call "Zaachila-style slabs."

Of painted glyphs we have relatively few from Period IIIB proper. Perhaps the most important ones are those of Tomb 125 at Monte Alban. On the other hand, carved jambs and lintels are numerous, as well as a different style of slab, on which appears a god or priest, or at times a feminine personage, seated on a kind of hand-barrow (Lápidas 8, 9, 10, and 11) (Caso, 1928).

Lastly, I know of two slabs which suggest certain Mixtec traits incorporated into Zapotec writing. The first of these was published with the others in the same work (Caso, 1928, fig. 92); on it the glyph for "house" appears twice, with numbers and a representation of a vessel with long tripod legs, like the ones used by the Mixtecs. The second, which has also been published (Caso and Bernal, 1952, fig. 350-II), is a stela from San Juanito, at the foot of Monte Alban, on which appear the glyph for the year in the Mixtec style and an individual that appears kneeling or running, as represented in the Mixtec and Mexican codices.

This covers the information we have on the Zapotec writing system, for most of the preserved documents from after the conquest are of other origins: Mixtec, Cuicatec, Chinantec. We have, nevertheless, the so-called "Lienzo de Guevea" in which is contained the genealogy of the lords who reigned in Zaachila and who still reigned at the time of arrival of the Spaniards (fig. 19). It was studied and reproduced by Seler (1908, 3: 157 et seq.). Many of the topographic glyphs, as well as name glyphs, are remote from the Zapotec glyphic system. For example, among all the names not one is accompanied by numbers, and consequently they cannot be considered calendrical.

Much more important is the information given by Córdova in his "Arte" about the names for days, periods of time, the *tonalpohualli,* the year, and the manner of computing time (Córdova, 1578a, p. 187 et seq.). We shall summarize his information briefly.

The year was called *yza*; the month *peo,* which is also the name for the moon; the day *chij, chee,* or *copijcha,* which is the name for the sun. He adds that "the Indians do not count the year or the day in which they are living." That is, time is reckoned as we do when we read a clock, so that, "when the actual year, month or day in which they are living is reckoned it is said that it is pending and they say: *nazabi yza, nazabi peo, nazabi chij*. Thus, when the month or year is running they say that it is performing its function, and to count so much of the month they say: *cochij copijchalacipeo* August, ten days of the month of August, etc. . . ."

Further on Córdova tells us of the existence of the *tonalpohualli,* which they called *pije* or *piye* and consisted of 260 days divided into four periods of 65 days each, each one a "sign" or "planet" also called *pije* or *piye* "time" or "time duration"; but Córdova also calls this 65-day-period *cocijo.* These 65 days were divided into five parts of 13 days each, which were called *cocij* or *tobicocij,* as if we were to say one "month," or a time period; each day had its name. The four planets, which presided over the main divisions and were the cause of everything, were called *cocijos* or *pitaos,* that is,

FIG. 19—LIENZO OF GUEVEA

TABLE 1—TABLE OF DAYS

Mexican		*Zapotec*	
Cipactli	Crocodile or Alligator	Chilla, Chilja	Crocodile, bean *patol*
Ehecatl	Wind	Quij, laa	Wind
Calli	House	Guela, ela, ala, Gueche, quiche	Night
Cuetzpallin	Lizard	Ache, achi, ichi	Iguana
Coatl	Snake	Zee, Zij	Snake
Miquiztli	Death	Lana, laana	Black
Mazatl	Deer	China	Deer
Tochtli	Rabbit	Lapa	Rabbit
Atl	Water	Niza, queza	Water
Itzcuintli	Dog	Tella	Dog
Ozomatli	Monkey	Loo, goloo	Monkey (fem.)
Malinalli	Twisted Grass	Pija	Sun, drought
Acatl	Cane	Quij, ij, laa	Cane
Ocelotl	Tiger	Geche, eche, ache	Jaguar
Cuauhtli	Eagle	Naa, ñaa	Mother, eagle
Cozcacuauhtli	Buzzard or Owl	Loo, guilloo	Crow, face
Ollin	Earthquake	Xoo	Earthquake
Tecpatl	Flint	Opa, gopa	Cold
Quiahuitl	Rain	Ape, gappe	Cloudy, drop
Xochitl	Flower	Lao, loo	Flower, eye, face

gods; they were given offerings, each one at their proper time, and blood was drawn in their honor. Each *piye* or *cocijo,* or 65-day-period, was called by the same name of the day of the 13-day unit which began them.

The *pije* or *piye* were managed by special priests called *colanij* or *peni colanij,* "agoreros," who had the same functions as the Mexican *tonalpouque.*

Of the 260 names of the *piye* some were of good fortune and some of bad. A child was given the name of the day he was born as his first name, then given another that we have called the surname.

The names of the days, according to the Vocabulary of Córdova (1578b) and the studies by Seler (1904c) and Cruz (1935), and their comparisons with Mexican name lists, are listed in Table 1.

Besides the day names and numbers there are some particles that vary slightly and that were joined to the day name and the number, as seen in Table 2.

From this information it is to be noted

TABLE 2

Number	*Particles*				
1. Tobi or chaga	– Quia	Que			
2. Topa or cato	– Pil	Pala	Pel	Pi	Pe
3. Chona or cayo	– Pela	Peo	Pel		
4. Topa or taa	– Nel	Cala	Cale	La	
5. Caayo	– Peci	Pel	Pet	Peo	
6. Xopa	– Que	Qua			
7. Caache	– Pilla				
8. Xoone	– Ne	Ni	La		
9. Caa or gaa	– Pela	Peo	Pel	Pilla	Pi
10. Chij	– Pilla		Nel		
11. Chijbitobi	– Ne	La	Ni		
12. Chijibitopa or Chijbicato	– Piño	Piña	Pini	Peñe	
13. Chijño or Chijbichona	– Pici	Pece	Piza	Pizo	

that, generally speaking, the Zapotec calendar has the same characteristics of the Mesoamerican calendar that are known from the Mayas, Mixtecs, Matlatzincas, and Nahuas; but it also has certain traits that are peculiar to it and seem to exhibit a great antiquity. For example, particles are used with the day sign and number, and these particles, of which there are thirteen, accompany the day as the thirteen lords of the days. Another characteristic trait is the breakdown into periods of 65 days and the naming of these periods by the day on which they begin.

Seler (1904c) rightly said that there is reason to believe that the Mesoamerican calendar, or at least the *tonalpohualli,* was invented in Oaxaca.

It seems interesting, therefore, to look at a type of Zapotec calendar recently discovered.

Calendar of the Southern Zapotec

From the data made available by Weitlaner (1958, 1961), we can briefly describe this calendar and examine its similarities with the *piye* or Zapotec *tonalpohualli.*

This calendar is founded on two series, one of nine day names and the other of the numerals from 1 to 13. "Both series repeat themselves until they arrive at the sum of 260." The nine day names are of deities which represent objects or natural forces.

1. Mdi	Lightning, god of water
2. Ndozin	Death, messenger of Ndan
3. Ndo'yet	Death
4. Beydo	Wind, seeds (not maize)
5. Dubdo	Maize
6. Kedo	Judge, dependent of Dubdo
7. Ndan	Supreme god
8. Mse	Evil spirit
9. Mbaz	Goddess of earth

The numbers from 1 to 13 run parallel to the days, but they do not combine to name the day. Each series of 13 numbers (joined by a series of 9+4 day names) are called a "time." Each "time" has its own name. Four "times" form a "period" which has its own name beginning with the particle *ze,* or "day." The name of the first "time" of a "period" is also the name of the "period."

The calendar of 260 days is made up of the union of the five "periods" of four "times" each one of 13 days.

When a period of 260 days has elapsed, it is immediately followed by another and so on indefinitely; but the first day is made up of the day names of the first two days—Mdi and Ndozin—so that in the first nine-day group the first day, Mdi, is repeated, and there are really only eight different names. This is an indispensable artifice so that the nine-day groups will fall exactly in the 260-day period. This calendar may thus be expressed with the formula

$$8 + 9 \times 28 = 260$$

and this is the same procedure followed by the *Tonalamatl de Aubin,* so that the nine "Lords of the Night" fit exactly in the *tonalpohualli;* but instead of repeating the first two names in the beginning, the last two are repeated (Seler, 1900–01).

In order to understand how this calendar functions let us place in continuation the days of the first "times" of the period called *Ze gon.*

The first day of the year, as we have

Table 3

	Time		Time		Time		Time	
Period	1	Ze gon	2	Sgablodios	3	Sgabgabil	4	Sgablyn
Period	5	Ze Blazgac	6	Sgablodios	7	Sgabgabil	8	Sgablyn
Period	9	Ze Yate tan	10	Sgablodios	11	Sgabgabil	12	Sgablyn
Period	13	Ze we	14	Sgablodios	15	Sgabgabil	16	Sgablyn
Period	17	Ze Blogay	18	Sgablodios	19	Sgabgabil	20	Sgablyn

TABLE 4

	Ze gon		*Sgablodios*		*Sgabgabil*
1	Mdi, ndozin*	1	Kedo	1	Mdi
2	Ndo'yet	2	Ndan	2	Ndozin
3	Beydo	3	Mse	3	Ndo'yet
4	Dubdo	4	Mbaz	4	Beydo
5	Kedo	5	Mdi	5	Dubdo
6	Ndan	6	Ndozin	6	etc.
7	Mse	7	Do'yet		
8	Mbaz	8	Beydo		
9	Mdi	9	Dubdo		
10	Ndozin	10	Kedo		
11	Ndo'yet	11	Ndan		
12	Beydo	12	Mse		
13	Dubdo widzin	13	Mbaz		

*Names of the first *two* days.

said, carries two names, Mdi and Ndozin, so that the name of the first day is repeated again in nine places, instead of in the tenth.

We can see that this calendar exhibits traits found also in the *tonalpohualli,* in general in Mesoamerica and especially in the Zapotec *piye* or *pije.* It is a computation of 260 days repeated indefinitely without taking into account the year or the century, just as our week repeats itself. This computation is divided into five "periods" of 52 days each, as the Zapotec *piye* is divided into four *cocijos* of 65 days each. Each "period" is divided into four "times," or time units, of 13 days each; the Zapotec *cocijo* is divided into 65 days, divided into five *cocij* of 13 days each. The name of each "period" is the same as that of the first "time" of that "period" just as the name of each *cocijo* in the *piye* is the same as the name of the first day.

The numbers that intervene in the formation of this calendar are the same as those that intervene in the *piye* and the *tonalpohualli*: 9, 13, 20, and 260.

The names of the days are the names of gods; as I have shown elsewhere (Caso, 1961), all the names of the days in the Mexican *tonalpohualli* are sacred, precisely because they are names of gods.

The nine day names are related to the "Lords of the Night."

Mdi	–	Tlaloc (Lightning, rain, water)
Ndozin	–	Mictlantecuhtli (Death)
Ndoyet	–	Mictlantecuhtli (Death)
Dubdo	–	Centeotl (Maize)
Kedo	–	Iztapaltotec (Sin, Justice)
Mdan	–	Tonacatecuhtli (Supreme god) (Pilzintecuhtli)
Baz	–	Tlazolteotl (The Earth)

The differences pointed out by Weitlaner are very important, but there is no doubt that between the ancient Zapotec calendar described by Córdova and used during the 16th century and that still used in the region of the Loxichas there is a relationship of origin. Is it merely the survival of an ancient calendar, earlier than the Mesoamerican *tonalpohualli,* and does it originate in this? Or is it the remnant of what is still left of the *tonalpohualli* after many of its elements have been forgotten or changed? We are inclined toward the second explanation, but it is possible that the publication of all the results of Weitlaner and his coworkers will help solve the question.

In any event, we are left with the impressive suggestion that a calendar already in use in Oaxaca during the 6th century before Christ is still used today in the same region after 2600 years have elapsed.

REFERENCES

Acosta, 1958–59
Arnold and Libby, 1950
Carrasco, 1951
Caso, 1928, 1935, 1938, 1939b, 1947, 1956, 1961
—— and Bernal, 1952
Córdova, 1578a, 1578b
Covarrubias, 1957
Cruz, 1935
Kelemen, 1943
Kidder, Jennings, and Shook, 1946
Seler, 1900–01, 1904c, 1908
Stirling, 1940, 1943
Weitlaner, 1958, 1961

38. Mixtec Writing and Calendar

ALFONSO CASO

Writing

FROM THE Mixtec region, which includes western Oaxaca, southern Puebla, and eastern Guerrero, comes a type of native writing that seems to be related to that of the neighboring area of Puebla and Tlaxcala, but which also has its own peculiar characteristics. This type of writing is not only recorded in several manuscripts of pre-Hispanic origin and in painted *lienzos* of the conquest period, but also is carved in sculptures, engraved on stone, wood or bone, painted on pottery, and even incised on ornaments of jade and gold jewelry.

Of the pre- and post-Hispanic codices containing this style of writing, the most important are: Codex Vindobonensis in Vienna, together with Codices Becker I (or "Manuscrit du Cacique") and Becker II; the Zouche-Nuttall Codex in the British Museum; the Colombino in the National Museum of Mexico; the Bodley 2858 and the Selden I and II in the Bodleian Library, Oxford University; the Fragment Gómez de Orozco; and several important lienzos, such as that of Antonio León in the Toronto Museum, the Map of Teozacoalco in Austin, and the Lienzo of Ihuitlan in the Brooklyn Museum (Caso, 1958a).

The subject matter of these manuscripts is mainly historical. Only the obverse of the Vindobonensis, the Selden Roll or Selden I, and the Fragment Gómez de Orozco contain references to mythological dates or to ritual. Generally, the pre-Hispanic codices, as well as those painted after the conquest, and the lienzos deal with the history of a place or with the history and the genealogies of the lords of various places. In addition, they include geographical data, particularly the lienzos which were painted after the conquest (fig. 1).

Two schools have attempted to interpret these manuscripts: the German, with Seler, Lehmann, and Beyer, which considers them religious, astronomical, and mythological statements; and the Anglo-American school, which considers their content to be historical.

The latter school began when Zelia Nuttall discovered that the codex that bears her name related to the lives and conquests of certain personages whom she believed to

FIG. 1—LIENZO DE IHUITLAN. Brooklyn Museum C

a b c d e f g

4
3
2
1
0
9
8
7
6
5
4
3
2
1

tlacotepec

tecuacu

cozcatla

yacatla

tecahuayac

mixtepec

tezopaztla

Aztatla

tecopa

xicotla

quauhtoco

tonalla

tlalixtlahuaca

tepenene

Santiago yuitla

tlalpitepec

Cuauxtlahuaca

pinoyalco yuitla

mixtepec

teczitepec

a b c d e f g

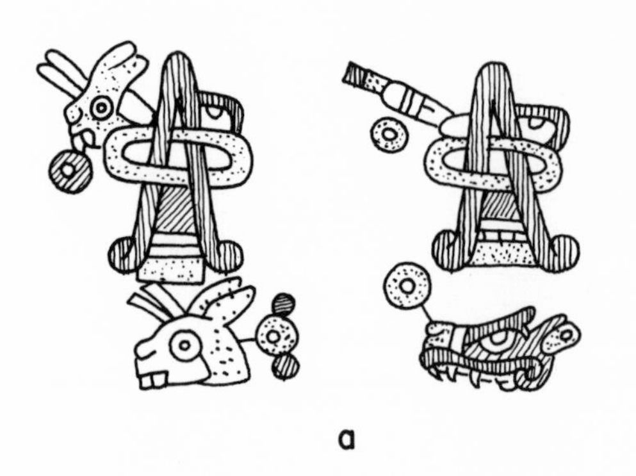

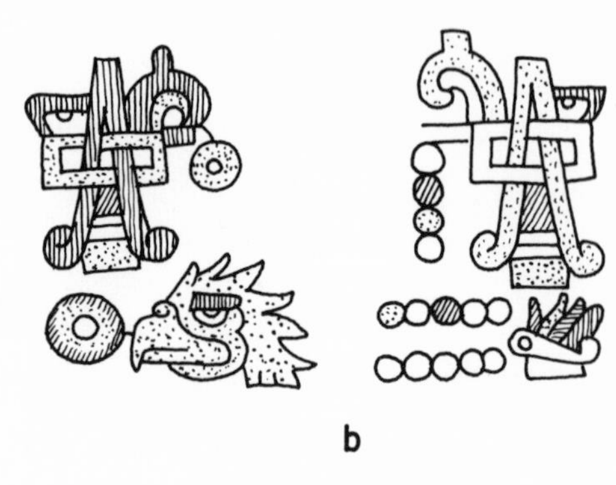

a b

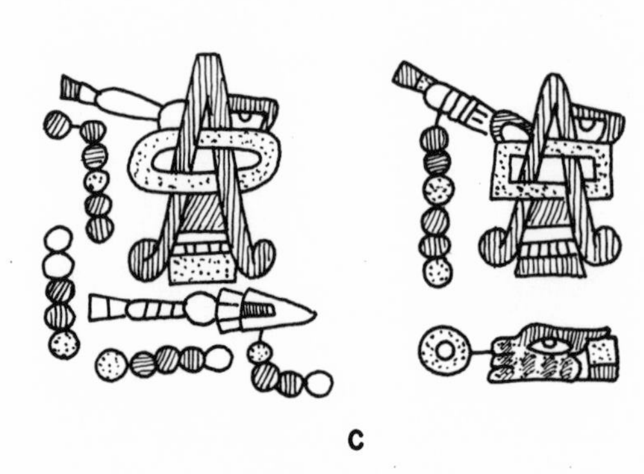

c d

FIG. 2—GLYPH FOR YEAR

be Aztec and Texcocan warriors (Nuttall, 1902). Later, Cooper-Clark noted (1912) that the codices we have called Mixtec constituted a group which, according to him, were elaborated by the Zapotecs. In his commentary on Codex Nuttall, Richard Long (1926) also considers it historical, and divides it into five parts which he says deal with 478 years of history. Spinden (1935), commenting on a portion of Selden II, also demonstrates the historical nature of these manuscripts and reconstructs the history of a princess mentioned in this codex. And lastly, in my article "El Mapa de Teozacoalco" (1949), I showed that the manuscripts are historical in character but begin by relating the divine ancestors of the kings and so constitute a true theogony. The earthly histories have a heavenly prologue. It was also demonstrated that they deal with the history of Mixtec principalities dating back to A.D. 692, the earliest date we have been able to read. In addition, the Map of Teozacoalco was the clue which permitted us to read all the Mixtec codices and lienzos.

We have said that the writing of the codices is related to the writing in the neighboring area of Puebla-Tlaxcala (Caso, 1927b), and it is this type of writing that characterizes a cultural complex which developed in Toltec times and which has been called the Mixtec-Puebla culture (Vaillant, 1941). Nevertheless, in spite of the similarities between the codices of the Puebla-Tlaxcala group (Borgia, Vatican B, Fejérváry-Mayer, Laud) and those of the Mixtec group, there are certain elements (for example, the year glyph in the form of an A and O intertwined [fig. 2]) which are found in the Mixtec codices and not in those of Puebla-Tlaxcala culture. For instance, the appearance of this year sign in Borgia exhibits different characteristics.

Even when the codices seem to be more painting than writing, because personages and scenes are represented, in most cases the representations of human figures, of geographic features, and of objects are more symbolic than real. In effect, they deal with presentation of ideas rather than of things and, as such, are more writing than painting. In fact, writing in the Mixtec codices has a threefold character. First, in certain cases it may be called iconographic, for it seems to be a representation of images. Second, it may be regarded as symbolic or ideographic, for it utilizes symbols to represent ideas rather than the things themselves. The symbol for place (a wall), the symbol for river (a vessel), and so forth are examples of ideographic representation. Third, it may be said that at least for the writing of toponyms—I believe for proper names as well—the Mixtecs used a series of symbols that had not ideographic but phonetic value. An example may make this clear. *Teozacoalco* in Nahuatl means "sacred pyramid"; it is also called *Hueyzacoalco,* which means "great pyramid." In Mixtec the name of this town is *Chiyocanu, Chiyo* meaning "base" or "pyramid," and *canu* meaning "great" or "doubled"; but in the Mixtec codices there appears a little man who doubles a base or foundation so that it is read not as "doubled base" but as "big base" or "foundation" (fig. 3).

Fig. 3—TEOZACOALCO

Another example of phonetics is evidenced by the identity of the Mixtec words for "plain" and "feathers"; both are *yodzo.* "Plain" in the codices is represented by a feather mantle. Thus, the name for Coixtlahuaca, or *Yodzo Coo,* is translated as "Plain of the serpent," and is represented by a serpent on a kind of feather mantle.

But, even though there is a phonetic principle, as well as realistic representations, most Mixtec writing undoubtedly consists fundamentally of symbols. Even the representations of men and women do not have the qualities of portraits but are symbolic figures drawn within certain stylistic canons which appear almost invariably uniform (Robertson, 1959).

By means of this type of writing in the pre-Hispanic codices and in the postconquest codices and lienzos the Mixtecs were able to record historical events and, above all, to present considerable data about the genealogy of their rulers. These genealogical codices were called *naandeye* or *tonindeye* in Mixtec. By this glyphic system they were able to set down information from A.D. 692 (Bodley Codex) until well into the 17th century (Muro Codex). Thus, as in no other part of the New World and in few parts of the world at large, we have ten centuries of continuous genealogical history recorded by the Mixtecs in the system of writing they invented.

This system allowed them to state specifically the names of individuals and their surnames (there were only 260 names from the calendar for men and women, which necessitated surnames for princes and princesses); names of places; dates marking the year and the day; representations of sun, moon, and stars; geographical localities; animals and vegetables; and houses, temples, palaces, furniture, weapons, rank, dress, and ornaments.

The name of an individual is always indicated in the Mixtec codices by the day of his

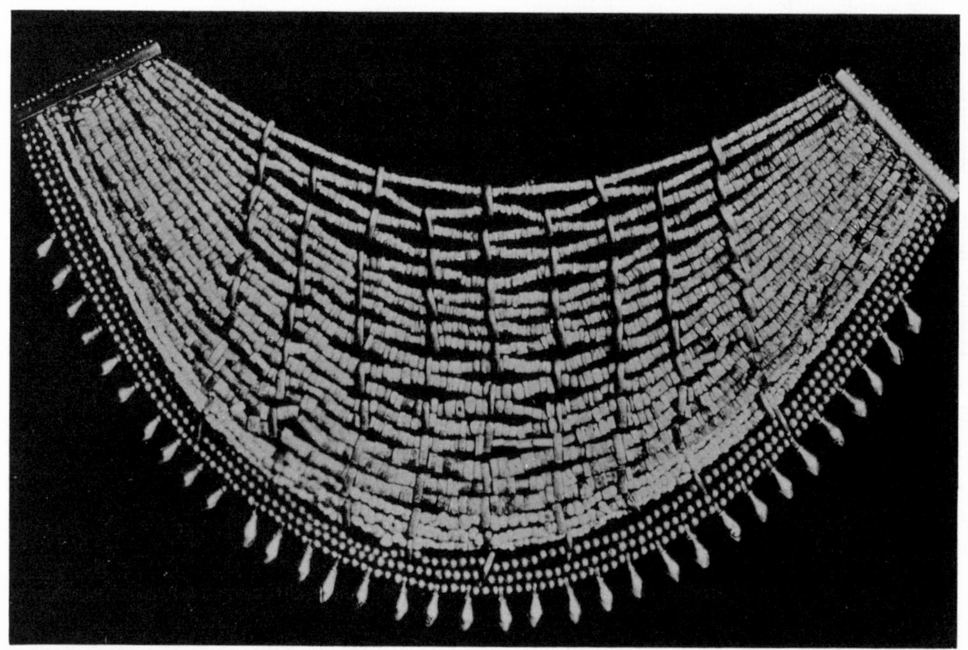

FIG. 4—PECTORAL, TOMB 7, MONTE ALBAN Turquoise, shell, coral, pearls, and gold.

birth, one of the 260 days of the *tonalpohualli*. Besides this calendrical name, the princes and princesses had surnames appropriate, even to our point of view, to their sex. Thus, men might be named "Bloody Tiger," "Tiger Claw," or "Stone Knife"; the women, "White Flower," "Golden Jewel," "Copal Ball," or "Flower Serpent."

The birth of an individual is indicated by a red line which connects with a year represented by a symbol consisting of an A and an O interlaced, which Spinden (1935) believes originally signified the umbilical cord. Other features that express rank or occupation are a white cloth with black designs, which the priests wear; a red cloth decorated with a stylized ear of maize and a feather fringe, characteristic of the king; special hair style for warriors; and so on.

Unlike those in the Mexican codices, men and women appear seated in the same manner, on small stools or big chairs with high backs that the Mexicans called *icpalli*. Men were generally covered with the *xicolli*, or long shirt; women wore the *huipil*, or blouse, called *xighu* or *dzico* in Mixtec. At other times men appear to wear the mantle called *tilmaitl* by the Mexicans and *dzoo* in Mixtec. When standing, the men are shown sometimes wearing the *maxtlatl* or loincloth; the women wear the skirt or *dziyo*. The feature that best distinguishes the sexes is the fact that the women wear their hair braided with colored ribbons, whereas the men usually wear a kind of headdress.

When the princes or princesses were shown walking, probably outside their houses, they usually wore sandals called *dzeñeya*.

Occasionally, we can see in the codices the weapons of the Mixtec kings and captains: the atlatl or dart-thrower, and the wooden sword edged with obsidian chips and sometimes curved like a boomerang. Lances or spears may be shown and, much less frequently, the bow and arrow. As a defensive weapon the shield is common. At times the warriors are clad in short shirts, possibly the quilted garment called by the Mexicans *ixcahuipilli*; however, the body is more often naked or covered with adornment. These ornaments are extraordinarily

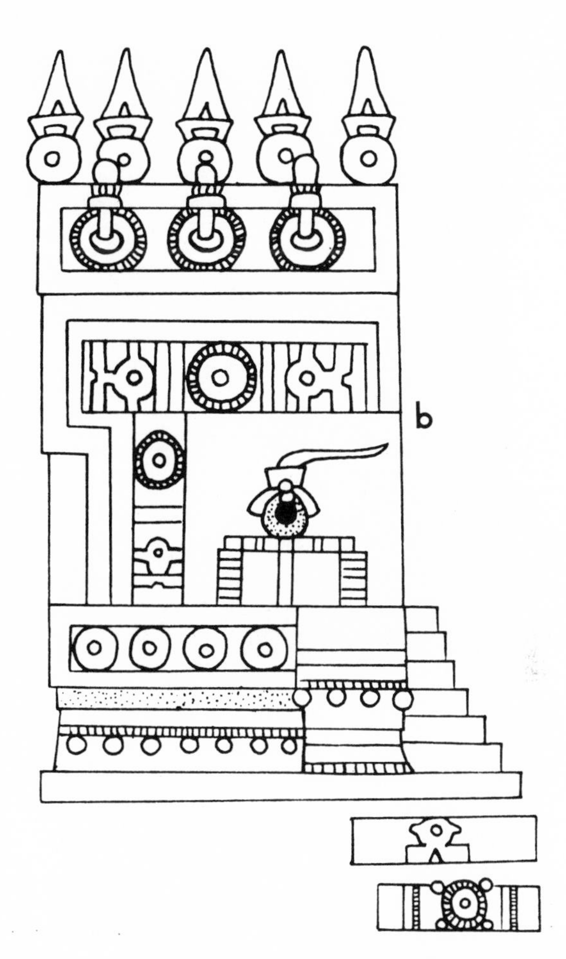

Fig. 5—PECTORAL ORNAMENTS DEPICTED IN CODICES. *a*, Human-figure pectoral of gold (Codex Nuttall 76-b II). *b*, Building with pectoral-shaped ornaments of gold and jade (Manuscrit du Cacique).

frequent and allow us to observe the ornamental art of the Mixtecs and to compare their jewels and adornments with those in other regions of Mexico, especially with those from Tomb 7 at Monte Alban (Caso, 1932d,e). Earplugs, noseplugs, and lip ornaments of jade and gold are common; examples occur in the ceremonies depicted in the codices whereby a cacique (or chief) was made a lord, when his lip was perforated by the claw of a tiger or an eagle, as the chroniclers described for Mexico and Tlaxcala. Also represented are necklaces strung with different sizes of beads and pectorals of the richest materials such as the turquoise, coral, pearls, and gold in Tomb 7 at Monte Alban (cf. fig. 4).

Also frequent are pectorals, sometimes shaped like human or animal heads and made of gold, at times in the style of those in Tomb 7, which probably derives from the frog-shaped pectorals of the Chiriqui art of Central America. There is one example of a person disguised as a gold pectoral, and little gold pectorals are represented as decoration on the walls of a building (fig. 5,*a*,*b*).

The ornament the Mexicans called *tezcacuitlapilli*, the brooch with which the *maxtlatl* was fastened at the back, is represented in the Mixtec codices in their usual manner of showing an object in profile, half of it seen in front view. This technique of representation is applied also in the depiction of buildings.

Bands were worn at the wrist and above the knee. Often they were of gold beads, of jade or turquoise, or of strips of jaguar skin from which hung gold bells.

Lastly, many women as well as men wore elaborate feather headdresses, with those of quetzal feathers predominating.

Houses are variously represented in the Mixtec codices. Of course, the most common house, which the Mexicans refer to as *xacalli*

FIG. 6—STRUCTURES DEPICTED IN CODICES. *a,* Temple with curtain, Tilontongo (Codex Nuttall). *b,* Sweat bath (Codex Nuttall 16).

(hence the Mexicanism "jacal," which still refers to a very humble house), was probably of wattle and daub, or perhaps adobe with a thatch roof. The foundation was either round or square. The name in Mixtec is *huahiita.*

Much more elaborate is the palace (*aniñe* or *tayu*) with sloping walls decorated with panels and topped with battlements. The palace generally had a masonry roof *(huahinehe)* although thatch roofs are quite frequent. The doorway is always painted red. When it is shown in profile, the representation follows the rule we have mentioned: only half of the front view is seen, given the shape of a T. It was closed by a curtain (fig. 6,*a*).

Besides the common house and the palace is the *temazcal* (*ñehe*), sweat bath, characterized by a kind of temple beside which is a triangular element from which fire and smoke frequently emanate (fig. 6,*b*).

The ball game (*yuhuasi cotota*) is pictured as in the Mexican codices, by a building in the form of an H. There are temples on pyramids; these temples are decorated with panels and frets which surely in several cases were formed by mosaics in the Mitla style or, in other instances, painted.

Other small buildings, such as altars, are frequently encountered in the codices.

On mountaintops walls with battlements probably depict fortifications.

Little furniture is shown in the codices. All we see are feather mantles, mats, benches covered with jaguar hide or painted red and decorated with gold, and some large chairs with high backs like thrones.

Utensils include stone knives, many kinds of pottery vessels, boxes containing objects, and bags. Instruments related to ceremonial cults or the arts are staffs, fans, brushes, chisels, masks, objects made from the bark of calabashes (*jicara* or *yasi*), torches, and balls of rubber for the ball game or for offerings (*tiñama* or *tinduu*).

Geographic features are represented symbolically rather than realistically. For example, a mountain range appears with the peaks decorated with scrolls, indicating a rugged place, and often bearing on their points their names: Mask Peak, Cacao Peak, Peak of the Legs, Broken Rock Peak, or Jaw Peak. In general, the hill or "cerro" is similar to that in the Puebla-Tlaxcala and the Mexican codices, incorporating the name of the "cerro" on the feature. Lakes and rivers are represented as if they were vessels, but the artist takes great care to distinguish a river by painting small waves (Nuttall 75), or the sea, by waves high and foamy at their peaks (Nuttall 80). Boats are like pottery vessels, i.e. in transverse section. Volcanoes spew fire and smoke; a plain may be a mantle of feathers, or a table-like element which simply indicates a place.

Animals and plants appear often and, though more realistic than the human beings, they do not lose their somewhat heraldic character. (See, for example, the jaguar with nose and claws painted blue, or the crocodile, fish, or shell in Nuttall 50, p. 75). Trees are never treated in a naturalistic manner, but are always drawn with their roots above the ground, the trunk clearly rugged, and the branches presented front view in almost perfect geometrical symmetry (Vindobonensis 39). Reeds and flowers are similarly shown in the symbolic and nonrealistic manner characteristic of Mixtec art.

Calendar

The Mixtec calendar is a regional aspect of the Mesoamerican calendar and so exhibits fundamentally the same structure and the same periods: the *tonalpohualli* of 260 days (we do not know its Mixtec name); the 365-day year, or *cuiya*; and the century of 52 years, which according to Alvarado's vocabulary was called *eedziya, eedzini,* or *eetoto* (*ee,* 1; *dziya* or *dzini,* crown or garland).

This Mesoamerican calendar definitely existed in the Mixteca since ancient times, but is not traceable to Monte Alban I or to Monte Negro, which is contemporaneous. In Huamelulpan it is associated with objects that correspond to Monte Alban II (Caso, 1956). The calendar is also found in Yucuñudahui, in a tomb contemporaneous with Monte Alban IIIA or early Monte Alban IIIB that yielded a radiocarbon date of A.D. 300–500.

But in this ancient Mixtec calendar almost all the symbols for days differ from those in the codices or on objects in use at the time of the conquest or a few centuries before. Many of these day signs are more like those of the Zapotec calendar, as are the numerals, which employ the bar or dash for number 5, whereas in the manuscripts and on later Mixtec objects numerals up to 13 are written with only dots. However, the glyph for the year is in an angular or trapezoid form characteristically Mixtec and is used in these earlier periods with the days that appear as year bearers among the Zapotecs.

In the most recent period, to which the manuscripts and wooden and bone objects belong, the symbols of the calendar change radically and look more like those of the Mexicans even though somehow maintaining their own style. When did this change from the older system, similar to that of the Zapotecs, to the new system resembling that of the Mexican plateau, come about?

We have advanced the hypothesis that it was the father of the great conqueror, 8 Deer "Tiger's Claw," the so-called 5 Crocodile "Tlaloc-Sun Dead" or "*Tlachitonatiuh,*" founder of the second dynasty of Tilantongo, who made this calendrical reform in the year 12 or 13 House, of the Mixtec computation which corresponds to the year 13 Owl of the Zapotec, on the day 7 Motion. These years would be A.D. 973 or 985, or when the Tula culture flourished on the Mexican plateau and when the Tepeu style was coming to an end in the Maya area. In Monte Alban this was the Period III-B (Caso, 1941).

Thus, if our hypothesis is correct, the Mixteca adopted the Toltec calendar towards the end of the 10th century, and since then the Mixtec glyphs have been closely linked with those of the Mexicans, and the years are called Cane, Stone, House, and Rabbit.

The Tonalpohualli

From the genealogical and historical codices of the Mixtecs we learn that the signs for the days were represented in a form very similar to that used by the Mexicans. On the other hand, the geographical relaciones of Oaxaca, 1579–80, give us names of gods and rulers whose first names were those of the day of their birth. With these facts we can make up the list on Table 1.

The Mixtec day names have been obtained mostly from the Relaciones Geográficas, the Codex of Yanhuitlan (Jiménez Moreno, 1940), the Map of Xochitepec (Caso, 1958a) preserved in the Museum of Copenhagen, Codex 36 of the National Museum of Mexico (Rosado Ojeda, 1945), and, above all, from the Lienzo de Nativitas. The last two documents are unedited. Some names are also found in Codex Muro, and some translations of names of gods and rulers have been published (Caso, 1928). In Codex Yanhuitlan, and in the portion discovered by Berlin, there are several names of individuals and rulers. Berlin (1947b) also has published a genealogy of San Miguel Tecomatlan with Mixtec names that can be translated.

The translations of all the above are based principally on Alvarado's vocabulary (1593) and, to some extent, on Reyes' statements (1593).

In dealing with calendrical names (whether of men or women), the prefixes *Ya* and *Ñu* are generally employed. Often the reverential masculine form is written *Yya* or *Yia*, used also for the feminine form as in *Yaa ni cuu*, of Tejupan, or *Ya ji mane*, of Mitlantongo, and as seen also in the word "prince," *Yya yevua*, and in that for "princess," *Yyadzehe Yevua*, according to Alvarado.

In the magnificent collection of carved bone found in 1932 in Tomb 7 at Monte Alban (Caso, 1932d,e) there are numerous examples of day and year glyphs. Some of these bones represent the beginning of the *tonalpohualli*; in them we see not only the day glyphs but also the numerals which accompanied them in the first group of thirteen (fig. 7,*a,b*). But there are also abundant day signs, used, surely, for their religious and magical significance. These do not appear in order (fig. 7,*c*), or else they are represented as complete dates of years and days on bones of historical char-

Table 1—TONALPOHUALLI

Cipactli (Crocodile) Quehui	1	8	2	9	3	10	4	11	5	12	6	13	7
Ehecatl (Wind) Chi	2	9	3	10	4	11	5	12	6	13	7	1	8
Calli (House) Cuau, Huahi	3	10	4	11	5	12	6	13	7	1	8	2	9
Cuetzpallin (Lizard) Quu	4	11	5	12	6	13	7	1	8	2	9	3	10
Coatl (Serpent) Yo, Coo, Yucoco	5	12	6	13	7	1	8	2	9	3	10	4	11
Miquiztli (Death) Moku	6	13	7	1	8	2	9	3	10	4	11	5	12
Mazatl (Deer) Cuaa, Cuav	7	1	8	2	9	3	10	4	11	5	12	6	13
Tochtli (Rabbit) Sayu, Xay	8	2	9	3	10	4	11	5	12	6	13	7	1
Atl (Water) Cuta, Duta	9	3	10	4	11	5	12	6	13	7	1	8	2
Itzcuintli (Dog) Ua, Huaa	10	4	11	5	12	6	13	7	1	8	2	9	3
Ozomatli (Monkey) Ñuu, Ñooy	11	5	12	6	13	7	1	8	2	9	3	10	4
Malinalli (Grass) Cuañe	12	6	13	7	1	8	2	9	3	10	4	11	5
Acatl (Reed) Huiyo	13	7	1	8	2	9	3	10	4	11	5	12	6
Ocelotl (Jaguar) Vidzu	1	8	2	9	3	10	4	11	5	12	6	13	7
Cuauhtli (Eagle) Xa, Sayacu	2	9	3	10	4	11	5	12	6	13	7	1	8
Cozcacuauhtli (Buzzard) Cuij	3	10	4	11	5	12	6	13	7	1	8	2	9
Ollin (Motion) Qhi	4	11	5	12	6	13	7	1	8	2	9	3	10
Tecpatl (Flint) Si, Cuxi	5	12	6	13	7	1	8	2	9	3	10	4	11
Quiahuitl (Rain) Dzahui, Co	6	13	7	1	8	2	9	3	10	4	11	5	12
Xochitl (Flower) Uaco, Coo, Coy	7	1	8	2	9	3	10	4	11	5	12	6	13

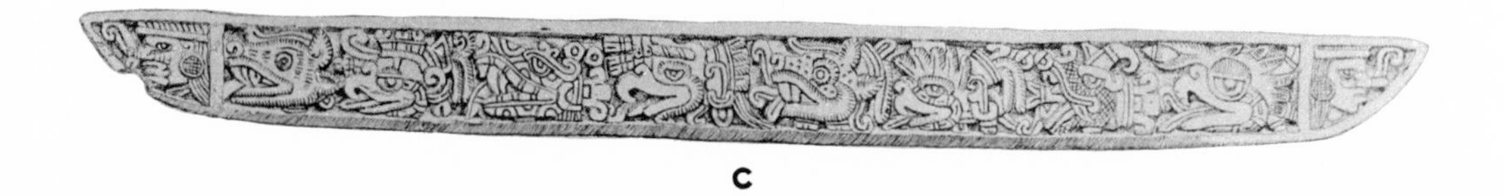

Fig. 7—CARVED BONES, TOMB 7, MONTE ALBAN. *a,b,* Bones 172 and 203 K. *c,* Bone 114.

Fig. 8—CARVED BONES, TOMB 7, MONTE ALBAN. *a,* Bone 174a, Tomb 7. *b,* Bone 37a.

Fig. 9—GOLD PECTORAL, TOMB 7, MONTE ALBAN

acter (fig. 8,*a*), or as names for years (fig. 8,*b*).

The Year

The Mixtec year is represented by a characteristic glyph for this writing; it appears as an interlaced A and O (fig. 2). There are several forms of this glyph but they do not seem to indicate any regional or temporal differences, for variations appear not only in the same manuscript but on the same page.

The 365-day year that the Mixtec called *cuiya* must have followed the same structure of the year as in other Mesoamerican calendars, and was surely organized into 18 periods of 20 days each, commonly called months, plus the five left-over days which were placed at the end of the year. As yet we have not been able to prove that certain symbols, found on various monuments, in manuscripts, or on carved stones, are really "months," although it seems quite probable, for example, that they occur on the Lápida de Cuilapan (Caso, 1928).

The year began the 16th of March, according to Ríos (1900), or the 12th day of March, according to Burgoa (1674). On the other hand, Jiménez Moreno believes that it began with a month such as the *Atemoztli* of the Aztecs, which fell in November or December.

Correlation with the Zapotec Calendar

We believe we have found a correlation between the Mixtec and Zapotec calendars on a gold jewel from Tomb 7 in Monte Alban (fig. 9) (Caso, 1932d).

We know that the Zapotecs had a system of calling the years by day names corresponding with "Wind," "Deer," "Grass," and "Motion." It is the oldest system we know of, and the Maya used it in the Classic period; it is found on the monolith of Tenango, in the Cuicatec codices, in the Dehesa, in the codices of Azoyú, and among the Matlatzincas (Caso, 1928).

However, the Mixtecs, probably starting from the reforms carried out by 5 Crocodile "Tlachitonatiuh," the father of 8 Deer "Tiger's Claw," followed the system of calling the years by the day names "Cane," "Stone," "House," and "Rabbit," that we also find in the Dresden and Peresiano Codices, in Xochicalco and among Mexicans, Tlaxcalans, Otomies, and the other groups of conquest times.

On the gold pectoral from Tomb 7 that represents a god with jaguar-skin garment and a mask of a fleshless jaw, we have two dates on the plaque attached below. On the left side there is a symbol for year and the sign "wind" represented by the Ehecatl head and accompanied by 10 dot numerals, and the day "stone" accompanied by two points or dots. This is read as year 10 Wind, day 2 Stone. On the right plaque on the right side there is the glyph for the year with the sign "House" surrounded by 11 dots, but

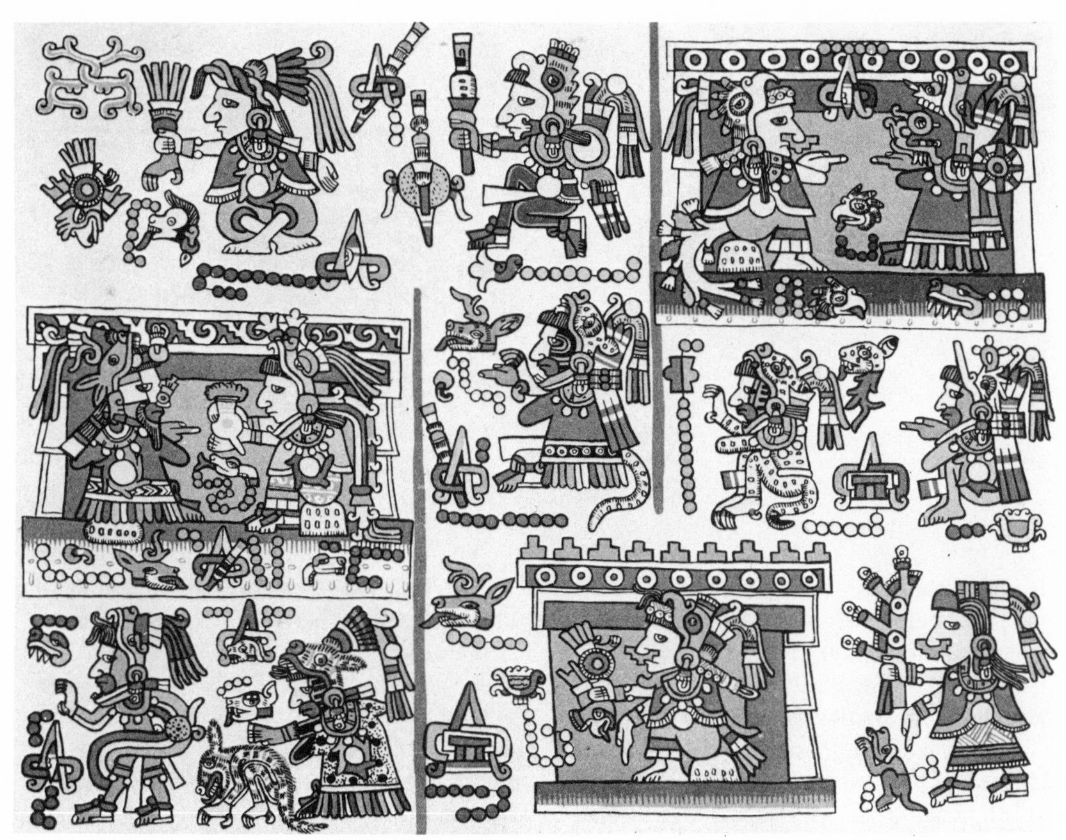

FIG. 10—PAGE 26, CODEX NUTTALL (ZOUCHE)

there is no sign to indicate day. This is read as year 11 House.

From our point of view, the dates on the pectoral may establish a correlation between the Zapotec and Mixtec calendars as to the years, but since the day was the same in both calendars it was not necessary to repeat it. This correlation fixes the year called 11 House in Mixtec as the year that the Zapotecs called 10 Wind; that is, the year bearer was passed on to the next day, a modification similar to that effected by the Maya on passing 0 Pop to 1 Pop.

Whether the Mixtecs began their year with the day of its name, or if this remained as the last day of the last month, the analysis of consecutive dates within the several years of Codex Nuttall does not allow us to decide (Caso, 1955b). Nevertheless, if the two dates 11 Serpent and 6 Cane in the year 10 Cane of the Lápida of Cuilapan fall within the same month, as seems most probable, then the Mixtec year could not begin with the day of its name.

Since the Mixteca is still largely unknown archaeologically, explorations may eventually solve these problems.

READING THE CODICES

The reading of the Mixtec codices is carried out in *bustrofedon* form, that is, scanning over the same page, or two or more consecutive pages, upward or downward, or from right to left, or vice versa. Incomplete red lines in the text allow passing from one column to another, or from one line to another, where the lines are interrupted. When a chapter ends, as for example in the Bodley,

FIG. 11—PAGES 83 AND 84, CODEX NUTTALL (ZOUCHE)

or when two notes relate to the content of the page but which should not be read in conjunction with the text, then the red line marks a definite separation (cf. for example, Nuttall 33 or Bodley 28 and 40–34).

As we have said, most of the pre-Hispanic Mixtec codices, excepting some we call ritualistic, have a historical-genealogical character. Thus, there are in these codices lists of rulers who reigned over a locality, as for example, Tilantongo, on the reverse of the Codex Vindobonensis, or Teozacoalco, on the reverse of the Codex Zouche-Nuttall, or a place which may have been called "Green Carpet" in Codex Becker II. The codices may also be lists of the genealogies of several places, as, for example, the obverse of the Zouche-Nuttall or of the Bodley.

The Mixtec scribes offer considerable information about the rulers of each place. First they gave the name and the surname, the day and year of birth, their parents, and their wife. Also cited are the names of the parents of their wives and their birthplaces, the names of their brothers and sisters and whom they had married, and the names of their sons and daughters. Let us read a page from the Codex Zouche-Nuttall which contains genealogical data and another page which contains historical data.

On page 26 of Zouche-Nuttall (fig. 10) the reader begins in the upper right corner and goes down this column, passes to the second column which is between two red lines, ascends this column to where the red line is interrupted, and then descends the left-hand column.

In the first column is a palace in which is seated a lord, called ♂ 5 Crocodile (the 6 is mistaken), and a lady, ♀ 9 Eagle. He is wearing a mask of Tlaloc, the god of rain, and is carrying the sun on his back. His surname would be "Sun of Rain." From her comes her surname, "Garland of Cacao Flowers." Facing each other indicates they are married. The date is the year 6 Stone and the day 7 Eagle. According to our calculations, this year would be A.D. 992. Below appear the three children of this couple: the first son ♂ 12 Motion "Bloody Tiger," born the year following their marriage, in 7 House, A.D. 993; the second son ♂ 3 Water "Heron"; and a daughter ♀ 3 Lizard "Jade Ornament."

Turning to the second column, we see another palace in which is seated a lone lady called ♀ 11 Water "Bluebird-Jewel." She is the second wife of ♀ 5 Crocodile "Sun of Water"; the date of their wedding was the day 6 Deer of the year 10 House, A.D. 1009, or 17 years after his first marriage. In the year 12 Cane, A.D. 1011, in the day 8 Deer, their first son was born, called ♂ 8 Deer "Tiger's Claw," the most famous king the Mixtecs had, who reigned in Tilantongo and Teozacoalco and conquered many places. Then come the births of his younger brother, ♂ 9 Flower "Copal Ball with an Arrow," in the year 3 Cane, A.D. 1015, and his sister ♀ 9 Monkey "Clouds–Quetzal of Jade," in the year 13 Stone, A.D. 1012. Although older than ♂ 9 Flower, she is mentioned last, being a woman.

Descending the third column of this page, we see another palace and in it the lord ♂ 8 Deer "Tiger's Claw" and the lady ♀ 13 Serpent "Serpent of Flowers" who is offering him a bowl of chocolate, symbolic of marriage. The date of this is the day 12 Serpent of the year 13 Cane, A.D. 1051; thus, when "Tiger's Claw" married he was already 40 years old. The page ends with mention of the birth of his two sons: ♂ 4 Dog "Tame Coyote" in the year 7 Rabbit, A.D. 1058, and ♂ 4 Crocodile "Serpent Ball of Fire" two years later in 9 Stone, A.D. 1060. Thus ends page 26 of the Zouche-Nuttall codex.

On page 83 and 84 of the same codex (fig. 11) we see an example of a nongenealogical narrative. The reading is in the same manner, beginning in the lower right corner. The year 11 House and the day 12 Monkey is A.D. 1049. On the day 12 Monkey, ♂ 8 Deer "Tiger's Claw" conquers a place whose name we do not know, but whose glyph is called "God Xipe's bundle." The conquest of this place, which appears also in other codices (Colombino, Becker II, and Bodley), puts to an end a long dynastic war. Here we see ♂ 8 Deer "Tiger's Claw" making prisoner the youngest prince of this place, only nine years old and called ♂ 4 Wind "Serpent of Fire." He also captures the older brothers, the princes called ♂ 10 Dog "Eagle Copal Burning" and ♂ 6 House "Row of Flint Knives." In the following year, 12 Rabbit, A.D. 1060, on the day 6 Serpent ♂ 8 Deer, disguised as a red tiger, and probably his brother, ♂ 9 Flower, disguised as a yellow tiger, engage in a sacrificial gladiatorial combat with the prince ♂ 10 Dog "Eagle Copal Burning" and another warrior disguised as death. He (♂ 8 Deer) kills the other prince, ♂ 6 House "Row of Flint Knives," by shooting him eight days later, on 1 Cane (Caso, 1955a).

Besides the ceremonies mentioned on page 84 of the codex are those that occur on the days 9 Wind and 2 Buzzard and consist of the decapitation of quail, ritual offerings of pulque and cacao, and the burning of bones, probably those of the sacrificed princes.

REFERENCES

Alvarado, 1593
Berlin, 1947b
Burgoa, 1674
Caso, 1927b, 1928, 1932d, 1932e, 1941, 1949a, 1955a, 1955b, 1956, 1958a, 1960
Cooper-Clark, 1912
Jiménez Moreno, 1940
Long, 1926
Nuttall, 1902
Reyes, 1593
Ríos, 1900
Robertson, 1959
Rosado Ojeda, 1945
Spinden, 1935
Vaillant, 1941

39. The Zapotec and Mixtec at Spanish Contact

RONALD SPORES

THE PRESENT article[1] describes the native cultures of Oaxaca as they appeared during the period of early contact with Europeans from 1519 to early 1522. Five major regions have been distinguished for specific treatment: (1) Valley of Oaxaca, (2) southeast Oaxaca comprising the territory from the vicinity of Miahuatlan to Tehuantepec, (3) the northern mountains running from the Valley of Oaxaca north to Teotitlan del Camino on the Oaxaca-Puebla border, (4) the Mixteca Alta, and (5) the Mixteca Baja and regions bordering on the southwest Pacific coast. Zapotec cultures predominated in the first two regions, and Mixtec-speaking peoples were in the majority in the Mixteca Alta and Mixteca Baja. The third region was the most linguistically diversified, containing Zapotec, Mixe, Chinantec, Cuicatec, Mazatec, and Nahuatl elements. Huave, Chontal (of Oaxaca), Mixe, and Nahuatl groups resided within the southern Zapotec zone east of Miahuatlan. The predominantly Mixtec region contained communities speaking Nahuatl, Chatino, Amuzgo, Trique, Chocho, and Popoloca.

Documentary evidence for many of these groups was either inadequate or unavailable for the present discussion. Much of the accessible material contains very specific data, particularly on Zapotec and Mixtec communities, allowing for fairly good ethnographic reconstruction. Although there was a rich diversity at the time of the Spanish conquest, a number of themes were common to all Oaxacan culture. The variations on the theme, the divergent paths to the solution of life's problems, the differential adjustments and orientations, present a patterned mosaic, but one secured by the common bond of the Mesoamerican tradition.

SOURCES

The documentary and secondary sources will be discussed in other volumes of the *Handbook*, but brief comment is required here on the *relaciones geográficas* of 1579–

[1] This paper was prepared with the assistance of a grant from the National Institutes of Health, U. S. Public Health Service. The author is most grateful for this aid and for the direction of F. V. Scholes, who provided a number of unpublished documents, G. R. Willey, and E. Z. Vogt.

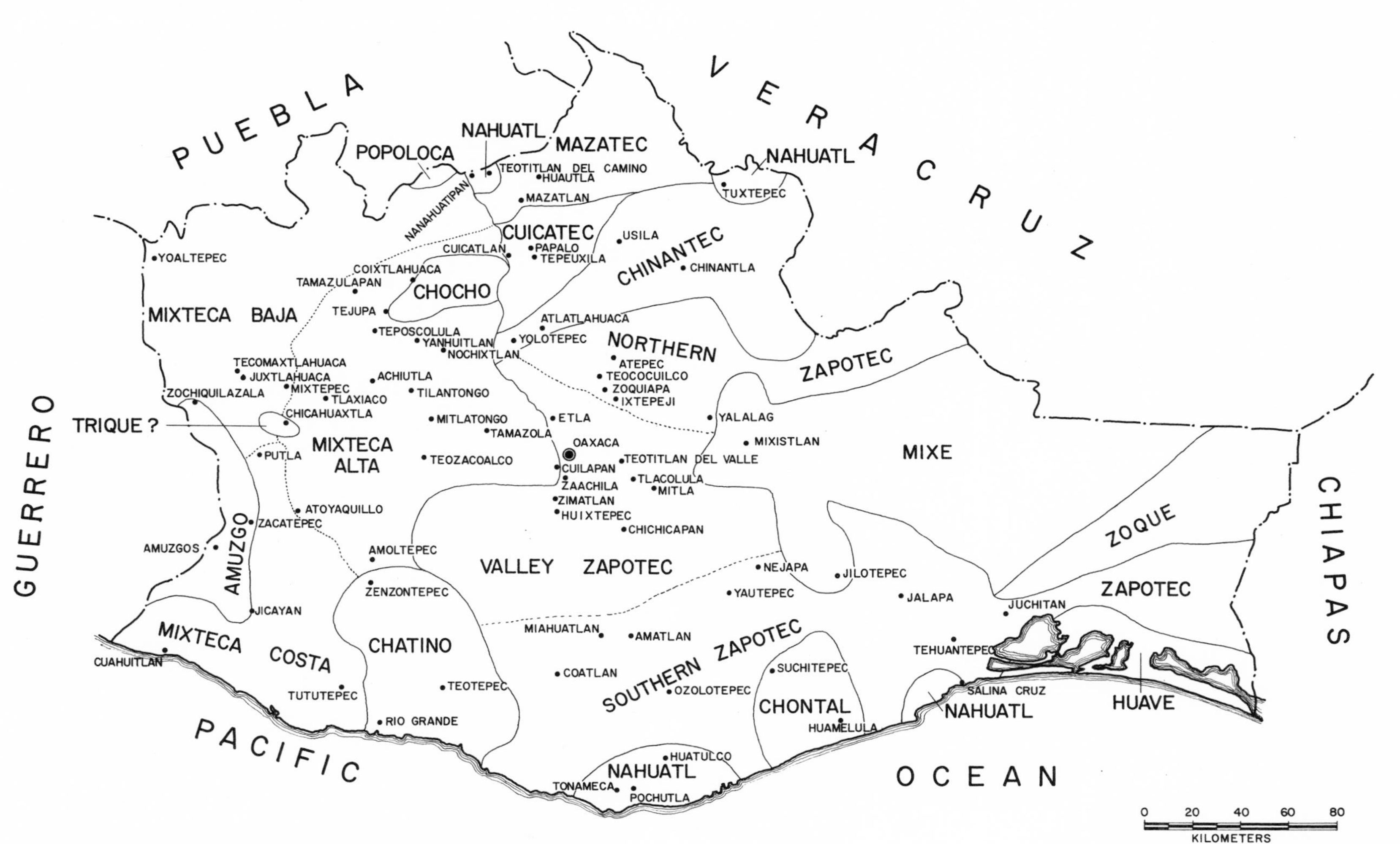

Linguistic distributions approximate. Map based on: American Geographical Society 1:1,000,000; García Granados, 1935; Mendizabal and Jiménez Moreno, 1937; Johnson, 1940; Dahlgren de Jordan, 1954; Papeles de Nueva España, 1905; Borah and Cook, 1960; RMEH.

81 published by Francisco del Paso y Troncoso (PNE, 4).[2] At the request of King Philip II of Spain elderly inhabitants of many Indian communities were asked a series of standardized questions on conditions prior to the conquest. Their answers constitute the bulk of our direct ethnographic evidence on the conditions of native life at the time of the arrival of the Spaniards. These relaciones serve as the basic source for the present study. Other materials are derived from published works and from the resources of the Archivo General de la Nación, Mexico (AGN), and the Archivo de Indias, Sevilla.

Population

Borah and Cook (1960), in a recent study of population in 16th-century New Spain, estimate the total population at the time of the conquest as 11,022,450. This figure agrees with the earlier estimate of Cook and Simpson (1948) but is substantially below the figure of 25,000,000 given by Cook and Borah in 1963. Basing their more reasonable 1960 estimates on the great *Suma de visitas* (PNE, 1), Borah and Cook have computed a figure of 7,800,000 for 1548 for all of New Spain. The 1548 figure is well below that of the estimated aboriginal population because it comes after the great pestilence of 1545–47 which attacked an already rapidly declining native population with almost universal severity. By 1565, however, there had been a steady recovery from this low point (Borah and Cook, 1960, p. 6). George Kubler (1942, p. 641; 1948, pp. 556–59) has discussed the matter of fluctuation in the native population during the 16th century, arguing against earlier views that there had been a steady decline until late in the century. According to this interpretation there was periodic decline and recovery throughout the century. Analysis of census records from a number of towns in the Mixteca Alta lends support to Kubler's view.

Further computation is necessary in estimating the population of Oaxaca at the conquest. In 1548 a total of 2,939,383 tribute payers (the base-point for population estimates, each tribute payer being equivalent to 3.3 people in the Borah-Cook scheme) were listed by the Suma for all of New Spain. Although Borah and Cook have taken care to add many non-tribute-paying subjects to the final estimate, it is assumed for present purposes that the distribution of tribute payers and the ratio of tribute payers to non-payers were fairly uniform throughout the area represented by the Suma lists.

Oaxaca provided 477,267 of the 2,939,383, or approximately 16 per cent of the total tribute payers. Since Oaxaca was subject to the same general trends and influences as the rest of New Spain during the early years of colonization and probably lost a proportionate segment of her population, we can assume that she held approximately 16 per cent of the total population in 1519, or approximately 1,760,000. A more conservative estimate is achieved by applying the same sort of computation to the 1565 figures of Cook and Simpson (4,409,180 for all of New Spain; 693,680, or scarcely 13 per cent for Oaxaca). The result is a 1519 population of approximately 1,430,000. It should be apparent that these estimates, if by nothing more than the disparity between the 1548 and 1565 figures, are to be considered provisional. Regardless of which set of figures is selected or the manner of their interpretation, it is safe to estimate the 1519 population of Oaxaca at 1,500,000 people.

Zapotec of the Valley of Oaxaca

The valleys of Tlacolula, Etla, and Zimatlan converge at Oaxaca City to form the great central complex known as the Valley of Oaxaca. The area is drained by the Atoyac and its affluents and is roughly a triangle with corners lying just southeast of Mitla, slightly

[2] Abbreviations: PNE, *Papeles de Nueva España;* RMEH, *Revista mexicana de estudios históricos,* vol. 2, nos. 5–6, pp. 113–19; AGN, Archivo General de la Nación, Mexico.

TABLE 1—ZAPOTEC OF THE VALLEY OF OAXACA

Communities	*Latitude North*	*Longitude West*	*Language*
Oaxaca	17° 4′	96°44′	Zapotec
Zimatlan	16°53′	96°47′	Zapotec
Etla	17°12′	96°47′	Zapotec
Huixtepec	16°48′	96°46′	Zapotec
Cuilapan	17° 0′	96°47′	Mixtec
Zaachila (Teotzapotlan)	16°55′	96°45′	Zapotec
Teotitlan del Valle	17° 3′	96°31′	Zapotec
Macuilxochitl	17° 2′	96°32′	Zapotec
Tlacolula	16°56′	96°28′	Zapotec
Mitla	16°55′	96°24′	Zapotec
Teitipac	16°57′	96°36′	Zapotec
Chichicapan	16°45′	96°29′	Zapotec
Taliztaca	17° 5′	96°40′	Zapotec

northwest of Etla, and in the vicinity of San Pablo Huixtepec to the south of Zimatlan. Steep-sided hills punctuate the level or somewhat undulating countryside. Abruptly rising mountain ranges delimit and define the several valleys. The altitude of the valley floor ranges from 5000 to 6000 feet above sea level.

Cuilapan, on the western border of the Valley zone, stands on the dividing line between the Mixtec and Zapotec areas. This community was under Mixtec control at the time of the conquest but historically has been very much involved in the culture of the Valley. The important archaeological sites of Cuilapan, Mitla, and Yagul testify to the era of Mixtec occupation of the classic heartland of Zapotec culture (Paddock, 1958, 1960; Bernal, 1958a–c; Iturribarría, 1960). At the Spanish conquest in November, 1521, Cuilapan constituted the principal outpost of receding Mixtec influence which had been so pronounced in the Valley (Caso, 1942).

The Valley had for many centuries been the traditional center of Zapotec culture. Zapotec occupation dated with certainty to around A.D. 400, the beginning of Monte Alban IIIA of the Mesoamerican Classic horizon (Bernal, 1958b).

During the late Postclassic the Mixtecs pushed into the area, and the carriers of two distinct cultures were living in the Valley. Bernal estimates that by 1521 Mixtec influence had been in evidence at approximately 75 per cent of the more than 200 Valley sites (Bernal, 1958b). The Mixtec strain (Monte Alban V) seems to have been dominant, but it did not displace the Zapotec tradition. The two existed side by side but with little or no visible blending.

Although Iturribarría (1960) is convinced that pockets of Mixtec-speakers continued to occupy the central portion of the Valley up to the time of the conquest, documentary evidence suggests that by 1521 cultural and linguistic coexistence had ceased to characterize the life of the area. None of the materials mention a contemporary Mixtec occupation in any part of the Valley outside of Cuilapan. By that time the Zapotec, after allying themselves with the Mexicans, had reasserted control. Although there are positive indications in the relaciones of 1579–81 that many of the towns had once been under Mixtec control, there is little hint of their having played a significant role in the local cultures. The Mixtec appear to have come in, built or taken over communities, occupied them for a period, and then moved out, leaving Zapotec culture relatively unaffected.

Political Organization

Political control of most of the important Valley towns during the period of Zapotec reassertion was centered at Teotzapotlan (Zaachila). Teotitlan del Valle, Mitla, Taliztaca, Tlacolula, Chichicapan, Macuilxochitl, and Teitipac were some of the towns included in the Teotzapotlan sphere. These towns offered tribute and services, the characteristic emblem of subjugation in precolonial central Mexico, to the Zapotec rulers seated in the capital. It is certain that Teotzapotlan had some kind of political control, but the precise nature of that control is not yet well known. This may reflect a convenient alliance of weaker towns to a militarily powerful one, a necessity in the face of the ever-present danger of Mexican, Mixtecan, and probably Mixe encroachment (PNE, 4: 190–95). It may, however, connote allegiance to an ancient native tradition. That service was normally specified as "assistance in war" and that local government tended to reside in the hands of local lords (PNE, 4: 104–08, 115–19, 144–47) reinforce the argument that this was an involuntary alliance.

A number of years before the conquest, the Valley Zapotec entered into an alliance with their traditional enemies, the Mixtec, to fend off the Mexican armies at Tehuantepec (Burgoa, 1674, 2: 341–45; Gay, 1881, 2: 185–203). The enlightened military leadership of the Zapotec king, Cosijoeza, his timely marriage to a near relative of Montezuma, the subsequent alliance of the Zapotec with the Mexicans, and the activities of Cosijopij, the son of Cosijoeza and his Mexican wife, were important themes in the native oral tradition at the time of the conquest. The seat of Zapotec political power shifted from Teotzapotlan to Tehuantepec probably during the time of the concentration of military force in that area (PNE, 4: 104–08; Gay, 1881, 2: 201).

Higher authority was recognized by the Valley communities through their tribute and services to either Teotzapotlan, Tehuantepec, Tenochtitlan, or to the Mixtec, but local political control was vested in local ruling dynasties. Teotitlan was governed by a local *señor natural* (a native or "natural born" lord) (PNE, 4: 104–08). Chichicapan recognized as its local ruler the cacique Coquilguany, "lord who illuminates the world." His descendents remained in effective power in the community until at least 1580 (PNE, 4: 115–19).

Tlacolula (PNE, 4: 144–47) was governed by a local lord but at the same time recognized the authority of the Lords of Teotzapotlan. Caso (1942, p. 26) believes that Mitla had no cacique but was under the authority of a priest whose religious authority extended over the entire Valley. The relación from that community indicates, however, that although the king of Teotzapotlan was recognized, the local government was in the hands of Coqui Cualaniza, a *señor natural*. In the other towns of the Valley there was a clear distinction between religious and secular authority, and the instance in Mitla would constitute something of an anomaly.

The lord of Teotzapotlan, according to the relación of Macuilxochitl (PNE, 4: 100–04), ordered the citizens of the latter town to obey a local *principal* (a member of the local nobility) in all things. Macuilxochitl denies having paid tribute to Teotzapotlan but admits to contributing services in war. The relaciones of Tlacolula and Mitla (PNE, 4: 144–54) also state that no tribute was given. Mitleños, however, went to work the maize fields of the lord of Teotzapotlan, and they "presented" him with honey and turkeys. Taliztaca (PNE, 4: 177–82) gave feathers, mantles, and service in war. Teotitlan del Valle, a town closely related to Macuilxochitl, contributed either to Teotzapotlan, Tehuantepec, or to the Mixtec of Cuilapan gold dust, cotton mantles, turkeys, chile, and slaves (PNE, 4: 104–08). Teitipac gave to the cacique of Teotzapotlan, and later to Montezuma, turkeys, rabbits, and honey.

The pattern of tribute and services in recognition of higher political authority is well established for the communities of the

Valley of Oaxaca. Another well-defined pattern is that local rule was in the hands of members of the local nobility. This group saw to the government and maintenance of order in the community—which usually included a number of outlying dependencies of varying size—and to the collection of tribute and recruitment for service.

All sources indicate the existence of a hereditary aristocracy in each community, the members of which were clearly distinguished from the remainder of the population. There was within this body a royal lineage which possessed, guarded, and passed from generation to generation the title of cacique, or "ruling lord," and the privileges and possessions adhering to that title.

Economic Systems and Subsistence Patterns

The fertile soils, the ample rainfall and friendly climate, and the level topography of the Valley furnished a favorable natural setting for the forging of an advanced culture based on permanent agriculture. The great productivity of the region must have accelerated the rise of the great cultures of the Monte Alban tradition and ensured their persistence in time.

Crops under cultivation at the conquest included the classic Mesoamerican agricultural complex of maize, beans, chile, and squash. Maguey, the great multipurpose plant of the Mexican upland, was grown on the less productive lands and exploited in a variety of ways. Among its more important products were maguey-fiber cloth and nectar for the preparation of the fermented drink known variously as *pulque, pulcre, octli,* or *nectli.*

A great variety of wild herbs, roots, and fruits, some of which were probably domesticated or partially so, were gathered for food and medicinal purposes. Although agriculture furnished the bulk of subsistence items, the gathering of wild plants, roots, fruits, and berries must have played a very important subsidiary role.

Hunting was of some importance in the food quest but generally only as concerned the upper class, since the lower class, the *macehuales,* was permitted to eat meat rarely, if at all. The consumption of meat very often reflected class lines. In Teitipac, for example, only principales ate the meat of rabbits, turkeys, deer, and other animals. Macehuales ate only herbs, roots, and locally produced commodities (PNE, 4: 109–14).

Only four animals were under domestication in the Valley of Oaxaca at the time of the conquest. These were the dog (probably the fattened "voiceless" variety), the turkey, the bee, and the tiny cochineal (*Coccus cacti*), a rich dyestuff. Cochineal females were gathered periodically from cactus plants on which they were raised, then dried and placed in small bags. The Valley of Oaxaca settlements annually produced 20 "bags" of this microscopic insect for tribute to the empire of the Culhua-Mexica (Barlow, 1949, pp. 118–25). Possibly the duck should be added to the list of domesticates, but the animal is mentioned only once in the relaciones (PNE, 4: 100–04) and could represent a postconquest acquisition. Domestication of animals in Oaxaca, as in the rest of Mesoamerica, was never an important factor in the economy. The few animals which were domesticated were utilized primarily in ritual feasting and sacrifice and for tribute purposes.

There were no draft animals, and the wheel was unknown. The only form of communication and conveyance was human. Individual carriers transported heavy loads over great distances, many professional *cargadores* spending most of their lives in this occupation. The universal device for securing the load to the back of the carrier in preconquest times was the tumpline, or head-strap. There is no mention of the litter being employed in the Valley.

A number of materials were imported from outside the Valley. Cotton was obtained from Tehuantepec, Jalapa, and Nejapa many miles to the south and east (PNE, 4: 100–04, 109–14). Tehuantepec seems to have furnished the bulk of the salt consumed in the Valley. It is likely that many commodities—metals, precious stones, feathers, fish, animal skins—were imported from outside. The entire problem of preconquest commerce, however, requires additional detailed study before definite patterns can be perceived.

Tribute figured prominently in the economy of the Valley on the eve of the conquest. Barlow's study of the Matrícula de Tributos and the Códice Mendocino indicates that the following items were sent in tribute to the empire of the Culhua-Mexica (Barlow, 1949, p. 123):

800 bundles of richly worked mantles
1600 bundles of large mantles
4 wooden cribs (2 of maize, 1 of beans, and 1 of *chian*)
20 gold discs, the size of an average plate and as thick as one's forefinger
20 bags of cochineal

Settlement Patterns

Houses in the majority of communities were of mud and thatch or of wood, mud, and clay with gabled thatch roofs. There is little mention of public buildings except at Mitla, but archaeological investigations at the late Valley sites show a variety of sophisticated masonry and adobe buildings.

Schmieder (1930, pp. 48–76) contrasts the settlement patterns of the valley and mountain Zapotec to that of the Mixe. It is indicated that the Spanish conquerors introduced no fundamental changes in either the mountain Zapotec or Mixe systems of settlement. The latter two groups occupy roughly similar mountain terrain (*ibid.*, p. 76). Both the mountain Zapotec and the valley Zapotec, although differing in certain aspects of culture and language, occupied compact, or nucleated, communities. The Mixe, practicing a type of mountain agriculture not greatly unlike that of the mountain Zapotec, maintained diffuse settlements of isolated farms or tiny hamlets which were scattered about the countryside.

Where the diffuse settlement pattern prevailed the houses of the families owning the land would be located on or adjacent to the scattered plots themselves. In the case of the nucleated pattern, houses are clustered in village centers, and fields are scattered about the surrounding area. The various plots in possession of a particular family need not necessarily be contiguous. Schmieder (1930, pp. 76–77) suggests that the Zapotec cooperated in clearing extensive areas of land, then divided it among those taking part in the enterprise. The result was the dispersion of a family's lands.

As the settlements grew and the cultivated area around them extended, this condition was augmented and kept the inhabitants from moving out of the village and building up isolated farmsteads on their increasingly distant and scattered fields. Among the Tzapotec, therefore, field dispersion resulted in the growth of larger, more compact settlements, in which a differentiation of activities became possible. Crafts, art, and science developed and were maintained by the mass of the population which nevertheless remained agricultural.

Warfare

War was undertaken in most cases for the taking of captives and for exacting tribute. This was of course the Mexican pattern, but it seems to have typified warfare in the Valley of Oaxaca as well. On a number of occasions, however, the Zapotec were forced to defend themselves against the encroachment of other groups. Boundary disputes probably occurred with some frequency, but such contests over land are not mentioned prominently in the record.

Most often warfare was conducted as a series of raids or ambushes which were initiated on the basis of opportunity or, perhaps, dictated by the need for sacrificial victims. It is known, on the other hand, that

Zapotec and Mixtec troops fortified and defended a hilltop near Tehuantepec and from this static position were able to administer a serious defeat to the Mexicans (Burgoa, 1674, 2: 341–45; Caso, 1942; Gay, 1881, 1: 187–96).

Armaments are of surprising uniformity throughout the Valley, and indeed throughout Oaxaca. The most characteristic implements were the flint-edged double broadsword known as the *macana,* padded cotton armor composed of three or four layers of quilted fabric and stuffing and called *ixcahuipiles* (Nahuatl) or *pelaga* (Zapotec), shields made of reeds, and bows and arrows. No mention is made of the atlatl, or spearthrower. Headdresses are mentioned as part of the war paraphernalia in Macuilxochitl.

The Spaniards arrived in the Valley of Oaxaca after a long period of generalized warfare. Many communities were constantly at war with their neighbors (PNE, 4: 117–18). Some of the towns are listed below with their opponents:

Macuilxochitl	opposed	Mitla (probably Mixtecs) and as ordered by the Lord of Teotzapotlan
Teotitlan del Valle	opposed	Mexicans
Teitipac	opposed	"the people of the mountains" and as ordered by the lord of Teotzapotlan
Mitla	opposed	Tututepec; Mexicans
Taliztaca	opposed	"the people of the mountains"
Tlacolula	opposed	Mixe; Mitla (probably Mixtecs)
Teotzapotlan (and allies)	opposed	Tututepec, Mixtecs of Tlaxiaco and Cuilapa; Mexicans (PNE, 4: 190–95; Barlow, 1949, 23)

Social Organization

It is not known what marriage prescriptions were in effect. Certain royal marriages to the contrary, there seems to have been general community endogamy. There was strict adherence to class lines in the selection of a mate. Patrilineality and patrilocality appeared as the characteristic patterns of kinship reckoning and residence. Lateral ties of kinship seem to have been weak. It was direct lineal ancestry that was constantly stressed in matters of inheritance of land, goods, and prerogatives in the legal encounters of the 16th century. In these matters lateral ties were of definitely secondary importance and were seldom stressed. The order of inheritance seems to have been: oldest son, other sons, daughters, grandchildren, and, lacking these, the next closest kin, probably a brother or nephew. Primogeniture does not appear to have been customary.

As to the social implications of residence patterns, it is not certain whether a man and his married sons would occupy adjoining dwelling complexes or maintain noncontiguous residences. Polygyny was common, both nobles and commoners being allowed to take as many wives as they could maintain (RMEH, pp. 121–32). In the case of cacique succession, however, only the offspring of the principal wife were eligible.

The most clearly emerging feature was the stress laid on social class. This was a two-class society composed of (1) a privileged nobility—the principales, and the caciques, or señores naturales, and (2) the common, or macehual, class. Distinctions are frequently drawn between the common mass and the aristocratic minority. Only the nobility could wear brightly woven and decorated cotton and feathered mantles and skirts; the commoner wore maguey-fiber garments devoid of ornamentation. Lip plugs, earrings, brightly colored feathers, and gold and stone beads were adornments restricted to the upper class. In war the principales were equipped with better weapons and armor than were the macehuales. In most communities meat and cacao consumption was limited to the privileged group, being denied to the macehuales except possibly on special occasions. The range of social interaction within and between the classes was framed in a variety of prescriptive and proscriptive rules.

Religion

Zapotec religion in the Valley of Oaxaca was characterized by seven major themes: (1) the possession and adoration of wooden and stone idols; (2) ritual sacrifice of dogs, birds, and human beings; (3) blood offering by piercing tongue, ears, nostrils, and other body parts; (4) fasting and penance; (5) feasting, ritual dancing, and intoxication; (6) a formalized, and probably full-time, priesthood; and (7) ritual cannibalism.

In Taliztaca (PNE, 4: 179) an idol representing Coquihuani, "god of light," was worshipped. Boys and men were sacrificed; quail feathers, dogs, parrot feathers and blood were offered. There were ceremonial drunkenness and dancing before the idol to the accompaniment of musical instruments. Pulque was consumed in enormous quantities.

An idol called Coquebila was worshipped in Macuilxochitl. There was fasting for periods of 40 or 80 days, during which time the celebrant consumed only a quantity of *picietl* (Nahuatl), or native tobacco, every four days and offered blood from the tongue and ears. At the time of religious feasting there was dancing and intoxication.

Dogs, turkeys, and humans were sacrificed in Tlacolula. The principal idol was Coque Cehuiyo. Children, slaves, and dogs were sacrified before the idols of Teitipac, followed by dancing and consumption of narcotic mushrooms which produced "frightful visions."

Chichicapan recognized many gods and worshipped figures of them. Pichanagobeche, the major deity, was regarded with the greatest reverence "because he took away sickness." Another god was Pichanto who acted as intercessor for the god Pichanagobeche. To these were offered blood taken from the ears, nose, tongue, and other parts of the body. Quail, dogs, and other animals were sacrificed. The heart of any animal taken in the hunt had to be offered to the gods before the flesh could be consumed. The hearts of war captives were torn out and the bodies eaten.

In Mitla the chief deities were Xonaxi Quecuya and her husband Coqui Bezelao, "Señor Diablo." The relación of the community states that all pueblos of the Valley worshipped these gods, made sacrifices to them, and danced before them. Caso (1942) identifies these as the god and goddess of death. The usage of the time (Córdova, 1942, p. 141,*r*), however, would favor "lord and mistress of the underworld." Mitla had a priest called *vigaña,* whose authority apparently extended beyond Mitla (Caso, 1942). He is likened to a bishop by the relación. The designation *vigaña* appears to mean "priest," since it occurs in reference to the local priests at Ozolotepec and at Miahuatlan among the southern Zapotec.

The number of names attributed to the deities of the various communities, as Caso (1942, p. 26) has suggested, do not necessarily designate separate gods. The individual names could very well be different appellations for the same god, for separate aspects of the same god, or they may refer to an intercessor between the deity and man. As has been indicated, each village had its own patron deity which may account for the numerous entities that appear to constitute the Zapotec pantheon. It is probable that the concept of a supreme god was well formulated in the Valley prior to the arrival of the Spaniards. Córdova (1942, p. 140*v*) gives the name Coquixee or Coquicilla for the supreme god. Mitla may well have been the focal point of a cult dedicated to ancestor worship, death, or the underworld as symbolized by Coqui Bezelao.

Southern Zapotec

By the time of the conquest, Zapotec-speaking peoples had distributed themselves over the varied terrain running from the torrid

TABLE 2—SOUTHERN ZAPOTEC

Communities	*Latitude North*	*Longitude West*	*Language*
Miahuatlan	16°21′	96°35′	Zapotec
Amatlan	16°20′	96°28′	Zapotec
Ozolotepec	16° 8′	96°20′	Zapotec
Coatlan	16°12′	96°46′	Zapotec
Nejapa	16°38′	95°58′	Zapotec, Mixe, Chontal
Suchitepec	16°12′	95°55′	Zapotec, Chontal
Jalapa	16°30′	95°26′	Zapotec, Mixe, Mixtec
Tehuantepec (vicinity)	16°20′	95°14′	Zapotec, Huave, Nahuatl, Mixe, Mixtec, Zoque (RMEH, pp. 164–80; Burgoa, 1674, 2: 338–43)

tropical plain of Tehuantepec up through the humid steep-sided valleys and ridges to the rugged 8000–10,000-foot heights of the cool coast range of southern Oaxaca. The region was sprinkled with islands of Nahuatl-, Chontal- (of Oaxaca), Huave-, Mixtec-, and Mixe-speakers, and was bordered on the east by the Zoque tribes which were allied linguistically to the great Zoque-Maya stock. Zapotec peoples, however, were clearly dominant. It would be possible to divide further the Zapotec into (1) Miahuatlan, (2) coastal mountain, and (3) Tehuantepec groups. The distinctions have not been adequately appraised by specific comparative studies of language and culture, however, and the larger grouping employed here is adequate for general descriptive purposes. Very little is known of the Mixe, Chontal, Zoque, Huave, and Nahuatl groups residing in this area at the conquest, and they are mentioned in the documents only in an incidental way.

Political Organization

Both the Mexicans and the Mixtec of Tututepec attempted to bring much of this area under control. Coatlan was perpetually at war with Tututepec but paid tribute to Montezuma in return for military "protection" (PNE, 4: 133–34). Ozolotepec (PNE, 4: 138) and Miahuatlan (PNE, 4: 127) also paid tribute to the Mexicans. The remainder of the Zapotec communities seem to have been independent or somehow allied with Tehuantepec or Teotzapotlan. Local rule remained in the hands of a hereditary aristocracy just as it had in the Valley of Oaxaca. Amatlan, Ozolotepec, Miahuatlan, and Coatlan had their own ruling caciques, as did Tehuantepec and Jalapa, the latter two combined within the cacicazgo of Tehuantepec at the time of the conquest (RMEH, pp. 164–80). All caciques were the recipients of tribute and/or services.

Economic Systems and Patterns of Subsistence and Settlement

The principal crops being cultivated in Tehuantepec at the conquest were maize, chile, beans, squash, and sweet potatoes (RMEH, pp. 164–80). Fields were irrigated by diverting water from running streams onto farm plots. Turkeys, bees, and dogs were under domestication. A great variety of wild animals—armadillos, wild pigs, rabbits, iguanas—and birds were taken for food, and fish and shellfish were collected from sea and stream. In addition, many wild fruits, herbs, and roots were gathered. The area was reported to be extremely rich in a variety of resources, including precious stones and metals.

Suchitepec (PNE, 4: 25), in the hot mountain valleys to the west of Tehuantepec, harvested two crops of maize and cacao a year. Bananas, pineapple, zapotes, and sweet potatoes were also raised. Nearby Nejapa raised maize, cotton, and chile which were said to have been irrigated from passing streams (PNE, 4: 37–42). A variety of herbs, plants, and trees were employed for food and medicine, and a number of wild animals, including snakes, were eaten. Nejapa was adjacent to gold- and silver-producing areas. Ozolotepec raised maize, chile, and beans on high mountain terraces (PNE, 4: 141). Miahuatlan raised these crops and others including maguey (PNE, 4: 128). Amatlan was a *pulque*-producing center (PNE, 4: 121). Cochineal was raised around Miahuatlan.

The entire southern Zapotec area was devoted to extensive commercial enterprise. A great weekly market was held in Miahuatlan, to which goods, merchants, and patrons came from many miles distant. This was also a center for the slave trade. Slaves were sent from here to Mexico, Tlaxcala, Tepeaca, and to the Mixteca, the going rate per head being the equivalent of 1 peso or 1½ pesos in gold. Nearby Amatlan seems to have been a village that was largely devoted to commerce. Merchants from here brought salt and fish from Tehuantepec and maize, chile, cotton, and other products from Tehuantepec and elsewhere, carrying them from market to market. Tehuantepec was of course a great market center, and goods and traders went from here to all parts of preconquest Mesoamerica.

Houses were most generally made of mud and thatch. There is insufficient evidence at this time to make definite statements regarding settlement patterns. The general commercial complexion of the region would seem to favor clustering in compact centers in certain areas, but there is not yet any convincing evidence that this "Zapotec pattern" was uniform throughout the area.

Native Medicine: Use of Tobacco

A rich pharmacopoeia and curing lore were important components of the Mesoamerican tradition. The relaciones of the various communities of Oaxaca list a great variety of medicinal products and methods of treatment. From Miahuatlan (PNE, 4: 130) comes an interesting example of the early use of native tobacco in curing.

The leaf, *picietl,* was gathered from the plant (apparently wild) and left in the sun to dry. It was then mixed with a little lime and placed in the mouth between the gums and the lips and chewed all day.

> With it they say they don't feel the cold, and that it strengthens and fortifies the body. They cure ulcers with it and enjoy inhaling the smoke which they take in a small pipe. They also mix it with the leaf of another plant which they call *nanctzi,* that is, "madre," which they burn and inhale the smoke and eject it through the nostrils. They say it eases headache and hay fever. They call this mixture *suchietl,* which is to say, "flower that smells."

The Spanish author of the relación of 1580 remarks that "we have had the experience of it and find it to be, as they say, very beneficial. It is in general use, especially among those afflicted with asthma for which it is a notable remedy."

Warfare

The major wars fought in Tehuantepec were those against the Mexicans. Suchitepec is said to have fought with "Chichimecs" (PNE, 4: 27). In addition to their struggles with the great powers, Miahuatlan, Ozolotepec, and Coatlan, even though they were "all of one language and custom," seem to have fought among themselves (PNE, 4: 126–28). Ozolotepec made war on the Chontal and Mixe, a warfare which continued to 1580 (PNE, 4: 140). Amatlan did not fight with her neighbors, but the cacique and his appointed captains did lead a battle against the Mexican garrison at Oaxaca (PNE, 4: 120–21). Nejapa battled neighboring groups, which appear to have been composed of Mixe and Chontal (PNE, 4: 35).

The warriors of Nejapa used bows and arrows, the *macana,* and shields; cotton armor was worn by the nobility. These were standard equipment throughout the southern Zapotec region. Feathered headdresses were worn in Ozolotepec. The Mixe and Chontal are reported to have fought exclusively with spears (PNE, 4: 35).

Prisoners were taken in war either as slaves or as sacrificial victims. Again, warfare appears to have consisted mostly of short skirmishes initiated from ambush or quick raids with the intent of taking prisoners. This was the pattern in Ozolotepec (PNE, 4: 140). The prisoners taken in war by Ozolotepec were divided into three groups: the boys and girls were made slaves, some captives were "sent to Montezuma" as sacrificial victims, the remainder was sacrificed and eaten.

Social Organization

Information is extremely scarce, but these patterns do emerge: (1) Polygyny was commonly practiced (RMEH, pp. 164–80). (2) Marriage was delayed until the male was 30–40 years of age (PNE, 4: 141). (3) There were puberty rites for boys, at which time the celebrant was presented with a symbolic loincloth (PNE, 4: 34). (4) There was rigid stratification into two social classes: a dominant aristocracy, and the common class. Class differences were evident in dress, religious observances, food consumption, and differential extension of privilege by the ruling element.

Note on Native Law

One of the few statements on native law in Oaxaca comes from Nejapa (PNE, 4: 34). Adultery, wife-stealing, theft, and dishonesty were severely punished. For lying the mouth was laid open to the molars. Illicit fornication was punished by slitting the nostrils and the genitals. In the case of adultery the parties were separated and stoned. The relación of that community states that it was seldom necessary to carry out such punishments since children were raised from childhood to conform with the laws.

Religion

Information on religion is very good from this area. One of the most adequately described religious complexes is at Ozolotepec (PNE, 4: 138–39). Here a temple containing the idols was maintained by a group of priests, the vigañas. They performed all sacrifices of animals and prisoners, and all offerings passed through their hands. In carrying out the sacrifice of a human being they "took out the hearts and placed them on a stone altar with the blood spilling over the edge, and they ate the flesh of the victim with great relish." The lords and nobles of the town took blood from their ears, nose, and tongue with very thin stone blades and "offered it by hand to the vigañas who never left the temple."

The principal idol of Ozolotepec was called *Bezalao,* "The Devil."

> They recognized this as the universal god who protected them from death and aided them in war. He was invoked for all their crops, dealings, and activities. And there were also others, called in their language *Cozichacozee,* who acted as mediators. This was the god of war for whom they had much need since they were constantly engaged in warfare. They pictured him thus, as very ferocious, holding bows and arrows in his hands. They feared him and had great reverence for him, and above all for *Bezalao,* who was the devil, the supreme universal god."

How precisely such a pattern represents the southern Zapotec region as a whole remains in question. It seems likely, however, that local complexes did not vary appreciably from that of Ozolotepec. In Miahuatlan (PNE, 4: 127) there was a temple wherein the priests prayed and sacrificed to Gozío (Cozío), the rain god, at planting time. Tlacatecolotl was invoked for all their "necessities and works." Miahuatlan practiced customs of sacrifice and offering identical to those at Ozolotepec.

Coatlan (PNE, 4: 134) observed rights in a great cave. Legend held that sacrifice was not practiced until one of the caciques visited the Mixteca Alta, where he learned the custom. Returning to his community, an idol called Benelaba ("Seven Rabbit") and his wife, Jonaji Belachina ("Three Deer"), were "invented" and placed in the great cave. Benelaba was approached only by male worshipers; only women appealed to Jonaji Belachina.

Nejapa (PNE, 4: 34) is reported to have had gods of waters, winds, agriculture, hunting, fishing, childbirth or fertility, war, peace, "a god for all works," and a god of gods. There was a 40-day fast in which only meat from the hunt was consumed, and penance and confession were practiced. Sacrifice was carried out among some ancient buildings atop nearby Mt. Quiatoni.

Tehuantepec, Suchitepec, and Jalapa appear to have had the conventional temple-priest-sacrificial complex as described for the other communities. The over-all complex, including the names of the deities, is very similar to that reported for the Valley Zapotec.

Mountain Zapotec

Political Organization

Ixtepeji (PNE, 4: 16), a mountain Zapotec community, Chinantla (PNE, 4: 60–61), traditional center of Chinantec peoples, the Cuicatec centers of Tepeuxila (PNE, 4: 98), Papaloticpac (PNE, 4: 90), Cuicatlan (PNE, 4: 185–86), Atlatlahuaca (PNE, 4: 165–66), and Malinaltepec (PNE, 4: 168–69), and Chinantec-speaking Usila (PNE, 4: 48–49) were under Mexican control at the conquest. *Calpixquis* were sent out from the Mexican stronghold of Tuxtepec to supervise the collection of tribute in each of the tributaries. All pueblos maintained local ruling lineages and noble classes, the effective social and political leadership thus residing in local hands.

Teotitlan del Camino on the Oaxaca-Puebla border was a Nahuatl-speaking community allied with, but independent of, Tenochtitlan. This important town controlled a territory composed primarily of Mazatec groups in and around Mazatlan (PNE, 4: 223–25) and Huautla (PNE, 4: 225–27) and mixed Mazatec and Nahuatl communities around Nextepec (PNE, 4: 227–29), Nanahuaticpac (PNE, 4: 229–30),

Table 3—MOUNTAIN ZAPOTEC AND OTHER TRIBES OF THE NORTHERN SIERRA

Communities	*Latitude North*	*Longitude West*	*Language*
Teotitlan del Camino	18° 8′	97° 4′	Nahuatl
Nanahuatipan	18° 7′	97° 6′	Nahuatl, Mazatec
Tecolutla	(near Teotitlan, but exact location unknown)		Nahuatl, Mazatec
Nextepec	(near Teotitlan, but exact location unknown)		Nahuatl, Mazatec
Huautla	18° 8′	96°51′	Mazatec
Mazatlan	18° 2′	96°55′	Mazatec
Tepeuxila	17°47′	96°50′	Cuicatec
Papalo (Papaloticpac)	17°48′	96°52′	Cuicatec
Cuicatlan	17°47′	96°57′	Cuicatec
Atlatlahuaca	17°32′	96°49′	Cuicatec
Malinaltepec	(near Atlatlahuaca, but location unknown)		Cuicatec
Chinantla	17°47′	96°17′	Chinantec
Usila	17°52′	96°32′	Chinantec
Tuxtepec	18° 6′	96° 7′	Nahautl
Atepec	17°25′	96°34′	Zapotec
Teococuilco	17°20′	96°51′	Zapotec
Zoquiapa	17°18′	96°37′	Zapotec
Ixtepeji	17°15′	96°34′	Zapotec

and Tecolutla (PNE, 4: 230–31). All towns were tributaries of Teotitlan. It is indicated that the lord of Teotitlan appointed governors to handle local affairs and to see to the collection of tribute in the subject towns.

Teococuilco (RMEH, pp. 121–32) had a supreme native lord who was assisted by two or more elderly advisors. The cacique had absolute power over the life and goods of his subjects and held them in a high degree of servitude. Complete respect and obedience were required of his people. A group of assistants called *tequitlatos* enforced compliance with the cacique's orders. Anyone appearing before the lord was required to remove his shoes and to keep his head bowed throughout the interview. Although there had been some curtailment of power, it is mentioned that the cacique of Teococuilco continued to be regarded with the greatest respect in 1580 (RMEH, p. 128).

Economic Systems and Subsistence Patterns

The Chinantec and Cuicatec communities (PNE, 4: 49–51, 62–66, 91–92, 95) cultivated maize, squash, beans, chile, and alligator pears. In the flatlands around Usila cotton and cacao were raised; achiote, cacao, and zapotes were grown by the Chinantla farmers. A variety of fruits, herbs, and roots were gathered in the countryside. Fish, turkeys, armadillos, rabbits, and rats were the principal meat animals.

Three crops of maize yearly were possible on the moist soils around Chinantla, and two annual crops were customary in Usila. Iztepeji (PNE, 4: 19–20), however, was cursed with sterile soils which would yield only small amounts of maize, beans, and squash. The diet in this Zapotec community was heavily supplemented with wild game. Much of the food had to be imported from outside the community. Teotitlan del Camino (PNE, 4: 213–23) grew maize, chile, beans, and squash on somewhat marginal lands. The diet of the macehuales was restricted to tortillas, chile, and *pinole* (a kind of cornmeal porridge). Only the principales were permitted to eat meat from the hunt in Teotitlan.

Ixtepeji paid in tribute to the Mexicans imported gold dust, imported green feathers, deer, maize, wood, and personal services (PNE, 4: 16–17). Chinantla, Usila, Tepeuxila, and other communities contributed large quantities of goods to Tuxtepec, the capital of an immensely rich tribute province that included southern Veracruz, parts of Tabasco, and this section of Oaxaca (Barlow, 1949, pp. 93–97). The little Teotitlan "empire" was actively involved in the production of clothing, which was traded as far as Guatemala (PNE, 4: p. 215). Pottery, reed mats, and clothing were also manufactured in Chinantla (PNE, 4: 68).

Wearing apparel for males was the cotton breechclout and a mantle knotted at the shoulder; the cotton *huipil* and wrap-around skirt were standard feminine garments. This standardized dress overrode linguistic boundaries and was characteristic for the entire area from Ixtepeji to Teotitlan del Camino.

Settlement Patterns

Houses were of mud and thatch or of adobe, stone, and wood.

Diffuse settlement patterns seem to have been typical of non-Zapotec areas. The relación of Chinantla comments on the almost vacant ceremonial center, the bulk of the population being scattered over "50 square leagues" of countryside on farms or in hamlets (PNE, 4: 59). The Chinantecs were said to be poor builders, accustomed to constructing impermanent dwellings since they "moved freely from one place to another."

It is reported that the Nahuatl and Mazatec peoples around Teotitlan del Camino did not reside in permanent formally organized villages (PNE, 4: 228). The relación of Atlatlahuaca conveys the impression that the houses were grouped along "streets" in compact centers (PNE, 4: 175).

In this Cuicatec community the macehuales resided in one- and two-room huts and the principales in large residences with two and three patios.

As mentioned previously, the mountain Zapotec lived in compact settlements. This contrasts sharply with the dispersed patterns of the Chinantec and Mixe. The Mixe apparently lacked large settlements in preconquest times. Schmieder (1930, p. 63) states that preconquest ruins in the Mixe area suggest "a loose nucleus of dwellings around that of a leader, on a naturally fortified site, the rest of the population spread about on isolated ranchos in the surrounding forest." The arrangement of dwellings in the Mixe area was without apparent over-all plan. Schmieder, in discussing the rather inferior achievement of Mixe culture when contrasted to that of neighboring Zapotec groups, states (1930, p. 63) that among the Mixe "the extremely rugged country and the scattered little patches of really good land formed an obstacle to the formation of larger, compact settlements. Urban culture in all its multiple aspects never developed among them."

Warfare

Tepeuxila (PNE, 4: 98) and Usila (PNE, 4: 49) fought neighboring communities for the purpose of gaining captives for sacrifice. The Mazatec (PNE, 4: 226) warred with the Mixtec, and before being reduced to Mexican control, Atlatlahuaca (PNE, 4: 169) did battle with Teococuilco and Ixtepeji; the enemies of Malinaltepec were Yolox and the Chinantec. When summoned, Chinantla fought on the side of the Mexicans.

Warfare was initiated for the purpose of capturing slaves and/or acquiring tribute. The Ixtepeji Zapotec went into battle singing to the accompaniment of the *teponaztli* (Nahuatl: a wooden drum) and carrying an idol. A favored tactic in battles between Atlatlahuaca and Teococuilco was to form a squadron into two companies on the highest accessible terrain. As the enemy advanced the combined elements would descend the hill and engage their opponents in hand-to-hand combat. Face and leg paint "to make them appear more fierce and terrifying" was worn by the troops of Atepec (RMEH, pp. 128–29). Implements of war included padded cotton armor, clubs, *macanas,* shields of reed or skins, long and short wooden swords, and bows and arrows. Rocks and slings are reported for Tepeuxila and Papaloticpac. The Mixe are believed to have gone to war armed with especially long pikes (PNE, 4: 35).

Social Organization

Two or three married couples with their children resided in the same one- or two-room house in Atlatlahuaca (PNE, 4: 175). It is not possible to determine from the published documents the relationship of the different nuclear families; the most that could be implied is that some form of extended family may have been in practice.

There is a report from Chinantla (PNE, 4: 67) that houses were abandoned on the death of one of the members of the household. This is the only indication of this practice noted for preconquest Oaxaca.

A man of Ixtepeji (PNE, 4: 17–18) contemplating marriage would inquire as to whether or not the woman of his choice was a virgin and eligible to be his wife. If the parents approved the match, he would take the girl away, by force or deceit if necessary, to his house. The couple would then return to the house of the girl's parents where there would be sacrifices before an image, feasting, and much drinking. A woman found guilty of adultery in Ixtepeji was not killed but was returned to her parents with the report that "she was a bad woman."

Religion

A fast of 140 days was prescribed for those engaging in the principal feast of the year at Usila (PNE, 4: 48). During this time the celebrant could indulge in no act which might be ritually unclean. Salt, chile, or other "dainties" could not be consumed. Only tortillas, a little cooked maize, and some tobacco could be taken once daily. One of the ceremonies practiced in Usila required the sacrifice of a child without sin, a turkey, a dog, and a cat. Great amounts of copal were burned, and there was much dancing and feasting on the flesh of slaves purchased for the occasion. This ritual was practiced twice yearly, in the spring and in the fall.

The communities around Teococuilco (RMEH, p. 121–32) had idols of wood and stone. These were dedicated to rain, fertility, health, and to the satisfaction of other basic needs. Further, each community had an individual patron deity which "they revered above all." In Teococuilco there was a god Coquebezelao, "prince of devils," to whom sacrifices and offerings were made from a nearby hilltop. This town also observed a periodic celebration at each renewal of the calendric cycle of 260 days. Human sacrifices were begun on the eve of the first day of the new year and continued through the hours of darkness. This was followed on the succeeding day by great feasting. Nearby Zoquiapa observed ceremonies dedicated to Coquenexo, "lord of multiplication," every 260 days.

The priests at Teococuilco were taken into the temple or special houses of instruction at seven years of age. Here they learned the rituals and prepared for life-long service in the priesthood. During tenure they were required to observe rules of chastity and sobriety and to endure frequent periods of fasting. Violation of the proscriptions was punishable by death. The priests played a vital role in the life of the community where nothing was possible or undertaken without the intercession of the gods. The caciques did not enter into war, marriage, any important negotiation, or even go hunting without consulting the community priests.

Chinantla (PNE, 4: 60–61) had a tower-like temple with 100 steps leading to the top, and adjacent to the temple was a cave where a group of images was kept.

They sacrificed at the top of the tower, and those doing penance entered the cave. This penance was in accord with what their priests had ordered. They did not leave the cave, nor did they communicate with women during the time of penance. They fasted 100 days, eating only once a day, and for three days they ate nothing except one tortilla of the size and thickness ordered by the priest. To more easily endure the hunger they chewed the resin of a tree called *uli*.

Teotitlan del Camino (PNE, 4: 217), following the Mexican ceremonial cycle, observed 18 yearly festivals, one every 20 days. There was, in addition, a great celebration every four years. The relación of Teotitlan states that a "new fire" was lit every four years and that great quantities of copal were burned before the idols and in the houses at that time. The Mexican religious complex was also observed in the Mazatec and Nahuatl communities subject to Teotitlan (PNE, 4: 224–31).

Mixteca Alta

Political Organization

The concept of absolute monarchy in preconquest Oaxaca had its classic expression among the caciques of the Mixteca Alta. A cacicazgo (the rights, properties, duties, and prerogatives pertaining to the hereditary title of cacique) was a rigorously guarded possession; there were precisely defined requirements for establishing a valid claim. After the conquest an individual's right to a title depended on his ability to prove that he was the rightful heir by "linea recta y derecha sucesión." A number of suits presented to the Spanish courts in the middle and late 16th century most adequately point up the importance of this concept both before and after the arrival of the Spaniards.

One of the great cacicazgos during the 16th century was that of Yanhuitlan located in the very heart of the Mixteca Alta. Ex-

TABLE 4—MIXTECA ALTA

Communities	*Latitude North*	*Longitude West*	*Language*
Teozacoalco	17° 2′	97°18′	Mixtec
Tamazola	17° 8′	97° 5′	Mixtec
Mitlatongo	17°10′	97°15′	Mixtec
Tlaxiaco	17°16′	97°42′	Mixtec
Tilantongo	17°16′	97°20′	Mixtec
Achiutla	17°20′	97°31′	Mixtec
Nochixtlan	17°27′	97°14′	Mixtec
Teposcolula	17°31′	97°29′	Mixtec
Yanhuitlan	17°32′	97°21′	Mixtec
Tejupa	17°39′	97°28′	Mixtec, Chocho
Coixtlahuaca	17°42′	97°22′	Mixtec, Chocho
Tamazulapan	17°40′	97°35′	Mixtec

amination of a number of sources (AGN, Civil, 516; AGN, Tierras, 400, exp. 1; AGN, Indios, 3, exp. 540) indicates that the title carried with it 980 acres of farm and grazing land, many houses and buildings, tribute from subject communities, personal services for the cacique's houses and fields, great amounts of movable property, and a number of privileges extended by the Spanish Crown. These included commercial monopolies, a salary of 400 pesos a year, the title of Don, a coat of arms, permits to raise livestock, to wear Spanish habit and ride on horseback, and to bear firearms, and other concessions and privileges. Sixteen witnesses, many of them born before the conquest, testified in 1580 that these privileges—except for those specially extended by the Spaniards—had been accorded to Numahu and Cauaco, preconquest caciques of Yanhuitlan. This group of natives further testified that one Don Gabriel de Guzmán, grandson of Numahu and Cauaco, was the only legitimate heir to the title that he had assumed some 30 years previously by virtue of the fact that he was the legitimate son of María Coquahu, former cacica, and grandson of Numahu and Cauaco (AGN, Civil, 516).

The cacicazgo of Teposcolula (AGN, Tierras, 24, exp. 6), an average-size cacicazgo for the period following the conquest, held many parcels of land, houses, crops, a share of tribute, labor services, custody of 6000 pesos' worth of jewelry (probably not typical), and a number of other rights, properties, and privileges. Each of the important communities of the Mixteca Alta was somehow involved as part of such a cacicazgo.

Tilantongo was an extremely important center around the time of the conquest. It was said to be ruled by "the most noble lineage in all the Mixteca Alta" (AGN, Tierras, 24, exp. 6). Caso (1960, pp. 21–22) has concluded, on the basis of documentary evidence, that the lords of Tilantongo ranked supreme in the region and that the cacique of Tilantongo reserved the right to appoint a member of the royal lineage of Tilantongo to vacancies in certain towns where the caciques had produced no legitimate offspring. It is certain that descent from the lords of Tilantongo was mentioned in cases of cacique succession in the 16th century at Yanhuitlan (AGN, Civil, 516), Tamazola-Chachuapa (AGN, Tierras, 3343), Teposcolula (AGN, Tierras, 24, exp. 6), and Tejupa (AGN, Tierras, 34, exp. 1).

The lord of Tilantongo (PNE, 4: 73–74) had a great kingdom (*señorío*) that included the provinces of Teposcolula, Tlaxiaco, Atoyaquillo, and Teozacoalco, "the most important pueblos of all the Mixteca Alta." These communities are said to have contributed gold jewels, precious stones, plumes, and mantles to the Cacique. The relación states that these pueblos were "divided among brothers" in ancient times. The native lord is said to have had four *regidores* who governed the entire kingdom. They were aware of everything which occurred in the area and gave accounts of events to the cacique. The most "gifted" of the group was designated the leader and the remainder were "associates." They determined when and what to sacrifice and handled other business. The priest and the cacique ruled on such important matters as making war.

The Tilantongo relación indicates that the first lord in the Mixteca was Yoqhque, or Nahui Cipactli (Nahuatl: "Four Crocodile"), who was born on the nearby hill of Tilantongo. From this lord was descended Yaq Quaa, or Nahui Mazatzin (Nahuatl: "Four Deer"), who was cacique at the conquest. Yay Quaa was not baptized, but his oldest son was converted and was called Don Juan de Mendoza. The lord of Tilantongo received gold, precious jewels, feathers, and mantles at the major festivals. His subjects also worked his fields and gave the cacique deer and turkeys for food.

Mitlantongo (PNE, 4: 78) was divided into two cabeceras with no additional dependencies. Legend states that the people of Mitlantongo were in ancient times vassals of a Lord Yacoñooy, or Ceozomatli (Nahuatl: "One Monkey"), who was born on the hill of Yucucuy, or Xoxotepec (Nahuatl: "Green Mountain"), in Tilantongo. This lord produced two sons. The older took Santa Cruz Mitlantongo as his cacicazgo and the younger was given Santiago Mitlantongo. Both of them succeeded to their titles by "linea recta" and were in power at the conquest. Both were baptized, the older, Yaqhii, as Don Francisco de Mendoza, and the younger, Nucoy, as Don Diego de Rojas. These lords were given mantles in tribute and their fields were worked for them, "and that is all."

Similar patterns of recognition of hereditary lords and customs of tribute and service were evident in Nochixtlan (PNE, 4: 208). Tejupa (PNE, 4: 55) had as "lord and cacique" at the conquest Yesa Huyya, and his wife was Yaanicuin. The community was subject to Montezuma, as was Nochixtlan, and gave slaves, parrot feathers, and cochineal in tribute to the Empire. The cacique of Tejupa received "copal and all other necessary items for rites and for the temple of the devil where sacrifices were made."

According to local legend, Yacocuuñi, lord of Tamazola, had come from heaven. His wife, Yajimañe, came forth from a stone that had broken open. Their descendent by "linea recta," Yasimeni, Don Diego de Velasco, was cacique of Tamazola at the conquest (PNE, 4: 83; see also AGN, Civil, 516; AGN, Tierras, 3343). Don Diego is said to have governed through four counsels, "the wisest men from the pueblos." This community was "friendly" toward Montezuma, but it was denied that tribute was paid to the Empire. Barlow (1949, pp. 114–15), however, indicates that Tamazola was one of the towns listed in the Códice Mendocino as having paid tribute to the Culhua-Mexica and that a Mexican garrison was quartered there. The relación mentions that the cacique of the community received mantles, gold beads, precious stones, and had his fields worked.

Barlow's (1949) careful study of tribute to the Empire of the Culhua-Mexica based on materials derived from the Matrícula de Tributos and Códice Mendocino has determined that there were two main tribute provinces in the Mixteca Alta. These were Tlaxiaco, and Coixtlahuaca.

The winning of Coixtlahuaca was one of the great conquering achievements of the Culhua-Mexica in the 15th century. The conquest was made under the reign of Montezuma I, who ruled Mexico-Tenochtitlan from 1440 to 1468 (Códice Chimalpopoca, 1945, pp. 66–67). The Anales de Tlatelolco (1948, pp. 56–57) gives 5 Tochtli (1458) as the year of the overthrow of what may have been at that time the chief city-state of the Mixteca Alta. Herrera (1726, dec. 3, lib. 3, cap. 13) states that the Mixteca Alta, and Yanhuitlan under Lord Three Monkey in particular, fell to Montezuma I. The Anales de Cuauhtitlán (Códice Chimalpopoca, 1945, p. 67) and Clavijero (1958, 1: 306) attribute the fall of Yanhuitlan to the reign of Tizoc around 1486. There is little doubt that the greater part of the Mixteca Alta was under the political domination of the Mexicans during the four decades that preceded the Spanish conquest.

It is well documented that the Mexicans undertook a punitive expedition to Yanhuitlan and Zozollan—a "rebellious situation" involving Mexican merchants had taken place—in 1506. Yanhuitlan was sacked and 1000 prisoners were taken and later sacrificed in the festival of Tlacaxipehualistli in Tenochtitlan (Durán, 1941, 1: 454–56; Tezozomoc, 1944, pp. 447–51).

Despite the Mexican overlordship, virtual local autonomy continued in the major centers of the Mixteca Alta. The Mexicans were interested more in acquiring tribute than in physical domination or acquisition of land. The desired end could best be obtained by maintaining traditional lines of authority, and there seems to have been little effort on the part of the Mexicans to upset traditional local patterns. Ruling lineages were allowed to carry on probably much as they had previously.

That there were ruling lineages of native lords within the various communities is beyond question. There is little doubt, moreover, that members of a dynastic family might be distributed in a number of communities, as is indicated in the case of Tilantongo. Caso (1960, p. 22) has suggested that all the caciques of the Mixteca Alta were part of a great dynastic family. This conclusion is borne out by 16th-century testimony from Mitlantongo, Tilantongo, Yanhuitlan, Tamazola, and Teposcolula, where descent from the lords of Tilantongo is mentioned. An emergent pattern is that caciques married only the legitimate daughters of caciques if they wished to have their children inherit the title. Every effort was extended to ensure the purity of the ruling lineages, and the concept of inheritance of title by direct succession was defended at all costs.

Economic Systems and Subsistence Patterns

The agriculturalists of the Mixteca Alta cultivated maize, chile, beans, and squash. A variety of wild plants, roots, fruits, and herbs were gathered for dietary and medicinal purposes. There was considerable hunting of wild animals; dogs, turkeys, and the cochineal appear to have been under domestication. The general pattern of subsistence was one of agriculture strongly supplemented by gathering and, to a lesser extent, hunting.

In Tejupa the diet was comprised of tortillas, chile, beans, vermin, rats, snakes, and lizards (PNE, 4: 55). Turkeys, deer, dogs, and human flesh were reserved for the consumption of the principales. The basic preconquest diet in Tilantongo consisted of maize, beans, chile, squash, tuna (a palatable fruit from a cactus), herbs, and dogs. The principales ate birds and deer. Approximately the same diet is reported for Mitlantongo (PNE, 4: p. 79) and Nochixtlan (PNE, 4: 208).

Some indication of the economic potential of the Mixteca Alta is derived from an itemization of the goods exacted from the area by the Mexican overlords. Tlaxiaco-Achiutla (Barlow, 1949, pp. 112–13) gave 800 large mantles, a warrior's costume with shield, 20 vessels of gold dust, five sacks of cochineal, and 400 bunches of quetzal feathers yearly. The economic value of Coixtlahuaca Province is implied by its yearly tribute which was constituted as follows (Barlow, 1949, pp. 116–18):

800 bundles of quilted mantles, richly decorated
800 bundles of mantles, striped red and white
800 bundles of black-and-white mantles
800 bundles of loincloths
800 bundles of women's blouses and skirts
2 warrior's costumes with shields
2 strings of chalchihuitl (precious green stones)

800 bunches of quetzal feathers
1 royal emblem called *tlalpiloni*
40 sacks of cochineal
20 bowls of gold dust

Dress and personal adornment is discussed in detail by Dahlgren (1954). The common people of Mitlantongo and Tejupa wore maguey-fiber mantles usually open down the front. The usual dress, however, was the wrap-around skirt and huipil for women and the breechclout and cape for men (RMEH, p. 143). The regidores of Tilantongo were reported to have worn long cape-mantles colored like lawyers' gowns (PNE, 4: 74). Priests on the day of a sacrifice wore many plumes, elegantly painted mantles, and mitres like that worn by a bishop. War captains of Tilantongo were reported to have worn their hair piled high on their heads with plumes inserted, gold earplugs, nose and lip plugs, necklaces, bracelets of gold, and red ochre body paint (PNE, 4: p. 74).

Settlement Patterns

There are several indications of what the settlement patterns might have been on the eve of the conquest. Bernal in excavating a late site at Coixtlahuaca states (1948–49, pp. 75–77) that unlike the great cities of the Mesoamerican Classic period with their separated ceremonial center and residential quarter, the residences of the populace were immediately adjacent to the ceremonial structures. Bernal indicates that the seven houses excavated showed a "typical Mixtec" construction with walls made of large stones interspaced with small ones. All floors were of stucco.

The relación of Tilantongo (PNE, 4: 81) states that the houses were small flat "cells" of adobe and white stone. The same type of house is reported for Tamazola, Mitlantongo, and Tejupa. In possible contrast to the pattern found in Coixtlahuaca, the houses in Tilantongo were said to be situated *far apart* and located *next to the fields.*

One gains the impression that the pattern of dispersal of dwellings and buildings over the terrain may fall somewhere between that reported for the Zapotec on the one hand and that of the Mixe and Chinantec on the other. The picture is one of a ceremonial center that was sparsely or periodically occupied with a scattering of hamlets or groups of farm-ranches clustered around it. However, far more work of the type initiated by Bernal coupled with archaeological survey and documentary analysis is required to determine the nature of settlement in the Mixteca Alta just prior to the arrival of the Spaniards.

Arts and Crafts

The Mixtec were noted both before and after the conquest for their unexcelled ability in the production of extraordinary artistic works in miniature. Favored media for this refined expression were gold, bone, wood, semiprecious stone, and obsidian. Fine polychromes were applied to beautifully designed pottery vessels, and excellent pictorial manuscripts—the codices—were produced in quantity. The remarkable Mixtec codices, frequently mentioned in the relaciones, in the lawsuits of the middle and late 16th century, and by such chroniclers as Burgoa (1674, 1: 288–89), have been described and analyzed with regard to their historical content and technique of execution in this volume of the *Handbook* by Caso and elsewhere by Robertson (1959) and others. The general artistic abilities and productions of the Mixtec have been discussed in some detail by Dahlgren (1954, pp. 353–61).

Warfare

There were well-developed patterns of warfare in the Mixteca Alta. Intervillage war, most probably provoked by boundary disputes, was common. In addition to the previously mentioned encounters with Mexican armies during the last half of the 15th century, there was warfare between such towns as Mitlantongo and Tlaxiaco, Mitlantongo and Tututepec in the coastal region of the Mixteca, Tamazola and Tututepec, Tejupa and Chocho-speaking peoples, and Tilantongo carried on warfare against Teposcolula and the Zapotec. The weapons of war were the *macana,* cane shields, and cotton armor. Throwing darts are reported for Mitlantongo and Tilantongo.

Social Organization

What little information there is on Mixtec social organization has been discussed in some detail by Dahlgren (1954). Little can at present be added to her account. Far greater study of unpublished documents, lexicons, and codical materials is required before significant results can be obtained.

No direct evidence of extra-familial kin organization is present. In the case of cacique marriage, the principales and priests would be consulted prior to the marriage to determine the advisability of the match and to decide on the question of succession (AGN, Civil, 516). There was rigid social stratification with two elements, a hereditary aristocracy lead by the dynastic families and a commoner class, the macehuales, being recognized. Inferences may be drawn from patterns emerging in other closely related parts of the Mixtec zone, and these will be described in the following section.

Religion

The matter of religion in the Mixteca Alta of preconquest times has been treated by Jiménez-Moreno (Códice de Yanhuitlán, 1940), Caso (1942), and Dahlgren (1954). Important features were the worship of various stone and wooden idols; ritual sacrifice of turkeys, dogs, quail, and human beings; autosacrifice; fasting and penance; offering of stones, plumes, and other items to the idols or gods; ritual cannibalism; burning of incense; maintenance of a formally trained and probably full-time priesthood; sacred temples, hills, and caves. The flying pole, or *voladores,* ceremony and the eating of sacred mushrooms were mentioned for Yanhuitlan (Códice de Yanhuitlán, 1940, pp. 38–39; AGN, Inquisición, 37).

There is a rich documentary body pertaining to native religion in the Mixteca Alta. Much of the presently known detail comes from a case before the Holy Inquisition (AGN, Inquisición, 37) involving two native principales and a cacique from Yanhuitlan. This extraordinary account of native religious belief and custom is partially printed and discussed in the Códice de Yanhuitlán (1940). Jiménez-Moreno, Caso, and Dahlgren have listed and identified many of the sacred images and deities of the area.

The over-all pattern varies little from that described for the Zapotec of the Valley of Oaxaca and the south. Future study in depth, however, will probably reveal significant divergences.

MIXTECA BAJA AND THE SOUTHWEST COAST

Political Organization

Most of this area was under the domination of the kingdom of Tututepec, a tribute empire similar to that of the Culhua-Mexica but entirely independent of Mexico. Tututepec controlled Tonameca, Pochutla, Huatulco port, and Huatulco pueblo to the south and east; extracted tribute from Amoltepec, Tetiquipa (RMEH, pp. 114–17), and Cocautepec (RMEH, pp. 117–20); and was endeavoring to extend control over the towns of Peñoles (RMEH, p. 187), Coatlan (PNE, 4: 133–34), Tamazola, Achiutla (Burgoa, 1674, 1, p. 352), Tlaxiaco, and Mitlantongo (PNE, 4: 79). The composition and great wealth of the "empire" of Tututepec has been discussed in detail by Berlin (1947a, pp. 17–49).

Tonameca, Pochutla, Huatulco port and pueblo, and other small communities in the surrounding area (PNE, 4: 232–51) spoke a dialect of Nahuatl but were subject to the lord of Tututepec. The ruler at Tututepec was said to have named the chief *principal* of each community as its gov-

TABLE 5–MIXTECA BAJA AND SOUTHWEST COAST

Communities	*Latitude North*	*Longitude West*	*Language*
Huatulco Port	15°47′	96°18′	Nahuatl
Huatulco Pueblo	15° 9′	96°22′	Nahuatl
Pochutla	15°43′	96°27′	Nahuatl
Tonameca	15°42′	96°34′	Nahuatl
Tututepec	16° 8′	97°38′	Mixtec
Cuahuitlan (estimated location)	16°17′	98°18′	Mixtec
Jicayan	16°26′	97°58′	Amuzgo, Mixtec
Zacatepec	16°47′	97°59′	Amuzgo, Mixtec
Putla	17° 3′	97°57′	Mixtec, Nahuatl
Zochiquilazala	17°14′	98°12′	Mixtec, Amuzgo
Mixtepec	17°18′	97°52′	Mixtec
Justlahuaca	17°20′	98° 2′	Mixtec
Tecomaxtlahuaca	17°22′	98° 4′	Mixtec
Yoaltepec (estimated location)	17°47′	98°22′	Mixtec

ernor. The governor would then designate a *principal* and a *tequilato,* or tribute collector (Molina, 1944, 105*v*), for each *barrio* or dependency. These three individuals constituted the effective local government at the community level.

Prior to the arrival of the Spaniards, Zacatepec (RMEH, pp. 160–61), a Mixtec- and Amuzgo-speaking community, recognized Yyachihuyzu as cacique and gave him in tribute mantles, jewels, and green stones; the macehuales of the cacicazgo worked his fields. The cacique is said to have recognized no higher authority and to have had complete control over the community. Whatever the cacique ordered was done without question. Those found guilty of adultery and theft had their goods confiscated by the lord and were made his perpetual slaves.

Cuahuitlan (PNE, 4: 158), also a Mixtec community, was located on the Pacific shore. The community was governed in preconquest times by native lords who continued to be obeyed and respected in 1580. Either Tututepec or Mexico dominated the community and its dependencies, but the relación is not clear as to which was in control and at what time.

Zacatepec (RMEH, pp. 160–61) remained independent of both Tututepec and Mexico. Tecomastlahuaca (RMEH, p. 137) and the Amuzgo centers of Jicayan (RMEH, p. 151) and Zochiquilazala (RMEH, pp. 148–49), to the north of Zacatepec, were under Mexican control but maintained their own local governments under native lords.

Economic Systems and Patterns of Subsistence and Settlement

All cultures in the region were based on permanent agriculture. The diet in Zacatepec consisted of maize, beans, chile, squash, sweet potatoes, a variety of herbs and roots, and the meat of deer, rabbits, and iguanas. Herbs, roots, bark, and leaves were made into medicinal powders, inhalants, and drinks. The main garments were the white cotton mantle for men and the wrap-around skirt and huipil for women. This same general complex is reported for the Amuzgo center of Jicayan (RMEH, p. 152).

Cuahuitlan on the south coast cultivated maize, beans, chile, squash, cacao, and cotton on very fertile lands (PNE, 4: 155–60). Salt was derived by boiling water from ocean lagoons. The cotton mantle was the principal garment.

Citizens of Pochutla, Tonameca, and the Huatulcos produced and consumed maize, tamales, tortillas, chile, beans, cacao, squash, great quantities of salt, and fish and game. A variety of fruit was gathered from the countryside. *Pozole,* or corn gruel, was consumed in Huatulco. Houses were small, low-roofed, windowless, and constructed of mud and thatch. The breechclout and cape are mentioned as items of male clothing. Tribute to Tututepec consisted of pieces of imported copper, mantles, imported cochineal, feathers, gold dust, and precious stones.

Information on tribute to the empire of the Culhua-Mexica as listed by Barlow comes only from the towns in the north. Yoaltepec Province which included several of the towns of the Mixteca Baja contributed each year 800 large mantles, one warrior's costume with shield, 80 jars of honey, 40 gold discs, and ten medium-sized turquoise mosaic masks (Barlow, 1949, pp. 106–07). Military service, certain vegetables, and feathers were also given.

Houses in this area were of one or two rooms and constructed of combinations of wood, mud, and thatch or, in some cases, of stone and wood. Unfortunately, there is too little information at present to draw honest conclusions on settlement patterns.

Warfare

All the communities of the region had been at war with either Mexico or Tututepec. There was constant intervillage warfare as well. Zacatepec had three major battles with the Mexicans and two with Tututepec but was never defeated. After their reduction by Tututepec, the subject towns of Tonameca, Pochutla, and Huatulco fought on the side of their overlords against Tehuantepec and other enemy towns.

Warriors of Zacatepec went to war with bows and arrows, shields, macanas, carried white and striped flags, and wore gold nose rings and bells on their legs. Those of Tonameca, Huatulco, and Pochutla used bows and arrows, macanas, and shields, and wore loincloths. Cotton armor is reported only for the soldiers of Putla (RMEH, p. 158).

Arts and Crafts

Berlin (1947a, pp. 31–34) has listed some of the great handicrafted materials from this area that were in the hands of the cacique of Tututepec around the time of the conquest. Among the items were necklaces of coral and gold beads, other necklaces of gold beads, of pearls and gold, of turquoise and of semiprecious green stone. Beautifully worked and inlaid gold discs, pendants, pectorals, other finely executed pieces of jewelry, and fine featherwork are also described.

Social Organization

The stratified social pyramid, with the cacique at the pinnacle, the nobility immediately below, and the great mass of population distributed in undifferentiated fashion at the base, is clearly the appropriate pattern for this region. Direct information on other aspects of the social structure is far from satisfactory.

The most substantial evidence on at least one social institution, marriage, comes from Zacatepec (RMEH, pp. 160–61).

> When a cacique wanted to marry he first took up the matter with the priests. He then sent his messengers to deal with the girl's parents and sent to them presents of mantles, jewelry, and feathers. These were given to the parents of the girl. Three or four times messengers took presents to the girl's parents. Later the girl consented to be taken to the cacique. When she left her parents' home this cacica was accompanied by two priests, many old people, and her relatives. The two priests carried an incensory and bits of pine wood with which they illuminated the road. This flame could not be extinguished until she had served in the house of the cacique, and they did not wish to burn the light which the cacique had in his house but only the one she had brought from her home. And she arrived at the house of the husband together with many people and among these the two priests. They made their parley and ate and drank and amused themselves a day or two, and thus was the marriage consummated. And the children of these

señores were recognized as legitimate and inherited the seigniory, and if they had no male son the daughters inherited, and if the couple had no children the cacique's nearest relatives inherited.

When a cacique of Justlahuaca (RMEH, pp. 138–39) wished to marry he made preliminary overtures to the girl and her parents and consulted the priests. Then a group of principales would take many presents to the house of the prospective bride. The principales would escort the cacica to the house of the cacique, and during the night there would be a gathering of priests and other principales. In the actual ceremony the mantles of the man and woman would be tied together. The cacique then divided a tortilla and a piece of meat. He placed the bits of food in her mouth and the cacica reciprocated. This completed the act of marriage, and the ceremony was followed by great feasting. As to the matter of succession, it made no difference whether sons or daughters inherited the title, "there being no difference in the lineages, because he who was a cacique married a cacica and the principal married a principala, and thus some caciques accommodated others." In the case of caciques in both Justlahuaca and Zacatepec, polygyny was practiced, but there could be legitimate succession only by the children of the principal wife, the legitimate cacica.

In Tututepec (Berlin, 1947a, p. 30) it was stated that both the cacique and his wife had to be of a cacique lineage. A son of a cacique was by the tenets of ancient custom prohibited from succession to the cacicazgo of Tututepec because his mother "had not been of the lineage of señores, but of a lineage of principales, and it was determined that he was "no more than half lineage, and that he could not inherit if he was only half lineage."

Religion

The natives of Zacatepec (RMEH, p. 160) worshipped two stone idols called Yahatujyuty and Ñañahuconuhu. Priests in charge of the idols were selected by the local cacique and occupied office for 15 or 20 years. When the cacique desired that there be a feast the priests would fast for five or six days, eating nothing but inhaling only quantities of tobacco smoke. They were required to observe rules of chastity and abstinence. Violations of the proscriptions were punished with death by stoning. Priests were sons of caciques, principales, and macehuales, and were selected according to their ability. They advised the cacique in all things. The Zacatepec religious pattern also holds for Jicayan (RMEH, pp. 151–55) and Putla (RMEH, pp. 156–59).

Among the Nahuatl-speaking communities, Huatulco (PNE, 4: pp. 234–35) had an idol called Coatepetl ("Hill of the Snake"). There was a temple where copal, richly colored feathers, precious stones, and blood from tongue and ears were offered and animals and prisoners sacrificed. Tonameca (PNE, 4: p. 243) observed the same type of rituals before an idol called Telpochtli ("Young Man"). Natives of Pochutla (PNE, 4: p. 239) are said to have worshipped a goddess called Izpapalotl ("Butterfly with a mouth like a thorn") and to have made all types of offerings and sacrifices and to have practiced cannibalism.

General Conclusions

There was a highly developed religious complex centered around curing, agriculture, and fertility. It was characterized by a trained priesthood, sacrifice of animals and human beings, highly diversified iconography, temples and sacred shrines in caves and on mountains, autosacrifice, worship of the dead or a well-developed ancestor cult, a calendrical cycle of feasts closely connected with general religious expression, well-developed concepts of penance-fasting, and highly characteristic ritual intoxication and narcotization. The idea of a supreme deity seems to have been well established in preconquest times. There were many aspects of ancient Oaxacan religion, when shorn of certain more violent and objectionable tendencies, which were most compatible with Spanish Catholicism and its rich iconography, greatly facilitating the syncretism of the 16th century.

The entire area had economies based on settled agriculture, but gathering of wild plant products was a most important subsidiary enterprise in the subsistence quest. Hunting was of only tertiary importance, and animal domestication of slight significance. The Zapotec were a commercially minded people with well-developed markets, extensive lines of trade, and groups of specialized traders being recognized. Technology as applied to the practical necessities of life was poorly developed. Practical metalworking did not evolve, and in the inventory of tools, armor, transportation, and general industrial achievement Oaxaca was at a "Neolithic" level at the conquest.

Three generalized settlement patterns emerge for the Oaxaca area. The Mixe, Chinantec, and probably the Mazatec followed a diffuse or vacant-center type of settlement. The valley, southern, and mountain Zapotec, and possibly the Cuicatec tended toward nucleated or compact centers. The Mixtec fell somewhere between the two extremes with a sparsely occupied center and the majority of the population occupying contiguous ranch-farms or hamlets. There is too little information presently available to determine coastal Mixtec and Nahuatl patterns.

In the Zapotec areas, and probably in the Mixtec region, the bond of kinship was submerged by overriding ties to the community. Clans or other kin organization above the extended family do not emerge. The important considerations of the individual are his immediate family and his community. Without this sense of communal responsibility it is unlikely that the urban or semiurban centers typifying Zapotec and Mixtec culture could have arisen. The communal tie seems much less pronounced among such groups as the Mixe and Chinantec, but the evidence is very limited.

There was a strong expression of the lineage principle among the nobility as they sought to preserve their positions and prerogatives. This awareness does not appear to have descended to the level of the common class, however. Whatever extra-familial affiliations and allegiances were evident at the macehual level appear moreover not to have extended beyond the boundaries of the immediate community.

The social configuration was characterized by a high degree of fusion and centripitality. There was no expression of a positive value on individualism, striking out on one's own, or other forms of innovation. The social group within which one functioned and the world of practical existence were pretty well defined by the boundaries of the community in which one dwelled.

During the years immediately preceding the conquest there were five foci of political power for the peoples of Oaxaca. These were Tenochtitlan, Teotzapotlan, Tehuantepec, Tututepec, and Teotitlan del Camino. Depending on its location, the community was at one time or another part of the political macrostructure radiating from one of these centers. For the traditionally important considerations of life, however, for matters bearing on social custom, religion, economy, and subsistence, the citizen of the community was guided by the traditional leaders, the cacique, the priest, and the local nobility. Except for a substitution of Catholic friar for pagan priest the same pattern within the broader framework of the Mesoamerican tradition continued into the centuries of Spanish domination.

REFERENCES

Anales de Tlatelolco, 1948
Archivo de la Nación, Mexico
Barlow, 1949
Berlin, 1947a
Bernal, 1948–49, 1958a–c
Borah and Cook, 1960
Burgoa, 1674
Caso, 1942, 1960
Clavijero, 1958
Códice Chimalpopoca, 1945
Códice de Yanhuitlan, 1940
Cook and Simpson, 1948
Córdova, 1942
Dahlgren, 1954
Descripción de la Ciudad de Antequera, 1946
Dos relaciones . . . de Cuilapa, 1945
Durán, 1951
García Granados, 1935
Gay, 1881
Herrera, 1726
Iturribarría, 1960
Johnson, F., 1940
Kubler, 1942, 1948
Mendizabal and Jiménez Moreno, 1937
Molina, 1944
Paddock, 1958, 1960
Papeles de Nueva España, 1905
Relación . . . de Tlaxcala, 1904
Robertson, 1959
Schmieder, 1930
Tezozomoc, 1944

REFERENCES AND INDEX

REFERENCES

Acosta, J. R.
1949 El pectoral de jade de Monte Alban. *An. Inst. Nac. Antr. Hist.*, 3: 17–26.
1956 Resumen de los informes de las exploraciones arqueológicas en Tula, Hgo., durante la VI, VII y VIII temporadas. *Ibid.*, vol. 7.
1956–57 Interpretación de algunos de los datos obtenidos en Tula relativos a la época tolteca. *Rev. Mex. Estud. Antr.*, 14: 75–110.
1957 Exploraciones arqueológicas en Tula, Hgo. *An. Inst. Antr. Hist.*, vol. 9.
1958–59 Exploraciones arqueológicas en Monte Alban, XVIII temporada. *Rev. Mex. Estud. Antr.*, 15: 7–50.
1959 Técnicas de la construcción. *In* Esplendor del Mexico Antiguo, 2: 501–18.

—— and H. Moedano K.
1946 Los juegos de pelota. *In* Vivó, 1946a, pp. 365–84.

Adams, E. B.
n.d. Tabulation of the encomiendas, encomenderos, and principal items of the tribute in the 1549 tax list. MS. Archivo General de Indias, Guatemala 128.

Adams, R. E. W.
1962 The ceramic sequence at Altar de Sacrificios and its implications. *35th Int. Cong. Amer.*
1963 The ceramic sequence at Altar de Sacrificios, Guatemala. Ph.D. thesis, Harvard Univ.

—— and A. S. Trik
1961 Temple I: post-constructional activities. *Mus. Monogr., Univ. Pennsylvania,* Tikal Reports, no. 7.

Adams, R. M., Jr.
1953 Some small ceremonial structures of Mayapan. *Carnegie Inst. Wash., Current Reports,* no. 9.
1960 Changing patterns of territorial organization in the central highlands of Chiapas, Mexico. Mimeographed.

Adán, E.
1927 Nota acerca de unas piedras talladas de aspecto prehistórico, procedentes de Mitla, estado de Oaxaca. *An. Mus. Nac. Mex.*, 5: 157–67.

Agrinier, P.
1960 The carved human femurs from Tomb 1, Chiapa de Corzo, Chiapas, Mexico. *Papers New World Archaeol. Found.*, no. 6.

Aguirre Beltrán, G.
1953 Formas de gobierno indígena. Mexico.

Alvarado, F. de
1593 Vocabulario en lengua mixteca. Mexico.

Alvarado, P. de
1924 An account of the conquest of Guatemala in 1524. Ed. and tr. by S. J. Mackie. *Cortés Soc.*, no. 3.

Alvarez, M. F.
1900 Las ruinas de Mitla y la arquitectura. Mexico.

Anales de Tlatelolco
1948 Anales de Tlatelolco y códice de Tlatelolco. Ed. by H. Berlin and R. H. Barlow, Mexico.

Anderson, A. H., and H. J. Cook
1944 Archaeological finds near Douglas, British Honduras. *Carnegie Inst. Wash., Notes Middle Amer. Archaeol. Ethnol.*, no. 40.

Anderson, A. J. O., and C. E. Dibble
1959 The Florentine codex, parts 9 and 10. Santa Fe.

Andrews, E. W.
1939 A group of related sculptures from Yucatan. *Carnegie Inst. Wash.*, Pub. 509, Contrib. 26.
1940 Chronology and astronomy in the Maya area. *In* The Maya and their Neighbors, pp. 150–61.
1942 Yucatan: architecture. *Carnegie Inst. Wash.*, Year Book 41, pp. 257–63.
1943 The archaeology of southwestern Campeche. *Carnegie Inst. Wash.*, Pub. 546, Contrib. 40.
1951 The Maya supplementary series. *In* Tax, 1951, pp. 123–41.
1959 Dzibilchaltun: lost city of the Maya. *Nat. Geog. Mag.*, 115: 90-109.

1960 Excavations at Dzibilchaltun, northwestern Yucatan, Mexico. *Proc. Amer. Phil. Soc.*, 104: 254–65.
1961a Excavations at the Gruta de Balankanche, 1959. *Tulane Univ., Middle Amer. Research Inst., Misc. Ser.*, no. 11.
1961b Preliminary report on the 1959–60 field season, National Geographic Society–Tulane University Dzibilchaltun program. *Ibid.*, no. 11.
1962 Excavaciones en Dzibilchaltun, Yucatan, 1956–1962. *Univ. Nac. Autónoma Mex., Estud. Cultura Maya*, 2: 149–83.
in press Progress report on the 1960–64 field seasons, National Geographic Society –Tulane University Dzibilchaltun program. *Tulane Univ., Middle Amer. Research Inst.*

ANGHIERA, P. M. D'
1912 De orbe novo, the eight decades of Peter Martyr d'Anghiera. Tr. with notes and introduction by F. A. MacNutt. New York.

ANNALS OF THE CAKCHIQUELS
1953 The annals of the Cakchiquels. Tr. from the Cakchiquel Maya by A. Recinos and D. Goetz. Title of the lords of Totonicapan. Tr. from the Quiche text into Spanish by D. J. Chonay; English version by D. Goetz. Norman, Okla.

ANONYMOUS
ca. 1580 Vocabulario en lengua Cakchiquel y Quiche. Photographic copy by W. E. Gates in Bowditch Coll., Peabody Mus., Harvard Univ.

ARCHIVO GENERAL DE INDIAS, SEVILLE
1548–51 Un libro de tasaciones de los naturales de las provincias de Guatemala, Nicaragua, Yucatan, y pueblos de Comayagua. Guatemala, leg. 128.
1604–07 Salinas. . . . Mexico, leg. 72. Extracted by E. B. Adams.

ARCHIVO DE LA NACIÓN, MEXICO
Documents: Civil, 516; Inquisición, 37; Indios, 3, exp. 540; Tierras: 24, exp. 6; 34, exp. 1; 400, exp. 1; 3343.

ARMILLAS, P.
1951 Mesoamerican fortifications. *Antiquity*, 25: 77–86.
——, A. PALERM, AND E. R. WOLF
1956 A small irrigation system in the valley of Teotihuacan. *Amer. Antiquity*, 21: 396–99.

ARNOLD, J. R., AND W. F. LIBBY
1950 Radiocarbon dates (September 1, 1950). Univ. Chicago, Inst. Nuclear Studies.
1951 Radiocarbon dates. *Science*, 113: 111–20.

ARSANDAUX, H., AND P. RIVET
1921 Contribution à l'étude de la métallurgie mexicaine. *Jour. Soc. Amer. Paris*, vol. 13.

AVELEYRA ARROYO DE ANDA, L.
1950 Prehistoria de Mexico. Mexico.
1959 Los cazadores del mamut, primeras habitantes de Mexico. *In* Esplendor del Mexico Antiguo, 1: 53–72.

AVENDAÑO Y LOYOLA, A. DE
1696 Relación de las dos entradas que hize a la conversión de los gentiles itzaex y cehaches. MS in Ayer Coll., Newberry Library, Chicago.

AYMÉ, L. H.
1882 Notes on Mitla. *Proc. Amer. Antiquarian Soc.*, n.s., 2: 82–100.

BACABS, RITUAL OF THE
n.d. Medical incantations and prescriptions. MS. Gates reproduction.

BALL, S. H.
1941 The mining of gems and ornamental stones by American Indians. *Smithsonian Inst., Bur. Amer. Ethnol.*, Bull. 128, Anthr. Papers, no. 13.

BALSALOBRE, G. DE
1892 Relación auténtica de las idolatrías, supersticiones, vanas observaciones de los indios del Obispado de Oaxaca. *An. Mus. Nac. Mex.*, 6: 225–60.

BANCROFT, H. H.
1882 The native races. 5 vols. San Francisco.

BANDELIER, A. F.
1884 Report of an archaeological tour in Mexico. *Papers Archaeol. Inst. Amer., Amer. Ser.*, no. 2.

BARBOUR, G. B.
1957 A note on jadeite from Manzanal, Guatemala. *Amer. Antiquity*, 22: 411–12.

BARLOW, R. H.
1949 The extent of the empire of the Culhua Mexica. *Ibero-Amer.*, no. 28.

BARRERA VÁSQUEZ, A.
1957 Códice de Calkini. *Bib. Campechana*, no. 4. Campeche.

BARTHEL, T. S.
1951 Maya-astronomie: lunare Inschriften aus dem Südreich. *Zeit. für Ethnol.*, 76: 216–38.

1952 Der Morgensternkult in den Darstellungen der Dresdener Maya-Handschrift. *Ethnos,* 17: 73–112.
1954 Maya epigraphy: some remarks on the affix 'al.' *Proc. 30th Int. Cong. Amer.,* pp. 45–49.
1955a Maya-Palaeographik: die Hieroglyphe Strafe. *Ethnos,* 20: 146–51.
1955b Versuch über die Inschriften von Chichen Itza viejo. *Baessler Archiv,* n.s., 3:5–33.

Batres, L.
1902 Exploraciones de Monte Alban. Mexico.

Beals, R. L.
1932 Unilateral organizations in Mexico. *Amer. Anthr.,* 34: 467–75.
1934 A possible culture sequence at Mitla, Oaxaca. *Ibid.,* 36: 89–93.

Beltrán de Santa Rosa, P.
1859 Arte del idioma maya reducido a succintas reglas y semilexicón yucateco. Merida. (Originally published 1746, Mexico.)

Bennett, W. C.
1948 A reappraisal of Peruvian archaeology. *Mem. Soc. Amer. Archaeol.,* no. 4.

Bergsøe, P.
1937 The metallurgy and technology of gold and platinum among the pre-Columbian Indians. *Ingeniørvidenskabelige skrifter,* nr. A. 44. Copenhagen.
1938 The gilding process and the metallurgy of copper and lead among the pre-Columbian Indians. *Ibid.,* nr. A. 46.

Berlin, H.
1943 Notes on Glyph C of the lunar series at Palenque. *Carnegie Inst. Wash., Notes Middle Amer. Archaeol. Ethnol.,* no. 24.
1946a Archaeological excavations in Chiapas. *Amer. Antiquity,* 12: 19–28.
1946b Three Zapotec stones. *Carnegie Inst. Wash., Notes Middle Amer. Archaeol. Ethnol.,* no. 66.
1947a Fragmentos desconocidos del códice de Yanhuitlan y otras investigaciones mixtecas. Mexico.
1947b Nota bibliográfica. *Bol. Bib. Antr. Amer.,* 9: 200–01.
1950 La historia de los Xpantzay. *Antr. Hist. Guatemala,* 2 (2): 40–53.
1951 The calendar of the Tzotzil Indians. *In* Tax, 1951, pp. 155–61.
1952 Excavaciones en Kaminal Juyu: Montículo D-III-13. *Antr. Hist. Guatemala,* 4 (1): 3–18.
1953 Archaeological reconnaissance in Tabasco. *Carnegie Inst. Wash., Current Reports,* no. 7.
1955a Selected pottery from Tabasco. *Carnegie Inst. Wash., Notes Middle Amer. Archaeol. Ethnol.,* no. 126.
1955b Apuntes sobre vasijas de Flores (El Peten). *Antr. Hist. Guatemala,* 7 (1): 15–17.
1956 Late pottery horizons of Tabasco, Mexico. *Carnegie Inst. Wash.,* Pub. 606, Contrib. 59.
1957 Las antiguas creencias en San Miguel Sola, Oaxaca, Mexico. *Beiträge zur mittelamerikanischen Völkerkunde, Herausgegeben vom Hamburgischen Museum für Völkerkunde und Vorgeschichte,* no. 4.
1958 El glifo "emblema" en las inscripciones mayas. *Jour. Soc. Amer. Paris,* 47: 111–19.
1963 The Palenque triad: a study in method. *Jour. Soc. Amer. Paris,* 52: 91–99.

Bernal, I.
1946 La cerámica preclásica de Monte Alban. Thesis, Escuela Nac. Anthr. Hist. MS. Mexico.
1948–49 *See* his 1949a.
1949a Exploraciones en Coixtlahuaca. *Rev. Mex. Estud. Antr.,* 10: 5–76.
1949b La cerámica grabada de Monte Alban. *An. Inst. Nac. Antr. Hist.,* 3: 59–78.
1949c La cerámica de Monte Alban III-A. Thesis, Univ. Nac. Autónoma de Mex.
1949d Distribución geográfica de las culturas de Monte Alban. *El Mexico Antiguo,* 7: 209–16.
1950 Compendio de arte mesoamericano. *Enciclopedia Mex. Arte,* vol. 7. Mexico.
1953 Excavations in the Mixteca Alta. *Mesoamer. Notes,* no. 3. Mexico.
1955 Excavations at Yagul, I. *Ibid.,* no. 4.
1958a Monte Alban and the Zapotecs. *Bol. Estud. Oaxaqueños,* no. 1. Mexico.
1958b Archaeology of the Mixteca. *Ibid.,* no. 7. Mexico.
1958c Exploraciones en Cuilapan de Gue-

rrero, 1902–1954. *Inst. Nac. Antr. Hist.*, Informe 7. Mexico.
1958d Mexico: pinturas prehispánicas. New York Geog. Soc. Col. UNESCO de Arte Mundial.
1960a Exploraciones arqueológicas en Noriega, Oaxaca. *In* Homenaje a Rafael García Granados, pp. 83–88. Mexico.
1960b El palacio de los seis patios en Yagul. Mexico.

BETJEMAN, J., ed.
1959 Collins guide to English parish churches. London.

BEYER, H.
1922 Sobre una plaqueta con una deidad teotihuacana. *Mem. Soc. Cien. Antonio Alzate*, 40: 549. Mexico.
1926 Die Verdopplung in der Hieroglyphenschrift der Maya. *Anthropos*, 21: 580–82. St. Gabriel Mödling bei Wien.
1932a Mayan hieroglyphs: some tun signs. *Tulane Univ., Middle Amer. Research Inst.*, Pub. 4, pp. 103–30.
1932b The stylistic history of the Maya hieroglyphs. *Ibid.*, Pub. 4, pp. 71–102.
1934–36 The position of the affixes in Maya writing. *Maya Research*, 1: 20–29, 101–08; 3: 102–04.
1937a Lunar glyphs of the supplementary series. *El Mexico Antiguo*, 4: 75–82.
1937b Studies on the inscriptions of Chichen Itza. *Carnegie Inst. Wash.*, Pub. 483, Contrib. 21.
1945 An incised Maya inscription in the Metropolitan Museum of Art, New York. *Tulane Univ., Middle Amer. Research Rec.*, 1: 85–88.

BIERHENKE, W., W. HABERLAND, U. JOHANSEN, AND G. ZIMMERMANN, eds.
1959 Amerikanistische miszellen. Festband Franz Termer. *Mitteilungen aus dem Museum für Völkerkunde in Hamburg*, no. 25.

BLOM, F.
1927 Masterpieces of Maya art: the tomb at Comalcalco in the state of Chiapas, Mexico. *Art Soc. Washington*, vol. 24, no. 6.
1929 Preliminary report of the John Geddings Gray memorial expedition. Tulane Univ.
1930 Preliminary notes on two important Maya finds. *Proc. 23d Int. Cong. Amer.*, pp. 165–71.
1932a The Maya ball-game *pok-ta-pok*. *Tulane Univ., Middle Amer. Research Inst.*, Pub. 4, no. 13.
1932b Commerce, trade and monetary units of the Maya. *Ibid.*, Pub. 4, no. 14.
1934 Short summary of recent explorations in the ruins of Uxmal, Yucatan. *Proc. 24th Int. Cong. Amer.*, pp. 55–59.
1954 Ossuaries, cremation and secondary burials among the Maya of Chiapas, Mexico. *Jour. Soc. Amer. Paris*, 43: 123–35.
1959 Historical notes relating to the pre-Columbian amber trade from Chiapas. *In* Bierhenke, 1959, pp. 24–27.

—— AND O. LAFARGE
1926–27 Tribes and temples. *Tulane Univ., Middle Amer. Research Inst.*, Pub. 1. 2 vols.

BOGGS, S. H.
1950 "Olmec" pictographs in the Las Victorias group, Chalchuapa archaeological zone, El Salvador. *Carnegie Inst. Wash., Notes Middle Amer. Archaeol. Ethnol.*, no. 99.

BOOK OF THE PEOPLE
1954 The book of the people: Popol Vuh, the national book of the ancient Quiche Maya. English version by D. Goetz and S. G. Morley from tr. into Spanish by A. Recinos, with pronouncing dictionary comp. by L. K. Weil and with illus. by E. G. Jackson. Los Angeles. *See* Popol Vuh.

BORAH, W., AND S. F. COOK
1960 The population of central Mexico in 1548: an analysis of the Suma de visitas de pueblos. *Ibero-Amer.*, no. 43.

BORBOLLA, D. F.
See Rubín de la Borbolla, D. F.

BORHEGYI, S. F.
1950a Estudio arqueológico en la falda norte del Volcán de Agua. *Antr. Hist. Guatemala*, 2 (1): 3–22.
1950b Rim-head vessels and cone-shaped effigy prongs of the preclassic period at Kaminaljuyu, Guatemala. *Carnegie Inst. Wash., Notes Middle Amer. Archaeol. Ethnol.*, no. 97.

1950c Tlaloc effigy jar from the Guatemala National Museum. *Ibid.*, no. 96.
1950d A group of jointed figurines in the Guatemala National Museum. *Ibid.*, no. 100.
1950e Notas sobre sellos de barro existentes en el Museo Nacional de Arqueología y Etnología de Guatemala. *Antr. Hist. Guatemala,* 2 (1): 16–26.
1951a A study of three-pronged incense burners from Guatemala and adjacent areas. *Carnegie Inst. Wash., Notes Middle Amer. Archaeol. Ethnol.*, no. 101.
1951b Further notes on three-pronged incense burners and rimhead vessels in Guatemala. *Ibid.*, no. 105.
1951c "Loop-nose" incense burners in the Guatemala National Museum. *Ibid.*, no. 103.
1952a Notes and comments on "duck-pots" from Guatemala. *Tulane Univ., Middle Amer. Research Rec.*, 2: 1–16.
1952b Travertine vase in the Guatemala National Museum. *Amer. Antiquity,* 17: 254–56.
1953 The miraculous shrines of Our Lord of Esquipulas in Guatemala and Chimayo, New Mexico. *El Palacio,* 60: 83–111.
1954a Jointed figurines in Mesoamerica and their cultural implications. *SW. Jour. Anthr.*, 10: 268–77.
1954b The cult of Our Lord of Esquipulas in Middle America and New Mexico. *El Palacio,* 61: 387–401.
1954c Figurinas articuladas de Mesoamerica. *Antr. Hist. Guatemala,* 6 (2): 3–9.
1955 Pottery mask tradition in Mesoamerica. *SW. Jour. Anthr.*, 11: 205–13.
1956a Settlement patterns in the Guatemala highlands: past and present. *In* Willey, 1956c, pp. 101–06.
1956b The development of folk and complex cultures in the southern Maya area. *Amer. Antiquity,* 21: 343–56.
1956c Summer excavations in Guatemala. *Archaeology,* 9: 286–87.
1956d El incensario de "tres asas" de Kaminaljuyu, Guatemala. *Antr. Hist. Guatemala,* 8 (2): 3–7.
1957a Un raro cascabel de barro del período primitivo pre-clásico en Guatemala. *Ibid.*, 9 (1): 9–11.
1957b "Mushroom stones" of Middle America, arranged . . . geographically and chronologically by type. *In* Wasson and Wasson, 1957, vol. 2, folded leaf in pocket.
1957c Incensario de Purulha, Guatemala. *Antr. Hist. Guatemala,* 9 (1): 3–7.
1958a Figuras de incensarios de tres picos de la colección "Raul Moreno," Guatemala. *Ibid.*, 10 (2): 13–15.
1958b Aqualung archaeology. *Natural Hist.*, 67: 120–25.
1959a The composite or "assemble-it-yourself" censer: a new lowland Maya variety of the three-pronged incense burner. *Amer. Antiquity,* 25: 51–58.
1959b Underwater archaeology in the Maya highlands. *Sci. Amer.*, 200: 100–13.
1960a Underwater archaeology in Guatemala. *Acts 33d Int. Cong. Amer.*, 2: 229–40.
1960b America's ball game. *Natural Hist.*, 69: 48–59.
1961a Miniature mushroom stones from Guatemala. *Amer. Antiquity,* 26: 498–504.
1961b Ball-game handstones and ball-game gloves. *In* Lothrop and others, 1961, pp. 126–51.
1961c Shark teeth, stingray spines, and shark fishing in ancient Mexico and Central America. *SW. Jour. Anthr.*, 17: 273–98.
1961d Underwater archaeological studies in Lake Amatitlan, highland Guatemala. *Amer. Phil. Soc.*, Year Book 1960, pp. 547–51.
1963 Pre-Columbian pottery mushrooms from Mesoamerica. *Amer. Antiquity,* 28: 328–38.

—— and N. S. Scrimshaw
1957 Evidence for pre-Columbian goiter in Guatemala. *Amer. Antiquity,* 23: 174–76.

Bowditch, C. P.
1904 [ed.] Mexican and Central American antiquities, calendar systems, and history. *Smithsonian Inst., Bur. Amer. Ethnol.*, Bull. 28.
1910 The numeration, calendar systems and astronomical knowledge of the Mayas. Cambridge.

Brainerd, G. W.
1951 Early ceramic horizons in Yucatan. *In* Tax, 1951, pp. 72–78.
1954 The Maya civilization. SW. Mus. Los Angeles.

1956 Changing living patterns of the Yucatan Maya. *Amer. Antiquity*, 22: 162–64.
1958 The archaeological ceramics of Yucatan. *Univ. California, Anthr. Rec.*, vol. 19.

BRASSEUR DE BOURBOURG, C. E.
1857–59 Histoire des nations civilisées du Mexique et de l'Amérique-Centrale durant les siècles antérieurs à Cristophe Colomb. 4 vols. Paris.
1862 Grammaire de la langue Quichée servant d'introduction au Rabinal-Achi. Paris.
1864 Relation des choses de Yucatan de Diego de Landa . . . accompagné de documents divers historiques et chronologiques. . . . Paris.

BRETON, A. C.
1908 Archaeology in Mexico. *Man*, 8 (17): 34–37.
1917 Relationships in ancient Guatemala. *Ibid.*, Art. 119.

BRINTON, D. G.
1882 The Maya chronicles. *Library Aboriginal Amer. Lit.*, no. 1. Philadelphia.
1897 The pillars of Ben. *Bull. Free Mus. Sci. and Art*, 1: 3-10.

BROCKINGTON, D.
1955 Brief report on the tombs at Yagul. *Mesoamer. Notes*, no. 4, pp. 70–71.

BROMAN, V. L.
1958 Jarmo figurines. M.A. thesis, Radcliffe College.

BULLARD, W. R., JR.
1960a Archaeological investigation of the Maya ruin of Topoxte, Peten, Guatemala. *Amer. Phil. Soc.*, Year Book, pp. 551–54.
1960b Maya settlement pattern in northeastern Peten, Guatemala. *Amer. Antiquity*, 25: 355–72.

BUNZEL, R.
1952 Chichicastenango: a Guatemalan village. *Amer. Ethnol. Soc.*, Pub. 22.

BURGOA, F. DE
1670 Palestra historial de virtudes, y exemplares apostólicos. . . . Pub. Archivo General de la Nación (Mexico, 1934).
1674 Geográfica descripción. Pub. Archivo General de la Nación, vols. 25, 26 (Mexico, 1934).

BURKITT, R.
1924 A journey in northern Guatemala. *Mus. Jour., Univ. Pennsylvania*, 15: 115–44.
1930a Excavations at Chocola. *Ibid.*, 21: 5–40.
1930b Explorations in the highlands of western Guatemala. *Ibid.*, 21: 41–72.
1933 Two stones in Guatemala. *Anthropos*, 28: 9–26.

BURLAND, C. A.
1958 The inscription on Stela 1, El Castillo, region of Santa Lucia Cotzumalhuapa, Guatemala. *Proc. 32d Int. Cong. Amer.*, pp. 326–30.

BUTLER, M.
1935a A study of Maya mouldmade figurines. *Amer. Anthr.*, 37: 636–72.
1935b Piedras Negras pottery. *Univ. Pennsylvania Mus., Piedras Negras Prelim. Papers*, no. 4.
1940 A pottery sequence from the Alta Verapaz, Guatemala. *In* The Maya and their Neighbors, p. 250–67.
1959 Spanish contact at Chipal. *In* Bierhenke, pp. 28–35.

CACALCH'EN, LIBRO DE
n.d. [Collection of wills, statutes, and other legal documents in Maya.] MS. Gates reproduction.

CALKINI, CRÓNICA DE
n.d. [Chronicle and geographical description of the Province of Ah Canul in Maya.] MS. Gates reproduction. *See also* Barrera V., 1957.

CANBY, J. S.
1951 Possible chronological implications of the long ceramic sequence recovered at Yarumela, Spanish Honduras. *In* Tax, 1951, pp. 79–85.

CANGAS Y QUIÑONES, S. DE
1580 Descriptión de la Villa de Espíritu Santo. MS in Univ. Texas Library.

CANSECO, A. DE
1905 Relación de Tlacolula y Mitla. *In* Paso y Troncoso, 1905, 4: 144–54.

CARNEGIE INSTITUTION OF WASHINGTON
1935–51 Annual reports of the chairman of the Division of Historical Research or the Department of Archaeology. Year Books 34–50.
1952–57 Current reports. Dept. Archaeol.

CARR, R. F., AND J. E. HAZARD
1961 Map of the ruins of Tikal, El Peten, Guatemala. *Mus. Monogr., Univ. Pennsylvania, Tikal Reports*, no. 11.

CARRASCO, P.
1951 Una cuenta ritual entre los Zapotecos

del sur. *In* Homenaje Caso, pp. 91–100.
1959 Kinship and territorial groups in pre-Spanish Guatemala. MS of paper delivered at meeting of Amer. Anthr. Assoc., 1959.
1961 The civil-religious hierarchy in Meso-american communities: pre-Spanish background and colonial development. *Amer. Anthr.,* 63: 483–97.

CARRIEDO, J. B.
1846 Estudios históricos y estadísticos del estado libre de Oaxaca. (2nd ed. 1949.)
1851 Los palacios antiguos de Mitla. *Ilustración Mex.,* 2: 493–500.

CARTAS DE INDIAS
1877 Publícalas por primera vez el ministro de fomento. Madrid.

CASE, H. A.
1911 Views on and of Yucatan. Merida.

CASO, A.
1927a Una pintura desconocida en Mitla. *Rev. Mex. Estud. Hist.,* 1: 243–47.
1927b Las pinturas de Tizatlan, Tlaxcala. *Ibid.,* 1: 139–72.
1928 Las estelas zapotecas. *Monogr. Mus. Nac. Arqueol., Hist., Etnog.* Mexico.
1932a Las exploraciones de Monte Alban, temporada 1931–32. *Inst. Panamer. Geog. Hist.,* Pub. 7.
1932b Las últimas exploraciones de Monte Alban. *Univ. Mexico,* 26: 100–07.
1932c La tumba de Monte Alban en Mixteca. *Ibid.,* 26: 117–50.
1932d Monte Alban, richest archaeological find in America. *Nat. Geog. Mag.,* 62: 487–512.
1932e Reading the riddle of ancient jewels. *Natural Hist.,* 32: 464–80.
1933 Las tumbas de Monte Alban. *An. Mus. Nac. Mex.,* 8: 578–82.
1935 Las exploraciones en Monte Alban, temporada 1934–35. *Inst. Panamer. Geog. Hist.,* Pub. 18.
1936 Culturas mixteca y zapoteca. *Libro Cultura,* 6: 227–62. Barcelona.
1938 Exploraciones en Oaxaca, quinta y sexta temporadas, 1936–37. *Inst. Panamer. Geog. Hist.,* Pub. 34.
1939a La correlación de los años azteca y cristiano. *Rev. Mex. Estud. Antr.,* 3: 11–45.
1939b Resumen del informe de las exploraciones en Oaxaca durante la 7a y 8a temporadas, 1937–38 y 1938–39. *Acts 27th Int. Cong. Amer.,* 2: 159–87.
1941 El complejo arqueológico de Tula y las grandes culturas indígenas de Mexico. *Rev. Mex. Estud. Antr.,* vol. 5.
1942 Culturas mixtecas y zapotecas. Bib. del Maestro, "El Nacional."
1946 Contribución de las culturas indígenas de Mexico a la cultura mundial. Mexico en la Cultura.
1947 Calendario y escritura de las antiguas culturas de Monte Alban. *In* Obras completas de Miguel O. de Mendizábal, vol. 1.
1949a El mapa de Teozacoalco. *Cuad. Amer.,* 8: 145–81.
1949b Una urna con el dios Mariposa. *El* Mexico Antiguo, 7:78–95.
1950 Explicación del reverso del Codex Vindobonensis. *Mem. Col. Nac.,* vol. 5, no. 5. Mexico.
1955a Vida y aventuras de 4 Viento "Serpiente de Fuego." *Misc. Estud. Fernando Ortíz,* 1: 289–97. Havana.
1955b Der Jahresanfang bei den Mixteken. *Baessler Archiv,* n.s., 3: 4–7.
1955c La orfebrería prehispánica. *Artes de Mexico,* año 3, no. 10.
1956 El calendario mixteco. *Hist. Mex.,* 5: 481–97.
1958a El mapa de Xochitepec. *Proc. 32d Int. Cong. Amer.,* pp. 458–66.
1958b El calendario mexicano. *Mem. Acad. Mex. Hist.,* 1: 41–95.
1959 Glifos teotihuacanos. *Rev. Mex. Estud. Antr.,* 15: 51–70.
1960 Interpretación del Cōdice Bodley 2858. Soc. Mex. Antr.
1961 Nombres calendáricos de los dioses. *El Mexico Antiguo,* vol. 8.
1962 La pintura mural en Mesoamérica. *In* Cuarenta siglos de plástica mexicana. Mexico.

—— AND I. BERNAL
1952 Urnas de Oaxaca. *Mem. Inst. Nac. Antr. Hist.,* no. 2.

——, ——, AND J. R. ACOSTA
1965 La cerámica de Monte Alban. *Ibid.,* no. 3.

—— AND L. GAMIO
1961 Informe de exploraciones en Huamelulpan. MS. in Archivo Inst. Nac. Antr. Hist.

—— and D. F. Rubín de la Borbolla
1936 Exploraciones en Mitla, 1934–35. *Inst. Panamer. Geog. Hist.*, Pub. 21.

Castañeda, F. de
1581 Relación de Teutitlan del Camino. *In* Paso ye Troncoso, 1905, pp. 213–31.

Castells, F. de P.
1904 The ruins of Indian Church in British Honduras. *Amer. Antiquarian and Oriental Jour.*, 26: 32–37.

Catherwood, F.
1844 Views of ancient monuments in Central America, Chiapas, and Yucatan. . . . London and New York.

Charnay, D.
1863 Le Mexique: souvenirs et impressions de voyage. Paris.
1885 Les anciennes villes du Nouveau Monde: voyages d'explorations au Mexique et dans l'Amérique Centrale. Paris.
1887 The ancient cities of the New World, being travels and explorations in Mexico and Central America from 1857 to 1882. London.

Chi, G. A.
1941 Relación. *In* Landa, 1941, pp. 230–32.

Childe, V. G.
1950 The urban revolution. *Town Planning Rev.*, 21: 3–17. Univ. Liverpool.

Chimalpahin Quauhtlehuanitzin, F. de
1889 Annales de . . . sixième et septième relations (1258–1612). Rémi Siméon tr. and ed. *Bib. Linguistique Amer.*, vol. 12.

Chonay, D. J., and D. Goetz
1953 Titles of the lords of Totonicapan. Norman, Okla.

Chowning, A.
1956 A round temple and its shrine at Mayapan. *Carnegie Inst. Wash., Current Reports*, no. 34.

—— and D. E. Thompson
1956 A dwelling and shrine at Mayapan. *Ibid.*, no. 33.

Ciudad Real, A. de
See Noyes, 1932; Ponce, 1873.

Clavijero, F. J.
1958 Historia antigua de Mexico. 4 vols. Mexico.

Cline, H. F.
1959a The Patiño maps of 1580 and related documents: analysis of 16th century cartographic sources for the gulf coast of Mexico. *El Mexico Antiguo*, 9: 633–84.
1959b A preliminary report on Chinantec archaeology: excavations in Oaxaca, Mexico, 1951. *Acts 33d Int. Cong. Amer.*, 2: 158–70.

Codex Dresden
1880 Die Maya-Handschrift der Königlichen Bibliothek zu Dresden. Herausgegeben von Prof. Dr. E. Förstemann. Leipzig.

Codex Madrid (Cortesiano section)
1892 Códice maya denominado Cortesiano que se conserva en el Museo Arqueológico Nacional (Madrid). . . . Hecha y publicada bajo la dirección de D. Juan de Dios de la Rada y Delgado y D. Jerónimo López de Ayala y del Hierro. Madrid.

Codex Madrid (Troano section)
1869–70 Manuscrit Troano. Etudes sur le système graphique et la langue des Mayas. By C. E. Brasseur de Bourbourg. 2 vols. Paris.

Codex Mendoza
1938 Codex Mendoza. Ed. and tr. by J. Cooper-Clark. 3 vols. London.

Codex Nuttall (Codex Zouche)
1902 Facsimile of an ancient Mexican codex belonging to Lord Zouche of Harynworth, England, with an introduction by Zelia Nuttall. Peabody Mus., Harvard Univ.

Codex Paris
1887 Codex Peresianus. Manuscrit hiératique des anciens Indiens de l'Amérique Centrale conservé à la Bibliothèque Nationale de Paris, avec une introduction par Léon de Rosny. Publié en couleurs. Paris.

Codex Pérez
ca. 1837 MS owned in Yucatan. Photograph made for Carnegie Inst. Wash. *See also* Solís Alcalá, 1949.

Códice Chimalpopoca
1945 Anales de Cuauhtitlan y leyenda de los soles. Mexico.

Códice de Yanhuitlan
1940 Ed. by W. Jiménez Moreno and S. Mateos Higuera. Mexico.

Coe, M. D.
1956 The funerary temple among the classic Maya. *SW. Jour. Anthr.*, 12: 387–94.
1957a Preclassic cultures in Mesoamerica: a comparative survey. *Papers Kroeber Anthr. Soc.*, 17: 7–37.

1957b Cycle 7 monuments in Middle America: a reconsideration. *Amer. Anthr.*, 59: 597–611.
1957c The Khmer settlement pattern: a possible analogy with that of the Maya. *Amer. Antiquity*, 22: 409–10.
1959a La Victoria, an early site on the Pacific coast of Guatemala. Ph.D. thesis, Harvard Univ.
1959b Una investigación arqueológica en la costa del Pacífico de Guatemala. *Antr. Hist. Guatemala*, 11 (1): 5–15.
1960a Archaeological linkages with North and South America at La Victoria, Guatemala. *Amer. Anthr.*, 62: 363–93.
1960b A fluted point from highland Guatemala. *Amer. Antiquity*, 25: 412–13.
1961 La Victoria, an early site on the Pacific coast of Guatemala. *Papers Peabody Mus., Harvard Univ.*, vol. 53.

COE, W. R.
n.d. Tikal caches 1–56. *Mus. Monogr., Univ. Pennsylvania, Tikal Reports*, no. 13.
1955 Early man in the Maya area. *Amer. Antiquity*, 20: 271–73.
1959 Piedras Negras archaeology: artifacts, caches, and burials. *Mus. Monogr., Univ. Pennsylvania.*
1961 A summary of excavation and research at Tikal, Guatemala: 1956–1961. Univ. Pennsylvania Mus. Mimeographed. *See* 1962b.
1962a Maya mystery in Tikal. *Natural Hist.*, 71: 10–21, 44–53.
1962b A summary of excavation and research at Tikal, Guatemala: 1956–1961. *Amer. Antiquity*, 27: 479–507.

—— AND V. L. BROMAN
1958 Excavations in the Stela 23 group. *Mus. Monogr., Univ. Pennsylvania, Tikal Reports*, no. 2.

—— AND J. J. MCGINN
1963 Tikal: the north acropolis and an early tomb. *Expedition, Bull. Univ. Pennsylvania Mus.*, 5 (2): 24–32.

——, E. M. SHOOK, AND L. SATTERTHWAITE
1961 The carved wooden lintels of Tikal. *Mus. Monogr., Univ. Pennsylvania, Tikal Reports*, no. 6.

COGHLAN, H. H.
1951 Notes on the prehistoric metallurgy of copper and bronze in the Old World. Pitt Rivers Mus., Oxford Univ.

COGOLLUDO, D. L. DE
See López de Cogolludo, D.

COOK, S. F.
1949 Soil erosion and population in central Mexico. *Ibero-Amer.*, no. 34.

—— AND W. BORAH
1960 The Indian population of central Mexico, 1531–1610. *Ibid.*, no. 44.

—— AND L. B. SIMPSON
1948 The population of central Mexico in the sixteenth century *Ibid.* no. 31.

COOK DE LEONARD, C.
1959a El arte y sus técnicas: la escultura. In her 1959c, 2:519–606.
1959b Archäologisch-geographische Probleme der Insel Jaina, Campeche, Mexiko. *In* Bierhenke, 1959, pp. 44–47.
1959c [ed.] Esplendor del Mexico antiguo. 2 vols. Centro Invest. Antr. Mex.

COOKE, C. W.
1931 Why the Mayan cities of the Peten district, Guatemala, were abandoned. *Jour. Wash. Acad. Sci.*, 21: 283–87.

COOPER-CLARK, J.
1912 The story of 8 Deer in Codex Colombino. London.

CÓRDOVA, J. DE
1578a Arte en lengua zapoteca. Pedro Balli, Mexico. (Reprinted 1886, Morelia.)
1578b Vocabulario en lengua zapoteca. Pedro Charte y Antonio Ricardo, Mexico. (Reprinted 1942.)
1942 Vocabulario castellano-zapoteco. Mexico.

CORDRY, D. B., AND D. M. CORDRY
1941 Costumes and weaving of the Zoque Indians of Chiapas, Mexico. *SW. Mus. Papers*, no. 15.

CORTÉS, H.
1922 Cartas de relación de la conquista de Mexico. (Calpe ed.) Madrid.

COVARRUBIAS, M.
1943 Tlatilco, archaic Mexican art and culture. *DYN*, 4–5: 40–46.
1946 El arte "Olmeca" o de La Venta. *Cuad. Amer.*, año 5, pp. 153–79.
1947 Mexico south: the isthmus of Tehuantepec. New York.
1954 The eagle, the jaguar, and the serpent: Indian art of the Americas. New York.
1957 Indian art of Mexico and Central America. New York.

COWGILL, G. L.
1959 Postclassic cultures in the southern Maya lowlands. MS of paper read at meeting of Amer. Anthr. Assoc.

COWGILL, U. M.
1959 Agriculture and population density in the southern Maya lowlands. MS of paper read at meeting of Amer. Anthr. Assoc.
1960 Soil fertility, population, and the ancient Maya. *Proc. Nat. Acad. Sci.*, 46: 1009–11.

CRUZ, W. C.
1935 El *tonalamatl* zapoteco. Oaxaca.

CULEBRO, C. A.
1937 Reseña histórico de Soconusco. Huixtla, Chiapas.
1939 Chiapas prehistórico: su arqueología. Folleto no. 1. Huixtla, Chiapas.

DAHLGREN DE JORDAN, B.
1954 La Mixteca: su cultura e historia prehispánicas. *Col. Cultura Mex.*, no. 1. Mexico.

DANZEL, T. W., AND E. FUHRMANN
1923 Mexiko. Vol. 3. *Kulturen der Erde*, 13. Hagen, Darmstadt.

DECICCO, G., AND D. BROCKINGTON
1956 Reconocimiento arqueológico en el suroeste de Oaxaca. *Inst. Nac. Antr. Hist.*, Informe 6.

DE LA FUENTE, J.
1942a Un reporte sobre los sitios arqueológicos existentes en los distritos de Villa Alta, Choapam, Ixtlan y Tlacolula. MS in Archivo Inst. Nac. Antr. Hist.
1942b Los Zapotecos de Choapam, Oaxaca. *An. Inst. Nac. Antr. Hist.*, 2: 143–205.

DELGADO, A.
1957 Exploración de tumbas en la Chinantla. MS in Archivo Inst. Nac. Antr. Hist.
1960a Investigaciones en la parte alta de la Chinantla. *Bol. Inst. Nac. Antr. Hist.*, 2: 7.
1960b Exploraciones en la Chinantla. *Rev. Mex. Estud. Antr.*, 16: 105–23.
1961 Exploraciones en Tehuantepec. *In* Los Mayas del sur y sus relaciones con los Nahuas meridionales, pp. 93–104. Soc. Mex. Antr.

DESCRIPCIÓN . . . ANTEQUERA
1946 Descripción de la ciudad de Antequera. *Tlalocan*, 2: 134–37.

DE TERRA, H.
1949 Early man in Mexico. *In* De Terra, Romero, and Stewart, 1949, pp. 11–86.

——, J. ROMERO, AND T. D. STEWART
1949 Tepexpan man. *Viking Fund Pub. Anthr.*, no. 11.

D'HARCOURT, R.
1958 Representation de textiles dans la statuaire Maya. *Proc. 32d Int. Cong. Amer.*, pp. 415–21.

DÍAZ DEL CASTILLO, B.
1908–16 The true history of the conquest of New Spain. Tr. by A. P. Maudslay. 5 vols. Hakluyt Soc. London.
1933–34 Verdadera y notable relación del descubrimiento y conquista de la Nueva España y Guatemala. 2 vols. Guatemala.
1939 Historia verdadera de la conquista de la Nueva España. 2 vols. Mexico.

DIBBLE, C. E., AND A. J. O. ANDERSON
See Anderson, A. J. O., and C. E. Dibble.

DIESELDORFF, E. P.
1903 Old titles of the Queccki Indians. MS in Peabody Mus., Harvard Univ.
1904 A pottery vase with figure painting from a grave in Chama. *Smithsonian Inst., Bur. Amer. Ethnol.*, Bull. 28, pp. 639–50.
1926–33 Kunst und Religion der Mayavölker im alten und heutigen Mittelamerika. 3 vols. Berlin.

DIRINGER, D.
[1948] The alphabet, a key to the history of mankind. London.

DIXON, K. A.
1958 Two masterpieces of Middle American bone sculpture. *Amer. Antiquity*, 24: 53–62.
1959a Two carved human bones from Chiapas. *Archaeology*, 12: 106–10.
1959b Ceramics from two preclassic periods at Chiapa de Corzo, Chiapas, Mexico. *Papers New World Archaeol. Found.*, no. 5.

DOS RELACIONES . . . CUILAPA
1945 Dos relaciones antiguos del pueblo de Cuilapa, estado de Oaxaca. *Tlalocan*, 2: 18–28.

DOUTRELAINE, COLONEL
1867 Rapport sur les ruines de Mitla. *In* Archives de la Commission Scientifique du Mexique, 3: 104–11. Paris.

DRUCKER, P.
n.d. Field and laboratory notes, Soconus-

co survey of 1947. MS in Smithsonian Inst. Washington.
1943a Ceramic stratigraphy at Cerro de las Mesas, Veracruz, Mexico. *Smithsonian Inst., Bur. Amer. Ethnol.,* Bull. 141.
1943b Ceramic sequences at Tres Zapotes, Veracruz, Mexico. *Ibid.,* Bull. 140.
1948 Preliminary notes on an archaeological survey of the Chiapas coast. *Tulane Univ., Middle Amer. Research Rec.,* vol. 1, no. 11.
1952a La Venta, Tabasco: a study of Olmec ceramics and art. *Smithsonian Inst., Bur. Amer. Ethnol.,* Bull. 153.
1952b Two aboriginal works of art from the Veracruz coast. *Smithsonian Misc. Coll.,* 117: 1–7.
1955 The Cerro de las Mesas offering of jade and other materials. *Smithsonian Inst., Bur. Amer. Ethnol.,* Bull. 157, pp. 25–68.

—— AND R. F. HEIZER
1960 A study of the milpa system of the La Venta island and its archaeological implications. *SW. Jour. Anthr.,* 16: 36–45.

——, ——, AND R. J. SQUIER
1959 Excavations at La Venta, Tabasco, 1955. *Smithsonian Inst., Bur. Amer. Ethnol.,* Bull. 170.

DUPAIX, CAPITAINE
1834 Antiquités Méxicaines: relation des trois expéditions du Capitaine Dupaix, ordonnées en 1805, 1806 et 1807 pour la recherches des antiquités du pays notamment celles de Mitla et de Palenque; accompagnés des dessins de Castañeda. . . . 2 vols. Paris.

DURÁN, D.
1951 Historia de las Indias de Nueva-España y Islas de Tierra Firme. 2 vols. and atlas. Mexico.

DU SOLIER, W.
1950 Ancient Mexican costume. Mexico.

DUTTON, B. P.
1943 A history of plumbate ware. *Papers School Amer. Research,* no. 31. Santa Fe. (Reprinted from *El Palacio,* 49: 205–19, 229–47, 257–71.)
1955 Tula of the Toltecs. *El Palacio,* 62: 195–251.
1956 A brief discussion of Chichen Itza. *Ibid.,* 63: 202–32.
1958 Studies in ancient Soconusco. *Archaeology,* 11: 48–54.

—— AND H. R. HOBBS
1943 Excavations at Tajumulco, Guatemala. *Monogr. School Amer. Research,* no. 9.

EASBY, D. T.
1956 Orfebrería y orfebres precolombinos. *An. Inst. Arte Amer.,* no. 9. Buenos Aires.
1957 Sahagún y los orfebres precolombinos de Mexico. *An. Inst. Nac. Antr. Hist.,* 9: 85–117.

EASBY, E. K.
1961 The Squier jades from Tonina, Chiapas. *In* Lothrop and others, 1961, pp. 60–80.

—— AND D. T. EASBY
1953 Apuntes sobre la técnica de tallar el jade en Mesoamerica. *An. Inst. Arte Amer.,* no. 6. Buenos Aires.

EGGAN, F.
1934 The Maya kinship system and cross-cousin marriage. *Amer. Anthr.,* 36: 188–202.

EKHOLM, G. F.
1944 Excavations at Tampico and Panuco in the Huasteca, Mexico. *Amer. Mus. Natural Hist., Anthr. Papers,* vol. 38, pt. 5.
1946 The probable use of Mexican stone yokes. *Amer. Anthr.,* 48: 593–606.
1949 Palmate stones and thin stone heads: suggestions on their possible use. *Amer. Antiquity,* 15: 1–9.

EMMONS, G. T.
1923 Jade in British Columbia and Alaska, and its use by the natives. *Mus. Amer. Indian, Heye Found., Indian Notes and Monogr.,* no. 35.

ENCICLOPEDIA YUCATANENSE
1944–47 Ed. by C. A. Echánove Trujillo. 8 vols. Mexico.

EROSA P., J. A.
1948 Guide book to the ruins of Uxmal. Merida.

ESCALONA R., A.
1946 Algunas ruinas prehispánicas en Quintana Roo. *Bol. Soc. Mex. Geog. Estad.,* 61: 513–628.

ESPINOSA, M.
1910 Apuntes históricos de las tribus chinantecas, matzatecas y popolucas. Mexico.

ESPINOZA, G.
1934–35 Ruinas de Guaytan. *Rev. Agrícola,* 7: 215–64; 8: 54–58. Guatemala.

ESPLENDOR DEL MEXICO ANTIGUO
See Cook de Leonard, 1959c.

ESTADO ACTUAL . . .
1928 Estado actual de los principales edificios arqueológicos de Mexico. Sec. Educ. Pub. Mexico.

ESTADO . . . COATZACOALCOS
1945 Estado en que se hallaba la provincia de Coatzacoalcos en el año de 1599. *Bol. Archivo General Nación,* 16: 195–246, 429–79.

EVANS, C., AND B. J. MEGGERS
1960 A new dating method using obsidian. Pt. 2: an archaeological evaluation of the method. *Amer. Antiquity,* 25: 523–37.

FERDON, E. N.
1953 Tonala, Mexico: an archaeological survey. *Monogr. School Amer. Research,* no. 16. Santa Fe.

FERNÁNDEZ, M. A.
1941 El templo num. 5 de Tulum, Quintana Roo. *In* Los Mayas Antiguos, pp. 155–80.
1943 New discoveries in the Temple of the Sun in Palenque. *DYN,* 4–5: 55–58.
1945a Las ruinas de Tulum, I. *An. Mus. Nac. Arqueol. Hist.,* 3: 109–15.
1945b La ruinas de Tulum, II. *Ibid.,* 1: 95–105.
1945c Exploraciones arqueológicas en la Isla Cozumel. *Ibid.,* 1: 107–20.

——, C. LIZARDI R., AND R. ROZO
1945 Las pinturas de la galería sur del Templo de los Frescos, Tulum. *Ibid.,* 3: 117–31.

FERNÁNDEZ DE MIRANDA, M. T., M. SWADESH, AND R. WEITLANER
1960 El panorama etno-linguístico de Oaxaca y el istmo. *Rev. Mex. Estud. Antr.,* 16: 137–57.

FLINT, F. R., AND E. S. DEEVEY
1959 Radiocarbon supplement. *Amer. Jour. Sci.,* vol. 1.

FÖRSTEMANN, E. W.
1904 Various papers *in* Bowditch, 1904, pp. 393–590.
1906 Commentary on the Maya manuscript in the Royal Public Library of Dresden. *Papers Peabody Mus., Harvard Univ.,* vol. 4, no. 2.

FOLLETT, P. H. F.
1932 War and weapons of the Maya. *Tulane Univ., Middle Amer. Research Inst.,* Pub. 4, pp. 375–410.

FONCERRADA DE MOLINA, M.
1962 La arquitectura Puuc dentro de los estilos de Yucatan. *Univ. Nac. Autónoma Mex., Estud. Cultura Maya,* 2: 225–38.

FOR THE DEAN
1950 For the dean: essays in anthropology in honor of Byron Cummings. Ed. by E. K. Reed and D. S. King. Tucson and Santa Fe.

FORBES, R. J.
1950 Metallurgy in antiquity. Leiden.

FORSTER, J. R.
1955 Notas sobre la arqueología de Tehuantepec. *An. Inst. Nac. Antr. Hist.,* 7: 77–100.

FOSHAG, W. F.
1954 Estudios mineralógicos sobre el jade de Guatemala. *Antr. Hist. Guatemala,* 6 (1): 3–47.
1957 Mineralogical studies on Guatemalan jade. *Smithsonian Misc. Coll.,* vol. 135, no. 5.

—— AND R. LESLIE
1955 Jadeite from Manzanal, Guatemala. *Amer. Antiquity,* 21: 81–83.

FOSTER, G. M.
1943 The geographical, linguistic, and cultural position of the Popoluca of Veracruz. *Amer. Anthr.,* 45: 531–46.

FRANCO C., J. L.
1959 La escritura y los códices. *In* Esplendor del Mexico Antiguo, pp. 361–78.

FRY, E. I.
1956 Skeletal remains from Mayapan. *Carnegie Inst. Wash., Current Reports,* no. 38.

FUENTES Y GUZMÁN, F. A. DE
1882–83 Historia de Guatemala o recordación florida escrita el siglo XVII. 2 vols. Madrid.
1932–33 Recordación florida discurso historial y demonstración natural material, military política del reyno de Guatemala. *Bib. Goathemala,* vols. 6–8. Guatemala.

GADOW, H.
1908 Through southern Mexico. London.

GAMIO, L.
1950 Informe relacionado con la zona de Quiotepec. MS in Archivo Inst. Nac. Antr. Hist.
1954 Inspección de las zonas arqueológicas de la Costa Rica. MS *ibid.*

1957 Zona arqueológica de San Martin Huamelulpan. MS *ibid.*

GAMIO, M.
1922 La población del valle de Teotihuacan, Mexico. 3 vols. Sec. Agricultura y Fomento. Mexico.
1926–27 Cultural evolution in Guatemala and its geographic and historic handicaps. *Art and Archaeol.*, 22: 203–22; 23: 17–32, 71–78, 129–33.
1946 Exploración económico-cultural en la región oncocercosa de Chiapas, Mexico. *Amer. Indig.*, vol. 6, no. 3.

GANN, T. W. F.
1900 Mounds in northern Honduras. *Smithsonian Inst., Bur. Amer. Ethnol.*, 19th ann. rept., pt. 2, pp. 655–92.
1914–16 Report on some excavations in British Honduras. *Univ. Liverpool, Ann. Archaeol. Anthr.*, 7: 28–42.
1918 The Maya Indians of southern Yucatan and northern British Honduras. *Smithsonian Inst., Bur. Amer. Ethnol.*, Bull. 64.
1925a Mystery cities: exploration and adventure in Lubaantun. London.
1925b Maya jades. *Proc. 21st Int. Cong. Amer.*, pp. 274–82.
1926 Ancient cities and modern tribes: exploration and adventure in Maya lands. London.
1928a Discoveries and adventures in Central America. London.
1928b Maya cities. New York.
1932 Worshippers of the long-nosed god. *Illustr. London News*, 101: 1006–07.
1939 Glories of the Maya. London.

—— AND M. GANN
1939 Archaeological investigations in the Corozal district of British Honduras. *Smithsonian Inst., Bur. Amer. Ethnol.*, Bull. 123, pp. 1–66.

—— AND J. E. S. THOMPSON
1931 The history of the Maya from the earliest times to the present day. New York.

GARCÍA, J. M.
1859 Apéndice a José María Murguía y Galardi. *Bol. Soc. Mex. Geog. Estad.*, 7: 159–275.

GARCÍA GRANADOS, R.
1935 Contribución para la geografía, etnográfica y lingüistica de Oaxaca. *Ibid.*, 44: 401–10.
1942 Antigüedades mexicanas en Europa. *Mem. Acad. Mex. Hist.*, vol. 1, no. 2.

GARCÍA PIMENTEL, L., ed.
1904 Relación de los obispados de Tlaxcala, Michoacan, Oaxaca y otros lugares en el siglo XVI. Paris and Madrid.

GARIBAY K., A. M., ed. and tr.
1961 Vida económica de Tenochtitlan. I: Pochtecayotl (arte de traficar). Fuentes indígenas de la cultura nahuatl. *Informantes de Sahagún*, no. 3. Mexico.

GATES, W.
1932 The Mayance nations. *Maya Soc. Quar.*, 1: 97–106.

GAY, J. A.
1881 Historia de Oaxaca. 2 vols. Mexico.

GAYANGOS, P. DE, ed.
1866 Cartas y relaciones de Hernán Cortés al emperador Carlos V. Paris.

GENIN, A. M. A.
1928 Note sur les objets précorteziens nommés indûments yugas ou jougs. *Proc. 22d Int. Cong. Amer.*, 1: 521–28.

GIBSON, C.
1960 The Aztec aristocracy in colonial Mexico. *Comparative Studies in Society and Hist.*, 2: 169–196.

GIFFORD, J. C.
1960 The type-variety method of ceramic classification as an indicator of cultural phenomena. *Amer. Antiquity*, 25: 341–47.

GIRARD, R.
1962 Los Mayas eternos. Mexico.

GOETZ, D., AND S. G. MORLEY
1950 Popol Vuh: the sacred book of the ancient Quiche Maya. Norman, Okla.

GOGGIN, J. M.
1960 The Spanish olive jar, an introductory study. *Yale Univ. Pub. Anthr.*, no. 62.

GÓMEZ DE OROZCO, F.
1928 Relaciones histórico-geográficas del obispado de Oaxaca. *Rev. Mex. Estud. Hist.*, 2: 113–91.

GONZÁLEZ DE COSSÍO, F.
1952 El libro de las tasaciones de pueblos de la Nueva España, siglo XVI. Mexico.

GOODMAN, J. T.
1897 The archaic Maya inscriptions. *In* appendix to Maudslay, 1889–1902.

Gordon, G. B.
1896 Prehistoric ruins of Copan, Honduras. *Mem. Peabody Mus., Harvard Univ.*, vol. 1, no. 1.
1898 Caverns of Copan, Honduras. *Ibid.*, vol. 1, no. 5.

—— and J. A. Mason
1925–43 Examples of Maya pottery in the museum and other collections. 3 pts. *Univ. Pennsylvania Mus.*

Goubaud Carrera, A.
1949 Problemas etnológicos del Popol Vuh. I: Procedencia y lenguaje de los Quiches. *Antr. Hist. Guatemala,* 1 (1): 35–42.

Granlund, J.
1953 Birdskin caps: a cultural element of the Arctic and northern countries. *Ethnos,* 18: 125–42.

Greengo, R. E.
1952 The Olmec phase in eastern Mexico. *Bull. Texas Archaeol. Paleontol. Soc.,* 23: 260–92.

Groth-Kimball, I.
1953 Kunst im alten Mexiko. Atlantis Verlag. Zürich.

Gruning, E. L.
1930 Report on the British Museum expedition to British Honduras, 1930. *Jour. Royal Anthr. Inst.,* 60: 477–83.

Guillemin, J. F.
1958 La pirámide B-6 de Mixco Viejo y el sacrificatorio de Utatlan. *Antr. Hist. Guatemala,* 10 (1): 21–28.
1959 Iximche. *Ibid.,* 11 (2): 22–64.

Guiteras Holmes, C.
1947 Clan es y sistema de parentesco de Cancuc (Mexico). *Acta Amer.,* 5: 1–18.
1960 Background of a changing kinship system among the Tzotzil Indians of Chiapas. MS.

Guthe, C. E.
1921 A possible solution of the number series on pages 51 to 58 of the Dresden Codex. *Papers Peabody Mus., Harvard Univ.,* vol. 6, no. 2.

Guzmán, E.
1934 Exploración arqueológica en la Mixteca alta. *An. Mus. Nac. Arqueol. Hist. Etnog.,* 1: 17–42.

Guzman, L. E.
1958 The agricultural terraces of the ancient highland Maya. *Ann. Assoc. Amer. Geog.,* 48: 266.

Haberland, W.
1953 Die regionale Verteilung von Schmuckelementen im Bereiche der klassichen Maya-Kultur. *Beitrage zur mittelamerikanischen Völkerkunde,* no. 2.
1960 Ceramic sequences in El Salvador. *Amer. Antiquity,* 26: 21–29.

Hamy, E. T.
1897 Galerie Américaine du Musée d'ethnographie au Trocadéro: choix de pièces archéologiques et ethnographiques, décrites et figurées. Paris.

Hay, C. L., and others, eds.
1940 The Maya and their neighbors. New York.

Healey, G. G.
1950 The Lacanja valley. *Archaeology,* 3: 12–15.

Heath-Jones *[no given name]*
1959 Definition of an ancestral Maya civilization in Miraflores phase: Kaminaljuyu. *In* Suhm, 1959, p. 37.

Helbrüger, E.
1874 Album de vistas fotográficas de las antiguas ruinas de los palacios de Mitla. Oaxaca.

Hendrichs Perez, P. R.
1943 Tlachtemalacates y otros monumentos de la zona arqueológica de La Soledad, Gro. *El Mexico Antiguo,* 6: 120–30.

Henning, P.
1912 Informe del colector de documentos etnológicos sobre su excursión a Tuxtepec. *Bol. Mus. Nac. Arqueol. Hist. Etnol.,* 1: 229–35.

Hernández, F.
1959–60 Obras completas. Vols. 1–3. Mexico.

Herrera y Tordesillas, A. de
1725–26 The general history of the vast continent and islands of America. . . . Tr. by Capt. John Stevens. London.
1726 Historia general de los hechos de los castellanos en las islas i tierra firma del mar océano. 2 vols. Madrid.
1941 *In* Landa, 1941, pp. 213–20.

Hester, J. A.
1952 Agriculture, economy and population densities of the Maya. *Carnegie Inst. Wash.,* Year Book 51, pp. 266–71.
1953 Agriculture, economy and population densities of the Maya. *Ibid.,* Year Book 52, pp. 289–92.

HEWETT, E. L.
1913 The excavation of Quirigua, Guatemala, by the School of American Archaeology. *Proc. 18th Int. Cong. Amer.*, pp. 241–48.
1936 Ancient life in Mexico and Central America. Indianapolis.

HICKS, F., AND C. E. ROZAIRE
1960 Mound 13, Chiapa de Corzo, Chiapas, Mexico. *Papers New World Archaeol. Found.*, no. 10.

HISSINK, K.
1934 Masken als fassadenschmuk. *Akad. Abh. Kulturgeschichte*, vol. 3, no. 2.

HOLDEN, J.
1957 The postclassic stage in Mesoamerica. *Papers Kroeber Anthr. Soc.*, no. 17, pp. 75–108.

HOLMES, W. H.
1887 The use of gold and other metals among the ancient inhabitants of Chiriqui, Isthmus of Darien. *Smithsonian Inst., Bur. Amer. Ethnol.*, Bull. 3.
1888 Ancient art of the province of Chiriqui. *Ibid.*, 6th ann. rept., pp. 13–187.
1895–97 Archaeological studies among the ancient cities of Mexico. *Field Columbian Mus., Anthr. Ser.*, vol. 1, no. 1.
1907 On a nephrite statuette from San Andres Tuxtla, Vera Cruz, Mexico. *Amer. Anthr.*, 9: 691–701.

HOMENAJE CASO
1951 Homenaje al doctor Alfonso Caso. Nuevo Mundo. Mexico.

HUBBS, C. L., G. S. BIEN, AND H. E. SUESS
1963 The La Jolla natural radiocarbon measurements III. *Radiocarbon*, 5: 254–72.

HUMBOLDT, A. DE
1810 Vues des cordillères et monuments des peuples indigènes de l'Amérique. Paris.

ICAZA, F. A. DE
1928 Miscelánea histórica. *Bib. Rev. Mex. Estud. Hist.*, 2: 15.

ITURRIBARRÍA, J. F.
1960 Yagul: mestizo product of Mixtecs and Zapotecs. *Bol. Estud. Oaxaqueños*, no. 17.

IXTLILXOCHITL, F. DE A.
1892 Historia de la nación chichimeca. Ed. by A. Chavero. Mexico.

JAKEMAN, M. W.
1947 The ancient Middle American calendar system: its origin and development. *Brigham Young Univ., Pub. Archaeol. and Hist.*, no. 1.

JIMÉNEZ, T. F.
1957 El monolito de Cayagunca. *An. Mus. Nac. "David J. Guzmán,"* 7: 11–17. El Salvador.

JIMÉNEZ MORENO, W.
1940 El códice de Yanhuitlan. Mexico.
1941 Tula y los Toltecas según las fuentes históricas. *Rev. Mex. Estud. Antr.*, 5: 79–83.
1942 El enigma de los Olmecas. *Cuad. Amer.*, 1: 113–45.
1954–55 Síntesis de la historia precolonial del Valle de Mexico. *Rev. Mex. Estud. Antr.*, 14: 219–36.
1959 Síntesis de la historia pretolteca de Mesoamerica. *In* Esplendor del Mexico Antiguo, 2: 1019–1108.

JOHNSON, F.
1940 The linguistic map of Mexico and Central America. *In* The Maya and their Neighbors, pp. 88–114.
1951 Radiocarbon dating. *Mem. Soc. Amer. Archaeol.*, no. 8.

JOHNSON, I. W.
1954 Chiptic cave textiles from Chiapas, Mexico. *Jour. Soc. Amer. Paris*, 43: 137–47.
1959 Hilado y tejido. *In* Esplendor del Mexico Antiguo.

JONES, M. R.
1952 Map of the ruins of Mayapan, Yucatan, Mexico. *Carnegie Inst. Wash., Current Reports*, no. 1.

JOYCE, T. A.
1916 Central American and West Indian archaeology. London.
1926 Report on the investigations at Lubaantun, British Honduras, in 1926. *Jour. Royal Anthr. Inst.*, 56: 207–30.
1933 The pottery whistle-figurines of Lubaantun. *Ibid.*, 63: xv–xxv.

——, J. COOPER-CLARK, AND J. E. S. THOMPSON
1927 Report on the British Museum expedition to British Honduras, 1927. *Ibid.*, 57: 295–323.

JUARROS, D.
1823 A statistical and commercial history of the kingdom of Guatemala in Spanish America. Tr. by J. Baily. London.

KELEMEN, P.
1939 Pre-Columbian jades. *Parnassus*, vol. 11, no. 4, pp. 4–10.

1943 Medieval American art. 2 vols. New York.
1956 *Idem*, 2d ed.

KELLEY, D. H.
1955 Quetzalcoatl and his coyote origins. *El Mexico Antiguo,* 8: 397–413.
1960 Calendar animals and deities. *SW. Jour. Anthr.,* 16: 317–37.

KEMPTON, J. H.
1935 Preliminary report of the agricultural survey of Yucatan of 1935. Mimeographed. Carnegie Inst. Wash.

KIDDER, A., AND C. SAMAYOA CHINCHILLA
1959 The art of the ancient Maya. New York.

KIDDER, A. V.
1935 Notes on the ruins of San Agustin Acasaguastlan, Guatemala. *Carnegie Inst. Wash.,* Pub. 456, Contrib. 15.
1940 Clay heads from Chiapas, Mexico. *Carnegie Inst. Wash., Notes on Middle Amer. Archaeol. Ethnol.,* no. 1.
1942 Archaeological specimens from Yucatan and Guatemala. *Ibid.,* no. 9.
1943 Grooved stone axes from Central America. *Ibid.,* no. 29.
1945 Excavations at Kaminaljuyu, Guatemala. *Amer. Antiquity,* 11: 65–75.
1947 The artifacts of Uaxactun, Guatemala. *Carnegie Inst. Wash.,* Pub. 576.
1948 Kaminaljuyu, Guatemala: addenda and corrigenda. *Carnegie Inst. Wash., Notes on Middle Amer. Archaeol. Ethnol.,* no. 89.
1949a Jades from Guatemala. *Ibid.,* no. 91.
1949b Certain archaeological specimens from Guatemala, I. *Ibid.,* no. 92.
1950 Certain archaeological specimens from Guatemala, II. *Ibid.,* no. 95.
1954 Miscellaneous archaeological specimens from Mesoamerica. *Ibid.,* no. 117.
1961 Archaeological investigations at Kaminaljuyu, Guatemala. *Proc. Amer. Phil. Soc.,* 105: 559–70.

—— AND G. F. EKHOLM
1951 Some archaeological specimens from Pomona, British Honduras. *Carnegie Inst. Wash., Notes on Middle Amer. Archaeol. Ethnol.,* no. 102.

——, J. D. JENNINGS, AND E. M. SHOOK
1946 Excavations at Kaminaljuyu, Guatemala. *Carnegie Inst. Wash.,* Pub. 561.

—— AND A. O. SHEPARD
1944 Stucco decoration of early Guatemala pottery. *Carnegie Inst. Wash., Notes on Middle Amer. Archaeol. Ethnol.,* no. 35.

—— AND E. M. SHOOK
1946 "Rim-head" vessels from Kaminaljuyu, Guatemala. *Ibid.,* no. 69.
1959 A unique ancient Maya sweathouse, Guatemala. *In* Bierhenke, 1959, pp. 70–74.
1961 A possibly unique type of formative figurine from Guatemala. *In* Lothrop and others, 1961, pp. 176–81.

KING, A. R.
1955 Archaeological remains from the Cintalapa region, Chiapas, Mexico. *Tulane Univ., Middle Amer. Research Rec.,* vol. 2, no. 4.

KIRCHHOFF, P.
1954–55 Calendarios Tenochca, Tlatelolca y otros. *Rev. Mex. Estud. Antr.,* 14: 257–67.

KNAUTH, L.
1961 El juego de pelota y el rito de la decapitación. *Univ. Nac. Autónoma Mex., Estud. Cultura Maya,* 1: 183–98.

KNOROZOV, Y. V.
1952 Drevnyaya Pis'menost Tsentralnoy Ameriki [The ancient script of Central America]. *Sovietskaya Etnografiya,* no. 3, pp. 100–18. Moscow.
1955 La escritura de los antiguos Mayas (ensayo de descrifado). In Russian and Spanish. Inst. Etnografi Akad. Nauk. Moscow.
1958a The problem of the study of the Maya hieroglyphic writing. *Amer. Antiquity,* 23: 284–91.
1958b New data on the Maya written language. *Proc. 32d Int. Cong. Amer.,* pp. 467–75.

KROEBER, A. L.
1948 Anthropology. New York.
1953 [ed.] Anthropology today. Chicago.

KUBLER, G.
1942 Population movements in Mexico, 1520–1600. *Hisp. Amer. Hist. Rev.,* 22: 606–43.
1948 *Review of* The population of central Mexico in the sixteenth century, by S. F. Cook and L. B. Simpson. *Ibid.,* 28: 556–59.
1958 The design of space in Maya architecture. *Univ. Nac. Autónoma Mex., Misc. Paul Rivet,* 1: 515–31.
1961 Chichen Itza y Tula. *Univ. Nac.*

Autónoma Mex., Estud. Cultura Maya, 1: 47–80.
1962 The art and architecture of ancient America: the Mexican, Maya, and Andean peoples. Penguin Books.
—— and C. Gibson
1951 The Tovar calendar. *Mem. Connecticut Acad. Arts and Sci.,* vol. 11.
Kulp, J. L., H. W. Feely, and L. E. Tryon
1951 Lamont natural radiocarbon measurements, I. *Science,* 114: 565–68.
Kunz, G. F.
1907 Gems and precious stones of Mexico. *In* Compt rendu, 10th sess., Cong. Geol. Int. Mexico.
LaFarge, O.
1931 Post-Columbian dates and the Maya correlation problem. *Maya Research,* 1: 109–24.
1947 Santa Eulalia: the religion of a Cuchumatan Indian Town. Chicago.
—— and D. Byers
1931 The year bearer's people. *Tulane Univ., Middle Amer. Research Inst.,* Pub. 3.
Landa, D. de
1864 Relation des choses de Yucatan de Diego de Landa . . . accompagné de documents divers historiques et chronologiques. . . . Ed. by C. E. Brasseur de Bourbourg. Paris.
1938 Relación de las cosas de Yucatan (1566). Ed. Pérez Martínez. Mexico.
1941 Landa's relación de las cosas de Yucatan. Tr. and ed. with notes by A. M. Tozzer. *Papers Peabody Mus., Harvard Univ.,* vol. 18.
Las Casas, B. de
1909 Apologética historia de las Indias. Madrid.
Lathrap, D. W.
1957 The classic stage in Mesoamerica. *Papers Kroeber Anthr. Soc.,* 17: 38–74.
Lehmann, W.
1920 Zentral-Amerika: die Sprachen Zentral-Amerikas in ihren Beziehungen Zueinander sowie zu Süd-Amerika und Mexiko. 2 vols. Berlin.
1922 [ed.] Festschrift Eduard Seler. Stuttgart.
Leigh, H.
1961 Head shrinking in ancient Mexico. *Sci. Man,* 2: 4–7.
Lejeal, L.
1903 Campagnes archéologiques récentes dans l'Oaxaca (Mitla et les "mogotes" de Xoxo). *Jour. Soc. Amer. Paris,* 4: 174–89.
León, N.
1901 Lyobaa o Mictlan. Guia históricodescriptiva. Mexico.
1907 Bibliografía mexicana del siglo XVIII. *Bol. Inst. Bib.,* vol. 8.
León-Portilla, M.
1962 La institución cultural del comercio prehispánico. *Estud. Cultura Nahuatl,* 3: 23–54.
Libby, W. F.
1952 Radiocarbon dating. Chicago.
1954 Chicago radiocarbon dates, V. *Science,* 120: 733–42.
Life en Español
1959 Issue of November 16, pp. 84–87.
Life Magazine
1959 Issue of October 26, pp. 93–96.
Lincoln, J. S.
1942 The Maya calendar of the Ixil of Guatemala. *Carnegie Inst. Wash.,* Pub. 528, Contrib. 38.
Linné, S.
1934 Archaeological researches at Teotihuacan, Mexico. *Ethnog. Mus. Sweden,* n.s., Pub. 1.
1938 Zapotecan antiquities and the Paulson collection in the Ethnographical Museum of Sweden. *Ibid.,* Pub. 4.
1941 Teotihuacan symbols. *Ethnos,* 6: 174–86.
1942 Mexican highland cultures: archaeological researches at Teotihuacan, Calpulalpan and Chalchicomula in 1934–35. *Ethnog. Mus. Sweden,* n.s., Pub. 7.
1947 The thin orange pottery of Mexico and Guatemala. *Ethnos,* 12: 127–36.
1956 Treasures of Mexican art. Tr. by A. Read. Swedish-Mexican Exhibition Comm. Stockholm.
Linton, R.
1922 The sacrifice to the morning star by the Skidi Pawnee. *Field Mus. Natural Hist.,* Leaflet 6.
1936 The study of man. New York.
Lister, R. H.
1955 The present status of the archaeology of western Mexico: a distributional study. *Univ. Colorado Studies, Anthr. Ser.,* no. 5.
Littmann, E. R.
1958 Ancient Mesoamerican mortars, plasters, and stuccos: the composition

and origin of *sascab*. *Amer. Antiquity,* 24: 172–76.

LIZANA, B. DE
1893 Historia de Yucatan. Devocionario de Ntra. Sra. de Izamal y conquista espiritual. Mexico. (1st ed. 1633.)

LIZARDI R., C.
1939 Exploraciones arqueológicas en Quintana Roo. *Rev. Mex. Estud. Antr.,* 3: 46–53.
1940 Exploraciones en Quintana Roo. Mexico.
1941 [ed.] Los Mayas antiguos: monografías de arqueología, etnografía y lingüística mayas. . . . Colegio de Mexico.
1949 Mas fechas mayas. *El Mexico Antiguo,* 7: 238–60.
1955 ¿Conocían el xihuitl los teotihuacanos? *El Mexico Antiguo,* 8: 219–23.
1959 El calendario maya-mexicano. *In* Esplendor del Mexico Antiguo, pp. 221–42.

LOCKE, L. L.
1923 The ancient Quipu or Peruvian knot record. Amer. Mus. Nat. Hist.

LONG, R. C. E.
1926 The Zouche codex. *Jour. Royal Anthr. Inst.,* 56: 239–58.
1948 Some remarks on Maya arithmetic. *Carnegie Inst. Wash., Notes Middle Amer. Archaeol. Ethnol.,* no. 88.

LONGYEAR, J. M.
1944 Archaeological investigations in El Salvador. *Mem. Peabody Mus., Harvard Univ.,* vol. 9, no. 2.
1952 Copan ceramics: a study of southeastern Maya pottery. *Carnegie Inst. Wash.,* Pub. 597.

LÓPEZ DE COGOLLUDO, D.
1867–68 Historia de Yucatan. 2 vols. 3d ed. Merida. (1st ed. 1688, Madrid.)
1955 *Idem,* 4th ed. Campeche.

LÓPEZ DE GÓMARA, F.
1931 Hispania victrix. Primera y segunda parte de la historia general de las Indias. *In* Historiadores primitivos de Indias, pp. 155–455. Madrid.

LÓPEZ DE LLERGO, R.
1960 Principales rasgos fisiográficos de la región comprendida entre el paralelo 19° y el istmo de Tehuantepec. *Rev. Mex. Estud. Antr.,* 16: 21–29.

LÓPEZ MEDEL, T.
1941 Relación. *In* Landa, 1941, pp. 221–29.

LORENZO, J. L.
1955 Los concheros de la costa de Chiapas. *An. Inst. Antr. Hist.,* 7: 41–50.
1958 Un sitio precerámico en Yanhuitlan, Oaxaca. *Inst. Nac. Antr. Hist., Dir. Prehistoria,* Pub. 6.
1961 La revolución neolítica en Mesoamerica. *Ibid.,* Pub. 11.

LOTHROP, S. K.
1923 Stone yokes from Mexico and Central America. *Man,* 23: 97–98.
1924 Tulum: an archaeological study of the east coast of Yucatan. *Carnegie Inst. Wash.,* Pub. 335.
1926a Stone sculptures from the Finca Arevalo ruins, Guatemala. *Mus. Amer. Indian, Heye Found., Indian Notes,* 3: 147–71.
1926b Pottery of Costa Rica and Nicaragua. *Mus. Amer. Indian, Heye Found., Contrib.,* no. 8.
1927a The museum Central American expedition, 1925–26. *Mus. Amer. Indian, Heye Found., Indian Notes,* 4: 12–33.
1927b Pottery types and their sequence in El Salvador. *Mus. Amer. Indian, Heye Found., Indian Notes and Monogr.,* vol. 1, no. 4.
1933 Atitlan: an archaeological study of ancient remains on the borders of Lake Atitlan, Guatemala. *Carnegie Inst. Wash.,* Pub. 444.
1936 Zacualpa: a study of ancient Quiche artifacts. *Ibid.,* Pub. 472.
1937 Cocle: an archaeological study of central Panama. Pt. I: Historical background, excavations at the Sitio Conte, artifacts and ornaments. *Mem. Peabody Mus., Harvard Univ.,* vol. 7.
1942 Cocle. Pt. II: Pottery of the Sitio Conte and other archaeological sites. *Ibid.,* vol. 8.
1950a Archaeology of southern Veraguas, Panama. *Ibid.,* vol. 9, no. 3.
1950b An exhibition of ancient American gold and jade. Taft Mus. Cincinnati.
1952 Metals from the cenote of sacrifice, Chichen Itza, Yucatan. *Mem. Peabody Mus., Harvard Univ.,* vol. 10, no. 2.

——, W. F. Foshag, and J. Mahler
1957 Pre-Columbian art: Robert Woods Bliss Collection. Phaidon Press. London.

—— and others
1961 Essays in pre-Columbian art and archaeology. Cambridge.

Lowe, G. W.
1956 Summary of New World Archaeological Foundation investigations at Chiapa de Corzo, Chiapas, 1955. *New World Archaeol. Found.*, Pub. 1, pp. 38–42.
1959a The Chiapas project, 1955–1958: report of the field director. *Papers New World Archaeol. Found.*, no. 1.
1959b Archaeological exploration of the upper Grijalva River, Chiapas, Mexico. *Ibid.*, no. 2.
1962 Mound 5 and minor excavations, Chiapa de Corzo, Chiapas, Mexico. *Ibid.*, no. 12.

Lundell, C. L.
1934 Preliminary sketch of the phytogeography of the Yucatan peninsula. *Carnegie Inst. Wash.*, Pub. 436, Contrib. 12.

McBryde, F. W.
1947 Cultural and historical geography of southwest Guatemala. *Smithsonian Inst., Inst. Social Anthr.*, Pub. 4.

McDougall, E.
1946 Observations on altar sites in the Quiche region, Guatemala. *Carnegie Inst. Wash., Notes Middle Amer. Archaeol. Ethnol.*, no. 62.

MacKie, E. W.
1961 New light on the end of the classic Maya culture at Benque Viejo, British Honduras. *Amer. Antiquity*, 27: 216–24.

MacNeish, R. S.
1954 An early archaeological site near Panuco, Vera Cruz. *Trans. Amer. Phil. Soc.*, 44: 539–641.
1961 Restos precerámicos de la cueva de Coxcatlan en el sur de Puebla. *Inst. Nac. Antr. Hist., Dir. Prehistoria*, Pub. 10.
1964 The origins of New World civilization. *Sci. Amer.*, 211: 29–37.

—— and F. A. Peterson
1962 The Santa Marta rock shelter, Ocozocoautla, Chiapas, Mexico. *Papers New World Archaeol. Found.*, no. 14.

McQuown, N. A.
1956 The classification of the Maya languages. *Int. Jour. Amer. Ling.*, 22: 191–95.
1959 [ed.] Report on the "Man-in-Nature" project of the Department of Anthropology of the University of Chicago in the Tzeltal-Tzotzil-speaking region of the state of Chiapas, Mexico. 3 vols. Hectographed.

Mahoney, R.
1961 Caballito Blanco (Oaxaca) again. *Katunob*, 2: 12.

Makemson, M. W.
1943 The astronomical tables of the Maya. *Carnegie Inst. Wash.*, Pub. 546, Contrib. 42.
1946 The Maya correlation problem. *Vassar College Observatory*, Pub. 5.

Maler, T.
1895 Yukatekische forschungen. *Globus*, 68: 247–60, 277–92.
1901–03 Researches in the central portion of the Usumatsintla valley. *Mem. Peabody Mus., Harvard Univ.*, vol. 2, nos. 1, 2.
1902 Yukatekische forshungen. *Globus*, 82: 197–230.
1908a Explorations of the upper Usumatsintla and adjacent region: Altar de Sacrificios; Seibal; Itsimte-Sacluk; Cancuen. *Mem. Peabody Mus., Harvard Univ.*, vol. 4, no. 1.
1908b Explorations in the Department of Peten, Guatemala, and adjacent region: Topoxte; Yaxha; Benque Viejo; Naranjo. *Ibid.*, vol. 4, no. 2.
1911 Explorations in the Department of Peten, Guatemala: Tikal. *Ibid.*, vol. 5, no. 1.
1912 Lista de las ilustraciones para una proyectada publicación, de Teobert Maler, en el libro de recuerdos del Congreso Americanistas, 1910. *Reseña 2d ses., 17 Cong. Int. Amer.*
1942 Descubrimiento de una tumba real zapoteca en Tehuantepec, en el año de 1875. *El Mexico Antiguo*, 6: 1–5.

Marden, L.
1959 Dzibilchaltun: up from the well of time. *Nat. Geog. Mag.*, 115: 110–29.

Mariscal, F.
1928 Estudio arquitectónico de las ruinas mayas: Yucatan y Campeche. Sec. Educ. Púb. Mexico.

MARQUINA, I.
1928 Estudio arquitectónico comparativo de los monumentos arqueológicos de Mexico. Sec. Educ. Púb. Mexico.
1939 Atlas arqueológico de la República Mexicana. *Inst. Panamer. Geog. Hist.*, Pub. 41.
1951 Arquitectura prehispánica. *Mem. Inst. Nac. Antr. Hist.*, vol. 1.

MARTÍ, S.
1955 Instrumentos musicales precortesianos. Inst. Nac. Antr. Hist.

MARTÍNEZ ESPINOSA, E.
1959 Una nueva escultura olmeca de Tonala, Chiapas. *Inst. Cien. Artes Chiapas,* 1: 79–81. Tuxtla Gutierrez.

MARTÍNEZ GRACIDA, M.
1895 Minería y su industria. *Proc. 6th Int. Cong. Amer.*

MARTÍNEZ HERNÁNDEZ, J.
1926 Crónicas mayas: crónica de Yaxkukul. Merida.
1929 Diccionario de Motul: Maya-Español. Merida.

MARTYR, P.
1612 De nouo orbe *or* The historie of the West Indies. Tr. by R. Eden and M. Lok. London.

MASON, G.
1927 Silver cities of Yucatan. New York.

MASON, J. A.
1927 Native American jades. *Mus. Jour., Univ. Pennsylvania,* 18: 47–73.
1935 Preserving ancient America's finest sculptures. *Nat. Geog. Mag.,* 68: 537–70.
1940 The native languages of Middle America. *In* The Maya and their Neighbors, pp. 52–87.
1943 The American collection of the University Museum: the ancient civilizations of Middle America. *Bull. Univ. Pennsylvania Mus.,* 10: 1–2.
1960a Mound 12, Chiapa de Corzo, Chiapas, Mexico. *Papers New World Archaeol. Found.,* no. 9.
1960b The terrace to north of Mound 13, Chiapa de Corzo, Chiapas, Mexico. *Ibid.,* no. 11.

MAUDSLAY, A. C. AND A. P.
1899 A glimpse at Guatemala and some notes on the ancient monuments of Central America. London.

MAUDSLAY, A. P.
1889–1902 Archaeology. *In* Biologia Centrali-Americana. 5 vols. London.

MAYA AND THEIR NEIGHBORS, THE
1940 Ed. C. L. Hay and others. New York.

MAYAS ANTIGUOS, LOS
See Lizardi, 1941.

MAYAS Y OLMECAS
1942 Segunda reunión de mesa redonda sobre problemas antropológicos de Mexico y Centro America. Soc. Mex. Antropol. Tuxtla Gutierrez.

MAYER, B.
1857 Observations on Mexican history and archaeology, with a special notice of Zapotec remains. *Smithsonian Contrib. Knowledge,* 9: 1–33.

MEANS, P. A.
1917 History of the Spanish conquest of Yucatan and of the Itzas. *Papers Peabody Mus., Harvard Univ.,* vol. 7.

MEDELLÍN ZENIL, A.
1960a Cerámicas del Totonacapan. Jalapa.
1960b Nopiloa, un sitio clásico del Veracruz central. *Palabra y Hombre,* 4 (13): 37–48.
1960c Monolitos inéditos olmecas. *Ibid.,* 4 (16): pp. 75–98.

—— AND F. A. PETERSON
1954 A smiling head complex from central Veracruz, Mexico. *Amer. Antiquity,* 20: 162–69.

MEDINA, J. T.
1912 Monedas usadas por los Indios de América al tiempo del descubrimiento según los antiguos documentos y cronistas españoles. *Proc. 17th Int. Cong. Amer.,* pp. 556–57.

MÉDIONI, G.
1950 Art Maya du Mexique et du Guatemala. Ancien Empire. Paris.

MELHUS, I. E., ed.
1949 Plant research in the tropics. Agricultural Exp. Station, Iowa State College.

MEMORIA . . . SANTA ANA
1565 Memoria título de Santa Ana. MSS in Pokom, no. 6 in volume of photographs of Kekchi documents prepared by W. Gates.

MEMORIAL DE SOLOLA
1950 Memorial de Solola. Anales de los Cakchiqueles. Bib. Amer., Ser. Lit. Indígena.

MENDELSON, M. E.
1958 A Guatemalan sacred bundle. *Man,* 58: 1–6.

MÉNDEZ, A. C. DE
1959 El comercio de los Mayas antiguos. *Acta Anthr.,* vol. 2, no. 1.

MENDIZABAL, M. O.
1928 Influencia de la sal en la distribución geográfica de los grupos indígenas de Mexico. Mexico.
—— AND W. JIMÉNEZ MORENO
1937 Distribución geográfica de las lenguas indígenas de Mexico conforme al censo de 1930. Map. Mexico.
MERCER, H. C.
1896 The hill caves of Yucatan. Philadelphia.
MERRILL, R. H.
1945 Maya sun calendar dictum disproved. *Amer. Antiquity,* 10: 307–11.
MERWIN, R. E.
1909–10 Note book no. 4. Peabody Mus., Harvard Univ.
1913 The ruins of the southern part of the peninsula of Yucatan with special reference to their place in the Maya area. Ph.D. thesis, Harvard Univ. MS in Peabody Mus.
—— AND G. C. VAILLANT
1932 The ruins of Holmul, Guatemala. *Mem. Peabody Mus., Harvard Univ.,* vol. 3, no. 2.
MEXICO CITY COLLEGIAN
1960 Issue of August 4.
MEXICO PREHISPÁNICO
See Vivó, 1946a.
MILES, S. W.
1957a Maya settlement patterns: a problem for ethnology and archaeology. *SW. Jour. Anthr.,* 13: 239–48.
1957b The 16th century Pokom-Maya: a documentary analysis of social structure and archaeological setting. *Trans. Amer. Phil. Soc.,* 47: 731–81.
1958 An urban type: extended boundary towns. *SW. Jour. Anthr.,* 14: 339–51.
MILLON, R. F.
1954 Irrigation at Teotihuacan. *Amer. Antiquity,* 20: 176–80.
1957 Irrigation systems in the valley of Teotihuacan. *Ibid.,* 23: 160–66.
MOEDANO KÖER, H.
1946 Jaina: un cementerio maya. *Rev. Mex. Estud. Antr.,* 8: 217–42.
1948 Breve noticia sobre la zona de Oztotitlan, Guerrero. *In* El Occidente de Mexico, pp. 105–06.
MOLINA, A. DE
1944 Vocabulario en lengua mexicana y castellana. *Col. Incunables Amer.,* vol. 4. Madrid.
MORLEY, S. G.
1915 An introduction to the study of the Maya hieroglyphs. *Smithsonian Inst., Bur. Amer. Ethnol.,* Bull. 57.
1916 The supplementary series in the Maya inscriptions. *In* Holmes Anniv. Vol., pp. 366–96.
1920 The inscriptions at Copan. *Carnegie Inst. Wash.,* Pub. 219.
1935 Guide book to the ruins of Quirigua. *Ibid.,* Supp. Pub. 16.
1937–38 The inscriptions of Peten. 5 vols. *Ibid.,* Pub. 437.
1946 The ancient Maya. Stanford.
1956 The ancient Maya. (3d ed. rev. by G. W. Brainerd.) Stanford.
—— AND F. R. MORLEY
1938 The age and provenance of the Leyden Plate. *Carnegie Inst. Wash.,* Pub. 509, Contrib. 24.
MORRIS, E. H., J. CHARLOT, AND A. A. MORRIS
1931 The Temple of the Warriors at Chichen Itza, Yucatan. 2 vols. *Ibid.,* Pub. 406.
MOTOLINÍA, T. DE B.
1858 Historia de los Indios de la Nueva España. *In* J. García Icazbalceta, Col. Doc. para la Historia de Mexico, 1: 1–249.
MOTUL DICTIONARY
See Martínez Hernández, 1929.
MÜLLERRIED, F. K. G.
1957 La geología de Chiapas. Tuxtla Gutierrez.
MURGUÍA Y GALARDI, J. M. DE
1859 Apuntamientos estadísticos de la provincia de Oaxaca en esta Nueva España, que comprenden dos partes: la primera sobre sus antigüedades y la segunda sobre su actual estado. Año de 1818. Oaxaca.
NAVARRETE, C.
n.d. Investigaciones arqueológicas acerca del problema chiapaneco. MS of paper presented to VII Mesa Redonda, Soc. Mex. Antropol. (1959).
1959a Explorations at San Agustin, Chiapas, Mexico. *Papers New World Archaeol. Found.,* no. 3.
1959b A brief reconnaissance in the region of Tonala, Chiapas. *Ibid.,* no. 4.
1960 Archaeological explorations in the region of the Frailesca, Chiapas, Mexico. *Ibid.,* no. 7.
NICHOLSON, H. B.
1961 The use of the term "Mixtec" in

Mesoamerican archaeology. *Amer. Antiquity,* 26: 431–33.

Noguera, E.
1940 Excavations at Tehuacan. *In* The Maya and their Neighbors, pp. 306–19.
1942 Exploraciones en "El Opeño," Michoacan. *Proc. 27th Int. Cong. Amer.,* 1: 574–86.
1946 Cultura de El Opeño. *In* Mexico Prehispánico, pp. 150–54.
1954 La cerámica arqueológica de Cholula. Mexico.

Nottebohm, K. H.
1945 A second Tlaloc gold plaque from Guatemala. *Carnegie Inst. Wash., Notes Middle Amer. Archaeol. Ethnol.,* no. 51.

Noyes, E., ed. and tr.
1932 Fray Alonso Ponce in Yucatan, 1588. *Tulane Univ., Middle Amer. Research Inst.,* Pub. 4, pp. 297–372.

Núñez de la Vega, F.
1702 Constituciones diocesanas del obispado de Chiapa. Rome.

Nuttall, Z.
1901 Chalchihuitl in ancient Mexico. *Amer. Anthr.,* 3: 227–38.
1902 *See* Codex Nuttall.

Ober, F. A.
1884 Travels in Mexico and life among the Mexicans. Boston.

Occidente de Mexico, el
1948 El occidente de Mexico. Cuarta reunión de mesa redonda sobre problemas antropológicos de Mexico y Centro America. . . . Soc. Mex. Antr.

Oliver, J. P.
1955 Architectural similarities of Mitla and Yagul. *Mesoamer. Notes,* 4: 49–67.

O'Neale, L. M.
1942 Early textiles from Chiapas, Mexico. *Tulane Univ., Middle Amer. Research Rec.,* vol. 1, no. 1.
1945 Textiles of highland Guatemala. *Carnegie Inst. Wash.,* Pub. 567.

Orchard, W. C.
1925 Minute gold bead from La Tolita, Ecuador. *Mus. Amer. Indian, Heye Found., Indian Notes,* vol. 2, no. 1.

Ordóñez y Aguiar, R. de
1907 Historia de la creación del cielo, y de la tierre, conforme al systema de la gentilidad americana. *In* León, 1907.

Orellana Tapia, R.
1952 Zona arqueológica de Izapa. *Tlatoani,* 1: 17–25.
1954a El vaso de Ixtapa, Chiapas. *Yan,* no. 3, pp. 114–18.
1954b Ixtapa, Chinkultic, Tenam-Puente, Mox. y Tonina. *Ibid.,* no. 3, pp. 125–26.
1955 Nueva lápida olmecoide de Izapa, Chiapas, Estela 21. *El Mexico Antiguo,* 8: 157–68.

Outwater, J. O., Jr.
1957 The pre-Columbian stonecutting techniques of the Mexican plateau. *Amer. Antiquity,* 22: 258–64.

Oviedo y Valdés, G. F. de
1851–55 Historia general y natural de las Indias, islas y tierra-firme del Mar Océano. 4 vols. Madrid.

Paddock, J.
1957 The 1956 season at Yagul. *Mesoamer. Notes,* 5:13–36.
1958 Comments on some problems of Oaxaca archeology. *Bol. Estud. Oaxaqueños,* no. 4.
1960 Exploración en Yagul, Oaxaca. *Rev. Mex. Estud. Antr.,* 16: 91–96.

Palacios, E. J.
1928a En los confines de la selva lacandona. Sec. Educ. Púb. Mexico.
1928b Monumentos de Etzna-Tixmucuy. *In* Estado Actual, pp. 167–78.
1937 Mas gemas del arte maya en Palenque. *An. Mus. Nac. Arqueol. Hist. Etnog.,* 2: 193–225.
1941 Cien años después de Stephens. *In* Los Mayas Antiguos, pp. 275–342.
1945a Guia arqueológica de Chacmultun, Labna, Sayil, Kabah, Uxmal, Chichen Itza y Tulum. *In* Enciclopedia Yucatanese, 2: 405–554.
1945b Arquitectura, escultura, pintura, orfebrería y lapidaria. *Ibid.,* 2: 343–404.

Palerm, A.
1957 Ecological potential and cultural development in Mesoamerica. *In* Studies in Human Ecology, pp. 1–37. *Pan Amer. Union, Social Sci. Monogr.,* no. 3.

Papeles de Nueva España (PNE)
See Paso y Troncoso, 1905.

Pareyón Moreno, E.
1960 Exploraciones arqueológicas en Ciudad Vieja de Quiotepec, Oaxaca. *Rev. Mex. Estud. Antr.,* 16: 97–104.

PARSONS, L. A., S. F. BORHEGYI, P. JENSON, AND R. RITZENTHALER
1963 Excavaciones en Bilbao, Santa Lucia Cotzumalhuapa: informe preliminar. *Antr. Hist. Guatemala,* 15 (1): 3–14.

PASO Y TRONCOSO, F. DEL
1905 Papeles de Nueva España. 7 vols. Madrid.
1939–42 [comp.] Epistolario de Nueva España. 16 vols. Mexico.

PEABODY MUSEUM
1896 Prehistoric ruins of Copan, Honduras. *Mem. Peabody Mus., Harvard Univ.,* vol. 1, no. 1.

PEÑAFIEL, A.
1890 Monumentos del arte mexicano antiguo. 3 vols. in 5 bindings. Berlin.

PÉREZ, J. P.
1843 Cronología antigua de Yucatan y examen del método con que los indios contaban el tiempo, sacados de varios documentos antiguos. Peto. (Copies published in Registro Yucateco and in Brasseur de Bourbourg, 1864.)

PÉREZ GARCÍA, R.
1956 La Sierra Juarez. 2 vols. Mexico.

PÉRIGNY, M. DE
1908 Yucatan inconnu. *Jour. Soc. Amer. Paris,* 5: 67–84.

PETERSON, F. A.
1952 Caritas sonrientes de la región maya. *Tlatoani,* 1: 63–64.
1963 Some ceramics from Mirador, Chiapas, Mexico. *Papers New World Archaeol. Found.,* no. 15.

PHILLIPS, P., AND J. C. GIFFORD
1959 A review of the taxonomic nomenclature essential to ceramic analysis in archaeology. MS in Peabody Mus., Harvard Univ. (Mimeographed.)

PIJOAN, J.
1946 Arte precolombiano, mexicano y maya. *In* Summa artis: historial general del arte, vol. 10. Madrid.

PIÑA CHAN, R.
1948 Breve estudio sobre la funeraria de Jaina, Campeche. *Mus. Arqueol. Etnog. Hist.,* Cuad. 7. Campeche.
1955 Chalcatzingo, Morelos. *Dir. Monumentos Pre-Hispánicos,* Informe 4.
1958 Tlatilco. 2 vols. *Inst. Nac. Antr. Hist., Ser. Invest.,* nos. 1, 2.
1960a Mesoamerica: ensayo histórico cultural. *Mem. Inst. Nac. Antr. Hist.,* vol. 6.
1960b Algunos sitios arqueológicos de Oaxaca y Guerrero. *Rev. Mex. Estud. Antr.,* 16: 65–76.
1960c Reconocimientos arqueológicos en el estado de Chiapas. MS, VII Mesa Redonda, Soc. Mex. Antr. San Cristobal las Casas.

PINEDA, E.
1845 Descripción geográfica de Chiapas. Mexico.

POLLOCK, H. E. D.
1936 Round structures of aboriginal Middle America. *Carnegie Inst. Wash.,* Pub. 471.
1940a Sources and methods in the study of Maya architecture. *In* The Maya and their Neighbors, pp. 179–201.
1940b Architectural survey of Yucatan. *Carnegie Inst. Wash.,* Year Book 39, pp. 265–67.
1952 Department of archaeology. *Ibid.,* Year Book 51, pp. 235–43.

——, R. L. ROYS, T. PROSKOURIAKOFF, AND A. L. SMITH
1962 Mayapan, Yucatan, Mexico. *Carnegie Inst. Wash.,* Pub. 619.

—— AND G. STROMSVIK
1953 Chacchob, Yucatan. *Carnegie Inst. Wash., Current Reports,* no. 6.

PONCE, A.
1873 Relación breve y verdadera de algunas cosas de las muchas que sucedieron al Padre Fray Alonso Ponce. 2 vols. Madrid. [Almost certainly the work of Antonio Ciudad Real.]

PONCE DE LEÓN, L.
1882 Relación de la provincia de Soconusco, together with a covering letter dated 1574. *In* Fuentes y Guzmán, 1882, 1: 423–28.

POPOL VUH
1950 Popol Vuh: the sacred book of the ancient Quiche Maya. Norman, Okla. *See* Book of the People.

PORTER, M. N.
1948 Pipas precortesianas. *Acta Anthr.,* 3: 130–251.
1953 Tlatilco and the pre-classic cultures of the New World. *Viking Fund Pub. Anthr.,* no. 19.

PREUSS, K. T.
1955 El concepto de la estrella matutina según textos recogidos entre los Mexicanos del estado de Durango,

Mexico. *El Mexico Antiguo,* 8: 375–93.

PRICE, H. W.
1899 Excavations on the Sittee River, British Honduras. Proc. Soc. Antiquaries.

PROSKOURIAKOFF, T.
1944 An inscription on a jade probably carved at Piedras Negras. *Carnegie Inst. Wash., Notes Middle Amer. Archaeol. Ethnol.,* no. 47.
1946 An album of Maya architecture. *Carnegie Inst. Wash.,* Pub. 558.
1950 A study of classic Maya sculpture. *Ibid.,* Pub. 593.
1951 Some non-classic traits in the sculpture of Yucatan. *In* Tax, 1951, pp. 108–18.
1952a Sculpture and artifacts of Mayapan. *Carnegie Inst. Wash.,* Year Book 51, pp. 256–59.
1952b The survival of the Maya tun count in colonial times. *Carnegie Inst. Wash., Notes Middle Amer. Archaeol. Ethnol.,* no. 112.
1954 Varieties of classic central Veracruz sculpture. *Carnegie Inst. Wash.,* Pub. 606, Contrib. 58.
1957a Notes and news: Middle America. *Amer. Antiquity,* 22: 333–34.
1957b Notes and news: Middle America. *Ibid.,* 23: 218–20.
1960 Historical implications of a pattern of dates at Piedras Negras, Guatemala. *Ibid.,* 25: 454–75.
1961 Portraits of women in Maya art. *In* Lothrop and others, 1961, pp. 81–99.
1962a Civic and religious structures of Mayapan. *Carnegie Inst. Wash.,* Pub. 619, pp. 87–164.
1962b The artifacts of Mayapan. *Ibid.,* pp. 321–442.
1962c *Review of* More human than divine, by William Spratling. *Amer. Antiquity,* 27: 439.

—— AND C. R. TEMPLE
1955 A residential quadrangle: Structures R-85 to R-90. *Carnegie Inst. Wash., Current Reports,* no. 29.

—— AND J. E. S. THOMPSON
1947 Maya calendar round dates such as 9 Ahau 3 Mol. *Carnegie Inst. Wash., Notes Middle Amer. Archaeol. Ethnol.,* no. 79.

RANDS, B. C.
1954 Ceramics associated with the Temple of the Inscriptions, Palenque, Chiapas, Mexico. M.A. thesis, Univ. New Mexico.

—— AND R. L. RANDS
1959 Preliminary notes on Group 4, Pit 5, Palenque, Chiapas: burials 1959. MS.

RANDS, R. L.
1952 Some evidences of warfare in classic Maya art. Ph.D. thesis, Columbia Univ.
1953 The water lily in Maya art: a complex of alleged Asiatic origin. *Smithsonian Inst., Bur. Amer. Ethnol.,* Bull. 151, pp. 75–153.
1954 Artistic connections between the Chichen Itza Toltec and the classic Maya. *Amer. Antiquity,* 19: 281–82.
1955 Some manifestations of water in Mesoamerican art. *Smithsonian Inst., Bur. Amer. Ethnol.,* Bull. 157, pp. 265–393.
1961a Elaboration and invention in ceramic traditions. *Amer. Antiquity,* 26: 331–40.
1961b The ceramic history of Palenque, Chiapas, Mexico. *Amer. Phil. Soc.,* Year Book 1960, pp. 566–68.

—— AND B. C. RANDS
1957 The ceramic position of Palenque, Chiapas. *Amer. Antiquity,* 23: 140–50.
1959 The incensario complex of Palenque, Chiapas. *Ibid.,* 25: 225–36.
1960 Ceramic investigations at Palenque, Mexico. *Bol. Bib. Antr. Amer.,* vol. 21-22, pt. 1, pp. 218–20.

RAVICZ, R.
1961 La Mixteca en el estudio comparativo del hongo alucinante. *An. Inst. Nac. Antr. Hist.,* 13: 73–92.

RECINOS, A.
1913 Monografía del departamento de Huehuetenango, República de Guatemala. Guatemala.
1947 Popol Vuh: las historias antiguas del Quiche. Tr. from original with introduction and notes. Mexico.
1957 Crónicas indígenas de Guatemala. Guatemala.

—— AND D. GOETZ
1953 The annals of the Cakchiquels. Norman, Okla.

——, ——, AND S. G. MORLEY
1950 Popol Vuh. Norman.

REDFIELD, R.
1950 A village that chose progress: Chan Kom revisited. Chicago.
—— AND M. P. REDFIELD
1940 Disease and its treatment in Dzitas, Yucatan. *Carnegie Inst. Wash.*, Pub. 523, Contrib. 32.
—— AND A. VILLA R.
1934 Chan Kom, a Maya village. *Ibid.*, Pub. 448.
REICHEL-DOLMATOFF, G.
1961 Anthropomorphic figurines from Colombia, their magic and art. *In* Lothrop and others, 1961, pp. 229–41.
RELACIÓN . . . DE TLAXCALA
See García Pimentel, 1904.
RELACIONES DE YUCATAN
1898–1900 *In* Colección de documentos inéditos relativos al descubrimiento, conquista y organización de las antiguas posesiones españolas de ultramar. 2d ser., vols. 11, 13. Madrid.
REYES, A. DE LOS
1593 Arte de la lengua mixteca. Mexico. (Reprinted 1750, Puebla; 1890, Paris.)
REYGADAS V., J.
1928 Chacmultun, Chacbolay y Kom, Kiuic, Labna, Zayi, Kabah, Uxmal. *In* Estado Actual, pp. 179–235.
REYNOSO, D. DE
1644 Arte y vocabulario en lengua mame. Mexico. (Charencey reprint, 1892.)
RICHARDSON, F. B.
1940 Non-Maya monumental sculpture of Central America. *In* The Maya and their Neighbors, pp. 395–416.
RICKARDS, C. G.
1910 The ruins of Mexico. London.
RICKETSON, O. G., JR.
1925 Burials in the Maya area. *Amer. Anthr.*, 27: 381–401.
1929 Excavations at Baking Pot, British Honduras. *Carnegie Inst. Wash.*, Pub. 403, Contrib. 1.
1935 Maya pottery well from Quirigua farm, Guatemala. *Maya Research*, 2: 103–05.
1936 Ruins of Tzalcani, Guatemala. *Ibid.*, 3: 18–23.
—— AND A. V. KIDDER
1930 An archaeological reconnaissance by air in Central America. *Geog. Rev.*, 20: 177–206.
—— AND E. B. RICKETSON
1937 Uaxactun, Guatemala, Group E, 1926–1931. *Carnegie Inst. Wash.*, Pub. 477.
RIDGWAY, R.
1912 Color standards and color nomenclature. Washington.
RÍO, A. DEL
1822 Description of the ruins of an ancient city, discovered near Palenque, in the kingdom of Guatemala, in Spanish America. London.
RÍOS, P. DE
1900 Il manoscritto Messicano. Vaticano 3738 detto il codice Rios. Rome.
RIVET, P., AND H. ARSANDAUX
1946 La métallurgie en Amérique précolombienne. *Travaux et Mem. Inst. Ethnol.*, vol. 39. Paris.
ROBERTSON, D.
1959 Mexican manuscript painting of the early colonial period. New Haven.
ROBINA, R. DE
1956 Estudio preliminar de las ruinas de Hochob, municipio de Hopelchen, Campeche. Mexico.
1959 La arquitectura. *In* Esplendor del Mexico Antiguo, 2: 607–50.
ROMERO, J.
1951 Monte Negro, centro de interés antropológico. *In* Homenaje Caso, pp. 317–29.
1958 Mutilaciones dentarias prehispánicas de Mexico y America en general. *Inst. Nac. Antr. Hist., Ser. Invest.*, no. 3.
ROOT, W. C.
1951 Gold-copper alloys in ancient America. *In* Symposium on Archaeological Chemistry. *Jour. Chem. Educ.*, vol. 28, no. 2.
ROSADO OJEDA, V.
1945 Estudio del códice mixteco post-cortesiano, no. 36. *An. Inst. Nac. Antr. Hist.*, 1: 147–55.
ROYS, L.
1933 The Maya correlation problem today. *Amer. Anthr.*, 35: 403–17.
1934 The engineering knowledge of the Maya. *Carnegie Inst. Wash.*, Pub. 436, Contrib. 6.
1958 The use of the term "classic" in Maya archaeology. *Davenport Public Mus. Quar.*, 3: 1–5.
ROYS, R. L.
1931 The ethno-botany of the Maya. *Tu-*

lane Univ., Middle Amer. Research Inst., Pub. 2.
1933 The book of Chilam Balam of Chumayel. *Carnegie Inst. Wash.*, Pub. 438.
1939 The titles of Ebtun. *Ibid.*, Pub. 505.
1940 Personal names of the Maya of Yucatan. *Ibid.*, Pub. 523, Contrib. 31.
1941 The Xiu chronicle, pt. 2. MS in Peabody Mus., Harvard Univ.
1943 The Indian background of colonial Yucatan. *Carnegie Inst. Wash.*, Pub. 548.
1949a Guide to the Codex Pérez. *Ibid.*, Pub. 585, Contrib. 49.
1949b The prophecies for the Maya tuns or years in the books of Chilam Balam of Tizimin and Mani. *Ibid.*, Pub. 585, Contrib. 51.
1954 The Maya katun prophecies of the books of Chilam Balam, Series I. *Ibid.*, Pub. 606, Contrib. 57.
1957 Political geography of the Yucatan Maya. *Ibid.*, Pub. 613.

——, F. V. Scholes, and E. B. Adams
1940 Report and census of the Indians of Cozumel, 1570. *Ibid.*, Pub. 523, Contrib. 30.
1959 Census and inspection of the town of Pencuyut, Yucatan, in 1583 by Diego García de Palacio, oidor of the audiencia of Guatemala. *Ethnohistory*, 6: 195–225.

Rubín de la Borbolla, D. F.
1944 Orfebrería tarasca. *Cuad. Amer.*, vol. 3, no. 15.
1947 Teotihuacan: ofrendas de los templos de Quetzalcoatl. *An. Inst. Nac. Antr. Hist.*, vol. 2.
1953 Mexico: monumentos históricos y arqueológicos. *Inst. Panamer. Geog. Hist.*, Pub. 145.

Ruppert, K.
1931 The Temple of the Wall Panels, Chichen Itza. *Carnegie Inst. Wash.*, Pub. 403, Contrib. 3.
1935 The Caracol at Chichen Itza, Yucatan, Mexico. *Ibid.*, Pub. 454.
1940 A special assemblage of Maya structures. *In* The Maya and their Neighbors, pp. 222–31.
1943 The Mercado, Chichen Itza, Yucatan. *Carnegie Inst. Wash.*, Pub. 546, Contrib. 43.
1950 Gallery-patio type structures at Chichen Itza. *In* For the Dean, pp. 249–58.
1952 Chichen Itza: architectural notes and plans. *Carnegie Inst. Wash.*, Pub. 595.

—— and J. H. Denison
1943 Archaeological reconnaissance in Campeche, Quintana Roo, and Peten. *Ibid.*, Pub. 543.

—— and A. L. Smith
1952 Excávations in house mounds at Mayapan: I. *Carnegie Inst. Wash., Current Reports*, no. 4.
1954 Excavations in house mounds at Mayapan: III. *Ibid.*, no. 17.
1957 House types in the environs of Mayapan and at Uxmal, Kabah, Sayil, Chichen Itza, and Chacchob. *Ibid.*, no. 39.

——, J. E. S. Thompson, and T. Proskouriakoff
1955 Bonampak, Chiapas, Mexico. *Carnegie Inst. Wash.*, Pub. 602.

Russell, S. R.
1954 A new type of archaic ruins in Chiapas, Mexico. *Amer. Antiquity*, 20: 62–64.

Ruz Lhuillier, A.
1945a La costa de Campeche en los tiempos prehispánicos. M.S. thesis, Univ. Nac. Autónoma de Mexico.
1945b Campeche en la arqueología maya. *Acta Anthr.*, vol. 1, nos. 2, 3.
1945c Guía arqueológica de Tula. Mexico.
1948 Exploraciones arqueológicas en Kabah y Uxmal, Yucatan. MS in Archivo Inst. Nac. Antr. Hist.
1952a Exploraciones arqueológicas en Palenque (1949). *An. Inst. Nac. Antr. Hist.*, 4: 49–60.
1952b Exploraciones en Palenque: 1950. *Ibid.*, 5: 25–46.
1952c Exploraciones en Palenque: 1951. *Ibid.*, 5: 47–66.
1952d Estudio de la cripta del Templo de las Inscripciones en Palenque. *Tlatoani*, vol. 1, no. 5.
1953 Presencia atlántica en Palenque. *Rev. Mex. Estud. Antr.*, 13: 455–62.
1955a Exploraciones en Palenque: 1952. *An. Inst. Nac. Antr. Hist.*, 6: 79–110.
1955b Uxmal-Kabah-Sayil: temporada 1953. *Inst. Nac. Antr. Hist., Dir. Monumentos Prehispánicos*, Informe 1.
1955c Uxmal: temporada de trabajos 1951–1952. *An. Inst. Nac. Antr. Hist.*, 6: 49–67.

1956 Uxmal: official guide. Inst. Nac. Antr. Hist.
1958 Exploraciones arqueológicas en Palenque: 1953–56. *An. Inst. Nac. Antr. Hist.*, 10: 69–299.
1959 Estudio preliminar de los tipos de enterramientos en el area maya. *Acts 33d Int. Cong. Amer.*, 2: 183–99.
1962a Chichen Itza y Tula: comentarios a un ensayo. *Univ. Nac. Autónoma Mex., Estud. Cultura Maya*, 2: 205–20.
1962b Exploraciones arqueológicas en Palenque: 1957. *An. Inst. Nac. Antr. Hist.*, 14: 35–90.

SÁENZ, C. A.
1956 Exploraciones en la Pirámide de la Cruz Foliada y en los Templos XVIII y XXI. *Inst. Nac. Antr. Hist., Dir. Monumentos Prehispánicos*, Informe 5.
1957 Informe sobre reconocimientos en algunos sitios de Guerrero. MS in Archivo Inst. Nac. Antr. Hist.

SAHAGÚN, B. DE
1905 Codex Florentino. Illustrations to Sahagún's Historia general de las cosas de Nueva España. Madrid.
1938 Historia general de las cosas de Nueva España. Ed. P. Robredo. Mexico.
1946 *Idem*, lib. 6, cap. 29.
1956 *Idem*, ed. A. M. Garibay K. Mexico.
1959 *See* Anderson and Dibble.

SÁNCHEZ DE AGUILAR, P.
1937 Informe contra idolorum cultores del obispado de Yucatan. . . . Merida. (Originally published 1639, Madrid.)

SANDERS, W. T.
1955 An archaeological reconnaissance of northern Quintana Roo. *Carnegie Inst. Wash., Current Reports*, no. 24.
1956 The central Mexican symbiotic region: a study in prehistoric settlement patterns. *In* Willey, 1956c, pp. 115–27.
1960 Prehistoric ceramics and settlement patterns in Quintana Roo, Mexico. *Carnegie Inst. Wash.*, Pub. 606, Contrib. 60.
1961 Ceramic stratigraphy at Santa Cruz, Chiapas, Mexico. *Papers New World Archaeol. Found.*, no. 13.

SAN FRANCISCO, DICCIONARIO DE
n.d. MS, 17th century; original missing. Copy by J. Pío Pérez. Gates reproduction. Copy by H. Berendt. *Univ. Pennsylvania Mus., Berendt Ling. Coll.*, no. 3.

SAPPER, K.
1895 Altindianische Ansiedelungen in Guatemala und Chiapas. *Veroffentlichen aus dem Königlichen Mus. Völkerkunde*, 4: 13–20.
1897 Das nördliche Mittel-Amerika. Nebst einem Ausflug nach dem Hochland von Anahuac. Reisen und Studien aus den Jahren 1888–95.
1898 Die Ruinen von Mixco (Guatemala). *Inc. Archeofun Ethnog.*, 11:1–6.

SATTERTHWAITE, L.
1937 Thrones at Piedras Negras. *Bull. Univ. Pennsylvania Mus.*, 7 (1): 18–23.
1939 Evolution of a Maya temple, pt. 1. *Ibid.*, 7 (4): 3–14.
1941 Some central Peten Maya architectural traits at Piedras Negras. *In* Los Mayas Antiguos, pp. 182–208.
1943a Notes on sculpture and architecture at Tonala, Chiapas. *Carnegie Inst. Wash., Notes Middle Amer. Archaeol. Ethnol.*, no. 21.
1943b Animal-head feet and a bark-beater in the middle Usumacinta region. *Ibid.*, no. 27.
1943–54 Piedras Negras archaeology: architecture. Univ. Pennsylvania Mus.
1946 *Review of* An incised Maya inscription in the Metropolitan Museum of Art, New York, by H. Beyer. *Amer. Antiquity*, 12: 131.
1947 Concepts and structures of Maya calendrical arithmetics. *Joint Pub., Univ. Pennsylvania Mus., Philadelphia Anthr. Soc.*, no. 3.
1948 Further implications of Thompson's readings of Maya inscriptions at Copan. *Acts 28th Int. Cong. Amer.*, pp. 467–93.
1951a Moon ages of the Maya inscriptions: the problem of their seven-day range of deviation from calculated mean ages. *In* Tax, 1951, pp. 142–54.
1951b Reconnaissance in British Honduras. *Bull. Univ. Pennsylvania Mus.*, 16 (1): 21–36.
1952 Piedras Negras archaeology: architecture. Pt. 5: Sweathouses, nos. 1–4. Univ. Pennsylvania Mus.
1954 Sculptured monuments from Cara-

col, British Honduras. *Bull. Univ. Pennsylvania Mus.*, 18 (1,2): 1–45.
1956a Maya dates on stelae in Tikal "enclosures." *Ibid.*, 20 (4): 25–40.
1956b Radiocarbon dates and the Maya correlation problem. *Amer. Antiquity*, 21: 416–19.
1958a The problem of abnormal stela placements at Tikal and elsewhere. *Mus. Monogr., Univ. Pennsylvania, Tikal Reports*, no. 3.
1958b Five newly discovered carved monuments at Tikal and new data on four others. *Ibid.*, no. 4.
1958c Early "uniformity" moon numbers at Tikal and elsewhere. MS of paper presented to 33d Int. Cong. Amer.
1961a Maya long count. *El Mexico Antiguo*, 9: 125–33.
1961b The mounds and monuments at Xutilha, Peten, Guatemala. *Mus. Monogr., Univ. Pennsylvania, Tikal Reports*, no. 9.

—— AND E. K. RALPH
1960 Radiocarbon dates and the Maya correlation problem. *Amer. Antiquity*, 26: 165–84.

SAUER, C. O.
1936 American agricultural origins: a consideration of nature and culture. *In* Essays in Anthropology in Honor of Alfred Louis Kroeber, pp. 279–97.
1950 Cultivated plants of South and Central America. *In* Handbook of South American Indians, 6: 487–543. *Smithsonian Inst., Bur. Amer. Ethnol.*, Bull. 143.

SAVILLE, M. H.
1899 Exploration of Zapotecan tombs in southern Mexico. *Amer. Anthr.*, 1: 350–62.
1900 Cruciform structures near Mitla. *Bull. Amer. Mus. Natural Hist.*, 13: 201–18.
1909 The cruciform structure of Mitla and vicinity. *In* Anthropological Essays Presented to Frederick Ward Putnam, pp. 151–90.
1920 The goldsmith's art in ancient Mexico. *Mus. Amer. Indian, Heye Found., Indian Notes and Monogr.*, no. 7.
1921 Bibliographic notes on Uxmal, Yucatan. *Ibid.*, vol. 9, no. 2.
1922 Turquoise mosaic art in ancient Mexico. *Mus. Amer. Indian, Heye Found.*, Contrib., vol. 6.
1928 Bibliographic notes on Palenque, Chiapas. *Ibid.*, vol. 6, no. 5.
1929 Votive axes from ancient Mexico. *Mus. Amer. Indian, Heye Found., Indian Notes*, 6: 266–99.
1935 The ancient Maya causeways of Yucatan. *Antiquity*, 9: 67–73.

SAYRE, E. V., A. MURRENHOFF, AND C. F. WEICK
1958 The nondestructive analysis of ancient potsherds through neutron activation. Brookhaven Nat. Lab.

SCHAPIRO, M.
1953 Style. *In* Kroeber, 1953, pp. 287–312.

SCHELLHAS, P.
1945 Die Entzifferung der Mayahieroglyphen ein unlösbares Problem? *Ethnos*, 10: 44–53.

SCHMIEDER, O.
1930 The settlements of the Tzapotec and Mije Indians, state of Oaxaca, Mexico. *Univ. California Pub. Geog.*, vol. 4.

SCHOLES, F. V., AND E. B. ADAMS
1938 Don Diego Quijada, alcalde mayor de Yucatan. 2 vols. *Bib. Hist. Mex.*, vols. 14, 15. Mexico.
1957 [eds.] Documentos para la historia del Mexico colonial, IV. Mexico.

——, C. R. MENENDEZ, J. I. RUBIO MAÑÉ, AND E. B. ADAMS, eds.
1936–38 Documentos para la historia de Yucatan. Mexico.

—— AND R. L. ROYS
1938 Fray Diego de Landa and the problem of idolatry in Yucatan. *Carnegie Inst. Wash.*, Pub. 501, pp. 585–620.
1948 The Maya Chontal Indians of Acalan-Tixchel: a contribution to the history and ethnography of the Yucatan peninsula. *Ibid.*, Pub. 560.

SCHUCHERT, C.
1935 Historical geology of the Antillean-Caribbean region. New York.

SCHUFELDT, P. W.
1950 Reminiscences of a chiclero. *In* Morleyana, a collection of writings in memoriam, Sylvanus Griswold Morley, 1883–1948, pp. 224–29.

SCHULZ, R. P. C.
1936 Beiträge zur chronologie und astronomie des alten Zentralamerika. *Anthropos*, 31: 758–88.
1942 Apuntes sobre cálculos relativos al

calendario de los indígenas de Chiapas. *El Mexico Antiguo,* 6: 6–14.
1944 Los sistemas cronológicos de los libros de Chilam Balam. *Ibid.,* 6: 239–60.

SCHUMANN, E. A., JR.
1936 A recent visit to southern Mexico. *Maya Research,* 3: 396–405.

SCHUSTER, C.
1951 Joint-marks: a possible index of cultural contact between America, Oceania and the Far East. *Mededeling no. 94, Afdeling Culturele en Physische Anthropologie,* 39. Koninklijk Inst. Tropen. Amsterdam.

SEARS, P. B.
1951 Pollen profiles and culture horizons in the basin of Mexico. *In* Tax, 1951, pp. 57–61.

SÉJOURNÉ, L.
1952a Palenque, una ciudad maya. Mexico.
1952b Una interpretación de las figurillas del arcaico. *Rev. Mex. Estud. Antr.,* 13: 49–63.
1956 Identificación de una diosa zapoteca. *An. Inst. Nac. Antr. Hist.,* 7: 111–16.
1959 Un palacio en la ciudad de los dioses, Teotihuacan. Mexico.
1960 Burning water: thought and religion in ancient Mexico. New York. (Evergreen Book E-241.)

SELER, E.
n.d. The stucco façade of Acanceh in Yucatan. *In* his 1902–23, 5: 389–404.
1888 Die archäologischen Ergebnisse meiner ersten mexikanischen Reise. *Proc. 7th Int. Cong. Amer.,* pp. 111–95.
1890a Die sogennanten sakralen Gefässe der Zapoteken. Altmexikanische Studien. *Veröff. Koniglichen Mus. für Völkerkunde,* 1: 181–88.
1890b L'orfévrerie des anciens Mexicains et leur art de travailler la pierre et de faire des ornements en plumes. *Proc. 8th Int. Cong. Amer.* (Also in his 1902–23, vol. 2.)
1891 Zur mexikanischen Chronologie mit besonderer Berücksichtitung des zapotekischen Kalenders. *Zeit. für Ethnol.,* 23: 89–133.
1894 Beile aus Kupfer (nicht aus Bronce) in Mexiko (Zapoteken), aus der Mixteca (Pueblo del Zapote, Distr. Jamiltepec). *Proc. 10th Int. Cong. Amer.,* pp. 7–8.
1895 Wandmalerei von Mitla: eine mexikanische Bilderschrift in Fresko, nach eigenen, an Ort und Stelle aufgenommenen Zeichnungen herausgegeben und arläutert. Berlin.
1896 Die Ruinen auf dem Quiengola. *In* Festschrift für Adolf Bastian, pp. 419–33.
1900–01 The tonalamatl of the Aubin Collection. Berlin and London.
1901 Die alten Ansiedelungen von Chacula. Berlin.
1902–23 Gesammelte Abhandlungen zur amerikanischen Sprach- und Alterthumskunde. 5 vols. Berlin.
1904a Wall paintings at Mitla. *Smithsonian Inst., Bur. Amer. Ethnol.,* Bull. 28, pp. 243–324.
1904b Antiquities of Guatemala. *Ibid.,* pp. 75–122.
1904c The Mexican chronology, with special reference to the Zapotec calendar. *Ibid.,* pp. 11–56.
1908 Das Dorfbuch von Santiago Guevea. *In* his 1902–23, 3: 157–93.
1916 Die Quetzalcouatl-fassaden yukatekischer Bauten. *Konigl. Akad. Wissenschaften,* no. 2.

SELER-SACHS, C.
1900 Auf alten Wegen in Mexiko und Guatemala. Berlin.

SHEPARD, A. O.
1947 Ceramic technology. *Carnegie Inst. Wash.,* Year Book 46, pp. 190–92.
1948 Plumbate: a Mesoamerican trade ware. *Carnegie Inst. Wash.,* Pub. 573.
1965 Notas sobre la cerámica de Monte Alban. *In* Caso, Bernal, and Acosta, 1965.

SHOOK, E. M.
1940 Exploration in the ruins of Oxkintok, Yucatan. *Rev. Mex. Estud. Antr.,* 4: 165–71.
1945 Archaeological discovery at Finca Arizona, Guatemala. *Carnegie Inst. Wash., Notes Middle Amer. Archaeol. Ethnol.,* no. 57.
1947 Guatemala highlands. *Carnegie Inst. Wash.,* Year Book 46, pp. 179–84.
1948 Guatemala highlands. *Ibid.,* Year Book 47, pp. 214–18.
1949a Guatemala highlands. *Ibid.,* Year Book 48, pp. 219–24.
1949b Historia arqueológica de Puerto de San Jose, Guatemala. *Antr. Hist. Guatemala,* 1 (2): 3–22.

1949c Some recent aspects of Mayan civilization and maize culture on the Pacific coast of Guatemala. *In* Melhus, 1949, pp. 503–09.
1950a Guatemala. *Carnegie Inst. Wash.*, Year Book 49, pp. 197–98.
1950b The ruins of Sin Cabezas, Tiquisate, Dept. of Escuintla, Guatemala. *Unifruitco,* August.
1950c Tiquisate UFers scoop archaeological world. *Ibid.*
1951a The present status of research on the pre-classic horizons in Guatemala. *In* Tax, 1951, pp. 93–100.
1951b Guatemala. *Carnegie Inst. Wash.*, Year Book 50, pp. 240–41.
1951c Investigaciones arqueológicas en las ruinas de Tikal, Departamento de El Peten, Guatemala. *Antr. Hist. Guatemala,* 3 (1): 9–32.
1952a The ruins of Cotio, Department of Guatemala, Guatemala. *Carnegie Inst. Wash., Notes Middle Amer. Archaeol. Ethnol.*, no. 107.
1952b Lugares arqueológicos del altiplano meridional central de Guatemala. *Antr. Hist. Guatemala,* 4 (2): 3–40.
1952c The great wall of Mayapan. *Carnegie Inst. Wash., Current Reports,* no. 2.
1953 The X-Coton temples at Mayapan. *Ibid.*, no. 11.
1954a Three temples and their associated structures at Mayapan. *Ibid.*, no. 14.
1954b A round temple at Mayapan, Yucatan. *Ibid.*, no. 16.
1954c The temple of Kukulcan at Mayapan. *Ibid.*, no. 20.
1955a Yucatan and Chiapas. *Carnegie Inst. Wash.*, Year Book 54, pp. 289–95.
1955b Another round temple at Mayapan. *Carnegie Inst. Wash., Current Reports,* no. 27.
1956a An Olmec sculpture from Guatemala. *Archaeology,* 9: 260–62.
1956b An archaeological reconnaissance in Chiapas, Mexico. *New World Archaeol. Found.*, Pub. 1, pp. 20–37.
1957 The Tikal project. *Bull. Univ. Pennsylvania Mus.*, 21: 36–52.
1958 Field director's report: the 1956 and 1957 seasons. *Mus. Monogr., Univ. Pennsylvania, Tikal Reports,* no. 1.
1960 Tikal Stela 29. *Expedition, Bull. Univ. Pennsylvania Mus.*, 2 (2): 29–35.

—— AND W. N. IRVING
1955 Colonnaded buildings at Mayapan. *Carnegie Inst. Wash., Current Reports,* no. 22.

—— AND A. V. KIDDER
1952 Mound E-III-3, Kaminaljuyu, Guatemala. *Carnegie Inst. Wash.*, Pub. 596, Contrib. 53.

—— AND T. PROSKOURIAKOFF
1951 Yucatan. *Carnegie Inst. Wash.*, Year Book 50, pp. 239–40.
1956 Settlement patterns in Mesoamerica and the sequence in the Guatemalan highlands. *In* Willey, 1956c, pp. 93–100.

—— AND R. E. SMITH
1950 Descubrimientos arqueológicos en Poptun. *Antr. Hist. Guatemala,* 2 (2): 3–15.

SKINNER, A.
1920 An image of an amulet of nephrite from Costa Rica. *Mus. Amer. Indian, Heye Found., Indian Notes and Monogr.*, vol. 6, no. 4.

SMILEY, C. H.
1960 The antiquity and precision of Maya astronomy. *Jour. Royal Astron. Soc. Canada,* 54: 222–26.

SMITH, A. L.
1937 Structure A-XVIII, Uaxactun. *Carnegie Inst. Wash.*, Pub. 483, Contrib. 20.
1940 The corbeled arch in the New World. *In* The Maya and their Neighbors, pp. 202–21.
1950 Uxactun, Guatemala: excavations of 1931–1937. *Carnegie Inst Wash.*, Pub. 588.
1955 Archaeological reconnaissance in central Guatemala. *Ibid.*, Pub. 608.
1961 Types of ball courts in the highlands of Guatemala. *In* Lothrop and others, 1961, pp. 100–25.
1962 Residential and associated structures at Mayapan. *Carnegie Inst. Wash.*, Pub. 619, pp. 165–320.

—— AND A. V. KIDDER
1943 Explorations in the Motagua valley, Guatemala. *Ibid.*, Pub. 546, Contrib. 41.
1951 Excavations at Nebaj, Guatemala. *Ibid.*, Pub. 594.

—— AND K. RUPPERT
1953 Excavations in house mounds at Mayapan: II. *Carnegie Inst. Wash., Current Reports,* no. 10.
1954a Ceremonial or formal archway, Ux-

mal. *Carnegie Inst. Wash., Notes Middle Amer. Archaeol. Ethnol.,* no. 116.
1954b Excavations in house mounds at Mayapan: III. *Carnegie Inst. Wash., Current Reports,* no. 17.
1956 Excavations in house mounds at Mayapan: IV. *Ibid.,* no. 36.

—— AND G. R. WILLEY
1962 Preliminary report on excavations at Altar de Sacrificios, 1959–1960. *Proc. 34th Int. Cong. Amer.,* pp. 318–25.

SMITH, R. E.
1936 Ceramics of Uaxactun: a preliminary analysis of decorative techniques and design. Mimeographed. Guatemala.
1937 A study of Structure A-I complex at Uaxactun, Peten, Guatemala. *Carnegie Inst. Wash.,* Pub. 456, Contrib. 19.
1944 Archaeological specimens from Guatemala. *Carnegie Inst. Wash., Notes Middle Amer. Archaeol. Ethnol.,* no. 37.
1949a Cerámica elaborada sin torno, Chinautla, Guatemala. *Antr. Hist. Guatemala,* 1 (2): 58–61.
1949b Guatemala highlands. *Carnegie Inst. Wash.,* Year Book 48, pp. 229–31.
1952 Pottery from Chipoc, Alta Verapaz, Guatemala. *Carnegie Inst. Wash.,* Pub. 596, Contrib. 56.
1953 Cenote X-Coton at Mayapan. *Carnegie Inst. Wash., Current Reports,* no. 5.
1954a Exploration on the outskirts of Mayapan. *Ibid.,* no. 18.
1954b Pottery specimens from Guatemala: I. *Carnegie Inst. Wash., Notes Middle Amer. Archaeol. Ethnol.,* no. 118.
1955a Early ceramic horizons at Mayapan and Santa Cruz. *Carnegie Inst. Wash., Current Reports,* no. 26.
1955b Ceramic sequence at Uaxactun, Guatemala. 2 vols. *Tulane Univ., Middle Amer. Research Inst.,* Pub. 20.
1955c A correction on "preclassic metal." *Amer. Antiquity,* 20: 379–80.
1955d Pottery specimens from Guatemala: II. *Carnegie Inst. Wash., Notes Middle Amer. Archaeol. Ethnol.,* no. 124.
1957 The Marquez collection of X fine orange and fine orange polychrome vessels. *Ibid.,* no. 131.
1958 The place of fine orange pottery in Mesoamerican archaeology. *Amer. Antiquity,* 24: 151–60.

—— AND J. C. GIFFORD
1959 A check list of prehistoric Maya pottery types and varieties. Mimeographed. Peabody Mus., Harvard Univ.
in press Maya ceramic varieties, types, and wares at Uaxactun: supplement to "Ceramic Sequence at Uaxactun, Guatemala." *Tulane Univ., Middle Amer. Research Inst.,* Pub. 28.

——, G. R. WILLEY, AND J. C. GIFFORD
1960 The type-variety concept as a basis for the analysis of Maya pottery. *Amer. Antiquity,* 25: 330–40.

SOCIEDAD MEXICANA DE ANTROPOLOGÍA
1942 *See* Mayas y Olmecas.

SOLÍS ALCALA, E.
1949 Códice Pérez. Tr. libre del Maya al Castellano. Merida.

SORENSON, J. L.
1955 A chronological ordering of the Mesoamerican preclassic. *Tulane Univ., Middle Amer. Research Rec.,* 2: 43–68.
1956 An archaeological reconnaissance of west-central Chiapas, Mexico. *New World Archaeol. Found.,* Pub. 1, pp. 7–19.

SPINDEN, H. J.
1913 A study of Maya art: its subject matter and historical development. *Mem. Peabody Mus., Harvard Univ.,* vol. 6.
1924 The reduction of Maya dates. *Papers Peabody Mus., Harvard Univ.,* vol. 6, no. 4.
1928 Ancient civilizations of Mexico and Central America. *Amer. Mus. Natural Hist., Handbook Ser.,* no. 3.
1930 Maya dates and what they reveal. *Brooklyn Inst. Arts Sci.,* vol. 4, no. 1.
1935 Indian manuscripts of southern Mexico. *Smithsonian Inst.,* ann. rept. for 1933, pp. 429–51.
1957a Art of the Maya civilization. Martin Widdifield Gallery. New York.
1957b Maya art and civilization. Revised and enlarged with added illustrations. Pt. 1: A study of Maya art. Pt. 2: The nuclear civilization of the Maya and related cultures. Indian Hills, Colo.

SQUIER, E. G.
1870 Observations on a collection of chal-

chihuitls from Mexico and Central America. *Ann. Lyceum Natural Hist.*, 9: 246–65.

STANDLEY, P. C.
1930 Flora of Yucatan. *Field Mus. Natural Hist.*, Pub. 279, *Bot. Ser.*, vol. 3, no. 3.

STARR, F.
1897 The little pottery objects of Lake Chapala, Mexico. Univ. Chicago, Dept. Anthr., Bull. 2.

STENDAHL, A. E.
1957 *Foreword to* Art of the Maya civilization. Martin Widdifield Gallery. New York.

STEPHENS, J. L.
1841 Incidents of travel in Central America, Chiapas and Yucatan. 2 vols. New York.
1843 Incidents of travel in Yucatan. 2 vols. New York.

STERN, T.
1950 The rubber-ball games of the Americas. *Amer. Ethnol. Soc.*, Monogr. 17.

STIRLING, M. W.
1940 An initial series from Tres Zapotes, Vera Cruz, Mexico. *Nat. Geog. Soc., Contributed Technical Papers, Mex. Archaeol. Ser.*, vol. 1, no. 1.
1941 Expedition unearths buried masterpieces of carved jade. *Nat. Geog. Mag.*, 80: 278–302.
1943 Stone monuments of southern Mexico. *Smithsonian Inst., Bur. Amer. Ethnol.*, Bull. 138.
1945 Letter quoted in "News and Notes." *Amer. Antiquity*, 11:137.
1947 On the trail of La Venta man. *Nat. Geog. Mag.*, 91: 137–72.
1955 Stone monuments of the Rio Chiquito, Veracruz, Mexico. *Smithsonian Inst., Bur. Amer. Ethnol.*, Bull. 157.
1957 An archaeological reconnaissance in southeastern Mexico. *Ibid.*, Bull. 164, pp. 213–40.

STONE, D.
1949 Los grupos mexicanos en la America Central y su importancia. *Antr. Hist. Guatemala*, 1 (1): 43–47.
1957 The archaeology of central and southern Honduras. *Papers Peabody Mus., Harvard Univ.*, vol. 49, no. 3.

—— AND C. BALSER
1958 The aboriginal metalwork in the Isthmian region of America. Museo Nacional, San Jose, Costa Rica.

STROMSVIK, G.
1931 Notes on the metates of Chichen Itza, Yucatan. *Carnegie Inst. Wash.*, Pub. 403, Contrib. 4.
1941 Honduras. *Carnegie Inst. Wash.*, Year Book 40, pp. 292–95.
1942a Honduras. *Ibid.*, Year Book 41, pp. 249–50.
1942b Substela caches and stela foundations at Copan and Quirigua. *Carnegie Inst. Wash.*, Pub. 528, Contrib. 37.
1947 Guide book to the ruins of Copan. *Ibid.*, Pub. 577.
1950 Las ruinas de Asuncion Mita, informe de su reconocimiento. *Antr. Hist. Guatemala*, 2 (1): 21–29.
1952 The ball courts at Copan, with notes on courts at La Union, Quirigua, San Pedro Pinula and Asuncion Mita. *Carnegie Inst. Wash.*, Pub. 596, Contrib. 55.
1956 Exploration of the cave of Dzab-Na, Tecoh, Yucatan. *Carnegie Inst. Wash., Current Reports*, no. 35.

STRONG, W. D.
1947 Finding the tomb of a warrior-god. *Nat. Geog. Mag.*, 91: 453–82.

——, A. KIDDER II, AND A. J. D. PAUL, JR.
1938 Preliminary report on the Smithsonian Institution–Harvard University archeological expedition to northwestern Honduras. *Smithsonian Misc. Coll.*, vol. 97, no. 1.

SUÁREZ, L.
1960 Pellicer denuncia: las palas mecánicas destruyen en Tabasco un cementerio maya del siglo 7. "Novedades" suplemento dominical Mexico en la cultura, no. 592.

SUHM, D. A., ed.
1959 Abstracts of papers, 24th ann. meeting of Soc. Amer. Archaeol.

SWADESH, M.
1953 The language of the archaeologic Huastecs. *Carnegie Inst. Wash., Notes Middle Amer. Archaeol Ethnol.*, no. 114.
1954–55 Algunas fechas glotocronológicas importantes para la historia nahua. *Rev. Mex. Estud. Antr.*, 14: 173–92.

TABI, DOCUMENTOS DE
n.d. Documentos de tierras de la hacienda Sn. Juan Bautista Tavi en idioma maya o yucateca. MS in Tulane Univ.

TAMAYO, J. L.
1949 Atlas geográfico general de Mexico. Mexico.

TAX, S., ed.
1951 The civilizations of ancient America. Selected papers of the 29th Int. Cong. Amer. Chicago.

TEEPLE, J. E.
1930 Maya astronomy. *Carnegie Inst. Wash.*, Pub. 403, Contrib. 2.

TEJEDA, A.
1947 Drawings of Tajumulco sculptures. *Carnegie Inst. Wash., Notes Middle Amer. Archaeol. Ethnol.*, no. 77.

TEMPSKY, G. F. VON
1858 Mitla: a narrative of incidents and personal adventure. London.

TERMER, F.
1930a Über die Mayasprache von Chicomucelo. *Proc. 23d Int. Cong. Amer.*, pp. 926–36.
1930b Archäologische Studien und Beobachtungen in Guatemala in den Jahren 1925–29. *Tagungsberichte der Gesellschaft für Völkerkunde*, pp. 85–102.
1931 Zur Archäologie von Guatemala. *Baessler Archiv*, 14: 167–91.
1936 Die Bedeutung der Pipiles für die Kulturgestaltung in Guatemala. *Ibid.*, 19: 108–13.
1948 Récit d'un voyage archéologique dans le sud-est de la République de Guatemala. *Proc. 28th Int. Cong. Amer.*, pp. 511–28.
1951 The density of population in the southern and northern Maya empires as an archaeological and geographical problem. *In* Tax, 1951, pp. 101–07.
1952 Die Mayaforschung. *Nova Acta Leopoldina*, 15: 93–164.

TEZOZOMOC, H. A.
1944 Crónica mexicana. Mexico.

THOMPSON, D. E., AND J. E. S. THOMPSON
1955 A noble's residence and its dependencies at Mayapan. *Carnegie Inst. Wash., Current Reports*, no. 25.

THOMPSON, E. H.
1892 The ancient structures of Yucatan not communal dwellings. *Proc. Amer. Antiquarian Soc.*, 8: 262–69.
1895 Ancient tombs of Palenque. *Amer. Anthr. Soc.*, 10: 418–21.
1897a Explorations in the cave of Loltun, Yucatan. *Mem. Peabody Mus., Harvard Univ.*, vol. 1, no. 2.
1897b The chultunes of Labna, Yucatan. *Ibid.*, vol. 1, no. 3.
1898 Ruins of Xkichmook, Yucatan. *Field Columbian Mus., Anthr. Ser.*, 2: 209–29.
1904 Archaeological researches in Yucatan. *Mem. Peabody Mus., Harvard Univ.*, vol. 3, no. 1.
1938 The high priest's grave, Chichen Itza, Yucatan, Mexico. Prepared for publication, with notes and introduction, by J. E. S. Thompson. *Field Mus. Natural Hist., Anthr. Ser.*, vol. 27, no. 1.

THOMPSON, J. E. S.
1928 Some new dates from Pusilha. *Man*, vol. 28, no. 70.
1930 Ethnology of the Mayas of southern and central British Honduras. *Field Mus. Natural Hist., Anthr. Ser.*, vol. 17, no. 2.
1931 Archaeological investigations in the southern Cayo district, British Honduras. *Ibid.*, vol. 17, no. 3.
1932 The humming bird and the flower. *Maya Soc. Quar.*, 1: 120–22.
1934 Sky bearers, colors and directions in Maya and Mexican religion. *Carnegie Inst. Wash.*, Pub. 436, Contrib. 10.
1935 Maya chronology: the correlation question. *Ibid.*, Pub. 456, Contrib. 14.
1936 The civilization of the Mayas. *Field Mus. Natural Hist., Anthropol. Leafl.* no. 25. 3d ed.
1937 A new method of deciphering Yucatecan dates, with special reference to Chichen Itza. *Carnegie Inst. Wash.*, Pub. 483, Contrib. 22.
1938 Sixteenth and seventeenth century reports on the Chol Mayas. *Amer. Anthr.*, 40: 584–604.
1939a Excavations at San Jose, British Honduras. *Carnegie Inst. Wash.*, Pub. 506.
1939b The moon goddess in Middle America, with notes on related deities. *Ibid.*, Pub. 509, Contrib. 29.
1940 Late ceramic horizons at Benque Viejo, British Honduras. *Ibid.*, Pub. 528, Contrib. 35.
1941a Dating of certain inscriptions of non-Maya origin. *Carnegie Inst. Wash., Theoretical Approaches to Problems*, no. 1.

1941b Maya arithmetic. *Carnegie Inst. Wash.*, Pub. 528, Contrib. 36.
1941c Yokes or ball game belts? *Amer. Antiquity*, 6: 320–26.
1942 Las llamadas "Fachadas de Quetzalcouatl." *Proc. 27th Int. Cong. Amer.*, 1: 391–400.
1943a A trial survey of the southern Maya area. *Amer. Antiquity*, 9: 106–34.
1943b A figurine whistle representing a ballgame player. *Carnegie Inst. Wash., Notes Middle Amer. Archaeol. Ethnol.*, no. 25.
1943c Some sculptures from southeastern Quezaltenango, Guatemala. *Ibid.*, no. 17.
1943d Representations of Tlalchitonatiuh at Chichen Itza, Yucatan, and at El Baul, Escuintla. *Ibid.*, no. 19.
1943e Pitfalls and stimuli in the interpretation of history through loan words. *Tulane Univ., Middle Amer. Research Inst., Philol. and Documentary Studies*, vol. 1, no. 2.
1945 A survey of the northern Maya area. *Amer. Antiquity*, 11: 2–24.
1946 Tattooing and scarification among the Maya. *Carnegie Inst. Wash., Notes Middle Amer. Archaeol. Ethnol.*, no. 63.
1948 An archaeological reconnaissance in the Cotzumalhuapa region, Escuintla, Guatemala. *Carnegie Inst. Wash.*, Pub. 574, Contrib. 44.
1949 Tentativa de reconocimiento en el área maya meridional. *Antr. Hist. Guatemala*, 1 (2): 23–48.
1950 Maya hieroglyphic writing. *Carnegie Inst. Wash.*, Pub. 589. (2d ed. 1960, Norman, Okla.)
1951 The Itza of Tayasal, Peten. *In* Homenaje Caso, pp. 389–400.
1952a The introduction of Puuc style of dating at Yaxchilan. *Carnegie Inst. Wash., Notes Middle Amer. Archaeol. Ethnol.*, no. 110.
1952b La inscripción jeroglífica del tablero de El Palacio, Palenque. *An. Inst. Nac. Antr. Hist.*, 4: 61–68.
1953 Relaciones entre Veracruz y la región maya. *Rev. Mex. Estud. Antr.*, 13: 447–54.
1954a The rise and fall of Maya civilization. Norman, Okla.
1954b A presumed residence of the nobility at Mayapan. *Carnegie Inst. Wash., Current Reports*, no. 19
1956 Notes on the use of cacao in Middle America. *Carnegie Inst. Wash., Notes Middle Amer. Archaeol. Ethnol.*, no. 128.
1957 Deities portrayed on censers at Mayapan. *Carnegie Inst. Wash., Current Reports*, no. 40.
1958a Research in Maya hieroglyphic writing. *Pan Amer. Union, Social Sci. Monogr.*, no. 5, pp. 43–52.
1958b Symbols, glyphs, and divinatory almanacs for diseases in the Maya Dresden and Madrid codices. *Amer. Antiquity*, 23: 297–308.
1959a Systems of hieroglyphic writing in Middle America and methods of deciphering them. *Ibid.*, 24: 349–64.
1959b The role of caves in Maya culture. *In* Bierhenke, 1959, pp. 122–29.
1960 Maya hieroglyphic writing. 2d ed., with original pagination, new preface, and additional bibliography. Norman, Okla. (*See also* his 1950.)
1961 A blood-drawing ceremony painted on a Maya vase. *Univ. Nac. Autónoma Mex., Estud. Cultura Maya*, vol. 1.
1962 A catalog of Maya hieroglyphs. Norman, Okla.

——, H. E. D. Pollock, and J. Charlot
1932 A preliminary study of the ruins of Coba, Quintana Roo, Mexico. *Carnegie Inst. Wash.*, Pub. 424.

Thompson, R. H.
1958 Modern Yucatecan Maya pottery making. *Mem. Soc. Amer. Archaeol.*, no. 15.

Torquemada, J. de
1723 Los veinte i un libros rituales i monarchia indiana. 3 vols. Madrid.
1943 *Idem*, 3d ed. Mexico.

Toscano, S.
1944 Arte precolombino de Mexico y de la América Central. Mexico.
1945 Informe sobre la existencia de jugadores de pelota mayas en la cerámica escultórica de Jaina. *Carnegie Inst. Wash., Notes Middle Amer. Archaeol. Ethnol.*, no. 54.

Totten, G. O.
1926 Maya architecture. Washington.

Tozzer, A. M.
1907 A comparative study of the Mayas and the Lacandones. New York.
1911 A preliminary study of the prehistoric ruins of Tikal, Guatemala. *Mem.*

Peabody Mus., Harvard Univ., vol. 5, no. 2.
1913 A preliminary study of the ruins of Nakum, Guatemala. *Ibid.*, vol. 5, no. 3.
1921 Excavation of a site at Santiago Ahuitzotla, D. F., Mexico. *Smithsonian Inst., Bur. Amer. Ethnol.*, Bull. 74.
1930 Maya and Toltec figures at Chichen Itza. *Proc. 23d Int. Cong. Amer.*, pp. 155–64.
1941a Landa's Relación de las cosas de Yucatan: a translation. *Papers Peabody Mus., Harvard Univ.*, vol. 18.
1941b Stephens and Prescott, Bancroft and others. *In* Los Mayas Antiguos, pp. 35–60.
1957 Chichen Itza and its cenote of sacrifice: a comparative study of contemporaneous Maya and Toltec. *Mem. Peabody Mus., Harvard Univ.*, vols. 11, 12.

—— AND G. M. ALLEN
1910 Animal figures in the Maya codices. *Papers Peabody Mus., Harvard Univ.*, vol. 4, no. 3.

TRENS, M. B.
1947 Historia de Veracruz. Vol. 2. Jalapa.

TRIK, A. S.
1939 Temple XXII at Copan. *Carnegie Inst. Wash.*, Pub. 509, Contrib. 27.

VAILLANT, G. C.
1927 The chronological significance of Maya ceramics. Ph.D. thesis, Harvard Univ.
1928 The native art of Middle America. *Natural Hist.*, 28: 562–76.
1930 Excavations at Zacatenco. *Amer. Mus. Natural Hist., Anthr. Papers*, vol. 32, pt. 1.
1931 Excavations at Ticoman. *Ibid.*, vol. 32, pt. 2.
1932 A pre-Columbian jade. *Natural Hist.*, 32: 512–20, 556–58.
1935a Excavations at El Arbolillo. *Amer. Mus. Natural Hist., Anthr. Papers*, vol. 35, pt. 2.
1935b Early cultures of the valley of Mexico: results of the stratigraphical project of the American Museum of Natural History in the valley of Mexico, 1928–1933. *Ibid.*, vol. 35, pt. 3.
1935c Chronology and stratigraphy in the Maya area. *Maya Research*, 2: 119–43.
1940 Patterns in Middle American archaeology. *In* The Maya and their Neighbors, pp. 295–305.
1941 Aztecs of Mexico. New York.

VAILLANT, S. B., AND G. C. VAILLANT
1934 Excavations at Gualupita. *Amer. Mus. Natural Hist., Anthr. Papers*, vol. 35, pt. 1.

VALENZUELA, J.
1942 Informe de la primera temporada de exploraciones en Arroyo Tlacuache, municipio de Ojitlan. MS in Archivo Inst. Nac. Antr. Hist.
1945a Las exploraciones efectuadas en Los Tuxtlas, Veracruz. *An. Mus. Nac. Arqueol. Hist. Etnog.*, 3: 83–107.
1945b La segunda temporada de exploraciones en la región de Los Tuxtlas, estado de Veracruz. *An. Inst. Nac. Antr. Hist.*, 1: 81–94.

VÁSQUEZ, F.
1937–44 Crónica de la provincia del Santísimo Nombre de Jesus de Guatemala. *Bib. Goathemala*, vols. 14–17. Guatemala.

VIENNA DICTIONARY
n.d. Bocabulario de mayathan por su abeceario (Spanish Maya). MS in National Bibliothek. Vienna.

VILLA R., A.
1934 The Yaxuna-Coba causeway. *Carnegie Inst. Wash.*, Pub. 436, Contrib. 9.
1945 The Maya of east central Quintana Roo. *Ibid.*, Pub. 559.

VILLACORTA C., J. A.
1938 Prehistoria e historia antigua de Guatemala. Guatemala.

—— AND C. A. VILLACORTA R.
1927 Arqueología guatemalteca. Guatemala.
1930 Códices mayas: Dresdensis, Peresianus, Tro-Cortesianus. Guatemala.

VILLAGRA CALETI, A.
1947 Los danzantes: piedras grabadas del montículo "L," Monte Alban, Oax. *Proc. 27th Int. Cong. Amer.*, 2: 143–58.
1949 Bonampak, la ciudad de los muros pintados. *An. Inst. Nac. Antr. Hist.*, suppl. to vol. 3.

VINCENT, J. E.
1960 Some comments about Oaxaca. *Katunob*, 1: 40–41.

VINSON, G. L.
1960 Two important recent archaeological discoveries in Esso concessions, Guatemala. Exploration Newsl., Standard Oil Co., New Jersey.

VIVÓ, J. A.
1942 Geografía, lingüística y política prehispánica de Chiapas y secuencia histórica de sus pobladores. *Rev. Geog., Inst. Panamer. Geog. Hist.,* 2: 121–57.
1946a [ed.] Mexico prehispánico: culturas, deidades, monumentos. Mexico.
1946b Culturas de Chiapas. *In* his 1946a.

VOGT, E. Z.
1959 Zinacantan settlement patterns and ceremonial organization. MS of paper presented at 58th ann. meeting, Amer. Anthr. Assoc.

VON WEBER, F.
1922 Zur Archäologie Salvador. *In* Lehmann, 1922, pp. 619–44.

VON WINNING, H.
1948 The Teotihuacan owl-and-weapon symbol and its association with "Serpent Head X" at Kaminaljuyu. *Amer. Antiquity,* 14: 129–32.
1958 Figurines with movable limbs from ancient Mexico. *Ethnos,* 23: 1–60.
1961 Teotihuacan symbols: the reptile's eye glyph. *Ibid.,* 26: 121–66.

WAGNER, H. R., tr. and ed.
1942 The discovery of New Spain in 1518, by Juan de Grijalva. Cortés Soc.

WAIBEL, L.
1946 La Sierra Madre de Chiapas. Soc. Mex. Geog. Estad.

WALDECK, F.
1866 Monuments anciens du Mexique: Palenque et autres ruines de l'ancienne civilisation du Mexique. Paris.

WARREN, B. W.
1959 New discoveries in Chiapas, southern Mexico. *Archaeology,* 12: 98–105.
1961 The archaeological sequence at Chiapa de Crozo. *In* Los Mayas del sur y sus relaciones con los Nahuas Mendionales, pp. 75–83.

WASHINGTON, H. S.
1922 The jades of Middle America. *Proc. Nat. Acad. Sci.,* 8: 319–26.

WASSON, V. P., AND R. G. WASSON
1957 Mushrooms, Russia and history. 2 vols. New York.

WAUCHOPE, R.
1934 House mounds of Uaxactun, Guatemala. *Carnegie Inst. Wash.,* Pub. 436, Contrib. 7.
1938 Modern Maya houses: a study of their archaeological significance. *Ibid.,* Pub. 502.
1941 Effigy head supports from Zacualpa, Guatemala. *In* Los Mayas Antiguos, pp. 211–31.
1942a Cremations at Zacualpa, Guatemala. *Proc. 27th Int. Cong. Amer.,* 1: 564–73.
1942b Notes on the age of the Cieneguilla cave textiles from Chiapas. *Tulane Univ., Middle Amer. Research Rec.,* 1: 7–8.
1948a Excavations at Zacualpa, Guatemala. *Tulane Univ., Middle Amer. Research Inst.,* Pub. 14.
1948b Surface collection at Chiche, Guatemala. *Tulane Univ., Middle Amer. Research Rec.,* 1: 123–50.
1949 Las edades de Utatlan e Iximche. *Antr. Hist. Guatemala,* 1 (1): 10–22.
1950 A tentative sequence of pre-classic ceramics in Middle America. *Tulane Univ., Middle Amer. Research Rec.,* 1: 211–50.
1954 Implications of radiocarbon dates from Middle and South America. *Ibid.,* 2: 17–40.

WEIANT, C. W.
1943 An introduction to the ceramics of Tres Zapotes, Veracruz, Mexico. *Smithsonian Inst., Bur. Amer. Ethnol.,* Bull. 139.

WEITLANER, R. J.
1948 Exploración arqueológica en Guerrero. *In* El Occidente de Mexico, pp. 77–85.
1958 Un calendario de los Zapotecos del sur. *Proc. 32d Int. Cong. Amer.,* pp. 296–99.
1961 La jerarquía de los dioses zapotecos del sur. *Acts 34th Int. Cong. Amer.*

WEITZEL, R. B.
1949 Mean new moons. *Pop. Astron.,* 57: 283–85.

WESTHEIM, P.
1957 Ideas fundamentales del arte prehispánico en Mexico. Mexico.

WEYERSTALL, A.
1932 Some observations on Indian mounds, idols, and pottery in the lower Papa-

loapan basin, state of Vera Cruz, Mexico. *Tulane Univ., Middle Amer. Research Ser.,* 4: 23–69.

WHORF, B. L.
1933 The phonetic value of certain characters in Maya writing. *Papers Peabody Mus., Harvard Univ.,* vol. 13, no. 2.
1942 Decipherment of the linguistic portion of the Maya hieroglyphs. *Smithsonian Inst.,* ann. rept. for 1941, pp. 479–502.

WICKE, C. R.
1956 Los murales de Tepantitla y el arte campesino. *An. Inst. Nac. Antr. Hist.,* 8: 117–22.
1957 The ball court at Yagul, Oaxaca: a comparative study. *Mesoamer. Notes,* 5: 37–78.

WILLARD, T. A.
1926 The city of the sacred well. London.

WILLEY, G. R.
1945 Horizon styles and pottery traditions in Peruvian archaeology. *Amer. Antiquity,* 11: 49–56.
1948 A functional analysis of "horizon styles" in Peruvian archaeology. *In* Bennett, 1948, pp. 8–15.
1956a Problems concerning prehistoric settlement patterns in the Maya lowlands. *In* his 1956c, pp. 107–14.
1956b The structure of ancient Maya society: evidence from the southern lowlands. *Amer. Anthr.,* 58:777–82.
1956c [ed.] Prehistoric settlement patterns in the New World. *Viking Fund Pub. Anthr.,* no. 23.
1960 New World prehistory. *Science,* 131: 73–86.

—— AND W. R. BULLARD, JR.
1956 The Melhado site: a house mound group in British Honduras. *Amer. Antiquity,* 22: 29–44.
1961 Altar de Sacrificios, Guatemala: mapa preliminar y resumen de las excavaciones. *Univ. Nac. Autónoma Mex., Estud. Cultura Maya,* 1: 81–85.
1955 The Maya community of prehistoric times. *Archaeology,* 8: 18–25.

——, ——, AND J. B. GLASS

——, ——, ——, AND J. C. GIFFORD
in press Prehistoric Maya settlements in the Belize Valley. *Papers Peabody Mus., Harvard Univ.,* vol. 54.

—— AND J. C. GIFFORD
1961 Pottery of the Holmul I style from Barton Ramie, British Honduras. *In* Lothrop and others, 1961, pp. 152–70.

—— AND A. L. SMITH
1963 New discoveries at Altar de Sacrificios, Guatemala. *Archaeology,* 16: 83–89.

——, ——, W. R. BULLARD JR., AND J. A. GRAHAM
1960a Informe preliminar, Altar de Sacrificios, 1959. *Antr. Hist. Guatemala,* 12 (1): 5–24.
1960b Altar de Sacrificios, a prehistoric Maya crossroads. *Archaeology,* 13: 110–117.

WILLIAMS, H.
1952 Geologic observations on the ancient human footprints near Managua, Nicaragua. *Carnegie Inst. Wash.,* Pub. 596, Contrib. 52.

WILSON, J. A.
1951 The burden of Egypt. Chicago.

WÖLFFLIN, H.
n.d. Principles of art history, the problem of the development of style in later art. New York. (Dover ed.)

WOLF, E. R.
1959 Sons of the shaking earth. Chicago.

—— AND A. PALERM
1955 Irrigation in the old Acolhua domain, Mexico. *SW. Jour. Anthr.,* 11: 265–81.

WOODBURY, R. B., AND A. S. TRIK
1953 The ruins of Zaculeu, Guatemala. 2 vols. Richmond.

XIMÉNEZ, F.
1929–31 Historia de la provincia de San Vicente de Chiapa y Guatemala de la Orden de Predicadores. *Bib. Goathemala,* vols. 1–3. Guatemala.

YDE, J. M.
1932 Architectural remains along the coast of Quintana Roo: a report of the Peabody Museum expedition, 1913–1914, compiled from the field notes of R. E. Merwin. MS in Peabody Mus., Harvard Univ.
1938 An archaeological reconnaissance of northwestern Honduras. *Tulane Univ., Middle Amer. Research Inst.,* Pub. 9. (Reprinted from Acta Archaeol., vol. 9, Copenhagen.)

ZAVALA, L. J.
1949 Exploraciones arqueológicas en Palenque, Chiapas, 1949. MS in Inst. Nac. Antr. Hist., Archivo Monumentos Prehispánicos.

ZIMMERMAN, G.
1956 Die Hieroglyphen der Maya-Handschriften. *Abh. Gebeit der Auslandkunde,* vol. 62. Hamburg.

INDEX